The
Journal of Infectious Diseases

Published by the John McCormick Institute for Infectious Diseases

Volume 33

1923

Chicago, 1923

Composed and Printed by
American Medical Association Press
Chicago, Illinois, U. S. A.

HYDROGEN-ION CONCENTRATION VS. TITRATABLE ACIDITY IN CULTURE MEDIUMS

AGNES J. QUIRK AND EDNA H. FAWCETT
WITH AN INTRODUCTION BY ERWIN F. SMITH

From Laboratory of Plant Pathology, Bureau of Plant Industry, United States Department of Agriculture, Washington, D. C.

Since the general principles underlying the interpretation of Fuller's scale in terms of hydrogen potential, as here published, were set forth by McIntosh and Smart[1] in 1919, and there is no mention of their work in the text, a few words of introduction to this paper seem necessary.

Soon after the appearance of Clarke and Lubs' paper of 1915 questioning the value of chemical titration methods for the standardization of bacterial culture mediums and advising their discard in favor of his colorimetric P_H method, I suggested to Miss Quirk the advisability of making a series of comparisons to ascertain whether we must discard the work of twenty years and begin all over again. This she undertook in intervals of other work and had progressed far enough by the autumn of 1918 to know that by our methods, and within the range of growth of our pathogens, it was possible to get Fuller's scale results which could be interpreted in terms of P_H, and on Nov. 5, 1918, she filed with the United States Civil Service Commission, as part of an examination paper, a preliminary table of transfers with 8.1 P_H = zero Fuller's scale and other values nearly like those given on page 20. We knew long before this, for that matter for a whole series of years, by the behavior of our organisms in our mediums, that starting from our phenolphthalein neutral point (a faint but distinct pink—not a bright or deep pink), it was not only possible but easy and customary to make one batch of beef infusion peptone bouillon or agar like any other batch.

I am specific because the reader should know that all of the work submitted in this paper was done independently of anything done by McIntosh and Smart. We did not know of the existence of their first paper[1] until Oct. 2, 1922, after the manuscript of this paper was completed, nor of their second paper[2] until two weeks later, their titles not including any reference to H-ions and neither of these journals being included in the many coming regularly to my desk or elsewhere in this laboratory.

The results as detailed in this paper, therefore, are a summary of wholly independent researches covering a period of more than six years and are all the more interesting because arrived at independently. They will serve in many ways to confirm the interesting conclusion of the English authors. They add also much new data and will, I trust, be welcomed by many laboratory workers.

From the beginning I suspected that inordinate claims were being made for the colorimetric P_H system. Having had a good deal of experience with various indicators, I knew something about their defects and the

Received for publication, March 14, 1923.

[1] Lancet, 1919, 197, p. 723.
[2] Brit. Jour. Exper. Path., 1920, 1, p. 9.

difficulties of getting any two persons to read color scales exactly alike, even one color scale (see p. 6), much more half a dozen. I felt, therefore, that all our comparisons should be checked on the potentiometer. Fortunately, Dr. R. B. Harvey, then of Dr. Rodney H. True's Laboratory (B. P. I.), had fitted up a specially insulated room in the west marble wing of the Department of Agriculture with an Otto Wolff potentiometer and all its accessories for his own physiologic needs and, learning what we desired to do, he kindly made some preliminary determinations for us and taught Miss Quirk how to use the beautiful instrument. When he left the Department of Agriculture in August, 1920, this instrument was turned over to us, and we have kept it in repair and used it a great deal during the last three years.

In May, 1919, Miss Edna Fawcett was added to the culture medium department of this laboratory and since that time she and Miss Quirk have worked together putting into these researches all the time available, after that consumed in the necessary routine preparation of laboratory mediums for other workers. The latter labor, naturally has considerably delayed the completion of this paper. Other delays have been due to the fact that for a year or more we could use the potentiometer only three days in the week. In certain ways, however, the delays have been an advantage to the work rather than a detriment, since it is now more exact and rests on a much greater body of data than it did in 1918.

The cultural work underlying the preparation of Charts 8, 9 and 10 was done by other members of the laboratory force. The colored plate and all of the charts were made by James F. Brewer.

My own part in this work has consisted only in making suggestions now and then and in continually supporting, criticizing and stimulating it all I could.

The manuscript of this paper first came into my hands in the spring of 1921, but after carefully studying it I returned it to the authors suggesting that they make additional comparisons so as to fill certain gaps and strengthen or eliminate insufficiently supported statements. Since that time the authors have worked continuously on the problems involved, and the paper now appears to me to be logical and worthy of general consideration. It has involved an enormous amount of painstaking labor, the positive and practical results of which I believe deserve the highest praise, since as McIntosh and Smart have said, and as every one knows:

"The importance of a correct adjustment of the reaction of bacteriological media cannot be over-estimated if one wishes to obtain uniform growths or constant toxin production."

E. F. S.

HISTORICAL

Standard methods for making and adjusting beef broth, the fundamental culture medium used in bacteriologic work, may be said to begin with George W. Fuller. His report published in 1895[3] gives the methods which have been in general use, with some modifications, until the present time.

Fuller's method of titration is in brief: Add 45 c c. distilled water to 5 c c. culture medium in porcelain capsule. Boil 3 minutes. Add 1 c c. phenolphthalein solution (a 0.5% solution of the powder in 50% alcohol). Titrate with 1/20 normal NaOH. End-point not described.

In regard to the expression of acidity, Fuller says: "For accuracy and convenience, the expression of acidity or alkalinity of culture media in numbers

[3] Jour. Public Health Assn., 1895, 20, p. 381.

of cubic centimeters of a normal solution per liter is by far the best, and I recommend its universal adoption as a standard method (Jour. Pub. Health Assn., p. 388)." His scale was constructed as follows: Beginning with zero as representing the neutral point of phenolphthalein, acidity was expressed by increasing integers while alkalinity was expressed in the same way, the integers preceded by the minus sign. The optimum reaction for bacterial growth was given as 15.

Fuller's method of making meat infusion is substantially that subsequently given in the Report of the Committee of the American Public Health Association on Standard Methods (1898), of which he was a member. Since these directions are more concise, they are summarized below in an abstract of the Report.

The following is a brief chronologic survey of the development of standard methods for making beef mediums from 1895 to the present time as they have been worked out by American bacteriologists.

In 1895, the first convention of American Bacteriologists assembled in New York and appointed a committee to study bacteria in a uniform manner. This committee made a report in 1897 to the American Public Health Association, embodying provisional recommendations. (Report published in 1898.)

In 1898, appeared the Report of the Committee of American Bacteriologists to the American Public Health Association.[4] (The committee consisted of J. George Adami, W. T. Sedgwick, George W. Fuller, Charles Smart, A. C. Abbott, T. M. Cheesman, Theobald Smith, and W. H. Welch.)

The following directions for preparing beef infusion broth were recommended by this committee:

"Nutrient Broth" (Cold Infusion).—1. To one part fresh lean meat finely chopped, add 2 parts distilled water. Place in ice chest 18 to 24 hours. 2. Strain infusion while cold through a fine cloth and to the clear filtrate add 1% peptone and 0.5% NaCl. 3. Heat mixture over a water-bath until all ingredients are dissolved.* 4. Titrate and make neutral to phenolphthalein with NaOH. 5. Heat over water-bath 30 minutes and boil over free flame 5 minutes. 6. Filter while hot. 7. Add enough normal HCl to give the medium the reaction of "+ 1.5."

Titration.—Add 45 c c. distilled water to 5 c c. medium. Boil 3 minutes. Add 1 c c. phenolphthalein (0.5% solution of the powder in 50% alcohol).

End-point: First change is a "faint darkening." Next appears " a more evident color," which "may be described as an Italian pink." A still further addition of alkali suddenly develops a "clear, bright pink, and this is the reaction always to be obtained."

Expression of Acidity.—The degree of acidity or alkalinity shall be noted in parts per hundred; "thus a medium marked + 1.5 would indicate that the medium was acid and that 1.5% of N/1 NaOH is required to make it neutral to phenolphthalein, while —1.5 would indicate that the medium was alkaline." "Optimum degree for reaction" for bacterial development + 1.5 ("bulk of available evidence from Europe and America.")

In 1899, at a meeting in Minneapolis of the American Public Health Association, a new committee, consisting of George W. Fuller, H. C. Whipple, H. W.

[4] Public Health Papers and Reports of Am. Public Health Assn., 1898, 23, p. 60.

* The first titration and adjustment is evidently made before coagulation of the albumins by heat, i. e., while the solution is still reddish from the blood corpuscles and cloudy from the peptone.

Clark, Edwin O. Jordan, H. L. Russell, J. W. Ellms and Robert Spurr Weston, was appointed for further study of standard procedures involved in the analysis of water including bacteriologic examination. This committee was at work for five years, issuing progress reports from time to time. The final report was made in 1905.

In 1905, the Report of the Committee of the American Public Health Association appeared on Standard Methods of Water Analysis.[5]

Titration Method.—The method recommended was Fuller's. Only modification: Boil material in capsule only 1 minute instead of 3 minutes.

End-point: "Faint but distinct pink" instead of "clear bright pink."

Method of Expressing Acidity or Alkalinity.—Same as in 1898 report.

"Nutrient Broth" (Cold Infusion).—Infuse 500 gm. chopped lean meat 24 hours with 1,000 c c. distilled water, in ice chest. Restore loss by evaporation. Strain through cotton flannel. Add 1% peptone. Warm on water-bath until peptone is dissolved. Steam 30 minutes. Restore loss. Titrate.[6] Adjust to + 1.0% by adding normal HCl or normal NaOH as required. Boil two minutes over open flame, stirring. Restore loss. Filter through cotton and cotton flannel.

While the Committee on Water Analysis of the American Public Health Association were standardizing their methods, the Society of American Bacteriologists were devising methods for classification of species according to cultural characteristics.

In 1903, the Society of American Bacteriologists appointed a committee consisting of F. D. Chester, F. P. Gorham and Erwin F. Smith, to study the problem of classification.

In 1905, the first "society card" (or descriptive chart) was issued. (This was entirely the work of Chester.)

In this year also appeared Erwin F. Smith's "Bacteria in Relation to Plant Diseases," Carnegie Institution of Washington, vol. 1. For method of making standard peptonized beef bouillon and agar see page 195. Chester's card, p. 175.

In 1906, the second "society card" was issued—also the work of Chester.

In 1907, the third society card[7] was issued. Chiefly the work of Dr. Erwin F. Smith, but Dr. Gorham collaborated. Chester did not collaborate although his name was retained because he was the author of the earlier cards. This was the first card endorsed by the Society (December, 1907).

Recommendations Concerning Mediums and Titration on Third Descriptive Chart.—"To secure uniformity in cultures, in all cases preliminary cultivation shall be practiced as described in the revised Report of the Committee on Standard Methods of the Laboratory Section of the American Public Health Association 1905."

"All media shall be made according to the same standard methods."

"Titrate with N/20 NaOH, using phenolphthalein as an indicator: Make titrations at the same time from blanks. The difference gives the amount of acid produced."

"The titration should be done after boiling to drive off any CO_2 present in the culture."

[5] Jour. Infect. Dis., 1905, Suppl. 1, p. 1.

[6] Here the first titration and adjustment of the mediums is evidently made after coagulation of the albumins by 30 minutes' heating at a temperature of 100 C.

[7] Society of Am. Bacteriologists, Descriptive Chart, 1907.

In 1917, "Standard Methods for the Examination of Water and Sewage," 3d edition appeared. This was revised by the Committee of the American Public Health Association, American Chemical Society, and referees of the Association of Official Agricultural Chemists.[8]

"Nutrient Broth."—Beef extract broth is recommended in preference to Beef Infusion.

1. Add 3 gm. of beef extract and 5 gm. of peptone to 1,000 c c. distilled water.
2. Heat slowly on a steam-bath to at least 65 C.
3. Make up lost weight, titrate and if reaction is not already between + 0.5 and + 1.0 adjust to + 1.0.
4. Cool to 25 degrees and filter through filter paper until clear.

Titration Methods Recommended.—These were, identical with those given in the 1905 Report of the Committee on Water Analysis.

Optimum reaction given as + 1.0.

In 1919, "Progress Report for 1918 of the New Committee on the Descriptive Chart of the Society of American Bacteriologists appeared.[9] (The committee consisted of H. J. Conn, H. A. Harding, I. J. Kligler, W. D. Frost, M. J. Prucha and H. N. Atkins.)

A colorimetric system of determining H-ion concentration recommended in place of the older titration methods which are said to be "illogical." Barnett and Chapman drop-system highly recommended to students as simple and easy.

In 1920, the "Report of the Committee of the Society of American Bacteriologists on the Descriptive Chart for 1919" appeared. (Same committee as above.) [10]

Beef Extract Mediums Recommended.—Adjustment of media to "a distinct grass green (neither yellow green nor blue green)." Indicator, brom thymol blue. "This color indicates approximately true neutrality—i. e., a hydrogen-ion concentration between P_H 6.6 and P_H 7.4."

The fourth edition of the standard methods for examination of water and sewage by the American Public Health Association appeared in 1920.

Preparation of Culture Mediums.—(a) Adjustment of Reaction.

"aa. Phenol red method for adjustment to a hydrogen-ion concentration of $P_H+ = 6.8—8.4$. Withdraw 5 c c. of the medium, dilute with 5 c c. of distilled water, and add 5 drops of a solution of phenol red (phenolsulphonephthalein). This solution is made by dissolving 0.04 gram of phenol red in 30 c c. of alcohol and diluting to 100 c c. with distilled water.

"Titrate with a 1:10 dilution of a standard solution of NaOH (which need not be of known normality) until the phenol red shows a slight but distinct pink color. Calculate the amount of the standard NaOH solution which must be added to the medium to reach this reaction. After the addition check the reaction by adding 5 drops of phenol red to 5 c c. of the medium and 5 c c. of water.

"bb. Titration with phenolphthalein. (For the convenience of those who wish to retain the use of this method for the present it is given here, but it is recommended that as soon as possible the more accurate method of determining the hydrogen-ion concentration be substituted.)"

(b) Beef Extract Broth again Recommended.

[8] Am. Pub. Health Assn., Boston, 1917.
[9] Jour. Bacteriol., 1919, 4, p. 107.
[10] Ibid., 1920, 5, p. 127.

Twelve standard American textbooks,[11] in their latest editions, dating from 1916 to 1922, were examined as to methods of making and adjusting beef mediums. Their recommendations are summarized as follows:

Methods of Making Beef Bouillon.—All except one give directions for making meat infusion broth.

Nine of these prefer the cold infusion method as described by the American Public Health Association (1898) with or without modifications. Five of the 9 follow the old practice of dissolving the peptone at a temperature below 60 C. and adjust at this point, i. e., before coagulating the albumins; 3 of them recommend coagulating the albumins by heating to boiling point before adding peptone or adjusting; 2 coagulate by heat after adding peptone but before adjusting; 2 of them distinctly mention bringing the mediums to neutrality of phenolphthalein and subsequently adding HCl. Three give hot infusion methods. Only 3 give beef extract broth as preferred to meat infusion, while 2 give it as equally good.

Methods of Titration.—Each one of the twelve gives Fuller's method with a slight modification in some cases. All titrate in porcelain capsule (5 c c. of medium added to 45 c c. H_2O—boiled to drive off CO_2). One advocates bringing to a boil; 2, recommend boiling for 1 min.; 1, for 2 min.; 5, for 3 min.

The end-point is described by, one as "bright pink"; by one, as "clear bright pink"; by one, as "the appearance of a pink color"; by one as "first pale pink—(P_H 8.3 given as equivalent value)"; by one, as "faint but distinct pink not dissipated on boiling"—(P_H 8.48 given as equivalent value); by 5 as "faint but distinct pink" (one gives P_H 8.0 as equivalent value).

Expression of Titratable Acidity.—All use the percentage system (e. g., $+1.0$ or $+1.0\% = 1$ c c. normal acid per 100 c c.).

H-ion Method of Determining Acidity.—Four give it as the preferred method; three others mention or describe it; the remainder recommend titration methods.

The reader now has in mind the main facts concerning the efforts of American bacteriologists to standardize methods of preparing beef infusion culture mediums. A survey of the summary of methods recommended in the various textbooks indicates to what extent uniformity had been attained as well as to what extent variations in method exist at the present time.

The disagreement found among them as to the point in the process at which adjustment should be made gives much room for variation in reaction of the end-product unless the mediums are carefully checked and readjusted after thorough boiling or autoclaving.

The variety of end-points described by different workers also gives room for considerable variation in the reaction of finished mediums since $+1.0$ or

[11] Abbott, Alexander C.: The Principles of Bacteriology, Ed. 10, 1921. Eyre, J. W. H.: The Elements of Bacteriological Technique, Ed. 2, 1916. McFarland, Joseph: Text-Book upon the Pathogenic Bacteria and Protozoa, Ed. 9, 1919. Zinnser, Hans: A Text-Book of Bacteriology, Ed. 5, 1922. Jordan, Edwin Oaks: A Text-Book of General Bacteriology, Ed. 7, 1921. Kendall, Arthur Isaac: Bacteriology, General, Pathological and Intestinal, Ed. 2, 1921. Mallory, Frank Burr and Wright, James Homer: Pathological Technique; a Practical Manual for Workers in Pathological Histology and Bacteriology, Ed. 7, 1918. Morrey, Charles Bradfield: The Fundamentals of Bacteriology, Ed. 2, 1921. Muir, Robert and Ritchie, James: Manual of Bacteriology, Ed. 7, 1919. Park, W. Hallock and Williams, Anna Wessels, assisted by Charles Krumwiede: Pathogenic Microorganisms; a Practical Manual for Students, Physicians and Health Officers, Ed. 7, 1920. Stitt, Edward Rhodes: Practical Bacteriology, Blood Work and Animal Parasitology, Including Bacteriological Keys, Zoological Tables and Explanatory Clinical Notes, Ed. 6, 1920. Laboratory Methods of the United States Army Compiled by the Division of Infectious Diseases and Laboratories, Office of the Surgeon General, etc. Medical War Manual No. 6, Ed. 2, 1919.

+ 1.5 may mean different things according to depth of color chosen in the capsule. (See under "end point" (p. 6), the variation in P_H values given by different authors for neutrality phenolphthalein).

As to manner of expressing titratable acidity, bacteriologists are divided into two camps, those who with Dr. Smith, including many plant pathologists, have adhered to Fuller's original scale, based on number of cubic centimeters of normal acid or alkali required to bring a liter of material to phenolphthalein neutrality, e. g.,

$$+10 = 10 \text{ c c. normal acid per } 1{,}000$$
$$-10 = 10 \text{ c c. normal alkali per } 1{,}000$$

and those who use the percentage system also vouched for by Fuller and his co-workers on the Committee of the American Public Health Association, 1898, and based on the number of cubic centimeters of normal acid or alkali required to bring 100 c c. of material to neutrality, e. g.,

$$+1.0 \text{ or } +1.0\% = 1 \text{ c c. normal acid per } 100$$
$$-1.0 \text{ or } -1.0\% = 1 \text{ c c. normal alkali per } 100$$

The latter method has been universally used by the medical profession and by many others, hence its adoption by the writers of bacteriologic textbooks.

Those who are accustomed to using the scale based on 1,000 should carefully note the foregoing distinction, since + 1.0 or + 1.5, etc., is sometimes used without the percentage sign. To avoid confusion, the percentage should always be indicated when the scale of 100 is used.

Since a considerable number of laboratories are either adopting H-ion methods of adjusting culture mediums or are doubting the value and true significance of the older titration methods (in use since 1898) it would seem that a correlation of the two methods of determining acidity which would make it possible to interpret Fuller's scale readings on standard beef mediums in terms of P_H would be a timely service. This should have a double value, for if it can be done, even approximately, it will not only enable workers to continue the use of titration methods and to know where they stand, when equipment for H-ion work is not available, but will also afford a means of interpreting the work of the past and connecting the past with the present.

GENERAL CONSIDERATIONS

The purpose of this paper is to show by direct experimentation on beef infusion mediums, as prepared in the Laboratory of Plant Pathology, Bureau of Plant Industry, U. S. Department of Agriculture, the relationship which exists between the long accepted method of titration, and the new hydrogen-ion, or P_H, method of determining acidity or alkalinity.

The fact that the senior author has prepared or been responsible for the preparation under Dr. Erwin F. Smith of all culture mediums used in this laboratory covering the period of the publication of the major part of the literature pertaining to the science of bacteriology in relation to plant diseases (1901-22), gives an unusually broad experience from which to speak. Since in all publications emanating from the Laboratory of Plant Pathology beginning with the year 1901 acidity has been recorded in terms of Fuller's scale, and since this is likewise the case with all other plant pathologic work until recently and also with an enormous mass of medicobacteriologic and sanitary work, a device which helps the investigator to visualize and transpose the values cited in literature expressing acidity or alkalinity of standard culture mediums should be welcomed no matter how specific or limited its usage. Such a device is incorporated in the text.

It is the hope of the authors that this paper will form a link in the chain connecting the monumental research work of Dr. Smith with the work of future investigators and that it will leave no doubt as to what Fuller's scale determinations on beef broth mean in his own contributions. A survey of his writings will show that records of the final determinations on mediums were always cited, and the practice of adding an excess amount of alkali to beef broth to allow for the change that takes place during sterilization, etc., was always followed. This principle must be applied where either method is used if a desired plus (+) or minus (—) degree, or P_H, is to be reached when adjusting beef infusion mediums. That such mediums can be prepared and reproduced at will with Fuller's scale and P_H values which are interchangeable with a fair amount of accuracy, will be shown in the text.

Abandonment of the titrimetric methods (measuring quantity or total available acidity) and the adoption of the colorimetric or P_H scale only (which measures intensity of acid) is advocated by Clark in his earlier writings 1915 [12] and 1917 [13] and by the Committee of American Society of Bacteriologists in the Progress Report on the Descriptive Chart in 1918. It is believed by the authors that the stressing of this point will detract from the true importance of the estimation of total acidity, and Clark calls attention to this fact in his latest book on the "Determination of Hydrogen-Ions," page 211. The estimation of the total acidity is a necessary part of the procedure when adjusting culture mediums, i. e., in the process of adjustment the total acidity must be measured in terms of the number of c c. of normal acid or alkali which must be added to the bulk to reach the desired end-reaction, whether that reaction is a given Fuller scale or P_H value.

If the data here presented furnish a logical means of interpreting Fuller's scale in terms of P_H values within the range of growth of most bacterial plant parasites, it is believed that a real service will have

[12] Jour. Infect. Dis., 1915, 17, p. 109.
[13] Jour. Bacteriol., 1917, 2, p. 1, 109, 191.

been rendered the science of plant pathology. It is believed further that the data will also be of service to animal pathology and to medicine, since the same culture mediums are used and the plus (+) and minus (—) range of growth of animal and plant pathogens falls for the most part within common limits.

No claim is made that the same relation exists between titratable acidity and hydrogen-ion concentration in any other than standard beef-infusion mediums, for experience has shown that that relation is materially affected by the nature and amount of buffer substances present, or by the kind or amount of acid present. For this reason it would be valuable to determine both titratable acidity and H-ion concentration when plant juices or beef extract or other unusual mediums are used. In these cases, the potentiometer renders a real service, and its use marks a distinct advance over purely chemical methods.

It should be stated in this connection that beef extract medium, which is seldom used in this laboratory, yields very different results from beef-infusion mediums when treated with hydrochloric acid or sodium-hydroxid, on account of its deficiency in buffer substances which in beef infusion hold ionization in check. (Chart 6, extract curve.) This has also been worked out by Clark. Beef extract was rejected by Dr. Smith many years ago on account of its variable composition, salt content, spore content, etc.

It is obvious that the present paper is concerned primarily with the study of beef infusion which for more than twenty years has been the basis of those kinds of mediums most frequently used in the research work of the Laboratory of Plant Pathology, as well as in that of many other laboratories.[14]

In making plant infusion mediums, the practice of this laboratory has been to regulate acidity by dilution as related to the solidification of agar. Systematic work on the relation of titratable acidity to P_H values in this field is also planned.

SECTION 1

TECHNIC

Glassware.—Resistant glass, either pyrex or Jena, was used in all of this work.

Titration Methods.—(1) Formula for Phenolphthalein Solution: 1 gm. phenolphthalein, 200 c c. 50% alcohol.

[14] Jordan gives the following list of mediums compounded from beef infusion: (1) nutrient broth, (2) nutrient agar, (3) litmus lactose agar, (4) beef gelatin, (5) nitrate broth, (6) fermentation tubes (bouillon with sugars and alcohols), and (7) graded series (broth plus acid or alkali).

(2) General Procedure for Titration and Adjustment of Standard Beef Broth:

(a) 50 c c. of distilled water are placed in a white porcelain capsule and brought to boiling over a bunsen flame.

(b) The dish is removed from the flame and 5 c c. of the material to be titrated are added from a pipet.[15]

(c) From the stock bottle 0.5 c c. of the phenolphthalein solution is then added.

(d) The capsule is immediately placed under a calibrated buret containing 1/20 normal NaOH solution. The buret is carefully read and recorded, the solution is then allowed to drip into the dish slowly stirring meanwhile until a "faint but distinct pink" is obtained.

(e) The buret is read again, and the difference between the initial and final readings recorded.

(f) The acidity or alkalinity, reckoned in degrees on Fuller's scale, is then calculated in terms of the number of c c. of normal acid or alkali required to bring 1 liter of the material to phenolphthalein neutrality.

(g) Adjustment of beef infusion, which is always acid, to a desired degree (i. e., + 15 or + 10, Fuller's scale) for standard mediums is accomplished by adding a sufficient quantity of N/1 or 5/N NaOH to neutralize only a part of the acid, i. e., the difference in number of c c. between the initial value obtained by the above titration method and the desired degree. Since a final determination on the sterilized broth to which this calculated quantity of alkali has been added always shows a greater degree of acidity than would be expected, an excess above the calculated quantity must be added to the bulk before sterilization. Experience has shown that in adjusting beef infusion broth to + 15, an excess of 2 or 3 c c. normal NaOH to the liter is required. Ex.—If we desire to adjust a medium titrating + 25 to + 15, we add 10 c c. N/1 NaOH to the liter or its equivalent of a stronger alkali plus the excess necessary to allow for changes on sterilization. The practice of first reducing the infusion to neutrality recommended in the 1898 report of the American Public Health Association and still followed in some textbooks has never been used in the Laboratory of Plant Pathology and is thought undesirable.

(3) Special Titration Procedure Used in the Work Under Discussion.

(*a*) *Titration of Acid Mediums.*—For the titration of acid mediums n/20 NaOH was used. This was standardized against n/20 acid potassium phthalate of known accuracy (the same used for titration of alkaline mediums and having a known P_H value.[16] The n/20 alkali was added drop by drop to a capsule prepared as described until a "faint but distinct pink" appeared. The calculations were then made from the buret readings as stated under "General Procedure."

(*b*) *Titration of Alkaline Mediums.* For the titration of alkaline mediums, n/20 acid potassium phthalate solution made in the laboratory according to

[15] Our own method of titrating was studied in comparison with Fuller's 3-minute method of boiling, and repeated trials showed that the same number of c c of N/20 NaOH were required in either case to reach the "first faint but distinct pink." The value of the comparison lies in showing that where the Fuller method of titrating has been used in the past results are capable of the same interpretation in terms of P_H, provided the same degree of color intensity has been chosen for the end-point. Our method seems to have an advantage in that the first appearance of a pink color is more easily detected and consistency of choice is thus more readily secured than in the Fuller method in which a concentration of the mediums and consequent browning is brought about by boiling medium and water together.

[16] Acid potassium phthalate (N/5) obtained from the LaMotte Chemical Company, Baltimore, was used as a standard for checking most of our normal solutions. No solution having an error greater than 0.5 per cent. was accepted. The normal solutions (HCl and NaOH) used for additions to the mediums were always obtained from the Bureau of Chemistry and checked against each other, as well as against our N/5 phthalate.

Clark's method was used. On account of the difficulty of choosing consistent end-points in passing from deep red to faint pink, residual titrations were made. In making the backward titrations, the n/20 NaOH was added cautiously until the accepted "faint but distinct pink" was obtained. Calculations were made accordingly.

(*c*) *Standardization of End-Points.*—In order to discover whether the end-points arrived at in making a series of titrations were consistent, P_H determinations were made on the contents of the capsules by the Clarke and Lubs' colorimetric method as follows: The porcelain capsules covering the entire series (made at one time) were kept, and when the contents had cooled, a 10 c c. sample from each dish was placed in a test tube and 5 drops of phenol red were added. Each tube was then compared with the color standard tubes of the phenol red series, using a check (faint pink as in the dish) behind the standard. The P_H was thus obtained and recorded for each capsule. The end-points were found to vary between P_H 8.0 and P_H 8.2. Anything distinctly greater than P_H 8.2 or less than P_H 8.0 was considered a faulty titration and when possible another trial was made. In this way, the chance for error was lessened.

Determination of the Electrometric P_H Value of Phenolphthalein Neutrality.—In order to establish a starting point for the comparison of the P_H scale and Fuller's scale in our experiments, it was necessary to determine accurately by means of a potentiometer the P_H value for the "faint but distinct pink" habitually chosen for many years as the end-point in our phenolphthalein titrations. This was done in the following way:

A flask of unadjusted 1% peptone beef broth (laboratory no. 10,521 hot infusion A) was titrated as above in a porcelain capsule with N/20 NaOH and both Clarke and Lubs' color scale and potentiometer tests were made on (1) the first change of color detectable, (2) the "first faint but distinct pink," and (3) a rose pink (see colored chart).

The following method was used in making the tests compiled in table 1:

1. A titration was made in capsule as usual with 0.5 c c. phenolphthalein solution carrying it to the desired color (faint but disinct pink).
2. On cooling, the selected end-point was checked colorimetrically (C. and L.) as described above under (c).
3. The same quantity of N/20 NaOH as that added in no. 1 was added to 5 c c. of diluted broth in capsule prepared in exactly the same way as the first, but omitting phenolphthalein.
4. When the above solution (3) had cooled to the temperature of the potientiometer room, it was tested electrometrically.

All of the tests included in the table were made on the same batch of uncorrected 1% peptone-beef infusion.

Note that the *first change* was observed, at one time, on the addition of 17 c c. N/1 NaOH per liter, and at another time not until addition of 18 c c.; also that the "first faint but distinct pink" was chosen sometimes on the addition of 22 c c., and at others not until

23 c c. had been added. Thus the electrometric value of our "faint but distinct pink" end-point falls in the one case slightly to the acid side, in the other slightly to the alkaline side of P_H 8.2.

The figures separated by dashes (4th column) represent two successive potentiometer readings on the same material.

TABLE 1

END-POINT TESTS ON 1% PEPTONE BEEF INFUSION BOUILLON 10,521

Date	C c. N/1 NaOH per Liter	Colorimetric Reading	Potentiometer Reading
Nov. 12..................	17	7.8	7.87 – 7.85
Nov. 15..................	17	7.8	7.76 – 7.78 av. 7.81
Nov. 17..................	18	7.8	7.80 – 7.79 av. 7.79 7.8 first change
Nov. 12..................	22	8.2	8.12 – 8.06
Nov. 15..................	22	8.2	8.16 – 8.16 av. 8.12
Nov. 15..................	22	8.2	8.08 – 8.12 "Faint but
			8.2 distinct
Nov. 12..................	23	8.2	8.28 pink"
Nov. 15..................	23	8.2	8.31 – 8.30 av. 8.28 (Color chart)
Nov. 17..................	23	8.2	8.26 – 8.26
Nov. 12..................	27	8.4	8.43 8.43
Nov. 15..................	26	8.4	8.45 – 8.38 8.42 rose pink
Nov. 17..................	26	8.4	8.44 – 8.38 av. 8.41

The color chart gives the colors to which the values in round numbers (7.8, 8.2 and 8.4) may be attached. For example, if broth is titrated to the shade of pink shown in circle no. 3, the contents of the capsule representing the end-point will have the value of approximately P_H 8.2.

The figures given in table 1 warrant the conclusion that in the ordinary titration tests as described on page 10 the phenolphthalein end-point commonly chosen by the workers presenting this paper is P_H 8.2. Therefore, P_H 8.2 was accepted as the equivalent of zero, Fuller's scale, in constructing all charts and tables.

In order to discover the dilution factor, if there was any, which entered into the comparative tests on which transposition values were based (i. e., electrometric P_H, colorimetric P_H and Fuller's scale determinations), potentiometer tests were made on 1% peptone beef infusion broth no. 10,521 treated in the following ways:

(1) On broth diluted in capsule, 1 part to 10 as in routine titration (i. e., 5 c c. broth to 50 c c. H_2O) and rendered neutral to phenolphthalein by adding $\frac{N}{20}$ NaOH until a "faint but distinct pink" was obtained.

COLOR CHART FOR PHENOLPHTHALEIN END POINTS.

LABORATORY OF PLANT PATHOLOGY,

BUREAU OF PLANT INDUSTRY,

U. S. DEPART. OF AGRICULTURE.

1. Check

2. First Change
pH 7.8

3. Faint, but decided, Pink
pH 8.2

4. Rose Pink
pH 8.4

(2) On broth diluted in capsule, 1 part to 4 (2 c c. bouillon to 8 c c. H_2O), the proportion used in colorimetric tests and neutralized by adding the same number of c c. of $\frac{N}{20}$ NaOH per liter as in (1).

(3) On undiluted broth to which the same number of c c. of NaOH per liter were added as in (1) and (2).

Table 2 shows the amount of variation obtained in 4 repetitions of the experiment described above.

TABLE 2

DILUTION EXPERIMENT 1% PEPTONE BEEF INFUSION BOUILLON NO. 10,521

Date	C c. N/1 NaOH per Liter	Amount of Dilution	Potentiometer Readings	Variation
Nov. 14	23	1 to 10 Undiluted	8.31 - 8.30 av. 8.30 8.33 - 8.38 av. 8.35	0.05
Nov. 15	22	1 to 10 1 to 4 Undiluted	8.08 - 8.16 av. 8.12 8.15 - 8.10 av. 8.12 8.28 - 8.22 av. 8.25	0.13
Nov. 16	22	1 to 10 1 to 4 Undiluted	8.23 - 8.16 - 8.19 av. 8.19 8.24 - 8.25 - 8.22 av. 8.23 8.30 - 8.30 - 8.26 av. 8.29	0.10
Nov. 17	23	1 to 10 1 to 4 Undiluted	8.26 - 8.26 av. 8.26 8.24 - 8.20 - 8.15 av. 8.19 8.30 - 8.31 - 8.25 av. 8.29	0.10

Table 2 shows that there is probably little, if any, error due to dilution. Therefore the question which might arise later in regard to transposing P_H values to Fuller's scale values when the former were determined on undiluted and the latter on diluted broth may be considered eliminated, since the differences found between diluted and undiluted would average less than 0.1 P_H, and as a rule were not greater than differences found in repeated readings on the same material.

Colorimetric Methods.—In making colorimetric tests, the LaMotte Standard Buffer mixtures were used, and the Clarke and Lubs' dilution method was followed. The "comparator" was always used with the "compensation" tube behind the color standard tube.[13] All determinations were made in daylight, and ordinary distilled water (the same used for titration purposes) was used. Where possible, determinations were made with more than one indicator and if results varied, as they sometimes did, to the extent of 0.2 P_H, the reading nearest to the potentiometer reading was chosen. In making determinations, the material was always used at room temperature (approximately 26 C.).

It was assumed that the buffers were correct, care being taken to make up fresh color standards at frequent intervals. The results obtained, however, together with a few tests made on buffers led to the conclusion that the boric acid series is not dependable, probably owing to the fact that it does not keep well. Possible inaccuracy of standards, however, was disregarded in presenting colorimetric data, allowing the method as it stands, including its commercial aspect, to speak for itself.

Electrometric Methods, Apparatus Used and Procedures Followed in Making Electrometric Determinations.—1. Room: The special room in which the work was done was kept at a temperature between 24 and 26 C. throughout the experiments. It is a room lined with pipes through which hydrant water circulates and the temperature is controlled by a thermoregulator and a fan.

2. Apparatus: The principal apparatus and accessories used were as follows:

(a) Potentiometer—Otto Wolff.

(b) Weston cell, value 1.0183 (Bureau of Standards determination).

(c) Standard with motor-driven shaker, complete with calomel electrode vessel (see below how calomel cell was prepared), connecting vessel or "bridge" for saturated potassium chloride, and two Clark hydrogen electrode vessels with platinum electrodes (Cat. 75, no. 7690, Northrup and Leeds Co., Philadelphia).

(d) Three Columbia dry cells for supplying current to each of the two vials containing solutions used in platinizing the electrode.

(e) Two small glass vials, one containing the platinic chloride solution (50 c c. distilled water plus 1 gm. of Merck's platinic chloride plus a trace of c. p. lead acetate), the other containing a 10% solution of c. p. sulphuric acid.

(f) A tank of pure hydrogen. (This hydrogen was further purified by heating it with a resistance coil as it passed over into the vessel which contained the broth.)

(g) A stock bottle of saturated KCl for flushing the contact tube before and after each determination.

3. Methods for Cleaning and Platinizing the Electrode: (a) The platinum electrode was immersed in hot aqua regia until the metal was bright, rinsed under running tap water and then in distilled water.

(b) The clean bright platinum was immersed in the platinic chloride solution for one minute or until a thin even coat of platinum black was deposited on the electrode, and then it was rinsed well with a stream of distilled water.

(c) The platinized electrode was immersed in the 10% H_2SO_4 solution and rinsed well in streaming distilled water. (It is easy to see electrolysis taking place in the vials by looking for tiny bubbles at the surface of the solution around the electrode.) Time 30 sec.

(d) The platinized electrode was placed in the glass vessel attached to the shaking apparatus taking care to fasten the rubber stopper tightly.

(e) The same platinum electrode was used throughout each experiment to eliminate any possible error due to the use of different electrodes. It was found possible to clean the electrode in boiling aqua regia by having the platinum inserted in resistant (pyrex) glass.

4. Manipulation: For manipulating the electrode vessels devised by W. M. Clark.[17] Attention is called to the importance of saturating the electrode with hydrogen by allowing the latter to flow abundantly through the vessel before the test solution is let in. The importance of the shaking apparatus is not to be minimized. In our judgment, accurate results cannot be obtained without it, since otherwise proteins in the broth are deposited, thereby interfering with hydrogen saturation of the electrode.

5. The Calomel Electrode and Its Use: (a) The saturated calomel electrode was prepared as follows: (1) A layer of triple distilled mercury especially prepared for this purpose by the Bureau of Standards was put into the bottom bulb of the vessel. (2) A layer of calomel was added which was prepared by shaking well together about equal volumes of Merck's c. p. dry mercurous chloride (Hg_2Cl_2) and purified mercury (the same as above) with a slightly larger quantity of saturated KCl solution. The finer precipitation left after decanting the supernatant liquid was used. (3) A deeper layer of saturated c. p. KCl solution (with some crystals in excess) was added filling the vessel about three-fourths full. This forms only a "half cell," but when the KCl solution is connected by means of a "bridge" of the same KCl solution with the test solution surrounding a hydrogen electrode, it forms a complete cell.

(b) The potential produced by this calomel electrode was entirely reproducible and held throughout the experiments, as indicated by

[17] The Determination of Hydrogen Ions, 1920, pp. 124-133.

testing with standard n/20 acid potassium phthalate solution from time to time. The solution used was checked by 2 workers on 2 potentiometer systems with the following substantial agreement between them:

N/20 KH phthalate—test 1	P_H 3.969	Laboratory of Plant
N/20 KH phthalate—test 2	P_H 3.976	Laboratory of Plant
N/20 KH phthalate—test 3	P_H 3.98	Pathology

The last test was made in another laboratory of the department by H. F. Zoller (formerly of B. A. I., Dairy Division) to whom thanks are due for many courtesies.

6. Routine Procedure in Making Tests: (a) For each determination on broth a trial test was made in order to wash thoroughly the vessel and the electrode. The material was kept in motion for 5 minutes by adjusting the shaking apparatus, taking care to see that the medium was washed on and off the electrode throughout that time.

(b) A second test was made immediately after the washing as follows:

Without removing the electrode from the glass vessel, the tested material was removed and more material from the same sample was let into the vessel. The same precautions were taken in manipulating the apparatus and extreme care was observed in recording the values as registered on the potentiometer system. The values given by Michaelis [18] were used in making calomel cell and temperature corrections.

(c) The manner in which records were made in the effort to maintain uniformity was as follows:

Sample Record—Beef infusion (uncorrected)

May 27, 1921. Potentiometer system at balance ("nullpoint")
Temperature 26 C.

Wash Test

5 min.	1:49 p. m.	Started shaking
	1:54 p. m.	Contact
5 min.	1:59 p. m.	Reading in millivolts 6174

Final Test

10 min.	2:04 p. m.	New material (same sample) added and started shaking again
	2:14 p. m.	Contact
5 min.	2:19 p. m.	Reading in millivolts 6210—P_H 6.34
10 min.	2:24 p. m.	Reading in millivolts 6209
15 min.	2:29 p. m.	Reading in millivolts 6207

[18] Die Wasserstoffionenkonzentration. Ihre Bedeutung für die Biologie und die Methoden ihre Messung, 1914, p. 157.

The highest register of millivolts was taken for calculating the P_H, and in most cases this point was reached between 2 and 5 minutes after the contact was made. After this time, there was usually a gradual fall in potential as the foregoing figures show.

Note that since saturated KC1 was used in both calomel-cell and "bridge," the liquid potential was considered eliminated.

The probable amount of variation or limit of error possible in repeating readings on the same material is shown by the following figures, which include all the P_H determinations made on the uncorrected broth used as the basis for the graded series in Exper. 28.

March 29, P_H 6.25	6.25
April 5, P_H 6.25	6.16
April 12, P_H 6.16	——
April 19, P_H 6.21	0.09 = limit of variation.

This variation in P_H is hardly detectable on the colorimetric scale, which progresses in increments of 0.2 P_H.

SECTION 2.

METHODS OF PRESENTING DATA

1. *Charts.*—In presenting in graphic form a series of parallel tests comparing titratable acidity with P_H values on mediums to which acid and alkali have been added, it has seemed advisable for the sake of simplicity to plot the Fuller's scale readings on the same sheets with the P_H readings. Fuller's scale appears on the left, the P_H scale on the right, as ordinates, and the c c. of acid or alkali added to broth as abcissas. The same space which represents 5 degrees on Fuller's scale also represents in these charts 0.5 P_H.

This discussion presupposes an acquaintance on the part of the reader with the main facts of the hydrogen-ion theory and the meaning of P_H. Those who are not familiar with the subject will find a simple exposition in the Progress Report for 1918 [9] of the Committee on the Descriptive Chart of the Society of American Bacteriologists.

Park and Williams' textbook, 1920 edition, pp. 99-100, gives the following brief explanation of the meaning of the symbol P_H and its relation to actual hydrogen-ion concentration values.

The figures (P_H value) which are used to represent the H-ion concentration are obtained as follows: Distilled water ($H_2O = H + OH$) represents true neutrality, for the positive [acid] hydrogen (H) ions and negative [alkaline] hydroxyl (OH) ions are present in balanced amounts. As fast as dissociation

TABLE 3
Hydrogen-Ion Concentration

	P_H Values*	Acid and Alkali Normalities	Ch† Values or Gm. per Liter of Hydrogen ions
Acid	P_H 0.0	$\frac{N}{1}$	1
	P_H 1.0	$\frac{N}{10}$	$\frac{1}{10}$
	P_H 2.0	$\frac{N}{100}$	$\frac{1}{100}$
	P_H 3.0	$\frac{N}{1,000}$	$\frac{1}{1,000}$
	P_H 4.0	$\frac{N}{10,000}$	$\frac{1}{10,000}$
	P_H 4.5	Color change—methyl orange	$\frac{3.2}{100,000}$
	P_H 5.0	$\frac{N}{100,000}$	$\frac{1}{100,000}$
	P_H 6.0	$\frac{N}{1,000,000}$	$\frac{1}{1,000,000}$
	P_H 6.8	Color change—litmus	$\frac{1.6}{10,000,000}$
Neutral	P_H 7.0	$\frac{N}{10,000,000}$	$\frac{1}{10,000,000}$
Alkaline	P_H 7.5	Blood	$\frac{3.2}{100,000,000}$
	P_H 8.0	$\frac{N}{1,000,000}$	$\frac{1}{100,000,000}$
	P_H 8.5	Color change—phenolphthalein	$\frac{3.2}{1,000,000,000}$
	P_H 9.0	$\frac{N}{100,000}$	$\frac{1}{1,000,000,000}$
	P_H 10.0	$\frac{N}{10,000}$	$\frac{1}{10,000,000,000}$
	P_H 11.0	$\frac{N}{1,000}$	$\frac{1}{100,000,000,000}$
	P_H 12.0	$\frac{N}{100}$	$\frac{1}{1,000,000,000,000}$
	P_H 13.0	$\frac{N}{10}$	$\frac{1}{10,000,000,000,000}$
	P_H 14.0	$\frac{N}{1}$	$\frac{1}{100,000,000,000,000}$

* The P_H values given as the points of color change for the indicators recorded are, of course, only approximations. In the table as a whole, absolute accuracy has been sacrificed for simplicity of presentation.

† Ch is the symbol used for "concentration of hydrogen."

occurs, the H-ions and OH-ions recombine. One liter of distilled water contains $\frac{1}{10,000,000}$ gm. of ionizable hydrogen. This awkward fraction may be written 0.0000001 or 1×10^{-7} = log. $^{-7}$ (minus exponent because of the decimal). The "log" is dropped, together with the minus sign, and for convenience the term P_H, as suggested by Sörensen, substituted. Therefore, the amount of ionizable hydrogen present in distilled water is represented by P_H7 (see below). The other values are obtained in a like manner. Since P_H is an invert logarithm or the reciprocal of H-ion concentration, it decreases with an increasing H-ion concentration. Therefore, acid solutions have a P_H value less than 7, and basic solutions a P_H value greater than 7; or, a solution containing an amount of H-ions greater than $\frac{1}{10,000,000}$ gm. per liter is acid; one containing less than $\frac{1}{10,000,000}$ gm. per liter is alkaline.

In the middle column of the preceding chart, the values refer to a normality strength based on grams of ionizable H or OH per liter and should not be confused with normal solutions (gram-equivalent) nor with gram-molecular (molar) solutions.

2. *Discussion of Fuller's Scale vs. P_H Scale.*—Transposition of P_H scale determinations to Fuller's scale determinations and vice versa has been found to be possible with a fair degree of accuracy [19] for beef infusion bouillon throughout a range covering the limits of growth of nearly all bacterial plant parasites.

In order to visualize the relationship between these two arbitrary scales when applied to peptone beef infusion broth, we may say that within the limits to be defined later a degree on Fuller's scale is approximately comparable to a degree (P_H 0.1) on the P_H scale, because for every increase or decrease in titratable acidity there is a corresponding change in the same direction in H-ion concentration when acid or alkali is added to it.

One degree or unit on the Fuller's scale = 1 c c. normal acid or alkali to the liter.

One degree or unit on the P_H scale = 0.1 P_H.

Neutrality or zero on Fuller's scale indicates a balance between normal acid and alkali as determined by phenolphthalein.

Neutrality by H-ion determination = P_H 7.0, the P_H obtained when the conductivity of pure water is determined by means of the potentiometer at a temperature of 25° C. and indicates the nearest point to equilibrium between H-ions and OH-ions.

Hydrogen-ion neutrality, P_H 7.0 = + 12 on Fuller's scale.

Phenolphthalein neutrality (zero on Fuller's scale) = P_H 8.2.

[19] The limits of error will be discussed after presentation of the experiments (see p. 44).

Table 4 and the two formulas are based on a comparison of electrometric P_H determinations with Fuller's scale determinations:

TABLE 4

RELATIONSHIP OF SCALES WHEN 1% PEPTONE BEEF INFUSION IS USED

P_H Scale		Fuller's Scale
5.0		+32
5.2		+30
5.4		+28
5.6		+26
5.8		+24
6.0		+22
6.2		+20
6.4		+18
6.6		+16
6.8		+14
7.0	Neutrality-H-ions	**+12**
7.2		+10
7.4		+ 8
7.6		+ 6
7.8		+ 4
8.0		+ 2
8.2	Neutrality-Phenolphthalein	**0**
8.4		— 2
8.6		— 4
8.8		— 6
9.0		— 8
9.2		—10

Formulas for Transposing Fuller's Scale Determinations to P_H Determinations and Vice Versa.

I. GIVEN ANY FULLER'S SCALE VALUE, TO FIND THE P_H VALUE: LET F BE THE GIVEN FULLER VALUE, THEN $8.2 - \frac{F}{10} = P_H$.

II. GIVEN ANY P_H VALUE TO FIND THE FULLER'S SCALE VALUE: LET P_H REPRESENT THE P_H VALUE, THEN $10(8.2 - P_H) = F$.

SECTION 3

DESCRIPTION OF EXPERIMENTS

1. *On the Preparation of a Uniform Beef Infusion Broth.*—Having established a starting point for comparison of titratable acidity with H-ion concentration in peptone beef infusion broth by determining a fixed P_H value for zero phenolphthalein (viz., P_H 8.2), it is plain that we must have equivalent or approximately equivalent values (Fuller's scale and P_H) in the unadjusted broth, if the relationship of scales, as given on page 20, is maintained on the addition of acid or alkali in the process of adjusting mediums.

During a series of years there has been considerable variability in the initial acidity of broth made in the Laboratory of Plant Pathology. Records on routine broths show a variation of from + 18 to + 30

Fuller's scale, or 12 degrees, while the variation in H-ion concentration has been from P_H 6.4 to P_H 5.8, a range of only 6 degrees. This means that some of our uncorrected broths may have shown a discrepancy of 6 degrees in comparing Fuller's scale with P_H values. For instance, in the case of a broth titrating + 30 and having a H-ion concentration of P_H 5.8, + 30 would be 6 degrees (Fuller's scale) too high for the "equivalent" value of P_H 5.8, which is + 24. This, however, is an extreme case and does not occur often in actual practice. The discrepancy, moreover, becomes much less when the same broth is adjusted by the addition of NaOH to reach the customary + 15 for general laboratory use. In practice, + 15 has been found to have P_H values ranging from P_H 6.6 to P_H 7.0, a more limited range than that specified by the Committee on the Descriptive Chart for 1919, as indicating "approximately true neutrality, i. e., a hydrogen-ion concentration between P_H 6.6 and P_H 7.4" (a "grass green" color with brom thymol blue).

In order to determine how great a variation in initial values may be expected and to what extent this variation may be controlled, a great many experiments were carried on in which various methods of preparing the broth were carefully studied.

Outline of Methods Used.—Up to the time of these experiments, a hot infusion method, essentially that described by Dr. Smith in "Bacteria in Relation to Plant Diseases," vol. 1, 1905, page 195, was used, and this was the type of broth used in Exper. 28, page 31. This will be designated as "hot infusion A" and was prepared by us as follows:

Hot Infusion A

(a) Added distilled water to finely chopped beef (initial proportion varied experimentally).

(b) Placed in water-bath and kept at a temperature between 50 and 55 C. for 1 hour.

(c) Steamed in Arnold sterilizer for 1 hour to coagulate albumins.

(d) Filtered through surgeon's gauze using pressure (meat press).

(e) Cooled and filtered through S and S filter paper to remove fat.

(f) Made up to desired volume by adding more water.

(g) Added 1% peptone ("Difco").

(h) Steamed ½ hour and filtered through paper.

Hot Infusion B

Another method studied for comparison will be designated as "hot infusion B." This was exactly like A except that the infusion was put through the meat press on removing from water-bath and the extract then placed in the steamer for 1 hour to coagulate the albumins. It was treated from this point on as in A.

These two hot infusion methods were compared with a cold infusion made as follows:

Cold Infusion

(a) Added distilled water (quantity varied experimentally) to finely chopped lean beef.
(b) Placed in ice chest overnight.
(c) Strained through clean surgeon's gauze with pressure.
(d) Filtered through absorbent cotton with suction.
(e) Steamed in Arnold sterilizer 1 hour to coagulate albumins.
(f) Filtered through paper.
(g) Made up to volume by adding more water.
(h) Added 1% peptone ("Difco")
(i) Steamed ½ hour in Arnold sterilizer and filtered through paper.

These broths were sterilized and stored in large Jena flasks ready to be used in making routine culture mediums or graded series for experimental purposes.

Our mediums are never adjusted until after the albumins have been coagulated by heat and removed by filtration, the peptone dissolved, and the broth again filtered as described above.

A Study of the Effect of Variation in Method on the Relation of Titratable Acidity to P_H Values.—Results of a few of these experiments are given in table 5, in which volumes as they changed throughout the process were carefully recorded and the percentage of total volume of water to the weight of the beef correlated in each case with the titratable acidity of the finished medium.

It is plain that it is not the method itself so much as the dilution factor incident to the method which controls the titratable acidity. Generally speaking, it will be seen that the latter varies inversely with the total volume of water added, while the P_H values change little, if at all. This is in accord with the well-known principle that, within limits, P_H is not affected by dilution in well-buffered solutions such as beef infusion.

The importance of uniform dilution and in sufficient amount, if comparable values are to be obtained, is brought out by these experiments. In hot infusions A, with a total dilution of only about 175%, it will be seen that comparable values are not obtained, although this has been, in the main, our routine method. But the fact that the method used in past years has been to filter through absorbent cotton before filtering through paper allows for considerably more dilution than is here recorded, especially as the cotton was frequently changed when filtering large bulks, thus losing a good deal of the strong infusion. It is easy to see how more dilution could have crept in when making up to volume, and it is quite probable that in the majority of

TABLE 5

FULLER'S SCALE AND PH DETERMINATIONS ON UNADJUSTED 1% PEPTONE BEEF INFUSION BROTHS SHOWING EFFECT OF DILUTION ON TITRATABLE ACIDITY. (EACH GROUP OF BROTHS WAS MADE FROM A SINGLE SAMPLE OF BEEF)

1 Method of Making Infusion	2 Weight of Beef, Gm.	3 Volume of Water Added in Beginning, C c.	4 Volume of Extract Obtained on First Filtering	5 Volume of Extract after Coagulation and Second Filtering	6 Volume of Water Added to Make up Loss	7 Final Volume of Infusion	8 Total Volume of Water Added During Whole Process	9 Percentage of Total Water Added to Weight of Beef	10 Fuller's Scale Values on Autoclaved Mediums (Actual)	11 Fuller's Scale Values Calculated by Formula from P_H Values	12 Difference Between Actual and Calculated Fuller	13 P_H Values on Autoclaved Mediums
Exper. 1 (Cheap cut of beef)												
Cold infusion..........	500	800	890	670	330	1,000	1,130	226	+20	+20	0	6.23*
Hot infusion B........	500	800	925	780	220	1,000	1,020	204	+23	+20	3	6.18*
Hot infusion A........ (squeezed by hand)	500	800	925	900	100	1,000	900	180	+25	+20	5	6.2*
Hot infusion A........ (meat press)	500	800	930	920	80	1,000	880	176	+26	+20	6	6.18*
Exper. 2 (Cheap cut of beef)												
Cold infusion..........	400	600	600	460	340	800	940	235	+17	+18	1	6.4†
Hot infusion B........	400	600	660	560	240	800	840	210	+21	+19	2	6.2+†
Hot infusion A........ (squeezed by hand)	400	600	730	690	110	800	710	177	+26	+20	6	6.2†
Hot infusion A........ (meat press)	400	600	745	700	100	800	700	175	+26	+20	6	6.2†
Exper. 3 (Round steak)												
Cold infusion..........	400	600	600	480	320	800	920	230	+21	+21	0	6.15*
Cold infusion..........	400	600	630	...	280	800	880	220	+24	+22	2	6.05*
Hot infusion B........	400	600	730	610	190	800	790	197	+29	+22	7	6.05*
Hot infusion A........	400	600	...	710	90	800	690	172	+35	+22	13	6.03*

* Electrometric readings. † Colorimetric readings.

cases the total dilution was sufficient to reduce titratable acidity to values low enough to compare with the usual P_H values obtained on beef infusion. This we know to be the case in the broth used for exper. 28 and in a number of tested broths used in preliminary experiments.

The cold infusions, on the other hand, with a total dilution of approximately 230%, did give comparable values in every case.

In another series of experiments, comparable values were also obtained on cold infusions made by adding an initial volume of water equal to 2 times the weight of the beef, as directed in the textbooks, and also on hot infusion B, made by adding an initial volume of water equal to 2½ times the weight of the beef.

These 2 kinds of infusion were made from each sample of beef. Each group of 2 in table 6 represents a different sample; all samples were shoulder beef.

It will be seen that a total dilution of 252% (average) was necessary in making a hot infusion in order to obtain comparable values, while an average dilution of only 227% was required to obtain comparable values in the cold. Even then the values were slightly higher in titratable acidity for the hot infusion. This reverses the general relation of titratable acidity to dilution found in table 5. But there are two good reasons for these higher values: (1) A greater amount of juice proportionately to the volume of water added in the beginning is extracted from the beef in a hot infusion than in a cold (compare columns 4 and 5), a fact which is also apparent in the earlier experiments. (If the figures in table 5 are studied with regard to the mathematical ratio of volumes, it will be seen that the titratable acidity as it stands cannot be deduced from the volumes with exactness and that in most cases the titration figures are higher for hot infusions than the volumes would warrant.)

(2) A comparison of columns 4 and 9 in table 6 will show that in the case of hot infusion the volume of water added in the beginning is almost as great as the total dilution, while in the cold infusions it is very much less, meaning that in the hot infusion a greater proportion of the water of the final product has been in direct contact with the meat.

The two factors working together tend to extract more acid from the beef, and the amount thus extracted is sufficient to outweigh the dilution factor.

TABLE 6

FULLER'S SCALE AND PH DETERMINATIONS ON 10 UNADJUSTED 1% PEPTONE BEEF INFUSION BROTHS MADE FROM 5 SAMPLES OF SHOULDER BEEF. COMPARISON OF HOT AND COLD METHODS

1 No. of Exper.	2 Method	3 Weight of Beef in Gm.	4 Water Added in Beginning, C c.	5 Volume of Extract Obtained on First Filtering	6 Volume of Extract after Coagulation and Second Filtering	7 Water Added to Make up Loss, C c.	8 Final Volume of Infusion	9 Total Water Added During Whole Process	10 Total Water Added to Weight of Beef, %	11 Fuller's Scale Values on Autoclaved Mediums (Actual)	12 Fuller's Scale Values Calculated by Formula from P_H Values	13 Error in Transference	14 P_H Values*
4	Hot infusion B..	480	1,200	1,275	1,185	15	1,200	1,215	253	+20	+19	1	6.34
	Cold infusion...	400	800	780	680	120	800	920	230	+18	+18	0	6.36
5	Hot infusion B..	400	1,000	1,090	1,000	0	1,000	1,000	250	+20	+19	1	6.4
	Cold infusion...	400	800	815	685	115	800	915	229	+19	+19	0	6.4—
6	Hot infusion B..	400	1,000	1,065	980	20	1,000	1,020	254	+19	+20	1	6.2
	Cold infusion...	400	800	785	690	110	800	910	227	+18	+19	1	6.2+†
7	Hot infusion B..	400	1,000	1,075	985	15	1,000	1,015	253	+22	+20	2	6.2
	Cold infusion...	400	800	820	710	90	800	890	222	+20	+21	1	6.2—
8	Hot infusion B..	400	1,000	1,110	1,000	0	1,000	1,000	250	+22	+20	2	6.2
	Cold infusion...	400	800	785	690	110	800	910	227	+20	+19	1	6.2—

* All determinations were made colorimetrically except in exper. 4 which was done on the potentiometer.

† The minus and plus signs are used in connection with colorimetric values to indicate determinations falling a little short of or slightly exceeding the standard in color intensity.

Since a 2:1 proportion is simpler to work with and is the one recommended in all manuals, the cold infusion method was now chosen for a long series of broths made from 4 different cuts of beef to discover whether uniform results could be obtained when care was taken to keep the method uniform.

The results are given in table 7. Volumes were carefully recorded throughout these experiments, but for the sake of brevity only the total percentage of dilution is given.

The readings in table 7 are arranged in order of the amount of total dilution, which, it will be seen, varied considerably even with the greatest care to keep uniformity. The average total dilution, however, is about the same as it was for the cold infusion broth in the earlier experiments.

One notices in glancing up and down the columns that there is no apparent relation between dilution and titratable acidity. This is due to an inherent variability in samples of beef even when the same cut is used. In the majority of cases, the P_H values seem to vary in the same direction as the Fuller's scale values.

No doubt the dilution factor is at work here in controlling titratable acidity just as it was in the other experiments, but since the broths in table 7 were made from different samples of meat, another variable factor has been introduced confusing the data from the dilution standpoint. That there is another cause for variation is plain from a study of the figures, which often show broths having equal dilution percentages but different Fuller's scale readings.[20] Frequently in such cases the P_H reading, which is a constant unaffected by small dilution differences, varies with the Fuller's scale value, i. e., the higher titratable acidity values are usually found with the more acid P_H values.

In order to obtain exact data on this point, the following experiment was carried on:

A short series of cold infusion broths (table 8) was made by adding the same percentage of water to equal weights of different samples of beef representing different cuts and not making up the loss due to filtration or any other cause. (Loss due to evaporation in the icebox or in the Arnold sterilizer was found by weighing to be negligible.) Great care was taken to treat all samples alike and by refraining from adding any more water after the initial amount variation, due to dilution, was eliminated.

[20] This variation in the reaction of beef infusion broths in spite of uniformity of method corroborates the work of Gage and Adams, who found range of from +16.5 to +29 (average +21.8) in 15 samples (Jour. Infect. Dis., 1904, 1, p. 358).

TABLE 7

Fuller's Scale and P_H Determinations on Unadjusted 1% Peptone Beef Infusion Broth Made from 57 Different Samples of Beef—4 Distinct Cuts—Cold Method. (All P_H Readings Were Made Colorimetrically.)

Exper No.	Round					Shoulder					Bouillon Piece					Chuck				
	Percentage of Total Water Added to Weight of Beef	Fuller's Scale Values on Autoclaved Mediums (Actual)	Fuller's Scale Values Calculated by Formula from P_H Values	Difference Between Actual and Calculated Fuller's Scale Values	P_H Values on Autoclaved Mediums	Percentage of Total Water Added to Weight of Beef	Fuller's Scale Values on Autoclaved Mediums (Actual)	Fuller's Scale Values Calculated by Formula from P_H Values	Difference Between Actual and Calculated Fuller's Scale Values	P_H Values on Autoclaved Mediums	Percentage of Total Water Added to Weight of Beef	Fuller's Scale Values on Autoclaved Mediums (Actual)	Fuller's Scale Values Calculated by Formula from P_H Values	Difference Between Actual and Calculated Fuller's Scale Values	P_H Values on Autoclaved Mediums	Percentage of Total Water Added to Weight of Beef	Fuller's Scale Values on Autoclaved Mediums (Actual)	Fuller's Scale Values Calculated by Formula from P_H Values	Difference Between Actual and Calculated Fuller's Scale Values	P_H Values on Autoclaved Mediums
9	250	+26	+26	0	5.6															
10	235	+26	+22	4	6.0	235	+20	+21	1	6.0+										
11	235	+24	+23	1	6.0—	235	+23	+21	2	6.0+										
12	232	+22	+22	0	6.0	231	+19	+19	0	6.4—										
13	227	+28	+23	5	6.0—	230	+18	+18	0	6.4										
14	227	+24	+23	1	6.0—	229	+19	+19	0	6.4—										
15	225	+29	+25	4	5.8—	227	+18	+19	1	6.2+										
16	225	+26	+23	3	6.0—	227	+23	+23	0	5.8+	247	+25	+23	2	6.0—	247	+25	+24	1	5.8
17	225	+21	+21	0	6.0+	227	+21	+21	0	6.1	240	+26	+21	5	6.0+	244	+21	+21	0	6.0+
18	223	+30	+25	5	5.8—	227	+20	+21	1	6.2—	240	+25	+23	2	6.0—	232	+21	+21	0	6.0+
19	222	+22	+21	1	6.0+	225	+21	+21	0	6.0+	231	+28	+27	1	5.6	233	+23	+23	0	6.0—
20	222	+22	+21	1	6.0+	225	+25	+23	2	5.8+	230	+28	+26	2	5.6	227	+21	+21	0	5.2—
21	220	+26	+23	3	6.0—	222	+24	+21	3	6.0+	227	+23	+23	0	6.0—	227	+24	+23	1	5.8+
22	220	+28	+22	6	6.0	222	+20	+21	1	6.2—	227	+23	+23	0	6.0—	227	+22	+22	0	6.0
23	220	+24	+23	1	6.0—	221	+22	+20	2	6.2	226	+25	+23	2	6.0—	225	+23	+21	2	6.0+
24	220	+24	+23	1	6.0—	220	+28	+24	4	5.8	225	+26	+21	5	6.0+	225	+24	+21	3	6.1
25	220	+24	+21	3	6 0+	215	+26	+23	3	5.8+	225	+25	+23	2	6 0—	225	+25	+23	2	6.0—
26	219	+25	+22	3	6.0	215	+27	+23	4	5.8+	212	+24	+22	2	6 0	225	+22	+22	0	6.0
Aver...	225	+25.4	....	..	5.9	225.5	+22	....	..	6.09	230	+25	....	..	5.9	230	+22	....	0	6.0

Total number of samples, 57; total average titratable acidity, +23.8 (range from +30 to +18); total average P_H acidity, 5.97 (range from P_H 5.6 to P_H 6.4)

A study of any one line of figures from left to right in table 8 shows that the P_H acidity varies consistently in the same direction as the titratable acidity, although not, as a rule, to the same extent.

In series 1, the variation in Fuller's scale readings is 6 degrees as against a possible 3 degrees on the P_H scale. In series 2 and 4, we find a variation of 5 degrees Fuller's scale against 3 degrees P_H, while in series 3 there is a variation of 4 to 4.

The interesting point is that there are no inconsistencies in direction and that the highest titratable acidity is always found with the greatest P_H acidity and the lowest titratable acidity with the lowest P_H acidity, as noted in a general way in the other experiments when dilution was not entirely controlled.

In order to obtain comparable values, it is necessary to add water at the rate of 250% when the total dilution is made at the start.

The following conclusions are drawn from the data contained in exper. 4 to 26:

The average titratable acidity as well as the average P_H value for broth made from round steak and bouillon piece is higher than that made from the shoulder or chuck. (That the cuts so group themselves is probably due to the fact that the two former and the two latter are adjacent to each other on the animal.) Average P_H values for the groups tested vary in the same direction as the average titration values, e. g., the average titratable acidity for round steak is $+25.4$, while the average titratable acidity for shoulder is $+22$; the average P_H for round steak is 5.9, while the average P_H for shoulder is 6.1.

A comparison of P_H with Fuller's scale values as it is brought out in the columns which record the differences computed by formula, gives a rather satisfactory impression from the point of view of transferable values, for, if we regard 2 degrees on either scale as a possible variation due to optical error, we find that 70% of the readings are comparable, i. e., can be transposed one for the other; 84% show no greater discrepancy than 3 degrees in transposing; 91% fall within 4 degrees of being equivalents and less than 1% show a greater discrepancy than 4 degrees.

Tests on Broths from Other Laboratories.—Determinations were also made on 16 samples of unadjusted meat infusion broth sent to us from 4 different laboratories in Washington. These were obtained at different times covering periods of from 1 to 3 months and hence ought to be representative of the routine broth of these laboratories. The results of tests are given in table 9.

TABLE 8

EXPER. 27, SHOWING RELATION OF P_H TO FULLER'S SCALE READINGS IN UNADJUSTED 1% PEPTONE BEEF INFUSION (COLD) MADE FROM 4 DIFFERENT CUTS WITH ABSOLUTELY UNIFORM DILUTION FOR EACH SERIES

Series No.	Dilution. Water to Weight of Beef, %	Round				Bouillon Piece				Shoulder				Chuck			
		Fuller's Scale Values (Actual)	Fuller's Scale Values (Calculated)*	Colorimetric P_H Values	Difference Between Actual and Calculated Fuller	Fuller's Scale Values (Actual)	Fuller's Scale Values (Calculated)*	Colorimetric P_H Values	Difference Between Actual and Calculated Fuller	Fuller's Scale Values (Actual)	Fuller's Scale Values (Calculated)*	Colorimetric P_H Values	Difference Between Actual and Calculated Fuller	Fuller's Scale Values (Actual)	Fuller's Scale Values (Calculated)*	Colorimetric P_H Values	Difference Between Actual and Calculated Fuller
1	200	+30	+25	5.8—	5	+27	+24	5.8	3	+27	+24	5.8	3	+24	+22	6.0	2
2	200	+29	+25	5.8—	4	+27	+25	5.8—	2	+28	+25	5.8—	3	+24	+22	6.0	2
3	250	+24	+24	5.8	0	+23	+22	6.0	1	+20	+20	6.2	0	+20	+20	6.2	0
4	250	+26	+24	5.8	2	+24	+24	5.8	0	+23	+23	5.9	0	+21	+21	6.1	0

* From P_H values. Note: The minus sign indicates that the actual value was somewhat less than the recorded value.

The average titratable acidity and the average P_H readings on these broths resemble our own broth averages very closely, as do the limits of variation.

Comparable values were obtained throughout on the broths from the Navy Medical School Laboratory and from the Hygienic Laboratory, and this is particularly interesting in view of the fact that these

TABLE 9

FULLER'S SCALE AND P_H DETERMINATIONS ON UNADJUSTED 1% PEPTONE BEEF INFUSION BROTHS FROM 4 OTHER LABORATORIES IN WASHINGTON

Samples from	Colorimetric P_H Values on Autoclaved Mediums	Fuller's Scale Values on Autoclaved Mediums (Actual)	Fuller's Scale Values Calculated from Colorimetric P_H by Formula	Difference Between Actual and Calculated Fuller Based on Colorimetric P_H	Electrometric P_H Values on Autoclaved Mediums	Fuller's Scale Values Calculated from Electrometric by Formula	Difference Between Actual and Calculated Fuller Based on Electrometric P_H
Navy Med. Sch. Lab.							
2/16/22...........	5.8	+26	+24	2	5.73	+25	1
2/13/22...........	6.1	+21	+21	0	6.05	+20	1
2/17/22...........	6.3	+18	+19	1	6.27	+19	1
2/24/22...........	5.8	+24	+24	0	5.83	+24	0
Hygienic Lab.							
2/ 6/22...........	5.6	+26	+26	0	5.61	+26	0
2/13/22...........	5.6	+25	+26	1	5.67	+25	0
2/17/22...........	5.8	+24	+24	0	5.83	+24	0
2/22/22...........	5.6	+24	+26	2	5.78	+24	0
B.A.I. Biochem. Lab.							
2/ 6/22...........	6.1	+26	+21	5	6.0	+22	4
2/13/22...........	6.3	+24	+19	5	6.18	+20	4
2/17/22...........	6.3	+24	+19	5	6.2	+20	4
3/1 /22...........	6.6	+20	+16	4	6.62	+16	4
Army Med. Sch. Lab.							
2/ 4/22...........	6.0	+26	+22	4	5.95	+22	4
3/19/22...........	5.4	+33	+28	5	5.41	+28	5
4/13/22...........	5.6	+26	+26	0	5.64	+26	0
5/ 5/22...........	6.0	+27	+22	5	....	....	...
Average.........	5.9	+24.6	....	...	5.9	....	...

two laboratories use cold infusion methods involving considerable dilution through making up to volume the loss due to filtration. It is thus probable that their total dilution percentage was very much like that in our cold infusion. The other two laboratories, Biochemical Laboratory (Bureau of Animal Industry) and the Army Medical School Laboratory, use hot infusion methods, and their broths show comparatively higher titratable values in reference to P_H. Although here we do not get comparable values, the discrepancy is such that when adjusting the mediums for use (Fuller's scale) the P_H values would merely be thrown a few degrees lower (i. e., to the alkaline side) than they would have been if the initial values had been equivalents; for instance, at + 10 the P_H value instead of being 7.2 (see page 20) would still show a discrepancy in the same direction as did the initial broth but to a lesser degree and would be perhaps P_H 7.3 or 7.4, H-ion concentrations which are most favorable to the growth of animal pathogens.

3. *On the Addition of Acid and Alkali to Beef Infusion Bouillon in Graded Series.*—General Procedure: 1. For each experiment recorded in this section, fresh 1% peptone beef infusion broth was prepared in sufficient quantity to cover the entire series.

2. Small quantities of the uniform medium were placed in beakers, when a series was to be made, and given amounts of hydrochloric acid or of sodium hydroxid were added from a graduated pipet. In the tables, all additions are recorded in c c. of normal acid or alkali per liter. The broths were steamed in the Arnold sterilizer for one-half hour, filtered, tubed and autoclaved for 15 minutes at 115 C.

In order to handle the work conveniently and make the tests with sufficient care and accuracy, each experiment was divided into sections, the whole series sometimes covering a period of several days or weeks. Parallel tests on the same mediums (including titrations according to Fuller's scale, colorimetric determinations and electrometric determinations), were made as nearly as possible at the same time. The time which elapsed between sterilization and the making of determinations was always noted, since in some cases this factor was found to be of great importance, due to the instability of mediums to which large quantities of alkali have been added.

Exper. 28: Graded Series—Beef Broth—Hot Infusion A: Exper. 28 was carried on for the purpose of observing the relationship between Fuller scale and P_H values in a graded series made by adding normal acid or alkali in steps of 5 c c. per liter to 1% peptone beef broth. Hot infusion A was used as a basis in this case. In table 10, the P_H values and Fuller's scale determinations are arranged in such a way that the two may be compared and correlated in each case with the number of c c. of acid or alkali added.

Enough tubes of each grade of broth were sterilized so that 3 sets of determinations could be made as follows: One set immediately after autoclaving (taking care that the mediums had cooled to room temperature), a second set 1 week later and a third set 2 weeks after sterilization.

In running the 3 kinds of tests, one worker made electrometric determinations while another made colorimetric and titrimetric readings.

A study of any one set of determinations made on the same day in table 10 will bring out the relationship of Fuller's scale to P_H values.

TABLE 10

EXPER. 28, SHOWING PARALLEL TITRIMETRIC, COLORIMETRIC AND ELECTROMETRIC READINGS ON BEEF BROTH (HOT INFUSION A)* WITH ADDITIONS OF NORMAL ACID AND ALKALI IN STEPS OF 5 C C. PER LITER, ALSO INCREASE IN ACIDITY OF THE ALKALINE MEDIUMS ON STANDING

(Side label: Normal NaOH ←—0—→ Normal HCl)

C c. Added to Liter	Titration (Fuller's Scale)			Colorimetric P_H (Clarke and Lubs' Scale)			Electrometric P_H		
	Same Day	One Week	Two Weeks	Same Day	One Week	Two Weeks	Same Day	One Week	Two Weeks
40	+60	+62	+63	3.8	3.8	3.8	3.7	3.7	3.7
35	+54	+56	+58	4.0	4.0	4.0	3.8	3.8	3.9
30	+50	+50	+54	4.2	4.2	4.2	4.0	4.0	4.0
25	+44	+42	+46	4.6	4.8	4.8	4.3	4.3	4.4
20	+41	+40	+42	4.8	4.8	4.8	4.5	4.3	4.3
15	+37	+38	+39	5.0	5.0	5.0	4.8	4.8	4.8
10	+32	+34	+33	5.4	5.4	5.4	5.2	5.3	5.2
5	+28	+28	+28	5.8	5.8	5.8	5.7	5.7	5.6
0	+22	+23	+24	6.3	6.2	6.2	6.2	6.2	6.1
5	+17	+17	+18	6.5	6.5	6.6	6.5	6.5	6.4
10	+12	+13	+13	6.9	6.9	6.9	6.9	6.9	6.8
15	+ 9	+10	+10	7.3	7.2	7.2	7.3	7.2	7.1
20	+ 5	+ 6	+ 6	7.6	7.6	7.4	7.7	7.6	7.6
25	0	+ 2	+ 3	8.3	8.1	7.9	8.1	7.9	7.9
				—Phenolphthalein Zero Line—					
30	— 3	0	+ 1	8.6	8.3	8.2	8.4	8.2	8.0
35	— 6	— 3	— 1	8.8	8.6	8.4	8.7	8.3	8.2
40	— 9	— 6	— 3	9.1	8.7	8.6	9.0	8.5	8.3
45	—14	— 8	— 5	9.4	8.8	8.8	9.2	8.6	8.4
50	—18	—10	— 6	9.6	9.0	8.8	9.4	8.8	8.6
55	—22	—12	— 9	9.7	9.2	8.8	9.6	8.9	8.7
60	—25	—13	—11	9.8	9.2	9.0	9.7	9.0	...
65	—30	—15	—13	9.8	9.6	9.0	9.9	9.1	...
70	—32	—18	—14	9.8	9.6	9.1	10.1	9.2	...
75	—38	—21	—16	9.9	9.8	9.1	10.2	9.3	...
80	—40	—24	—19	10.0	9.9	9.2	10.4	9.6	...
85	—44	—26	—21	10.0	9.9	9.2	10.6	9.6	...

* The initial volume of water added was 1½ × weight of beef—made up to volume 2 × weight of beef after filtration.

A comparison of consecutive readings on each grade of broth below the phenolphthalein zero line, whether Fuller's scale or P_H, shows clearly an increase in acidity on standing (particularly in the lower alkaline range) and that there is a parallel increase as measured by both scales. This change in reaction on standing was observed by Grace and Highberger [21] and by Foster and Randall.[22] From the 25 c c. NaOH addition which is required to bring the beef infusion down to the neutral point of phenolphthalein up to the end of the acid range, the medium was found to be comparatively stable (although there is

[21] Jour. Infect. Dis., 1920, 26, p. 457.
[22] Jour. Bacteriol., 1921, 6, p. 143.

a slight increase in titratable acidity in the extreme upper range), while below the neutral point there is a steady increase in amount of change as the lower limits of the series are approached.

This gradual change is perhaps due to the hydrolysis of proteins and is always observed when the medium is retested after standing. There is usually a slight increase in acidity even in unadjusted beef infusion, but the phenomenon is always more marked when alkali has been added, and the change becomes greater as the proportion of alkali is increased.

TABLE 11

EXPER. 28. FULLER'S SCALE AND PH DETERMINATIONS ON BEEF BROTH (HOT INFUSION A) WITH ADDITIONS OF NORMAL ACID AND ALKALI IN STEPS OF 5 C C. PER LITER. READINGS MADE SAME DAY BROTH WAS AUTOCLAVED

Normal NaOH←—0—→Normal HCl

			Titration (Fuller's Scale)		Points of Error	
C c. Added to 1 Liter	Electro-metric P_H	Colori-metric P_H	Calculated*	Actual	Between Actual and Calculated Fuller	Between Colorimetric and Electrometric P_H
40	3.7	3.8	+45	+60	15	1
35	3.8	4.0	+44	+54	10	2
30	4.0	4.2	+42	+50	8	2
25	4.3	4.6	+39	+44	5	3
20	4.5	4.8	+37	+41	4	3
15	4.8	5.0	+34	+37	3	2
10	5.2	5.4	+30	+32	2	2
5	5.7	5.8	+25	+28	3	1
0	6.2	6.3	+20	+22	2	1
5	6.5	6.5	+17	+17	0	0
10	6.9	6.9	+13	+12	1	0
15	7.3	7.3	+ 9	+ 9	0	0
20	7.7	7.6	+ 5	+ 5	0	1
25	8.1	8.3	+ 1	0	1	2
30	8.4	8.6	— 2	— 3	1	2
35	8.7	8.8	— 5	— 6	1	1
40	9.0	9.1	— 8	— 9	1	1
45	9.2	9.4	—10	—14	4	2
50	9.4	9.6	—12	—18	6	2
55	9.6	9.7	—14	—22	8	1
60	9.7	9.8	—15	—25	10	1
65	9.9	9.8	—17	—30	13	1
70	10.1	9.8	—19	—32	13	3
75	10.2	9.9	—20	—38	18	3
80	10.4	10.0	—22	—40	18	4
85	10.6	10.0 (?)	—24	—44	20	6 (?)

(Rows 10 to 40 of the middle section, Actual column: Limits within which error is small in transposition)

* From the potentiometer readings.

Table 11 brings out the close parallel existing between changes in titratable acidity and H-ion concentration resulting from the addition of given amounts of acid or alkali to the broth (hot infusion A). The parallel becomes more striking when the data are reduced to a "common denominator," so to speak. This is really what we have done in transposing electrometric determinations to equivalent Fuller's scale readings as calculated by the formula already given (see p. 20) and recording the difference between actual and calculated Fuller's scale determinations. Colorimetric readings are also given and the points of difference shown between them and true electrometric P_H values. This tabulation, of course, is only another way of showing what is expressed in chart 1, i. e., the figures in column 6, table 11, represent

EXPERIMENT XXVIII CHART 1

BEEF INFUSION MEDIUM* WITH ADDITIONS OF ACID AND ALKALI

DETERMINATIONS MADE SAME DAY AS AUTOCLAVING

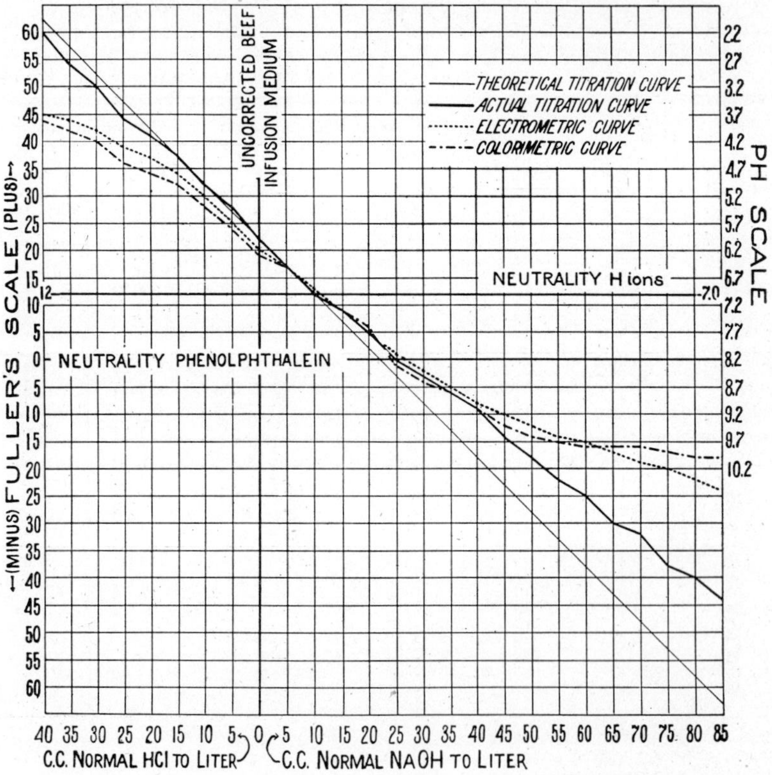

*HOT INFUSION A

the space in degrees between the electrometric and the titration curves at each point of addition of the acid or alkali.

The approximate agreement of values in the middle range, which is the range of growth of most bacterial plant and animal parasites and the divergence, especially in the alkaline range beyond these points, is strikingly brought out by both the tables and the curves (see charts).

Attention is called to the relation which the curves bear to the theoretical titration line,[23] based on the actual quantity of acid or alkali that would be required if no buffers were present. It will be noticed that the titration, colorimetric and electrometric curves all deviate considerably from this theoretical line in the alkaline range even when

EXPERIMENT XXVIII *CHART 2*

BEEF INFUSION MEDIUM* WITH ADDITIONS OF ACID AND ALKALI
DETERMINATIONS MADE 1 WEEK AFTER AUTOCLAVING

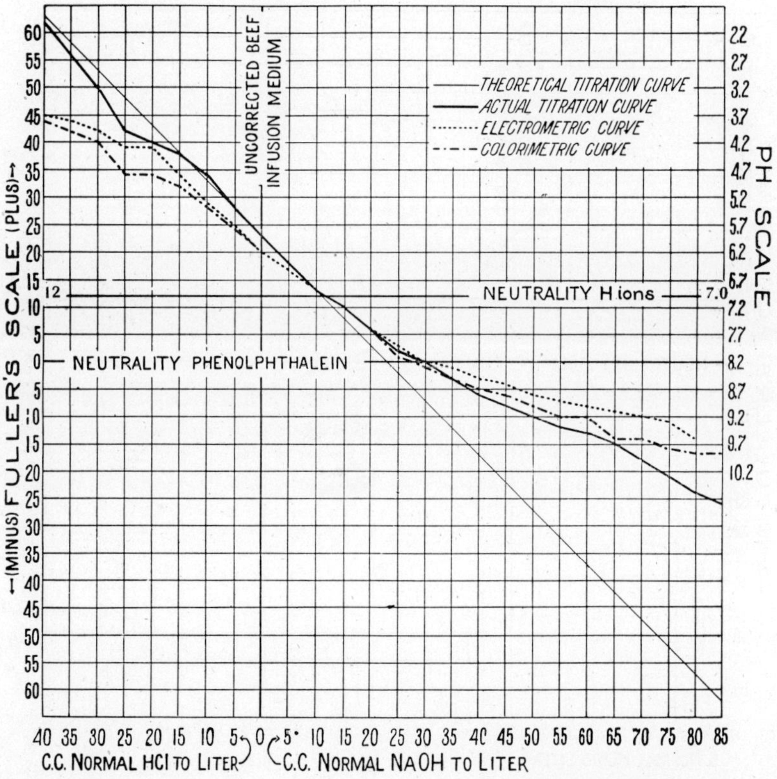

**HOT INFUSION A*

they represent determinations made immediately after sterilization, but that in the acid range they follow it more closely, the titration curve approaching nearest of all to the theoretical curve in both cases.

[23] It must be clearly understood that this "line" is only a theoretical titration line and that no assumption is made as to the form which a theoretical PH curve might take.

Comparing the 3 charts, we see that the distance between all the curves and the theoretical line becomes greater in the alkaline range as time elapses, but that the general relationship of the curves (titration and P_H) to each other is the same, i. e., the changes are parallel, as has been brought out in connection with table 10.

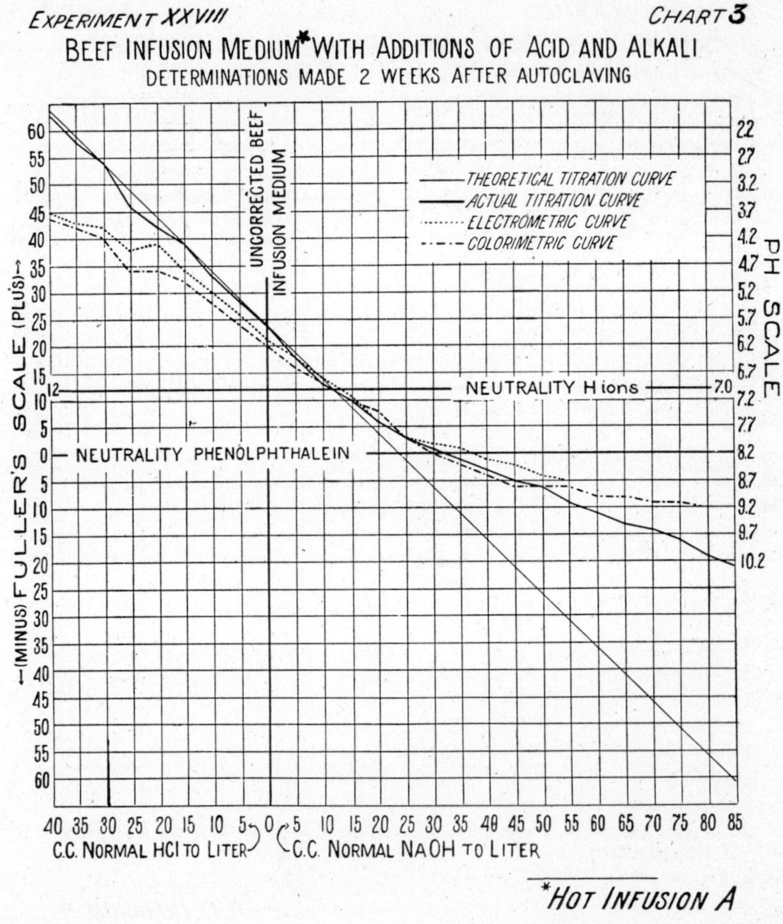

The fact that we do not find the "reaction" changing at a rate equal to the increase in amount of acid or alkali added, whether the reaction is measured by Fuller's scale or by the P_H scale, is striking. That a marked buffer effect is exerted by the broth in the case of the P_H readings and that some principle, perhaps the same, is acting to prevent a complete register of the acid or alkali added when the titration method is used is evident. This principle has long been recognized in this laboratory owing to the discovered necessity of adding an excess of alkali over the calculated amount when adjusting mediums to a desired Fuller's scale value.

For the sake of those who are not familiar with the literature on H-ion concentration, it may be well to explain the term "buffer."

Clark gives the following simple definition: "Any substance which tends to preserve the original H-ion concentration of its solution upon the addition of an acid or a base is called a 'buffer' or 'regulator.'" Again he defines buffer action as "the ability of a solution to resist change in P_H through the addition or loss of acid or alkali." More specifically, it is a matter of chemical equilibrium and is brought about by the reaction of part of the H or OH-ions of the acid or alkali added with substances which have the power to hold ionization in check. In other words, the resultant chemical compounds are of a more weakly dissociated character than are the acids or bases added to the solution. The principal buffers in beef infusion are proteins and salts of organic acids, e. g., phosphates.

It is evident from the strong odor that considerable quantities of free ammonia are given off from the broth to which large amounts of alkali have been added, and this may be accountable for the partial failure to obtain an accurate register in the lower ranges by titration, since ammonia and ammonium salts have a disturbing influence on phenolphthalein.

Even where P_H readings are concerned, ammonia may enter into the problem, and some of the supposed buffer effect may be due to a "poisoning" of the electrode.[24]

Exper. 29: Comparison of Buffer Effect in Hot and Cold Infusions: A more careful study of the buffer effect of hot and cold infusions was made in exper. 29. Both kinds of infusion were made at the same time from the same piece of shoulder beef. In the cold infusion, water equal in quantity to two times the weight of the beef was added in the beginning. In the hot infusion, water equal to 2½ times the weight of the beef was added, and the directions for "hot infusion B" (p 21) were followed. Both were made up to the original volume after filtration. Determinations were made immediately after adding the alkali and compared with another set made immediately after

24. Clark: The Determinations of H-ions, 1920, p. 185.

autoclaving, i. e., on cooling to room temperature. In this way it was possible to ascertain how much of the apparent loss of alkali added is due to the buffer effect of the broth without the application of heat and how much is due to changes brought about by heating.

Both tables and curves bring out the fact that considerable buffer effect is exerted by the broths before the application of heat, but that the change brought about by sterilization is still greater.

TABLE 12

EXPER. 29, FULLER'S SCALE AND PH DETERMINATIONS BEFORE AND AFTER STERILIZATION ON 1% PEPTONE BEEF BROTH (COLD INFUSION) WITH ADDITIONS OF NORMAL ALKALI IN STEPS OF 20 C C.

C c. Normal NaOH per 1,000 C c.	Colorimetric PH		Electrometric PH		Fuller's Scale Readings	
	Before	After	Before	After	Before	After
Unadjusted	6.0	6.0+	6.02	5.98	+20	+21
20	8.2	8.0—	8.14	7.86	+ 1	+ 3
40	9.8	9.2	9.51	9.19	—17	—12
60	10.0	9.8	11.02	10.01	—36	—26

TABLE 13

EXPER. 29, FULLER'S SCALE AND PH DETERMINATIONS BEFORE AND AFTER STERILIZATION ON 1% PEPTONE BEEF BROTH (HOT INFUSION B) WITH ADDITIONS OF NORMAL ALKALI IN STEPS OF 20 C C.

C c. Normal NaOH per 1,000 C c.	Colorimetric PH		Electrometric PH		Fuller's Scale Readings	
	Before	After	Before	After	Before	After
Unadjusted	6.2—	6.1	6.08	6.03	+23	+24
20	7.8	7.6	7.80	7.55	+ 4	+ 7
40	9.6	9.4	9.20	8.95	—14	— 9
60	10.0	10.0—	10.40	9.75	—32	—23

It is of practical importance to compare the loss of titratable alkali in reducing the 2 broths to phenolphthalein neutrality by noting where the titration curves cross the zero line, that is, the amount of alkali necessary to bring them respectively to this line before and after sterilization. The heavy horizontal lines in the lower half of charts 4 and 5, between the arrows, bring this out more clearly than it is possible to do by words. It is plain that in the case of the sterilized hot infusion there is a loss of 6 degrees (6 c c. of normal alkali per liter), if only the exact amount calculated, 23 c c., is added in an attempt to reduce it to neutrality—in other words, an excess of 6 c c. is necessary, if we are actually to reach neutrality in the autoclaved broth. In the cold infusion there is a loss of only 4 degrees after autoclaving, hence an excess of 4 c c. only is needed.

The heavy vertical lines between the arrows at the right and left of the charts show the total buffer effect of the infusion both before and after sterilization, as do also the ratios expressed at the top of the lines. In comparing the length of the two lines representing the total progress on the Fuller's scale and on the P_H scale made by adding 60

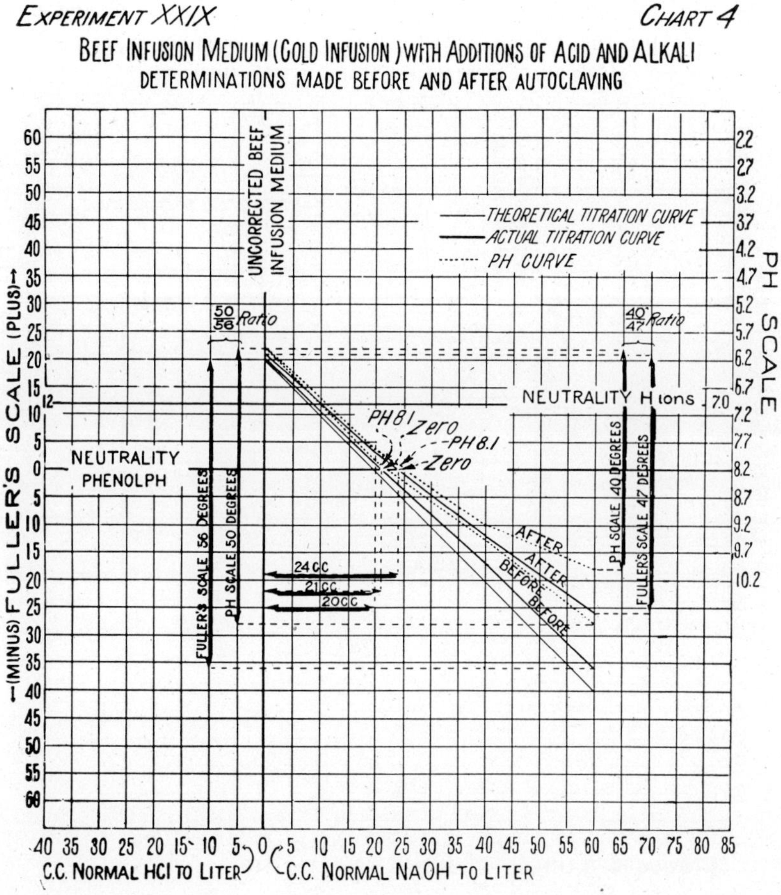

c.c. of normal alkali, we see that the two are more nearly of the same length in the case of the cold infusion than in that of the hot. Comparing the two ratios $\frac{40\ P_H}{47\ \text{Fuller}}$ and $\frac{37\ P_H}{47\ \text{Fuller}}$ we have the same thing expressed numerically. Either method brings out the fact that the P_H readings progress more slowly in proportion to the Fuller's scale readings in the hot infusion than in the cold, in other words, that the hot infusion has a slightly greater buffer effect than the cold. In case of this particular broth, the electrometric determination was P_H 8.14 at the phenolphthalein zero point.

In reference to the inner heavy vertical lines on the two charts, "P_H scale—50 degrees," etc., no confusion need result if it is remem-

EXPERIMENT XXIX *CHART 5*

BEEF INFUSION MEDIUM (HOT INFUSION B) WITH ADDITIONS OF ALKALI

DETERMINATIONS MADE BEFORE AND AFTER AUTOCLAVING

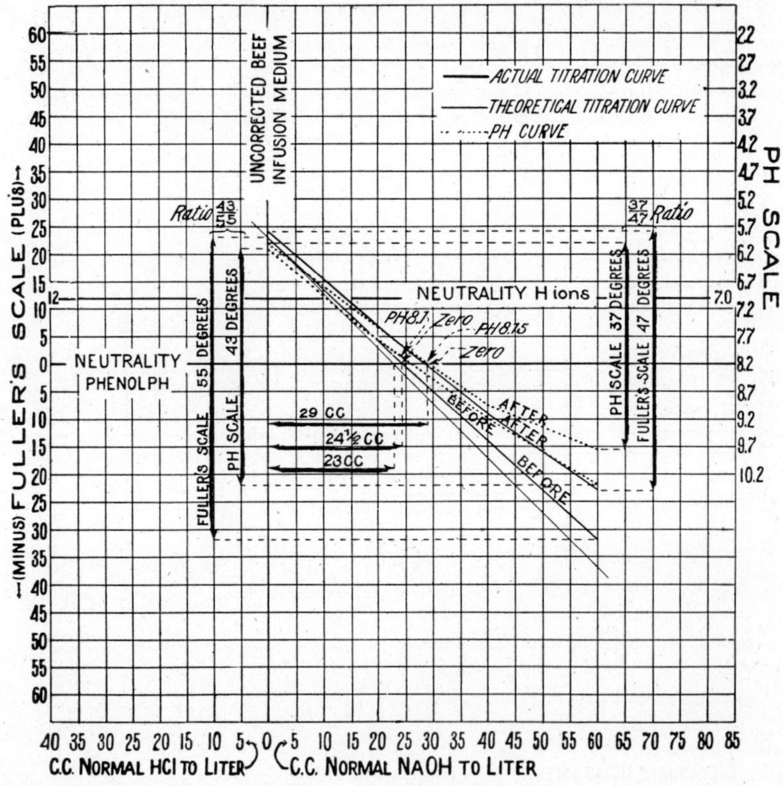

bered that 1 degree on this P_H scale = 1/10 P_H, as stated in the beginning (p. 19).

The true "buffer index," as the term is used by Brown,[25] may be computed readily for the two broths by noting the amount of alkali required to progress from one fixed point on the P_H curve to another,

[25] Jour. Bacteriol., 1921, 6, p. 555.

say P_H 6.0 to P_H 9.2. We find at once that 46 c c. are required in the case of the hot infusion and only 40 c c. in the case of the cold. The "buffer index," or "acid reserve," is therefore greater for the former than for the latter.

Exper. 30: Graded Series—Cold Infusion: Exper. 30 is a graded series made by adding normal acid and alkali in steps of 10 c c. to a cold infusion which had comparable P_H and Fuller's scale values before adjustment. Here the P_H and Fuller's scale curves are almost identical from P_H 4.2 to P_H 9.2 (chart 6). Only after we pass 20 c c. of normal

TABLE 14

EXPER. 30, FULLER'S SCALE AND P_H DETERMINATIONS ON 1% PEPTONE BEEF BROTH (COLD INFUSION*) WITH ADDITIONS OF NORMAL ACID AND ALKALI IN STEPS OF 10 C C. PER LITER

	C c. Added to 1 Liter (Nor. NaOH←0→Normal HCl)	Readings Made Same Day: Electrometric P_H	Readings Made Same Day: Colorimetric P_H	Titration Fuller's Scale: Calculated	Titration Fuller's Scale: Actual	Points of Error†: Between Actual and Calculated Fuller	Points of Error†: Between Colorimetric and Electrometric P_H	Readings Made 24 Hours after Sterilization: Fuller	Readings Made 24 Hours after Sterilization: Colorimetric P_H	Readings Made 1 Week after Sterilization: Fuller	Readings Made 1 Week after Sterilization: Colorimetric P_H
Normal HCl	30	3.82	4.0—	+44	+49	5	1	+47	4.0—	+51	4.5‡
	20	4.25	4.2+	+39	+40	0	1	+39	4.2	+42	4.4‡
	10	4.94	5.0	+33	+30	3	1	+29	5.0	+31	5.0
0	0	6.15	6.2—	+21	+21	0	0	+21	6.2—	+21	6 2—
Nor. NaOH	10	7.05	7.0+	+12	+12	0	1	+12	7.0—	—	—
	20	8.05	8.0	+ 2	+ 3	1	0	+ 3	8.0	+ 5	7.9
	30	8.72	8.8—	— 5	— 5	0	0	— 5	8.8—	— 2	8 4
	40	9.27	9.4	—11	—11	0	1	—10	9.2	— 6	9.0—
	50	9.71	9.6	—15	—20	5	1	—17	9.4	—11	9.4
	60	10.19	10.0	—20	—26	6	2	—23	9.6—	—16	9.6—

* Volume of water added in beginning, 2 times weight of beef. See p. 22.

† In comparing electrometric values with Fuller's scale, 5 or less in the hundredth's place was dropped; over 5 hundredths was considered as adding 1 to the tenth's place.

In comparing colorimetric P_H values with electrometric P_H values, the minus sign was interpreted as taking 0.1 from the here recorded value, and the plus sign as adding 0.1 to the recorded value.

‡ The two readings on the two scales are contradictory and one or the other (Fuller or P_H) is probably a misreading.

acid or 40 c c. of normal alkali per liter do we find any discrepancy between the two curves worthy of note. The table for exper. 30 shows the same hydrolysis phenomena as in exper. 28, with the additional fact that some increase in acidity takes place in the lower range even on standing 24 hours.

The "buffer index" is the same in this cold infusion as it was for the cold infusion of exper. 28, i. e., 40 c c. of normal alkali are required to progress from P_H 6.0 to P_H 9.2, when determinations made the same day the medium was autoclaved are taken as a basis for computing.

Exper. 31: Graded Series—Beef Extract Broth: Exper. 31 was planned (after some preliminary work) to carry a beef extract broth, in graded series, over about the same P_H range as had been covered in the case of the infusion broths. The broth was made with 0.3% Liebig's extract and 1% "Difco" peptone, and the additions of acid and alkali were made to the sterilized broth in steps of 5 c c. Table 15 gives the results.

The curves for beef extract broth were plotted on the same chart with those for cold infusions (exper. 31, chart 6) in order to bring

TABLE 15

EXPER. 31, FULLER'S SCALE AND PH DETERMINATIONS ON 1% PEPTONE BEEF EXTRACT BROTH WITH ADDITIONS OF NORMAL ACID AND ALKALI IN STEPS OF 5 C C. PER LITER

		Readings Made 24 Hours after Sterilization						Readings Made 1 Week after Sterilization	
						Points of Error Between			
	C c. Added to 1 Liter	Electrometric P_H	Colorimetric P_H	Fuller Calculated*	Fuller Actual	Actual and Calculated† Fuller	Colorimetric and Electrometric P_H	Colorimetric P_H	Fuller's Scale
Normal HCl	20	3.43	3.4	+48	+28	20	0	3.4	+29
	15	3.84	3.9	+44	+22	22	1	3.9	+24
	10	4.35	4.4	+39	+17	22	1	4.3	+18
	5	5.08	5.2	+31	+12	19	1	5.2	+13
←0→	0	6.7	6.7	+15	+ 8	7	0	6.7	+ 7
Nor. NaOH	5	7.87	7.8	− 5	+ 3	8	1	7.7	+ 4
	10	8.59	8.6	− 4	− 1	5	0	8.4	− 1
	15	9.08	9.5	− 9	− 6	3	4	9.0	− 4
	20	9.39	10.0	−12	−10	2	6	9.4	− 7

* Calculated from electrometric P_H.
† Note that the transferrence formulas cannot be used in case of beef extract.

out the contrast between the two. Note how precipitously the P_H curve of the extract broth moved on the addition of the first 5 c c. of acid or alkali and how it slows up on subsequent additions of either acid or alkali. Notice also that the whole direction of the P_H curve of the extract broth is entirely different from that of the P_H curve of the cold infusion, while the two titration curves are nearly parallel. In the extract broth, the widest discrepancy between the two curves (P_H and Fuller's scale) is found in the acid range, and the effect of adding acid to such a broth is strikingly brought out.

Comparing the "buffer index" of the two broths, we see that only 18.5 c c. of normal alkali are required to carry the beef extract broth from P_H 6.0 to P_H 9.2, as against 40 c c. for the infusion broth.

It is evident that the whole relationship of Fuller's scale values to P_H values is changed in beef extract medium, and that the formulas

EXPERIMENTS XXX AND XXXI — CHART 6

COMPARISON OF BEEF INFUSION (COLD) AND BEEF EXTRACT BOUILLON WITH ADDITIONS OF ACID AND ALKALI
DETERMINATIONS MADE DAY FOLLOWING STERILIZATION

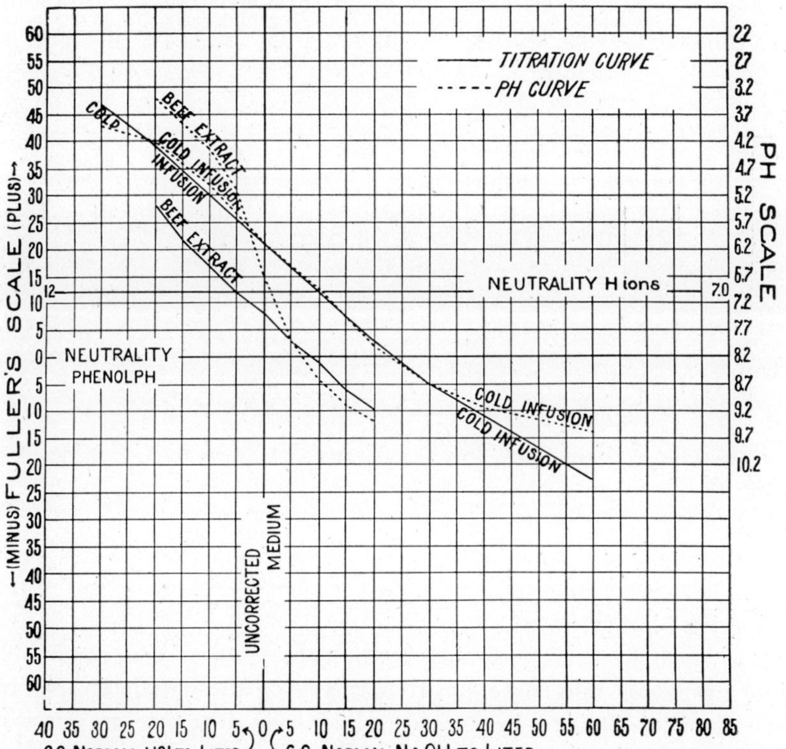

(p 20) cannot be used at all as a means of interpreting Fuller's scale readings in terms of P_H where beef extract medium is concerned.

Comment on the Foregoing Experiments: A comparison of all the experiments made on peptone beef infusion by addition of acid and alkali in graded series, as recorded in this paper (table 16), shows remarkable consistency between the values obtained and seems to prove beyond a doubt that uniform infusions, behaving in the same way toward additions of acid or alkali, can be prepared.

The difference in buffer effect between the hot and cold infusions is noteworthy only at the extremes, i. e., beyond the heavy horizontal lines marking the limits within which transposition is possible. Between these lines, with one exception, no greater error than 2 occurs in any series, whether hot or cold infusion is used—a discrepancy which is often found between colorimetric and electrometric determinations on the same material. A glance at the original tables from which table 16 was compiled (tables 11, 12, 13 and 14) will show that the average

TABLE 16

COMPARISON OF FULLER'S SCALE AND P_H VALUES IN 4 BEEF INFUSION SERIES

	C c. per Liter	Exper. 28 Hot Infusion A			Exper. 29 Hot Infusion B			Exper. 29 Cold Infusion			Exper. 30 Cold Infusion		
		Electrometric P_H	Fuller's Scale	Transposition Difference	Electrometric P_H	Fuller's Scale	Transposition Difference	Electrometric P_H	Fuller's Scale	Transposition Difference	Electrometric P_H	Fuller's Scale	Transposition Difference
HCl	30	4.0	+50	8	....	....	...	...	....	...	3.8	+49	5
HCl	20	4.5	+41	4	....	....	...	...	....	...	4.25	+40	0
HCl	10	5.2	+32	2	....	....	...	...	....	...	4.94	+30	3
NaOH←0→HCl	0	6.2	+22	2	6.0	+24	2	6.0	+21	1	6.15	+21	0
NaOH	10	6.9	+12	1	....	....	...	...	....	...	7.05	+12	0
NaOH	20	7.7	+ 5	0	7.55	+ 7	0	7.9	+ 3	0	8.05	+ 3	1
NaOH	30	8.4	— 3	1	....	....	...	...	....	...	8.7	— 5	0
NaOH	40	9.0	— 9	1	8.95	— 9	2	9.2	—12	2	9.3	—11	0
NaOH	50	9.4	—18	6	....	....	...	...	....	...	9.7	—20	5
NaOH	60	9.7	—25	10	9.75	—23	8	10.0	—26	8	10.2	—26	6

"error" is about the same between colorimetric and electrometric readings as between actual and calculated Fuller's scale readings, within the specified limits.

We conclude, therefore, that if comparable or nearly comparable values (Fuller's scale and P_H) are obtained on the initial broths—and these may be obtained by preparing the cold infusion as given on page 22 or the hot infusion as in "hot infusion B" (p. 21)—our formulas may be used between + 30 and — 10 Fuller's scale to obtain equivalent P_H values.

In making cold infusion, add water equal to 2 times the weight of the beef and make up to volume after filtering, or add water equal to 2½ times the weight of the beef in beginning, and do not make up to volume.

In making hot infusion, add water equal to 2½ times the weight of the beef and make up to volume after filtering.

Exper. 32: Graded Series of Beef Infusion Plus Gelatin and Agar: Exper. 32 was carried on to determine whether the values obtained on peptone beef infusions would hold good for the same broths plus the

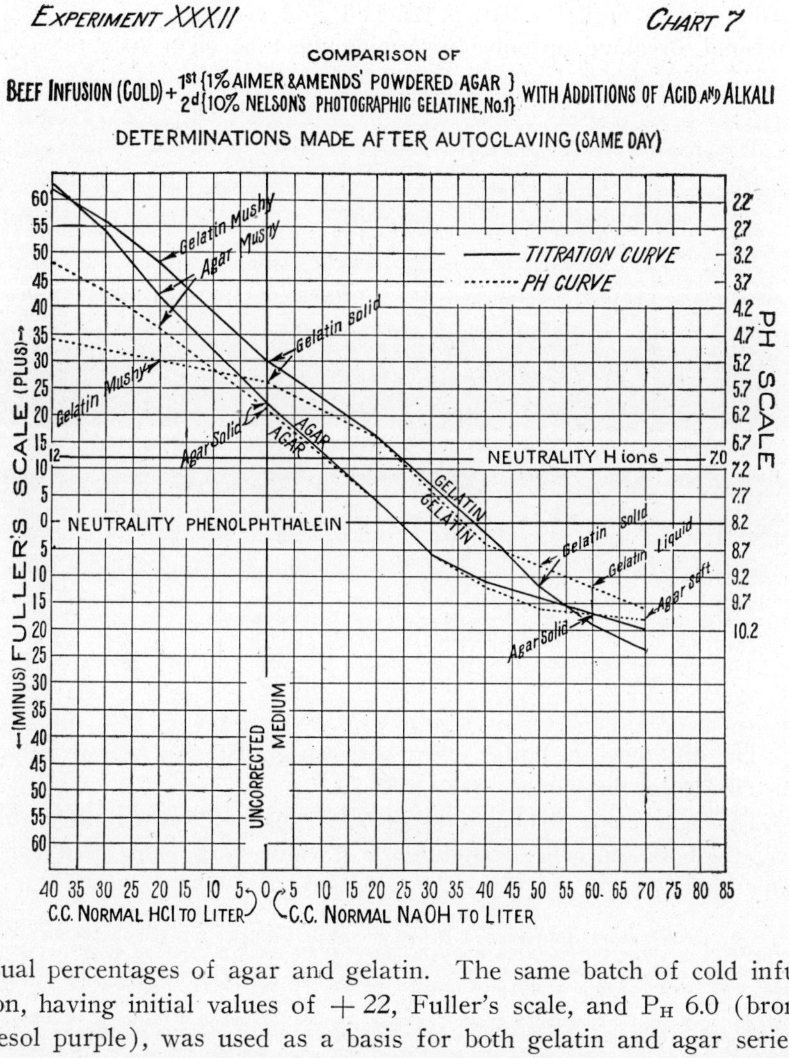

usual percentages of agar and gelatin. The same batch of cold infusion, having initial values of + 22, Fuller's scale, and P_H 6.0 (brom cresol purple), was used as a basis for both gelatin and agar series.

Ten per cent. of Nelson's photographic gelatin No. 1 was added to one half of the broth and 1% of Eimer and Amend's powdered agar to the other. They were steamed ½ hour, strained through cotton and then subdivided as usual for the addition of acid and alkali.

Gelatin begins to break down at about P_H 5.2 or between 5.6 and 5.2, and again between 9.0 and 9.4 P_H in the alkaline range. Agar evidently breaks down at about the same P_H acidity, i. e., between 6.1 and 4.6,[26] but does not begin to show signs of breaking down in the alkaline range until P_H 10.0 is reached, and even at this point it was semisolid, breaking up only on tapping the tube vigorously.

TABLE 17

EXPER. 32, FULLER'S SCALE AND PH DETERMINATIONS ON 1% PEPTONE BEEF INFUSION PLUS GELATIN AND AGAR WITH ADDITIONS OF ACID AND ALKALI. (READINGS MADE SAME DAY AS STERILIZED

C c. Normal NaOH←—0—→C c. Normal HCl

Beef Broth (Cold Infusion) + 10% Nelson's Photographic Gelatin No. 1							Same + 1% Eimer and Amend's Powdered Agar		
C c. Added to 1 Liter	Fuller's Scale	Colorimetric P_H	State of Medium after Two 15 Min. Steamings		State of Medium after Autoclaving		Fuller's Scale	Colorimetric P_H	State of Medium after Autoclaving
			Ice Box 15 C.	Room 22 C.	Ice Box 15 C.	Room 22 C.			
40	+62	4.8	Solid	Liquid, thin	Solid	Liquid, thin	+63	3.4	Liquid
30	+56	5.0	Solid	Liquid, thin	Solid	Liquid, thin	+54	3.9	Semiliquid
20	+48	5.2	Solid	Mushy	Solid	Liquid, thin	+42	4.6	Mushy
Unadjusted	+30	5.6	Solid	Solid, firm	Solid	Liquid, thick	+22	6.1	Solid
20	+16	6.6	Solid	Solid, firm	Solid	Solid, shaky	+ 4	7.8	Solid
30	+ 7	7.6	Solid	Solid, firm	Solid	Mushy	— 6	8.8	Solid
40	— 2	8.6	Solid	Solid, firm	Solid	Mushy	—11	9.4	Solid
50	—12	9.0	Solid	Solid, shaky	Solid	Liquid, thick	—14	9.8	Solid
60	—19	9.4	Solid	Liquid, thick	Solid	Liquid, thin	—17	9.9	Solid
70	—24	9.8	Solid	Liquid, thin	Solid	Liquid, thin	—20	10.0	Solid, soft

The difference in buffer effect between gelatin and agar is brought out clearly by the curves (see chart 7).

The agar evidently has very little, if any, additional buffer effect over the bouillon, hence transference of values is possible between the same limits.

[26] In another series, 1% agar was found to remain solid on the addition of 10 c c. of normal HCl per liter, P_H 5.4, while it was semisolid at P_H 5.0. A paper by Wolf and Shunk, J. Bacteriol., 1921, 6, p. 325, describes a method of adding acid and alkali to agar and gelatin under cold sterile conditions at concentrations far beyond the limits of growth of any plant pathogenic organism. This might be valuable to workers desiring to find the limits of acid tolerance for organisms having a greater tolerance or not well adapted to liquid mediums, for it will be seen from our data that both agar and gelatin break down in the acid range just before or just at the critical point for some organisms when the medium is sterilized after the acid has been added. In the alkaline range, however, agar remains solid beyond the limits of all the plant parasites tested and in gelatin below the limits of many.

Gelatin, on the other hand, has quite a strong buffer effect, as has been pointed out by Clark,[12] but even here the formula may be applied from + 20 to zero, Fuller's scale, which would naturally be the most useful range.

Exper. 33: Nitrate and Salt Broths: The addition of 1% potassium nitrate to peptone beef infusion does not change the P_H or the Fuller's scale readings.

Example: Beef broth no. 10,306.................... + 13 P_H 6.8
Beef broth no. 10,306 + 1% KNO_3....... + 13 P_H 6.8

The addition of sodium chloride seemed to cause a slight alkalinity as measured by Fuller's scale, but showed no change in P_H as determined by colorimetric tests. Several trials showed about the same grading as is given in table 18.

TABLE 18
RESULTS OF ADDITION OF SODIUM CHLORIDE TO BEEF BROTH

Beef broth No. 10306	+13	P_H 6.8
Beef broth No. 10306 + ½% NaCl	+13	P_H 6.8
Beef broth No. 10306 + 1% NaCl	+13	P_H 6.8
Beef broth No. 10306 + 2% NaCl	+12	P_H 6.8
Beef broth No. 10306 + 3% NaCl	+12	P_H 6.8
Beef broth No. 10306 + 4% NaCl	+11	P_H 6.8
Beef broth No. 10306 + 5% NaCl	+11	P_H 6.8

SECTION 4

GROWTH OF BACTERIAL PLANT PARASITES IN 1% PEPTONE BEEF INFUSION WITH ADDITIONS OF HYDROCHLORIC ACID AND SODIUM HYDROXIDE

The following charts show the behavior of 26 plant pathogens tested in 1% peptone beef broth (hot infusion A) with additions of HCl or NaOH. The relative arrangement of the two scales in these charts is the one on which transposition of values is based, while the blocks themselves represent actual determinations, that is, the limits of growth of organisms in mediums both titrated and P_H tested. Charts 8 and 9 bring out clearly the limits of acidity and alkalinity which the various organisms tested will tolerate in 1% peptone beef infusion as measured by the two scales (see also tables 19 and 20). Since the medium was graded in steps of 5 c c. additions of acid or alkali per liter, the exact "critical point" could not be determined for each organism. In chart 8 the blocks were extended by dotted lines in the case of the white blocks and by half-tinted sections in the case of the black blocks, to indicate the values of the next grades of broth in which no growth appeared.

CHART 8

SHOWING RANGE OF GROWTH OF 10 BACTERIAL PLANT PARASITES BY FULLER'S SCALE AND BY PH DETERMINATIONS.

(PH VALUES WERE DETERMINED BY MEANS OF THE POTENTIOMETER)

[hatched] [dotted] SHOW VALUES OBTAINED FOR THE NEXT GRADE OF BOUILLON IN WHICH THE ORGANISM WAS INOCULATED BUT DID NOT GROW.

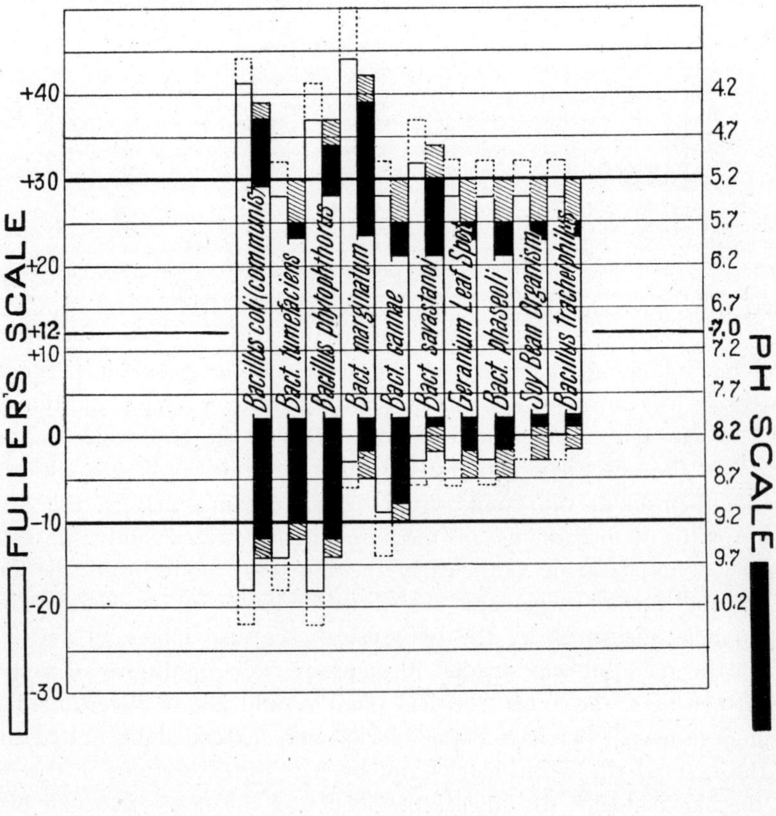

CHART 9

SHOWING RANGE OF GROWTH OF 18 BACTERIAL PLANT PARASITES BY FULLER'S SCALE AND BY PH DETERMINATIONS.

(PH DETERMINATIONS WERE MADE COLORIMETRICALLY)

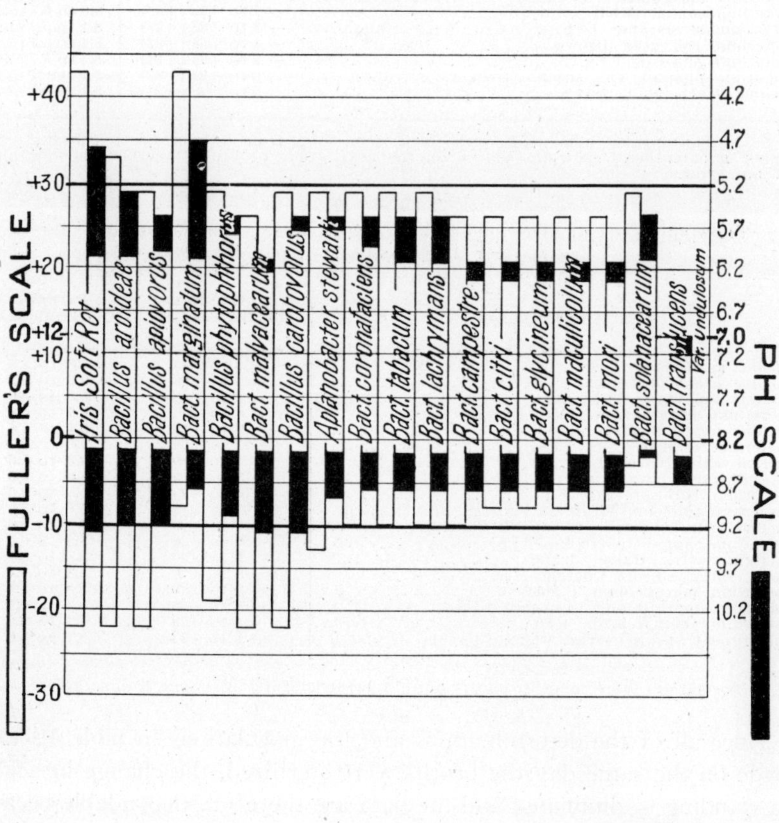

We note at once, in spite of the fact that the blocks representing P_H and Fuller's scale ranges for the same organism sometimes show considerable discrepancy in their lengths, the organisms having long titration ranges always have comparatively long P_H ranges, and those having short titration ranges always have comparatively short P_H ranges.

TABLE 19*

SHOWING RANGES OF 10 PLANT PATHOGENS IN 1% PEPTONE BEEF BROTH (HOT INFUSION A). SEE CHART 8

Name of Organism	Titration Range (Fuller's Scale)	P_H Range (Potentiometer)
Bacillus coli (Escher.) Migula	—18 to +41 (+44)	9.4 to 4.5 (4.3)
Bacterium tumefaciens Sm. and T.	—14 to +28 (+32)	9.2 to 5.7 (5.2)
Bacillus phytophthorus Appel	—18 to +37 (+41)	9.4 to 4.8 (4.5)
Bacterium marginatum L. McC.	— 3 to +44 (+50)	8.4 to 4.3 (4.0)
Bacterium cannae MKB	— 9 to +28 (+32)	9.0 to 5.7 (5.2)
Bacterium savastanoi EFS	— 3 to +32 (+37)	8.1 to 5.2 (4.8)
Bacterium pelargoni Brown	— 3 to +28 (+32)	8.4 to 5.7 (5.2)
Bacterium phaseoli EFS	— 3 to +28 (+32)	8.4 to 5.7 (5.2)
Bacterium phaseoli var. sojense Hedges	0 to +28 (+32)	8.1 to 5.7 (5.2)
Bacillus tracheiphilus EFS	0 to +28 (+32)	8.1 to 5.7 (5.2)

* The inoculations were made with one 3 mm. loop from 24-hour broth cultures. The figures in parentheses show the values on the next grade of broth in which the organisms did not grow.

TABLE 20

SHOWING RANGE OF GROWTH OF 18 PLANT PATHOGENS IN 1% PEPTONE BEEF BROTH (HOT INFUSION A).* SEE CHART 9

Name of Organism	Titration Range (Fuller's Scale)	P_H Range (Clarke and Lubs' Scale)
Bacillus sp. (Iris soft rot)	—22 to +43	9.3 to 4.8
Bacillus aroideae Towns	—22 to +33	9.2 to 5.3
Bacillus apiovorus Wormald	—22 to +29	9.2 to 5.6
Bacterium marginatum L.McC.	— 8 to +43	8.8 to 4.8
Bacillus phytophthorus Appel	—19 to +29	9.1 to 5.6
Bacterium malvacearum EFS	—22 to +26	9.3 to 6.1
Bacillus carotovorus LRJ	—22 to +29	9.3 to 5.6
Aplanobacter stewarti (EFS) L.McC.	—13 to +29	8.9 to 5.6
Bacterium coronafaciens Elliott	—10 to +29	8.8 to 5.6
Bacterium tabacum Wolf and Foster	—10 to +29	8.8 to 5.6
Bacterium lachrymans Sm. and Bryan	—10 to +29	8.8 to 5.6
Bacterium campestre (Pam.) EFS	—10 to +26	8.8 to 6.1
Bacterium citri (Hasse) Jehle	— 8 to +26	8.8 to 6.1
Bacterium glycineum Coerper	— 8 to +26	8.8 to 6.1
Bacterium maculicolum L.McC.	— 8 to +26	8.8 to 6.1
Bacterium mori B and L emend. EFS	— 8 to +26	8.8 to 6.1
Bacterium solanacearum EFS	— 3 to +29	8.4 to 5.6
Bacterium translucens var. undulosum Sm. J. and R.	— 5 to +12	8.7 to 7.0

* Inoculations were made from 24-hour-old broth cultures with one 3 mm. loop.

Since all of the determinations and the inoculations in table 19 were made on the same day the broths were sterilized, the change in acidity on standing is eliminated and the data are therefore dependable because no record of growth appearing after the second day was accepted for any given grade of broth below the phenolphthalein zero.

The fact that the P_H determinations included in table 20 were only colorimetric makes the values less dependable than the figures in table 19, especially in the extreme alkaline range covered by the thymol

CHART 10. SHOWING RELATION BETWEEN FULLER'S SCALE AND PH VALUES WITHIN RANGE OF GROWTH OF BACILLUS PHYTOPHTHORUS

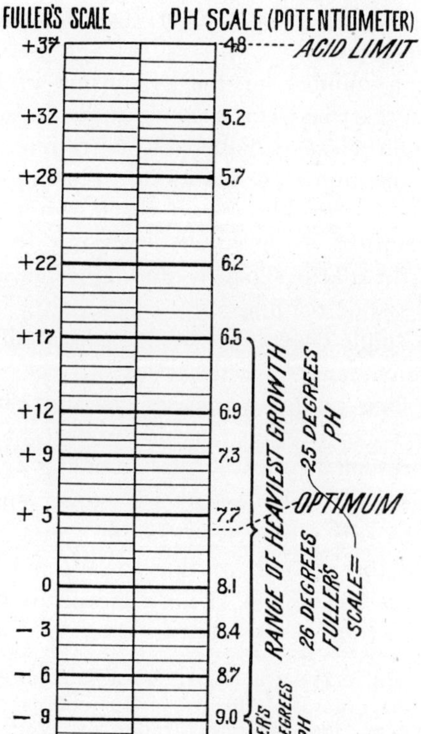

blue boric acid series. Neither tests on medium nor inoculations were made the same day the broths were sterilized, but extended over a period of several days. The ranges, however, are approximately correct. Some variation on the part of the organism is to be expected.

The organisms shown on chart 8, table 19, were a representative group of plant parasitic bacteria, including those known to have either unusually short or unusually long ranges.

Chart 9 and table 20 represent a test of the acid and alkali tolerance of a larger number of plant organisms, including 2 of the first group.

A survey of the two charts brings out the fact that a majority of the ranges (15 out of the 26) fall entirely within the transposition limits, i. e., the line drawn through + 30 and its equivalent P_H 5.2 and that drawn through — 10 and its equivalent P_H 9.2, while only 7 strongly project beyond these lines.

The fact that a number of the organisms in both charts grow beyond the limits prescribed for transposition of values need not disturb the worker who wishes to adhere to tritration methods in adjusting beef infusion mediums by additions of acid or alkali, since its strong buffer content holds the P_H in check, while the Fuller's scale values slightly outrun the P_H in either direction. In the critical region for the organism, the alarm signal is thus given in a more compelling way by the Fuller's scale readings.

Let us select a single organism, for the sake of illustration, Bacillus phytophthorus, which causes a widespread soft rot of the Irish potato, and which has a long range so that its P_H and Fuller's scale blocks show a wide discrepancy in their alkaline limits (chart 8).

If now we represent the two blocks (standing for P_H and Fuller's scale ranges diagrammatically as of the same length but with the degrees on each having relatively different values, a clearer picture may be formed of the relation of that organism to titratable acidity as compared with its relation to H-ion concentration.

An explanation of chart 10 follows:

A Fuller's scale with degrees of equal value was constructed covering the titration range of this organism's growth from — 18 to + 37. The Fuller's scale determinations on the different grades of broth in which *Bacillus phytophthorus* grew (see exper. 28, table 11) were noted on this scale and from these points heavy horizontal lines were ruled to intersect the companion block representing its P_H range (P_H 9.4 to P_H 4.8). The actual P_H readings as determined by the potentiometer were recorded opposite the corresponding titration values. The spaces between the heavy lines in the P_H block were then divided into as many equal parts as there were P_H "degrees" or tenths of P_H between one recorded P_H value and the next.

Note how strikingly comparable the values are within the range of best growth. Below this point 1 degree on the P_H scale is comparable to 2¼ degrees on the Fuller's scale. In other words, if P_H methods are used as various persons have recommended for bacteriologic work, we must have a much more coarsely graded scale, so to speak, in this part of the range if we are using the colorimetric system, and those who are familiar with the thymol blue boric acid series know that the color gradations are often difficult to distinguish in practice even in steps of 0.2 P_H on which the Clarke and Lubs' scale is constructed. This fact together with the possibility of inaccuracy of the boric acid buffer mixtures themselves makes it easily possible to have an error of from 2 to 4 degrees in this part of the colorimetric P_H scale. This would mean an error of from 5 to 10 degrees on Fuller's scale (see chart 10). Even 5 degrees on Fuller's scale is a difference which could not escape detection with careful titrimetric work, for instance, in preparing a graded series of broths.

The inference is that after passing the point at which this organism begins to be hampered by increase in alkalinity of the medium (— 9 or P_H 9.0) the danger point may be detected with more definiteness and greater accuracy by the titration method than by the colorimetric.

It is only when we are dealing with mediums in which the buffer content is low as compared with beef infusion and the P_H acidity or alkalinity increases at a more rapid rate than the titratable acidity or alkalinity, a point well illustrated by the curves for beef extract broth (see page 43), that there is danger in using the older titration method in preference to H-ion concentration methods.

It follows, therefore, that the titration method of determining the reaction of mediums based on peptone beef infusion is not illogical and unusable as Clark [12] and others, including the Committee on Methods of the Society of American Bacteriologists,[9] have claimed. On the contrary, it is justifiable to continue this method within the limits here assigned, when so desired, for reasons both of simplicity and economy.

In order to determine the best reaction of beef broth for the growth of plant organisms, a study of the complete records was made. Table 21, in which minus (—) means no growth, plus (+)slight growth, and (+ +) good growth, is a sample of the way in which all the records were kept.

Table 22 shows the limits of heaviest growth for each organism and the assumed optima, obtained by finding the mean between these limits.

The data in the preceding table should not be taken as final but as a guide to further experimentation, since it represents only a single trial for each organism, and only one tube was used for each grade of broth. Inoculations in all cases were made with a 3-mm. loop from 24-hour-old broth cultures.

TABLE 21

Sample Record Sheet, Showing Growth of Bacterium Cannae MKB in Graded Series (Hot Infusion A)

Normal NaOH←0→Normal HCl: C c. Added to 1 Liter	Titration Fuller's Scale	Electrometric P_H	Growth: 24 Hours	48 Hours	1 Week	2 Weeks
40	+60	3.7	—	—	—	—
35	+54	3.8	—	—	—	—
30	+50	4.0	—	—	—	—
25	+44	4.3	—	—	—	—
20	+41	4.5	—	—	—	—
15	+37	4.8	—	—	—	—
10	+32	5.2	—	—	—	—
5	+28	5.7	+	+	++	++
0	+22	6.2	+	++	++	++
5	+17	6.5	+	++	++	++
10	+12	6.9	+	++	++	++
15	+ 9	7.3	+	++	++	++
20	+ 5	7.7	+	+	+	++
25	0	8.1	+	+	+	++
30	— 3	8.4	+	+	+	++
35	— 6	8.7	+	+	+	++
40	— 9	9.0	+	+	+	++
45	—14	9.2	—	—	+	++
50	—18	9.4	—	—	—	—
55	—22	9.6	—	—	—	—
60	—25	9.7	—	—	—	—
65	—30	9.9	—	—	—	—
70	—32	10.1	—	—	—	—
75	—38	10.2	—	—	—	—
80	—40	10.4	—	—	—	—
85	—44	10.6	—	—	—	—

TABLE 22

Showing Range of Best Growth of Organisms in 1% Peptone Beef Infusion Broth by Fuller's Scale and Ph

Name of Organism	Limits of Best Growth P_H	Mean P_H	Limits of Best Growth Titration (Fuller's Scale)	Mean (Fuller's Scale)
B. sp. (iris soft rot)	6.8 - 7.3	7.1	+13 to + 7	+10
B. coli (Escher) Mig	4.8 - 9.2	7.0	+37 to —14	+12
Bact. tumefaciens (Sm. & T.) (hop strain)	5.7 - 9.0	7.3	+28 to — 9	+10
B. phytophthorus Appel (Ap-I)	6.5 - 9.0	7.7	+17 to — 9	+ 4
B. aroideae Towns	5.3 - 9.2	7.2	+33 to —22	+ 5
Bact. savastanoi EFS	6.3 - 7.6	6.9	+25 to + 7	+15
Bact. marginatum L.McC.	6.5 - 8.1	7.3	+17 to 0	+ 8
B. apiovorus Wormald	5.6 - 8.7	7.1	+29 to — 5	+12
B. carotovorus LRJ	6.1 - 8.2	7.1	+26 to 0	+13
Bact. cannae MKB	6.2 - 7.3	6.7	+23 to + 9	+16
Bact. malvacearum EFS	6.7 - 7.0	6.8	+15 to +12	+13
Apl. stewarti (EFS) L.McC	5.6 - 7.0	6.3	+29 to +12	+20
Bact. coronafaciens Elliott	6.1 - 7.3	6.7	+26 to + 7	+16
Bact. tabacum Wolf & Foster	6.8 - 7.6	7.2	+13 to + 5	+ 9
Bact. lachrymans Sm. & Bryan	6.1 - 7.6	6.8	+26 to + 5	+16
Bact. pelargoni Brown	6.5 - 8.1	7.3	+17 to 0	+ 8
Bact. campestre (Pam.) EFS	7.2 - 7.6	7.4	+ 8 to + 5	+ 6
Bact. citri (Hasse) Jehle	6.1 - 7.2	6.6	+26 to + 8	+17
Bact. glycineum Coerper	6.1 - 8.1	7.1	+26 to + 1	+13
Bact. maculicolum L.McC	7.1 - 7.3	7.2	+10 to + 7	+ 8
Bact. mori B & L emend. EFS	6.7 - 7.1	6.9	+15 to +10	+12
Bact. solanacearum EFS	6.1 - 7.3	6.7	+26 to + 7	+16
Bact. phaseoli EFS	6.5 - 8.1	7.3	+17 to 0	+ 8
Bact. phaseoli var. sojense Hedges	6.5 - 8.1	7.3	+17 to 0	+ 9
B. tracheiphilus EFS	6.5 - 7.3	6.9	+17 to + 9	+13
Bact. translucens var. undulosum Sm. J. & R.	7.2 - 7.6	7.4	+ 8 to + 5	+ 6
Average	....	7.05	....	+11.34

Twelve organisms (table 22 last column) have means falling below + 12, + 4 being the lowest, while 14 have means at + 12 or higher, + 20 being the highest. It will be seen that the mean for the majority (18 out of 26) falls between + 9 and + 20, i. e., a few degrees either way from H-ion neutrality.

Note that the average mean of the Fuller's scale readings (+ 11.34) and the average mean of the P_H readings (7.05), given at the end of the table, are almost equivalent values (see page 20, table 4).

We conclude, therefore, that beef infusion mediums should be adjusted to about + 12 or P_H 7.0 in order to meet the average requirement for the growth of plant disease bacteria.

SECTION 5

GENERAL CONCLUSIONS

The experiments described in this paper have made it clear that a striking parallelism exists between the rate of progress made on the P_H scale (representing free hydrogen-ions) and on Fuller's scale (representing titratable acidity) when acid or alkali are added to 1% peptone beef infusion broth. This makes it possible, within the limits prescribed, to translate Fuller's scale values into P_H values.

The great expense, or great labor, involved in maintaining an accurate set of buffer solutions makes the colorimetric method at present a much more difficult one to apply than the titration method. Since both are optical methods, dependent on the use of indicators and normal solutions, the one is liable to as much inaccuracy as the other. It seems justifiable, therefore, to adhere to the older method in determining the reaction of beef infusion mediums.

The colorimetric method is most valuable, perhaps, for determining changes brought about by growing organisms in culture mediums on account of the rapidity with which the tests may be made and the ease with which the eye can make comparative estimates in a long series, but even here chemical methods are necessary to determine total product formed. And in any event all are not agreed, for F. S. Jones [27] in a recent paper dealing with the production of acids by streptococci in culture mediums concludes that:

> From these experiments one is inclined to believe that titration is equally as satisfactory as the newer method for the study of the fermentive activity of streptococci.

[27] Jour. Exper. Med., 1920, 32, p. 273.

There are already several kinds of buffer mixtures on the market, and a number of more or less valuable adaptations of the colorimetric method have been worked out.[28]

Tentative work with plant decoctions and plant juices which form the natural habitat of parasitic organisms has shown that in some cases, at least, a different relationship exists between H-ion concentration and titratable acidity from that found in beef infusion broth, though titratable acidity was always found to vary in the same direction as the P_H acidity.

Haas[29] has done some interesting and valuable work along this line using electrode methods to determine "total acidity" in correlating the latter with P_H. He finds that the "total acidity" tends to fluctuate in the same direction as the "actual acidity."

That it is also possible to titrate correctly some plant juices, using phenolphthalein as an indicator, has been demonstrated in our laboratory. This was done by first centrifuging the expressed juice to remove part of the chlorophyll and then titrating it in capsule with n/20 NaOH without heating. A striking agreement of results was obtained when chemical titrations of certain freshly extracted plant juices (wheat seedlings) were compared with electrometric titrations made at the same time by a worker in another laboratory.

If, as has been found at times, slight or no appreciable differences in P_H are correlated with striking differences in titratable acidity, may it not be possible that the latter rather than the former is the important factor in the study of a given phenomenon? On the other hand, there are cases in which the P_H values are the striking and therefore probably the important things. Until much more work has been done along these lines, it does not seem fair to conclude that hydrogen-ion concentration is the all important phase of acidity as applied to pathologic bacteriology, nor that the titration methods must be discarded from bacteriology. It is evident that both titratable acidity and hydrogen-ion concentration are important in the study of biologic phenomena.

SUMMARY

A uniform method must be used in the preparation of peptone beef infusion broth if titratable acidity is to be interpreted in terms of P_H. Beef extracts cannot be used.

[28] Medalia, Leon S.: Jour. Bacteriol., 1920, 5, p. 441; Gillespie, Louis J.: Soil Science, 1920, 9, p. 115; Barnett, George D., and Chapman, Herbert S.: Jour. Am. Med. Assn., 1918, 70, p. 1062; Gillespie, Louis J.: Jour. Bacteriol., 1921, 6, p. 399; Michaelis, L.: Deutsch. med. Wchnschr., 1921, 47, p. 465; Chem. Abst., 1922, 16, p. 1101.

[29] Soil Science, 1920, 9, p. 341.

Fuller's scale values may be translated into P_H values by means of the formula incorporated in the text (p. 20), provided beef infusion is prepared as a cold infusion (p. 22) by adding water equal to 2 times the weight of the beef, or as a hot infusion B (p. 21) by adding water equal to 2½ times the weight of the beef, making up to volume after filtering in either case.

In titrating mediums, the carefully standardized methods described in this paper under technic, are as essential to consistent results as are accurate methods in making colorimetric P_H or electrometric determinations.

If P_H equivalents are to be obtained for Fuller's scale values as on p. 20, our directions for titrating should be followed, and the first "faint but distinct pink" reaction (see color chart) must be chosen as the end point. Too much emphasis cannot be placed on the necessity of a consistent choice of color in determining the end point in phenolphthalein titrations. A deep pink should never be used. Since the lithographer has used a fugitive color (Eosin Blush), the color chart must be carefully protected from the light. The present color of no. 3 is about one-half as deep as Ridgway's Cameo Pink, and no. 4 about his Venetian Pink. If Ridgway's first edition is used, no. 4 is approximately his Rose Pink and no. 3 one-half or one-third that deep.

If the methods herein recommended for the preparation and the titration of beef infusion medium are followed, the medium may be adjusted by the addition of acid or alkali over a range broad enough to cover almost any need of the plant or animal pathologist and titratable values transposed to P_H values by means of the formula.

In order to reach any given Fuller's scale value in finished, i. e., autoclaved beef infusion broth, an excess amount of alkali above the calculated quantity must be added to make up for the loss due to the buffer effect of the broth and the changes brought about by heating. To avoid the necessity of readjusting, the required excess may be readily ascertained by referring to the charts and the whole amount necessary added in the beginning. This excess will be the distance horizontally, i. e., the number of c c. of normal NaOH between the desired titrimetric point or degree of Fuller's scale and the theoretical titration line. Within the limits defined by + 30 and — 10 any Fuller's scale value thus arrived at will have an approximate P_H "equivalent."

The fact that the titration curve as based on sterilized mediums does not coincide with the theoretical titration curve based on the number of c c. of alkali added, should be carefully noted. Confusion has arisen in the minds of many persons because of a failure to make this distinction and because of an assumption that the number of c c. added represents actual titratable values.

Additions of large amounts of alkali to beef infusion cause markedly unstable mediums. Such mediums gradually become more acid on standing after sterilization. This is true whether the reaction is measured by titration or P_H determination. Mediums liable to become more acid on standing should be used at once, and statements as to the age of such medium should accompany all special experiments.

So far as tested, the same relation of scales (see p. 20) holds good for all standard mediums based on a 1% peptone beef infusion with the exception of gelatin in the extreme ranges especially on the acid side.

When 1% Eimer and Amend's powdered agar is added to peptone beef infusion broth, the agar may be adjusted by the addition of acid or alkali with practically the same resulting reactions (Fuller's scale and P_H), as obtained for the broth alone. Hence the same rules may be applied.

One per cent. agar does not solidify firmly when autoclaved in the presence of more than 10 c c. normal HCl per liter (giving a P_H value of 5.2 to 5.4) but will stand 60 c c. of normal NaOH giving a P_H value of about 9.8.

When 10% Nelson's photographic gelatin No. 1 is added to the broth, it exerts a considerable buffer effect, and the rules for transference of values can be applied only between zero and + 20 Fuller's scale.

The tests made showed 10% gelatin breaking down after sterilization by steam at about the same P_H in the acid range as the agar but not tolerating as much alkali, breaking down at 60 c c. normal NaoH per liter or P_H 9.4.

The greatest degree of acidity tolerated by any organism tested was + 44 (Fuller's scale), and P_H 4.3.

The greatest degree of alkalinity tolerated by any organism tested was — 22 (Fuller's scale) and P_H 9.4.

A consideration of the optima for all the organisms tested, obtained by finding the median points between limits of best growth, gave an average mean of + 11.3 Fuller's scale and P_H 7.05 (nearly equivalent values).

Thus the correction of beef broth to H-ion neutrality (P_H 7.0) or + 12 Fuller's scale leaves the medium at a point favorable to the growth of the majority of plant pathogenic bacteria, and the time-honored custom of adjusting beef broth to a point "slightly acid to phenolphthalein" (+ 10 to + 15) appears entirely justifiable.

The same principles which govern the correction of beef infusion mediums do not apply to beef extract mediums, for in order to adjust the latter to + 15, acid must be added. This brings the P_H proportionately much higher, owing no doubt to the absence of certain buffer substances in the extract which are present in the infusion. The fact that beef infusion is so rich in natural buffers makes it an especially valuable medium for bacteriologic work. That this fact is not always understood is plain from a statement made by Meacham, Hopfield and Acree, who class beef among the "usual unbuffered culture media." If beef extract is meant, it is not so stated.[30] The data here presented show clearly its adaptability to adjustment with acid or alkali without bringing about too great a concentration of the hydrogen-ions (acid) or the hydroxyl-ions (alkali) for the well being of the organism. The fact that beef extract broth is not so well buffered may be one reason why it has been abandoned by many for medical work. The adjustment of beef extract medium is an instance in which knowledge of the P_H value is undoubtedly useful.

Fuller's scale readings on beef infusion mediums made as recommended in this paper may be converted into P_H readings within the prescribed limits (+ 30 to — 10) by means of the following formula in which F is the Fuller's scale reading.

Formula: $8.2 - \frac{F}{10} = P_H$.

Within the limits defined by P_H 5.2 and P_H 9.2, P_H readings may be converted into Fuller's scale readings by a second formula as follows:

Formula: $10\ (8.2 - P_H) = F$.

[30] Jour. Bacteriol., 1920, 5, p. 491.

EXPERIMENTAL STUDIES ON INFECTION AND IMMUNITY IN TYPHUS

E. Weil and F. Breinl

From Department of Hygiene, German University, Prague

The following experiments were made to study the nature of infection and immunity in typhus fever. Questions of etiology, especially everything relating to Rickettsia prowazeki, were not considered. Most of our experiments were made on guinea-pigs, the rest on rabbits. Unfortunately, we had no monkeys. We owe the possibility of studying typhus experimentally to Nicolle and to Gaviño and Girard, whose fundamental discoveries enabled them to transmit the virus from typhus patients to guinea-pigs. The animals reacted after a period of latency of 1-2 weeks with fever of an average duration of a week and loss of weight, but they completely recovered. The virus could be transferred by the blood of infected animals as long as they had fever, and produced again the same symptoms. After the first infection, the animals became immunized against a new injection of the virus. Various authors mention that after the injection of blood from patients, only some guinea-pigs develop fever, which statement is corroborated by us. These negative cases, however, are not caused by a natural resistance of the animals, but by the small quantity of virus in the blood. The passage of the virus from animal to animal is, according to Landsteiner's suggestion, best effected by using a brain emulsion, in which case the infection is successful every time. We always used this method in our work. Dörr showed that the rabbit is susceptible to typhus virus; this animal, when infected with virulent guinea-pig brain, gives no outward signs of disease, and successful infection can only be proved by transmitting the virus or by demonstrating the immunity which follows the infection. Weil and Felix showed that two weeks after the infection agglutinins against the bacillus OX19 are present in the rabbits' blood. This did away with the doubt as to the nature of animal typhus, expressed by Friedberger, by showing that the same antigen is the cause of animal and human typhus.

Nicolle's discovery of infection not manifested by any symptoms was of the utmost importance. He was able to show that typhus

Received for publication, April 2, 1923.

infection in guinea-pigs can run its course without any fever. The presence of the virus in this case can be proved only by transmission to another animal.

In the following experiments, two strains were used (virus 1 and 2), which have been cultivated in guinea-pigs for several years. The transmission of the virus is effected in the following manner: On the fourth day after the beginning of the fever, the guinea-pig is bled from the carotid, the brain is removed asceptically and emulsified in 20 c c. of physiologic salt solution. One c c. of this emulsion is injected intraperitoneally into a fresh animal. With this procedure fever sets in as follows, according to the results in 379 passage animals:

In 5 days after the injection in 11% of the animals.
In 6 days after the injection in 63% of the animals.
In 7 days after the injection in 25% of the animals.
In 8 days after the injection in 1% of the animals.

In 99% of the cases the fever appeared within 7 days after the infection. The average period of latency is thus 6.11 days. If an animal has fever before the end of the fifth day after injection, this is certainly due to a nonspecific complication. If the period of latency is longer than 8 days, it shows that the quantity of virus was smaller than that which is contained in 1/20 of a brain, as will be shown later. Even after infection with a whole brain, the average period of latency is as long as after using 1/20 of a brain. The fever lasts 7-9 days, a duration of 5 days being a rare exception. The fever curve varies little, and usually the temperature rises only 1-1.5 C. above normal. In taking the temperature, attention must be paid to the fact that the normal winter temperature of the animals when fed with hay and turnips is lower than the summer temperature when fed with cabbages, grass, etc. As long as winter food is given, 39.1 C. can be considered as normal. When summer food is given, the normal temperature rises to 39.6 C.

Our aim was to ascertain the quantity of virus contained in the brain and blood at various times after the infection. For this purpose the brain of an animal which has been infected with 1/20 of a brain is diluted with 10 c c. of physiologic salt solution and pressed through a fine wire sieve. With this emulsion, further dilutions of 1:100, 1:1,000, etc., are made. Five guinea-pigs are injected with 1 c c. of each dilution, and their temperatures controlled during 3 weeks.

As illustration we give Charts 1 and 2. The brain was studied three days after inoculation. The thick horizontal line drawn at 39.6 C. shows the limit of the normal temperature — this experi-

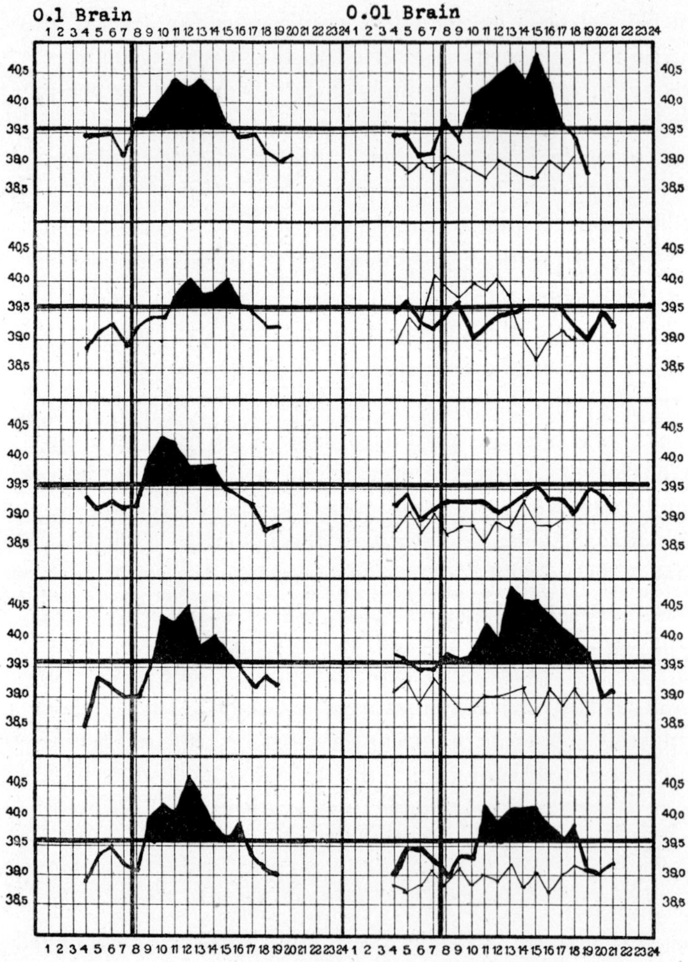

Chart 1.—Content of virus in brain of guinea-pig 72 hours after infection.

ment was made in summer; the thick vertical line between 7 and 8 shows the normal period of latency after an infection with 1/20 of a brain or more. We begin to take the temperature 72 hours after inoculation. The thin temperature line is the curve of the second infection (immunity test). The charts show that in 72 hours after infection 0.1 of the brain suffices to transmit a new infection in every case, but to be sure, the period of latency is prolonged by 1-3 days. After infection with 0.01 of a brain, 3 animals reacted with fever after a delay of 1-3 days, one animal had symptomless infection, one remained negative; 0.001 of brain was able to infect 1 animal only of 5, and represents the smallest efficient quantity of the brain emulsion. The animals inoculated with 0.0001 had no reaction as the following positive reinfection proved. Thus the brain of guinea-pigs contains 1,000 doses capable of causing infection 72 hours after injection. By "infecting dose" we mean the smallest quantity of virus which just suffices to infect a guinea-pig. The quantity of virus contained in the brain and the blood was tested on the days following injection with results given in table 1.

TABLE 1

VIRUS CONTAINED IN BRAIN AND BLOOD

Days	Infecting Doses	
	Brain	Blood
Period of Latency:		
1		
2	10	
3	1,000	
4	1,000	100
5		
Period of Fever:		
6	10,000	
7		
8		
9	100,000	1,000
10		
11		
12		
13	10,000	
Apyrexia:		
14		
15	10,000	1,000
16		
17		
18	1,000	
19		
20	1,000	

It is clear that the brain contains far more virus than the blood. The virus multiplies slowly; to increase 100,000 fold 9 days are required, while usual pathogenic germs multiply to such an extent in a few hours. This slow growth probably explains the long period of latency in typhus. The virus increases still more slowly in the blood. This seems to indicate that typhus is not really a septic disease in which the primary growth of the germ takes place in the blood, but that the tissues are the real soil for the virus. The histologic findings make it probable that the virus is present in the endothelium of the capillaries. The comparative tests, furthermore, show that 10,000 doses must be

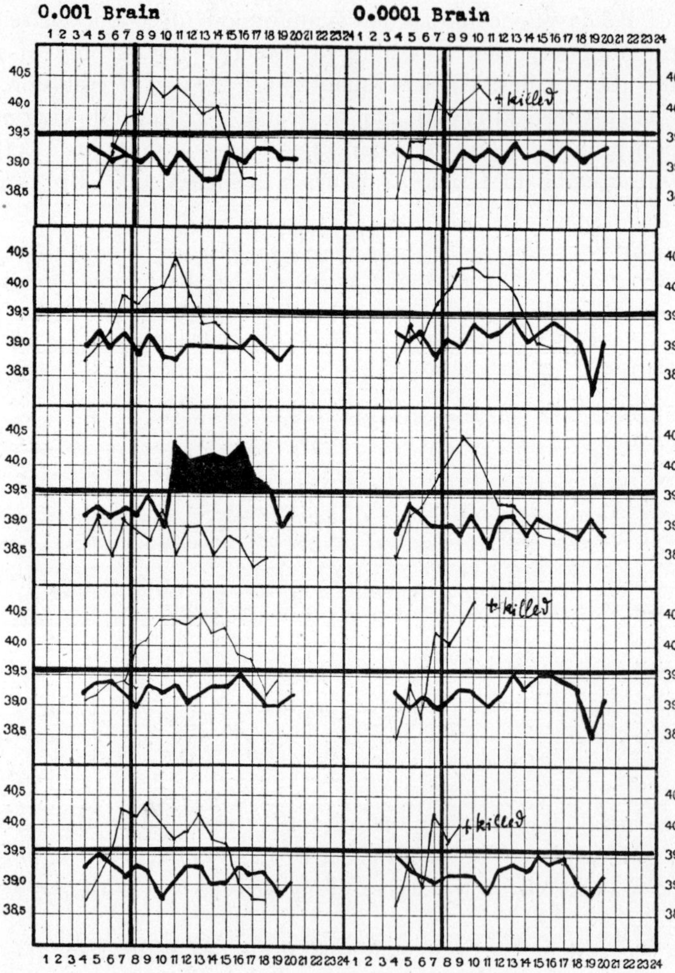

Chart 2.—Content of virus in brain of guinea-pig 72 hours after infection.

present in the brain for the temperature to rise above normal, for when there are only 1,000 doses in the brain, the animal is still afebrile. The blood and the organs remain virulent after the fever has ceased, and in spite of immunity, 7 days after the temperature has returned to normal the brain still contains 1,000 doses—a fact which is of epidemiologic importance. This series of experiments shows that the period of latency depends on the quantity of the infecting virus; the smaller the infecting dose, the longer is the latent period. In using minute doses of virus we have observed periods of latency that were 6-8 days longer than normal.

Latent or symptomless infections were noticed, but only when the quantity of virus injected was not far above the limit of efficiency. Efforts at reinfection failed in all these cases.

So long as the micro-organism causing typhus remains unknown, it will not be possible to say how many germs are necessary for infection. In spite of this, we can get an approximate idea of how many germs constitute one infectious dose by the following consideration: Rabbits react with an agglutinating titer of 1:200 to an inoculation of a guinea-pig brain. The same titer can be reached by injecting 1/200 of the quantity of dead OX19 culture that can be taken up with the loop of a platinum wire, a quantity that contains about 7,000,000 germs. The injection of a whole guinea-pig brain, however, whose virus has been killed by 60 C., and which contains 100,000 doses, does not induce the production of any agglutinins. Therefore 100,000 doses must consist of less than 7,000,000 germs, one dose of less than 70 germs. For this calculation it was presupposed that one typhus germ has the same power of causing the production of agglutinins as one bacillus OX19.

Rabbits are less susceptible to the virus than guinea-pigs. To infect the former, 100 infecting doses at least are necessary; when the production of agglutinins is at its height, the brain contains at the most 100 infecting doses. The rabbit susceptibility is thus 100 times smaller than the guinea-pig, and its brain contains 1,000 times less virus.

IMMUNITY

Active Immunity.—It is generally accepted that after a normal infection active immunity is found in all cases. We, too, used reinfection as an absolutely reliably means of proving a preceding typhus infection. The duration of active immunity in rabbits and guinea-pigs is at least a year. In a series of guinea-pigs, which we reinfected 13 months after their first infection, we noticed slight fever in one case, but it is uncertain whether this was due to typhus. In order to study the behavior of typhus in actively immune animals, we injected a series of actively immunized guinea-pigs intraperitoneally with large quantities of virulent brain emulsion and then tested the brains of these animals at various moments as to the content of virus. The brain was always free from virus; therefore neither an increase of the virus takes place in the immune organism nor is the virus absorbed by the tissues; the injected virus is destroyed in the peritoneal cavity of the immune animal. This result was surprising, since it had been previously noticed that the virus can be found in the brain in great quantity 7 days after the fever has ceased, that is to say, at a time when immunity is fully developed. Whether active immunity sets in after abortive or symptomless infection is a question that has not been decided. The authors who have worked in this direction incline to the opinion that this is only rarely or never the case, and that, on the contrary, a normal infection is necessary for producing active immunity. Supported by more than 200 animal experiments, we can maintain that abortive or symptomless infections are followed by complete active immunity in every case without exception, a fact that is of importance for the understanding of the subsequent experiments.

Passive Immunity.—The elementary fact that the serum of animals that have become apyretic possesses protecting powers had been discovered by Nicolle. But as no detailed statements as to the action of typhus immune serum exists, a thorough investigation of these questions seemed necessary. The following experiments were made on passive immunity: Five c c. of immune serum were injected subcutaneously into an animal which was infected intraperitoneally 24 hours later. This method is preferable to the intraperitoneal injection of a mixture of virus and immune serum, for in this way a disturbing nonspecific resistance of the peritoneal cavity may easily develop. The effect of the immune serum is shown by the lengthened period of latency and by suppression or at least reduction of fever, as has been ascertained by Dörr and Pick. We have been able to show in detailed experiments that all guinea-pigs are equally susceptible to the action of immune serum. On the other hand, every animal produces an efficient serum if it has gone through a normal attack of typhus. This phenomenon appears so regularly that we can acknowledge a fever of 7-9 days duration as being typhus only if it is followed by a distinct production of antibodies.

First of all we ascertained the earliest appearance and the gradual increase of the immune bodies in the serum. A series of infected guinea-pigs was bled on the first, third, seventh and thirtieth days after the temperature had returned to normal; 5 guinea-pigs were injected with 5 c c. of the serum of each group; 24 hours later they were infected with 0.01 of brain (charts 3 and 4).

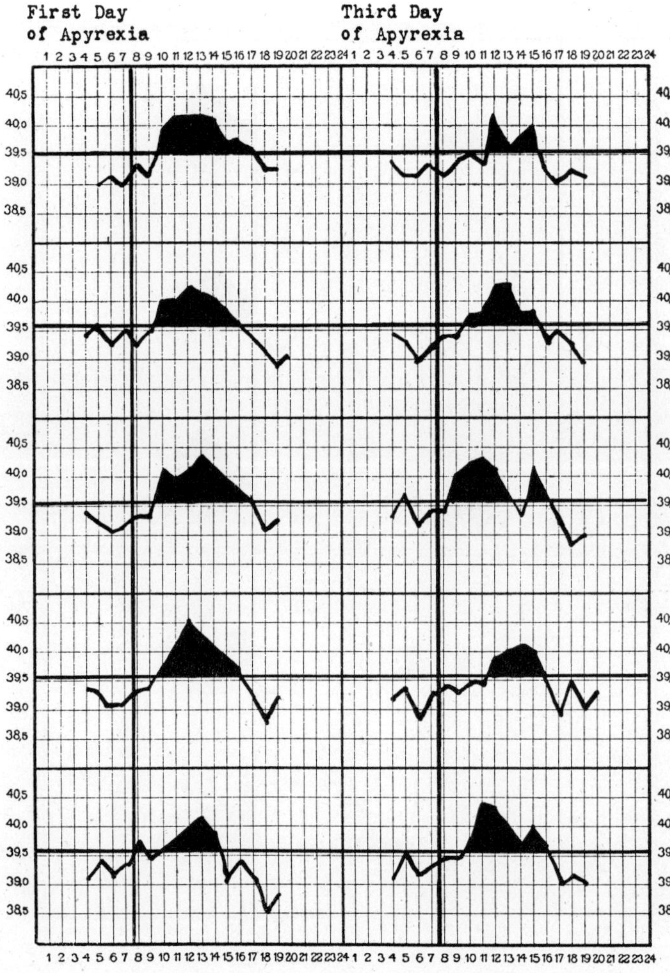

Chart 3.—Action of typhus immune serum.

The serum of animals bled on the first day of apyrexia shows its action only through a slight prolongation of the period of latency. The serum of the third day shows more definitely a delay in the development of fever, and in some cases an abbreviation of the febrile period. On the seventh day, the serum has reached its maximum efficiency; after a period of latency which is lengthened by 10-12 days

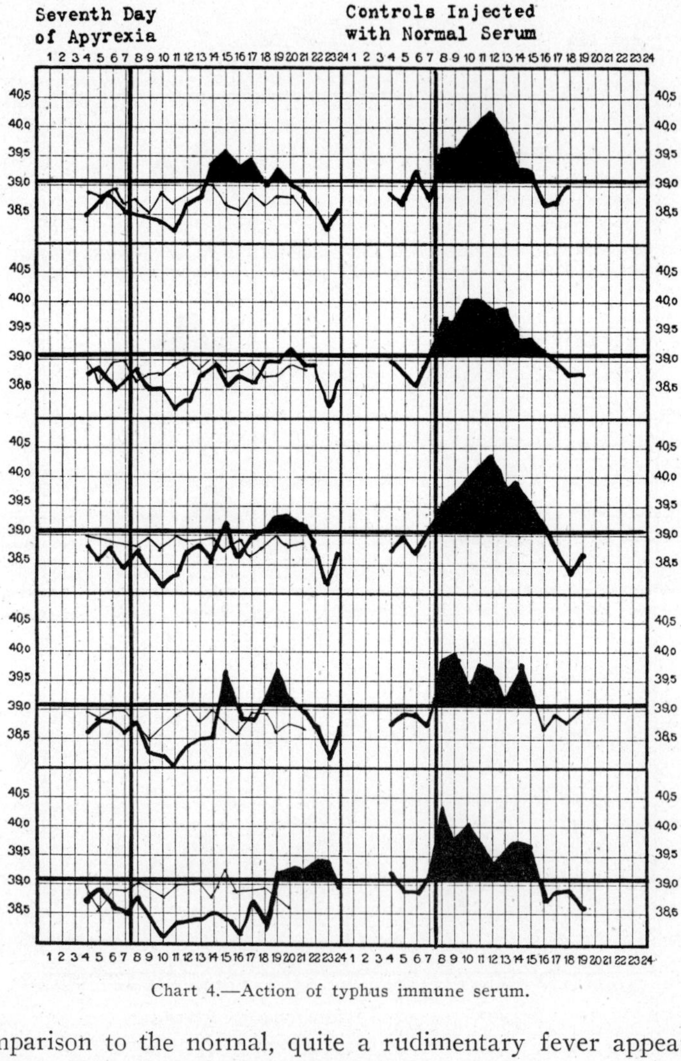

Chart 4.—Action of typhus immune serum.

in comparison to the normal, quite a rudimentary fever appears; the infection is often practically symptomless. The same can be said of the serum taken 4 weeks after apyrexia sets in; in this series, we saw 2 cases of symptomless infection. After about the eighth week, the protecting power of the serum begins to wane; after 8 months, it is found only exceptionally in one or the other of the immune animals, and after a year it has disappeared completely. We could obtain a renewed augmentation of immune bodies only by reinfection in old immune animals. The quantity of immune bodies present in the blood 4 months after immunization is not influenced by reinfection, but among guinea-pigs immunized 8-10 months previously about twice as many serums efficient for protection are found in reinfected animals. We were able to induce a new production of antibodies by reinfection in all animals that had been immune for a year. Probably reinfection is successful only when active immunity has decreased to such an extent that a renewed development of the virus in the organism—in the form of a symptomless infection—is possible.

To learn the way the immune serum acts, it was necessary to study the increase of the virus in the organism of a passively immunized animal. The virulence of an animal's brain during the abortive fever was tested in the way described and was found to contain 10,000 infecting doses. It was still more important to study the behavior of the virus in the organism of treated animals that had developed no fever after the infection. The brain of such an animal was free from virus on the tenth day after infection, but it is true that one cannot say for certain whether this guinea-pig would not have had fever if it had lived longer. An apyretic animal on the eighteenth and another on the nineteenth day after infection contained 10,000 infectious doses. This shows that the increase of the virus is undoubtedly delayed by the immune serum, but that later on it reaches approximately the same degree as in a normal animal; this explains the fact that all animals that had an abortive fever or symptomless infection showed active immunity.

Since the prolongation of the period of latency is a constant attribute of the immune serum's action, and as we had shown before that long periods of latency are seen when small quantities of virus are used, the question whether the immune serum kills part of the injected virus had to be considered. The immune serum had therefore to be examined for its virulicidal power. If virulent brain is added to active serum in a proportion of 1:100, the emulsion being allowed to stand for 3 hours at 37 C. and the brain matter finally separated by centrifugation and washed, the latter will be found to be just as virulent as a control brain treated with normal guinea-pig serum or salt solution.

An insignificant decrease in virulence, which is manifested by a slightly prolonged period of latency, is caused by 3 hours' standing in the incubator. Typhus immune serum therefore does not contain virulicidal matter.

Similar experiments were made with normal serum of other animals to ascertain whether typhus virus is susceptible to the nonspecific virulicidal properties of serum. Active serum of cattle, goat and sheep proved highly effective, killing large quantities of virus; dog and pig serum acted only moderately, whereas horse, goose and rabbit serum was totally inefficient. When these experiments were repeated with inactive normal serum, no virulicidal action could be discovered in any of them. In the same way, these virulicidal normal serums are inefficient in animal experiments even if they are used in an active condition; if a guinea-pig is injected subcutaneously with 5 c c. of virulicidal serum and the next day with 0.01 of virulent brain, a fever of normal duration will set in on the seventh or eighth day. The mechanism of virulicidal action of normal serum is thus totally different from that of typhus immune serum. The lengthening of the period of latency provoked by the immune serum is shown to be due, not to a partial destruction of the virus, but must be supposed to consist in an inhibitory effect on its development. Nothing definite can be said at present in relation to the immune bodies that lower or suppress the fever. Possibly they are related to the antitoxins.

The production of antibodies is not the same in all animals. Generally 0.5 c c. of immune serum produces a distinct prolongation of the period of latency and has a slight influence on the course of the fever in guinea-pigs 300-400 gm. in weight. The action is more apparent when 1 c c. is used, but only when a dose of 3 c c. is applied does the protecting power of the serum reach its full height. This is the case only when the animal supplying the serum has passed through a fever of normal length and intensity, and it appears that guinea-pigs that have an abortive fever only generally give weaker antibodies or none at all. Symptomless infections—whether they are caused by slight doses of virus or by the action of immune serum—give rise to an efficient immune serum in exceptional cases only. Although these animals are actively immune without exception, their serum usually contains no immune bodies; neither can the production of the same ever be induced by reinfection. These results show that immunity in typhus is an immunity of the tissues, it needs the stimulant of disease—i. e., fever—to bring the protective substance from its localization in the tissues into the blood. In concordance with this view, the serum of immune rabbits, which never have fever during the infection, never contains immune bodies. There is thus a distinct parallelism between the violence of the fever reaction and the quantity of immune bodies in the serum.

A dose of 5 c c. of immune serum remains effective for several weeks in the guinea-pig organism. If an animal that has been treated subcutaneously is infected 3 weeks after having received the serum, it still proves to be strongly protected in the majority of cases; even after 4 weeks a prolonged period of latency and rudimentary fever can be observed, but after this the influence of the serum disappears quickly. If the protecting serum is injected after the infection, it proves to be just as effective, provided it is given during the period of latency, but if the fever has once set in, its course no longer can be influenced by serum injections. Serotherapy of typhus is therefore absolutely hopeless, and the immune serum will have its value in prophylaxis only. The titer of immune bodies which the guinea-pig acquires by passing through a normal typhus infection cannot be raised by repeated injections of virulent organ emulsions; these findings are explained by the experiment mentioned, according to which an increase of the virus does not take place in an immune organism. Likewise, rabbit serum remains free from immune bodies after renewed infections.

Repeatedly, and in divers ways, immunization of human beings against typhus has been attempted, but the methods tried have not led to success. The preceding experiments show that the production of a lasting active immunity in man is not an unattainable aim. According to the present state of our knowledge, only the production of a symptomless infection can be taken into consideration; for this kind of infection, so far as can be deduced from animal experiments, causes no clinical symptoms and is followed by active immunity in all cases. A symptomless infection can be produced (1) by infection with small quantities of virus, and (2) by injection of immune serum and virus. The first method is impracticable because there is no direct relation between the quantity of the virus and the symptomless infection. But in view of the experiments described, the second method cannot be considered as practicable, for in the majority of our attempts a more or less distinct rise of fever was noticed, while an absolutely symptomless infection could be observed only in a few cases. Only a method by means of which it is possible to make the course of infection free from all symptoms with absolute certainty would be fit for a practically useful immunization. We have elaborated such a method. The symp-

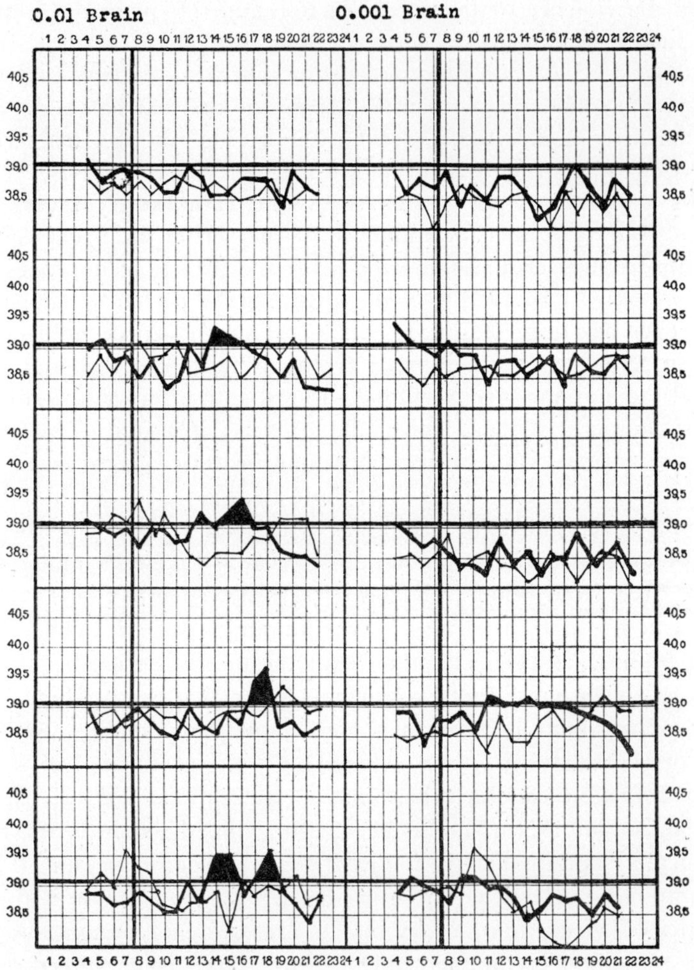

Chart 5.—Influence of immune serum on typhus infection of guinea-pigs (groups 2 and 3).

tomless infection is, so to speak, a condition of equilibrium between the protecting power of the serum and the attacking force of the virus, which always causes symptomless infection in cooperation with an unvarying quantity of immune serum. In all former experiments undertaken to protect animals against typhus, the dose used for infection was 0.01 of brain, but preceding investigations had shown that when the fever culminates even 0.00001 of brain causes an infection.

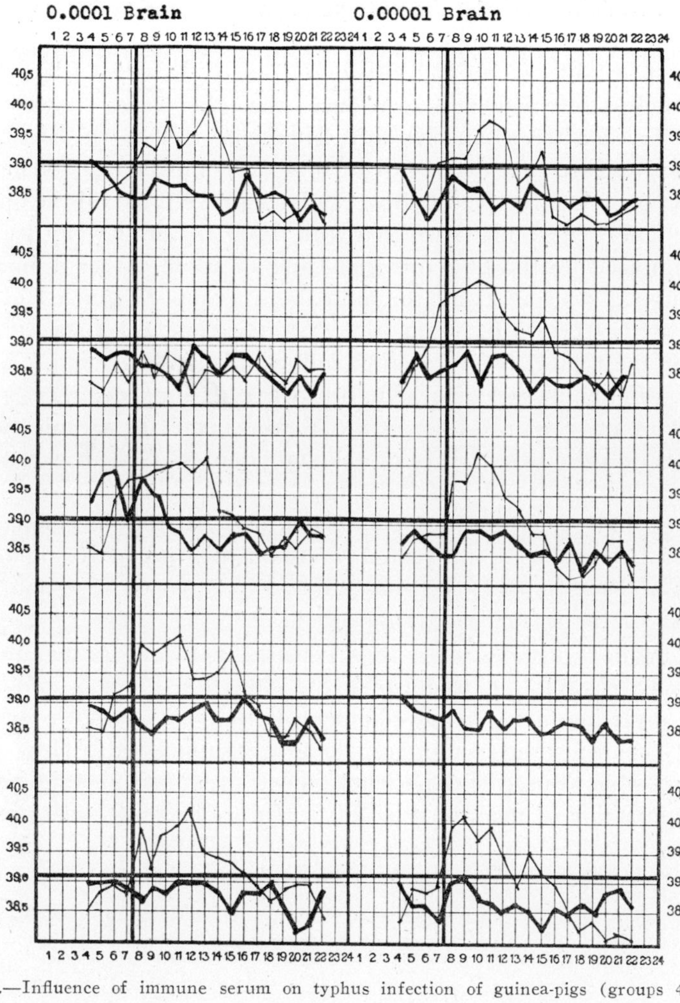

Chart 6.—Influence of immune serum on typhus infection of guinea-pigs (groups 4 and 5).

Experiment.—Twenty-five guinea-pigs of equal size were treated subcutaneously with 5 c c. of immune serum each. The next day groups of 5 animals each were infected intraperitoneally with decreasing doses of virus: Group 1 received 0.1 of guinea-pig brain; group 2,

0.01; group 3, 0.001; group 4, 0.0001; group 5, 0.00001. At the same time, 5 animals that had not been treated with serum were infected with the same doses of virus. All the animals showed typical fever after the corresponding period of latency (tables are omitted for want of space). The animals were reinfected 8 weeks later (tables 5 and 6). The action of the immune serum was moderate when 0.1 of brain was used for infection (group 1); in group 2, infected with 0.01 of brain, a symptomless infection was seen once; the other cases showed rudimentary fever after a considerably lengthened period of latency; in group 3, after infection with 0.001 of brain, all animals had a symptomless infection. The reinfection 8 weeks later proved that all the animals were immune. In group 4, infected with 0.0001 of brain, only 1 animal was immunized by the first infection, and in all the other animals of this group, as well as in all the animals in group 5, which had been infected with 0.00001 of brain, the first infection was ineffective, as shown by the typical fever reaction following the reinfection. A dose of 5 c c. of immune serum is thus too weak to suppress fever totally after an infection with 0.1 or 0.01 of brain, but after an injection of 0.001 of brain the infection is of the symptomless type in every case. When smaller doses of virus are used, the inhibitory action of the immune serum preponderates so considerably that the development of the virus is completely prevented, consequently no active immunity develops and the animals are susceptible to a renewed infection when the action of the serum has disappeared.

The method just described thus consists in incorporating immune serum and virus into the organism at the same time in such proportions that the infection, i. e., the development of the virus, is not prevented, but that the infectious symptoms alone are suppressed. How far it will be possible to use the experience gained in animal experiments for the immunization of man must be left to future investigations to settle.

STUDIES ON EPIDEMIOLOGY OF SCARLET FEVER IN A SCHOOL OUTBREAK

W. P. Shepard and H. S. Diehl

From the Students' Health Service and from the Department of Preventive Medicine and Public Health, University of Minnesota, Minneapolis

Between January 24 and March 26, 1922, there occurred among the 840 students of the School of Agriculture, University of Minnesota, a scarlet fever epidemic of rather unusual form and one which offered in some ways an exceptional opportunity for study. The majority of the students were slightly above high school age; 105 were girls and 735 boys. Of this group, 385 lived in 5 dormitories on the campus and ate at a common dining hall. The remaining 455 lived in private rooms near the campus and took meals at home or at public boarding places. Sixty-six and five tenths per cent. of the students came from farms or towns of less than 5,000 population. The entrance histories showed a surprisingly low incidence of the usual childhood diseases, and the entrance physical examinations showed a rather high percentage of minor defects, such as enlarged tonsils, nasal obstructions, refractive errors, etc.

ANALYSIS

Source.—The first case appeared on Jan. 24, and within 3 weeks there were 15 cases in spite of immediate and concerted efforts to locate and isolate all cases and contacts. At this time foci of numerous scarlet fever cases existed in both Minneapolis and St. Paul, between which cities this school is located, a fact which should receive consideration not only as a possible source of the epidemic, but also as a means of its prolongation.

Incidence.—1. There was a total of 59 cases occurring among 840 students, an incidence of 7%, or 702 per 10,000.

The epidemic extended over a period of 61 days and showed no peak, the largest number occurring in one day being 4, and the greatest number of days without the occurrence of a case being 3.

Incidence by current residence shows 42 cases among the 385 students living in dormitories, a rate of 10.9%, and 17 cases among the 455 students living in private rooms, a rate of 3.7%.

Received for publication, April 9, 1923.

The incidence of 10.9% among the dormitory students, as compared to 3.7% among students living in private rooms, is rather striking, even though data are not available for correlation of the more susceptible ages with this figure.

Chart 1 shows the incidence rate in percentage by ages.

The rise at the ages of 21 and 22 is interesting and may possibly be accounted for by the fact that the 3 lowest average age groups are 22.7 years in students coming from farms; 23.2 years in students from villages of 100 to 250 population; and 23.8 years in students from villages of 250 to 500 (table 4).

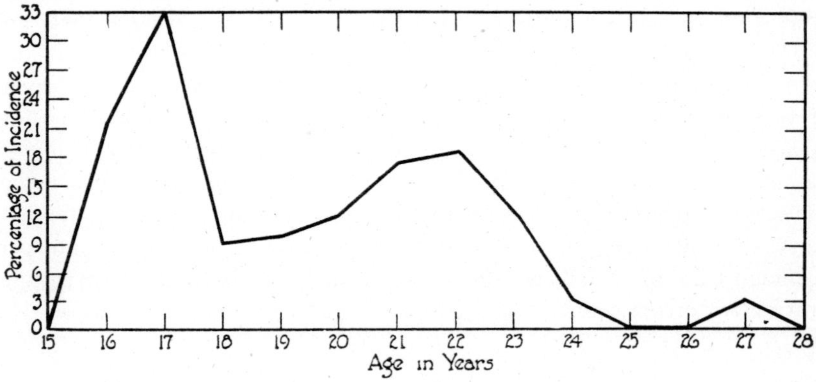

Chart 1.—Age incidence percentage.

There were 5 cases among 105 girls, a rate of 4.7%, and 54 cases among 735 boys, a rate of 7.3%. This low incidence among the girls was a remarkable feature, particularly as it was impossible to prevent a certain amount of intermingling of boys and girls in class rooms and corridors. The 4 secondary cases among the girls were probably all traceable to contact other than in the class room.

It would seem from this that the danger of spread in class rooms is slight, and that schools may be left open with safety during an epidemic, providing social intercourse at parties, entertainments and eating places is strictly prohibited.

Incidence among known exposures disclosed the interesting fact that among 66 men intimately exposed to roommates in the early stages of scarlet fever, only one case of this disease developed. This is the one potent observation made which seems to support the theory of

Rosenau,[1] Vaughan [2] and Forchheimer [3] that scarlet fever is of low infectivity in its earliest stages.

Following the observations made in army training camps, notably by Vaughan and Palmer [4] on the comparative rates of infectious diseases among men from urban and rural groups, this phase was given special attention and proved most interesting.

Table 1 shows the percentage of incidence in the first subdivision by residence that was made.

TABLE 1

INCIDENCE RURAL AND URBAN

Size of Community	Number of Students	Number of Cases	Percentage of Incidence
Rural districts	303	33	10.9
Towns under 100	41	4	9.8
Towns 100 - 250	36	2	5.5
Towns 250 - 500	56	4	7.1
Towns 500 - 1,000	61	3	4.9
Towns 1,000 - 2,500	49	4	8.2
Towns 2,500 - 5,000	23	3	13.0
Towns 5,000 -10.000	16	1	6.2
Cities over 10,000	255	5	1.9

TABLE 2

INCIDENCE RURAL AND URBAN

Size of Community	Number of Students	Number of Cases	Percentage of Incidence
Rural and under 100	344	37	10.7
Towns 100 - 1,000	153	9	5.9
Towns 1,000 - 5,000	72	7	9.7
Towns 5,000 -12,500	20	1	5.0
Towns over 12,500	251	5	1.9

A progressive decline of incidence is noted in inverse ratio to the size of the community in which the student lived, until towns of 1,000 to 10,000 are reached. Here, among the students coming from towns of 2,500 to 5,000, a second peak occurs. Combining this table, in order to get groups more nearly comparable as to size, we have table 2, where a rise is again noted in groups from towns of 1,000 to 5,000.

Combining again to conform with the U. S. Census standards of rural, small town and urban populations, we have table 3 in which

[1] Preventive Medicine and Hygiene, 1921, p. 220.
[2] Epidemiology and Public Health, 1922, p. 257.
[3] 20th Century Practice of Medicine, 1896, 14, p. 13.
[4] Jour. Lab. & Clin. Med., 1918, 3, p. 635 and 1919, 4, pp. 587 and 647.

the high incidence in both rural and small-town groups as compared to urban groups is emphasized. This is the only table in which the size of the groups is really comparable.

Whether the rise in small-town groups seen in tables 1 and 2 is apparent or real, and whether a similar rise might be observed in scarlet fever epidemics of larger proportions, cannot of course be determined in so small a number of cases. Closer scrutiny of these groups, however, resulted in a computation of average ages in an attempt to ascertain whether more susceptible ages were represented in any of the groups. The result is given in table 4.

TABLE 3

INCIDENCE RURAL AND URBAN

Size of Community	Number of Students	Number of Cases	Percentage of Incidence
Rural	303	33	10.9
Small towns, 50 - 5,000	266	20	7.5
Urban over 5,000	271	6	2.2

TABLE 4

AGE AND RESIDENCE CORRELATION

Size of Community	Average Age	Motile Age
Rural	22.7	20
Towns under 100	26.4	26
Towns 100 - 250	23.2	22
Towns 250 - 500	23.8	18
Towns 500 - 1,000	26.2	19 and 26
Towns 1,000 - 2,500	24.2	18
Towns 2,500 - 5,000	24.1	20
Towns 5,000 -10,000	24.2	27, 28 and 33
Cities over 10,000	26.3	27 and 33

In preparing this table, the unsuitability of all average age computations must be considered, hence motile age is also tabulated. It will be seen that on the basis of average ages alone, assuming those of younger ages to be more susceptible to scarlet fever, there is some slight additional reason here for the higher incidence among rural groups and small-town groups, and that the next most susceptible group according to average age would be from towns of 2,500 to 5,000. From the standpoint of motile age alone, we find the rural group and the 2,500 to 5,000 group of equal susceptibility but slightly less susceptible than the groups from 1,000 to 2,500 and from 250 to 500.

Correlation of age and residence shows, therefore, that the increased incidence rate in towns of 1,000 to 5,000 is probably only apparent and that the decreased rate in the urban group is probably not so great as shown in table 3. It is believed, however, that a difference in rate of 8.7% between urban and rural groups is too great to be attributed alone to 2.5 years difference in the average age. The increased rate noted in students from towns of 1,000 to 5,000 is presumably a chance distribution, since the Minnesota State Board of Health reports [5] do not show a decreased incidence rate of scarlet fever in towns of this size. Vaughan [2] points out that scarlet fever is a "neighborly" disease and thrives in small towns and villages more than in the city or country.

The incidence of second attacks of scarlet fever was high in this series, 2 out of the 59 having had previous attacks of scarlet fever 6 and 10 years before. The report of the previous attacks of these 2 patients were authenticated by correspondence with the family physicians and with the patients' parents. Two others of the series stated that they had had previous attacks but their statements could not be verified.

Morbidity.—Incidence rates have been given.

Fifty-nine patients with scarlet fever lost 2,169 days of school, an average of 36.2 days per patient.

Cases and contacts together lost a total of 2,400 school days.

A total of 1,976 school days were lost by suspects. The drastic isolation measures instituted on Feb. 28 and described below were responsible for this large number.

Mortality.—There were no deaths in this epidemic, although several of the cases were extremely severe. The clinical aspect of the series is presented in another paper.[6] In a large group of cases reported from an army training camp by Ludy, Hunt and Cogswell,[7] the mortality rate was 2.5%.

Known Exposure.—The relation of known exposure to incidence proved interesting and is illustrated in chart 2.

Assuming scarlet fever to be contagious from the time of the first symptoms, known exposure was reckoned by counting the number of patients who were at liberty each day after the onset of the first symptoms.

[5] Fourth Biennial Report (New Series), pp. 26 and 112.
[6] Jour. Am. Med. Assn., 1922, 79, p. 2079.
[7] Military Surgeon, 1919, 45, p. 414.

Vaughan,[2] Forchheimer [3] and Rosenau [1] were convinced that scarlet fever is of low infectivity in the preeruptive stage. Holt [8] and Griffith [9] believe that infectivity begins with the onset of the first symptoms, if not before. The evidence gathered here on this point is conflicting and permits no conclusions. From the standpoint of safety, however, it was necessary to assume that infectivity commenced with the earliest appearance of the first symptoms.

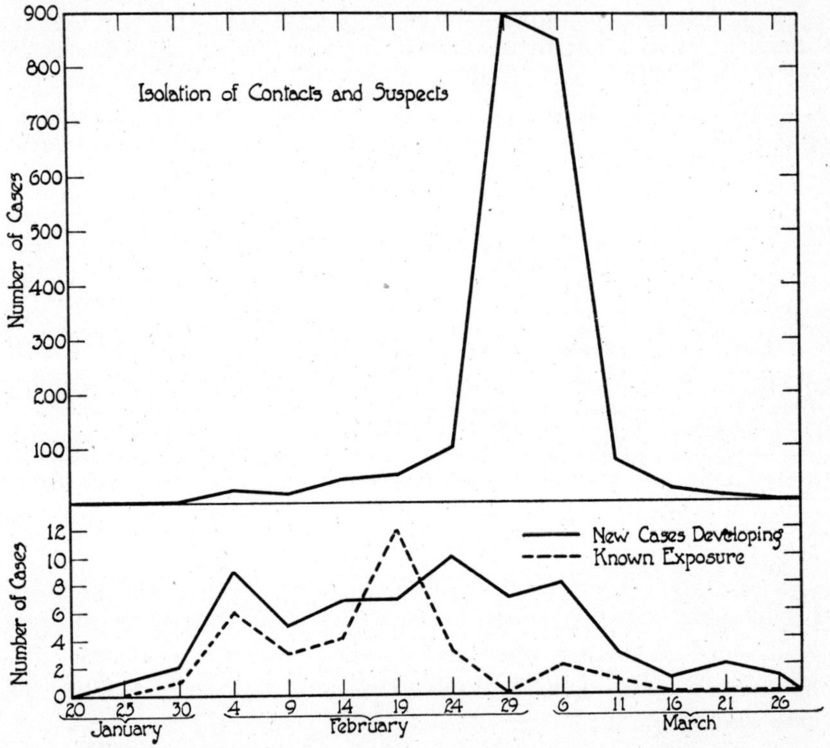

Chart 2.—Relationship of isolation, incidence and known exposure.

Seventy per cent. of our patients were isolated before development of the rash and of the remaining 30% only 5 were at liberty as long as 12 hours after the rash appeared. It appears that the number of such cases, or the amount of so-called "known exposure," had a direct bearing on the appearance of new cases. The radical isolation measures

[8] Diseases of Infancy and Childhood, 1919, p. 954.
[9] Forchheimer: Therapeusis of Internal Diseases, 1914, p. 117.

instituted on Feb. 28 eliminated practically all of the known exposure, and there was an immediate falling off of new cases. The effect of these radical isolation measures will be discussed below.

Concurrent Influenza.—From Feb. 13 to March 12 there occurred an epidemic of 58 cases of a mild form of influenza in the same group of students. There was no apparent effect of the one epidemic on the other.[6, 10]

Return Cases.—By a return case here is meant the occurrence of a secondary case of scarlet fever, presumably from exposure to a patient recently released from isolation. This bugbear of isolation hospitals was not altogether absent in this epidemic, in spite of the rigid precautions described below. There were two patients of the 59 who were believed to fall into this class.

As many of the students returned to their homes immediately after discharge from the hospital, it was thought these might be the source of some return cases. The reports of communicable diseases of the Minnesota State Board of Health show no cases which could possibly be called secondary to any of these discharged patients.

Assuming 2 to be return cases, we have a percentage rate of 3.4 after an average isolation period of 39 days. Considering the precautions taken against this misfortune (see below), this percentage seems unusually high. Osler[11] states that in a series of 15,000 cases submitted to an average isolation period of 49 days or less, the percentage of return cases was 1.86 and that the isolation period must be lengthened to between 57 and 65 days to reduce this rate to 1%. Chapin[12] states that among London hospitals this disease is found still infectious after 6 weeks' isolation in from 5 to 6%.

CONTROL MEASURES

Control measures employed were carried out with the Division of Preventable Diseases of the Minnesota State Board of Health acting in an advisory capacity. Briefly they were as follows:

Reduction of Direct Contact.—1. All patients with suspicious looking throats were immediately and carefully isolated in the Students' Health Service Hospital on the Agricultural Campus. That the technic employed here was adequate is evidenced by the fact that patients with

[10] Wohl, M. G., and Detwiler, A. K.: Interstate Med. Jour., 1916, 27, p. 729.
[11] Principles and Practice of Medicine, 1920, p. 345.
[12] Boston Med. & Surg. Jour., 1916, 175, p. 715.

diphtheria, mumps, pneumonia, bronchitis and numerous influenza patients were cared for in the same hospital simultaneously with patients who had scarlet fever, without one cross infection.

2. Isolation of contacts for 7 days each were carried out. As pointed out by Chesley [13] and others, this one point, together with isolation of positive cases, is the key to the control of epidemic scarlet fever. This is discussed later.

3. Daily examinations of all students in the dormitories showing the first cases of scarlet fever was extended on February 16 to include all of the 840 students. Examination consisted of noting the general appearance of each student, asking him whether he felt well, a careful inspection of the mouth and pharynx in good daylight, inspection of the ears, cheeks and neck for desquamation, inspection of the upper part of the chest for eruption and palpation of the neck for cervical lymph nodes. A student showing anything suspicious was picked out of line, his pulse and temperature were taken, and he was questioned more closely regarding symptoms and exposure. Absentees were reported to the Health Service and checked by telephone, and no student absent on account of illness was allowed to return to school without permission from the Health Service.

The difficulties immediately encountered were that: first, the typical enanthem of scarlet fever often does not appear until shortly before or coincident with the exanthem, even though the patient be already suffering from the earliest symptoms and therefore presumably is in the infectious stage; and, second, there were encountered a great number of people who showed a chronic or subacute inflammation of the pharynx which was indistinguishable from the earliest appearance of the scarlet fever throat; and, third, many of the scarlet fever cases were so mild that the symptoms and physical signs produced were almost negligible.

4. It was, therefore, decided on Feb. 28, after the epidemic had been in progress for 36 days, without signs of either abatement or increase, that all persons showing any abnormality in the mucous membranes of the throat should be placed in isolation for closer observation until such time as it could be made certain that they were not early cases or missed cases. This was accomplished by utilizing the gymnasium and resulted in excluding from school as many as 273 students in one day and a loss, between March 3 and March 13, of 1,839 school days.

[13] Am. Jour. Pub. Health, 1916, 6, p. 234.

5. All meetings, social functions, assemblies, gymnasiums, drill and swimming pools were closed Feb. 14.

6. Precautions were taken to prevent crowding in corridors, dining halls, etc., and all students living in the dormitories were restricted to the campus.

7. Boys and girls were separated in the dining hall on Feb. 14. Dining hall waitresses, being well instructed in the use of masks from previous epidemics, were required to wear masks for their own protection. Those handling dirty dishes, table cloths and napkins were instructed regarding the cleansing of their hands.

8. In accordance with the educational policy of the health service, every effort was made to instruct the students by public speeches and frequent bulletins in the manner of the spread of communicable diseases, the reasons for the rigid enforcement of irksome control measures, the necessity of reporting first symptoms early, etc. At the same time it was necessary, from experience with previous epidemics in this particular student group, to prevent a tendency toward a panic, resulting in a bolt for home by many students, by frequent reassurances and statements of the exact seriousness of the situation.

Reduction of Indirect Contact.—Whether scarlet fever is transmitted mainly by fomites or by direct contact is a much disputed question. Rosenau [1] believes that transmission by fomites is most important. Vaughan [2] is certain that the weight of our present evidence is in favor of transmission by fomites. On the other hand, Kobrak [14] after careful investigation of 87 cases, concludes that transmission is chiefly through direct contact with the nasopharyngeal secretions and not by fomites. Chapin [12] is convinced that transmission by fomites is negligible. McCollum and Place [15] state that in transmitting scarlet fever the contact must be fairly intimate to allow infection, in contrast to measles and pertussis. It seems likely that both modes of transmission are important and in planning control of the present epidemic efforts were made to reduce both direct and indirect contact.

To control indirect contact the following measures were instituted: (1) The daily thorough cleansing of all toilet rooms in dormitories was instituted Feb. 14. (2) Dishes were subjected to a minimum of two minutes in live, circulating steam. The maids handling dirty dishes were separated from those wiping clean dishes in the kitchen. Table

[14] Ztschr. f. Kinderh., 1920, 26, p. 150.
[15] Osler and McCrae: Modern Medicine, 1907, 1, p. 856.

linen was changed every other day and paper napkins were used and burned. (3) Immediately on the appearance of a new case a member of the Health Service staff was sent to the patient's room to gather up all clothing and bed clothing used by him and bring it to the hospital for disinfection.

Precautions Against Return Cases.—Careful measures to reduce return cases to a minimum were carried out. Each case was isolated in the hospital for a minimum of 28 days, then given an antiseptic bath and shampoo and clean clothes. No patients were released which showed any nasal, ear, throat or sinus discharges. Completion of desquamation was not deemed necessary before discharge. After release from the hospital patients were sent to the third floor of one of the dormitories set aside for convalescents and were allowed to attend classes only; not to attend any other meetings or to eat with the others in the dining hall. They were required to report to the infirmary daily for ear, nose and throat examinations and treatment of the nasopharynx with a mild antiseptic spray. At the end of 35 days, they were permitted to return to their rooms and resume all school activities.

DISCUSSION

Predisposing Causes.—Records in the Health Service show that among this particular group of students epidemic diseases have occurred more frequently and more extensively than in any other part of the University. This fact, together with the observations made here that the incidence rate among rural and small town groups was much greater than in urban groups, lead us to concur in the belief that mingling with the city crowds by urban residents in some way increases immunity to the respiratory contagions.

The studies of Bullowa [16] showing increased severity of scarlet fever in children having pathologic tonsils suggest the possibility that such persons may be more susceptible to scarlet fever. While there was a large percentage of pathologic tonsils in this group of students, examination of our records does not show scarlet fever to be any more frequent among such people.

Missed Cases and Carriers.—It is believed that the detection of missed cases and carriers is only second in importance to isolation of frank cases and contacts in the control of epidemic scarlet fever.

[16] Am. J. Dis. Child., 1921, 22, p. 29.

Chapin,[12] Kobrak,[14] Herrman[17] and Rosenau[1] emphasize this phase. T. Mironesco[18] reports experiences which show that during an epidemic some patients may have only a mild sore throat, but that these are capable of infecting others as well as do those with frank cases. In this connection we have three interesting cases to report.

During the daily examinations, 3 boys were found who had suspicious looking throats, but in whom no other signs could be detected. All 3 boys steadfastly and heatedly denied the slightest symptoms, but each was subjected to 2 separate 7 day isolation periods. Their throats showed absolutely no change in the entire 38 days, during which daily examinations were carried out. They were at liberty during the epidemic, except for these 2 isolation periods. In the case of 1 of these, A. W., his room-mate first reported with scarlet fever on Feb. 3 (Case 33); then a friend who ate at the same table daily (Case 32), appeared with a rash on Feb. 22; and finally his brother, who was also his room-mate (Case 58), appeared with a rash on March 23. No other exposure was known in any of these 3 cases. The second man, G. F., had an especially suspicious throat. On Feb. 12, his room-mate came down with scarlet fever, and no other exposure could be discovered. His other room-mate had already had the disease some years before. The third man, V. E., was picked out of the line almost daily by each of the several examiners on account of the appearance of his pharynx. On March 9, his only room-mate (Case 53) appeared with scarlet fever.

Efficacy of Control Measures.—Obviously, the first and most important measure is the detection and isolation of all cases and contacts.

Daily examinations of the entire personnel of an institution harboring an epidemic of scarlet fever are necessary and of great value. Examinations alone, however, were found inadequate to eliminate the known exposure and hence to control the epidemic until means were provided to isolate each and every person showing an abnormal pharyngeal mucous membrane. While positive conclusions can rarely be drawn as to the curative agent in disease or the successful preventive measure in epidemics, it is believed by the writers that these radical isolation measures instituted Feb. 28 were responsible for the subsidence of the epidemic. No other changes were made at this time in the manner of handling the epidemic. The outbreak had surely not "burned itself out," since the incidence rate was low throughout, and there was no peak preceding its subsidence. Due to incomplete entrance histories of students entering some years before, it was impossible to compute accurately the number of susceptibles. It was obvious, however, from the records available, that nowhere near the total number of susceptibles had been attacked. Meteorologic conditions have long been proved to have

[17] Arch. Pediat., 1909, 26, p. 112.
[18] Presse méd., 1921, 29, p. 176.

no bearing on the prevalence of scarlet fever. The rationale of the procedure adopted may be questioned and was severely criticized by some members fo the school. It was felt justified, however, by the health service from the standpoint of public health alone. The economic standpoint was, therefore, studied as follows:

Economic Aspect.—This was an institutional epidemic apparently under only partial control, extending without increase or abatement from Feb. 4 to March 10. This suggested the possibility of comparing the number of school days lost through the epidemic as it existed, including days lost by the many suspects isolated as well as those lost by cases and contacts, with the school days which would probably have been lost had the epidemic continued at the same rate for another 31 days; that is, until the time of closing of the school. While the figures obtained are only probable ones, the comparison is interesting.

Number of school days lost by patients and contacts	2,400
Number of school days lost by suspects (all abnormal throats)	1,976
Total days lost as epidemic was handled	4,376
Average number of days lost by each patient with scarlet fever	36.25
Average number of days lost by each contact	7
Average number of cases per day from Feb. 4 to March 6	1.54
Average number of contacts per day from Feb. 4 to March 6	1.80
Probable number of new cases from March 6 to April 6	48
Probable number of contacts from March 6 to April 6	56
School days lost by probable new patients from March 6 to April 6	1,740
School days lost by probable contacts from March 6 to April 6	392
Additional days lost if epidemic had continued for 31 days	2,132
Days actually lost by patients and contacts	2,400
Additional days lost if epidemic had continued 31 days	2,132
Total days lost if epidemic had continued 31 days	4,532
Total days lost as epidemic was handled	4,376
Estimated days saved by radical isolation of all suspects	156

Another economic loss to be avoided by a student health service whenever possible is the canceled registration on account of ill health. The failure of a health service to keep a student fit to carry his full amount of educational work is comparable to the failure of an army hospital to rehabilitate a soldier for front line duty. In this epidemic, 22 registrations were canceled out of 59 cases, or 35%. Had there been 48 additional cases of scarlet fever between March 6 and April 6, according to this rate there would have been 17 additional canceled registrations.

We see, therefore, that in spite of drastic isolation measures which at times decimated certain classes for short periods, in all probability, 156 school days were saved to the students and to the school, and 17 students were saved from an illness so severe that they could not have continued school work. This of course does not take into consideration the probable saving of 48 more students from scarlet fever, with consequent escape from danger of death and health impairing complications.

It is still more interesting to contemplate that on the basis of the same means of figuring, had radical isolation measures been instituted Feb. 7, as they should have been, instead of Feb. 28, 50 scarlet fever cases would probably have been prevented, 54 contacts would not have been isolated and a total of 2,190 school days would have been saved. Had the cooperation of the school management been as ready early in the outbreak as it was after a larger number of cases appeared, this measure would doubtless have been carried out Feb. 7.

SUMMARY

A school epidemic of 59 cases of scarlet fever among 840 students occurring over a period of 61 days is studied.

Features offering unusual opportunity for study were: The large percentage of students from rural or small town districts; the possibility of absolute enforcement of control measures; and a comparison of the economic loss incident to control measures alone and to the epidemic alone.

The incidence of scarlet fever was greater among students from farms and small towns than from cities.

A concurrent epidemic of a mild form of influenza had no apparent effect on the epidemic of scarlet fever.

Some evidence is offered to show the possibility of a person having a mild angina infecting others with scarlet fever.

Daily examinations of the entire group of students harboring an epidemic of scarlet fever were necessary but alone were not sufficient to control the epidemic.

Isolation of all persons showing the slightest abnormality suggestive of beginning scarlet fever was necessary for a short period to control the epidemic.

The economic loss alone occasioned by such drastic isolation measures was slightly less in this epidemic than the probable loss from the disease alone.

BACTERICIDAL ACTION OF BLOOD OF RABBITS IMMUNIZED AGAINST PNEUMOCOCCI *

H. Everett Smiley

From the Department of Preventive Medicine and Hygiene, Harvard Medical School, Boston

Among the factors which have been considered as playing a rôle in the mechanism of immunity to the pneumococcus, the property of bactericidal action of the blood has held a conspicuous place. While a complete survey of the early work done in studying this problem is not within the scope of this paper, there are certain investigations which are worthy of especial note. As early as 1906, Rosenow [1] called attention to the fact that pneumonic defibrinated blood was decidedly pneumococcidal, which action was more noticeable when the patient showed a high leukocytosis. He laid emphasis on the latter feature. Later, Eggers,[2] following along similar lines, demonstrated by the use of blood-agar plates the antipneumococcal action of the serum plus leukocytes of a pneumonia patient. This property reached the maximum with the crisis and then gradually decreased. In 1914, Hektoen,[3] in his discussion of the mechanism of the crisis in pneumonia, held that "the crisis is not a point at which the invading pneumococci suddenly became avirulent, but is rather the point at which a more or less complete and rapid destruction of the organism is accomplished."

In 1915,[4] Wright published observations in which he maintained that in some cases of pneumonia among the natives of South Africa he had been able to demonstrate the bactericidal action of whole blood against the pneumococcus. A little later, Heist and Solis-Cohen [5] published experiments with rabbits, in which they called attention to the bactericidal action of whole blood, and by a series of careful tests showed bactericidal properties present in the blood of animals immunized against pneumococci.

Received for publication, April 14, 1923.

* This is one of a series of studies carried out in part under a grant of the Influenza Commission of the Metropolitan Life Insurance Company.

1 Jour. Infect. Dis., 1906, 3, p. 683.

2 Ibid., 1912, 10, p. 48.

3 Jour. Am. Med. Assn., 1914, 62, p. 254.

4 On Pharmotherapy and Preventive Inoculation Applied to Pneumonia in the African Native, 1915, p. 78.

5 Jour. Immunol., 1918, 3, p. 261; 1919, 4, p. 147.

The method of immunizing used by Heist and Solis-Cohen was as follows: They made a "vaccine" of pneumococci grown for 14 hours in meat infusion broth containing 1% of dextrose. The culture was heated at 53 C. for one-half hour, centrifugalized, and the pneumococci suspended in salt solution. After heating again at 55 C. for half an hour, 0.3% tricresol was added. Four spaced injections of the vaccine were given the rabbits subcutaneously at weekly intervals, the total amount of the 4 doses varying for each rabbit from 1,500,000,000 to 24,000,000,000 organisms. As the rabbits showed no bactericidins in their blood, further injections were given, this time intravenously. Each received 3 additional doses at weekly intervals, the total amounting to from 60,000,000 to 1,200,000,000 pneumococci. Heist and Solis-Cohen again tested the blood of the immunized rabbits and found bactericidal action, using a modification of the Wright[6] capillary pipet.

Briefly, the Heist technic is as follows: Four capillary tubes are filled to a certain mark with diluted live culture of pneumococci (1:25, 1:125, 1:625, 1:3,125) and immediately emptied, leaving a film of culture adhering to the inside of the tubes. Whole blood from the punctured ear vein of a rabbit is drawn up to the mark, the tubes sealed with paraffin and incubated at 37 C. over night. After incubation, the contents are blown on to slides, smeared and stained, and then examined for the presence of pneumococci. If no organisms are found, it is assumed the blood had bactericidal action. However, in some experiments by Heist and Solis-Cohen, the contents of the capillary tubes were blown into test tubes containing broth, which were incubated and examined for growth the next day.

Bull and Bartual[7] questioned the conclusions of Heist and Solis-Cohen, holding that the ultimate test of bactericidal action was not the absence of organisms in smears, but rather their failure to grow when reintroduced into a favorable medium. Bull and Bartual therefore claimed that no distinction could be made by the Heist technic between bacteriostatic and bactericidal action. Their experiment showed that the activity of the blood was not bactericidal but bacteriostatic.

It is significant, however, to note that Bull and Bartual did not follow the scheme of immunizing used by Heist and Solis-Cohen, and therefore the comparison is not apt. In the experiment by Bull and Bartual, 2 rabbits were used. Killed cultures of 2 agar slants were given intravenously in a single injection, the total number of organisms being approximately 4,000,000,000. Tests of the blood were made every day up to the 6th day by the capillary tube method and subsequently cultures made. Inhibition in growth was noted, but no bactericidal action was observed.

It is thus seen that the two methods of immunization were dissimilar. and hence the results are not comparable; in fact, Heist and Solis-Cohen claimed that bactericidal action was demonstrable only in rabbits "suitably immunized," and it is noteworthy that they repeatedly injected the rabbits in their experiment until the bactericidal action appeared.

It is the purpose of this paper to give the results of experiments designed to study the bactericidal action of the whole blood of rabbits immunized against pneumococci. After seeking to establish a method of testing for this property that readily would differentiate between

[6] Technique of the Test and Capillary Glass Tube, 1908.

[7] Jour. Exper. Med., 1920, 31, p. 233.

bactericidal and bacteriostatic actions, it was desired to determine whether or not bactericidal substances could be demonstrated, and for how long a period they were present.

METHOD

For several months the Heist test was followed as an index of bactericidal action, and then was abandoned for these reasons: (1) The readings obtained were inconsistent and not constant; there was too great a variability even with normal rabbits. (2) It was not a true index of bactericidal action. To replace this test by one which would tell better whether or not bactericidal action was demonstrable, and be easy of application, recourse was had to the use of small test tubes. The technic follows:

Four dilutions of an 18-hour broth culture were used, namely, 1:1,000, 1:10,000, 1:100,000 and 1:1,000,000. One drop of each dilution was placed carefully at the bottom of a small sterile test tube. The rabbit's ear was shaved along the marginal vein. The upper and under sides were painted with tincture of iodine which was allowed to dry and then washed off with 70% alcohol. The vein was then pricked, and from 5 to 8 drops of blood collected in each tube. The tubes were shaken immediately so that the culture and blood were mixed thoroughly, corked to prevent evaporation, and incubated at 37.5 C. At the end of 24 hours, one loopful of the serum from each tube was transferred to the surface of a 4% blood agar slant and incubated over night. The number of colonies was noted. If any tube showed no growth for 24 hours, it was left in the incubator for 96 hours and cultures made again. The ratio of culture to blood within the limits used was found to be of slight import in this study of the qualitative determination of bactericidal action, for if present, it was demonstrable in the ratio of 1:5 as well as 1:20. It was found to be essential that the culture be in the tube before the addition of blood, and that both be thoroughly shaken before clotting occurs. If the culture be added to blood already clotted, or to serum only, or to plasma, no bactericidal action is indicated.

With this method, the readings have been consistent and in addition distinguish between bactericidal and bacteriostatic action. Table 1

TABLE 1
COMPARISON OF HEIST AND TEST TUBE METHODS

Normal Rabbits	Heist Method				Test Tube Method			
	1:10	1:100	1:500	1:1,000	1:10,000	1:100,000	1:1,000,000	1:10,000 000
151a	—	+	+	—	++++	++++	++++	++++
151b	+++	+	+	+	++++	++++	++++	++++
152a	+	++++	++++	—	++++	++++	++++	++++
152b	+	+	+	++++	++++	++++	++++	++++

— = no pneumococci in smears.
++++ = many pneumococci.

++++ = innumerable colonies in blood agar slants.

shows the results of comparative tests made in duplicate on the blood of 2 normal rabbits and illustrates the difficulty of drawing definite conclusions from the Heist test.

Exper. 1.—As a result of several months' work in immunizing rabbits, it was found that single or repeated small doses did not develop immune bodies to a high degree, at least so far as the titer of the agglutination and bactericidal tests indicated. If the doses were large, and if live organisms were used for immunizing, much better results were obtained. The relative value of small versus large doses is indicated by the following results: Rabbits were immunized by different routes with a vaccine made by washing down a blood-agar slant of pneumococci with salt solution and heating at 56 C. for 30 minutes. The rabbits received 4 single injections at intervals of 4 days, the doses being 1,000,000 for the first injection and 10,000,000 for each of the other three.

As the blood of these rabbits showed little or no bactericidal property, a second course of immunization was given. the doses being 10,000,000, 100,000,000, 1,000,000,000 and 2,000,000,000 organisms at 4-day intervals. Because the titer of the blood was still low, a third course was later followed, consisting of 9 injections over a period of 3 weeks, namely, 3 injections on 3 successive days, with 4-day intervals of rest. The amounts injected were 3,000,000,000 (total) for the 1st week, 3,000,000,000 for the 2d, and 6,000,000,000 for the 3rd. These experiments were made early in the work when the Heist technic was followed as an index of bactericidal action. As the results in this case were consistent, the experiments were not repeated. In later work, the test tube method was substituted for the reasons given. The Heist readings, it may be said in all instances, were made 10 days after the last injection. Table 2 shows the results of the readings in the case of 4 rabbits during the entire course; also the reading of results obtained with a control rabbit, which was given only the 3rd course of treatment.

TABLE 2

PNEMOCOCCIDAL ACTION OF BLOOD OF IMMUNIZED RABBITS, HEIST METHOD

Rabbits	Route of Injection	First Course				Second Course				Third Course			
		1:10	1:100	1:500	1:1000	1:10	1:100	1:500	1:1000	1:10	1:100	1:500	1:1000
273	Intra-tracheal	++	+	+++	+	+++	++++	++++	++++	±	±	±	±
275	Intra-pleural	+++	+++	+	++++	++	++++	+	±	±	±	±	±
278	Intra-venous	+	+	++	±	±	±	±	±	±	±	±	±
279	Subcu-taneous	+++	++++	++++	++++	+	±	±	±	±	±	—	—
283	Intra-venous	......	....	....	....	......	....	....	....	—	—	—	—

± = 1 or 2 organisms in several fields.

Exper. 2.—Having decided on the test tube method as an index of bactericidal action, experiments were made by again immunizing rabbits that had received killed cultures some time previously. At the outset, none of the rabbits showed any bactericidal property in the blood, as revealed by the test tube method. Large doses of vaccine (heat killed followed by live organisms) were given, and their blood tested for the presence of bactericidins.

In these experiments, the most satisfactory antigen was found to be live pneumococci; a preliminary injection of 2 or 3 doses of heat killed organisms lessened the chance of pneumococcic infection. The antigen was prepared by washing down a blood agar slant with salt solution or with Locke's solution. The latter decreases the rate of autolysis, and, furthermore, maintains the viability of the vaccine for a greater length of time. The schedule for immunizing these rabbits was as follows:

Three injections made intravenously on successive days of 500,000,000 heat killed pneumococci with a four day interim of rest.

Three injections on successive days of live organisms (500,000,000, 500,000,000 and 1,000,000,000) followed by a four day rest interim.

Three injections of live pneumococci (one, two and five billion) with an interim from 4 to 10 days before testing the blood.

Four routes of immunization were tried, namely, intratracheal, intrapleural, intravenous and subcutaneous. All were effective, differing only in the degree of bactericidal action produced. While sufficient experiments were not made to draw definite conclusions, the results suggested that the best results were obtainable by the intravenous route, with the intratracheal a close second. It is interesting to note in this connection that Bronfenbrenner and Knights[8] found the intratracheal route was preferable. The doses were large and pushed vigorously so that the rabbits showed a reaction following the injections. The amount of reaction seemed to be in direct relation to the amount of bactericidal action demonstrable.

During the course of immunization, the bactericidal action was not marked or constant, but appeared 10 to 14 days after the last injection and remained demonstrable in the blood for periods ranging from 30 to 70 days. Table 3 gives the results (no growth) in 4 of the rabbits used in this experiment. It is interesting to note that the 2 rabbits which earlier had the smaller doses of vaccine (table 3, no. 268, and 249) showed the persistence of bactericidins for a period of 30 days. While the other 2 rabbits, which had received more extensive injections (no. 228; no. 327) showed the bactericidins to persist for at least 70 days. It is also noteworthy that the 24-hour result did not always run parallel to the 96-hour result, indicating that the absence of growth for the first 24 hours was due to inhibiting influences rather than to bactericidal activity. All the rabbits showed this bactericidal property to be present even after 96 hours' incubation of the whole blood and culture. The degree of bactericidal action varied with the route of giving the vaccine, and to a certain extent with the individual rabbit.

Exper. 3.—In another experiment, 6 rabbits were selected for a trial of the effect of using live organisms as antigen, and also to determine whether or not the response to immunization would differ in rabbits with different histories. Two rabbits which were "sensitized," that is, received but a single injection several months previously, were contrasted to 2 rabbits that had undergone repeated injections in a course of immunization some months earlier, and also to 2 normal rabbits.

These 6 rabbits were tested before beginning the experiment, and the blood of none showed bactericidal property. All the rabbits received a similar course of treatment, as follows:

One-half billion live pneumococci intravenously on 3 successive days, followed by a 4-day interval of rest.

[8] Proc. Soc. Exp. Biol. and Med., 1922, 19, p. 336.

TABLE 3

PNEUMOCOCCIDAL ACTION OF BLOOD OF IMMUNIZED RABBITS, TEST TUBE METHOD

Number of Rabbits and Injections of Pneumococci	Dilutions of Broth Culture Mixed with the Blood						Incubation Hours	Days After Last Injection
	1 : 10,000,000	1 : 1,000,000	1 : 100,000	1 : 10,000	1 : 1,000	1 : 100		
Rabbit 268—Intrapleural injections 1 million heat killed, April 14 ½ billion heat killed, Sept. 26, 27 and 28 ½ billion living, Oct. 3, 4 and 5 2 billion living, Oct. 10, 11 and 12	—	++++	++++	++++	....	......	24	10
	—	++++	++++	++++	....	......	96	
	—	—	++++	++++	....	......	24	14
	—	—	....	....	....	......	96	
	—	—	—	+++	+++	......	24	32
	—	—	—	++	+++	......	96	
	....	....	++++	++++	++++	......	24	40
Rabbit 249—Intratracheal injections 1 million heat killed, April 14 ½ billion heat killed, Sept. 26, 27 and 28 ½ billion living, Oct. 3, 4 and 5 2 billion living, Oct. 10, 11 and 12	—	—	+++	++++	....	......	24	10
	—	—	++++	++++	....	......	96	
	—	—	—	++	....	......	24	14
	—	—	—	....	....	......	96	
	....	—	++	+++	+++	......	24	30
	....	—	+	—	+++	......	96	
	....	....	+++	+++	+++	......	24	37
Rabbit 327—Intrapleural injections 1 agar slant heat killed, Oct. 29 1 autolyzed culture, intratracheally, Feb. 17 ⅓ living culture, Feb. 17 1 living culture, March 2 1 billion living, June 8 ½ billion heat killed, Sept. 26, 27 and 28 ½ billion living, Oct. 3, 4 and 5 2 billion living, Oct. 10, 11 and 12	....	—	—	—	....	......	24	10
	....	—	—	—	....	......	96	
	....	—	—	—	....	......	24	14
	....	—	—	—	....	......	96	
	....	—	—	+	+++	......	24	24
	....	—	—	+	+	......	96	
	....	—	—	++	++	......	24	32
	....	—	+	+	++	......	96	
	....	....	—	+	+++	......	24	38
	....	....	—	+	+++	......	96	
	....	....	—	—	+++	......	24	45
	....	....	++	++	....	......	96	
	....	—	+++	++++	++++	......	24	72
	....	—	....	....	....	......	96	
	....	—	++	++	+++	......	24	90
	....	++++	....	....	....	......	96	
Rabbit 228—Intravenous injections 1 agar slant heat killed, Feb. 17, 21, 25 and April 8 1 billion heat killed, Sept. 13, 14 and 15 1½ million living, Sept. 20, 21 and 22 50 million living Sept. 27, 28 and 29 1 billion living, Oct. 4 and 5 2 billion living, Oct. 6	....	—	—	—	....	......	24	22
	....	—	—	—	....	......	96	
	....	—	—	—	....	......	24	30
	....	+++	++	+	....	......	96	
	....	—	—	+	+	......	24	38
	....	+++	—	+++	+++	......	96	
	....	....	—	—	—	+	24	45
	....	....	—	++	—	+++	96	
	....	—	—	+	—	......	24	65
	....	—	—	—	+	......	96	
	....	—	+++	++	+++	......	24	72
	....	—	....	....	....	......	96	
	....	—	—	++++	+++	......	24	90
	....	+	+	....	....	......	96	

—, no colonies; +, only occasional colonies; ++, few colonies; +++, many colonies; ++++, innumerable colonies.

TABLE 4

PNEUMOCOCCIDAL ACTION OF BLOOD OF RABBITS IMMUNIZED IN DIFFERENT WAYS, TEST TUBE METHOD

Number of Rabbits and Injections of Pneumococci	Dilutions of Broth Culture Mixed with the Blood						Incubation Hours	Days After Jan. 9, 1923
	1 : 1,000 000	1 : 100,000	1 : 10 000	1 : 1,000	1 : 100	1 : 10		
Rabbit 363—Intratracheal injections: 1 agar slant in bile, Dec. 8, 1921; ½ billion living, Jan. 9, 10, 11, 1923; 1 billion living, Jan. 16; 1½ billion living, Jan. 17 and 18; 2 billion living, Jan. 24 and 25; 3 billion living, Feb. 2	++++	++++	++++	++++	++++	......	24	6
	+++	+++	++++	+++	......	......	24	13
	—	++	—	+++	......	......	24	20
	—	+	—	......	......	......	96	
	—	—	+	+	+	......	24	28
	—	—	—	—	—	......	96	
	—	+	—	+	—	......	24	33
	—	—	—	—	—	......	96	
	—	—	++	+++	+++	......	24	38
	—	—	......	......	......	......	96	
	......	—	++	+++	+++	......	24	51
	......	—	......	......	......	......	96	
Rabbit 334—Intrapleural injections: ½ agar slant, heat killed, Nov. 1, 2, 3, 8, 9, 10, 1921; 1 agar slant, heat killed, Nov. 15, 16, 17, 22; 1 agar slant, heat killed, Dec. 14; 1 broth culture living, March 25, 1922; 1½ broth culture living, May 5; 1 billion living, June 8; ½ billion living, Jan. 9, 10 and 11, 1923; 1 billion living, Jan. 16; 1½ billion living, Jan. 17 and 18; 2 billion living, Jan. 24 and 25; 3 billion living, Feb. 2	+++	+++	++++	++++	......	......	24	6
	+++	+++	+++	++	......	......	24	13
	—	—	—	+	......	......	24	20
	—	—	—	+	......	......	96	
	—	—	—	—	—	......	24	28
	—	—	—	—	—	......	96	
	—	—	—	+	+	......	24	33
	—	—	—	......	......	......	96	
	+	—	—	++	++	......	24	38
	—	—	—	......	......	......	96	
	......	—	—	+	++	......	24	51
	......	—	—	......	......	......	96	
Rabbit 194—Intravenous injections: 1 billion heat killed, June 28, 29, 30, July 5, 6, 7, 12, 13 and 14; ½ billion living, Jan. 9, 10 and 11; 1 billion living, Jan. 16; 1½ billion living, Jan. 17 and 18; 2 billion living, Jan. 24 and 25; 3 billion living, Feb. 2	+++	++	++	+++	......	......	24	6
	++	+	++	++++	......	......	24	13
	—	—	—	—	......	......	24	20
	—	—	—	—	......	......	96	
	—	—	—	—	++	......	24	28
	—	—	—	—	+++	......	96	
	—	—	—	—	+	—	24	33
	—	—	—	—	—	—	96	
	—	—	+	++	++	......	24	38
	—	—	......	......	......	......	96	
	......	—	—	+	++	+	24	51
	......	—	—	......	......	......	96	

—, no colonies; +, only occasional colonies; ++, few colonies; +++, many colonies; ++++, innumerable colonies.

TABLE 4—*Continued*

PNEUMOCOCCIDAL ACTION OF BLOOD OF RABBITS IMMUNIZED IN DIFFERENT WAYS, TEST TUBE METHOD

Number of Rabbits and Injections of Pneumococci	Dilutions of Broth Culture Mixed with the Blood						Incubation Hours	Days After Jan. 9, 1923
	1 : 1,000,000	1 : 100,000	1 : 10,000	1 : 1,000	1 : 100	1 : 10		
Rabbit 192— ½ billion living, Jan. 9, 10 and 11 1 billion living, Jan. 16 1½ billion living, Jan. 17 and 18 2 billion living, Jan. 24 and 25 3 billion living, Feb. 2	+	+++	+++	+++	....	....	24	6
	+	++	++	+++	....	....	24	13
	—	—	+	—	....	....	24	20
	—	—	—	+	....	....	96	
	—	—	—	—	—	....	24	28
	—	—	—	—	—	....	96	
	—	—	—	+	—	....	24	33
	—	—	—	....	—	....	96	
	—	—	—	—	—	....	24	38
	—	—	+++	+++	—	....	96	
	....	—	—	—	+	....	24	51
	....	—	+	+	....	....	96	
Rabbit 193— ½ billion living, Jan. 9, 10 and 11 1 billion living, Jan. 16 1½ billion living, Jan. 17 and 18 2 billion living, Jan. 24 and 25 3 billion living, Feb. 2	++	++	+++	+++	....	....	24	6
	—	+	++	++++	....	....	24	13
	—	....	—	....	....	....	96	
	—	—	—	—	....	....	24	20
	—	—	—	—	....	....	96	
	—	—	—	—	—	....	24	28
	—	—	++	++	—	....	96	
	—	—	—	—	....	....	24	33
	—	—	—	++	....	....	96	
	—	—	—	—	—	....	24	38
	—	++	—	++	....	....	96	
	....	—	+	++	++	....	24	51
	....	—	....	....	....	....	96	

—, no colonies; +, only occasional colonies; ++, few colonies; +++, many colonies; ++++, innumerable colonies.

Three successive injections of live pneumococci, the doses being 1,000,000,000, 1,500,000,000 and 1,500,000,000 organisms, followed by a 6-day interval of rest.

Two successive injections of 2,000,000,000 organisms each.

During the immunization, the bactericidal test was made every week, but it was not until 6 days after the course had been finished that the bactericidal property appeared. It is interesting to note that one of the "sensitized" rabbits died following the initial injection with no lesions of pneumonia, suggesting that anaphylaxis might have been the cause of death. Moreover, the other "sensitized" rabbit, which survived the course of immunization, did not show as high a bactericidal titer as did the others. The titer of the bactericidins produced in the normal rabbits was not so high and was more irregular than in those rabbits that had received repeated injections previous to the present experiment. These results are shown in table 4.

There appears to be no question, as indicated in the experiments just described, that bactericidins can be produced and demonstrated in the blood of rabbits; and the fact that the titer of bactericidal activity increases in proportion to the amount of pneumococci introduced suggests that there may be some relationship between the bactericidal property of blood and active immunity. Experiments are now being made in an attempt to learn whether or not the bactericidal titer of blood will serve as an index of the amount of active immunity present.

CONCLUSIONS

The capillary tube method of indicating the bactericidal property of the blood of rabbits immunized against pneumococci, as described by Heist and Solis-Cohen, was found to be unsatisfactory, as the results obtained were not constant and did not distinguish between bactericidal and bacteriostatic action.

A test tube method has been substituted, and in our experience has given constant and conclusive results.

Bactericidins have been demonstrated in the blood of rabbits following the injection of pneumococci.

Although the best method of producing bactericidins in the blood against pneumococci has not as yet been determined, the method which we have used successfully was to give an initial injection of heat killed organisms followed by large and repeated doses of live organisms. The preliminary injection of heat killed organisms lessened the chance of pneumococcic infection.

In the rabbits thus "immunized," bactericidins appeared in the blood 10 days after the last injection and persisted in the blood for periods ranging from 30 to 70 days.

BACTERIOLOGIC STUDY OF PNEUMONIA IN SHEEP

Robb Spalding Spray

From the Department of Hygiene and Bacteriology, University of Chicago

A respiratory infection commonly called infectious pneumonia, or hemorrhagic septicemia, has long been known to affect sheep. In the typical form there is an acute pneumonia with hemorrhagic lesions most evident on the serous surfaces of the lungs and heart. An intense septicemia usually occurs at death, and a highly pathogenic organism of the pasteurella group may be almost constantly isolated from the heart blood either by direct inoculation on blood agar or by inoculation of rabbits, which are very susceptible to pasteurella infections.

A similar disease, however, at times assumes a chronic form among sheep. In this form there is usually an intense fibrinous pleuritis of one or both lungs and the adjacent tissues rendering it almost impossible to remove the lung intact from the carcass. Necrosis and extensive suppuration are constant. This type of infection occurs chiefly in old sheep, particularly among those from the West, and the affected animal may show no visible signs of the condition until at slaughter. Infections of the adjacent lymph nodes often accompany this chronic form of the disease, and the resulting condition is termed caseous lymphadenitis or pseudotuberculosis. Since the work of Nocard,[1] Preisz and Guinard,[2] Nocard and Leclainche,[3] Preisz,[4] Nörgaard and Mohler,[5] Cherry and Bull,[6] Roux,[7] Dammann and Freese [8] and others, the causative organism has been assumed to be the bacillus of pseudotuberculosis of Preisz-Nocard.

A third type of infection, occurring in market lambs, is herein described. In these cases, the lungs show areas of varying extent in all stages of consolidation or hepatization. More commonly, one or more of the small lateral lobes are in the stage of red hepatization.

Received for publication, April 17, 1923.

[1] Ann. de l'Inst. Pasteur, 1887, 1, p. 417.
[2] Jour. de méd. vét., 1891, p. 563.
[3] Maladies microbiennes des Animaux, 1903, pp. 166 and 327.
[4] Ann. de l'Inst. Pasteur, 1894, 8, p. 231.
[5] 16th Ann. Rept. Bur. Animal Ind., 1899, p. 678.
[6] The Veterinarian, 1899, 72, p. 523.
[7] Ann. de l'Inst. Past., 1887, 1, p. 56.
[8] Deutsche thierärtz. Wchnschr., 1907, 15, p. 165.

Such areas are quite uniformly edematous, heavy and soggy, and a sanguineous fluid exudes from the surface and from the bronchioles, a condition entirely different from that in pneumonia of older sheep, in which the bronchioles are plugged with a purulent secretion.

Since the studies of Löffler,[9] Schütz,[10] Hueppe,[11] Lignieres[12] and many others, it has been generally accepted that pasteurella infections are responsible for the acute hemorrhagic septicemias of various animals. However, there are many who regard the causal relationship as at least doubtful. The relationship is even less well established in the more chronic infections and in the milder types of pneumonias described above.

Furthermore, in recent literature frequent references are made to the occurrence of pure cultures of other organisms in conditions similar to those presumed to be caused by pasteurella infections. These references pertain chiefly to pneumonias of animals other than sheep. The literature on this subject has been reviewed recently by the writer.[13]

It is also a matter of common opinion that avirulent strains of pasteurellas occur in the mouth, throat and lungs of normal animals, and that such animals act as carriers of organisms which in some way gain virulence and establish infection. Specific citations, however, are scarce. Recently Hoskins[14] reported the occurrence of an avirulent strain of Bact. bovisepticus in the lungs and muscles of a calf, and Giltner[15] reports an atypical and relatively avirulent strain from a case of sheep pneumonia. He regards this organism as being probably a pasteurella variant.

With these observations in mind, it was considered advisable to study intensively the bacterial flora of a number of cases of pneumonia of the types described and to attempt to determine the relationship of any strains which might be regarded as variants from the pasteurella type. Arrangements were then made for access to the killing floors of Chicago packing houses, where an abundance of material was available. This paper presents the results of a bacteriologic study of such types of pneumonia as were found during the summer months under slaughterhouse conditions. Ten cases of the suppurative type and 36

[9] Arb. a. d. kais. Ges., 1886, 1, pp. 46 and 546; Mitt. a. d. kais. Ges., 1884, 2, p. 421.
[10] Arb. a. d. kais. Ges., 1885, 1, pp. 56 and 376.
[11] Berl. klin. Wchnschr., 1886, 44, p. 753; 45, p. 776.
[12] Bull. de la Soc. centr. de Méd. vét., 1898, pp. 761, 797, 836.
[13] Jour. Infect. Dis., 1922, 31, p. 11.
[14] Jour. Am. Vet. Med. Assn., 1922, 60, p. 453.
[15] Personal communication, L. T. Giltner, U. S. Bur. An. Ind.

cases of lamb pneumonia were studied. Later, during December, 20 more cases of lamb pneumonia were studied. In addition, cultures were made in several typical cases of caseous lymphadenitis, with results to be reported fully later.

Technic of Isolation.—Blood agar was used throughout the work both for isolating and for carrying of stock cultures. This was the only solid medium on which the strains under study could be safely stored. After several transfers on plain veal infusion agar, some of the cultures became fairly well established, but the habit of dying out even after apparent adaptation to the medium necessitated too frequent transfer and frequent return to an old stock culture on blood agar.

The selected lesions were seared on the surface, cut into with a heated scalpel, and the bronchial secretions were stroked on blood agar plates. Selected colonies were replated once when a pure culture was found on initial cultivation, and twice replated when a mixed culture on the first plate might lead to questionable purity after only a single isolation. During the course of the study the cultures were always replated, and diagnostic mediums were then inoculated from a culture proliferated from a single isolated colony.

The first few inoculations served to distinguish the characteristic flora, only five well defined types being encountered in significant numbers in this work:

(1) A true Past. ovisepticum (S8 type).

(2) A type similar to the pasteurella, but distinct (S3 type).

(3) A type similar to the S3 type, but distinct (S14 type).

(4) A gram-negative diplococcus of M. catarrhalis type (S1 type).

(5) A gram-positive diplococcus with short-chain tendency (S20 type).

These type strains were selected for comparison with about 95 strains isolated, and were reinoculated as controls whenever cultural tests were made on new strains. Control cultures were also made of type strains of Past. bulbasepticum, ovisepticum, and suisepticum from several sources.

The results of an extensive study of the cultural characteristics indicate the frequent occurrence of the true Past. ovisepticum, together with two well defined types of similar organisms which are undoubtedly closely related to each other, as well as to the true pasteurella type. A number of strains varying slightly from the types noted were isolated, and these apparently serve to link the atypical strains (S3 and S14 types) to the true pasteurella type. The results of this study indicate that: (1) The pasteurella type has a wider divergence of cultural characteristics than is ordinarily recognized; (2) it is a "group" similar to the "swine typhus-B. suipestifer group"; or (3) that hitherto undescribed pasteurella-like organisms may be associated with pneumonic lesions commonly ascribed solely to true pasteurella infections.

Similar variants have been noted in a previous study of strains of Past. suisepticum, and it seems that the cultural characteristics of the entire pasteurella group might well be intensively reviewed, using some of the recently developed mediums and methods as criteria for classification.

MORPHOLOGIC AND CULTURAL CHARACTERISTICS OF THE TRUE PAST. OVISEPTICUM

1. Past. ovisepticum (S8 type) is a tiny cocco-bacillus showing the well-known bipolar staining tendency; also with a tendency toward pleomorphism, swollen cells and short threads being common. An extended description of the morphology of the true pasteurella is unnecessary.

On veal infusion blood agar, deep, moist, pearly colonies reached a size of 2 mm. in 24 hours when well isolated. Characteristically, a moist confluent growth occurred. No trace of lysis or other alteration of the blood was evidenced by any of the strains of this type, including the control strains of pasteurellas from animals other than sheep.

Two characteristics were observed to be specific for all of the true pasteurellas: (1) A peculiar odor, undoubtedly that of indol, best obtained from plate cultures on either plain agar or blood agar. The fact that this is indol was readily demonstrated by moistening a bit of filter paper with the Ehrlich reagent and causing it to adhere to the inner surface of the lid of the plate culture. A strongly positive reaction developed in a few minutes, the paper taking a deep rose color. Mention of this odor has been encountered in the literature in only one instance [3] and no significance or value is ascribed to its occurrence, although it is possible to identify unknown cultures with practical certainty or to detect the presence of these organisms in mixed culture by this odor alone.

2. A peculiar appearance of the surface of colonies on plain or on blood agar plates. At 24 hours, the colonies were moist and slimy tenacious, but at 48 hours they looked as though they were dusted over with a refractive powder giving a dull ground-glass appearance to the surface. At the same time, the growth becomes more viscid tenacious to waxy. Under the low power lens, this surface appearance is seen to be due to the presence of unidentified crystals. After several days, the growth takes on a pearly cast very conspicuous and peculiar to this organism.

Veal infusion agar of P_H 7.5 did not favor growth and it was necessary to carry stock cultures on blood agar to insure against loss. Many strains would not transfer after 3 days on plain infusion agar in the incubator, or after 2 days in the incubator followed by 5 days in the refrigerator. In this respect, however, the true pasteurellas were more hardy than the atypical strains. All of the strains grew well on plain infusion agar if transferred every third day. All strains grew moderately well on plain meat extract agar after several transfers on blood agar, but after apparent adaptation to extract agar the cultures might die out within 48 hours in the incubator.

Veal infusion gelatin was not liquefied by cultivation at either 20 or 37 C. Gelatin to which brom-thymol-blue was added and titrated to P_H 7.4-7.5 was not visibly altered in its reaction within 15 days incubation, although a fairly abundant growth occurred.

Litmus milk was given a doubtful trace of acidity at 2 to 3 days by all strains, accompanied by slow and incomplete reduction of the litmus beginning at the bottom and progressing upward, so that even at 19 days only the lower 2/3 of the medium had lost its color, while the upper 1/3 was neutral and was not reduced. No further change was observed for at least 50 days, although tests of several cultures showed the presence of viable organisms.

Nitrites were formed in standard nitrate broth, and indol was produced in peptone water (Armour) by all typical strains of pasteurellas from sheep, as well as by the control strains from other animals.

Fermentation reactions were particularly unsatisfactory, owing to the fact that many strains grew barely perceptibly or not at all in the mediums commonly used in fermentation tests. Strains which grew well in veal infusion broth without fermenting a sugar might ferment the sugar if grown in a serum or ascitic fluid broth. Some produced traces of acid in medium sterilized by heat, but not when the sugar was sterilized by filtration, or more peculiarly, in one case fermented a sugar when filtered but not when heated.

It was evident that an enriched medium was necessary to assure growth and uniform results, and for this purpose 2 kinds of mediums were tried. Serum broth in which equal parts of serum water (1 part serum and 3 parts distilled water) and standard veal infusion broth were mixed and 1% of Andrade indicator and 1% of the desired sugar added. This medium was adjusted to P_H 7.4, sterilized in small agglutination tubes for 10 minutes at 15 pounds pressure, and was incubated before inoculation. In such small quantities this method of sterilization was perfectly effective.

In recent work, serum in quantity was not readily available, and the possible substitution of egg-white suggested itself. One part of egg-white added to 2 parts of distilled water will coagulate in autoclaving, but if 4 parts of distilled water are added to 1 part of egg-white the mixture may be autoclaved without coagulating and an opalescent, serum-like fluid is obtained. If a trace of acid is added before heating only clouding results, but if added after heating the fluid immediately coagulates. If equal parts of this egg-water and standard broth are mixed and 1% of Andrade indicator added, autoclaving leaves a perfectly clear or faintly opalescent fluid medium. Addition of a trace of acid gives a red coagulated medium. It should be emphasized that it is necessary to heat the egg-white and distilled water to boiling before adding the broth which contains salt, otherwise the medium will coagulate in autoclaving. The chemistry of the reactions has not been studied; it happens that a suitable medium may thus be prepared, and numerous tests of the organisms studied in this work, as well as of streptococci, pneumococci, and the various typhoid-paratyphoids, indicate that it may be substituted for the common serum-water or serum-broth.

Table 1 gives the result of repeated tests of the fermentation of various carbohydrates and represents the reactions under the best growth conditions obtainable:

TABLE 1

FERMENTATION REACTIONS OF THE TYPE STRAINS, ATYPICAL AND CONTROL STRAINS CONSIDERED IN THIS STUDY *

	Glucose	Levulose	Galactose	Xylose	Lactose	Saccharose	Maltose	Glycerol	Mannite	Sorbite
Past. ovisepticum (S8 Type); Past. ovisepticum (B. A. I.); Past. bubalisepticum (B. A. I.); Past. suisepticum (P408)	+	+	+	+ to ±	—	+	—	+‡	+	+
S3 type	+	+	+	+	+†	+	+	+	+	+
S14 type	+	+	+	+	—	+	+	+§	+	+
S18	+	+	+	+	—	+	—	—‖	±¶	—#
S21, S21x	+	+	+	+	—	+	—	—‖	+	+
S5j, S11j	+	—	—	—	—	—	—	—‖	—	—
S23	+	+	+	+	—	+	+	—‖	+	—
Diplococcus (S20 type)	+	+	+	±	+	+	+	—	—	—

* Arabinose, dextrin, salicin, inulin, and inosite were never fermented by any of the organisms tested.
† Delayed fermentation at 6-7 days; coagulation at 10-12 days.
‡ Pasteurellas as a group first show acid at about 30 days.
§ S14 type showed acid first at about 15 days.
‖ No acid for 40 days.
¶ Negative on 3 tests; moderately positive 6 months after isolation.
# Negative on 4 tests.

Certain variations were noted in the avidity with which a few strains attacked some sugars, while a few atypical strains did not ferment certain sugars characteristically fermented by this group. It was possible to separate sharply the true pasteurella from the related strains by the inability of the former to ferment maltose.

Glycerol (5% in serum-broth or egg-broth) gave excellent differentiation, not only separating the true pasteurellas from the related types, but also dividing these related forms into 2 groups, based on the avidity with which they attacked glycerol. All typical strains showed traces of acid (to Andrade) at 30 to 33 days, while the atypical strains S18, S21, and S21x did not show acid at 40 days, although still viable, as was shown by inoculation of blood agar slants. Control tubes of serum-broth without carbohydrate were not rendered perceptibly acid within 40 days by any of the organisms included in this study, and the late acidity in the glycerol medium can be interpreted only as the result of the action of the organisms on the glycerol.

One control strain of Past. suisepticum (P408) showed a trace of acid at 17 days, the earliest observed for the pasteurella group.

Atypical Past. ovisepticum Strains.—S18 differed from type in the absence of reaction on glycerol for at least 40 days, although it was alive at 33 days, as shown by transfer to agar. This same strain failed on 4 tests to ferment sorbite; on 3 tests mannite was not attacked, while recently, 6 months after isolation, it was slowly and moderately fermented, acid being evident but not sufficient to coagulate the medium.

S21, and S21x (identical with S21, but isolated after animal passage) had no action on glycerol within 40 days, and did not form indol in peptone water in an amount detectable by the Ehrlich test in 3 tests of each organism. In one series of tests, ascitic fluid was added aseptically to enhance growth. All of the typical strains of pasteurellas gave strong indol reaction by the Ehrlich method in both plain and ascitic peptone water.

S5j and S11j never became well adapted to any medium, growing poorly even on blood agar. These 2 strains fermented only glucose of all the carbohydrates tested. In other respects, they were typical. These 2 strains represent well the difficulties encountered in the study of this group of organisms. They grew well in certain sugar broths, while in others no perceptible multiplication occurred, although the tubes were heavily inoculated, and although they remained viable for several weeks. It is questionable whether the inactivity of these strains toward the sugars is to be attributed to inability to ferment, or to inability to grow in the basic medium.

MORPHOLOGIC AND CULTURAL CHARACTERISTICS OF THE RELATED (MALTOSE FERMENTING) STRAINS

(2) S3 Type: This group is apparently closely related to the true Past. ovisepticum type in cultural as well as in morphologic characteristics. These organisms are gram-negative, and are slightly larger than the S8 type, resembling more the size and proportions of B. suipestifer. They show less tendency toward bipolar staining, although many cells stain irregularly, while swollen shadowy cells and short filaments were abundant in both fluid and solid mediums. This type, like the true pasteurella, did not normally form chains, but occurred typically only singly and in pairs. The morphology of the S3 type strains was so similar to that of the pasteurella type that it was impossible to differentiate them by microscopic examination alone. None of the 26 strains of this group showed any trace of motility.

The first distinguishing character observed for the group was the appearance on blood agar plates of a distinct ring of partial hemolysis barely perceptible beyond the periphery of the rather flat, thin, translucent colony. On removing the growth, a pale area of partial hemolysis distinctly marked the outline of the colony. The colonies of the S3 type are easily distinguished from those of the pasteurella type which are slightly deeper, more opaque, and show no hemolysis even after removal of the growth.

The S3 type lacked the indol odor peculiar to the true pasteurellas, and never produced indol in amounts detectable by the Ehrlich test in peptone water, nor by the filter paper test described above. Nitrites were formed in nitrate broth by all strains, some more actively than others. Gelatin was not liquefied whether grown at 20 or 37 C.

Litmus milk remained neutral, or very doubtfully acid, for 2 to 3 days, when reduction began at the bottom of the tube, progressing slowly upward, until at 14 days the top layer of about 1 mm. was slightly acid, while the remainder was completely decolorized. At 6 to 10 days all of the S3 group were distinct from the true pasteurella type, while at 18 to 21 days certain of the atypical Past. ovisepticum strains approached the S3 type in the extent of reduction. The reaction in litmus milk served to differentiate sharply the S3 type from the true pasteurella on early observation, while later observation, particularly of the atypical strains of each type, served only to emphasize their close resemblance, if not a possible relationship.

As a group the S3 type actively fermented glucose, saccharose, galactose, and maltose, while with other carbohydrates irregularity was observed with some strains. All S3 strains attacked glycerol in 3 to 6 days. In 5% glycerol serum broth, a heavy flocculent sediment was formed which was not diffused even by vigorous shaking, and the medium remained fluid during the period of observation. When the test was repeated in egg-broth, coagulation occurred. The reaction in the serum broth is emphasized because of the differentiation of the S3 and S14 types evidenced in this medium. The fermentation of maltose served to separate sharply the S3 from the true pasteurellas.

All S3 strains evidenced a delayed action on lactose, showing a doubtful trace of acid not earlier than 7 to 8 days, and increasing to the point of coagulation at 10 to 12 days. According to the present methods of classification, the fermentation of lactose would remove this type from the region of the pasteurella group. However, typical pasteurellas are occasionally encountered which show slight but undoubted ability to attack lactose after prolonged incubation.

As a check on the fermentation tests, 20% solutions of maltose and galactose were filtered through a Mandler filter into sterile serum broth to make a 1% concentration of the sugar. Andrade indicator was added and the medium tubed aseptically. The results of the tests in this filtered medium were sharper than with the heated sugars, and strain S7, which had given 2 negative tests with heated galactose, actively fermented the filtered sugar.

(3) S14 Type: This group resembled the S3 type closely, differing only in the total absence of action on lactose, and in the reaction in glycerol serum broth. In the latter medium, acid appeared first at 14 days, increasing slowly until the end reaction was moderately acid at 20 to 22 days. The type of growth, however, was distinct from that of the S3 type. A moderate sediment formed before acidity was perceptible. This sediment was not flocculent, and diffused readily on slight agitation. This diffusible sediment was characteristic of all S14 strains, the flocculent sediment for all S3 strains, while the pasteurellas all gave a tenacious, nondiffusible sediment. In other respects, the S14 and S3 types were culturally alike.

Atypical Strain, S23: This organism appeared to be most closely related to the S14 type, but did not ferment glycerol up to 40 days, although transfer showed it to be still viable. In litmus milk, the reaction simulated that of the pasteurella type, reduction being less active than that of the S14 and S3 types.

(4) M. catarrhalis Type, S1 Type: A gram-negative diplococcus occurring typically in pairs, or frequently in tetrads, was isolated in pure culture from 2 cases of pneumonia in lambs, and was found in mixed culture in several other cases, as well as in 2 cases of the purulent type in old sheep.

The reactions were negative as to fermentation, liquefaction of gelatin, indol production, and nitrate reduction. Litmus milk was decolorized within 3 days by all strains, while the upper portion became distinctly alkaline, this reaction persisting for at least 20 days.

Except for the strong alkaline reaction in milk this type would be rgearded as a typical M. catarrhalis, and it is at present considered a member of this group.

(5) Gram-positive Diplococcus, S20 Type: Eight strains of a gram-positive organism were isolated from cases of pseudotuberculosis or from types of pneumonia which were either associated with caseous lymphadenitis or showed lung lesions which suggested a similar etiology. This disease is attributed, in the veterinary literature, entirely to the activity of the Preisz-Nocard bacillus, an organism related to B. pyogenes bovis and suis of similar diseases of cattle and swine.

Immediately on isolation all strains were gram-positive, and decidedly bacillary in appearance, with pleomorphic forms varying from coccoid to typical bacilli very common. It was at first assumed that these were strains of the Preisz-Nocard bacillus, but one reaction after another failed to check with the description. Type strains were obtained from the Pasteur Institute, from the British National Type Collection, and from the U. S. Bureau of Animal Industry. It was at once evident that these strains were not related to the Preisz-Nocard type.

This group is at present under intensive study, and will be only briefly described here, complete description being reserved for a later report.

Inoculation on blood agar produced a haze of pin-point colonies at 24 hours, which attained a maximum size of 1 mm. after 4 to 6 days' incubation. Cultures could be maintained only on blood agar, although traces of growth were induced on fresh infusion agar. Slight and incomplete hemolysis was apparent on original cultures on blood agar plates. Some strains were more active than others, simulating Strep.

viridans colonies at 24 hours and verging on typical hemolysis at 48 hours. Repeated cultivation on blood agar seemed to enhance their hemolytic ability, all strains becoming decidedly hemolytic after 6 months' cultivation.

A proteoclastic activity was first noted in serum broth which within 24 hours lost the opalescence of serum medium and became perfectly clear. This action was more evident on Loeffler's serum, which was completely liquefied by 2 strains within 7 days, while the other strains were but little less active. Gelatin was liquefied in 24 to 48 hours at either 20 or 37 C.

Neutral litmus milk became slightly acid at 24 hours, and peptonization was evident in the upper half of the medium. At 48 hours, the upper half of the medium was clear and acid. Within 3 to 4 days peptonization was practically complete, with a moderate acid reaction throughout, and with a considerable yellowish solid sediment which was not diffusible by the most vigorous shaking.

The fermentation study is incomplete, and the results tabulated in table 1 were based on only one comprehensive test and a few isolated inoculations.

Pathogenicity Tests

Representative strains of 2 types were selected for test on rabbits. One c c. of a 24-hour broth culture was inoculated subcutaneously on the abdomen:

S1 (M. catarrhalis-type), no reaction, well at 42 days.
S13 (M. catarrhalis-type), no reaction, well at 42 days.
S6 (S3 type), no reaction, well at 42 days.
S5 (S3 type), ill on 3rd day, died on 7th day.

At necropsy of the S5 rabbit, no organisms were found in stains of the heart blood, and inoculations from the heart, liver, kidney, and spleen failed to yield any growth. The gallbladder contained a whitish mucoid fluid, and from this an organism was isolated which corresponded in all cultural respects to a typical B. paratyphosus B. The rabbit had been previously caged with animals used in testing various paratyphoid cultures.

On the second test, 5 rabbits were inoculated intravenously with 1 c c. of a broth emulsion of a 24-hour blood-agar culture of the selected strains.

S14 (S14 type strain), ill on 4th day, died on 11th day.
S33 (pasteurella), no reaction, well at 39 days.
S21 (atypical pasteurella), ill on 3rd day, died on 10th day.
S20 (Diplococcus), no reaction, well at 39 days.
S22 (Diplococcus), no reaction, well at 39 days, (killed on 40th day).

At necropsy, the S14 rabbit showed no visible lesions other than a moderate congestion of the lungs. A very few organisms were seen in stains of the heart blood, but the organism inoculated was not recovered from the heart, liver, spleen, or kidney.

The S21 rabbit was visibly ill on the 4th day, became rapidly cachectic, and died on the 10th day. Except for slight congestion of the peritoneum and numerous petechiae on the surface of the lungs, the organs were visibly normal. Stain of the heart blood showed only a few typical bipolar bacilli. Culture from the heart yielded 15 colonies similar to those of the culture inoculated, and strain S21x isolated from one of these colonies proved identical with the original strain.

The S22 rabbit showed no visible reaction and was active at 40 days, when it was killed and examined for evidence of infection. No lesions could be found, and the animal was apparently perfectly normal.

On the third test, 7 representative strains were selected and inoculated at the same time into 7 each of white mice, guinea-pigs, and rabbits. The cultures were grown 24 hours on blood agar slants, washed off in 5 c c. of sterile broth, and each animal given 1 c c. or ⅕ of an agar slant intraperitoneally:

Results of Mouse Inoculations

S1 (M. catar.-type), ill at 24 hours, recovered, active at 8 days.
S8 (pasteurella), dead at 24 hours.
S33 (pasteurella), dead at 24 hours.
S10 (S3 type), dead at 24 hours.
S30 (S14 type), ill at 24 hours, died on 3rd day.
S20 (Diplococcus), ill at 24 hours, died on 3rd day.
S22 (Diplococcus), no reaction, well active at 8 days.

Necropsy and Inoculations.—S8 mouse showed no gross lesions. Stain of heart blood revealed an intense septicemia of typical bipolar bacilli. A pure culture was recovered from the heart, which was identified morphologically and culturally with the original strain.

S33 mouse showed no lesions other than slight pulmonary congestion. An intense septicemia was evident on staining the heart blood, and an organism identical with the strain inoculated was recovered from the heart in pure culture.

S10 and S30, conditions same as for S8 and S33; intense septicemia was evident and organisms recovered in pure culture from heart were identical respectively with the strains inoculated.

S20 mouse showed 4 small yellowish nodules in the liver, which were apparently in early stages of focal necrosis. Typical diplococci were abundant in stain from one of these foci, and inoculation from the same area yielded a heavy growth in pure culture of an organism identical with the original culture.

Results of Guinea-Pig Inoculations

S1, dead at 24 hours.
S8, dead at 24 hours.
S33, dead at 24 hours.
S10, dead at 24 hours.
S30, dead at 24 hours.
S20, well at 24 hours; active at 8 days; lame at 12 days; killed 14th day.
S22, well at 24 hours; ill at 48 hours; active at 3 to 8 days; killed on the 8th day.

S1, pig, displayed an intense hyperemia of lungs, other organs being visibly normal. No organisms were demonstrable in the heart blood, and inoculations from heart, liver, and spleen yielded no growth. Inoculation from kidney gave about 25 colonies of a gram-negative tiny bacillus entirely distinct from the organism inoculated. In this case the original strain was not recovered.

S8, pig, showed numerous petechiae on the surface of the liver. The other organs were visibly normal. No organisms were seen in stains from kidney and of heart blood. However, a moderate growth was obtained by inoculation both from heart and kidney. The organism isolated from the heart was a typical bipolar bacillus, which on later test conformed culturally to the original strain. A similar organism was recovered from the kidney in mixed culture with a few gram-positive cocci.

S33, pig, displayed only an intense hyperemia of the lungs. Stains of heart blood and kidney displayed many typical bipolar bacilli, and inoculation from the heart yielded a heavy pure culture of a similar organism. A heavy growth, practically pure, was also recovered from the kidney.

Neither S10 nor S30 showed any conspicuous lesions. The organisms were not seen in the heart blood stains in either case. From the S10 pig a heavy pure culture was recovered from the kidney, and 5 colonies of the same type from the heart. These organisms were culturally the same as the original S10 strain. The S30 strain was not recovered from the heart, liver, spleen, or kidney.

S22, pig, was killed on the 8th day, although it had recovered from the initial reaction. The intestines were adherent to the slightly congested peritoneum; a moderate amount of a sanguineous fluid was found in the peritoneal cavity; the liver showed several isolated necrotic areas which were almost similar to the typical lesions of caseous lymphadenitis in sheep. Stains from these caseous areas showed enormous numbers of typical diplococci, and inoculation yielded a pure and heavy growth of an organism identical with the original strain. It was quite evident that this animal would have died within a short time as a result of the inoculation.

The S20 pig was not visibly affected for 12 days, when it developed lameness in the hind quarters. This animal was killed on the 14th day and presented the same picture as the S22 pig. The culture was recovered from the liver.

RESULTS OF RABBIT INOCULATIONS

S1, no reaction, well at 8 days.
S8, apparently well at 24 hours, dead at about 50 hours.
S33, ill at 24 hours, dead at about 40 hours.
S10, no visible reaction, well at 8 days.[16]
S30, no visible reaction, well at 8 days.[16]
S20, no visible reaction, well at 8 days.
S22, no visible reaction, well at 8 days.

The lungs of S8, rabbit, were intensely hyperemic, otherwise the viscera were visibly normal. Stains of the heart blood revealed quite a few typical bipolar bacilli, and inoculation from the heart gave a moderately heavy pure culture of an organism later demonstrated to be identical with the original strain.

S33, rabbit, had been dead several hours when found, and putrefaction had set in. Stain of heart blood showed many typical bipolar organisms and many large gram-positive rods. Isolation was not attempted.

Interpretation of Pathogenicity Tests.—It is evident from the results of these tests that the strains described here as similar, or related, to the true pasteurella ovisepticum are capable of causing a septicemia and death in mice, guinea-pigs, and rabbits, in which the

[16] It was necessary to terminate observations on the 8th day. Recent tests indicate that S10 and S30 would probably have died on about the 12th day.

organisms cannot be microscopically distinguished with certainty from the true pasteurella type. The virulence toward mice and guinea-pigs is of the same degree for both types, while toward rabbits the true pasteurella is decidedly more active.

Agglutination and Agglutinin Absorption Tests.—An attempt was made to establish the degree of relationship by agglutination and absorption tests. No satisfactory results were obtained. In the first place, it was impossible to

TABLE 2

Showing Extent of Direct and Cross Agglutination of Selected Strains

Cultures	Serums				
	S8	S18	Atypical Past. ovisepticum (Giltner)	S3	S14
S8	1-400	1-100	None	None	None
S18	1-200	1-400	None	None	None
Atypical Past. ovisepticum (Giltner)	None	None	1-600	1-600	1-300
S21	1-200	1-300	None	None	None
S3	None	None	1-600	1-600	1-300
S14	None	None	1-400	1-300	1-400
S23	None	None	1-400	1-400	1-400
Past. suisepticum (P408)	1-300	1-100	None	None	None
Past. bubalisepticum (B. A. I.)	1-400	1-50	None	None	None

TABLE 3

Highest Serum Dilution Showing Agglutination of the Homologous Strain After Absorption by Other Types

After Absorption by	S8 Serum x-S8 Antigen	S18 Serum x-S18 Antigen	Atypical Past. ovisep. (Gilt.) x-same Antigen	S3 Serum x-S3 Antigen	S14 Serum x-S14 Antigen
S8	None	1-100	1-600	1-600	1-400
S18	1-200	None	1-600	1-600	1-400
Atypical Past. ovisep. (Giltner)	1-400	1-400	None	None	1-100
S21	1-200	1-100	1-600	1-600	1-400
S3	1-400	1-400	None	None	1-200
S14	1-400	1-400	1-400	1-500	None
Past. suisepticum (P408)	None	1-100	x*	x	x

* x indicates not absorbed.

bring the serum titer in any case beyond about 1:600, and in most cases not above 1:400, even after 14 injections. Some difficulty was experienced in the lack of tolerance of rabbits toward increasing doses, 5 rabbits dying after several injections. In all cases, the rabbits lost weight and showed evidence of toxicity of heat-killed suspensions. Another difficulty was due to the fact that these organisms tend toward spontaneous agglutination either in broth culture or when washed from blood-agar slants.

While no great degree of reliance may be placed on the results obtained with a low titer serum, especially with organisms showing a tendency toward spontaneous agglutination, the results of the cultural grouping are in general substantiated.

The agglutinations were made with broth suspensions washed from 24-hour blood agar cultures. Formalin (0.1%) was added as a preservative. Tests were incubated 1 hour at 37 C. and were read after 24 hours in the refrigerator.

Absorptions were made by taking 1 c c. of serum, adding 1 c c. of normal salt solution, and washing off the growth of one 24-hour blood-agar slant culture. This suspension was incubated 1 hour at 37 C., then centrifuged at high speed to clear. The process was repeated with the growth of a second slant. Complete absorption by the homologous strains was effected by this process.

SUMMARY

A detailed bacteriologic study is reported of 2 types of pneumonia in sheep under slaughter-house conditions: (1) A rather edematous type frequent in spring lambs, (2) A purulent, chronic type found only in older sheep, and often associated with lesions of caseous lymphadenitis (pseudotuberculosis).

Pasteurella ovisepticum was isolated in mixed culture from 4 cases of the lamb type, and in pure culture from a castration abscess in a lamb. It was isolated in pure culture in 1 case, and in mixed culture in 5 cases in the older sheep.

Two groups of organisms apparently closely related to each other, and very similar to the true pasteurella type, were frequently isolated in pure or mixed culture from lambs, and once from old sheep in mixed culture. These two types may be separated by a slight difference in growth in glycerol, and by the results of the direct agglutination and absorption tests. They may be separated from the true pasteurellas by their action on blood agar, maltose, and glycerol.

Intermediate strains were isolated which seemed to connect these 2 types (S3 and S14) together and to the true Past. ovisepticum.

Agglutination and absorption tests, while unsatisfactory due to certain technical difficulties, seem to support this idea of the relationship of these strains.

A gram-positive diplococcus was isolated a number of times from suppurative pneumonia associated with lesions of caseous lymphadenitis in older sheep. This organism has certain outstanding characteristics which sharply separate it from the common infectious streptococci, the most striking being its proteoclastic activity on milk, gelatin, and blood serum.

A gram-negative diplococcus of the M. catarrhalis type was isolated in pure culture from 2 cases of pneumonia in lambs; in mixed culture from 6 more cases, and from 2 cases of pneumonia in the older sheep in mixed culture.

The pathogenicity tests showed the true Past. ovisepticum to be highly pathogenic for mice, guinea-pigs, and rabbits. The 2 types (S3 and S14) described as being similar to the pasteurella type are likewise highly pathogenic for mice and guinea-pigs, but less so for rabbits. They are capable of causing a septicemia in which the organisms cannot be microscopically distinguished with certainty from the true pasteurella.

The occurrence of a nonvirulent organism called "Atypical B. ovisepticus" is reported by Giltner,[15] and a culture of this strain was identical in its cultural reactions with the S3 type isolated in the course of this study. These 2 strains cross-agglutinated to the full serum titer, and mutually cross-absorbed agglutinins.

ACID AGGLUTINATION OF PARATYPHOID BACILLI

WILLIS E. GOUWENS

From the Department of Hygiene and Bacteriology, The University of Chicago

The acid agglutination of bacteria, a phenomenon at first studied because of its possible practical use in the diagnosis of infectious diseases, has since been of interest chiefly because of the theoretical considerations involved in it. Michaelis'[1] work opened an interesting field to bacterial colloidal chemical investigations. His studies were based in part on those of several earlier workers.

In 1897, Malvoz[2] had already observed the agglutinating effect of acids on bacteria, but he did not continue this work with further theoretical studies. Hardy[3] showed that proteins are electro-amphoteric colloids, and that they can be precipitated out of either acid or alkaline solutions by the addition of ions of opposite charge. Wetham[4] advanced the theory that the electrical charges are carried at the surface of particles in solution or suspension, and that these charges determine the stability of the colloidal suspension. In the colloidal state the surface energy is at a minimum, and therefore the substance presents a maximum surface. A disturbance of the existing equilibrium of the electrical surface energy by the addition of ions results in an increase in the free surface energy of the particles, causing them to aggregate into larger masses, which, because of their weight must precipitate. This precipitation or flocculation takes place at the iso-electric point of the suspension. Bechhold[5] studied the effects of several acids on agglutination of bacteria, and showed that acetic acid was intermediate in its effect between the highly dissociated hydrochloric and the weak amidobenzoic acid. Neisser and Friedemann[6] observed that in slightly acid solutions bacteria were negatively charged. They attributed this to the protein content of the cells. Dryer and Jex-Blake[7] determined the agglutinating effect of HCl in various concentrations in unbuffered solutions, and also in the presence of several concentrations of blood serum. Buxton and Shaffer,[8] and Buxton and Teague[9] established the different behavior of several species of bacteria in acid solutions.

The problem assumed a different aspect when Michaelis attacked it. He showed that each protein has a definite iso-electric point as one of its physical characteristics. Suspensions of B. typhosus and B. paratyphosus B. were found to have a certain sharply defined $(H^{\bullet})$,[10] called the "optimum $(H^{\bullet})$," at which their agglutination in the absence of specific serum best takes place.

Received for publication, March 15, 1923.

[1] Deutsch. med. Wchnschr., 1911, 37, p. 969.
[2] Ann. de l'Inst. Pasteur, 1897, 11, p. 582.
[3] Jour. Physiol., 1900, 24, p. 288.
[4] Philosoph. Mag., 1899, 48, p. 474.
[5] Ztschr. f. physiol. Chem., 1904, 48, p. 385.
[6] München. med. Wchnschr., 1904, 51, pp. 465 and 827.
[7] Mém. de l'Acad. des Sc. et des Lettres de Danemark, 1905, 4, p. 217.
[8] Ztschr. f. physiol. Chem., 1906, 57, p. 47.
[9] Ibid., p. 64.
[10] Throughout this paper the symbol $(H^{\cdot})$ stands for hydrogen-ion concentration.

This agglutination is dependent only on the ($H^{\bullet}$) of the reacting mixture, and not on the absolute quantity or nature of the acid, except that only acids which do not effect some specific action on the protoplasm of the bacteria are usable. B. coli was found to be inagglutinable by acids. Beniasch,[11] one of Michaelis' pupils, extended the study of acid agglutination to a large number of cultures of the colon-typhoid group, and confirmed the findings of his teacher. He divided the so-called Gärtner group into two subgroups, (a) "rat" bacilli—optimum 1.1×10^{-4} (P_H 3.8) and (b) "real Gärtner" bacilli, optimum 2.2×10^{-3} (P_H 2.7). He also divided the B. paratyphosus B. strains into 2 groups.

Michaelis and Davidson[12] found that the flocculation of the oppositely charged colloids in these bacterial suspensions is dependent on the ($H^{\bullet}$) of the solution, and that 2 such colloids having their optimum ($H^{\bullet}$) for flocculation greatly different, have, when mixed, an optimum which lies intermediate between the 2. This point will be discussed later, when the effect of the addition of normal blood serum in the process of acid agglutination will be considered.

The use of mixed cultures in acid agglutination was first recorded by Rost[13] who, after plating out feces on Endo and Drigalski mediums, used the entire growth for his tests. He found this method successful even in the presence of the various products of metabolism, which, he states, may be eliminated by washing the organisms with salt solution. These facts are mentioned at this time because they are in direct contradiction to the findings of others. Jaffe[14] confirmed Rost's findings, and agreed with Michaelis that B. paratyphosus A and B cannot be differentiated by the method. Some of his strains of B. typhosus were not found to be typical in their reaction. Further discrepancies by other authors will be referred to presently, and a possible explanation for them will be given at that time. Undoubtedly Schidorsky and Rein[15] went a step too far when they reported their success in the direct acid agglutination of filtered fecal emulsions in the diagnosis of typhoid fever. Heimenn[16] was unable to confirm this work, even when large amounts of highly acid-agglutinable cultures of B. typhosus were added to the feces.

Beniasch[11] and Michaelis and Davidson[17] showed that the acid-agglutinable substances in a bacterial suspension are identical with the substances agglutinable by immune serum. This explains the fact that strains weak in their specific serum agglutination are, as a rule, also weak in their acid agglutination, a point first observed by Sgalitzer.[18] Contradictory evidence on this point will be brought out later.

Poppe,[19] using the technic of Michaelis, found considerable variation in the range of optimum ($H^{\bullet}$) at which his strains of paratyphoid bacilli agglutinated. All strains of B. paratyphosus B had an optimum of between 1.6×10^{-4} and 3.2×10^{-4} (P_H 3.8- 3.5). B. paratyphosus A had an optimum of 4×10^{-5} (P_H 4.4) although previous investigators had reported it inagglutinable by acids. No subgroups were found among the B. paratyphosus B and Gärtner bacilli. Sgaltizer[18] showed that higher concentration of HCl were required for agglutination than of organic acids. Michaelis and Adler[20] studied this

11 Ztschr. f. Immunitätsf. u. exper. Therap., 1912, 12, p. 268.
12 Biochem. Ztschr., 1912, 39, p. 496.
13 Centralbl. f. Bakteriol., I, O., 1911, 60, p. 324.
14 Arch. f. Hyg., 1912, 76, p. 2.
15 Deutsch. med. Wchnschr., 1912, 38, p. 1125.
16 Ztschr. f. Immunitätsf. u. exper. Therap., 1913, 16, p. 127.
17 Biochem. Ztschr., 1912, 47, p. 59.
18 Ztschr. f. Hyg. u. Infektionskr., 1914, 76, p. 209.
19 Ztschr. f. Immunitätsf. u. exper. Therap., 1912, 13, p. 185.
20 Ibid., 1914, 23, p. 327.

point and proved that HCl required the same ($H^{\bullet}$) in flocculating bacteria as other, organic acids did, if the binding power of HCl for the soluble impurities derived from the medium were suppressed.

The inagglutinability of certain strains of B. coli was not explainable on a basis of the flocculation of bacterial proteins at their iso-electric point. In 1914, Arkright showed that there were 2 distinct substances present in B. typhosus—one agglutinable in low, and the other in high hydrogen-ion concentrations. Three years later Michaelis[21] showed that by the addition of a trace (1:2,000) of normal blood serum to a suspension of otherwise acid inagglutinable B. coli, these organisms were rendered susceptible to the flocculating effects of acids. This he explained on a basis of the mutual precipitation of colloids at a definite ($H^{\bullet}$)—that B. coli normally has only one such colloid, while acid agglutinable organisms have both. According to this theory, then, the acid agglutination of bacteria is not a question of the precipitation of a single colloid at its iso-electric point, as was first supposed. Recent studies by Northrop and De Kruif[22] indicate that in agglutination of bacteria two factors take part—a reduction of the potential difference between the surface of the bacteria and the solution to less than 15 millivolts and the cohesive force of the bacterial cells. If the cohesive force is made small enough, the potential difference can be reduced to 0 and still no agglutination takes place.

The conflicting results obtained by different investigators who made use of the method of acid agglutination led Eisenberg,[23] and Kuster, Lange and Potthoff[24] to undertake critical studies of the phenomenon and the factors influencing it. The former showed that external agents affecting acid agglutination of bacteria do not always affect specific serum agglutination in the same way, for conditions are not entirely comparable. In the latter case is present the agglutinable substance plus serum agglutinin, a colloidal complex flocculable by electrolytes, while in simple acid agglutination the only factor influenced is the equilibrium of the colloidal complexes of the bacterial cell, or the complex represented by the bacteria as such in suspension. It is not surprising, therefore, that all conditions affecting the latter only do not necessarily affect the complex of which it is only a part. Instances are recorded in which serum-inagglutinable strains are acid agglutinable, and vice-versa, although on the whole, the agreement is good. A possible explanation is that at times perhaps the serum albumin plays the part of a protective colloid. Whether, as Porges[25] assumed, the nucleoprotein of the bacterial cell or other substances are acted on in the disturbance of equilibrium which results in flocculation, is still an open question. Any agent affecting a physicochemical change on the nucleo-albumin might at the same time affect other colloidal substances present, such as the other albumins or lipins, and it is therefore difficult to attribute to any one substance a change effected by external agents. Eisenberg's work on the effect of addition of normal serum to bacterial suspensions used in acid agglutinations can be summarized as follows: (a) agglutinable strains sometimes showed a more pronounced agglutinability when serum was added, but (b) most acid-inagglutinable strains did not become agglutinable, while (c) in the agglutinable strains there was uniformly a lowering of the ($H^{\bullet}$) at which flocculation took place. The last point can

[21] Deutsch. med. Wchnschr., 1917, 48, p. 1506.

[22] Jour. Gen. Physiol., 1922, 4, p. 639.

[23] Centralbl. f. Bakteriol., I, O., 1919, 83, pp. 70 and 561; Wien. klin. Wchnschr., 1919, 32, p. 222.

[24] Centralbl. f. Bakteriol., I, O., 1921, 85, p. 132.

[25] Ibid., 1905, 40, p. 133.

be explained by the fact that the iso-electric point of serum proteins is at a lower ($H^{\bullet}$) than that of the bacteria employed, or, the cohesiveness of the latter may have been increased by the serum.

Undoubtedly, external physical and chemical agents are at least in part responsible for the striking differences in optimum ($H^{\bullet}$) reported for the same species of bacteria by different observers. Seven workers, reporting on 167 strains of B. typhosus, record variations between the limits P_H 4.7 and 1.7. Similar irregularities were recorded for members of the paratyphoid group, and are explained by Eisenberg as being in part due to differences in the culture mediums employed. The reaction and composition of the mediums used were recorded only by Sgalitzer. Kuster, Lange and Potthoff made a careful study of the effect of various mediums on the acid agglutination of several highly agglutinable strains of B. typhosus. These cultures when grown on (a) Endo medium were uniformily negative, (b) Drigalski medium, very irregular, (c) serum agar, were enhanced in their acid agglutinability, and (d) an alkaline medium, lost their susceptibility to acid flocculation. They speak of these effects as "great influences of mediums, upon an already very variable reaction," and are in almost entire disagreement with Rost[13] and Sgalitzer.[18] The effects of crushing and of washing bacteria previous to acid agglutination were also studied by Kuster, Lange and Potthoff. The acid inagglutinablility of some strains is explained by them as being due to something, perhaps a lipoidal membrane, which prevents the necessary contact between the electropositive hydrogen ions and the electronegative ions which are bound to the bacterial protein. Acid agglutinable strains are assumed not to have such a lipoidal membrane, or, they have sufficient albumin in or on their membrane. The loss of the property of acid agglutination of strains during washing is due, then, to the removal of such albuminous material by the water or salt solution (Contray to Rost[13]). The crushing of cells that have lost their acid agglutinability through washing restores this property. It is, however, not unlikely that the cohesiveness of the cells is also increased by the crushing. No constant influence of either time or temperature of incubation on the acid agglutination of members of the colon-typhoid group was noticed by these investigators. In this they agree with Eisenberg.

The value of the method of acid agglutination in the differential diagnosis of disease and the identification of bacterial species has been variously estimated by different men. Michaelis, Beniasch, Sgalitzer, Rost and Schidorsky recommend it highly. Poppe and Heimenn consider it only an aid in the differentiation of species of bacteria. More recently, Eisenberg stated that there are too many factors influencing the point of optimum agglutination, such as the variability of cultures from different mediums, in vivo changes of the optimum ($H^{\bullet}$) required for the agglutination of a single strain, the inagglutinability of some strains of an otherwise agglutinable species, and the fact that some species have optimums identical with those of others. According to Kuster, Lange and Potthoff, the method is good for nothing, as the precipitation of albumin is dependent on too many factors.

In view of the many discrepancies recorded in the literature, it is apparent that further investigation is needed on the question of external, physical and chemical agents on the phenomenon of acid agglutination. This work was undertaken with the hope of clearing up some of these points.

The object of this investigation is (a) to determine the applicability of the method of acid agglutination to the species and strain differentiation of the paratyphoid bacilli—B. paratyphosus A, B, and C, suipestifer, enteritidis, and abortivo-equinus, and (b) to determine the effect of time and temperature of incubation, washing, crushing, and the composition of the culture medium on the agglutination of acid-agglutinable strains.

Apparatus.—All agglutination tests were made in 4 x ½ inch glass test tubes. Electrometric hydrogen-ion determinations were made by means of a Leeds and Northrup potentiometer, in which a saturated calomel electrode and N/10 potassium chloride were used. All incubations were made in a 37 C. air incubator for lengths of time stated in the tables. In the standardization of the bacterial suspensions the method of McFarland[26] was used. This consists in the preparation of a set of standard tubes, each of which contains a definite amount of barium sulphate, precipitated from solution by the addition of various amounts of 1% sulphuric acid to a 1% barium chloride solution. These suspensions are stable, the state of division of the precipitate is great, and they need only be shaken to effect immediate homogeneity of the mixture. The tubes are sealed.

Reagents.—The acid mixtures used in the tests were acetic acid—sodium hydroxide mixtures, made as shown in table 1, in which the (H·) determined by means of a potentiometer, is indicated back of each mixture.

TABLE 1

ACID MIXTURES IN AGGLUTINATION TESTS

Solution	NaOH N/1 C.c.	Acetic Acid N/1	H_2O	P_H First	P_H Second	P_H Average
1	12.5	18.75	218.75	4.85	4.88	4.86
2	12.5	25.0	212.5	4.61	4.61	4.61
3	12.5	37.5	200.0	4.31	4.31	4.31
4	12.5	50.0	187.5	4.15	4.15	4.15
5	12.5	62.5	175.0	4.04	4.04	4.04
6	12.5	75.0	162.5	3.99	3.95	3.97
7	12.5	87.5	150.0	3.86	3.86	3.86
8	12.5	100.0	137.5	3.78	3.78	3.78
9	4.0	50.0	196.0	3.60	3.60	3.60
10	5.0	80.0	165.0	3.40	3.38	3.39
11	5.0	150.0	95.0	3.20	3.21	3.20
12	2.5	100.0	147.5	3.00	3.05	3.02
13	1.0	100.0	149.0	2.84	2.81	2.82
14	1.0	150.0	99.0	2.58	2.58	2.58
15	0.5	175.0	74.5	2.27	2.24	2.25

In all cases 3 parts of an acid mixture were employed to 1 part of a bacterial suspension.

[26] Jour. Am. Med. Assn., 1907, 49, p. 1176.

Experiments—(1) The effect of various native cultural impurities on the final ($H^\bullet$) of a mixture of bacterial suspension and buffered acid.

One liter of "conductivity" water, P_H 7.0 has 10^{16} hydrogen ions in solution. This amounts to 10^{13} per c c. If a bacterial suspension such as is used in agglutination tests contains 10^8 cells per c c., it is at once apparent that even an unbuffered solution of P_H 7.0 must have the capacity of neutralizing thousands of negative charges per bacterial cell. (The ionization product constants of the substances under consideration would, however, not permit the reaction to proceed to this point in an unbuffered solution.) Whether, however, the products of metabolism of the organisms, or soluble products of the culture medium would affect the final ($H^\bullet$) of the buffered solutions employed, remained to be seen. Accordingly, the following tests were run, in which the bacterial suspensions were prepared as indicated, and in which 3 parts of each suspension was mixed with 1 part of the standard acetic acid—sodium hydroxide solution. In each case after mixing, the materials were allowed to stand for ½ hour at room temperature, and then, after centrifugalization, the supernatant liquid was tested by means of the potentiometer. The suspensions all had the same turbidity, and were labeled (a) to (e) as follows:

(a) The growth was carefully scraped off from the agar plate, and was suspended in distilled water.

(b) The growth was washed off by the application of water to the surface of the agar medium.

(c) Organisms obtained as in (a) were washed in distilled water by centrifugalization to rid them of the products of metabolism, and were then resuspended in distilled water.

(d) A 48-hour culture was used as in (a) instead of a 24-hour one.

(e) Two suspensions were employed, one of which contained about twice as many cells per unit of volume as the other. (x = the more concentrated). The results are shown in table 2.

TABLE 2

RESULTS OF EXPERIMENTS

Suspension	P_H of Acid Mixture Before Cells Added	P_H After Centrifugalization	Difference
(a)	4.61	4.63	+0.02
(b)	4.61	4.66	+0.05
(c)	4.61	4.62	+0.01
(d)	4.61	4.58	—0.03
(e)	4.61	4.63	+0.02
(x)	4.61	4.65	+0.04

From these results it is evident that the acid mixture employed in the tests, and it was one of my most weakly buffered mixtures, is buffered sufficiently to neutralize the negatively charged particles without affecting the final ($H^\bullet$) of the mixture. It is therefore unnecessary to determine the final ($H^\bullet$) of the mixtures after agglutination to determine the ($H^\bullet$) at which the "optimum" agglutination occurs.

(2) The optimum ($H^\bullet$) for agglutination of 24-hour cultures of the paratyphoid bacilli

In the determination of the optimum (H•) for agglutination, veal infusion agar, of P_H 7.0 was employed as the culture medium. (This is medium 1 described under another heading.) In order to avoid possible differences in agglutination due to variations in the medium, all of the tests recorded below were made on organisms grown on agar prepared in one batch. This was stored in small flasks, (150 c c.) to avoid unnecessary reheating of the medium. Buffer mixtures varying by 0.4 of a unit on the P_H scale were employed, as the use of solutions varying by less than this amount was found unnecessary because of the wide range over which the agglutination took place. That tube in which the first flocculi were visible through a hand lens magnifying 8 diameters was taken as the tube in which the optimum of agglutination occurred. Ordinarily this tube showed the most compact sediment and the clearest supernatant liquid after standing 18 hours. Table 3 shows in summary form, the optimum (H•) for agglutination of from 8 to 10 strains of each of the 6 species studied.

TABLE 3

OPTIMUM (H•) FOR AGGLUTINATION OF FROM 8 TO 10 STRAINS OF EACH OF THE 6 SPECIES STUDIED

In this table the optimum (H•) for acid agglutination is recorded below the number of the strain of the organism, in each case. The symbol "I" stands for inagglutinable at any (H•) when grown on this medium.

B. paratyphosus A.......	3	4	9	40	131	158	188	191	212	219	215
P_H....................	4.0	3.8	4.0	4.0	3.8	I	3.8	3.6	3.6	I	3.6
B. paratyphosus B.......	12	169	179	210	274	310	315	371	379	112	
P_H....................	3.6	3.2	3.2	I	3.6	3.2	3.2	3.6	3.6	3.2	
B. paratyphosus C.......	326	328	329	330	349	350	351	354			
P_H....................	3.6	3.6	2.6	2.6	2.2	2.2	2.2	2.2			
B. enteritidis.............	51	52	53	204	205	206	207	226	228	253	
P_H....................	3.6	3.6	3.6	3.6	3.6	3.6	3.6	3.2	3.6	3.2	
B. suipestifer.............	66	166	133	162	167	178	234	257	304	338	
P_H....................	3.2	4.0	2.8	3.4	3.6	2.8	3.4	3.6	3.6	3.6	
B. abortivo-equinus.......	268	195	266	267	196	271	270	269	336	367	
P_H....................	2.5	2.5	2.8	3.6	3.6	3.6	2.5	3.4	2.8	2.8	

Table 3 shows that not all strains of a given species have the same optimum (H•) for acid agglutination, even when every effort is made to have conditions comparable in all possible respects. B. paratyphosus C, suipestifer, and abortivo-equinus show the greatest variations. Organisms of the paratyphoid group cannot be differentiated on a basis of acid agglutination because of the irregularities above mentioned, and because the zone over which agglutination extends for all strains of one species overlaps that of all the other species. The suspensions were prepared by the method given as (b) in table 2. All had the same turbidity.

(3) The effect of age of the culture on acid agglutination.

For this study, 2 groups of cultures were employed, one of which consisted of highly agglutinable strains, and the other, strains that were but slightly agglutinable, if at all. The same medium as was employed in the work recorded in table 3 was used here. Three sets of cultures were inoculated at the same time. These were incubated at 37 C., for 24, 48, and 72 hours, respectively.

The age of the culture was found to have little to do with the optimum (H·) for acid agglutination. Some strains showed a slight shifting of the point to the alkaline side, and a few a change to the opposite direction, but most showed no effect.

(4) The effect of washing the cells in distilled water prior to acid agglutination.

The organisms used in these determinations were obtained from the same agar plates that furnished the growth employed in the study recorded in table 3. In each case, one half of the growth of an agar plate was suspended in from 50 to 60 c c. of distilled water. The mixture was then centrifugalized, the supernatant liquid was pipetted off, and the sediment was resuspended in a small amount of distilled water. One half of this was used in a series of such tests as are recorded in table 3, and the other half was in each case employed as described under (5) below. Of the 59 strains of paratyphoid bacilli subjected to this treatment, 9 became inagglutinable by acids, and many more had their capacity for acid agglutination greatly reduced. The fact that washing in distilled water has this effect can probably be explained better on a basis of loss of cohesiveness than on the assumption that this washing removes 1 of 2 mutually precipitating colloids.

(5) The effect of grinding on cells that have lost their property of acid agglutination through washing.

As stated, one half of the bacterial mass obtained in the centrifugalization described under part (4) above was ground in the moist condition and then resuspended in distilled water. Acid agglutination tests were then run as outlined above to determine whether bacteria that had partially or completely lost their property of acid agglutination by washing had this property restored to them by grinding. In every case they did, although not always to the same extent. In some cases (B. paratyphosus A 158 and 219, and paratyphosus B. 210) the suspensions were acid inagglutinable even before washing, but grinding of the cells caused them to agglutinate readily. Apparently the grinding increases the cohesiveness of the cell masses. The results of these experiments and those described under (4), are in agreement with the findings of Kuster, Lange and Potthoff.[24]

(6) The effect of differences in the composition of the medium.

All the mediums used in this study were prepared from one large batch of veal infusion broth, the reaction of which was adjusted to P_H 7.0. This broth contained, per liter: peptone (Difco) 10g., NaCl 5g., and the water soluble portion of 500g. lean veal (ground). This was distributed in 1 liter flasks, and served as a base for the preparation of 5 different mediums, called 1 to 5, and having the following composition: Medium 1—stock broth plus 1.5% agar—reaction adjusted to P_H 7.0. Medium 2—same as No. 1 except that reaction was adjusted to P_H 8.0. Medium 3—(Endo medium) stock broth plus 3% agar, reaction adjusted to P_H 7.6. To each 200 c c. of this medium was added the following mixture, just previous to the pouring of plates:

Saturated alcoholic solution of basic fuchsin, 1.0 c c. Anhydrous sodium sulphite, 0.5 gm. Lactose, 2.0 gm. All dissolved in 25 c c. distilled water.

Medium 4—stock broth, plus 1.5% agar, reaction adjusted to P_H 7.0—20% by volume of ascites fluid added just previous to the time of pouring of the plates.

Medium 5—Same as medium No. 1 except that 1% glycerol was added.

These mediums were stored in flasks containing 200 c c. so that unnecessary heating was avoided. With each strain of organism used, all of these mediums were inoculated at the same time from the same 24-hour culture, so as to eliminate the possibility of differences in results which might be due to the culture used in the inoculations. Here, as in all other acid agglutinations, 1 part of the standardized, distilled water suspension of bacteria was added to 3 parts of each buffer mixture. The incubation period was 1 hour, at 37 C., in an air incubator. Readings were made 1 and 18 hours after the tests were "set up." Table 4 shows the results of these tests with 10 strains of B. paratyphosus B, which show very little influence of the mediums, and, 10 strains of B. abortivo-equinus, which show a greater influence than any other species of paratyphoid bacilli studied.

TABLE 4

RESULTS OF AGGLUTINATION TESTS WITH STRAINS OF B. PARATYPHOSUS B AND B. ABORTUS EQUINUS

Only the optimum (H•) for the agglutination of each strain is recorded.

B. paratyphosus B						B. abortivo-equinus					
Strain	Medium					Strain	Medium				
	1	2	3	4	5		1	2	3	4	5
12	3.6	3.6	3.6	3.6	3.6	268	2.5	2.5	2.8	3.6	2.8
112	3.2	3.2	I	3.2	3.2	195	2.5	2.5	2.5	2.8	2.8
169	3.2	3.2	3.2	3.2	3.6	266	2.8	2.8	2.8	3.6	2.8
179	3.2	3.2	3.2	3.6	3.2	267	3.6	2.8	2.8	2.8	2.8
210	I	I	I	I	I	196	3.6	3.6	2.5	3.6	2.8
274	3.6	3.6	I	3.6	3.6	271	3.6	3.6	2.8	3.6	2.5
310	3.2	3.2	3.2	3.2	3.2	270	2.5	2.5	2.2	3.4	2.8
315	3.2	3.2	3.2	3.2	3.2	269	3.4	3.4	3.2	3.6	2.8
371	3.6	3.6	3.6	3.6	3.6	336	2.8	2.5	2.2	3.6	2.8
379	3.6	3.6	I	3.6	3.6	367	2.8	2.8	2.8	3.2	2.5

The ascites fluid agar (medium 4) yielded cultures which had a broader zone of acid agglutination than the others. This was probably due to an increase in the cohesiveness of the bacteria when grown on this medium. Strains of B. paratyphosus B showed no shifting of the optimum (H•) for agglutination when grown on this medium, although the zone of agglutination was broadened. The strains of B. abortivo-equinus, however, do show changes. Those strains having an optimum higher than P_H 3.0 in cultures grown on medium 1 show little or no shifting of the optimum when grown on 4. Strains having their optimum below P_H 3.0 on the other hand, show a shifting to the alkaline side. The iso-electric point of the proteins contained in ascites fluid is at a lower (H•) than the bacteria in question. The greater the difference, the greater should be the effect of those substances of the ascites fluid which are dissolved in the water used in washing loose the growth from the surface of the agar. The alternative explanation is that the increase in the cohesiveness of the cells due to the ascites fluid lessens the reduction of the potential difference required for flocculation. The presence of 1% of glycerol (medium 5) had no uniform effect on the optimum (H•) for agglutination. Many of the strains studied were partially or completely acid inagglutinable when grown on Endo medium. An attempt was made to determine the cause of this inhibition. Flasks of endo stock agar, prepared as described above, were employed in this study. Eleven different combinations of fuchsin and sodium sulphite were tried, as follows: in one series the fuchsin was kept constant at 1 c c. per 200 c c. of the stock agar, while the sulphite content varied from 0.5 gm. to 0.0 gm.; in a second series the sulphite was kept constant at 0.5 gm., and the fuchsin was varied from 1.0 c c. to 0 c c. The eleventh medium contained neither fuchsin nor sodium sulphite. There was no noticeable difference in susceptibility to acid flocculation among 24-hour cultures grown on these different mediums. Twelve Endo-inhibited strains were employed in this work.

(7) The effect of the addition of normal horse serum on acid agglutination.

Many of the organisms studied as a routine by the methods recorded in tables 3 and 4 showed little if any tendency to agglutinate at any (H•). The acid inagglutinable strains and those which showed only a trace of agglutination when examined by means of a hand lens magnifying 8 diameters were used in determining the effect of addition of normal horse serum. In addition to these, all of the Endo inhibited strains were employed, each grown on 11 different mediums, and all showing little or no tendency to agglutinate in acid. This work can be summarized by stating that every culture showed agglutination after the addition of 0.2 c c. of 1 : 100 horse serum to 2 c c. of a mixture of bacteria and buffered acid. In every case also, the zone over which agglutination occurred was widened by several tenths of a unit on the P_H scale. The explanations given above, under the effect of ascites fluid suffices here.

(8) The effect of repeated transfers on the susceptibility to agglutination by acids.

Five strains showing little tendency to agglutinate and 7 which were highly agglutinable were employed in this study. Transfers were made every 24 hours for 12 days. Acid agglutinations were run on the 24-hour cultures on the 1st., 2d., 3d., 4th., 6th., 8th., 10th., and 12th. days. No strains which were highly acid agglutinable became inagglutinable nor was there any tendency for inagglutinable strains to become agglutinable. A shifting in the optimum (H•) for agglutination from P_H 4.2 to 3.0 and back to 4.2 was noticed among the strains of B. suipestifer. B. enteritidis, paratyphosus A and B were remarkable in their constancy.

Throughout all of these studies, the suspensions were tested by means of specific immune serums to avoid overlooking a possible change in the serologic behavior of the organisms. The serums had titers ranging from 1 : 5,000 to 1 : 10,000 and were used in a final dilution of 1 : 500. These controls were run with suspensions of the organisms in 0.85% NaCl, with the exception of the strains of B. suipestifer, which were suspended in 0.2% salt because of their tendency to agglutinate "spontaneously" in the other solution.

SUMMARY AND CONCLUSIONS

The following statements are made on a basis of over 4,500 acid agglutination tests and apply only to the 59 cultures of paratyphoid bacilli employed in this study.

The water soluble products of metabolism and the ingredients of nutrient agar which become mixed with the bacterial suspension when the organisms are rubbed loose in distilled water do not alter the final P_H of the buffer mixtures used or affect the optimum (H•) for acid agglutination.

Not all strains of a species have the same optimum (H•) for acid agglutination. Organisms of the paratyphoid group cannot be differentiated on a basis of this test.

The age of the culture has little to do with the optimum (H•) for acid agglutination.

Washing bacteria in distilled water by centrifugalization was effective in rendering some acid agglutinable strains acid inagglutinable. This is probably due to a reduction in the cohesiveness of the cells.

Thorough grinding of cells that have lost their tendency to agglutinate in acid mixtures restores this property. Here the cohesiveness of the masses of protoplasm is probably increased.

The addition of ascites fluid to nutrient agar enhances the acid agglutination of bacteria. The flocculation is more complete and extends over a broader range of (H•). Probably the small amount of ascites fluid dissolved in the water used in removing the growth from the surface of the plates is responsible for this, in that its proteins have their iso-electric points at lower (H•) than the bacteria, and they also increase the cohesiveness of the cells.

Many strains show little or no tendency toward acid agglutination when grown on Endo medium. The fuchsin and the sodium sulphite were found not to be responsible for this.

Normal horse serum, when added to acid inagglutinable suspensions, causes these to agglutinate completely over a wide range of (H•). The explanation given in a previous paragraph is adequate here.

Repeated transfers were not effective in causing acid inagglutinable strains to become agglutinable, or vice versa.

DIPHTHERIC VAGINITIS IN CHILDREN

ANNA I. VAN SAUN

From the Bureau of Laboratories, Department of Health, New Haven, Conn.

A search of the available literature for the last 30 years yields but 26 cases of diphtheric vaginitis in children. Few of the cases have been confirmed by bacteriologic examination. Primary diphtheria of the genitals in children is apparently rare.

Coldstream,[1] reports a case of apparently primary diphtheria of the vulva in a girl 12 years old; there was high fever with swollen labia and discharge. The source of infection could not be determined. The throat was clear, and there was no paralysis, although the cardiac action continued feeble for a long time. No mention is made of nose or other cultures.

Gayton[2] mentions a case of possible primary diphtheria of the genitals in a child 4 years old. The skin of the groins, labia and vulva were chafed by the discharge, and the vulva was covered with a diphtheric membrane. No mention is made of any cultures. The child died of paralysis of the throat and palate. The urine contained albumin. Gayton says that cases of genital infection occur infrequently—in 2,733 hospital patients he had about 6 cases in 6 years.

Hewlett and Nolan[3] mention a case of diphtheria of the fauces and vagina, but no special account is given of it. Apparently no cultures were made.

Pearce,[4] in a study of 157 cases of diphtheria and scarlet fever, gives an account of a case of diphtheric vaginitis with extensive diphtheria of the respiratory tract. Diphtheria bacilli were present in large numbers in the membranes.

Coues[5] reports 3 cases of diphtheria of the vulva; all asylum cases. The first was that of a child 8 months old, recently admitted to the institution. A membrane was present on the labia minora and small spots on the labia majora. Diphtheria bacilli were found in cultures from the vulva. Apparently, a culture was not taken of the throat at that time. Later, cultures from the throat were positive. Antitoxin was given. The primary seat of infection could not be determined. The second case may have been primary. The child, 2 years old, had been an inmate of the asylum for 5 months, when she developed a membrane on the labia majora from which a culture yielded diphtheria bacilli. A throat culture was negative. Nose cultures are not mentioned. The child was sent to the hospital and discharged cured in 2 weeks, which is something of a record, as many cases of vaginal diphtheria have been intractable even when treated in the early stages. The third case was in a child, 21 months old, an inmate of the asylum for 2 months. A slight discharge from

Received for publication, April 18, 1923.

1 Brit. Med. Jour., 1891, 1, p. 1016.
2 Lancet, 1894, 1, p. 1301.
3 Brit. Med. Jour., 1896, 1, p. 266.
4 Med. & Surg. Rept. City Hosp., Boston, 1898, 9, p. 86.
5 Boston Med. and Surg. Jour., 1897, 137, p. 470; 1898, 138, p. 445.

the nose was noted, with some membrane. The throat was reddened. Positive cultures were obtained from the throat and vulva. The child died about a week after the beginning of the illness.

Freymouth and Petruschky[6] give an account of the case of a child of 3 who was admitted to the hospital with measles. On the 4th day after admission the genitals were found discolored greenish black. On examination, diphtheria bacilli were found as well as fusiform bacilli and spirochetes. The throat was free from membrane though swallowing was difficult. Mucus was discharged from the nose. Later a whitish membrane developed on the throat. Antitoxin was given. An extensive laboratory examination was made, including virulence tests. The latter did not give results quite typical for diphtheria. The authors conclude that the case was one of noma rather than of diphtheric vaginitis.

Müller[7] gives the case of a child of 10 who suffered from pains in the genitals and who 2 days later developed a sore throat. She had injured her foot 4 weeks previously, and this wound contained pus. She had also a felon on her left thumb. The vulva was ulcerated and the vagina covered with a membrane. Virulent diphtheria bacilli were found in the vulva and vagina, as well as in the throat. The felon also contained virulent diphtheria bacilli. No diphtheria bacilli were found in the wound on the foot. Antitoxin was given, and on the seventh day the membrane had disappeared as well as the irritation. Müller thinks that the case was one of primary diphtheria of the throat rather than of the genitals.

Leick[8] mentions the case of a girl of 16 who was brought to a clinic suffering with a swelling of the external genitals. When 12 years old she had had diphtheria. The inner surface of the labia was covered with a gray membrane. The throat was normal. Smears were made of the membrane, and nose and throat cultures were taken. Diphtheria bacilli were found in the membrane, but not in the nose and throat. Antitoxin was given. Virulence tests were not made. The patient recovered in 4 weeks. The author considers this a case of primary diphtheria of the vulva. The source of infection was not discovered.

Silberstein[9] cites the case of a child 4½ years of age who developed inflamed and swollen genitals. A diphtheria case had recently occurred in the same house; 24 hours after the appearance of the first symptoms, a yellow membrane was found in the vulva and another on both tonsils. Antitoxin was given. In a week the vulva was normal, but there was still a slight swelling of the tonsils. No bacteriologic examinations are mentioned.

Ware[10] gives an account of a case of apparently primary diphtheria of the vulva in a child of 4 who became unable to urinate. She also developed paralysis of the soft palate. Diphtheria bacilli were found in cultures from the vulva. Nothing is said of cultures from the nose or throat, but reference is made to there having been no infection of the throat or eyes. No virulence tests were made.

Williams[11] mentions a case of diphtheric vaginitis as having the same variety of bacillus in cultures from the throat and vagina.

[6] Deutsch. med. Wchnschr., 1898, 24, p. 232.
[7] Ibid., 1899, 25, p. 91.
[8] Ibid., 1900, 26, p. 196.
[9] Ibid.
[10] Lancet, 1900, 1, p. 382.
[11] Proc. New York Path. Soc., 1902, 1, p. 4.

Erikson[12] reports a case in a child of 8 years, in whose family there had been other cases of diphtheria. The child experienced pain when urinating. Examination revealed a thin gray membrane at the entrance to the vagina. There was a slight vaginal discharge. The child was admitted to the hospital, and 3 days after developed a sore throat. Diphtheria was suspected, and diphtheria bacilli were found in cultures made from the throat and vagina In 2 weeks the symptoms had cleared up, and in 3 weeks the patient had entirely recovered. Erikson compares gonorrheal and diphtheric vaginitis. He refers to the former as producing a profuse discharge and says that in his case of the latter the discharge was slight.

Schwab[13] gives two cases of prolonged ulcerative processes on the mouth and genitals caused by diphtheria bacilli. In the first, ulcers covered with a membrane were found in the vulva of a 16-year old girl. Ulcers also developed on the cheek and on the gums. From all these sources, diphtheria bacilli were obtained, nonpathogenic for animals. He believes, however, that the organisms were probably diphtheria bacilli. The second case was exactly like the first.

McCollum,[14] study of 800 cases of diphtheria, in a series of tabulated reports, the case of a child of 2 years, ill 3 days on admission to the hospital. Membranes were found on the vulva, tonsils and uvula. There was a septic odor and swollen glands. The child died in 4 days. Any bacteriologic work which may have been done is not mentioned.

Banks[15] gives an account of a case of multiple infection by the diphtheria bacillus in a child of 7. She was admitted to the hospital 3 months after the beginning of the infection. She had an ulcer which had begun at the extreme inner end of the lower eyelid. It then extended from the inner canthus to the middle of the nose. There was slight epiphora. The persistent condition had lead to suspicion of diphtheria. The throat was congested, but there was no exudate. The turbinates in the nose were much congested and swollen. The child had an adenoid expression. The vulva and labia majora showed a reddened, raised and indurated area with serpiginous margins which did not extend beyond the labia majora. Swabs from all 4 localities were examined and reported to contain diphtheria bacilli. No guinea-pigs were inoculated. Antitoxin was given. The condition responded to treatment in 3 weeks. The nose was still swollen after 2 negative cultures. The sequence of the infection was not determined but was probably primarily of the nose or throat.

de Oyarzabel[16] cites 3 cases of diphtheria of the skin and genitals. The children were 6, 1 and 3 years of age, and all had diphtheria of the skin of the face and secondary diphtheria of the genitals. An extensive clinical history is given. The cases were of long duration. Cultures were examined and positive virulence tests were obtained on organisms isolated from them.

Klimenko[17] reports the case of a child of 10 years who had difficult urination but no sore throat. Bacterial and animal tests proved the condition to be diphtheric vaginitis. There had been other cases of diphtheria in the family. It is probable that the bacilli had been transferred to the genital organs of the patient from linen, etc. Klimenko considers the case one of primary vaginal diphtheria. He thinks that the mortality is high in these cases and that this is due to the fact that they are recognized too late for serum therapy to be of use.

[12] Hygeia, 1903, 1, p. 651.
[13] Abst. in Centralbl. f. Bakteriol., I, Ref., 1904, 35, p. 480.
[14] Med. and Surg. Rep. City Hosp., Ser. 9, 1898, p. 1.
[15] Brit. Med. Jour., 1911, 2, p. 17.
[16] Rev. de med. y. cirug. práct., 1913, 98, p. 516.
[17] Russk. Vracth., 1913; abstr. Semaine méd., 1913, 35, p. 419.

Pape[18] gives the case of a child of 12 who had not been able to see well for two weeks. She had had a vaginal discharge and swelling of the labia as is seen with oxyuris, 8 weeks previously. The physician who treated the child did not think of diphtheria, as there were no general symptoms and no case of diphtheria in the neighborhood. The condition yielded to "tonic treatment" in a few weeks. Apparently no bacteriologic examinations were made.

Mondolfo[19] gives an account of a case of vaginitis in a child of 2 years. It was diagnosed first as erysipelas due to a lesion on the face. The fauces were normal and the voice unaltered. The labia majora were reddened and swollen, and the vulva was covered with a grayish exudate. Microscopic preparations from the vulva and nasopharynx showed diphtheria bacilli. Antitoxin was given, and guinea-pigs were inoculated with cultures from the vulva, with death in 18 hours, and from the nasopharynx, with death in 30 hours. The child died of cardiovascular collapse.

Cenci is quoted by Mondolfo[19] as reporting the case of an infant in whom he saw a white membrane protruding from the vulva mucosa. The infant had also a diphtheric angina as determined bacteriologically. There were other cases of diphtheria in the family.

Lundertz[20] cites the case of a child 5½ years of age who was sent to the clinic with diphtheria of the vagina on the 19th day of illness. Two children in the same family had died of diphtheria a few days before she had contracted the disease. Antitoxin was given immediately. The vulva was found to be inflamed, and the vagina contained a large, dark brown membrane as well as ulcers which were also found on the external genitals and on the left buttock. There was no pain in the throat. Typical diphtheria bacilli were found in the membrane and in the skin ulcers. On the 28th day of the illness the diphtheria bacilli had disappeared, and the epithelium of the vagina had regenerated. On the 30th day incontinence of urine began. The paralysis spread to the throat, arms and legs. Paralysis of the bladder followed on the ninth day after the sloughing of the membrane. The paralysis gradually disappeared.

REPORT OF CASE

In Dec. 1921, an interesting case came to the attention of the City Laboratory of New Haven. On Dec. 24, the 3 "B" children were admitted to an institution in the city. M. B., was a girl of 13, J. B., a boy of 8, and A. B., a girl of 6 years who was in poor health. Routine cultures were taken of the throats and noses of each of the children and sent to the City Laboratory for examination. The cultures from M. B. and J. B. were found to be negative, as was that from the throat of A. B. The nose culture from A. B., however, was found to contain diphtheria bacilli, and she was accordingly isolated. Further cultures from the throats and noses of the 3 children were negative until Dec. 31, when J. B. developed spots on the right tonsil. He was promptly isolated, antitoxin was given, and nose and throat cultures examined at the City Laboratory were found to contain diphtheria bacilli. The condition cleared up rapidly, and the patient was released from quarantine after two negative cultures, Jan. 10, 1922. His sisters still gave negative cultures. On Jan. 30, 1922, A. B. was found to have developed a vaginitis, which rapidly increased in severity and was at first thought to be due to the gonococcus. Smears were at once made and sent to the laboratory, where they were found to contain

[18] Am. Jour. Ophth., 1915, 32, p. 121.
[19] Riv. crit. di clin. med., 1918, 19, pp. 25-37.
[20] Med. Klin., 1920, 16, p. 151

diphtheria bacilli in large numbers. On further examination of the patient, a membrane was found which covered the vulva and extended to the external genitals and buttocks. A profuse greenish discharge was present. Cultuers and smears were then taken from the nose and throat, as well as from the external and internal genital tract. Diphtheria bacilli were again found in large numbers in cultures and smears from the genital tract and in the culture from the nose. Antitoxin was at once given and local treatment instituted. The child was very ill and was unable to walk for 3 months, although she did not seem to be paralyzed; 41 days after the beginning of the illness she developed an irregular heart action. The bacilli persisted in the genital tract for 42 days, when a negative culture was obtained from the vagina. Cultures from the throat were consistently negative until March 29, when diphtheria bacilli were found. No other positive culture was obtained from the throat. Occasional negative nose cultures were obtained, but the majority of these were positive until June 1 and 3, when negative cultures were obtained, thus releasing the patient from quarantine 5 months after the beginning of her illness. Through the kindness of Dr. Bartlett, Director of the Connecticut State Laboratory, and his staff, virulence tests were made with cultures isolated at the City Laboratory. These tests proved the organisms from both vagina and nose to be fully virulent. The cultures fermented dextrose. The child has remained in perfect health since her recovery. I am indebted to Dr. H. F. Keating for the clinical history of this case. Cultures taken from her nose. throat and vagina one year later showed no diphtheria bacilli. The sister and brother also remain free from diphtheria bacilli. The older sister, M. B., stated that A. B. had once before had vaginitis, type unknown. The child had been much neglected before her admission and had probably been a nasal carrier for some time. It is interesting to note that there was only one positive culture in all those taken for the month following her admission. The severity and long duration of this case is also worthy of note.

Another case which may be of interest in this connection is that of a negro girl, 18 years of age and pregnant, who was said to have developed a membrane over the entire vaginal mucosa. Preliminary smears and cultures were examined at the City Laboratory with negative results. It was suggested that more material be submitted for examination and that nose and throat cultures be taken also. But the physician, who had given antitoxin and was firmly convinced that the case was one of diphtheric vaginitis, said that the condition had cleared up at once, and further cultures were refused. Since vaginitis may be caused and membranes formed by other organisms than the diphtheria bacillus (for example, streptothrix or streptococcus), one might infer that the foregoing was not a case of diphtheric vaginitis, as bacteriologic proof is lacking.

A recapitulation of the cases of diphtheric vaginitis in children in the literature shows their relative infrequency as well as the rather indifferent reports of many of them. Primary diphtheria of the vagina is said to have occurred but 6 times in the series of 26 cases mentioned, and in some of these cases it is not quite clear that a more extended examination might not have revealed another avenue of infection. Apparently bacteriologic examinations were made in 15 of the cases; virulence tests were made in but 6 of these. A number of the cases occurred in children physically below par. The mortality does not seem to have been higher in diphtheric vaginitis than in other forms of diphtheria. Four deaths were reported in the series collected. The duration of the disease would seem to have been anywhere from 1 to 4 weeks as a rule. No mention is made of release cultures in any of the reported cases, although they may have been taken. Our experience with the New Haven case indicates that they are quite as advisable after diphtheric vaginitis as after any other form of diphtheric infection. That several negative cultures obtained from A. B. were followed by many positive cultures gives point to various articles on diphtheria carriers which have drawn attention to the well-known fact that two negative cultures are by no means conclusive evidence that the patient will remain free from diphtheria bacilli for even a short period of time.

STUDIES ON YEAST

VI. ON THE CONTINUOUS GROWTH OF SACCHAROMYCES CEREVISIAE IN SYNTHETIC MEDIUMS

Ellis I. Fulmer and Victor E. Nelson

From the Chemistry Department, Iowa State College, Ames, Iowa

In a recent article, Robertson and Davis [1] conclude that yeast will not grow continuously in a synthetic medium, a conclusion at variance with those of Fulmer, Nelson and Sherwood,[2] Nelson, Fulmer and Cessna,[3] and of MacDonald and McCollum.[4] It seemed that a restatement of the problem and of our position with reference to it should be made at this time.

It will not be necessary to make a detailed historical statement, except to say that up to the time of our first publication the ability of yeast to grow continuously, and in a state of good nutrition, on a medium of known materials, was not supposed possible. By methods, which we believe to be new, we developed a medium for the continuous growth of yeast. There were experimental reasons for the concentrations of each of the salts used, and we believe that the mediums developed are the best that can be made from the constituents employed. Our mediums are not arbitrary in composition but are the result of the systematic asking of the yeast as to its preference.

What is meant by continuous growth of an organism? By growth we refer to the phenomenon by which one cell becomes two, i. e., reproduction. The number of cells may or may not be parallel to the yeast crop as measured by the weight or the volume of the crop. Conditions favorable for the greatest number of cells may or may not be favorable for the greatest weight or volume of yeast. So by continuous growth we mean the continuous reproduction of yeast.

The ideal method of subculture would maintain the reproduction at the maximum rate, i. e., at the logarithmic phase of growth. Yeast has grown continuously in 3 of our mediums for 39 months, averaging a transfer every 3 days (table 1). This makes nearly 1,200 transfers or subcultures. During that time the yeast has undergone at least

Received for publication, April, 1923.

[1] Jour. Infect. Dis., 1923, 32, p. 153.
[2] Jour. Am. Chem. Soc., 1921, 43, pp. 186 and 191.
[3] Jour. Biol. Chem., 1921, 46, p. 77.
[4] Ibid., p. 525.

10,000 periods of reproduction or generations. Definite conclusions regarding the nutrition of animals are drawn from 3 and 5 generations. Surely, then, the yeast is growing continuously in our mediums.

What is meant by the statement that a substance is "necessary" for the growth of an organism? The period of reproduction in our best medium is much less than twice that in beer wort. There is present in wort and other materials a substance or substances not present in our medium which greatly accelerates the growth of yeast in that medium. That this acceleration is not due to the change in concentration of any constituent of our medium is shown by the fact that the extract will increase the growth of yeast in a medium containing too little and in a medium containing too much of the known constituents. Evidently there are unknown substances which accelerate the growth of yeast in our synthetic medium, and the cause of the acceleration cannot be duplicated with the known components of that medium. To this class of substances the generic name "bios" is given. However, bios is not necessary for the growth of yeast, but only makes it grow more rapidly. It is not necessary for the yeast to maintain a rapid growth. Only those materials are necessary which are needed for continuous growth. And we maintain that yeast does undergo continuous growth in our mediums at the specified temperature.

Robertson and Davis [1] attempted subculture of yeast in a medium of the composition indicated in table 1.

It seems to us that the failure of the authors to maintain continuous growth in their medium is in no wise a rebuttal of our statements as to the subculture of yeast in our mediums at 30 C.

These authors stress the carrying over of the stimulant, which is either shared with the new cells or serves as a stimulant to the production of that stimulant. In 10,000 generations, there can be no question as to the diluting out of any original constituents. Our only contention is that this material need not be a constituent of the yeast dietary.

The failure to secure continuous growth in a synthetic medium may be due to one or more of 4 causes. The medium may not be the best synthetic medium under the condition of the experiment; the wrong temperature may be used for a medium otherwise satisfactory; the culture is impure; the culture is subcultured too rapidly. The first 2 factors were mentioned in the foregoing.

The successful use of our mediums depends on the correct balance of salt concentrations at a given temperature. The presence of a foreign organism may lead, by its metabolic products, to the overturning of optimum conditions in the medium. We have found that even slight contaminations lead to decreased growth, contaminations which would lead to no such lessening of growth in wort or in synthetic mediums plus extracts.

TABLE 1

COMPOSITION OF MEDIUM EXPRESSED IN GRAMS OF THE CONSTITUENT PER 100 C C. OF MEDIUM

Constituents	Medium E	Medium F	Medium C	Robertson and Davis
Asparagin	.....	.....	.....	0.34
Ammonium chloride	0.188	0.188	0.188	....
Calcium chloride	0.10	0.10	.....	0.01
Dextrose	.....	.....	.....	2.0
Cane sugar	10	10	10	....
Magnesium sulphate	.....	.....	.....	0.02
Dipotassium phosphate	0.10	0.10	0.10	0.10
Sodium chloride	.....	.....	.....	0.50
Dextrin	.....	0.60	.....	....
Temperature	30 C	30 C	30 C	37.5 C

Too rapid a subculture leads to what we term the "dropping" of the culture. In fact, one of the workers in this laboratory reported that yeast would not grow continuously in our medium. An analysis of the case showed the following: He added to 49 c c. of a medium 1 c c. of a culture in which the count was 50. (When the "count" is 1, there are 250,000 cells per c c.) This would make the initial count in the new culture $\frac{1 \times 50}{50} = 1$. He adopted the plan of subculturing, with the dilution of 1 : 50 c c. each 24 hours. In this particular medium, the yeast increased 30 fold each 24 hours. Table 2 shows the source of his error.

TABLE 2

RESULTS IN SUBCULTURING OF YEAST TOO RAPIDLY

Subculture 1: 50	Count in New Culture	Count After 24 Hours
1	1	30
2	0.60	18
3	0.360	10.8
4	0.216	6.50
5	0.130	3.90
6	0.078	2.34
7	0.047	1.40
8	0.028	0.84

After the 8th subculture, the maximum count would be less than 1, an amount of yeast that would not even make the medium turbid. A microscopic examination would show only a few cells, and certainly the comparison would lead to the erroneous conclusion that the medium would not sustain continuous growth. When this too rapid subculture was remedied, marked success of subculture was reported in place of failure. Inoculation by specified volume at regular intervals will fail to maintain a culture if the organism is not growing rapidly enough to insure at least as large an initial seeding in each subculture. We believe that the error mentioned cannot be stressed too strongly in subculture work.

Robertson and Davis suggest that our success in subculture may have been due to the use of impure chemicals, in view of the fact that our publications did not discuss that point. The only material which might be questioned as a possible carrier of bios would be the cane sugar. In order to test this point we extracted cane sugar for 7 days with 95% alcohol in a continuous extractor. Yeast did not grow any more poorly on the extracted sugar, nor did the crop show any increase when grown on the extract. Subculture gave the same results. These results were obtained by one of the authors and by Sherwood. Heller successfully made subcultures of yeast by the use of the extracted sugar and our salt combination. The salts used were all tested and were found to be free from any interfering substances.

SUMMARY

Failure to secure continuous growth in synthetic mediums has been discussed and possible causes for such failure are outlined.

STUDIES OF FUSIFORM BACILLI AND SPIROCHETES

IV. OCCURRENCE IN TONSILS AND ADENOIDS

I. Pilot and J. Brams

From the Department of Pathology and Bacteriology, University of Illinois, College of Medicine, Chicago, Illinois

Fusiform bacilli and spirochetes in connection with actinomyces-like granules of the tonsils were noted by Davis [1] in 25% of extirpated tonsils. They were found in about the same percentage in another series of tonsils.[2] In the present series of 100 pairs of tonsils, these formations were observed in 19% and in the adenoids in only one instance. No studies have been made to determine their incidence in the naso-pharynx and in tonsils devoid of granules. Gross [3] found fusiform bacilli and spirilla on the normal tonsils of 11 of 13 persons, but these may have been derived from the mouth secretions as well as from the tonsillar crypts.

In determining the frequency of certain organisms of the mouth and pharynx it has been pointed out [4] that smears and cultures from the surfaces by the swab method give a considerably lower incidence than cultures of extirpated tonsils and adenoids of the same persons; that cultures of excised tonsils, showing no other condition but hyperplasia yielded about the same incidence of bacteria as the normal throat. We therefore undertook the study of the frequency of fusiform bacilli and spirochetes from this point of view, using excised tonsils and adenoids.

The tonsils and adenoids were removed at the Cook County Hospital during January and February, 1923, from 100 children 5 to 16 years of age, who were free from fever and acute respiratory infections. Grossly, the tonsils presented varying degrees of hyperplasia of the lymphoid tissue and only exceptionally slight increase in fibrous tissue. Actinomyces-like granules were visible to the naked eye in one or both tonsils in 19%. They were foul-smelling, yellow, from 1 to 5 mm. in diameter, single or more often multiple in the crypts of one or both tonsils. In the procedure of enucleation these granules are readily lost. We have also observed them being expelled from the throat following irritation of the pharynx. It is probable that at some time these granules form in the crypts of tonsils of every person. The adenoids were obtained in 46

Received for publication, April 20, 1923.

1 Jour. Infect. Dis., 1914, 14, p. 144.
2 Pilot and Davis: Ibid., 1918, 23, p. 231.
3 Jour. Am. Med. Assn., 1906, 46, p. 481.
4 Jour. Infect. Dis., 1921, 29, p. 47.

of the same children. They varied from 0.3 to 2 cm. in diameter; were made up largely of folds of lymphoid tissue which often adhered at their margins forming slits or crypt-like depressions; fatty débris, composed of cholesterol crystals, desquamated epithelial cells, appeared in a few vegetations; granules similar to those of the tonsils were found in only one adenoid. This vegetation measured 1 cm. in diameter, and revealed 2 folds and a true crypt. The circumference of the mouth of this crypt was distinctly less than that of the base. A single granule occurred within the crypt near the opening, as a firm, yellow spherical mass, 2 mm. in diameter, with a foul odor. The crushed preparation revealed bacteria in masses identical with those in tonsillar granules. We have been searching for such masses in adenoids, and this is the first granule seen in the course of the examination of several hundred adenoid vegetations. Apparently the nature of the structure of the adenoid, with its folds hanging free in the nasopharyngeal vault, permits excellent drainage with no tendency to the large collections of bacteria as in the tonsillar crypts. If the folds become adherent with resulting cryptlike structures, bacteria may collect, readily forming masses. Undoubtedly such masses do form more often than our results would indicate, but in the removal of the adenoids the tissue is often macerated so that the masses are lost.

The tonsils were incised with a sterile knife and the crypts examined for contents. Smears were made from the bottoms and sides of the crypts, and from the depths and sides of the folds of the adenoids. When the granules were encountered, they were crushed and examined in fresh and smear preparations. The smears were stained with dilute carbol fuchsin and the Fontana stain. In the granules we have verified previous observations as to structure and nature. Fusiform bacilli and spirochetes were found in enormous numbers clustered about central shafts of filamentous structures with brushlike terminals. The filaments were often segmented like fungi, with diplococcoid and short comma-shaped or fusiform bodies at the extremities, suggesting that these bodies may be spores of fungus. True branching organisms or actinomyces were not observed. Cocci were irregularly distributed in the general mass. The combination of these structures—the filaments, short fusiform bodies, typical fusiform and spirochetes, gram-positive cocci—is a constant, striking characteristic of these masses, illustrating a remarkable symbiotic relationship. Similar groups of bacteria were observed in a few instances independent of granule formations. Spirochetes were encountered only in connection with rich bacterial masses. Fusiform bacilli were found regardless of such formations, appearing in direct smears in 65% of one or both tonsils of the 100 persons, and in 12 of 46 adenoids. In the tonsils, the bacilli were decidedly more numerous than in the adenoids. In all of the smears, fusiform bacilli and spirochetes were always associated with cocci and bacillary forms of the diphtheroid, capsulatus and other groups.

In smear preparations the bacilli varied in morphology. Forms with tapering ends were most common. Some stained uniformly solid, while most revealed a granular or barred appearance; straight and curved forms occurred, while in a few the ends were blunt instead of pointed. They were weakly gram-positive and observed by dark field illumination, nonmotile. The spirochetes were variable in shape. In the dark field they appeared actively motile in enormous numbers; they were gram-negative, and methylene blue stained them faintly, while with dilute carbol fuchsin they were quite distinct. The Fontana method stained them black or dark brown and rendered them coarser in appearance. Short slender and coarse forms with 3 to 5 undulations were intermingled freely with longer, both slender and coarse forms, with 5 to 15 undulations. While found in largest numbers in the granules, they were demonstrated also in fewer numbers in 6 tonsils, without gross evidence of bacterial masses. In the adenoids, they were apparently scarce, appearing in only 2 specimens. In shape, they were identical with the spirochetes in Vincent's angina and about the teeth.

Cultures were made from the tonsils and adenoids by inoculating blood-agar slants. Macerated specimens were not used. At first dextrose-infusion agar, to which was added blood or ascites fluid, was used; but it was found that the fusiform bacilli grew well on plain infusion agar with a P_H 7.6, to which defibrinated human blood was added in proportion of 1 part of blood to 5 of agar. Material from several crypts of each tonsil was inoculated in different slants made anaerobic by the pyrogallic-alkali mixture; aerobic blood-agar slants were inoculated from the same sources and used as control cultures. In a few instances, tall tubes of ascites dextrose broth were used, but this medium did not yield fusiform bacilli as constantly as the blood agar owing to overgrowth by cocci. Tall tubes of ascites broth, to which sterile rabbit kidney was added, supported growth of spirochetes for a few days, but later yielded only fusiform bacilli and cocci with the production of an intense putrid odor about the tissue.

Fusiform bacilli appeared in the anaerobic slants in varying numbers; they did not grow in the aerobic tubes. The slants giving positive growths as a rule emitted a foul odor. The odor was slight or absent when the bacilli were few in number.

In cultures the bacilli, occurred in typical forms with tapering ends, granular or striated, varying in size. The ends often tended to be less pointed than in direct smears. Long filamentous organisms were frequently present, but were not considered as pleomorphic forms except in the presence of the more typical bacilli. Both tonsils contained the bacilli in 36%, one tonsil in 46% or one or both tonsils gave positive growth in 82%. Of the 46 adenoids cultivated, the bacilli appeared in 15 (32.65%). Spirochetes did not grow on the slants. Streptococci either of the hemolytic or viridans type or both were present constantly. In the absence of the granules, the hemolytic streptococcus was more profuse. The cultures of the tonsils which did not contain fusiform bacilli usually yielded pure hemolytic streptococci. In the adenoids, streptococci were also present constantly. Staphylococci, B. capsulatus and Micrococcus catarrhalis were encountered less often.

Pure cultures were obtained by using the method of Krumwiede and Pratt,[5] inoculating washed macerated granules into ascites-dextrose agar and pouring into inverted plates. In 48 to 72 hours, small gray irregular colonies appeared. The plates were torn apart and the colonies were identified as fusiform bacilli by smearing and making subcultures of the colonies.

The pathogenicity of fusiform bacilli and spirochetes of the tonsils has been demonstrated in various ways. Davis[1] introduced the tonsil granules intraperitoneally and produced putrid abscesses. If rabbits were injected intrapleurally with macerated granules, the cavity filled rapidly with thick foul pus, usually causing the death of animal in 6 to 8 days.[6] Early fusiform bacilli, spirochtes and cocci appeared in the exudate; later the spirochetes disappeared,

[5] Ibid., 1913, 12, p. 199.
[6] Davis, D. J., and Pilot, I., Jour. Am. Med. Assn., 1922, 79, p. 944.

and if the animal survived, only cocci remained. In the rabbits that died the associated streptococci appeared to be aggressive, causing serofibrinous pleuritis in the opposite pleural cavity, serofibrinous pericarditis and peritonitis. The bacilli and spirochetes remained localized in the injected pleural cavity. Pure cultures of streptococci produced an extensive empyema with no odor, demonstrating the rôle of the bacilli and spirochetes in the production of the putrid character of the exudate. Davis found the bacilli by themselves did not produce distinct lesions, but when combined with cocci the lesions usually produced by cocci were altered.[1] We have been unable to isolate the spirochetes to test their pathogenic properties.

The frequent occurrence of fusiform bacilli and spirochetes in the tonsils and adenoids is not surprising when we consider the huge numbers of these organisms about teeth. The tartar is made up largely of these bacteria combined with filamentous masses forming brushlike processes comparable to those of the tonsil granules.[6] In the crypts of the tonsils, instead of forming squamous plaques of tartar, the organisms tend to form globular structures. As about the teeth, when these organisms accumulate or if drainage from the crypts is poor, a distinct foul odor results, especially in those who have diseased tonsils.

Aside from the production of foul breath, these organisms often assume pathogenic properties. The beginning of the exudate in Vincent's angina is often at the mouths of the tonsillar crypts, suggesting that certain cases of angina may arise from the organisms already present. In fact, the fusiform bacilli and spirochetes in Vincent's angina are thus far indistinguishable morphologically or culturally from those present normally in the tonsils. In the condition known as pharyngomycosis, masses of these organisms seem to grow between the layers of the thickened epithelium.[6] We have observed these organisms in putrid ethmoiditis and otitis media. Another important point of attack is the lower respiratory tract. Abscess or gangrene of the lung is often the result of fusospirochete infection. The organisms about the tonsils are significant in this connection, as many of the lesions are the result of ether anesthesia, especially for tonsillectomy.

SUMMARY

Fusiform bacilli were found in the extirpated tonsils of 82 of 100 children, and in 15 of 46 (32.6%) adenoids. Spirochetes appeared in 25% of the tonsils, especially in the actinomyces-like granules. In the adenoids, they were demonstrated in only 2 instances. Associated with them in both tonsils and adenoids were streptococci of the hemolytic and viridans types, and other bacteria.

In morphology, the fusiform bacilli and spirochetes resemble those found about teeth and in certain putrid and gangrenous processes of the mouth and respiratory tract. The tonsils and adenoids may be important sources of infections with these organisms and associated bacteria.

STUDIES IN FUSIFORM BACILLI AND SPIROCHETES

V. OCCURRENCE IN OTITIS MEDIA CHRONICA

I. Pilot and S. J. Pearlman

From the Department of Pathology and Bacteriology, University of Illinois, College of Medicine, and from the Emanuel Mandel Dispensary of the Michael Reese Hospital, Chicago

Our attention was drawn to the character of the flora in the discharge from the ear, in the study of various putrid and gangrenous processes due to fusiform bacilli and spirochetes.[1] Further observations were made on chronic otitis media, with the result that foul discharges in such cases seemed to be due to these anaerobes. Krumwiede [2] cultivated fusiform bacilli from chronically discharging ears, but made no reference to the odor or the associated organisms. According to Holt,[3] in 7 cases of noma of the ear, the condition was preceded by otitis media, the noma beginning in the deeper portions of the canal with the production of a dirty brown discharge with gangrenous odor. Weaver and Tunnicliff [4] established the fusiform bacillus and associated spirochetes as the etiologic factors of such cases of noma.

In our study of middle ear discharges, fusiform bacilli usually together with spirochetes were found in 15 patients, in greatest numbers in the intensely fetid, purulent secretions. In the less offensive discharges, they were fewer. In 3 instances in which the odor was distinctly foul, the organisms were not demonstrated. Chronic nonfetid discharges in 12 instances did not reveal them, and in cases of acute otitis the organisms were not found.

The discharges were studied in smear preparations stained with 10% carbol fuchsin, or gentian violet or by the Fontana method. The fusiform bacilli appeared in variable numbers as long rods thicker in the central portion and tapering to pointed or slightly blunt ends. The length varied from 5 to 12 microns. The shorter forms were as a rule curved. They stained often unevenly as granular or striated bacilli. They tend to be gram-positive, depending on care in decolorizing. Cultures were obtained under anaerobic conditions in 2 instances. In the cultures, the bacilli appeared typical, together

Received for publication, May 2, 1923.

[1] Davis, D. J., and Pilot, I., Jour. Am. Med. Assn., 1922, 79, p. 944.

[2] Science, 1913, 38, p. 45.

[3] Diseases of Infancy and Childhood, 1914, p. 280.

[4] Jour. Infect. Dis., 1905, 2, p. 446.

with longer pleomorphic forms. In smears, the spirochetes usually were not as numerous as the bacilli, and in 3 instances they were absent while the bacilli were present. In others they were comparatively few, while in the very foul discharges large numbers occurred. Morphologically they varied in size, some presenting 2 to 5 turns, others 5 to 15. Both the short or long spirochetes were either slender or coarse. They were gram-negative and did not grow in the cultures. In their morphology, the bacilli and the associated spirochetes resembled those found in Vincent's angina, pulmonary gangrene, and about normal teeth and tonsils.[1]

Although in the very foul discharges these organisms appeared in large numbers, they never occurred in pure form, but invariably associated with various pyogenic bacteria. Most constant of all were gram-positive diplococci and short chains of cocci. Staphylococci, pneumococci, diphtheroids and B. capsulatus were less frequently encountered. In one instance, Streptococcus hemolyticus was obtained in aerobic culture, and in another Streptococcus viridans.

The patients from whom the smears were obtained varied in age from 8 to 35 years, of either sex. The chronicity of the discharge was often 10 to 20 years; in a few, the duration was from 3 to 12 months. Bone destruction and granulation tissue were frequently found. The discharge was chronic, often intermittent, with periods when the odor was decidedly less or absent. Often the same patient with fusiform bacilli and spirochetes in the foul discharge returned after treatment with an odorless secretion in which the organisms could not be found.

The association of these organisms with the fetid character of the discharge is striking and in accordance with our general conception of the etiologic rôle that these anaerobes play in gangrenous and putrid processes in the respiratory tract. These infections in most instances are autogenous, complicating the exanthematous or other specific infectious diseases or chronic debilitated states with lowered general resistance. The sources of infection are the fusiform bacilli and spirochetes found normally about the teeth and tonsils.

In the tartar of the teeth, these organisms appear in large numbers as constant inhabitants. In the tonsils, the bacilli are found in 82%, spirochetes in 25%. In the adenoids, the bacilli appear in 32.6%; spirochetes were demonstrated in 2 of 40 specimens. The associated streptococci are either of the green or hemolytic type, the green being constant.[5]

In our studies, the bacilli and spirochetes were observed in only chronic discharges and not in the pus from acute otitis. The acute condition may be complicated later by the anaerobes as secondary invaders in the subsequent subacute or chronic stages. The mode of infection is through the Eustachean tube from the naso-oropharynx. Extension from the external auditory canal is improbable, as the bacilli and spirochetes were not demonstrable in the normal canal. The ordinary pyogenic bacteria prepare the soil for the anaerobes which cause the fetid discharge.

[5] Pilot, I., and Davis, D. J., Ibid., 1918, 23, p. 562.

SUMMARY

Chronic fetid discharges from the middle ear contained fusiform bacilli, spirochetes together with streptococci, pneumococci and diphtheroids. Nonfetid discharges did not harbor the bacilli and spirochetes. The fusiform bacilli and spirochetes appeared identical with those about normal teeth, tonsils, adenoids and in putrid infections of the mouth and lungs.

APPEARANCE AND PERSISTENCE OF TYPHOID AGGLUTININS IN RABBITS *

T. D. Beckwith and E. M. Jones

From the Department of Bacteriology and Experimental Pathology, University of California

Although the amount of work dealing with the time of appearance and period of persistence of agglutinins for B. typhosus after injection is somewhat large, there seems to be lacking conformity as to results. Variation in methods of technic of course explains this in part. Differences in strains utilized is to be considered also.

A survey of the available literature reveals the following. Deutsch[1] reports that the subcutaneous injection of 1½ to 2 agar slants in rabbits yielded a serum titer of 1:80 in 55 hours and that 1 animal gave a reading of 1:500 in 72 hours. Jatta[2] states that an agar culture suspended in broth introduced intravenously in rabbits resulted in a titer of 1:30 in 60 hours and 1:300 in 102 hours. By Jörgensen[3] it is reported that after intravenous injection of "1 c c. of a 24-hour culture" in rabbits, agglutinins commenced to appear on the 3rd day. Gaehtgens[4] gave one half agar culture intravenously and obtained an agglutinin reading of 1:50 on the second day, which in turn became 1:250 on the third day. Fukuhara[5] suggests that the introduction intravenously of ¼ loop of agar culture likewise into rabbits causes agglutinins to appear on the 3rd day. Tsukahara[6] confirms certain preceding writers who state that agglutinins are evident on the third day following injection. Locke,[7] by repeated intravenous injection, was able to produce a high titer in 8 to 11 days. Apparently the slow passage of fluid through the wall of a celloidin capsule may result in the formation of agglutinins, since we are informed by McCrae[8] that such capsules containing the paracolon bacillus placed intraperitoneally results in agglutinin formation by the 8th day.

When guinea-pigs were used, even greater variation was noted, as may be learned from the work of Widal and Sicard,[9] Fodor and Rigler,[10] Deutsch,[1] and Rehms.[11] It is shown by Reiter and Silberstein[12] that when pigeons of 350-400 gm. are injected with 300,000,000 to 400,000,000 B. typhosus heated to 60 C. for 1 hour, agglutinins appear on the 7th day.

Regarding the comparative effectiveness of live and of dead organisms for agglutinogens, Widal and Sicard[9] believed that it requires double the dose and a period of 5 days to produce agglutinins in the guinea-pig when the antigen is heated to 60 C. for 45 minutes. With live antigen, the time was 3 days.

Received for publication, May 3, 1923.

1 Centralbl. f. Bakteriol., I, O., 1900, 28, p. 45.
2 Ztschr. f. Hyg. u. Infektionskr., 1900, 33, p. 185.
3 Centralbl. f. Bakteriol., I, O., 1905, 38, pp. 475, 556 and 679.
4 Ibid., 1908, 48, p. 223.
5 Ztschr. f. Immunitätsf., 1909, 2, p. 305.
6 Ibid., 1921, 33, p. 410.
7 Univ. Calif. Publ. in Pathol., 1912, 2, p. 91.
8 Jour. Exper. Med., 1901, 5, p. 635.
9 Ann. l'Inst. Pasteur, 1897, 11, p. 353.
10 Centralbl. f. Bakteriol., I, O., 1898, 23, p. 930.
11 Compt. rend. d. Soc. biol., 1901, 53, p. 687.
12 Ztschr. f. Immuntätsf., 1915, 22, p. 443.

Rodella,[13] with B. proteus, likewise using guinea-pigs, states that approximately twice as much time is required when dead forms are injected as when living bacteria are used. He states also that promptness in the reaction is obtained when injection is intravenous rather than subcutaneous.

The point of maximum titer with rabbits was determined by Tsukahara[6] to lie between the 6th and 8th day. With guinea-pigs, Fodor and Rigler[10] indicate it to be at the 12th day. Reiter and Silberstein[12] noted in experiments with pigeons that it lies at the 15th day.

Little is known concerning the persistence of actively formed agglutinins in animals. Fodor and Rigler[10] found that some of their guinea-pigs gave a titer reading 77-80 days after injection, and Jatta[2] states that 1 rabbit showed agglutinins 3 months later.

To determine more accurately some of these points, concerning which there appears to be a lack of uniformity, the following experiments were undertaken. An effort was made to find when agglutinins may be expected to appear and when the point of highest titer will be found. Knowledge concerning the comparative effectiveness for agglutinin formation of dead suspension of B. typhosus and of the same suspension living in salt solution was sought. An attempt was made to learn facts concerning the persistence of agglutinins in the circulation following a single intravenous injection of the bacilli.

For this work the strain of B. typhosus known as No. 3 was used. This is the one used by the author in previous work and by other members of this department in research dealing with typhoid. Cultures were made on rabbit blood agar according to the method of Gay and Claypole[14] for a 24-hour period at 37 C., growth covering the whole of the slant. Rabbits were selected from carefully fed stock and with weights varying between 2,500 and 3,500 gm. Injections were made from suspensions in salt solutions into the posterior ear vein. Dosages were recorded as fractions of the growth appearing within 24 hours at 37 C. on a rabbit blood-agar slant of the strain of B. typhosus used. The preparation of dead suspension was carried out by heating to 56 C. for 45 minutes, after which streaks on agar were made to determine sterility. Agglutination was carried out by the macroscopic method with tubes carefully cleaned. Samples of blood were obtained from the posterior ear vein. The agglutination series were incubated for 2 hours at 37 C. and then placed in the icebox over night, after which observations were made only on such tubes as showed complete precipitation. Thus no partial agglutination was included. In the tables no mention of the 1st or 2d day is included, since no reaction was detected on either one.

[13] Centralbl. f. Bakteriol., I, O., 1900, 27, p. 583.
[14] Archiv. Int. Med., 1913, 12, p. 613.

Exper. 1.—To determine the time of appearance following intravenous injection of living B. typhosus into rabbits; dosage ⅓ slant. The results are shown in table 1.

TABLE 1

Appearance in Rabbits of Agglutinins for B. Typhosus Following One Intravenous Injection of Living Bacilli

Rabbits	Days									
	3	4	5	6	7	8	9	10	13	15
393	15	20	120	300	800	600	800	400		
394	10	20	120	600	200	Dead	——	——		
344	0	40	320	1280	960	1280	2560	7680	3840	2560
336	0	480	1280	3840	7680	2560	3840	1280	1280	960

Exper. 2.—The procedure paralleled that of the preceding experiment, but the suspension had been killed by the application of heat for 45 minutes at 56 C.; dosage ⅓ slant. Table 2 shows the results obtained.

TABLE 2

Appearance in Rabbits of Agglutinins for B. Typhosus Following One Intravenous Injection of Killed Bacilli

Rabbits	Days									
	3	4	5	6	7	8	9	10	13	15
391	20	60	800	600	600	800	400	150		
392	10	120	120	600	300	400	400	300		
341	0	10	1280	5120	5120	5120	7680	3840		
345	0	30	160	960	480	480	480	640	1920	960
347	0	10	80	1280	960	1280	1280	1280	960	640

Exper. 3.—Animals were given one intravenous injection of living B. typhosus with an individual dosage of 1/10 tube (table 3).

TABLE 3

Appearance and Persistence of Agglutinins Following One Intravenous Injection into Rabbits of 1/10 Slant of B. Typhosus

Rabbits	Days							
	3	5	7	11	14	21	28	35
317	20	80	160	320	640	320	160	160
330	20	80	160	320	320	160	80	160
335	40	320	160	320	320	320	640	80
382	20	40	80	160	80	80	Dead	....
345	20	160	80	320	640	160	20	80
369	20	160	320	2560	320	320	160	80

Exper. 4.—The procedure followed that in exper. 3, except that the organisms had been killed by 45 minutes' exposure to 56 C.; dosage $\frac{1}{10}$ slant. The results appear in table 4.

TABLE 4

APPEARANCE AND PERSISTENCE OF AGGLUTININS FOLLOWING ONE INTRAVENOUS INJECTION INTO RABBITS OF KILLED B. TYPHOSUS

Rabbits	Days							
	3	5	7	11	14	21	28	35
311	20	80	160	1280	320	40	20	40
383	20	40	80	320	80	40	160	80
393	20	80	160	1280	160	160	160	40
365	20	80	160	1280	640	80	80	40
370	20	20	40	640	80	40	20	40
351	20	2560	1280	1280	320	160	80	80

Exper. 5.—As the results in the 2 preceding experiments indicate a considerable degree of persistence of agglutinins in rabbits, the following tests were carried out to learn somewhat more exactly the period of time during which agglutinins may be expected to be present in the circulation after introduction of $\frac{1}{3}$ slant B. typhosus. It will be noted that the antibodies, although feeble in concentration, nevertheless were discernible in all instances 14 weeks after injection. Table 5 indicates the results obtained from this experiment.

TABLE 5

PERSISTENCE OF AGGLUTININS FOR B. TYPHOSUS IN RABBITS FOLLOWING ONE INTRAVENOUS INJECTION OF LIVING B. TYPHOSUS

Rabbits	9 Days	Weeks								
		2	3	4	6	8	10	12	13	14
639	1600	6400	12800	6400	3200	1200	400	100	160	80
633	1600	6400	3200	1600	1200	600	600	100	80	40
303	9600	6400	1600	1600	600	400	400	50	40	20
304	6400	6400	1600	2400	800	200	150	50	40	40

Exper. 6.—The antigen was the same as that of the preceding experiment but with the difference that it had been killed by 45 minutes' exposure to 56 C. in the water bath. The outcome of this series is given in table 6. The same dosage was used.

TABLE 6

PERSISTENCE OF AGGLUTININS FOR B. TYPHOSUS IN RABBITS FOLLOWING ONE INTRAVENOUS INJECTION OF KILLED B. TYPHOSUS

Rabbits	9 Days	Weeks								
		2	3	4	6	8	10	12	13	14
301	1600	4800	6400	3200	600	200	400	100	160	40
302	1200	1600	800	1600	400	300	150	75	40	Dead
305	3200	800	600	600	400	150	25	40	10	10
306	3200	800	600	400	300	100	25	0	....	0

SUMMARY

The results of experiments indicate that there is a ready response on the part of the rabbit in agglutinin formation following intravenous injection of B. typhosus. When living organisms are used, agglutinins may be expected to be demonstrable on the third day, but when the bacilli have been killed by heat before injection, this response may be delayed for approximately 24 hours. The curve of agglutinin formation is characterized by an extremely steep ascent, so that the peak is reached between the fifth and the thirteenth days, ordinarily on the seventh or eighth. There appears to be little difference in this respect, whether the organisms used be living or killed by heat. The altitudes of the peaks of the curves produced by these two preparations are approximately the same. The descent of the agglutinin titer is comparatively slow, and agglutinins may be present in the circulation even 14 weeks after the injection.

THE LIFE CYCLE OF BACILLUS FUSIFORMIS

ONE PLATE

Ruth Tunnicliff

From the John McCormick Institute for Infectious Diseases, Chicago

The question whether fusiform bacilli and the spirilla with which they are practically always associated in normal, as well as in pathological, conditions, are separate organisms or parts of the life cycle of one, has long been a subject for discussion. The earlier workers who reached the conclusion that the two organisms were different forms of one, studied either sections of tissues or mixed cultures. The pure cultures of fusiform bacilli, obtained by Veillon and Zuber,[1] Ellermann,[2] Dr. Weaver and myself,[3] showed no spirilla. Later, in studying pure cultures of these bacilli from the normal mouth, I [4] found after 48 hours to 5 days that spiral forms were present which greatly resembled those seen in smear preparations from the mouth. Old dead cultures of the bacilli isolated by Dr. Weaver and myself were examined and spirilla were found similar to those in the living cultures. The spiral forms could be overlooked easily as often they are present for only a few days in any considerable number and require special staining, which was not employed in the earlier cultures. Neither the bacilli nor spiral forms could be demonstrated to have progressive motion.

Spiral forms were also seen by me [5] in pure cultures of fusiform bacilli, isolated from ulceromembranous angina (Vincent's angina), gingivitis and noma. In cultures containing sodium citrate, the spiral forms appeared shorter and more curved than in other mediums.

Since then, many strains of fusiform bacilli have been isolated. Larson and Barron,[6] and Klimenko [7] found spiral forms in their pure cultures, and they concluded that they were different forms of the same organism.

Krumwiede and Pratt,[8] on the other hand, found forms simulating spirochetes in their fixed preparations but not in the dark field and

Received for publication, May 3, 1923.

1 Arch. de méd. exper., 1908, 10, p. 517.
2 Centralbl. f. Bakteriol., I, O., 1904, 37, p. 729.
3 Jour. Infect. Dis., 1905, 2, p. 446.
4 Ibid., 1906, 3, p. 148.
5 Ibid., 1911, 8, p. 316.
6 Ibid., 1913, 13, p. 429.
7 Centralbl. f. Bakteriol., I, O., 1914, 74, p. 487.
8 Jour. Infect. Dis., 1913, 13, p. 438.

concluded they were not typical spirochetal forms. They express the opinion that it concerns two separate and distinct organisms, the motility of the spirochete and the lack of motility of the bacillus being the strongest evidence against their identity. However, another form of bacteria, Nitrosomonas, has been shown by Winogradsky [9] to have a definite life cycle, first growing in a compact zoöglea-like mass which is nonmotile, and later resolving themselves into separate motile ellipsoid cells, with a flagellum at one end. Mellon [9a] found true spirochete-like forms, having the specific staining reaction of real spirochetes, in his cultures, but concluded they were not genuine on account of lack of motility.

Undoubtedly, there are several different strains of fusiform bacilli. Knorr [10] describes 3 kinds: Fusobacterium of Plaut-Vincent, forming brush-like colonies; Fusobacterium nucleatum, forming orbicular colonies, with sharply defined edges, and Fusobacterium polymorphum, often growing in brushlike, hazy colonies. The colonies studied by Veillon and Zuber,[1] Ellermann,[2] Dr. Weaver and myself formed lenticular colonies with regular edges. Ellermann states that his small colonies had a felted appearance. The colonies described by Krumwiede and Pratt [8] were of a puff-ball appearance, those of Mellon [9a] were raised, moderately moist, fairly adherent, generally developing a lemon-yellow pigment, those of Brams, Pilot and Davis [11] small and irregular. As pointed out by Löhnis,[12] in his interesting and stimulating discussion of the life cycle of bacteria, it is probable that there are strains of fusiform bacilli which have nothing to do with spirilla. For instance, the culture isolated by Dick and Emge [13] from a cerebral abscess showed no spiral forms. It was obtained from material, which contained fusiform organisms alone, neither spirilla no cocci being present. This is the only case I know of, in which fusiform bacilli were not associated with cocci.

Mühlens,[14] Knorr [10] and others consider my cultures not pure, but mixtures of B. fusiformis and spirochetes. As separate colonies were repeatedly plated out on blood and ascites agar and the colonies were widely separated in ascites shake cultures, with and without fresh kid-

[9] Jordan: General Bacteriology, 1922, p. 640.

[9a] Jour. Bacteriol., 1919, 4, p. 505.

[10] Centralbl. f. Bakteriol., I, O., 1922, 89, p. 4.

[11] Jour. Infect. Dis., 1923, 32, p. 159.

[12] Studies upon the Life Cycle of the Bacteria, Part I. Review of the Literature 1838-1912. Memoirs of the National Academy of Sciences, 1921, 16, Second Memoir.

[13] Jour. Am. Med. Assn., 1914, 62, p. 446.

[14] Kolle-Wassermann: Handbuch der pathogenen Microorganismen, 1913, 7, p. 297.

ney tissue, there being no indications of other colonies, the chance of a mixed culture always has seemed to me as rather unlikely.

Spirillum sputigeneum and Treponema macrodentium are the 2 spiral organisms most frequently found in mixed cultures of B. fusiformis and are readily distinguished culturally and morphologically in stained preparations and dark field illumination. They both appear in mixed fluid cultures after about 2 weeks' incubation and produce hazy growth in ascites tissue agar. The spirillum grows in small dry whitish colonies on blood agar; in stained preparations, it is comma shaped in young cultures and possesses from 1 to 3 flagella. Treponema macrodentium has small regular curves and a long fine flagellum at one or both ends. In the dark field the spirillum refracts the light along its edges and has a swift progressive motion; the treponema refracts the light nearly throughout its whole body and shows a serpentine, swinging motion.

The present study deals with a pure culture of Bacillus fusiformis isolated from a normal tonsil. The material was grown anaerobically first for 4 days in ascites broth (1:3) then subcultures were made on goat blood agar slants. Single colonies of fusiform bacilli were isolated after 3 days' incubation. The culture was repeatedly plated out on blood and ascites agar, and the colonies were well separated in ascites agar with and without fresh kidney tissue to insure a pure culture.

CULTURAL PROPERTIES

The organism is an obligate anaerobe; it grows at 36 C., but not at room temperature. A slightly offensive odor is given off in successful cultures. The bacilli are nonmotile and insoluble in 10% saponin or bile.

Cultures were made anaerobic according to Wright's method, by saturating the cotton stopper with a 5% solution of sodium hydroxide, a piece of pyrogallic acid the size of a pea having been placed on the plug; the tube was closed with a cork and sealed with paraffin.

The colonies on blood agar are whitish with a slightly violet tinge, smooth, moist, edges regular, from 1 to 3 mm. in diameter. In ascites agar shake cultures, the colonies are lenticular, with even borders, and slightly brownish. When well separated, they may become larger. A puff-ball appearance of the colonies has not been observed.

The organisms grow well on Loeffler's blood serum, autoclaved rabbit brain 1% dextrose broth, distilled water and ascites fluid 1:3, plain and dextrose broth with ascites fluid 3:1, plain and dextrose agar to which blood or ascites fluid has been added in the proportion of 3:1.

It requires some body fluid for growth, but enough may be carried over on inoculation for one generation. In dextrose broth the growth is diffuse at first, later settling into clumps; in other fluid mediums it is flocculent. Cultures were also successful on blood agar and in ascites broth, to which was added solutions of either 5 drops of 20% sodium chloride solution, 1-2 drops of 10% sodium hydroxide, or 1-2 drops of 10% acetic acid to each 5 c.c. of medium. Larger amounts of these substances generally inhibited growth. The addition of fresh rabbit kidney tissue did not appear to enhance the growth. The hydrogen-ion concentration of the medium was 7.4 to 7.6.

The bacillus ferments lactose, dextrose, salicin and inulin, but not mannite, maltose, or saccharose.

MORPHOLOGY AND STAINING PROPERTIES

The organism was stained by the following methods: The specimen is dried in the air, fixed either with osmic acid vapor 1 minute alone or followed by absolute alcohol 30 minutes or fixed with methyl alcohol 2 minutes and then stained with Giemsa (1:10) for 2 minutes. The organisms stained more clearly after methyl alcohol fixation.

The organisms were stained vitally by suspending them in brilliant cresyl blue. The stain acted in a few minutes, the organisms not showing any sign of plasmolysis; in a few hours the stain faded.

Flagella were demonstrated as follows: The organisms were carefully suspended in distilled water, dried in the incubator, flamed, gently heated for 5 minutes with 2 parts of a 20% aqueous tannic acid and 1 part of a filtered saturated aqueous solution of ferrous sulphate; washed; dried; gently heated 1 to 2 minutes with carbol-gentian-violet; washed; treated with Gram's iodine solution 2 to 3 seconds; washed again and dried. The tannic acid and ferrous sulphate solution is stable for several weeks.

In routine work, the organisms were stained with carbol-gentian-violet a few seconds, washed, treated with Gram's iodine solution for the same length of time, washed and dried. I have found this method of staining useful for spiral organisms, which are difficult to stain.[15]

Special fixing as with flagellar stain was sometimes found necessary to stain spirilla and cultivated Treponema macrodentium, as pointed out by Mühlens and Hartmann.[16]

[15] Jour. Am. Med. Assn., 1922, 78, p. 191.
[16] Ztschr. f. Hyg. u. Infektionskr., 1906, 55, p. 81.

As other strains of fusiform bacilli, this one is extremely pleomorphic, differing in form and size with different mediums. During its early growth, the bacilli appear as delicate, pointed, straight, rarely curved, rods from 2-10 mikrons in length. The shortest forms show deeply staining bodies at the ends or only 1 near the center, the longer forms generally contain 2 in the body. Large, thick forms are seen sometimes on solid mediums. Definite branching has been observed twice. Vacuoles are occasionally observed. In 24 to 48 hours or later, filaments of various lengths are formed, which also contain many deeply staining bodies, often in pairs, sometimes in bands. Some threads are seen to be made up of strings of bacilli. Sometimes short bacillary forms are seen in contact with the edge of the thread. Twisted forms are rare. Some filaments are much broader than others and at times appear as if dividing longitudinally. Later spiral forms with from 2 to 20 curves are observed staining uniformly or showing bodies and vacuoles in the interior. Filaments and spiral forms are most numerous in mediums containing dextrose and acetic acid. No spores could be demonstrated. The different forms do not stain typically with the Gram method, but unless thoroughly decolorized with alcohol, retain a faint bluish color. The body of the bacilli, filaments and some spiral forms stain blue with the Giemsa method, other spirals stain pinkish blue, the bodies within the organisms bright pink. When stained for flagella, they often show a fine long straight unstrained projection, at one or both ends. None of these forms show any progressive motion but are flexible. While many of the spiral forms straighten out when suspended in fluids, many others retain their spiral shape.

After incubation from 1 to 2 weeks, shorter spiral forms, 5 mikrons in length, more sharply curved, and with pointed ends, are observed. They may have from 2-10 shallow, regular or irregular curves. They may be single, in pairs or radiate from a central mass. In the dark field they appear granular, refracting the light irregularly. When first formed, they are actively motile, with a progressive, whirling, serpentine motion. The body of the spirillum appears flexible. Only one long fine wavy flagellum has been demonstrated at the end. These spirilla were found in all the mediums used, but were most numerous on goat blood agar and in ascites broth to which acetic acid was added. They also are gram negative and stain pink or pinkish blue with the Giemsa stain. They are insoluble in saponin or bile, 10%.

The small spirilla appear to develop in two ways: The bodies inside the threads are occasionally seen to fall out and then seem to burst, forming comma forms, then spirilla of from 2-10 curves; straight or curved forms may be seen attached to one of the bodies. These different forms show up well when vitally stained with brilliant cresyl blue. They are most often observed in old blood agar cultures or in fluid medium containing sodium hydroxide.

The most common method of development of the spirilla seems to occur within the threads. Here also the bodies appear to break up, forming comma shaped spirilla, then spiral forms with 2 to 4 curves, until finally the whole filament is filled with spirals with definite rounded curves of great regularity. The thread may contain spirilla with as many as 20 continuous curves. The spirilla in one filament are generally all at the same stage of development. These spirals stain bright pink with Giemsa stain, the filaments blue. The spirals inside the threads are less easily seen when stained with carbol-gentian-violet, but become distinctly visible when vitally stained with brilliant cresyl blue, the spirilla taking the stain more deeply than the filament. The spirilla may be seen clearly inside the threads in the dark field also, but not always on account of the spirillum refracting the light irregularly.

In fixed and occasionally in vitally stained preparations the spirilla may be observed to emerge from the end of the filament. In some specimens the whole filament appears to dissolve leaving the spirilla free. They may now increase to 20 mikrons in length and the curves often become fewer and more shallow, the spirilla appearing more as they do in fresh specimens. I have looked repeatedly for evidence of longitudinal division but have seen it only once. The spirilla now stain irregularly and show inside and outside in Giemsa preparations, blue elongated slightly pointed bodies, 2 mikrons in length, with deeply staining granules at the ends. These bodies look not unlike spores, but do not stain as such; they strongly resemble the short fusiform bacilli seen in early cultures.

As in cultures of other spiral organisms, this organism may break up into masses of bodies of various sizes. This is seen especially well in old ascites broth cultures, containing sodium hydroxide. These bodies sometimes stain bluish in Giemsa preparations with pink bodies inside, or just masses of pink or blue bodies are seen. They do not pass through a Berkefeld N filter and survive heating at 58 C. one half hour. From these masses, bacilli and threads may be seen to emerge. The masses of bodies may be the symplastic stage described by Löhnis [12] as connecting the different cycles in the life of bacteria, in this instance the spirillar and bacillary stages.

The fluid culture mediums may not possess sufficient nutrient material or the reaction may become unfavorable for the spirilla to free themselves from the filaments, in which case, a pipet full of the culture, containing many spirilla inside threads, may be transferred to fresh medium, in which the spirilla may later be found free in large numbers.

The staining reactions of the spirilla inside the threads and their motility when free speaks against their being due to plasmolysis. The suggestion may be made that they are parasites inside the bacillus, but the development of bacilli from the spirilla makes this supposition unlikely.

The development of new spiral organisms from bodies fallen out of the mother cell or from degenerated spiral cells is well known. There is also evidence that motile organisms may develop inside the cell wall, which later dissolves. Finkler and Prior [17] described this phenomenon in their spirillum, and Ferràn [18] made similar observations with the cholera spirillum. The formation of motile organisms inside the old cell wall of nonmotile threads has also been described in Cladothrix dichotoma by Zopf in 1881 and later verified by Ellis.[19]

Mellon [9a] describes fusiform bacilli, in smear preparations from a renal and pleural abscess, as having the chromatin disposed in rod shapes, resembling vibrios; bodies of various sizes and very thin wavy pink staining forms, some of which were seen springing from the end of thicker blue staining vibrio forms. I also have seen in smears from sputum, spiral forms with from 1 to 4 curves, inside fusiform bacilli; bodies staining pink with Giemsa, separating from the bacilli and free spirilla attached to similar round and curved bodies, as if growing from them.

SUMMARY

The pure culture of Bacillus fusiformis under observation is extremely pleomorphic, forming straight and wavy, nonmotile threads of various lengths, the bacilli and filaments staining blue with Giemsa stain, and bodies inside the organism bright pink. Under certain conditions these bodies appear to fall out of the threads and develop into motile spirilla with from 1 to 10 curves; or more frequently the spirilla develop from the bodies in the interior of the cell and later emerge from the end of the thread, or the filament ruptures leaving them free. The spirilla now seem to degenerate, and when stained with Giemsa

[17] Deutsch. med. Wchnschr., 1884, 10, p. 632.
[18] Ztschr. f. klin. Med., 1885, 9, p. 361.
[19] Proc. Roy. Soc. Med., 1912, 85, p. 344.

show both within and without elongated, slightly pointed blue bodies containing deeply staining granules at their ends, resembling short fusiform bacilli, seen in early cultures. The spirillar and bacillary cycles appear to be connected also by a symplastic stage, when a mass of bodies is formed, due to changes in the organisms, from which bacilli and threads emerge. These observations tend to confirm the theory that fusiform bacilli and spirilla are different forms in the life cycle of one organism.

PLATE 1

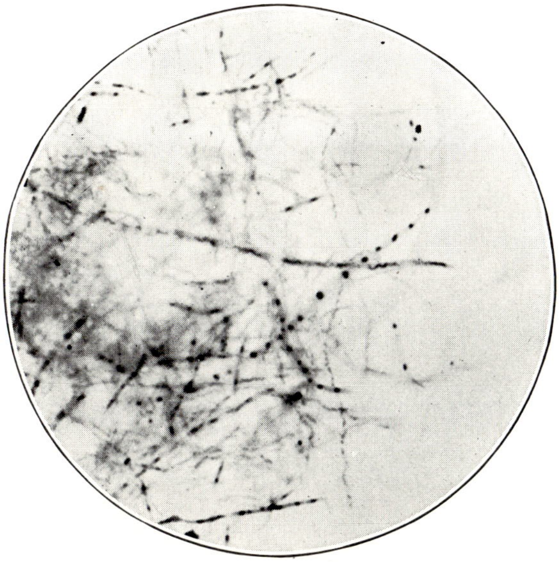

Fig. 1.—From a pure culture of fusiform bacilli grown one week in ascites broth with acetic acid. The preparation shows short fusiform bacilli, straight and wavy filaments, containing bodies, and a thread with spirilla inside. Giemsa stain; × 1200.

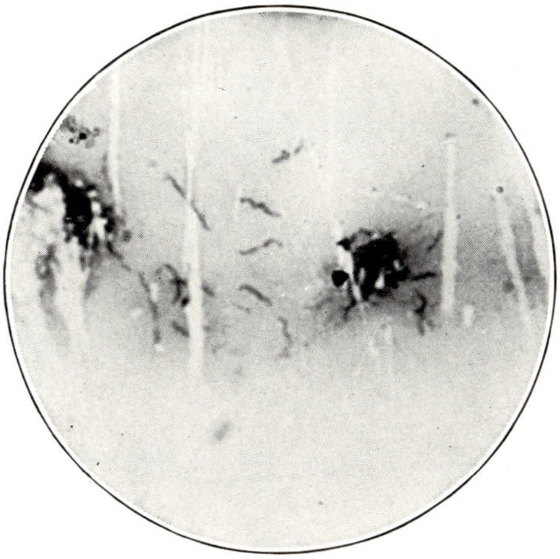

Fig. 2.—Pure culture of fusiform bacilli, grown 2 weeks in ascites broth with acetic acid. The specimen shows spirilla outside the filaments. Carbol-gentian-violet and Gram's iodine solution; × 1200.

STREPTOCOCCI OF FECES AND MOUTH OF COWS

V. STUDIES OF THE STREPTOCOCCI

From the Research Laboratories of the Dairy Division, U. S. Department of Agriculture, Washington, D. C.

S. Henry Ayers and Courtland S. Mudge

THE STREPTOCOCCI OF COW FECES

The streptococci of cow feces have been found by Winslow and Palmer,[1] Fuller and Armstrong,[2] Rogers and Dahlberg [3] and Jones [4] to be characterized by their ability to ferment raffinose. In this respect they differ from the human fecal type. The predominating cow fecal streptococcus is usually considered to be of Streptococcus salivarius type of Andrews and Horder.[5] The latter authors found this type most common in saliva.

Former studies of the streptococci of cow feces have been based largely on the fermentation to test substances. For this reason we have studied a number of cultures, using all the cultural characteristics described in a previous paper by the authors, on the streptococci of the bovine udder.[6]

Methods of Isolation.—Samples of fresh cow feces were collected on sterile cotton swabs, then brought to the laboratory and immediately plated on blood agar, after making suspensions in distilled water. This medium and cultural methods are described in a previous paper [6] of the series, with the exception of the medium for fermentation tests.

Because of a lack of supply of the yeast (cervisine) we were compelled to use the following medium: 15 gm. peptone (Bacto), 3 gm. meat extract, 5 gm. test substance and 1,000 c c. distilled water. The reaction was adjusted to P_H 7.5.

The peptone was increased from 1 to 1.5% in order to buffer the medium in a manner similar to the yeast peptone medium.

Our fecal cultures consisted of organisms isolated from 30 samples of cow feces from about 30 cows.

Received for publication, May 11, 1923.

[1] Jour. Infect. Dis., 1910, 7, p. 1.
[2] Ibid., 1913, 13, p. 442.
[3] Jour. Agric. Rec., 1914, 1, p. 491.
[4] Jour. Exper. Med., 1920, 31, p. 347.
[5] Lancet, 1906, 171, pp. 708, 775 and 852.
[6] Jour. Infect. Dis., 1922, 31, p. 40.

Differentiation of Cultures.—Our results confirm those of former investigators, as seen from table 1. Of the 78 cultures, 75 were found to be of the typical cow fecal type. Groups A and B varied only in their ability to ferment inulin. The 75 cultures showed only short chains averaging 6-10 cells in broth. On blood plates, the colonies had a slight hemolytic zone as a rule. They might be called weak Beta types, although some investigators might call them Gamma types. Methylene blue was reduced during 7 days' incubation in some cases. In litmus milk they did not grow at 10 C., at least not enough to cause any change in the color of the litmus indicator. It will be noted from the table that 54 of the cultures fermented raffinose and 21 inulin in addition.

The interesting features of the "majority cow fecal streptococcus" is the fact that no CO_2 or NH_3 was produced from peptone, no CO_2 from dextrose and that sodium hippurate was not hydrolized. We are indebted to Dr. Rupp of these laboratories for the determination of ammonia and the hydrolysis of sodium hippurate.

It is believed that these cultures represent the Streptococcus bovis type described by Jensen.[7] There seems to be two varieties, one which ferments inulin and one which does not. The typical raffinose-fermenting cow fecal type appears to be somewhat different from the raffinose-fermenting salivarius type of human saliva.

Group C, consisting of two cultures, was interesting because of characteristics which place the members of this group among the organisms of Streptococcus acidominimus type which were found in the udder and described in an earlier paper [6] of this series. It is possible that the udder occasionally becomes infected with this type of streptococcus.

The remaining culture agreed in many reactions with the typical cow fecal type and fermented raffinose but varied in the formation of CO_2 and NH_3 from peptone and in the positive hydrolysis of sodium hippurate. This culture is apparently not a typical fecal type.

THE STREPTOCOCCI OF THE MOUTH OF COWS

The streptococci of the mouth of cows have been included in this paper because it was found that the majority type was the same species as that of cow feces.

Methods of Isolation.—It must be pointed out that these cultures were isolated from the back of the mouth, toward the base of the tongue, and considerable care was taken in making swabs. In most

[7] Mém. l'Acad. Roy d. sc. et Lettres de Danemark, 1919, 5, ser. 8, No. 2.

TABLE 1

CHARACTERISTICS OF STREPTOCOCCI OF COW FECES

Group	Number of Cultures	Hemolysis	Methylene Blue Test	Litmus Milk Reaction		P_H in Fermentation Tests							C c. of CO_2 from		NH_3–N* Mg. per 100 C c. Excess over Control	Sodium Hippurate Hydrolyzed	
				30 C.	10 C.	Dextrose	Lactose	Saccharose	Salicin	Mannite	Raffinose	Inulin	Peptone Range	Dextrose Range			
A	54	Usually show a slight hemolytic zone about colony, not clear of blood corpuscles	May or may not be slightly decolorized	Very slight acid	No change	4.5 +	4.5 +	4.5 +	4.5 +	7.5 —	4.5 +	7.5 —	0.0-0.40 —	0.0-0.40 —	0.0-0.40 —	.... —	Streptococcus bovis, Var. A
B	21		May or may not be slightly decolorized	Very slight acid	No change	4.5 +	4.5 +	4.5 +	4.5 +	7.5 —	4.5 +	4.5 +	0.0-0.30 —	.... —	0.0-0.42 —	.... —	Streptococcus bovis, Var. B
C	2	Alpha................	—	No change	No change	6.5 +	6.5 +	6.5 +	6.5 +	7.5 —	7.5 —	6.5 +	7.4-8.5 +†	.... —	1.12-1.26 —‡	.... +	Streptococcus acidominimus
D	1	Gamma..............	¾ colorized	Decolorized, not coagulated	No change	4.4 +	4.4 +	4.4 +	4.5 +	7.7 —	5.5 +	7.5 —	3.9 +	.... —	20.74 +	+	

* Medium B used. See paper by Ayers, Rupp and Mudge, Jour. Infect. Dis., 1921, 29, p. 235.
† This CO_2 appears to come from organic acids and not peptone or dextrose.
‡ Produces from 24.10 – 24.94 mg. NH_3–N in infusion broth medium with 4% peptone.

cases a speculum was used to hold the jaw open. The speculum was held in a solution of a coal-tar disinfectant between swabs. Two men stood on either side of the cow and grasped her jaw behind the incisors, forcing her mouth open. A third man inserted the speculum and seized her tongue with a clean, dry towel. The tongue was pulled out and to one side, while a fourth man swabbed down the back of the tongue with a sterile piece of cotton bound to a long, stiff wire. Care was always taken to reach over the arch of the tongue to get a swab. These precautions in sampling were taken so as to obtain, if possible, the normal streptococcus flora of the back of the mouth.

Differentiation of Cultures.—The results of a study of 80 cultures isolated from the mouths of 26 cows are shown in table 2. It will be noted that 69 of the cultures were of the inulin fermenting variety B of Streptococcus bovis, the typical cow fecal type.

The remaining cultures were miscellaneous types which do not correspond with others studied in our work. Group B, consisting of 4 cultures, which did not ferment lactose, may be of Streptococcus equinus type, but we have not studied a sufficient number of such cultures to permit us to make a positive statement. Group D, consisting of 3 cultures, was of interest because of the large amount of gas produced from dextrose. The cultures may belong to Streptococcus kefir type, although others of this type in our collection produced only about one half as much gas in the same medium as used in this test.

Only 10 out of 80 cultures fermented mannite, which is quite different from the results obtained by Rogers and Dahlberg,[3] who found that 87.2% of these cultures from the mouth of the cow fermented this alcohol. They also found that about 82% of their cow mouth cultures reduced litmus, which is quite different from our results. Perhaps their cultures came from the front of the cow's mouth, and the flora there may be different from that of the back of the mouth where our cultures were isolated.

It was interesting to find that the characteristic streptococcus of the back of the mouth of the cow was the same as variety B of Streptococcus bovis, the typical streptococcus of cow feces. It seems that there may be a selective action in the stomach of the cow which determines the streptococci which pass into the intestinal tract, and that after this selective action the back of the mouth of the cow becomes contaminated through regurgitation of the stomach contents. This process seems possible because food remains in the first three stomachs of the cow for

TABLE 2

CHARACTERISTICS OF STREPTOCOCCI OF MOUTHS OF COWS

Group	Number of Cultures	Hemolysis	Methylene Blue Test	Litmus Milk Reaction		P_H in Fermentation Tests							C c. of CO_2 from		NH_3-N* Produced from Peptone	Sodium Hippurate Hydrolyzed	
				30 C.	10 C.	Dextrose	Lactose	Saccharose	Salicin	Mannite	Raffinose	Inulin	Peptone Range	Dextrose Range			
A	69	Usually show a slight hemolytic zone about colony, not clear of blood corpuscles	—	Very slight acid	No change	4.6 +	4.6 +	4.6 +	4.6 +	7.0 —	4.6 +	4.6 +	— —	— —	—	—	Streptococcus bovis, Var. B
B	4	Gamma, some green..	—	No change	No change	4.6 +	7.2 —	5.5 +	4.5 +	4.7 +	7.2 —	5.5 +	4.9-5.3 +	—	+	—	
C	3	Gamma..............	—	Slight acid	No change	4.5 +	4.6 +	4.5 +	4.6 +	4.5 +	4.5 +	6.8 —	1.5-3.1 +	—	+ little	Usually+	
D	3	Gamma..............	+ weak, slightly decolorized	Slight acid	No change	4.6 +	4.7 +	4.7 +	5.0 +	4.7 +	4.8 +	6.8 —	—	Over 12 c c.	—	—	
E	1	Gamma..............	+ decolorized	Very slight acid	No change	4.6 +	4.5 +	4.6 +	6.8 —	5.5 —	4.6 +	6.8 —	—	—	—	—	

* Medium A used. See Ayers, Rupp and Mudge, Jour. Infect. Dis., 1921, 29, p. 235.

quite a period and is subjected to a macerating, mixing and straining process before it passes into the fourth stomach for digestion. Whatever the conditions are, it is interesting that the majority of streptococci are of the same species at what might be said to be opposite ends of the digestive tract.

SUMMARY AND CONCLUSIONS

It has been shown that the characteristic streptococcus of cow feces is Streptococcus bovis. There are apparently two varieties, one of which ferments inulin.

Streptococcus bovis is characterized by the fermentation of raffinose and often inulin, by the inability to produce CO_2 from peptone or dextrose, NH_3 from peptone and lack of power to hydrolize sodium hippurate. The colonies on blood-agar plates seem to present a typical appearance.

It appears that the typical raffinose-fermenting streptococcus of bovine feces is somewhat different from the salivarius type of human saliva. The differences will be presented in a later paper.

Two cultures were found which were of the Streptococcus acidominimus type found in the udder.

The typical streptococcus of the back of the mouth of cows is the same as Streptococcus bovis variety B.

The studies of the streptococci of the mouth made by other investigators when compared with our results indicate that the streptococcus flora of the front and back of the mouth of the cow may be different.

A clear conception of the characteristics of Streptococcus bovis should assist those who may look on raffinose-fermenting streptococci in milk as evidence of contamination by cow feces. Particular attention is now called to the fact that Streptococcus bovis does not produce gas from dextrose and should not be mistaken for Streptococcus kefir, which ferments raffinose and produces gas from dextrose. Streptococcus kefir is often found in milk, but in our work it has not been isolated from cow feces.

A DIPLOCOCCUS ASSOCIATED WITH CASEOUS LYMPHADENITIS AND PNEUMONIA OF SHEEP

ROBB SPALDING SPRAY

From Department of Hygiene and Bacteriology of the University of Chicago

In a recent study of pneumonia of sheep, infection of the thoracic lymph nodules was observed frequently to accompany a chronic type of pneumonia. The condition was characterized by an accumulation of greenish, creamy to caseous pus enclosed by a thickened capsule of connective tissue which largely replaced the normal lymphatic tissue. Often the condition extended to the lungs, commonly leading to an extensive necrosis of practically an entire lung, which showed areas of encapsulation enclosing large quantities of a semifluid necrotic mass with many leukocytes and lung tissue in various stages of disintegration.

The lesions resembled "ovine caseous lymphadenitis" which commonly affects the external lymph nodes in sheep, but which may also affect visceral lymphatics. In view of the association with pneumonia, a study was made to determine which organisms might be associated with this condition and what etiologic relationship might exist between the closely related lymphatic and pulmonary lesions. A diplococcus with certain peculiar characteristics was isolated and its constant occurrence, together with certain characteristics, warrants a description as a hitherto probably undescribed pathogenic diplococcus.

Historical.—Attention was drawn to the lymphatic infection of sheep by Nocard,[1] Nocard and Masselin,[2] Preisz,[3] Preisz and Guinard,[4] Guinard and Morrey;[5] in Australia, by Cherry and Bull,[6] in New Zealand by Gilruth,[7] in Italy, by Cagnetto,[8] and Cipollina;[9] in South America, by Sivori,[10] and in the United States, by Nörgaard and Mohler.[11]

The disease at that time was common among sheep slaughtered for food. In Argentina 10%, in Australia 15%, and of sheep from southern California 5 to

Received for publication, May 3, 1923.

[1] Bull. Soc. Centralbl. de méd. vét., 1885, p. 207.
[2] Compt. rend. Soc. de biol., 1889, p. 177.
[3] Centralbl. f. Bakteriol., Ref., 1891, 10, p. 568.
[4] Jour. de méd. vét., 1891, 42, p. 563.
[5] Compt. rend. Soc. de biol., 1893, p. 893.
[6] The Veterinarian, 1899, 72, p. 525.
[7] Jour. Compar. Path. & Therap., 1902, p. 324.
[8] Ann. de l'Inst. Pasteur, 1905, 19, p. 449.
[9] Ann. d'ig. sper., 1900, 10, p. 1.
[10] Receuil de méd. vét., 1889, 76, p. 657.
[11] 16th Ann. Rept. U. S. Bur. An. Ind., 1899, p. 638.

8% showed lesions on postmortem examination. During the present study in June, July, and August, 1922, at the Chicago packing houses, from 1.5 to 3% of carcasses showed evidence of infection.

The work of Nocard and Preisz resulted in the isolation and identification of a small gram-positive bacillus apparently identical with B. pyogenes-bovis and B. pyogenes-suis of similar diseases of cattle and swine. Because of a similarity of the lesions with those of tuberculosis, the disease has been termed "pseudotuberculosis," and the organism isolated is usually referred to as the "Preisz-Nocard bacillus of pseudotuberculosis." Nörgaard and Mohler[11] proposed the name of "ovine caseous lymphadenitis" to indicate the predilection for the lymphatics, and now the disease is usually referred to by this name.

In the early part of this study, stains of material from the periphery of the lymphatic lesions showed large numbers of gram-positive organisms presumed to be the Preisz-Nocard bacilli. Inoculation on blood agar gave cultures, often pure, of a tiny gram-positive organism apparently a bacillus. It was at first assumed that this organism was the Preisz-Nocard bacillus, but on further study it was found that the characteristics failed to check with the description of the Preisz-Nocard bacillus in several important respects. The reactions were essentially typical of a streptococcus, and on further study of broth, serum, milk, and blood-agar cultures, it was evident that the organism was a diplococcus with short chains, and that the bacillary forms observed were the result of pleomorphism on mediums not well adapted to its growth.

In order to make direct comparison, strains of the Preisz-Nocard bacillus were obtained from the Bureau of Animal Industry, the Pasteur Institute, and from the British National Collection of Type Cultures. Comparative studies were made, and it was apparent that the diplococcus was in no way culturally related to the Preisz-Nocard bacillus. For purpose of direct comparison, the essential cultural differences are given in table 1.

The Diplococcus.—Three strains were isolated in the early part of the work by inoculation from thoracic lymph nodes showing typical lesions of caseous lymphadenitis. Five strains were isolated from lungs showing similar necrotic lesions. The 3 strains from lymph nodes were isolated in pure culture. Two strains from lung lesions were isolated in pure culture, while the other 3 were associated with Pasteurella ovisepticum in 2 cases and with a coccus of the catarrhalis type in one case. Later, 3 more strains were isolated in mixed culture together with Pasteurella ovisepticum from lungs, making a total of 11 strains isolated for study.

The isolation was effected in all cases by plating on blood agar after searing the surface of the tissue and incising with a heated scalpel. Direct inoculation of guinea-pigs was not made, and this may partly account for the failure to isolate the Preisz-Nocard bacillus, although it does not fully explain the absence of growth of the organism, which is easily cultivated on ordinary mediums.

Immediately on isolation the diplococcus strains were decidedly bacillary in appearance, owing to the pleomorphic characteristic of the growth on artificial medium in initial cultivation. Even on fresh blood agar these strains could scarcely be regarded as other than

TABLE 1

ESSENTIAL CULTURAL DIFFERENCES BETWEEN THE DIPLOCOCCUS AND THE PREISZ-NOCARD BACILLUS *

	Morphology	Plain Agar	Serum Agar	Blood Agar	Infusion Broth	Gelatin	Milk	Lactose, Saccharose, Xylose, Maltose
Preisz-Nocard Bacillus	Bacillus	Abundant, white, friable	Abundant, yellowish	No hemolysis, colonies 5 mm. in diameter	Turbid, pellicle	No liquefaction	No change	No gas, no acid
Diplococcus	Diplococcus	No growth	Scant growth	Hemoylsis evident, colonies 0.5 mm. in diameter	No growth	Liquefaction at 24 to 48 hours	Acid and rapid peptonization	Acid formed, no gas

* Mannite, inulin, salicin, arabinose, sorbite, inosite, dextrin, and glycerol not fermented by either organism; glucose, levulose, and galactose fermented by both.

bacilli when freshly isolated. When cultivated, however, in milk or in serum broth, the typical coccus form of these organisms was at once evident. In such fluids the characteristic shape was that of a diplococcus with short chains, the individual cells being practically spherical and about 0.7 mikrons in diameter. The diplococcus tendency was maintained even in the chains of 8 to 10 cells. They were nonmotile, nonflagellated, had no demonstrable capsule, and were insoluble in pig bile and in 10% sodium taurocholate.

On blood agar at the end of 24 hours the colonies were tiny and of a streptococcus type with a perceptible central papilla. At 48 hours they were about 0.25 to 0.5 mm. in diameter and surrounded by a narrow halo of incomplete hemolysis. Repeated cultivation on blood agar enhanced the ability to lake sheep blood, so that after 6 months' cultivation they could be described definitely as hemolytic. Repeated inoculation on plain agar failed to establish growth. On serum or ascitic fluid agar, growth was scant to moderate. Löffler's serum yielded moderate growth, and within 48 hours liquefaction of the medium was evident. Two strains completely liquefied within 7 days, while the other strains were slightly less active. Litmus milk at 24 hours was faintly acid and showed traces of peptonization at the surface. At 48 hours, the upper half of the milk was peptonized, and the lower half was moderately acid but not coagulated. Within 7 days the milk was completely peptonized with a clear, slightly acid whey and a considerable solidly caked yellowish precipitate. Gelatin was liquefied within 24 hours at 37 C., and within 48 hours at 20 C. by all strains. The liquefied gelatin was neutral to brom thymol blue (about P_H 6.9-7.0).

In sugar serum broth, the strains all fermented glucose, lactose, saccharose, xylose, and maltose without gas, and the serum was coagulated. Mannite, inulin, salicin, arabinose, inosite, sorbite, dextrin, and glycerol were not fermented, and the serum broth lost the characteristic opalescence due undoubtedly to the proteoclastic activity of the organism.

The Preisz-Nocard Bacillus (3 strains from the U. S. Bureau of Animal Industry, 2 strains from the Lister Institute, 2 strains from the Pasteur Institute).—The bacilli were single or in pairs, not in chains, rather short, 1.3 to 1.6 by 0.6 to 0.8 mikrons, plump, nonmotile and nonflagellated. All grew well on plain agar, producing whitish concentrically ringed colonies 3 to 4 mm. in diameter at 4 days. These colonies were brittle to the needle touch. On pig serum agar the growth took a yellowish tinge. Broth was rendered turbid at 24 hours with a faint pellicle, which was persistent for 7 to 8 days, when it seemed to break up and sink to the bottom of the tube, after which a second, and more persistent pellicle formed. Indol was not detected, and nitrates were not perceptibly reduced. Gelatin was not liquefied at either 20 or 37 C. Milk was not visibly altered, and the organisms did not grow well in this medium. Growth was abundant on Löffler's serum and was slightly yellowish, but the medium was not liquefied.

It is evident from the description that the diplococcus is distinct from the Preisz-Nocard bacillus, and a search of the literature pertaining to related pyogenic infections of sheep has failed to reveal any references to an organism answering to the description of the diplococcus here described.

A rather similar organism has been described by Nocard[13] from cases of gangrenous mammitis of sheep, a disease long known by the various names of "vulgo," "mammite septique," "d'araignée," and "mal de pis," and described before the era of bacteriology by Kotelmann[14] and Lafosse,[15] and later by Rivolta.[16] The organism is described as a "tiny micrococcus," aerobic or facultative anaerobic, gram-positive. It differs from the diplococcus herein described by the slower liquefaction of gelatin, abundant growth on plain agar and in broth, and in moderate growth on potato, and in the coagulation and lack of peptonization of milk with a strong acid reaction. The reaction on blood agar was not studied at that time, nor was the fermenting ability. Subcutaneous inoculation of the horse, calf, pig, cat, dog, hen, rabbit, and guinea-pig did not kill, except in the case of one rabbit.

Lucet,[17] in a study of a similar mammitis of sheep, reports the isolation and description of a motile bacillus.

Agglutination and Absorption Tests.—Agglutinating serum was prepared by intravenous inoculation of rabbits with cultures of 3 strains of the diplococcus. Six injections of killed blood-agar cultures were followed by 4 injections of live cultures. The highest titer obtained was 1:640. All 11 strains were agglutinated alike by 3 serums and could not be distinguished by direct agglutination.

One serum (S20) was absorbed by the growth of 1 blood-agar slant culture of each of the other 10 strains. Retest of the absorbed serum with the homologous antigen showed that all strains specifically absorbed agglutinins for the original antigen. Antiserums for the 3 strains (S20, S36, and S44) were cross-absorbed each by the other 2 antigens, which completely removed agglutinins for the homologous antigen in all instances.

None of the serums agglutinated the control strains of the Preisz-Nocard bacillus, and absorption with one strain (B. A. I. 572) did not affect the titer for the respective antigens. It is thus evident that the diplococcus is in no way related to the Preisz-Nocard bacillus of pseudotuberculosis.

Pathogenicity.—Two strains (S20, S22) were inoculated intravenously in rabbits, each receiving 1 c c. of a broth emulsion of a 24-hour blood-agar slant. Neither rabbit showed any visible reaction, and both were well at 39 days. On the 40th day, rabbit S22 was killed. No lesions were observed.

[13] Ann. de l'Inst. Past., 1887, 1, p. 417.

[14] Ztschr. f. d. ges. Thierheilk., 1836, p. 423.

[15] Jour. des vét. du Midi, 1836, p. 486.

[16] Gior. di anat. fisiol. e. patol., 1875, p. 139.

[17] Congestion des mammelles et des mammites aigues d'origine externe chez la vache Paris, 1891.

Two white mice were inoculated intraperitoneally with 1/5 of a 24-hour blood-agar culture of S20 and S22 in 1 c c. of broth. Mouse S22 showed no reaction and was normal at 8 days. Mouse S 20 was visibly ill at 24 hours and died on the 3rd day. The liver showed 4 small yellowish nodules apparently in early stages of focal necrosis. Typical diplococci were abundant in a Gram stain from one of these foci, and inoculation from the same area yielded a heavy growth in pure culture of an organism identical with the original culture.

Two guinea-pigs were inoculated intraperitoneally with the same suspension used for mice. Pig S20 was well at 24 hours and active at 8 days. Pig S22 was well at 24 hours, visibly ill at 48 hours, active from 3 to 8 days and was killed on the 8th day. Pig S22 was killed on the 8th day although it had recovered from the initial reaction. The intestines were adherent to the slightly congested peritoneum; a moderate amount of a sanguineous fluid was found in the peritoneal cavity; the liver showed several isolated necrotic areas which were similar to the typical early stages of caseous lymphadenitis in sheep. Stains from these caseous areas showed enormous numbers of typical diplococci, and inoculation yielded a pure and heavy growth of an organism identical with the original strain.

The S20 pig was not visibly affected for 12 days, when it developed lameness in the hind quarters. This animal was killed on the 14th day and presented essentially the same picture as Pig S22. A pure culture identical with the original strain was also isolated from the liver.

Two rabbits were inoculated intraperitoneally with 1/5 of a 24-hour blood-agar slant culture of S20 and S22 in 1 c c. of broth. Neither rabbit showed any visible reaction for 8 days, when it was necessary to terminate observation.

A kitten about 4 weeks old was inoculated intraperitoneally with 1 c c. of the suspension used on the rabbits. At the same time a mongrel pup about 8 weeks old was inoculated in the same manner. The kitten died on the 5th day and the pup died on the 10th day. Each animal showed the characteristic tiny necrotic areas in the liver. Stains showed the typical diplococci in large numbers, and pure cultures of the diplococcus were isolated from the livers of both animals.

Serum Protection.—Fresh antiserums were obtained aseptically from the rabbits immunized against strains S20, S36, and S44. These were preserved with 0.25% phenol.

Six white mice were inoculated intraperitoneally with 1/5 of a 24-hour blood-agar slant culture of the 3 strains, each strain being inoculated into 2 mice. One mouse of each pair was given immediately 1 c c. of the respective serum also intraperitoneally. All mice showed an initial reaction to the inoculations for about 6 hours. At 24 hours, they were all apparently normal. On the second day, 2 of the control mice which received no antiserum were ill. These 2 control mice died on the 4th day, and the 3rd control died on the 5th day. Necropsy revealed the typical liver lesions in all controls. The 3 serum treated mice were alive and apparently well on the 12th day, when they were killed and examined. No lesions were observed in any case.

Three mice were likewise inoculated, but the serum was given intravenously at the base of the tail. None of the mice died, and at necropsy on the 12th day showed no evidence of infection.

One mouse was given 1/5 of a 24-hour plain agar slant culture of the Preisz-Nocard bacillus (B. A. I. 572) intraperitoneally, and was immediately given 1 c c. of S20 antiserum intraperitoneally. The mouse was visibly ill on the 3rd day and died on the 5th day. Necropsy revealed numerous necrotic foci in the liver, spleen, and left kidney. Stain from the liver showed many typical gram-positive bacilli. On inoculation from the liver, the plates developed a growth of B. proteus, and the original culture was not recovered.

It was evident that the antiserum which was effective in protecting against the homologous strains of the diplococcus did not protect against infection wtih the Preisz-Nocard bacillus.

SUMMARY

In lesions of ovine caseous lymphadenitis in sheep with chronic pneumonia, a gram-positive diplococcus with certain peculiar characteristics was found frequently either in pure culture or, as in most instances, associated with Pasteurella ovisepticum. The diplococcus was isolated in pure culture from caseous lymph nodes in three instances, and twice from purulent pneumonia. The Preisz-Nocard bacillus was not recovered by direct plating from any of the lesions studied.

The diplococcus was slightly hemolytic when isolated and became more actively hemolytic on cultivation. It rapidly liquefied gelatin and Löffler's serum and peptonized milk without coagulation. Inoculations were fatal to white mice and guinea-pigs, and in one instance each to a kitten and a puppy. In all cases, lesions in the livers of the animals were similar to the lesions in sheep, from which the organisms were originally obtained. Rabbits apparently are not susceptible to infection judging from the negative results of a few inoculations. All strains were identical agglutinatively. Antiserum for three strains protected white mice against doses of the homologous strains fatal to unprotected mice.

From a review of the literature on pyogenic infections of sheep, it appears that this is probably an undescribed diplococcus which may be regarded as at least a complicating factor in ovine caseous lymphadenitis and in certain types of sheep pneumonia.

AGGLUTINATION STUDIES OF CLOSTRIDIUM BOTULINUM *

WILLIAM A. STARIN AND GAIL M. DACK

From the Department of Hygiene and Bacteriology of the University of Chicago

The agglutination reaction has been less frequently employed in the study of anaerobes than in that of aerobes, and its application has not been so satisfactory. The technical difficulties involved and the greater frequency of spontaneous clumping of cells are among the factors which have limited its use.

The literature reveals little information about agglutination of anaerobes in general and practically none as regards Cl botulinum. The confusion existing with reference to the identity of the different organisms, due to indefinite descriptions and differences in nomenclature, makes it difficult to interpret the findings of the various workers; especially is this true as regards the employment of the test with any particular organism.

Attempts to apply agglutination reactions to the study of Cl. welchii are most frequently noted. As early as 1903, Kamen[1] reported failure to demonstrate agglutinins in the serum of injected rabbits. Similar results were reported by Gaehtgens,[2] and by McIntosh and Fildes.[3] Positive results were reported by Bachmann.[4] who obtained a serum with which he was successful in differentiating Fränckel's gas bacillus from the B. edematous-maligni. Werner[5] prepared antiserum against various strains of B. phlegm. emphysematosae and of the Bulgaric acid bacilli, and secured agglutinins which were specific for the strain used in immunization, though of low titer. Simonds[6] obtained an antiserum which was active against the homologous strain of Cl. welchii in dilutions of 1:80, but against other heterologous strains of the same organism, he reports negative results. Pfeiffer and Bessau[7] state that only with great difficulty were they able to secure agglutinins against Fränckel's bacillus, and the serum obtained was specific for the strain used in immunization alone. Bull[8] reports similar results.

Agglutination of Vibrion septique is reported by Leclainche and Morel,[9] Meyer,[10] Robertson,[11] McIntosh and Fildes,[3] and Weinberg and Séguin.[12]. The

Received for publication, May 8, 1923.

* This study was aided by a grant from the National Canners' Association.

1 Centralbl. f. Bakteriol., I, O., 1903, 35, p. 686.
2 Ibid., 1917, 80, p. 166.
3 Brit. Med. Res. Com., Ser. 12, 1917, p. 74.
4 Centralbl. f. Bakteriol., I, O., 1904, 37, p. 353.
5 Arch. f. Hyg., 1905, 53, p. 128.
6 Monograph of the Rockefeller Inst. for Medical Research, No. 5, 1915.
7 Deutsch. med. Wchnschr., 1917, 43, p. 1255.
8 N. Y. Med. Jour., 1917, 106, p. 821.
9 Ann. l'Inst. Pasteur, 1901, 15, p. 1.
10 Jour. Infect. Dis., 1915, 17, p. 458.
11 Jour. Path. & Bacteriol., 1915, 20, p. 327.
12 Monographies l'Inst. Pasteur, 1918.

titer obtained was generally not high, but the reactions were quite specific. Robertson,[11] Weinberg and Séguin[12] were able to distinguish subgroups within the species.

Meyer[10] utilized the agglutination test in differentiating Cl. chauvœi from other anaerobes associated with symptomatic anthrax in swine, and is of the opinion that "for the identification of anaerobes, the agglutination test seems very reliable." By means of this test Leclainche and Vallée,[13] Grassberger and Schattenfroh,[14] Markoff,[15] Landau,[16] and Weinberg and Séguin[12] have been able to differentiate Cl. chauvœi from the Pseudorauschbrand bacillus, B. edemati-maligni, and the gas gangrene bacilli, although inconstant results were sometimes obtained.

Markoff[15] obtained specific agglutinins for B. edemati-maligni having a titer of 1 : 2500 to 1 : 5000, and suggested the use of agglutination as a means of differentiation of anaerobes. Gaehtgens,[2] and Pfeiffer and Bessau[7] secured specific agglutinins for this organism, but the specificity was limited to the particular strain injected, thus tending to limit the usefulness of the reaction.

Passini,[17] McIntosh and Fildes,[3] Henry,[18] and Weinberg and Séguin[12] have studied Cl. sporogenes and Cl. putrificum. Agglutinins were readily obtained against the former, but only with difficulty against the latter. Subgroups were indicated here also.

Application of the agglutination test to the group of organisms isolated from gaseous gangrene has been reported by many workers.

On the basis of this test, a large series of organisms have been designated as being involved. However, the marked specificity of the reaction minimizes its value in gaseous-gangrene. (Leclainche and Morel,[9] Fürth,[19] McIntosh and Fildes,[3] Weinberg and Séguin,[12] British Med. Research Committee.[18]

Tulloch[20] carried on extensive serologic work with Cl. tetani, and obtained interesting results. By agglutination, he demonstrated 4 distinct types of Cl. tetani, which he has designated I, II, III and IV. While it was not possible to differentiate these 4 groups of tetanus bacilli by means of antitoxin, there was some epidemiologic and clinical evidence of the existence of variations in the reaction to antitoxin on the part of patients infected with different agglutinative strains. Thus, while all commercially prepared antitoxin was apparently produced from type I strains, it was found that in patients given prophylactic treatment, whenever organisms were present in the wound subsequent to the introduction of the serum, the type recovered was type II, III, or IV. This would seem to indicate that protection against type I did not result in protection against infection with the other types. Likewise, he was able to differentiate toxigenic strains from morphologically indistinguishable nontoxin-producing strains (tetanoides) frequently found in wounds.

As regards agglutination of Cl. botulinum, little work has been reported. Hermann[21] demonstrated agglutinins against Cl. botulinum in serum which he prepared. Leuchs[22] states that the question of the production of antibodies

[13] Ann. l'Inst. Pasteur, 1900, 14, pp. 202 and 513.

[14] Kraus u. Levaditi's Handbuch. d. Immunitätsforsch., 1908, 1, p. 161.

[15] Central. f. Bakteriol., I, O., 1911, 60, p. 188.

[16] Ibid., 1917, 79, p. 417.

[17] München. med. Wchnschr., 1904, 51, p. 1283.

[18] Brit. Med. Res. Com., Special Rept. Series, 1919, No. 39, p. 54.

[19] München. med. Wchnschr., 1916, 63, p. 1169.

[20] Jour. Roy. Army Med. Corps, 1917, 29, p. 631; Proc. Roy. Soc. Lond., B, 1919, 90, p. 145; Jour. Hyg., 1919, 18, p. 103.

[21] Abst. Centralbl. f. Bakteriol., I, Ref., 1901, 29, p. 710.

[22] Kolle u. Wassermann's Handbuch der Path. Mikroorgan., 1912, 4, p. 944.

other than antitoxin had not been systematically investigated, but that antiserum which he prepared showed slight agglutinating and complement binding properties. Bronfenbrenner and Schlesinger [23] report it possible to utilize agglutination for the typing of Cl botulinum, and state that this method yields natural groups comparable to those obtained by the use of antitoxin. Cl. sporogenes was used as control, with which organism no cross reaction was ever observed Bitter,[24] in his general review of botulism in Europe, merely mentions the fact that complement binding and agglutinating substances are found in immune serum. Meyer [25] has observed indications of subgroups of Cl. botulinum, based on agglutination. Hall and Davis [26] state that they have been successful in preparing agglutinating serum against this organism.

Only meager descriptions of the methods employed have been given by the workers cited—either as regards the immunization of the animal or the technic of the test. Werner [5] states that young cells serve as the most satisfactory inoculum; this finding is in accord with the experience of most workers, although Footh [27] reports the demonstration of agglutinins in serum against symptomatic anthrax, in which immunization had been accomplished by injecting spores of Cl. chauvœi. McIntosh and Fildes,[3] and Tulloch [20] mention treatment given tetanus spores prior to injection. As a rule, the intravenous mode of injection has been used—a varying number of injections being necessary to obtain satisfactory antiserum. Rabbits were used generally, although Bachman's [4] experience was that guinea-pigs tolerated the injections better. Weinberg and Séguin [12] report a case of human hemothorax caused by Cl. welchii, in which the patient's serum agglutinated the organism in dilutions of 1:2,000.

The technic of the test as used for anaerobes is little different from that of ordinary agglutination tests. The macroscopic method is usually employed, although Bachman [4] obtained better results by the microscopic method. Fürth [19] checked his macroscopic methods with microscopic tests, and Plaut [28] describes a modified microscopic method yielding better results. The time of incubation has been most commonly from 2 to 3 hours at 50 C. Some workers have used a temperature of 70 C., while others have combined 2 to 3 hours at 50 C. with a further incubation of 24 hours at room temperature. Spontaneous agglutination, which has been reported frequently, may be explained in part by this prolonged period of incubation.

Tulloch [20] alone, in his work on Cl. tetani, employed absorption tests in studying the relationships among the members of this group. Satisfactory results were obtained.

Loss of specificity and even complete loss of the agglutination properties of some organisms are frequently reported. It is probable that these peculiarities are indicative of impurity of cultures and the ascendency of alien strains. As a rule, no details of the methods employed to secure pure cultures are given.

[23] Proc. Soc. Exper. Biol. and Med., 1921, 19, p. 21.
[24] Ergebn. d. allg. Path. u. path. Anat., 1921, 19, p. 733.
[25] Personal communication.
[26] Jour. Exper. Med., 1923, 37, p. 585.
[27] Ztschr. f. Infectionskr. d. Haustiere, 1911, 10, p. 1.
[28] Deut. med. Wchnschr., 1917, 43, p. 302.

Since the results of agglutination as applied to Cl. botulinum are especially meager, further study along this line is desirable. Conflicting results and nonspecific reactions are common in much of the early work. Probably this is due in a large part to the fact that immunizations were carried out with mixed cultures. Since the strains used in the present work were descendants of single cells, immunization should yield highly specific serums, and should furnish information as to whether subgroups really exist.

HISTORIES OF THE CULTURES USED

The cultures first selected for use in immunizing rabbits were Cl. sporogenes, Cl. putrificum and Cl. botulinum; of the latter, one culture of "type A" (A1) and one culture of "type B" (B201) were used. As the work progressed, it became necessary to immunize rabbits with other strains. To date the following strains have been employed: A39, A45, A55, A88, B207, and B220. All these cultures, with the exception of Cl. putrificum, represent growths from single cells isolated by the Barber technic. In the case of Cl. putrificum, attempts at single cell isolation were unsuccessful, and purification of the culture was accomplished by colony isolation, using shake cultures. Since subsequent tests showed no cross reactions with the antiserum prepared for this strain and other organisms, it is evident that it contained no Cl. botulinum or Cl. sporogenes contaminants. Thus it served the purpose of a heterologous type of antiserum.

A1 is a single cell isolation from a culture listed as No. 90 in the collection of Dr. K. F. Meyer. This organism was isolated from olives responsible for an outbreak of botulism at Greensburg, Pa., in July, 1921. The single cell isolations were made Aug. 13, 1922, and the resulting growths were tested for purity and typed shortly afterward. Tested against antitoxin, this culture was shown to be of type A. Cultivated in beef heart medium, it produces a potent toxin—0.00005 c c. being sufficient to kill a guinea-pig in less than 36 hours subsequent to intraperitoneal injection.

B201 was isolated from a stock furnished by Dr. R. S. Graham of the University of Illinois, who obtained it from corn ensilage. It is of type B, as shown by the reaction in mice in connection with specific antitoxin; it produces toxin readily, but with a relatively low potency. When grown in beef heart medium for 10 days at 37 C., 0.0005 c c. is the MLD for white mice. The culture used for the present work had been reisolated by the single cell method.

Cl. sporogenes is a subculture obtained by single cell isolation from a stock culture received from Reddish and Rettger. Cl. putrificum also is a strain received from the same source.

A39 is a culture from a stock obtained from the laboratory of the Ohio State Board of Health, in which it had been isolated from olives responsible for the Canton, O., outbreak in 1918. It is a highly toxigenic strain, whose toxin is neutralized by type A antitoxin.

A45 was isolated from a culture received from Dr. Graham, who isolated it from olives.

The stock from which A55 was isolated was received from Dr. W. G. Sackett, who had recovered it from spoiled canned corn responsible for an outbreak of botulism in Colorado. While the definite MLD has not been determined, relative tests show that cultures of this organism possess a higher degree of toxicity than do cultures of A1.

A88 was isolated from a culture obtained from Dr. Meyer, in whose collection it is listed as No. 19. It is a type A organism, and is a very resistant strain.

B207: the culture from which this strain was isolated was received from Dr. Meyer, in whose collection it is listed as No. 116. Its toxin is neutralized by type B antitoxin. The toxin production of this culture in beef heart medium is relatively small as compared with that of the type A strains used.

B220 was isolated from a culture also from Dr. Meyer, who recovered it from unbroken olives collected from the tree at La Mosa Ranch, Oroville, Calif., in Dec., 1920. It is a type B organism, and is listed in his collection as No. 53.

CULTIVATION

The organisms used for injection were grown in an ordinary veal infusion, plus 1% peptone, ½% sodium chloride, and 5% Wolf's casein digest.[29] The medium was carefully filtered to free it from any precipitated material. The reaction was adjusted to a P_H of 7.8 to 8. Growth of the various organisms in this medium was excellent. Cultivation was carried on at 37 C. In the early part of the work, cultures were allowed to incubate for from 7 to 10 days in order to secure large numbers of spores with a minimum of vegetative cells. It will be noted later that the use of spores for immunizing purposes was unsatisfactory, and as a consequence during the greater part of the work the cultures represented an 18- to 24- hour growth. This yielded an abundance of vegetative cells, and the cultures were practically free from spores. Aerobic controls were always made of all cultures prior to injection.

TREATMENT OF CULTURES

The cultures selected were filtered into sterile tubes through sterile absorbent cotton to free them from all gross cell sediment and clumps. They were then centrifuged until perfectly clear. The supernatant fluid was discarded and the sedimented cells resuspended in sterile salt solution and washed. This process was repeated several times, the cells finally being suspended in sterile salt solution. This suspension was then standardized for bacterial content, and served as the material for inoculation.

STANDARDIZATION

In the beginning of the work, standardization was made by direct count of the bacterial cells with the hemocytometer. This was too time consuming, and the accuracy of the reults of such practical insignificance that during the latter part of the work the number of the organisms was determined by comparing the density of the suspension with that of a previously standardized nephelometer tube. While this gave only approximate results, the variations played no detectable part in the results obtained.

DETOXIFICATION

Various methods were used to eliminate the danger of intoxication of the injected animals. In some instances, the animals were given preliminary injections of the homologous antitoxin. This method was discarded after a few trials, and detoxification limited to treatment of the organism used for injection. In one method, the well washed organisms were treated with a small

[29] Kahn, M. C.: Jour. Med. Research, 1922, 43, p. 155.

amount of the homologous antitoxin prior to the introduction. More commonly the cultures were detoxified by heating the well washed suspensions at 70 C. for from 10 to 15 minutes. · That the detoxification was adequate was shown by the injection of this heated material into mice, even in relatively large quantities. Cl. sporogenes and Cl. putrificum were subjected to no preliminary treatment.

IMMUNIZATION

In the beginning of the work, two cultures of Cl. botulinum were employed —A1 and B201—Cl. sporogenes, and Cl. putrificum. Four rabbits were injected with each organism. Two of each group received the injection intravenously; the remaining 2, intraperitoneally. The first tests of the serums for antibodies showed no apparent difference in the results, and the intraperitoneal method was used exclusively in the remainder of the work. Care was exercised to prevent extraneous infection during the process of immunization, and in no instance has there been any evidence that such infection occurred.

DOSAGE

The initial dose in the first series of rabbits was 20,000,000 spores, which was increased until 400,000000 to 600,000,000 cells were employed at each injection. The animals immunized later in the work were given 300,000,000 cells as an initial dose, which was afterward increased to 600,000,000 cells. Repeated injections of these large amounts were tolerated fairly well, although in the case of the larger doses there was considerable reaction, shown by the loss of weight.

NUMBER AND SPACING OF INJECTIONS

Two methods of spacing the injections were followed. In one, injections were made every 3rd to 5th day, depending on the condition of the animal. In the other method, injections were given on 3 consecutive days, followed by a rest period of from 4 to 5 days, after which another series of 3 daily injections was given. If there was any difference in the results, it was in favor of the second method, which was therefore used exclusively during the latter part of the work. The number of injections given varied greatly; some of the rabbits have received as many as 32 injections, others only 3 to 6. Animals receiving but 3 injections have yielded potent antiserum, although the titer was not high. The maximum titer has been obtained generally after from 6 to 8 injections. Additional injections served to maintain the maximum titer but did not result in any further increase.

REACTION OF THE ANIMALS

The reaction of the animals to spores and vegetative cells must be considered separately. When the spores, heated to complete detoxification for mice, were employed, there was no immediate reaction of any degree of severity. But when such material was continually introduced, death after the 4th to 6th injection occurred in from 4 of 8 rabbits receiving A1, and in 4 of 6 rabbits receiving B201. Autopsies generally revealed some secondary infective lesions, such as pneumonia or pulmonary abscesses. In every case, however, cultivation from the various organs and tissues resulted in the isolation of an organism morphologically and culturally similar to Cl. botulinum. The tolerance of the animals toward the injection of vegetative cells was much greater, and few deaths occurred among these rabbits. However, after prolonged immunization many of the rabbits developed chronic diarrhea and emaciation. Botulinus-like organisms have been isolated from the animals that have died.

BLEEDING

The animals were bled repeatedly during the period of immunization, as a rule from 5 to 7 days after the last injection. Five to 15 c c. of blood were drawn at each bleeding, and the serum preserved by the addition of 0.25% to 0.5% of phenol. The material was stored directly on ice. Each lot of serum was titrated within 2 days after it was obtained.

THE TEST

The macroscopic method was employed to determine the presence of agglutinins. At first the suspension of bacterial cells was obtained by growing the organisms from 18 to 20 hours in the casein-digest-peptone medium, centrifuging and washing cells, after which they were resuspended in sterile salt solution. Before using, they were diluted to a uniform density with salt solution. If any large clumps were present, the suspensions were filtered through sterile cotton. In some of the later tests, the cells were not washed, but the broth suspensions were filtered directly through cotton until uniformly turbid, and were diluted to the proper density with salt solution. This method proved equally satisfactory. Only suspensions of young vegetative cells have been employed, and always within 24 hours of their preparation. No tests have been made to note whether or not spores are agglutinable. In the test, 0.25 c c. of the suspension was added to 0.25 c c. of the desired dilution of the antiserum.

To determine the optimum temperature of incubation for the tests, triplicate tubes were incubated for 2 hours in water baths at 36 C., 45 C., and 54 C., respectively. While there was no marked difference in the results, the flocculation appeared more quickly and the aggregates were larger when incubation was carried on at 54 C. Following this observation, all tests were incubated at from 50 C. to 54 C. for 2 hours. Readings were made on the day subsequent to the test. During the interval between the removal from the incubation bath and the reading, the tubes were stored on ice. Four plus is used to indicate complete agglutination, with the supernatant perfectly clear following the period of sedimentation. The lesser degrees of agglutination are indicated by a decreasing number of plus marks. Controls of suspension of organisms plus salt solution were always made; controls of normal rabbit serum were also prepared, and in all cases gave negative results.

RESULTS

Animals receiving injections of spores failed to show any evidence of antibody formation. Twelve rabbits received 5 injections of spore cultures of A1, B201, Cl. sporogenes, and Cl. putrificum. Testing blood 5 days after the last injection failed to reveal any trace of antibodies.

The immunization with vegetative cells yielded agglutinins for all of the strains except A55. There seems to be some variation in the ability of the different strains to stimulate the production of agglutinins, and also in the ease with which they may be agglutinated. Cl. sporogenes induced the production of agglutinins readily, the serum uniformly giving a titer of 1 : 1200 to 1 : 2000. Cl. putrificum did not serve so well as antigen, producing a maximum titer of 1 : 750, and this in a single rabbit. In the case of Cl. botulinum, type B strains appeared capable of stimulating the production of antibodies more readily than type A strains. However, the mortality among the rabbits injected with type B strains was much higher. Serum with a titer greater than 1 : 2000 was obtained with both B201 and B207, both type B. The serum of rabbits immunized with most of type A strains had a titer of from 1 : 1000 to 1 : 1500. To date it has been impossible to obtain the slightest indication of antibodies for A55. The mode of injection and the quantity injected have been the same as in A1, A39, and A45, for which agglutinins were easily obtained. It is interesting also that no antiserum prepared with any other type A strain is capable

TABLE 1

SHOWING THE MAXIMUM TITER WHEN RABBITS WERE BLED AT VARYING INTERVALS AFTER THE LAST INJECTION

Rabbits and Cultures	Results			
	2d Day	5th Day	8th Day	10th Day
23—Cl. spor.	350	1,500	2,000	1,500
75—B201	750	1,250	1,500	1,200
12—A1	300	500	750	700
138—A1	100	200	500	350
27—Cl. put.	300	500	750	1,000
135—Cl. spor.	300	500	1,000	700
136—B201	300	500	750	500

of causing agglutination of A55, which appears to be nonantigenic and inagglutinable. As noted, its ability to produce toxin is marked, and this toxin is neutralized completely by type A antitoxin.

No appreciable difference was noted in the serum titer of rabbits injected intravenously or intraperitoneally.

Some who have worked with other anaerobes claim that the maximum amount of antibody is present within 3 days after injection, following which time there is a rapid decrease. Following one series of injections, tests were made to determine whether this is true in the case of Cl. botulinum. Blood was drawn 2, 5, 8, and 10 days subsequent to injection, and comparative tests were made.

Table 1 shows the maximum serum titers of animals bled at varying intervals after the last injection.

From a study of the table, it is evident that from 5 to 7 days after the last injection is the best time to bleed.

The number of organisms introduced did not seem to be very important. Some of the best antiserums were obtained from the injection of 90,000,000 to 125,000,00 cells, but since the animals tolerated the larger doses, these were used during the greater part of the work.

The number of injections necessary to secure a serum with satisfactory titer varied, but in several instances, a good serum was obtained after 3 injections. In practically all cases, the maximum antibody content was present after from 5 to 7 injections. These results are similar to those reported by other workers with anaerobes. There seems to be a maximum above which the antibody content cannot be forced. Some of the rabbits received as high as 32 injections, with no appreciable change in titer since the 7th to the 10th injections.

SPECIFICITY OF THE AGGLUTININS

The results consistently demonstrate a distinct specificity of agglutinins for type A and B cultures of Cl. botulinum. In no instance has there been any cross agglutination between the types. This indicates that serologically they represent separate groups (tables 2-4).

The agglutination reactions of Cl. sporogenes and Cl. putrificum were also specific, and showed no evidence of cross reactions with any of the strains of Cl. botulinum.

Ten cultures from the stocks on hand (6 type A, and 4 type B) were tested with homologous antiserums. It was found that among type B strains there were serologically at least 3 subgroups. Thus while cultures B201, B235, and B223 were agglutinated equally well by the B201 antiserum, cultures B207 and B220 were agglutinated but slightly, and this only in the lower dilutions. Among the type A strains, A1, A69, and A20 were agglutinated to an equal titer with the A1 antiserum; A45 showed complete agglutination in the lower dilutions only, while A55, A37 and A39 showed no agglutination. (It is interesting to note that history of the cultures shows that A37, which was received from Dr. Meyer, who in turn had obtained it from the Bureau of Chemistry, was originally isolated from the olives which were responsible for the outbreak of botulism at Canton, Ohio. A39 is a culture isolated from the same source, but by the Ohio State Board, from whom it was received.) These results indicate serologic subgroups among the 2 original antitoxic types of Cl. botulinum (table 5).

Rabbits were now immunized with cultures B207 and B220 of the type B strains, not agglutinable by the type serum obtained by

TABLE 2

Agglutination Reactions

Incubation 2 hours at 55 C. in water bath. 5 injections of spores; 2 injections of veg. cells.

Rabbits and Antiserum	A1	B201			Cl. spor.		Cl. put.	
	1:50	1:50	1:100	1:200	1:50	1:100	1:50	1:100
82—A1	++++	0	0	0	0	0	0	0
58—B201	0	++++	++++	++++	0	0	0	0
144—B201	0	++++	++++	++++	0	0	0	0
23—Cl. spor.	0	0	0	0	++++	++++	0	0
141—Cl. put.	0	0	0	0	0	0	++++	++

TABLE 3

Agglutination Reactions

Incubation 2 hours at 55 C. in water bath. 5 injections of spores; 4 injections of veg. cells.

Rabbits and Antiserum	A1		B201		Cl. spor.		Cl. put.	
	1:100	1:250	1:100	1:250	1:100	1:250	1:100	1:250
82—A1	++++	++++	0	0	0	0	0	0
12—A1	++++	++++	0	0	0	0	0	0
138—A1	++++	++++	0	0	0	0	0	0
75—B201	0	0	++++	++++	0	0	0	0
144—B201	0	0	++++	++++	0	0	0	0
23—Cl. spor.	0	0	0	0	++++	++++	0	0
135—Cl. spor	0	0	0	0	++++	++++	0	0
27—Cl. put.	0	0	0	0	0	0	++++	++

TABLE 4

Titer of Antiserums for Homologous and Heterologous Strains

Rabbits	Immunized with	Tested with	1:100	1:300	1:600	1:1,000	1:2,000
281	B207	B207	+++	++++	+++	++	0
281	B207	B201	0	0	0	0	0
133	B201	B201	++++	++++	++++	++++	0
133	B201	B207	0	0	0	0	0
150	A45	A45	++++	++++	++++	+++	+
150	A45	A1	++++	++++	+++	+	0
150	A45	A39	++++	++++	++++	++++	++++
283	A39	A1	++++	+++	+++	++	0
283	A39	A45	+++	0	0	0	0
283	A39	A39	++++	++++	++++	++++	+

TABLE 5

Agglutination of 8 Type A Strains with A 1 Antiserum, and of 5 Type B Strains with B 201 Antiserum

Culture	Results						
	1:100	1:200	1:375	1:750	1:1,000	1:1,250	1:1,500
A1	++++	++++	++++	+++	0	0	0
A39	++	+	0	0	0	0	0
A55	0	0	0	0	0	0	0
A69	++++	++++	++++	++++	+++	+++	0
A20	++++	++++	++++	++++	++++	++++	++++
A118	++++	++++	++++	+++	+++	+++	+++
A37	++	++	++	0	0	0	0
A45	++++	+++	0	0	0	0	0
B201	++++	++++	++++	++++	++++	++++	++++
B223	++++	++++	++++	++++	++++	++++	+++
B235	++++	++++	++++	++++	+++	+++	+++
B207	++	++	0	0	0	0	0
B220	++	0	0	0	0	0	0

immunizing animals with B201; with cultures A39, A45, and A55 of the type A strains, not agglutinable by the type serum obtained by immunizing animals with A1. Satisfactory antiserums were obtained for all of these strains except A55. When satisfactory antiserums were secured, 100 strains selected from isolated stocks were tested. Table 6 shows the results obtained.

It will be observed that the B201, B207, and B220 antiserums furnish agglutinins for all the type B strains tested except B254 and B255. Since the toxins of these 2 organisms are neutralized by the type B antitoxin, it is probable that they represent other subgroups. They are very weak toxin producers, differing from the others in this respect also. No further attempts to produce antiserums against these

TABLE 6

THE RELATIONSHIP OF 100 SINGLE CELL STRAINS OF CL. BOTULINUM AND ANTISERUMS OBTAINED BY IMMUNIZING RABBITS WITH REPRESENTATIVES OF DIFFERENT AGGLUTINATIVE TYPES

Type A strains as determined by the use of antitoxin:	
Strains agglutinated by A1 antiserum only	11
Strains agglutinated by A39 antiserum only	13
Strains agglutinated by A88 antiserum only	4
Nonagglutinable strains	16
Strains agglutinated by A1 and A39 antiserums, but not by A45	8
Strains agglutinated by A39 and A45 antiserums, but not by A1	12
Strains agglutinated by A1, A39, and A45 antiserums	9
Total	73
Type B strains as determined by the use of antitoxin	
Strains agglutinated by B201 but not by B207 or B220 antiserums	19
Strains agglutinated by B207 but not by B201 or B220 antiserums	4
Strains agglutinated by B220 but not by B201 or B207 antiserums	2
Nonagglutinable strains (B254 and B255)	2
Total	27

2 strains have been made. In the case of the type A strains, the relationship is not so clear. There are at least 4 well defined subgroups: Those agglutinated by A1, by A39, by A88, and those represented by A55 which are not agglutinated by any antiserum, and for which it has been impossible to obtain agglutinins by animal injections. In addition to these 4 subgroups, there are many type A strains which are partially agglutinated by one or more of the different antiserums. The antigenic constituents of each of these strains seem to be complex, comprising fractions that are common to the other strains; and the degree of agglutination is probably dependent on the relative amount of the different constituents present.

Each organism was also tested with the lowest dilutions of the heterologous serum to determine whether cross agglutination occurred.

In no case was there any agglutination of a type A organism by a type B antiserum, nor of a type B organism by a type A antiserum.

ABSORPTION TESTS

The absorption of antibodies as applied to anaerobic organisms has received little attention.

Massive cultures of the strains used were secured by growing the organisms in casein-digest-peptone broth for from 18 to 24 hours at 37 C. Ehrlenmeyer flasks with 100 c c. of this medium were inoculated with the desired organism, and rendered anaerobic by covering with paraffin. After from 18 to 24 hours' incubation, abundant growths were obtained. The organisms were separated from the medium by centrifugation, the cells resuspended in salt solution, and washed repeatedly. Following the last washing, they were suspended in a small volume of salt solution.

TABLE 7

ABSORPTION TESTS

Antiserum B201 Treated with	Results When Tested vs.					
	B201		B235		A1, A20, A39, A45, A55, B207, B220	
	1:250	1:500	1:250	1:500	1:250	1:500
B201	0	0	0	0	0	0
B235	0	0	0	0	0	0
B207	++++	++++	++++	++++	0	0
B220	++++	++++	++++	++++	0	0
A1	++++	++++	++++	++++	0	0
A20	++++	++++	++++	++++	0	0
A39	++++	++++	++++	++++	0	0
A45	++++	++++	++++	++++	0	0
A55	++++	++++	++++	++++	0	0

The serums were diluted 1 : 25 and a definite volume of cells added. After thorough mixing, the tubes were incubated at 50 C. for 25 minutes, with occasional shaking. The cells were removed by centrifuging, and a definite volume of fresh suspension added and the incubation carried out as before. It was found that 3 such absorptions were sufficient to remove completely all of the homologous antibody. The changes in dilution due to the addition of the cell suspension were calculated, and quantitative tests with varying organisms were carried out with treated serums (tables 7-9).

The absorption tests indicate that the 2 antitoxic types are specific, i. e., no absorption of any type A antiserum with a type B organism, or vice versa, resulted in any decrease of the agglutinin content for the homologous type. Some strains within the types are more inclusive than others. When culture B201 was added to B207 or B220 antiserum, it not only removed the agglutinins peculiar to itself, but also those for B207 and B220 strains as well. On the other hand, absorption of the agglutinins from B201 antiserum, which agglutinates B207 and B220 slightly in low dilutions, did not result in any measurable reduction in the agglutination titer for B201 when either of the B207 and B220 strains were added.

TABLE 8

ABSORPTION TESTS

Antiserum B207 Treated with	Results When Tested vs.				Antiserum B201 Treated with	Results When Tested vs.			
	B201		B207			B201		B207	
	1:250	1:500	1:250	1:500		1:250	1:500	1:250	1:500
B201	0	0	0	0	B201	0	0	0	0
B207	0	0	0	0	B207	++++	++++	0	0

TABLE 9

ABSORPTION TESTS

Anti-serum A45 Treated with	Results When Tested vs.						Anti-serum A39 Treated with	Results When Tested vs.					
	A45		A1		A39			A39		A1		A45	
	1:250	1:500	1:250	1:500	1:250	1:500		1:250	1:500	1:250	1:500	1:250	1:500
A45	0	0	0	0	0	0	A39	0	0	0	0	++	0
A1	+++	0	0	0	0	0	A1	++++	++++	0	0	0	0
A39	++++	++++	++++	++	0	0	A45	++++	++++	0	0	0	0

The absorption relations between B207 and B220 strains were not determined, although each antiserum was specific in its action against the other type when tested by ordinary agglutination.

Somewhat confusing relationships are revealed by the absorption tests of the type A group organisms. However, a number of definite subgroups are clearly indicated. That the technic of the absorption was satisfactory is indicated by the fact that in every case there was complete removal of the agglutinins specific for the absorbing strain.

A1 antiserum, when treated with strain A39, shows practically no diminution in titer for any of the other organisms of the group; absorption by A45 organisms removed only agglutinins peculiar to it. Agglutinins for each of the 3 strains mentioned seemed to be present in this antiserum, each being separate and distinct, and removed only by its homologous antigen. The addition of A55 to this antiserum did not result in the removal of any agglutinins.

The A45 antiserum showed complete absorption of all its agglutinins by the homologous antigen, and practically complete removal of all the agglutinins by A1 organisms. When strain A39 was used as the absorbing agent, however, there remained a definite amount of agglutinins for A1 and A45 organisms. This indicates a closer relationship between A45 and A1 strains than between either of these organisms and the subgroup A39.

The A39 antiserum showed complete absorption of all its agglutinins for all the strains when it was treated with the homologous antigen. A1 and A45 organisms absorbed only the agglutinins specific to each of them, leaving those peculiar to the strain A39 practically unchanged. This again indicates a closer relationship between A1 and A45 than between either of them and A39. That A1 and A45 are not identical was shown by cross agglutination reactions in which certain organisms were agglutinated by one antiserum and not by the other, or if by both, the titer was different.

SUMMARY

The immunization of rabbits by young vegetative cells of Cl. botulinum, Cl. sporogenes, and Cl. putrificum, results in the formation of specific agglutinins, three intraperitoneal injections being sufficient to call forth a considerable amount of agglutinins.

Similar injections of rabbits with spores of these strains did not result in the production of any agglutinins.

Rabbits tolerate the injection of vegetative cells well, but the injection of spores, detoxified so as to be harmless for mice, results in the death of a large proportion of the rabbits after from 5 to 7 injections.

From the bodies of the animals that died, it was possible to isolate cultures which were morphologically, culturally, and in the matter of toxin production, identical with Cl. botulinum.

The serum titer averaged 1:250 to 1:2000. Type B strains of Cl. botulinum, and Cl. sporogenes stimulated the production of agglutinins more readily than did Cl. putrificum or type A strains of Cl. botulinum.

It has been impossible to develop agglutinins against A55 organisms or to agglutinate this strain by bringing it in contact with any potent type A antiserum.

Agglutination tests of 100 single cell isolations using 8 antiserums showed that there are at least 3 distinct subgroups of Cl. botulinum, type B, and 4 distinct subgroups of Cl. botulinum, type A. In the case of the latter, there are also intermediate strains, partaking of the nature of more than 1 of the 4 distinct subgroups. The division into subgroups in this type is not so sharply defined as in type B, and certain strains are antigenically much more inclusive than others.

Absorption tests were successful and showed relationships among the various strains similar to those demonstrated by direct agglutination.

Agglutination showed distinct cleavage of all strains of Cl. botulinum into two distinct groups which are analogous to the division based on reactions with antitoxins.

No cross agglutination of Cl. botulinum, Cl. sporogenes, or Cl. putrificum was detected.

ANTICOMPLEMENTARY ACTION OF FRESH BOVINE SERUM

I. Forest Huddleson

From the Laboratory of Bacteriology and Hygiene, Michigan Agricultural Experiment Station, East Lansing

Complement fixation in conjunction with agglutination has been employed successfully in the diagnosis of bovine infectious abortion for a number of years. During the past few years, however, many investigators have abandoned the fixation test in favor of agglutination, for different reasons. One says there is too much work involved; another that the two tests agree so closely it is unnecessary to use both; another that the fixation test is unreliable because of the appearance of unexplained factors which interfere with accurate interpretations. The latter difficulty is the subject of this paper.

There seems to have been a wrong assumption in regard to the properties of bovine serum from the beginning of the use of the fixation test in the diagnosis of bovine infectious abortion, based on the belief that serum from all species of animals contains native complement in sufficient quantity to disturb the accuracy of the test, in case complement from another source is added also. This belief has led workers to heat all serum at 56 C. for 30 minutes to destroy native complement. There are no data available that show native complement in bovine serum or that the question of its presence has been studied. Of course, it is natural to assert, from experience with serum from other species, that bovine serum contains complement; nevertheless, the proof of its presence is lacking.

With this thought in mind, several hundred bovine serums were examined for complement, and of this number, only 2 were found to contain sufficient complement in 0.2 c c. to cause complete lysis of 0.5 c c. of a 2% suspension of sheep cells, in the presence of 2 units of hemolysin. In others, 0.6 c c. or more were required to produce complete lysis. It is a question whether the lysis induced was due to the action of complement. Since no technic lately described for the fixation test employs more than 0.1 c c. of serum for the accurate determination of specific antibodies for Bacterium abortus, it is evident that this amount of serum does not contain sufficient native complement to interfere with the accuracy of the test. Now the question raises, Why

Received for publication, May 14, 1923.

is bovine serum heated at 56 C. previous to the test, and why is not active serum used?

A preliminary study indicated that fresh bovine serum contains a complement-binding substance which is destroyed at 56 C. for 30 minutes.

An extended investigation has been made of the complement-binding or antilytic action of human serum by Noguchi,[1] Zinsser and Johnson[2] and Kuytoku.[3] The anticomplementary property, apparently, develops in human serum on standing and has not been found to exist preformed in the serum. A temperature of 56 C. for 15 to 30 minutes destroys the property. Kolmer and Trist[4] demonstrated anticomplementary property in active dog, rabbit and mule serums which increased at 56 C. for 30 minutes, but was removed at 70 C. for 30 minutes.

The anticomplementary property of bovine serum is apparently of a different nature than that observed in serum of other species, in that the time of standing after collection is not a factor in its appearance, nor is exposure to a high temperature necessary. It seems that little or no attention has been given to this action of bovine serum.

Thomsen[5] evidently encountered something of this nature when he began to apply the fixation test to the diagnosis of infectious abortion, as he says that a temperature of 56 C. for 30 minutes destroys the value of bovine serum for the test, and it is doubtful whether he was dealing with specific antibodies for Bacterium abortus. Moore and Fitch[6] also encountered some difficulty in applying the test to bovine serum. The cause of their trouble is not clearly stated, but they sum up the results in these words: "The complexity of the method itself, the additional complications noted by Surface and Thomsen, and the fact that a positive reaction does not give definite information as to whether the cow is infected and may abort or has been infected and already aborted seem to render this method of diagnosis of little practical value in the control of the disease."

In the light of our present knowledge of this property of bovine serum, of the constancy of its presence, and of the practical importance of its destruction in the fixation test, it seemed desirable to study the phenomenon more fully in order, if possible, to throw light on its nature and mechanism.

General Technic.—The bovine serum used in this study was collected aseptically in sterile containers from the jugular vein of animals of various ages, from the newly born to those 8 years of age. The

[1] Jour. Exper. Med., 1906, 8, p. 726.
[2] Ibid., 1911, 13, p. 31.
[3] Jour. Immunol., 1919, 4, p. 239.
[4] Jour. Infect. Dis., 1916, 18, p. 64.
[5] Ztschr. f. Infektionskrankh. d. Haustiere, 1913, 13, p. 175.
[6] Annual Rept. N. Y. State Vet. College, 1912-13, p. 82.

serum was tested always within 24 hours after collection, and none was used that showed hemolysis. The sheep-rabbit hemolytic system was used. The sheep cells were washed 10 times with physiological salt solution to free them from serum and cytozyme; a constant amount, 0.5 c c. of a 2% suspension, was put in each tube. The titer of the hemolysin was determined each day that tests were made. Two units in 0.1 c c. were used as indicated. The complement was obtained from the heart of anesthetized guinea-pigs. The blood was defibrinated immediately and centrifuged to remove the cells, thus preparing the complement on the day of the tests. The guinea-pig serum was diluted 1:10 with sterile physiologic salt solution and used in 2 units (0.1 c c.) in all titrations. All heating, whether at 56 C. or 37 C., was conducted in a water bath.

TABLE 1

ANTICOMPLEMENTARY ACTION OF UNHEATED BOVINE SERUM

Bovine Serum		Hemolysis	
Sample Number	Quantity in C c. in Each Tube	Unheated Bovine Serum	Bovine Serum Heated at 56 C. for 30 Minutes
11 999	0.2 0.1 0.05	None Slight Marked	Complete Complete Complete
11 A 1662	0.2 0.1 0.05	Slight Complete Complete	Complete Complete Complete
477 1656	0.2 0.1 0.05	None None Marked	Complete Complete Complete
1667	0.2 0.1 0.05	Marked Marked Complete	Complete Complete Complete
16	0.2 0.1 0.05	Complete Complete Complete	Complete Complete Complete

The Anticomplementary Property of Fresh Bovine Serum.—Tests were made by placing in sterile test tubes decreasing amounts of sterile bovine serum and adding 2 units (0.1 c c.) of complement and sufficient sterile salt solution to bring the quantity in each tube to a total volume of 0.9 c c. The mixtures were then placed in a water-bath at 37 C. for 30 minutes and the anticomplementary action demonstrated by adding to each tube 2 units of hemolysin and 0.5 c c. of a 2% suspension of sheep cells. The mixtures were again incubated at 37 C. for 40 minutes, and the degree of hemolysin noted. Table 1 shows the anticomplementary action of 12 serums in different quantities. It is seen that the degree of anticomplementary action varies with the serum, and may even be absent as in No. 16. This is, however, an exception rather than a rule. The right hand column of the table illustrates the absence of the binding property in the same serums after exposure at 56 C. for 30 minutes.

The Influence of Heat on the Anticomplementary Property of Bovine Serum.—Several serums were selected in which the anticomplementary property varied, and 0.2 c c. of each heated at 56 C. for 5, 10, 15, 20 and 30 minutes. To each tube were then added 2 units (0.1 c c.) of hemolysin, 0.5 c c. of a 2% suspension of sheep cells and sufficient salt solution to make the total volume in each tube 1.5 c c. The tubes were incubated at 37 C. for 40 minutes, and the degree of hemolysis noted. Table 2 shows that the anticomplementary property is reduced markedly in 5 minutes and destroyed completely in 15 minutes. The time of destruction has been repeatedly determined for a large number of serums, with identical results.

TABLE 2

THE INFLUENCE OF HEAT ON THE ANTICOMPLEMENTARY ACTION OF FRESH BOVINE SERUM (0.2 C C.)

Bovine Serum (Sample Number)	Hemolysis After Heating at 56 C. for			Unheated Control Serum
	5 Minutes	10 Minutes	15, 20 and 30 Minutes	
11, 1666	Slight	Marked	Complete	None
999, 477, 1656	Marked	Complete	Complete	None
1657, 11A, 1662, 200B	Complete	Complete	Complete	Slight
1667	Complete	Complete	Complete	Marked
16	Complete	Complete	Complete	Complete

The Effect of Concentration of Bovine Serum and the Time of Contact on the Degree of Anticomplimentary Action.—Three serums 11, 999 and 16 were selected for this experiment. Serum 16, as previously shown, possessed no anticomplementary property. The serums were used in amounts of 0.2, 0.1 and 0.05 c c. in 4 series of tests. To each tube of the first series were added 2 units (0.1 c c.) of complement, 2 units (0.1 c c.) of hemolysin and 0.5 c c. of a 2% suspension of sheep cells, and the mixtures immediately incubated at 37 C. for 40 minutes, and readings made. To each tube of the second series were added 2 units of complement. These were incubated at 37 C. for 30 minutes before adding hemolysin and sheep cells as indicated. In the third series, bovine serum plus complement remained in contact for 1 hour before the addition of hemolysin and sheep cells. In the fourth series, the primary incubation period was 2 hours. Table 3 illustrates clearly that the amount of complement taken up depends primarily on the concentration of the bovine serum and the time of contact between the bovine serum and the guinea-pig serum. As the time of contact increases, the amount of complement inhibited by decreasing amounts of serum increases.

The Influence of Time on the Rate of Anticomplementary Action of Bovine Serum.—A quantitative study of the amount of complement bound by a constant amount of fresh, active bovine serum was carried out in the following manner: To 0.2 c c. of each 2 bovine serums were added 10 units of complement (0.5 c c.) and 0.3 c c. of salt solution. Of this mixture, 0.1, 0.2, 0.3 and 0.4 c c. were added to each of 4 tubes.

TABLE 3

THE EFFECT OF THE CONCENTRATION OF BOVINE SERUM AND THE TIME OF CONTACT ON THE DEGREE OF ANTICOMPLEMENTARY ACTION

Bovine Serum		Hemolysis After Adding Hemolysin and Sheep Cells	
Sample Number	Quantity in C c. in Each Tube	Immediately	After 30 Minutes at 37 C.
	0.2	Slight	None
11	0.1	Marked	Slight
999	0.05	Complete	Marked
	0.2	Complete	Complete
16	0.1	Complete	Complete
	0.05	Complete	Marked

The amount of the mixture in the 1st tube contained 1 unit of complement; the 2d tube, 2 units; the 3d tube, 3 units; and the 4th tube, 4 units. To each of the tubes were immediately added 2 units of hemolysin (0.1 c c.), and 0.5 c c. of a 2% suspension of sheep cells, and sufficient salt solution to bring the total volume of each tube up to 1.5 c c. The tubes were incubated at 37 C. for 30 minutes and the degree of hemolysis recorded. The same procedure was carried out for 4 additional series of tubes, of which the primary incubation period was 10, 30, 60 and 120 minutes, respectively, before hemolysin and sheep cells were added. The results of this experiment are recorded in table 4. It is evident from the results that 0.2 c c. of serum inhibits the action of complement on immediate contact and 2 units after a contact of 30 minutes. Apparently there is little increase in inhibition after 30 minutes' contact. In other words, the number of units of complement inhibited by a constant amount of bovine serum in a given length of time is nearly constant. One might expect a decrease in the titer of the complement from the exposure to heat, but control titrations set up with each series showed no decrease.

The Action of Bovine Serum on Swine and Rabbit Complement.—In order to determine whether bovine serum alone possesses the property of inhibiting the action of complement or whether the anticomplementary action is due to an interaction of bovine serum and guinea-pig serum which would take up a certain quantity of complement, fresh, active rabbit and swine serums were substituted for guinea-pig serum as a source of complement. The complement titer of each serum was determined, and a quantity containing 2 units was added to tubes containing decreasing amounts of bovine serum, and incubated at 37 C. for 30 minutes before the addition of hemolysin and sheep cells. Readings were made at the end of the second incubation period of 40 minutes. The results of this experiment are illustrated in table 5, using 3 different serums, one of which (16) does not inhibit the action of complement. The results indicate that bovine serum alone does not inhibit the action of complement, and evidently guinea-pig serum plays an important rôle with the bovine serum in the anticomplementary phenomenon. Proof of the influence of this combination is shown in table 5. Here, inactive guinea-pig serum was incubated with bovine serum for 30 minutes, and then fresh complement, hemolysin and sheep cells were added at the same time. In comparing the results with the control column at the right of the table, it is clear that the bovine serum-guinea-pig serum complex is undoubtedly the factor concerned in the disappearance of complement, and that the rate at which complement disappears depends on the length of time these 2 serums are in contact.

TABLE 4

THE RATE OF THE ANTICOMPLEMENTARY ACTION OF BOVINE SERUMS 11 AND 999

Units of Complement	Duration of Contact Before Adding Hemolysin and Sheep Cells				
	Hemolysis				
	Immediately	10 Minutes	30 Minutes	1 Hour	2 Hours
1	None	None	None	None	None
2	Complete	Slight	None	None	None
3	Complete	Complete	Complete	Marked	Marked
4	Complete	Complete	Complete	Complete	Complete

In view of the fact that bovine serum agglutinates sheep cells, it seemed desirable to determine whether there was any relation between the agglutinating property and anticomplementary property.

Three serums—11, 999 and 16—used in previous experiments, were selected on account of the difference in their agglutinating powers for sheep cells. Three sets of tubes were prepared in 4 series for each serum. To each set of the series was added 0.2, 0.1 and 0.05 c c. of its respective serum. To the 1st series were immediately added 0.5 c c. of a 2% suspension of sheep cells and sufficient salt solution to make in each tube a total volume of 1.5 c c., and they were incubated at 37 C. for 1 hour, when the degree of agglutination in each tube was noted. The second series of tubes was incubated at 37 C. for 2 hours before sheep cells and salt solution were added. The 3rd series of tubes was incubated at 37 C. for 10 hours before sheep cells and salt solution were added. The 4th series of tubes was heated at 56 C. for 15 minutes

TABLE 5

THE ANTICOMPLEMENTARY ACTION OF AN ACTIVE BOVINE SERUM—INACTIVE GUINEA-PIG SERUM MIXTURE

Bovine Serum		Hemolysis	
Sample Number	Quantity in C c. in Each Tube	0.01 C c. Inactive Guinea-Pig Serum Added	No Inactive Guinea-Pig Serum Added
11 999	0.2 0.1 0.05	None None Marked	None Marked Complete
16	0.2 0.1 0.05	Complete Complete Complete	Complete Complete Complete

before sheep cells and salt solution were added. As in the 1st series, the 2d incubations were carried out for 1 hour, and the degree of agglutination noted.

The results of this experiment (table 6) indicate that the agglutinating property of bovine serum is more heat sensitive than the anticomplementary property. The agglutinating property disappeared in 2 hours at 37 C., while the anticomplimentary property (table 3) remained unchanged. Although not recorded in the tables, the anticomplementary property has been found unaffected after 10 hours at 37 C. Serum 16 (tables 3 and 7) had strong agglutinating properties but did not inhibit complement in the amounts of serum used. This appears to be conclusive evidence that the agglutinating property is distinct from the anticomplimentary property. Maltaner and Johnson [7] found that bovine serum continued to agglutinate after an exposure to

[7] Jour. Immunol., 1921, 6, p. 271.

56 C. for 30 minutes, but the data in table 6 do not corroborate this result. This is true not only with the serum recorded there, but also with a large number of serums studied with the same purpose in view.

The foregoing results reveal that fresh, active bovine serum possesses the property of inhibiting the action of complement in the presence of guinea-pig serum. The inhibitive power apparently exists, preformed in different degrees in the majority of serums, and is destroyed at 56 C. for 15 minutes. The inhibiting action is apparently due to the interaction of bovine and guinea-pig serum, as the amount of complement taken up in each case depends on the time of contact between the 2 serums.

TABLE 6

THE EFFECT OF TIME AND TEMPERATURE ON THE HEMAGGLUTINATING PROPERTY OF ACTIVE BOVINE SERUM

Sample Number	Quantity in C c. in Each Tube	Agglutination by Bovine Serum		
		Unheated	Heated at 37 C. for 2 and 10 Hours	Heated at 56 C. for 15 Minutes
11	0.2	Slight	None	None
	0.1	None	None	None
	0.05	None	None	None
999	0.2	Marked	None	None
	0.1	Slight	None	None
	0.05	None	None	None
16	0.2	Complete	None	None
	0.1	Marked	None	None
	0.05	Slight	None	None

The influence of serum-antiserum mixtures on the fixation of complement and the various factors concerned have been studied by Gengou,[8] Moreshi,[9] Gay,[10] Muir and Martin,[11] Dean [12] and many others. Muir and Martin [11] state that when a precipitate forms in a serum antiserum mixture, the fixing property is contained in it, and may be exclusively; that the fixation may occur without precipitation, and that the degree of fixation is not always in proportion to the amount of precipitate.

An effort was made to detect a precipitate resulting from mixing bovine and guinea-pig serum in various proportions and incubating for various lengths of time, but so far not even the most minute precipitate has been found. It is possible that the correct proportions of the two serums necessary for producing a visible precipitate have not been used.

[8] Ann. de l'Inst. Pasteur, 1902, 16, p. 734.
[9] Berl. klin. Wchnschr., 1905, 42, p. 1181.
[10] Centralbl. f. Bakteriol., I, O., 39, p. 603.
[11] Jour. Hyg., 1906, 6, p. 265.
[12] Proc. Roy. Soc. Med., 1911, 5, p. 62.

SUMMARY

Active bovine serum possesses a complement inhibiting property which is destroyed at 56 C. for 15 minutes.

It is necessary to destroy this property of bovine serum in order to apply the fixation test for Bacterium abortus antibodies.

The removal of complement appears to be due to the interaction of bovine and guinea-pig serum, and the amount of complement taken up by a bovine-guinea-pig serum mixture is nearly constant.

The complement-binding property of active bovine serum is not related to its agglutinins for sheep corpuscles.

Bovine serum has no action on complement derived from the rabbit or swine.

A STUDY OF THE COAGULUM OR PELLICLE AND OF THE FIBRINOGEN NITROGEN IN CEREBROSPINAL FLUID

A. Levinson and Dora Kirschenbaum

From the Nelson Morris Memorial Institute for Medical Research of the Michael Reese Hospital, Chicago

There is a general agreement among clinicians that the coagulum, also known as pellicle, film, web or sediment, when present in cerebrospinal fluid, is of value in the diagnosis of tuberculous meningitis. Tubercle bacilli are often found in the cerebrospinal fluid in no other way than by examination of the coagulum or pellicle. The mere presence of a coagulum is therefore spoken of in the literature as corroborative evidence of tuberculous meningitis.

So far as can be ascertained, Lichtheim[1] was the first to describe the presence of a coagulum or pellicle in cerebrospinal fluid. Discussing the various properties of the cerebrospinal fluid, he called attention to the coagulum in the fluid as follows: "The formation of a coagulum in the fluid should be observed. Transudates, in cases of brain tumors either do not coagulate at all or form only small flocculi containing very few leukocytes. Inflammatory fluids form larger flocculi which contain many white and red cells. This finding, however, should be used with reservation in diagnosis."

The author then quotes a case of sarcoma of the cerebellum with diffuse meningitic infiltration, which was first considered tuberculous meningitis because of the presence of a coagulum in the fluid. Connal,[2] Zaloziecky,[3] and Levinson[4] lay stress on the diagnostic importance of the coagulum or pellicle in suppurative meningitis, the latter going so far as to differentiate the type of coagulum or sediment in various forms of meningitis. Levinson[5] has also described small flocculi in the cerebrospinal fluid of syphilis of the central nervous system. Abt and Tumpeer,[6] however, believe the pellicle to be of no importance. Quincke,[7] in speaking of purulent meningitis, says, "On standing, the deposit of pus is light and only exceptionally is it coagulated by excreted fibrin."

The question of the fibrinogen content of normal and pathologic fluid would naturally be interesting in connection with a study of the pellicle, since the pellicle is supposed to consist of fibrin and cells. The data on this point, how-

Received for publication, May 22, 1923.

1 Deutsch. med. Wchnschr., 1893, 19, p. 1186.
2 Quart. Jour. Med., 1910, 3, p. 152.
3 Deutsch. Ztschr. f. Nervenheilk., 1913, 47, p. 783.
4 Jour. Lab. & Clin. Med., 1916, 1, p. 699.
5 Cerebrospinal Fluid in Health and in Disease, 1919.
6 Am. Jour. Dis. Child., 1920, 20, p. 153.
7 Modern Clin. Med., 1910.

ever, are meager. The early workers on cerebrospinal fluid, such as Hoppe[8] and Halliburton[9] do not mention any determination of fibrinogen in their chemical examination. Coriat[10] found no fibrinogen in fluid drawn post-mortem from a case of hydrocephalus. Mestrezat[11] also found no fibrinogen in normal fluid.

In view of these observations, it seemed desirable to study the question of coagulum or pellicle in cerebrospinal fluid with special reference to the content of fibrinogen nitrogen of the fluid. The points considered were:

1. Is pellicle formation in cerebrospinal fluid of pathologic significance?
2. Is pellicle formation limited to meningitis?
3. Does normal fluid contain any fibrinogen?
4. Does every fluid forming a pellicle contain an increased amount of fibrinogen?

It should be noted that we include under the term "pellicle" all forms of sediment or flocculi in the fluid.

METHOD

Pellicle formation was studied by allowing the fluid to stand undisturbed in the icebox or at room temperature. We found that it takes less time for a pellicle to form at room temperature than it does in the icebox. The fibrinogen content was studied by the method of Howe,[12] described by him for the determination of the amount of fibrinogen in blood. The method consists in precipitating fibrinogen in 0.5 c c. of cerebrospinal fluid by adding to it 1 c c. of 2.5% of calcium chloride and 14 c c. of 0.8% sodium chloride. This is allowed to stand for 3 hours; it is then filtered and the nitrogen in the filtrate determined. The resulting nitrogen figure is then subtracted from the total nitrogen as found in another portion of the fluid in which 0.5 c c. of cerebrospinal fluid is diluted with 15 c c. of 0.8% sodium chloride. The nitrogen determinations were made by the microkjeldahl method of Folin and Wu[13] by direct nesslerization.

The question of time element in the determination of fibrinogen is one to which we have paid a good deal of attention, but which we

[8] Virchows Arch. f. Path. Anat., 1859, 16, p. 391.
[9] Physiological Chemistry.
[10] Am. Jour. Physiol., 1903, 10, p. 111.
[11] Le liquide cephalo-rochidien normal et pathologique, 1912.
[12] Jour. Biol. Chem., 1921, 49, p. 109.
[13] Ibid., 1919, 38, p. 81.

have as yet not solved. It was shown by Levinson[14] and Felton, Hussey, and Jones[15] that in physicochemical examinations of cerebrospinal fluid, the time elapsing between the withdrawal of the fluid from the body, and the examination of the fluid plays a great rôle. It was natural to suppose that the same holds true in fibrinogen and that fibrinogen nitrogen would be lessened in the fluid after the pellicle separated out. It was found, however, that fluid from which the pellicle was removed, still contained a large amount of fibrinogen—this would speak for one of two possibilities: namely, either the pellicle does not consist of fibrinogen or not all of the fibrinogen in the fluid enters into the make-up of the pellicle. In the latter case, the incomplete precipitation of the fibrinogen might be due to an inadequate amount of calcium in the fluid.

That the pellicle does contain a larger amount of nitrogen than does the supernatant fluid was shown by determining the nitrogen in one portion of fluid in which part of the pellicle was removed and in another portion in which the pellicle was present in its entirety. It was found that the portion of the fluid containing the whole pellicle contained a greater amount of nitrogen than the supernatant fluid, the nitrogen most likely being fibrinogen nitrogen. Consequently we endeavored to begin the determination of each fluid immediately after it was withdrawn from the body, although we were not always able to do it, as our fluids had to be gathered from different parts of the city. Most of our fluids were obtained from the Sarah Morris Hospital for Children, and from the contagious and neurologic departments of the Cook County Hospital.

In addition to the chemical analysis, each fluid was examined for qualitative increase in globulin by the Pandy, Ross-Jones and Noguchi methods. The number and type of cells were determined and Wassermann and Lange tests were made of every fluid. The fluid was obtained by us in all cases but one by means of lumbar puncture. In one case, it was obtained by means of a cistern puncture.

RESULTS

As is seen from table 1, no pellicle or flocculi formed in any of the 18 fluids which gave negative cytologic, serologic and globulin tests. Only 4 of the 18 cases contained any fibrinogen. Of these 4 cases, one patient had been treated for syphilis of the central nervous

[14] Jour. Infect. Dis., 1917, 21, p. 556.
[15] Arch. Int. Med., 1917, 19, p. 1085.

system, although the blood and cerebrospinal fluid Wassermann reaction was negative. Furthermore, the amount of fibrinogen nitrogen in these 4 cases varied between 1.2 to 4.6 mg., or a very small amount. We, therefore, believe it right to state that no pellicle forms in what is commonly termed "normal" fluid and that no fibrinogen nitrogen or only a trace of it is contained in this type of fluid.

TABLE 1

NONMENINGITIC AND NONSYPHILITIC FLUIDS

Patient	Diagnosis	Total Nitrogen	Fibrinogen Nitrogen	Coagulum or Pellicle	Cells	Globulin Increase	Wassermann Test	Lange	Remarks
E. B. 1	Pneumonia	21.8	0	0	3	0	0	0	
E. B. 2	Pneumonia 3 days later	30.9	0	0	6	0	0	0	
M. M.	Pneumonia	28.0	0	0	27 60% polynuclears	0	Weakly positive with lipoid antigen	0123000000	
V. S.	Pneumonia	23.2	0	0	6	0	0	0	
S. K.	Penumonia	46.4	0	0	8	0	0	0	
H. E. I.	Endocarditis	38.7	0	0	640 16% polynuclears	0	0	0	Fluid slightly turbid
J. S.	Cerebral thrombosis	43.2	0	0	4	0	0	0	
L. M.	Spastic paraplegia	37.1	0	0	2	Faintly positive	0	0	
B. H.	Veronal poisoning	41.6	0	..	2	0	0	01111100000	
T. P. H.	Alcoholic	26.0	0	0	1	0	0	0	
M. R.	Paranoia	36.8	2.2	0	2	0	0	0	
T. O.	Paranoia	42.7	0	0	1	0	0	0	
A. J.	Dementia praecox	33.6	1.2	0	3	0	0	0	
R. C.	Mental deficiency	35.4	4.4	0	6	0	0	0002220000	
H. S.	Suspected lues	44.3	4.6	0	77 80% polynuclears	0	0	0	
T. Z.	Epidemic poliomyelitis of 2 weeks	37.9	0	0	16	0	0	0	
H. G.	Epilepsy	28.1	0	0	9	0	0	0	
L. E.	Epilepsy	26.0	0	0	6	0	0	0	

It may be worth while to note that the total nitrogen in our normal fluids were higher than those given by some other authors. Our figures ranged between 21.8 and 46.4 mg. per 100 c c. compared to 13 mg. found by Mestrezat,[11] and 13.2 to 25 mg. by Stanford.[16] However, even if we assume that our total nitrogen figures are too high, the accuracy of our fibrinogen nitrogen figures cannot be questioned, as the latter are obtained by subtracting the nitrogen figure obtained

[16] Repts. from Chemical Laboratory, Cardiff City Mental Hospital, 1919.

after calcium chloride precipitation from the total nitrogen, so that if the absolute values are incorrect, the relative values still hold good.

The 12 fluids in which the Wassermann and Lange reactions were positive showed no formation of pellicle such as is seen in various meningitides. However, 3 of the 8 fluids of general paresis, one of the two from cerebrospinal syphilis and one from tabes praecox, contained floating flocculi of small white particles, which formed a few minutes after the fluid had been withdrawn from the body.

TABLE 2
SYPHILITIC FLUIDS

Patient	Diagnosis	Total Nitrogen	Fibrinogen Nitrogen	Coagulum or Pellicle	Cells	Globulin Increase	Wassermann Test	Lange	Remarks
M. B.	General paresis	31.7	0	0	66 lymphocytes	++	+	5554300000	
V. G.	General paresis	58.7	5.2	Flocculi	42 lymphocytes	++	+	5555000000	
L. Q.	General paresis	56.9	0	Flocculi	160 90% lymphocytes	++	+	5455500000	
A. A.	General paresis	42.7	4.3	0	23	++	++	4455500000	
C. D.	General paresis	62.9	8.5	Flocculi	89	....	....	5555500000	
F. S.	General paresis	32.8	0	0	12	++	++	4444310000	
W. F.	General paresis	34.9	2.3	0	37	++	+	5554400000	
A. J. M.	General paresis (treated)	40.7	0	0	8	++	....	5555220000	
M. G.	Tabes praecox	47.5	7.1	Flocculi	15	++	+	0055400000	
L. W.	Cerebrospinal lues	86.0	0	0	92	....	....	0055550000	
J. O.	Cerebrospinal lues	53.9	8.2	Flocculi	73	....	....	2245500000	
F. H.	Congenital lues	25 5	0	0	11	....	Weakly positive	3224100000	Cistern puncture

Six specimens, or 50%, of the syphilitic fluids contained fibrinogen nitrogen and the other 6, or 50%, did not. The fibrinogen nitrogen varied between 2.3 mg. to 8.5 mg (table 2).

All of the fluids from cases of suppurative meningitis formed a heavy pellicle of a yellow or greenish yellow color. The pellicle was thicker than that formed in tuberculous meningitis. In most cases, the pellicle sank to the bottom after a lapse of 24 to 48 hours, and on standing 2 to 3 days more, the sediment became more compact. In a few cases, the sediment after standing 3 to 4 days, lost its yellow color and took on the appearance of coagulated egg albumin.

The 11 fluids from cases of suppurative meningitis all contained fibrinogen nitrogen, the amount varying between 6.2 and 51.1 mg. per 100 c c. of fluid (table 3). It may be noticed that the amount of fibrinogen nitrogen bore no direct relation to the number of cells in the fluid. Some fluids with a large number of cells contained less fibrinogen than others with a smaller number. The same is true in

TABLE 3

SUPPURATIVE MENINGITIS

Patient	Diagnosis	Total Nitrogen	Fibrinogen Nitrogen	Coagulum or Pellicle	Cells	Globulin Increase	Wassermann Test	Lange	Remarks
D. S.	Colon bacillus meningitis	333.6	37.5	++	12,000 99% polynuclears	++++	0	0000033444	Culture from fluid ante- and postmortem shows B. coli
H. E. 2	Pneumococcus type 1	64.3	28.0	+	1,060 75% polynuclears	++	0	0000012222	
H. E. 3	Same after serum	111.9	18.8	++	2,970 93% polynuclears	+	..	0000012333	Blood culture and spinal fluid give pneumococcus type 1
B. K.	Pneumococcus type 4	297.5	51.1	++	19,800 95% polynuclears	++	0	0000023455	Pneumococcus type 4
Mrs. M.	Pneumococcus	243.9	41.9	++	......	++	..	0000034444	
B. P. 1	Meningococcus meningitis	57.9	9.4	+	6,200 92% polynuclears	++	..	0000023333	
B. P. 2	Same after serum	129.8	23.6	+	1,500 95% polynuclears	++	..	0000000000	
H. N.	Meningococcus meningitis	67.7	10.0	+	1,400 95% polynuclears	++	..	0000023333	
J. A. 1	Meningococcus meningitis	73.6	8.2	+ sulphur granules	4,500	++	..	0000023344	
J. A. 2	Same after serum	58.0	6.2	+	150	++	..	0000022221	

relation to the total nitrogen. While all fluids had a high total nitrogen, fibrinogen did not increase in proportion to the total nitrogen.

The case of H. E. is interesting in connection with the fibrinogen nitrogen. The first fluid which was removed before the child presented any distinct signs of meningitis contained 38.7 mg. of total nitrogen per 100 c c. and no fibrinogen, although there were 640 cells per c. mm. When miningitic symptoms were manifested, the total nitrogen increased to 64.3 mg. and the fibrinogen nitrogen to 28.0 mg. per 100 c c. A few minutes before death, the fluid contained 111.9 mg. of total nitrogen and only 18.8 mg. of fibrinogen nitrogen, although the cell count was 2,970 c. mm. in the third fluid as compared to 1,060 in the second fluid.

Extremely puzzling are the 11 fluids from the series of cases of tuberculous meningitis (table 4). In all but one (S. S.) a pellicle

TABLE 4

TUBERCULOUS MENINGITIS

Patient	Diagnosis	Total Nitrogen	Fibrinogen Nitrogen	Coagulum or Pellicle	Cells	Globulin Increase	Wassermann Test	Lange	Remarks
R. K. 1	Tuberculous meningitis	35.0	0	+	250 95% mononuclears	Trace	0	0001233100	Tubercle bacilli found in pellicle
R. K. 2	Same 2 days later	37.6	0	+	240 85% mononuclears	+	0	0001233000	
R. K. 3	Same 6 days later	35.4	0	..	313 90% polynuclears	++	0	0000122310	Guinea-pig inoculation proves tuberculous nature of fluid
K. 1	Tuberculous meningitis	62.8	6.4	+ pellicle separated	......	+	0	0002220000	
K. 2	Tuberculous meningitis	65.5	3.1	pellicle separated	......	+	0	0002220000	
K. 3	Tuberculous meningitis	73.8	0	pellicle forming while setting up	......	+	0	0012230000	
E. B. 1	Tuberculous meningitis	38.9	5.2	+	43 lymphocytes	Ross-Jones neg., Noguchi +	0	0013330000	
E. B. 2	Tuberculous meningitis	41.6	0	+	43	Ross-Jones trace, Noguchi ++	0	0012221000	Subsequent Lange test showed 0000013330; necropsy showed secondary septic meningitis as well as tuberculous meningitis
S. S.	Tuberculous meningitis	74.6	0	..	..	+	0		
H. I.	Tuberculous meningitis	82.1	3.1	+	..	+	0	0001223333	Tests made of fluid after removal of pellicle; fluid obtained postmortem; yellow fibrous exudate found at necropsy
K. L.	Tuberculous meningitis	352.8	75.1	+ in ½ hour	6	++	0	0002221000	

formed on standing, and still only 5 fluids contained fibrinogen nitrogen and that in only small amounts. This series of 11 fluids makes one doubt the relation of fibrinogen to pellicle formation. At first the idea was entertained that some of the tuberculous fluids showed no fibrinogen because the pellicle had already separated. However, some of the fluids that were examined immediately after removal from the body also contained no fibrinogen, in spite of the fact that a different portion of the same fluids that was permitted to stand undisturbed did form a pellicle. Even a fluid that contained 73.8 mg. of total nitrogen contained no fibrinogen.

One fluid from a case of tuberculous meningitis drawn right after death (K. L.) contained 75.1 mg. of fibrinogen nitrogen, out of all proportion to the other cases of tuberculous meningitis. This case, however, presented a more chronic form of tuberculous meningitis, at least more chronic than the ordinary form. The patient was brought to the hospital with a history of fever and headache for 6 days. The patient was in a state of coma the 12 hours he stayed in the hospital. The fluid removed right after death was yellow, contained only 6 cells per c. mm. and formed a heavy pellicle in a few minutes. The globulin was markedly positive. The Lange test showed changes in the last 7 tubes, suggesting a suppurative meningitic curve. The small number of cells, the coagulation of the fluid in form of the pellicle and the markedly positively globulin, suggested the possibility of the case being a cord tumor. Necropsy revealed a thick fibrinous exudate at the base, with scattered tubercles. This case cannot, we believe, be taken as a criterion for the ordinary cases of tuberculous meningitis.

SUMMARY

No coagulum or pellicle forms in fluid that is not meningitic or syphilitic in character.

Fluid from cases of syphilis of the central nervous system forms no coagulum or pellicle, but often contains white flocculi.

Fluid from all cases of meningitis usually forms a coagulum, the color and size varying with the type and degree of the infection of the meninges.

The presence of a coagulum or pellicle indicates a pathologic condition, but not necessarily meningitis. The absence of a coagulum does not exclude meningitis.

Nonmeningitic and nonsyphilitic fluid contains either no fibrinogen nitrogen or small amounts of it. Only 4 of 18 such fluids contained any fibrinogen nitrogen, and the amount was small.

Fluid of syphilitic cases may or may not contain fibrinogen nitrogen; 50% contained no fibrinogen, and in the other 50% it varied between 2.3 mg. to 8.5 mg. per 100 c c.

Fluids from cases of suppurative meningitis have an increased amount of fibrinogen nitrogen. The amount in our series varied between 6.2 and 51.1 mg. per 100 c c.

Fifty per cent of our cases of tuberculous meningitis contained no fibrinogen, although they all contained a pellicle.

Fibrinogen nitrogen apparently bears no relation to the number of cells in the fluid.

Fibrinogen nitrogen in large amounts always indicates pathologic changes. An absence of fibrinogen nitrogen does not rule out pathologic changes.

Further study is necessary before it is possible to ascertain whether or not the pellicle is dependent on fibrinogen nitrogen.

THE INFLUENCE OF SURFACE TENSION DEPRESSANTS ON THE GROWTH OF STREPTOCOCCI

VI. STUDIES OF THE STREPTOCOCCI

S. Henry Ayers, Philp Rupp

and

William T. Johnson, Jr.

From Research Laboratories of the Dairy Division, United States Department of Agriculture

Bacteria, being single cell organisms capable of existence independent of other cells, offer an attractive field for the study of physiologic activities. The effect of certain substances on these activities may indicate fundamental differences which are of practical value even though the mechanism of the action may be obscure.

Interest in the relation of surface tension to the activity of living cells was stimulated by the work of Butschli [1] in 1876, in which he tried to connect surface tension with cell division. Those who are particularly interested in the relation of surface tension to vital phenomena will find a good review of the literature up to 1912 in a paper by Macallum.[2]

Apparently but little work has been done with surface tension in relation to bacteria. There are numerous papers which deal with the antiseptic properties of surface tension depressants and the influence of these substances on the efficiency of antiseptics. In this connection the work of Berczeller [3] may be cited. He showed that phenol acts more strongly than resorcin or hydroquinon and that it lowers the surface tension more in like concentrations. The action of thymol, he believed, was due to lowering of surface tension. He also pointed out that of the three cresols—ortho, meta, and para—the para had the strongest antiseptic action and was the most powerful depressor of the three. Berczeller concluded that there is a connection between physiologic activity and surface tension.

Hansen, [4] in studying the relation of surface tension to the bactericidal power of different disinfectants, found that by adding alcohol to

Received for publication, June 2, 1923.

[1] Abhandl. Senckenberg. Naturf. Gesell., 1876, 10, p. 213.
[2] Univ. of Toronto Studies, Physiol. Ser., 1912, 8, p. 82.
[3] Biochem. Ztschr. 1914, 66, p. 202.
[4] Compt. rend. Soc. biol., 1922, 86, p. 215.

N/10 HCl the bactericidal power was increased and the surface tension lowered. He did not believe, however, that the lowered surface tension was the reason for the increased power, because not all depressants increased the bactericidal property.

Kisch [5] found that substances which depress the surface tension of solutions to less than one half that of water (approximately 36 dynes) caused a permanent injury to yeast cells, but that a few bacteria which he studied were not affected as were yeasts and molds. He therefore concluded that the structure of their protoplasm must be different. On the other hand, Boeseken and Watterman [6] working with Penicillium glaucum believed that surface tension played a very subordinate rôle.

The work of Larson [7] and his associates was of particular interest to us because he found that the growth of pneumococci and streptococci was suppressed, or at least they did not grow well when the surface tension was lowered to about 50 dynes. Some preliminary experiments which we made with several different species of streptococci grown in plain infusion broth led to an agreement with the findings of Larson and his associates, but because of the rather wide limits in the surface tension in our experiments we were led to further studies, which are reported here.

METHOD OF MEASURING SURFACE TENSION

The surface tension, unless otherwise stated, was determined at room temperature by the drop method, taking the surface tension of water as 73 dynes, and was calculated in dynes according to the following formula:

$$\text{Surface tension in dynes} = \frac{\text{number of drops distilled water} \times 73 \text{ (surface tension of water)}}{\text{number of drops of medium}}$$

This method consists in dropping about 10 c c. of medium from a specially prepared pipet at a rate such that perfect, full-sized drops were formed. The same volume of liquid was used in all tests.

In our experiments it was found that the amount of surface tension depressants used did not change the specific gravity of the mediums sufficiently to have an appreciable effect on the surface tension measurements where the number of drops were counted.

When the surface tension is calculated according to the following formula:

$$\text{Surface tension in dynes} = \frac{\text{weight of number drops medium} \times 73}{\text{weight of same number drops water}}$$

more accurate results are obtained because the effect of specific gravity of the solution is a factor. In our experiments the surface tension, by number of drops, was a fraction of a dyne lower than when determined by weight of drops,

[5] Biochem. Ztschr., 1912, 40, p. 152.

[6] Ztschr. Chem. u. indust. Kolloide, 1912, 11, p. 58.

[7] Abstracts of Bacteriol., 1921, 5, p. 2; Larson, W. P.; Cantwell, W. F., and Hartzell, T. B.: Jour. Infect. Dis., 1919, 25, p. 41.

but the small difference was not considered important enough to compensate for the loss of time involved by the weight method.

We believe, however, that the weight of drops should be used in preference to the number of drops for general work, because under some conditions there may be a difference of 2 to 3 dynes in the surface tension when calculated by the two formulas.

EXPERIMENTAL METHODS

All mediums, unless otherwise noted, were steamed in the Arnold sterilizer on three successive days in order to prevent, or reduce to a minimum, the hydrolysis of the surface tension depressants.

Bacterial growth was measured by the change in hydrogen-ion concentration in dextrose mediums, the incubation period being 7 days at 30 C. In the preliminary experiments it was found that little reliance could be placed on the estimation of growth by the turbidity of the medium, because the depression of the surface tension affected it considerably. In all experiments inoculations were made from cultures 18 to 24 hours old.

RELATION OF MEDIUM TO THE EFFECT OF SURFACE TENSION DEPRESSION

Before selecting a basic medium for this work it was considered advisable to determine the effect of lowered surface tension on mediums of distinctly different composition.

For this comparison two mediums were selected, one a peptone-pepsin-dextrose medium and the other an infusion-peptone-dextrose medium. The peptone-pepsin-dextrose medium developed by one of us (Rupp) had been found to be particularly good for the growth of human hemolytic streptococci. Its composition was as follows:

	Gm. or C c.
Pepsin, Parke, Davis & Co.	5.0
Peptone, Parke, Davis & Co.	5.0
K_2HPO_4	3.0
NaCl	5.0
Dextrose	2.5
Distilled water	1000
Reaction adjusted to P_H 7.6	

The infusion peptone medium had the following composition:

	Gm. or C c.
Regular infusion broth	1000
Peptone, Parke, Davis & Co.	10.0
Dextrose	5.0
Reaction adjusted to p_H 7.5	

In this experiment the surface tension was lowered by adding castor oil soap (sodium ricinolate) in sufficient amounts to lower the surface tension to about 50 and 43 dynes.

As will be seen from table 1, the growth of several different cultures of different species of streptococci was studied in the 2 mediums at 2 different surface tensions. If a comparison of the final p_H is made in the 2 mediums at a surface tension of 50 dynes, it will be noted that lower and more consistent P_H values were obtained with the infusion medium. Similar results were obtained at a surface tension of 43 dynes.

It seems evident that the effect of surface tension depressants can be varied by the composition of the medium and that to obtain consistent and most accurate results a medium should be selected which is most favorable for the growth of the organisms studied. For this reason, infusion-peptone-dextrose broth was selected as the basic medium.

TABLE 1

GROWTH OF STREPTOCOCCI IN DIFFERENT MEDIUMS HAVING THE SAME SURFACE TENSION

Name or Source	Number	Pepsin-Peptone-Dextrose Medium		Infusion-Peptone-Dextrose Medium	
		50 Dynes	43 Dynes	50.1 Dynes	43.7 Dynes
		P_H	P_H	P_H	P_H
St. pyogenes	R 66	6.4	7.6	5.8	7.4
	A 34	5.8	7.6	5.2	7.4
	A 50	6.1	7.6	5.6	7.4
St. mastitidis	28 H-2	5.0	7.5	5.4	7.4
	67 H	5.6	7.1	4.6	7.1
	90 H-1	4.9	7.4	4.6	7.3
Typical streptococci of bovine feces	F 2-7	5.6	7.1	5.3	6.8
	F 5-1	5.6	7.0	5.3	6.8
St. kefir	X 4	6.4	7.5	5.5	6.0
St. lactis	53–2	4.8	...	4.5	4.5
	56–4	5.0	5.0	4.5	5.5
	62–4	4.9	5.4	4.5	6.0
	X 38	4.8	5.0	4.5	4.6
	X 48	4.6	5.5	4.5	4.6
Control	.....	7.5	7.5	7.4	7.4

Before leaving the results in table 1, attention must be called to the distinct difference in the ability of different species of streptococci to grow at lowered surface tensions as measured by the final P_H.

THE BASIC MEDIUM

It will not be necessary to repeat the composition of the infusion-peptone-dextrose medium, but it is desirable to show the buffer curve of this medium. The significance of difference in final P_H is of much more importance if it represents a considerable difference in the amount of acid produced. For this reason it was of advantage to have the basic medium quite heavily buffered. That such was the case is shown by the curve in chart 1. This curve should be kept in mind in connection with future discussion of the final P_H.

EFFECT OF SODIUM RICINOLATE ON GROWTH OF STREPTOCOCCI

Several different surface tension depressants have been studied in order to determine the surface tension which would prevent growth. Sodium ricinolate was first used. This soap has some advantages over

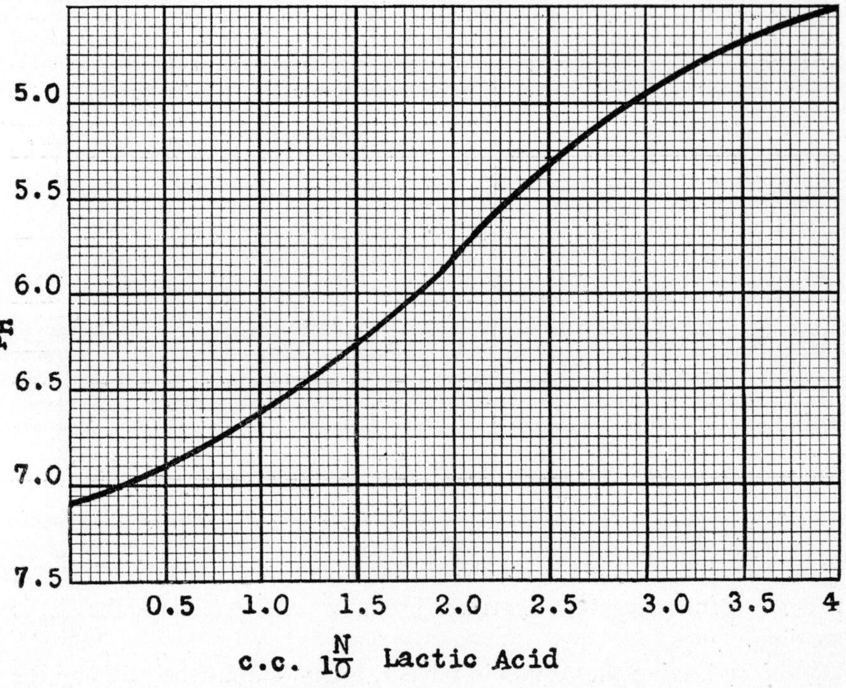

Chart 1.—Buffer curve of the basic medium.

other depressants in that it does not readily hydrolyze, as Larson found, and that it carries the surface tension to a low point.

The general effect on the streptococci from lowering the surface tension with this soap is of interest, particularly the effect on different species.

The results in table 2 show that reducing the surface tension to 50 dynes with ricinolate had some effect on the growth of Streptococcus pyogenes and also on the bovine fecal streptococci, but no effect on the other species as measured by the final P_H. At this point it may be well to mention that none of the surface tension depressants in the amounts used in the basic medium had any appreciable effect on the buffer curve. At the surface tension of 43.7 dynes there was no growth of Streptococcus pyogenes. There was a slight growth of Streptococcus mastitidis and the bovine fecal streptococci, with but little change in P_H. Streptococcus kefir was retarded in growth but cultures

TABLE 2

EFFECT OF SURFACE TENSION LOWERED BY SODIUM RICINOLATE ON THE GROWTH OF STREPTOCOCCI

Name or Source	Number	Basic Medium. No Ricinolate Surface Tension 59.6 Dynes	Surface Tension in Dynes, When Depressed by Sodium Ricinolate						
			56.3	54.2	52.8	50.1	43.7	38.8	35.9
		P_H	P_H	P_H	P_H	P_H	P_H	P_H	P_H
St. pyogenes	R 66	5.0	5.0	5.0	5.4	5.8	7.4	7.0	7.0
	A 34	5.0	5.0	5.0	5.0	5.2	7.4	7.0	7.0
	A 50	5.0	5.3	5.0	5.1	5.6	7.4	7.0	7.0
St. mastitidis	28 H-2	4.5	4.5	4.5	4.5	5.4	7.4	7.0	7.0
	67 H	4.5	4.5	4.5	4.5	4.6	7.1	7.0	7.0
	90 H-1	4.5	4.5	4.5	4.5	4.6	7.3	7.0	7.0
Typical streptococci of bovine feces	F 2-7	4.5	4.5	4.5	4.6	5.3	6.8	7.0	7.0
	F 5-1	4.5	4.5	4.5	4.6	5.3	6.8	7.0	7.0
St. kefir	X 4	5.3	5.5	5.5	5.5	5.5	6.0	7.0	7.0
	X 21	5.3	5.5	5.5	5.5	5.3	6.0	7.0	7.0
St. lactis	53-2	4.5	4.5	4.5	4.5	4.5	4.5	5.0	7.0
	56-4	4.5	4.5	4.5	4.5	4.5	5.5	7.0	7.0
	62-4	4.5	4.5	4.5	4.5	4.5	6.0	7.0	7.0
	X 38	4.5	4.5	4.5	4.5	4.5	4.6	7.0	7.0
	X 48	4.5	4.5	4.5	4.5	4.5	4.6	6.8	7.0
Control	.....	7.4	7.4	7.4	7.4	7.4	7.4	7.0	7.0

of Streptococcus lactis were but little affected. At a surface tension of 38.1 dynes one culture of Streptococcus lactis showed growth, and all were suppressed at 35.9 dynes.

Here again the possibility of using lowered surface tensions as a means of helping to differentiate streptococci is quite apparent.

We have purposely avoided giving the amounts of sodium ricinolate required to lower the surface tension, because the surface tension of the basic medium varied sufficiently to require slightly different amounts of the depressant. To give some idea of the amount required it was found that 11 mg. of pure sodium ricinolate per 100 c c. of the basic medium, or 0.011%, gave a surface tension of about 43 dynes.

EFFECT OF SODIUM GLYCOCHOLATE AND SODIUM TAUROCHOLATE ON THE GROWTH OF STREPTOCOCCI

In order to determine whether or not depressing the surface tension by other distinctly different substances would have the same effect as that of the ricinolate, sodium glycocholate and taurocholate were used. The salts were those prepared by the Digestive Ferments Company and, as they state, were not absolutely pure.

TABLE 3

EFFECT OF SURFACE TENSION LOWERED BY SODIUM GLYCOCHOLATE ON THE GROWTH OF STREPTOCOCCI

Name or Source	Number	Basic Medium. No Glycocholate. Surface Tension 59.6 Dynes	Surface Tension in Dynes, When Depressed by Sodium Glycocholate			
			53.1	50.9	45.8	42.8
		P_H	P_H	P_H	P_H	P_H
St. pyogenes	R 66	5.0	5.5	5.6	7.0	7.0
	A 34	5.0	5.0	5.3	7.4	7.4
	A 50	5.0	5.5	5.5	7.0	7.0
St. mastitidis	28 H-2	4.5	4.5	4.6	5.5	5.9
	67 H	4.5	4.5	4.6	5.9	6.0
	90 H-1	4.5	4.5	4.6	5.9	5.5
Typical streptococci of bovine feces	F 2-7	4.5	4.5	4.6	5.0	5.0
	F 5-1	4.5	4.5	4.6	5.0	5.0
St. kefir	X 4	5.3	5.2	5.2	5.3	5.2
	X 21	5.3	5.3	5.2	5.2	5.2
St. lactis	53–2	4.5	4.5	4.5	4.5	4.6
	56–4	4.5	4.5	4.5	4.5	4.6
	62–4	4.5	4.5	4.5	4.5	4.5
	X 38	4.5	4.5	4.5	4.5	4.7
	X 48	4.5	4.5	4.5	4.5	4.6
Control	.....	7.4	7.4	7.4	7.4	7.4

The same series of cultures was used as with ricinolate, but as will be seen from table 3 the results were not quite the same. A surface tension of 42.8 dynes generally permitted a slight visible growth with the pyogenes cultures, with, however, only a slight change in P_H. The mastitidis streptococci showed more growth and a distinct change in P_H. The rest of the cultures grew well, and, as the final P_H indicates, were not suppressed to any great extent, with the exception perhaps of bovine fecal streptococci. Quite different results were obtained, it will be remembered, with a surface tension of 43.7 dynes, using sodium ricinolate. The general uniformity of the final P_H among cultures of the same species is much better than in the medium with ricinolate. These results give promise of having distinct practical value in the differentiation of the streptococci.

Attempts were made to obtain lower surface tensions with the glycocholate, but it was found that about 42 dynes was the lowest point that could be reached. The amount of sodium glycocholate used to obtain about 42.7 dynes in the basic medium was 0.25%. Larger amounts had a tendency to increase surface tension.

The effect of sodium taurocholate on the growth of streptococci was the same as that of the glycocholate, and for that reason the results are not included in table 3.

GROWTH OF STREPTOCOCCI IN PEPTONE-BILE MEDIUM

Although not directly connected with the subject matter of this paper, it may be of interest to mention the growth in bacto-lactose-peptone bile of the streptococci used in the previous experiments. None of the streptococci grew, with the exception of some of the cultures of Streptococcus lactis. This fact may be of interest to those who use bile fermentation tubes in the routine examination of milk. There is also a tendency to long-chain formation by the lactic types when grown in mediums with low surface tension. This must also be recognized in milk work if confusion is to be avoided.

EFFECT OF VARIOUS SURFACE TENSION DEPRESSANTS AT ABOUT THE SAME SURFACE TENSION

Since it was found that there was a difference in the effect of sodium ricinolate and glycocholate at approximately the same surface tension, it was considered advisable to compare the effect of other depressants at about the same surface tension.

The results in table 4 show some interesting points. In addition to the ricinolate and glycocholate, iso-amyl alcohol and sodium oleate were used.

Before making comparisons between the effects of the different substances, the methods employed with the iso-amyl alcohol and oleate must be mentioned.

It was impossible to sterilize the medium after the addition of the iso-amyl alcohol by heat without volatilizing the alcohol. It was therefore necessary to sterilize by passing through a Berkefeld filter. Further trouble was encountered on incubation at 30 C., for the alcohol was volatile at this temperature. When the original surface tension, after filtration, was 43.1 dynes, it increased after 3 days' incubation at 30 C. to 46.5 dynes and after 7 days' incubation to 53.5 dynes.

In order to prevent the loss of the alcohol and the increase in surface tension, the medium in tubes was covered with a layer of about half an inch of melted petrolatum immediately after filtration through the Berkefeld filter and inoculation. This seal has proved satisfactory in all tests, for although there was sometimes a slight increase in the surface tension, the change was not of importance.

The use of sodium oleate also required special procedure, since it could not be sterilized by heat while in the basic infusion medium without undergoing some change. In one experiment with sodium oleate sterilized in the basic medium, the surface tension was reduced to

TABLE 4

COMPARISON OF THE EFFECT OF VARIOUS SURFACE TENSION DEPRESSANTS ON GROWTH OF STREPTOCOCCI

Name or Source	Number	Sodium Ricino-late, 43.7 Dynes	Sodium Glyco-cholate, 42.8 Dynes	Sodium Glyco-cholate, 45.8 Dynes	Iso-Amyl Alcohol, 42.5-45.2 Dynes	Sodium Oleate, 40.9-42.7 Dynes
		P_H	P_H	P_H	P_H	P_H
St. pyogenes	R 66	7.4	7.0	7.0	6.0	5.2
	A 34	7.4	7.4	7.4	5.6	7.3
	A 50	7.4	7.0	7.0	5.6	7.3
St. mastitidis	28 H-2	7.4	5.9	5.5	4.6	4.5
	67 H	7.1	6.0	5.9	5. 1	7.3
	90 H-1	7.3	5.5	5.9	5.1	4.5
Typical streptococci of bovine feces	F 2-7	6.8	5.0	5.0	4.6	4.5
	F 5-1	6.8	5.0	5.0	4.6	4.5
St. kefir	X 4	6.0	5.2	5.3	5.1	5.5
	X 21	6.0	5.2	5.2	5.2	5.5
St. lactis	53–2	4.5	4.6	4.5	4.6	4.5
	56–4	5.5	4.6	4.5	4.6	4.5
	62–4	6.0	4.5	4.5	4.6	4.5
	X 38	4.6	4.7	4.5	4.7	4.5
	X 48	4.6	4.6	4.5	4.6	4.5
Control	.....	7.4	7.4	7.4	7.4	7.3

42.4 dynes before sterilization, and after sterilization the surface tension was found to be 57.2 dynes. To overcome this difficulty the basic medium was sterilized in the autoclave in tubes containing 9.5 c c., and to this, at the time of inoculation, was added 0.5 c c. of a 2.0% solution of neutral sodium oleate which had been autoclaved.

Some general observations may now be made from the results in table 4. Let us consider first the pyogenes cultures. With ricinolate at 43.7 dynes, growth was prevented. With glycocholate at the slightly lower surface tension of 42.8 dynes, there was slight growth but little change in P_H. The same was true at 45.8 dynes, yet at 42.5 to 45.2 dynes with iso-amyl alcohol, good growth occurred. With sodium oleate, one of the 3 cultures showed growth at a surface tension of 40.9 to 42.7 dynes. In the case of the alcohol and oleate, the range in surface tension shows the number of dynes at the beginning and end of the 7 days' inoculation at 30 C.

The mastitidis cultures showed better growth with the glycocholate than with the ricinolate and still better with the iso-amyl alcohol. With oleate 2 of the 3 cultures grew well.

Even more striking were the results obtained with the bovine fecal streptococci. The rest of the cultures need no comment.

One fact seems evident from these results. It is not only the surface tension in dynes that is of importance, because the nature of the depressant seems to be an important factor.

We cannot get away from the fact, however, that at surface tensions below about 40 dynes the growth of streptococci, generally speaking, is prevented. This of course applies to the species of streptococci used in this work. There are probably many exceptions to this statement, for we have one culture which seems to grow at a surface tension as low as 34 dynes. This culture was isolated from the udder of a cow, but we have been unable to classify it.

The experiments with iso-amyl alcohol showed a further interesting fact. It was found that 0.8% of iso-amyl alcohol added to the basic infusion medium gave a surface tension of 42.5 dynes after filtration. In this concentration, all cultures grew well. When the amount was increased to 1.1%, the surface tension was reduced to 41 dynes, and only 3 cultures grew, one being F 2-7 and the others 62-4 and X 38.

The results obtained with sodium oleate need some further discussion. Avery,[8] in developing his oleate-hemoglobin agar, found that soaps of unsaturated fatty acids were bactericidal for certain bacteria. He used a 2% solution of neutral sodium oleate and added a sufficient amount to his medium to give a dilution of 1 : 1,000. This amount, he found, prevented the growth of certain gram-positive organisms, especially the pneumococcus and the streptococcus.

In our experiments we have used the same amount of neutral sodium oleate in a medium which was not exactly the same as his. Reference to table 4 shows that most of our species studied grew readily, with the exception of those of the pyogenes type. Of these, one culture grew well. One of the interesting points in connection with growth in mediums containing sodium oleate is that as soon as acid is formed the

[8] Jour. Am. Med. Assn., 1918, 71, p. 2050.

surface tension rises. The surface tension of a control tube after 7 days' incubation was found to be 42.7 dynes, while that of a culture of Streptococcus lactis was a final P_H after incubation of 4.5 was found to have increased to 55.3 dynes. The reason for this is undoubtedly the fact that in the presence of the acid formed by the fermentation of the sugar, the sodium oleate is changed into an insoluble form which is inert in the medium, as far as the surface tension is concerned.

It seems advisable to point out that, if the effect of sodium oleate observed by Avery [8] is due to the decreased surface tension, it may be possible to employ sodium ricinolate or glycocholate to better advantage, perhaps. These substances would at least have the advantage that they can be sterilized in the medium with but little, if any, hydrolysis.

EFFECT OF INCREASED AMOUNTS OF SODIUM GLYCOCHOLATE

The question whether the action of surface tension depressant is due to the lowering of the surface tension or to a toxic action is difficult to answer. From a practical standpoint, perhaps it is of no importance, provided the action of different depressants is recognized. From a strictly scientific standpoint the question is important. We do not wish to convey the idea that we can answer it. Too much depends on the definition of toxicity. If toxicity is considered to be an action similar to that of the corrosive poisons caused by heavy metals which lead to the disintegration of cells by coagulation of the protoplasm, that is one thing. If toxicity is considered as an action which is evidenced by abnormal changes in cell functions, then the question of the action of surface tension depressants becomes more complicated.

If the action is a toxic one in the sense of corrosive poisons, then increasing amounts of a surface tension depressant at the same surface tension should perhaps exert a greater toxic action.

Because of the fact that sodium glycocholate does not tend to decrease the surface tension below about 41 to 42 dynes it is possible to use large amounts in the medium.

Some experiments were arranged to test the effect, of large amounts of glycocholate. At first sodium glycocholate was tried in amounts of 0.25, 2.5 and 5% in a peptone-dextrose medium without infusion. The results shown in table 5 are rather striking, for in most cases the streptococci grew better in the medium with 5% sodium glycocholate than in the one with 0.25%. This may be due to some extent to the fact that the medium was lightly buffered and that the addition of 5% glycocholate about doubled the buffer, or it may be due to the fact that the surface tension was increased slightly by the large amounts of glycocholate. It seems evident that the depressant cannot be considered toxic in the sense of a corrosive poison.

The table also shows the results of the addition of 5% sodium glycocholate to the basic infusion medium. It will be noted that no growth occurred, except a slight growth with the lactic cultures. It was found that the addition of 5% glycocholate gave a higher surface tension, when calculated by weight of drops, than did small amounts of glycocholate, so that the prevention of growth could not be laid to surface tension alone. Other factors must have played a part.

TABLE 5

EFFECT OF INCREASING AMOUNTS OF SODIUM GLYCOCHOLATE

Name or Source	Number	Peptone-Dextrose Medium Plus Glycocholate			Infusion-Peptone-Dextrose Medium Plus Glycocholate 5.0%
		0.25%	2.5%	5.0%	
		PH	PH	PH	PH
St. pyogenes	R 66	7.2	7.3	7.5	7.0
	A 34	7.2	6.4	6.0	7.0
	A 50	7.2	7.2	7.5	7.0
St. mastitidis	28 H-2	6.2	5.9	6.0	7.0
	67 H	7.1	5.8	6.8	7.0
	90 H-1	6.0	6.0	6.4	7.0
Typical streptococci of bovine feces	F 2-7	7.1	5.5	5.5	7.0
	F 5-1	7.1	5.6	5.5	7.0
St. kefir	X 4	5.6	5.4	5.0	7.0
	X 21	5.4	5.1	5.0	7.0
St. lactis	53-2	5.3	5.0	4.8	6.0
	56-4	5.0	5.0	4.8	6.0
	62-4	5.6	5.1	4.6	6.0
	X 38	5.0	5.0	4.6	6.0
	X 48	5.3	5.0	4.7	5.6
Control	.....	7.2	7.4	7.6	7.2

It was realized that there was a distinct difference in the salt content of the peptone-dextrose and the infusion-peptone-dextrose medium due to the meat infusion. For this reason the effect of NaCl added to the basic medium was determined at both high and low surface tensions. For this work cultures of streptococci were selected which grew best at a low surface tension.

It was found that 5% salt had no apparent influence on the growth of cultures of Streptococcus lactis in the basic infusion medium at a surface tension of 55.1 dynes. However, the addition of 2.5% salt with sufficient sodium glycocholate to lower the surface tension to about

42 dynes, calculated by weight of drops, practically eliminated growth. Growth of cultures of Streptococcus kefir and the bovine fecal streptococci was even more strongly suppressed by the combined influence of NaCl and low surface tension. The cultures all grew in the basic medium with the same amount of glycocholate with no NaCl. Perhaps other salts in the basic infusion medium have more effect than NaCl, which together with salts of the impure sodium glycocholate may offer a possible explanation for the prevention of growth when 5% sodium glycocholate was added to the basic infusion medium.

TABLE 6

EFFECT OF INITIAL REACTION AND LOWERED SURFACE TENSION

Name or Source	Number	Initial P_H 6.0: No Glycocholate, Surface Tension 56.9 Dynes	Initial P_H 6.0: Glycocholate, Surface Tension 47.8 Dynes	Glycocholate P_H 7.4, Surface Tension 45.8 Dynes
		P_H	P_H	P_H
St. mastitidis	28 H-2	4.6	6.0	5.5
	67 H	4.6	6.0	5.9
	90 H-1	4.6	6.0	5.9
Typical streptococci of bovine feces	F 2-7	4.5	6.0	5.0
	F 5-1	4.5	6.0	5.0
St. kefir	X 4	4.5	5.7	5.3
	X 21	4.5	5.6	5.2
St. lactis	53-2	4.5	4.7	4.5
	56-4	4.5	5.0	4.5
	62-4	4.5	4.6	4.5
	X 38	4.5	4.7	4.5
	X 48	4.5	4.7	4.5
Control	......	6.0	6.0	7.4

RELATION OF INITIAL REACTION AND LOWERED SURFACE TENSION

With the exception of one experiment, the initial reaction of the basic infusion medium ranged from P_H 7 to 7.5. In one test the initial reaction was made P_H 6. The fact that the influence of sodium glycocholate in retarding growth is increased at a higher initial acidity is clearly shown in table 6. Here again the lactic streptococci were the least affected. In studying the table, the final P_H of the cultures must be compared with the initial P_H of the medium.

DISCUSSION OF RESULTS

Our results show that streptococci are in general suppressed at a higher surface tension than are intestinal bacteria, such as B. coli and B. aerogenes. These organisms were studied in almost all mediums used, although the results are not included in the tables. They grew readily when the surface tension was depressed by sodium ricinolate to 35 dynes. In a general way, therefore, our results agree with those of Larson [7] and his associates.

It would be most valuable if the mechanism of the action of surface tension could be fully explained. However, no attempt will be made to discuss the exact action of surface tension depressants, for the subject is probably bound up with many physicochemic phenomena. Probably the most important of these are the effects of adsorption and electrical charges. Substances which lower the surface tension according to the Gibbs-Thomson principle accumulate in the surface. They therefore are adsorbed on the bacterial cells, but in what way they interfere with the vital equilibrium necessary for the proper functioning of the cell is still a question. Perhaps by adsorption they tend to displace nutrient material, thus suppressing or preventing growth.

It appears evident that a definite surface tension of so many dynes cannot be considered a critical tension which exhibits its effect through influence on permeability. If such were the case, as Czapek believed to be the effect on plant cells, all depressants at a definite surface tension should exhibit the same effect. As has been shown in this paper, different substances act somewhat differently, so it is evident that the nature of the surface tension depressant as well as the actual surface tension in dynes must be taken into consideration.

Since the actual mechanism of the action of surface tension depressants cannot be explained at the present time, we must be satisfied to understand some of the conditions which affect its action in relation to the growth of bacteria, and if possible to make some practical application of surface tension effects. Some of these conditions have been discussed, and it appears quite likely that surface tension effects can be helpful in the classification of streptococci, for the retardation or suppression of growth at different surface tensions must be connected with fundamental differences in structure or physiologic activity.

SUMMARY AND CONCLUSIONS

Some species of streptococci are retarded in growth when the surface tension is lowered to about 53 dynes and are suppressed at about 45 dynes. Other species are retarded at about 43 dynes. Still other species are retarded in growth at 43 dynes and suppressed at 40 to 41 dynes. In general, when the surface tension is reduced to from 40 to 41 dynes the growth of streptococci is prevented. One exception to this statement was observed. These results were obtained when organisms were grown in an infusion-peptone-dextrose medium the normal surface tension of which ranged from 57 to 59 dynes.

Cultures of Streptococcus pyogenes were most susceptible to lowered surface tension and Streptococcus lactis the least.

Quite uniform results could be obtained in retarding or suppressing growth at a given surface tension when growth was measured by the decrease in P_H in a sugar medium.

The influence of the medium was important, best results being obtained in a medium most favorable for growth.

The initial P_H of the medium has been shown to exert an influence on the results, and a few experiments indicated that the salt content may play an important part.

By depressing the surface tension to the same point with different substances, the same results were not obtained. From the standpoint of the use of lowered surface tension and its effect on growth as measured by the final P_H, sodium glycocholate was found to give the best results.

It seems likely that the difference in growth of different species of streptococci at a given surface tension, with a definite depressant, a definite medium, and constant period and temperature of incubation, represents a fundamental difference in structure or metabolism of the cell which may be useful in classification. For this purpose the basic medium described in this paper is suggested, in which the surface tension is lowered to 43.0 to 43.5 dynes (calculated by weight of drops) by sodium glycocholate and the P_H used as a measure of growth after incubation for 7 days at 30 C.

When the effect of lowered surface tension is measured in the manner suggested, this effect seems to be correlated with other physiologic characteristics which have been used in classifying the streptococci used in this work. This surface tension test, as it may be termed, has been applied to a large number of cultures of each of the species mentioned in this paper, and the results have been quite uniform.

THE EFFECT OF SUPRARENALECTOMY IN RABBITS ON HEMOLYSIN FORMATION

N. Maximova Také and David Marine

From the Division of Laboratories, Montefiore Hospital, and Department of Pathology, Columbia University, New York

The active participation of the suprarenal cortex or interrenal gland in the defensive mechanism of the body, particularly against intoxications and infectious diseases, has long been suspected by pathologists. Hyperemia, edema, hemorrhage and focal necrosis occur particularly in cases of food poisoning, skin burns and acute infections. Examination with polarized light has shown that the anisotropic "lipoids" greatly decrease during acute infectious diseases, and chemical examination of the interrenal gland has shown that the "lipoid" loss consists mainly of cholesterol and its esters.

From these facts, the view that the interrenal gland is concerned directly or indirectly with the neutralization of toxins arose. This view has received experimental support from the fact that cholesterolized animals are more resistant to certain toxins and infections, and secondly, that animals in which the suprarenal glands have been removed or severely injured succumb to much smaller doses of a large variety of toxins than do normal animals.

This article deals with the influence of suprarenalectomy in rabbits on hemolysin formation. Immunologic studies bearing on this subject are limited. They may be divided into two groups: (a) The effect of epinephrin injections in the normal animal on opsonins, complement and antibody formation, and (b) the influence of partial suprarenalectomy on these substances.

Josué and Paillard[1] studied the opsonic properties of rabbits' blood after the intravenous injection of epinephrin and found that this drug was without effect. Sheep cell hemolysin and typhoid agglutinin production in rabbits following the subcutaneous and intravenous administration of epinephrin were studied by Bijlsma[2] and Hrma.[3] No appreciable effect was obtained. Bijlsma also observed that unilateral suprarenalectomy in rabbits was without influence on hemolysin and agglutinin production. A decrease in the complementing activity of guinea-pigs' blood after the administration of epinephrin and atropin was reported by Pinner.[4] Ecker and Rogoff[5] found no change in the com-

Received for publication, June 4, 1923.

[1] Compt. rend. Soc. de biol., 1910, 68, p. 657.
[2] Centralbl. f. Bakteriol., I, O., 1921, 86, p. 246.
[3] Casopsis Lekaruv Cesych, 1922, p. 1217; Abst. Jour. Am. Med. Assn., 1923, 80, p. 736.
[4] Beitr. z. klin. d. Tuberk., 1921, 46, p. 471.
[5] Jour. Immunol., 1921, 6, p. 355.

plementing power of the blood of rabbits which survived double suprarenalectomy. The observations of Ecker and Rogoff have been confirmed by us in the suprarenalectomized rabbits of this series. Hektoen and Curtis[6] removed the suprarenal glands from normal dogs and from dogs at the height of the antibody curve and found that no change in the curve followed. Gates[7] studied hemolysin and agglutinin formation in guinea-pigs and in three rabbits after the removal of from three-fourths to seven-eighths of the suprarenal glands. He observed no noteworthy effects.

EXPERIMENTS

As a result of the negative results of others following partial suprarenalectomy and of our own experience that it is rarely possible to produce a high grade functional insufficiency by partial removal, we resorted at once to double suprarenalectomy. Male and female adult rabbits were used. Suprarenalectomy was done in two stages in order to decrease the mortality. Double suprarenalectomy regularly produces a high grade and obvious clinical suprarenal insufficiency. Of the 31 rabbits operated on, 11 died within the first 3 weeks after removal of the second suprarenal. Those that were surviving and in good condition at the end of the 3rd week were used for sheep cell injections. On account of the greatly decreased resistance of suprarenalectomized rabbits to sheep cells, the injections were given intravenously in 0.25, 0.5, 0.75, 1.0, 1.25, 1.5 and 2.0 c c. doses of a 50% cell suspension every second day rather than in the usual doses. Severe shock followed each injection even in these doses. Of the 20 rabbits in which injections were started, 6 died from the direct toxic effects of the antigen. The rabbits died in from 8 to 12 hours after the injections and usually after the injections of the 1 c c. dose.

Natural antisheep hemolysin was determined in all instances before the injections were started, and in no instance was there any hemolysis in dilutions greater than 1 to 30. Thirty control rabbits were used. Cells from the same sheep were used in all injections, and all the rabbits were reared in the laboratory from our regular stock strain.

Titrations were made every 3rd day after the last injection. In all titrations 0.05 c c. inactivated serum with 2 units of complement and 0.1 c c. of a 5% suspension of sheep cells were used.

The general data, including the operations and their time intervals in relation to immunization, the titers and the amount of interrenal gland tissue found at necropsy are given in the table.

[6] Jour. Infect. Dis., 1915, 17, p. 409.
[7] Jour. Exper. Med., 1918, 27, p. 725.

TABLE 1

RESULTS OF SUPRARENALECTOMY IN RABBITS

Number and Sex	Interval Between Removal of 2d Suprarenal and Immunization in Days	Interval Between Splenectomy or Thyroidectomy and Immunization in Days	Condition of Animal Before Immunization	Titrations 1	2	3	4	Inter-renal Tissue at Necropsy	Major Cause of Death	Remarks
275 M	88	Splenectomy, 206	Diarrhea, dull	1,500	5,500	6,200	4,000	1 in spermatic cord	Killed	
283 F	69	Splenectomy, 270	Apparently normal	750	1,500	1,100	.....	1 near R. ovary 2×3 mm., 1 near L. ovary 1×2 mm.	Killed	
284 F	118	Thyroidectomy, 219	Dull, eats well	3,000	4,000	3,500	.....	R. ovary 1-5 mm. 2-1 mm., L. ovary 2-1 mm.	Typhoid* vaccine injection 0.25 c c.	Fragment of thyroid tissue 1 mm. in diameter on R. side
293 M	152	....	Diarrhea, dull	1,500	1,800	1,100	.....	1 small in L. epididymis	Killed	Subcutaneous abscess on R. side
323 M	55	Thyroidectomy, 123	Dull, eats well	3,000	1,600	1,400	.....	4 small in R. spermatic card, 1 small in L. spermatic cord	Killed	Thyroid fragment on R. side 3×2 mm.
349 F	62	....	Dull, losing weight, eats sparingly	2,500	2,500	2,000	.....	Small near L. ovary	Typhoid* vaccine injection 0.1 c c.	
352 M	24	....	Apparently normal	1,500	2,900	2,000	700	3-2×3 mm. in L. spermatic cord	Suprarenal insufficiency	
353 M	24	Thyroidectomy, 120	Dull, eats sparingly	1,000	2,500	1,000	950	2-1×1 mm. on L. kidney	Killed	No thyroid tissue found
357 M	60	....	Apparently normal	2,000	2,000	2,500	.....	1-1×2 mm. on vena cava R. ovary 2-2×2 mm.	Killed	
358 M	60	....	Soft stools	2,500	4,000	4,000	3,500	1-4×4 mm. on vena cava 1 small near R. ovary	Killed	Abscess of mammary gland
359 F	60	....	Apparently normal	1,500	2,000	2,000	1,200	2-2×2 mm. on inf. cava R. ovary 1-2×3 mm. L. ovary 1-1 mm.	Typhoid* vaccine injection 0.25 c c.	
369 M	20	....	Dull, eats sparingly	1,700	2,500	2,000	.....	1 large in spermatic cord	Typhoid* vaccine injection 0.2 c c.	
377 M	24	....	Apparently normal	1,400	2,500	1,900	1,000	....	Living	
402 F	24	....	Apparently normal	1,500	3,000	2,100	800	7 small near R. ovary 1 on vena cava	After metabolism exper.	
352 M	98	400	....	1,000	1,800	1,200	.....	....	....	Reimmunized
377 M	98	500	....	1,500	1,900	1,500	.....	....	....	Reimmunized
402 F	98	600	....	1,800	2,000	2,000	.....	....	....	Reimmunized

* Vaccine centained 2 billion bacilli per c c.

Fourteen rabbits survived all injections. The interval between removal of the second suprarenal and immunization varied between 20 and 152 days. No noteworthy difference in antibody formation was observed that might be related to the time interval between suprarenalectomy and immunization. Thyroidectomy was performed in 3 rabbits 120, 123 and 219 days before immunization and splenectomy in 2 rabbits 206 and 270 days before immunization. While 3 experiments are insufficient for any conclusion, particularly after such a long time interval, it may be pointed out that the absence of any noteworthy effect is in accord with the observations previously reported by one of us [8] for thyroidectomy alone. Of the 2 splenectomized rabbits, one (275) gave the highest titer, and the other (283) gave the lowest titer observed. It is fairly well established that antibody formation as a rule is decreased in recently splenectomized animals and without noteworthy effect if immunization is carried out a long time after splenectomy. It is possible that the low titer observed in rabbit 283 is an effect of a still uncompensated splenectomy.

The average titer for the 14 rabbits was 2700, while the lowest was 1500 and the highest 6200. In 30 control rabbits the average titer was 1100, while the lowest was 500 and the highest 1500. The average titer of the suprarenalectomized rabbits was, therefore, more than twice as high as that of the controls. Three of the rabbits (352, 377 and 402) were reimmunized 74 days after the first immunization and after the complete disappearance of hemolysin from the serum. The titers obtained in the 3 reimmunized rabbits were perhaps slightly lower than after the first immunization, but remained much higher than normal.

Accessory masses of interrenal tissue have been demonstrated at necropsy and checked by microscopic examination in the 13 rabbits which have come to necropsy. The amount of accessory interrenal tissue found shows wide variations. No relation between the amount of accessory interrenal tissue and the antibody titer could be made out. Sex is apparently without influence. No conclusions can be drawn concerning the influence of age, because all of the rabbits were adults but of unknown age.

DISCUSSION

Rabbits which survived removal of both suprarenal glands have been found to develop higher hemolysin titers than normal rabbits.

[8] Také, N. M.: Jour. Infect. Dis., 1923, 32, p. 138.

The highest titer in a series of 30 "normal" rabbits was 1500, or the same as the lowest titer of the 14 suprarenalectomized rabbits. The average titer for the "normals" was 1100, while for the suprarenalectomized it was 2700—approximately 2½ times as high. There is a great deal of indirect evidence that the increased antibody formation is associated with a loss of the interrenal rather than the suprarenal gland function. Epinephrin injections apparently do not influence the formation of hemolysins and agglutinins. On the other hand, profound anatomic and chemical changes are brought about in the interrenal gland by a great variety of toxins. The detoxication theory of interrenal gland function is based on these facts.

No explanation of the increase in hemolysin formation can be offered at present. Certain investigators, particularly Motohashi[9] working with splenectomized rabbits, claimed that the amount of antibody produced depends to some extent on the dosage of antigen. If this is the case and if the interrenal glands have a detoxifying function, it is possible that the effect of a given dose of antigen would be much greater in suprarenalectomized animals. Suprarenalectomized animals are more sensitive to a variety of poisons. This increased susceptibility is considered by some to depend in part on the loss of the power of the several body tissues to neutralize toxins—an influence believed to be exerted particularly by the interrenal gland.

Another factor should be mentioned which probably has a bearing on the high antibody titer produced in suprarenalectomized animals. While all body cells take part in antibody formation, it appears established that the lymphatic and hematopoietic tissues are particularly concerned. The lymphoid tissues of the body undergo hypertrophy after sufficient but sublethal injury to the suprarenal glands. It is possible that some biologic relation exists between the hypertrophy of the lymphoid tissue and the high antibody production in suprarenalectomized animals. Sublethal but sufficient injury to the interrenal glands increases the reactivity and irritability of the body tissues, as has been shown by the increased metabolism in rabbits, cats and dogs, by the increased sexual activity,[10] and it seems probable that the increased antibody formation is another manifestation of the increased tissue reactivity.

[9] Jour. Med. Res., 1923, 43, p. 473.
[10] Marine, D., and Baumann, E. J.: Am. Jour. Physiol., 1921, 57, p. 135.

Status lymphaticus, since the work of Wiesel,[11] Hedinger,[12] Paltauf [13] and others has some important relation to the suprarenal glands. We believe the disease is particularly associated with the interrenal portion, although others think the chromophil or suprarenal tissue is the one particularly involved. Both in status lymphaticus and in experimental suprarenal insufficiency there is a lowered resistance to poisons as well as many other conditions producing a physiologic strain on the organism. In reviewing the literature for studies on antibody formation in status lymphaticus only one reference has been found.

Tanabe [14] compared the reactions and antibody titers in cases of status lymphaticus with those of normal men in the Japanese army, to typhoid vaccination and came to the conclusion that while injections of the usual doses of typhoid vaccine were more dangerous and were followed by more severe reactions than in normal soldiers, the antibody production was just as high.

The possibility that the increased antibody titer in suprarenalectomized rabbits might be due to serum concentration was considered. It is true that rabbits dying of suprarenal insufficiency show a high grade of tissue dehydration, but this is not observed in animals surviving indefinitely.

With the data at present available, it would seem that rabbits with interrenal insufficiency have increased tissue reactivity and irritability, and that the increased antibody formation in such animals is only another manifestation of this increased susceptibility and capacity to react to stimuli. The "lipoid" substances of the body cells must play some important rôle in bringing about this striking immunologic reaction which follows suprarenal injury. It is possible that the increased reaction is in some way dependent on a loss of the cell "lipoids" which normally protect the cells from toxic injury and possibly from overstimulation and in this way bring about the increased susceptibility and tissue response to antigens.

CONCLUSIONS

Fourteen rabbits in which a high grade but sublethal suprarenal insufficiency was created (by removal of both main suprarenal glands) have been immunized with sheep cells.

[11] Internat. Clin., 1905, 15, p. 250.
[12] Ztschr. f. Pathol., 1907, 1, p. 527.
[13] Wien. klin. Wchnschr., 1889, 2, p. 877, and 1890, 3, p. 172.
[14] Mil. Surgeon, 1923, 52, p. 83.

These rabbits showed hemolysin titers averaging more than twice as high as the controls.

It is believed the increased antibody formation is due to the loss of some regulatory and inhibitory influence which the interrenal gland normally exerts on the irritability and susceptibility of the body cells. This influence may involve physical and chemical alterations in their "lipoid" mechanism.

ON SPECIFIC ERYTHROPRECIPITINS (HEMOGLOBIN PRECIPITINS?)

II. HEMOGLOBIN PRECIPITINS IN IDENTIFICATION OF BLOOD

LUDVIG HEKTOEN AND KAMIL SCHULHOF

From the John McCormick Institute for Infectious Diseases, Chicago

In our previous article [1] we considered the precipitin reaction of aqueous extracts of red corpuscles. The results of our experiments seemed to indicate that such extracts owe their precipitinogenic action to hemoglobin, so far as may be determined by the methods available, and that the precipitinogenic action of hemoglobin in turn depends on a distinct molecular group or groups which differ from globin. We now wish to record briefly further observations on the specificness of the precipitin reaction connected with hemoglobin, particularly because this reaction may be of practical value in the identification of blood under certain conditions.

For the production of precipitin serum for hemoglobin we have followed the method outlined previously,[1] using extracts of corpuscles thoroughly freed from all traces of serum by repeated and careful washing in large quantities of salt solution. Before injecting such extracts, the corpuscular stroma and all other proteins were removed completely by repeated treatment with aluminum cream. From 5 to 6 intravenous injections at 3-day intervals of gradually increasing quantities of hemoglobin solutions, prepared in this way, as a rule lead to the accumulation of goodly quantities of specific precipitin in the blood by the 4th or 5th day after the last injection. When the yield is insignificant, a 2d course of injections may increase the output greatly. A course of 3 daily injections, repeated after an interval of one week, also may give good results. To illustrate: Two rabbits were injected at 3-day intervals with 0.01, 0.02, 0.03, 0.04, and 0.05 gm. of recrystallized horse hemoglobin, 7 years old, dissolved in salt solution; on the fourth day after the last injection, the serum reacted well with hemoglobin from 1 in 2,000 up to 1 in 200,000 of salt solution. The failure to react of solutions of hemoglobin stronger than 1 to 2,000 emphasizes the importance of using serial dilutions of antigens in testing the strength of precipitin serum.

Received for publication, June 5, 1923.

[1] Jour. Infect. Dis., 1922, 31, p. 32.

The immunization with blood serum has been carried out along the same lines as with hemoglobin solutions. The quantities injected intravenously run from 1 or 2 c c. to 10 or 12, usually in increasing amounts at 3-day intervals, but in some cases 3 daily injections followed by a 2d series after 6 days or so have yielded the desired results.

Table 1 shows that after injections of hemoglobin solution in most cases precipitins for hemoglobin only developed and not for the serum. In these cases it is reasonable to assume that the antigenic solutions injected were free or nearly free from serum proteins. In the instances in which hemoglobin antiserum reacted with the corresponding normal serum, it is possible that the hemoglobin solution used as antigen contained serum proteins and induced the formation of specific hemoglobin and serum precipitins, or that the serum used in the tests contained a small amount of hemoglobin. Of course, a combination of these two possibilities is not impossible. As table 1 shows further, injections of blood serum, obtained in the usual way, in some cases may cause the production of precipitins for the homologous hemoglobin, manifestly due to the presence in the serum of more or less hemoglobin, as not rarely happens.

It is noteworthy that antihemoglobin serum may not contain any newly formed opsonins, agglutinins or lysins for the homologous corpuscles, and that the production of the antibodies just mentioned may follow injections of thoroughly washed corpuscular stroma. Clearly the hemoglobin and the stroma contain different antigens, and the immune reactions of erythrocytes are not dependent on various manifestations of the action of one general antibody.

Hemoglobin precipitin serums appear to contain specific complement-fixing bodies, but we have not studied their action in detail.

The only antihemoglobin serum with a wider range of action than illustrated in tables 1 and 2 came from a rabbit injected with beef hemoglobin. A solution containing in 20 c c. the hemoglobin in 1 c c. of fresh blood served as antigen, and 1, 2, 3, 4, and 5 c c. were injected intravenously at 3-day intervals. When tested on the 5th day after the last injection the serum reacted as follows, the figures indicating the greatest dilution in which a definite precipitate formed after 1 hour at room temperature: Beef hemoglobin, 256,000; sheep hemoglobin, 24,000; human hemoglobin, 32,000; swine hemoglobin, 0; horse hemoglobin, 0; guinea-pig hemoglobin, 0; rabbit hemoglobin, 0; monkey hemoglobin, 0; rat hemoglobin, 0; beef serum, 0. Later tests gave analogous results. Specific absorption experiments, in which the anti-

TABLE 1

TITERS OF HEMOGLOBIN AND SERUM PRECIPITIN SERUMS

Antigen	Precipitin Serums of Rabbits Injected with															
	Beef Hemoglobin	Beef Serum	Cat Hemoglobin	Cat Serum	Chicken Hemoglobin	Chicken Serum	Dog Hemoglobin	Dog Serum	Horse Hemoglobin	Horse Serum	Human Hemoglobin	Human Serum	Sheep Hemoglobin	Sheep Serum	Swine Hemoglobin	Swine Serum
Beef hemoglobin	160,000	64,000	0	0	0	0	0	0	0	0	0	0	0	10	0	0
Beef serum	0	64,000	0	0	0	0	0	0	0	0	0	0	0	0	0	0
Cat hemoglobin	0	0	25,000	12,800	0	0	0	0	0	0	0	0	0	0	0	0
Cat serum	0	0	100	8,000	0	0	0	0	0	0	0	0	0	0	0	0
Chicken hemoglobin	0	0	0	0	192,000	48,000	0	0	0	0	0	0	0	0	0	0
Chicken serum	0	0	0	0	20	3,200	0	0	0	0	0	0	0	0	0	0
Dog hemoglobin	0	0	0	0	0	0	4,000	112	0	0	0	0	0	0	0	0
Dog serum	0	0	0	0	0	0	0	3,200	0	0	0	0	0	0	0	0
Horse hemoglobin	0	0	0	0	0	0	0	0	200,000	0	0	0	0	0	0	0
Horse serum	0	0	0	0	0	0	0	0	10	800	0	0	0	0	0	0
Human hemoglobin	0	0	0	0	0	0	0	0	0	0	30,000	0	0	0	0	0
Human serum	0	0	0	0	0	0	0	0	0	0	100	32,000	0	0	0	0
Sheep hemoglobin	0	2,000	0	0	0	0	0	0	0	0	0	0	12,800	10	0	0
Sheep serum	0	160+	0	0	0	0	0	0	0	0	0	0	0	12,800	0	0
Swine hemoglobin	0	0	0	0	0	0	0	0	0	0	0	0	0	0	50,000	0
Swine serum	0	0	0	0	0	0	0	0	0	0	0	0	0	0	0	3,200

The figures for hemoglobin are based on solutions containing definite quantities by dry weight.

TABLE 2

PRECIPITIN TESTS WITH EXTRACTS OF SPOTS OF BLOOD MIXTURES

Blood Mixtures	Precipitin Serums of Rabbits Injected with											
	Beef Hemoglobin	Beef Serum	Dog Hemoglobin	Dog Serum	Horse Hemoglobin	Horse Serum	Human Hemoglobin	Human Serum	Sheep Hemoglobin	Sheep Serum	Swine Hemoglobin	Swine Serum
Beef, dog, swine	+	+	+	+	0	0	0	0	0	0	+	+
Dog, horse, man	0	0	+	+	+	+	+	+	0	0	0	0
Beef, horse, sheep	+	+	0	0	+	+	0	0	+	+	0	0
Beef, dog, sheep	+	+	+	+	0	0	0	0	+	+	0	0

TABLE 3

Tests of Extracts of Blood Spots with Hemoglobin and Serum Precipitin Serums

Extracts of Blood Spots		Precipitin Serums of Rabbits Injected with															
Kind	Age, Years	Beef Hemo-globin	Beef Serum	Cat Hemo-globin	Cat Serum	Chicken Hemo-globin	Chicken Serum	Dog Hemo-globin	Dog Serum	Horse Hemo-globin	Horse Serum	Human Hemo-globin	Human Serum	Sheep Hemo-globin	Sheep Serum	Swine Hemo-globin	Swine Serum
Beef..............	11	+	+	0	0	0	0	0	0	0	0	0	0	?	0	0	0
	4	+	+	0	0	0	0	0	0	0	0	0	0	?	0	0	0
Cat...............	11	0	0	+	+	0	0	0	0	0	0	0	0	0	0	0	0
	Recent	0	0	+	+	0	0	0	0	0	0	0	0	0	0	0	0
Chicken...........	11	0	0	0	0	+	0	0	0	0	0	0	0	0	0	0	0
	4	0	0	0	0	+	0	0	0	0	0	0	0	0	0	0	0
Dog...............	11	0	0	0	0	0	0	0	0	0	0	0	0	0	0	0	0
	Recent	0	0	0	0	0	0	+	+	0	0	0	0	0	0	0	0
Horse.............	11	0	0	0	0	0	0	0	0	+	+	0	0	0	0	0	0
	4	0	0	0	0	0	0	0	0	+	0	0	0	0	0	0	0
Human.............	11	0	0	0	0	0	0	0	0	0	0	+	+	0	0	0	0
	4	0	0	0	0	0	0	0	0	0	0	+	+	0	0	0	0
Monkey............	11	0	0	0	0	0	0	0	0	0	0	+	+	0	0	0	0
Sheep.............	11	0	0	0	0	0	0	0	0	0	0	0	0	+	0	0	0
	4	0	0	0	0	0	0	0	0	0	0	0	0	+	+	0	0
Swine.............	11	0	0	0	0	0	0	0	0	0	0	0	0	0	0	+	0
	4	0	0	0	0	0	0	0	0	0	0	0	0	0	0	0	+
Turkey, duck, pigeon...........	4	0	0	0	0	+	0	0	0	0	0	0	0	0	0	0	0
Goose............	4	0	0	0	0	0	0	0	0	0	0	0	0	0	0	0	0

serum was mixed with equal quantities of beef, human, or sheep hemoglobin 1:200, the precipitates that formed after standing some hours being removed by centrifugation, resulted in complete removal of all the precipitins by beef hemoglobin, while sheep and human hemoglobins each removed all precipitins for these 2 hemoglobins, but left the precipitin for beef hemoglobin almost as strong as in the original serum.

We offer no attempts at explanation of the results with this antiserum. It must be said, however, that the possibility that the rabbit may have been immunized before cannot be excluded with absolute certainty. The widened range of antibody production in allergic rabbits,[2] which may include antibodies for antigens of previous injections, consequently may have played a part in this case. Other precipitin serums for beef hemoglobin have not reacted with either human or sheep hemoglobin. In connection with this matter, it ought to be noted that we have been working with relatively strong precipitin serums which it is well known may seem to be rather less specific in their action than weaker serums.

No special effort has been made, however, to study the precipitin relationships of the hemoglobins of related species. That interactions occur is suggested by results in both tables 1 and 3: antibeef serum may react with solutions of sheep hemoglobin, but it is perhaps doubtful whether that was a true hemoglobin reaction; antiserum for chicken hemoglobin reacted with extracts of turkey, duck, and pigeon blood, but not with goose; and antiserum for human hemoglobin reacted with extract of monkey (rhesus) blood; sheep and goat appear to interact in precipitin reactions, as do the serums of these animals. The question of identity among antigenic elements in the hemoglobins of related species merits careful study.

Taking up now the identification of blood by the precipitin test for hemoglobin, we present first table 2, which shows that in fresh spots of mixed blood the hemoglobin precipitins pick out the homologous hemoglobin just as accurately as the corresponding serum precipitins pick out the homologous antigens. In table 3 are given the results of tests of extracts of older spots each of just one kind of blood. Here again the specificness of the precipitin reaction for hemoglobin holds good. It is noteworthy that in some cases the hemoglobin test is positive, while the serum test fails: chicken blood, 4 years old; horse blood, 4 years old; and swine blood, 11 years old. In the case of dog

[2] Hektoen, Ludvig: Jour. Infect. Dis., 1917, 21, p. 279.

blood, 11 years old, both the hemoglobin and the serum test failed. The 11-year blood spots were on pieces of cotton sheeting, the 4-year old on filter paper, and all had been kept in the laboratory at room temperature. In all cases the extracts gave the benzidin test for peroxidases. The extracts were made by simply soaking a bit of blood-stained cloth or paper for 2 or 3 days either in salt solution or in water to which 0.09% salt was added before testing. There seemed to be no advantage in using water for extraction, due perhaps to the fact that the dried corpuscles are hemolyzed in salt solution too.

Hemoglobin precipitin serums appear to keep as well as other precipitin serums.

SUMMARY

The precipitinogen in extracts of red corpuscles and purified hemoglobin differ from the antigens in the stroma.

The results presented in this article indicate that hemoglobin precipitins may be of value in the identification of blood. The precipitin test for hemoglobin is fully as specific and as sensitive as the precipitin test for serum, if not more so. The possible overlapping of the reaction in related species merits consideration and further study, and naturally careful control tests must be made in all cases. The advantage of the hemoglobin test should be that it is a direct test for blood only. The serum precipitin test is a test for species protein in general, and whether blood is present is determined by other and nonspecific tests. Now it is possible that a blood spot giving a precipitin reaction for human protein and therefore apparently human blood might be made or claimed to be made by animal blood falling on a place previously stained by human protein in sputum, albuminous urine or any kind of bloodless exudate. In problems of this kind, the precipitin test for hemoglobin may be of decisive value.

STUDIES IN COMPARATIVE IMMUNITY

II. RELATIVE IMPORTANCE OF THE LIVER AND SPLEEN IN DESTRUCTION OF FOREIGN BLOOD CELLS IN RABBITS

F. L. Pickof

From the Department of Pathology and Bacteriology, University of Illinois, College of Medicine, Chicago

We know of no method by means of which the site of antibody formation can be demonstrated conclusively. The results obtained by extracting organs to determine the concentration of antibodies are contradictory. An assumption quite generally accepted at present is that antibodies are formed in the organs where their antigens are destroyed. Therefore a method by means of which the site of destruction of antigens could be demonstrated should be of value. Microscopic evidences of the rôle of the phagocytic endothelial cells of the liver and spleen in the destruction of certain bacterial antigens are not lacking (Mesnil,[1] Kyes,[2] Berry and Melik,[3] Schilling,[4] Pickof [5] and others). Of course, it would be difficult to obtain microscopic evidences of the site of destruction of amorphus antigens, such as egg albumin or serum proteins.

However, the site of destruction of foreign blood cells lends itself more readily to microscopic observation, and this paper is concerned with a study of the site of foreign blood cell destruction in rabbits.

Recent reports on this subject by Cary [6] and Notohashi [7] state that certain iron containing endothelial cells of the spleen in rabbits are the structures concerned with the destruction of foreign red blood cells. Some of these iron containing cells of the spleen first described by Ecker in 1847,[8] and called macrophages by Metchnikoff,[9] erythrophages by Ebner,[10] and hemophages by Kyes,[11] have also been found to contain ingested red cells; therefore Kyes concluded that the iron in those

Received for publication, June 5, 1923.

1 Ann. de l'Inst. Pasteur, 1895, 9, p. 301.
2 Jour. Infect. Dis., 1916, 18, p. 125.
3 Jour. Immunol., 1916, 1, p. 47.
4 Virchows Arch. f. path. Anat., 1909, 196, p. 125.
5 Jour. Infect. Dis., 1923, 32, p. 232.
6 Ibid., 1915, 17, p. 432, and Jour. Med. Research, 1922, 43, p. 399.
7 Jour. Med. Research, 1922, 43, pp. 419 and 473.
8 Ztschr. f. rationell. Med., 1847.
9 Immunity, 1905.
10 Handbuch der Gewebelehreldes des Menschen., 1902.
11 Internat. Monatschr. f. Anat. & Phys., 1914, 31, p. 543.

cells must come from their hemophage activity. Because the number of iron containing cells is greatly increased in the spleen and liver of rabbits injected with sheep blood cells, Cary and Notohashi concluded that the injected corpuscles have been destroyed within the iron containing endothelial phagocytes.

That the increase in the number of iron containing cells in the spleen of rabbits injected with foreign blood cells does not necessarily indicate that the injected cells have been destroyed within the iron containing cells may be easily seen when the rôle of the spleen in iron metabolism is considered. As Eppinger had found,[12] intravenous injections of soluble iron will greatly increase the number of iron containing cells in the spleen and liver. Kahn[13] states that even feeding iron in normal animals results in an increase in iron in the spleen macrophages and in the Kupffer cells of the liver. Chevalier[14] considers the macrophages of the spleen and the Kupffer cells of the liver as concerned with the intermediary iron metabolism, and he named those cells siderocytes. The spleen, according to him, is the storehouse for siderocytes. Arnold[15] states that the iron in the macrophages of the spleen and the Kupffer cells comes from the circulating blood whence it is taken by the fixed tissue phagocytes in soluble form.

From this brief review of the literature on the source and significance of the iron in the endothelial phagocytes of the spleen it is evident that an increase in the number of iron containing cells in the spleen of rabbits which have received intravenous injections of foreign red blood corpuscles indicates only an increase in the intermediary iron metabolism, and that it would be necessary to obtain more direct evidences than those of Cary and Notohashi before the splenic phagocytes in rabbits could be rightly credited with the intracellular destruction of foreign blood cells.

As to the importance of the spleen in the destruction of red blood cells, there is a wide variation in various animals. Rous and Robertson state[16] that the number of red blood cells ingested in the large spleens of the rat, dog and guinea-pig is so considerable that, a priori, one might suppose phagocytosis to be the means whereby the destruction of erythrocytes is accomplished in these animals. But in the cat phagocytosis does not come in for consideration; in normal man, the

[12] Encykl. klin. Med., Die Hepato-Lienalen Erkrank., 1920.
[13] Amer. Jour. Med. Sc., 1923, 165, p. 214.
[14] La Rate: Organe de l'assimilation du fer, Thèse de Paris, 1913.
[15] Virchows Arch. f. path. Anat., 1900, 161, p. 284.
[16] Jour. Exper. Med., 1917, 25, p. 651.

rhesus monkey, and the rabbit it cannot be held responsible for the disappearance of any important amount of blood.

My own work revealed an increase in the number of iron containing cells in the spleen of rabbits killed 24 hours after one or more intravenous injections of sheep blood cells. But I have not been able to find any direct evidence of phagocytosis of red corpuscles by the iron containing cells. As the larger and nucleated red cells of birds are more easily demonstrable, I have injected rabbits with chicken washed blood cells. The results were the same as in rabbits injected with sheep blood cells, namely: in rabbits killed 24 hours after the injection there were no foreign red blood cells found in the spleen and no evidences of phagocytosis of the injected cells by the endothelial phagocytes of the spleen.

It was evident that in order to be able to demonstrate the site of destruction of foreign blood cells it would be necessary to kill the injected animals before the foreign blood cells have been completely destroyed. This was accomplished in the following experiments:

EXPER. 1.—Eight healthy rabbits of medium size, whose blood on preliminary examination had been found to contain no appreciable amount of natural hemolysins for chicken blood corpuscles, were injected intravenously with 5 c c. of a 50% suspension in normal saline solution of chicken washed corpuscles. At 10 minute intervals veins were punctured and blood films made and stained with Wright's stain. It was found that the injected red cells completely disappeared from the circulation of the injected rabbits in 40 to 60 minutes. It was also noted that even in the films in which only an occasional nucleated red blood cell remained, the foreign red cells showed no gross changes. Apparently the serum of the injected rabbits had no effect on the injected cells while in the general circulation; nor were there seen in the smears any nuclei which might have come from dissolved chicken corpuscles.

Accumulation of Foreign Red Blood Cells in the Capillaries of the Liver, Spleen and Bone Marrow.—The rabbits were killed 15 minutes, 30 minutes, 1, 1½, 2, 2½, 3 and 4 hours after injection. All animals killed 1½ hours after injection and later showed a marked hemoglobinuria. The liver, spleen, heart, kidney, lung and bone marrow (from long bones)were removed for microscopic examination. The sections were stained with hemotoxylin and eosin and with Pearl's Prussian blue stain for iron. The detailed results follow:

After 15 minutes: There were many nucleated red cells in the capillaries of the liver, spleen and marrow; few were seen in the larger blood vessels of those organs. Only an occasional nucleated red corpuscle was found in the sections of the rest of the organs.

After 30 minutes: The capillaries of the liver, spleen and marrow were filled with apparently uninjured nucleated red blood cells. None were found in the other organs.

After 1 hour: The foreign red cells were limited to the capillaries of the liver, spleen and marrow, there being field for field about equal number of injected cells in these organs. The foreign red cells were beginning to show dissolution of the cytoplasm. Nuclei of dissolved red corpuscles were seen. There were no evidences of phagocytosis of the injected cells.

After 1½ hours: The injected red cells appeared pale, irregular in shape, and in places had become agglutinated. The number of nuclei without cytoplasm was increasing. After 2 hours: There were fewer nucleated red cells and more nuclei without cytoplasm in the capillaries of the spleen and marrow. The liver capillaries still contained many nucleated red cells.

After 2½ hours: Almost all foreign red cells had disappeared from the spleen and marrow, only a few free nuclei still remaining. The capillaries of the liver contained few nucleated red cells and numerous nuclei of dissolved red cells. Some of the nuclei appeared as within Kupffer cells.

After 3 and 4 hours: No more nucleated red cells were found in any of the organs; occasional nuclei were seen in the spleen and marrow; more were seen in the liver, some of them in the Kupffer cells.

As seen from these results, the injected red cells disappeared from the general circulation within one hour after the injection, the cells having accumulated by that time in the capillaries of the liver, spleen and marrow. All injected cells were destroyed in these organs within 3 to 4 hours after injection. The destruction of the injected cells was definitely extracellular, only a comparatively small number of nuclei and no whole cells having been found inside the Kupffer cells of the liver. These results are in complete accord with the findings of M'Gowan.[17]

While field for field the spleen and marrow contained about as many foreign blood cells as the liver, if we take into consideration that the spleen in the rabbits I used weighed between 0.6 and 0.7 gm., while the average weight of the liver was 50 gm., or over 70 times the weight of the spleen, it becomes evident that in the rabbit the liver is many times more active in the destruction of foreign blood cells than the spleen.

Although the predominating rôle of the liver in the destruction of foreign red cells in rabbits is quite conclusive in the foregoing experiments, and although the destruction of the injected cells was definitely extracellular, the claims of Cary and Notohashi for the endothelial phagocytes of the spleen in rabbits might also be considered from the following largely philosophic point, namely: Since the endothelial phagocytes of the spleen in rabbits represent only a small part of 0.6 or 0.7 gm., the total weight of the spleen, and as about 2 gm. of blood cells have been injected, it would appear that the intracellular destruction of the injected cells by the fixed phagocytes of the spleen under the conditions of the experiment would be almost a physical

[17] Jour. Path. & Bacteriol., 1910, 14, p. 379.

impossibility. It might also be considered that the injected cells were about the same size as the endothelial phagocytes, and therefore the phagocytes hardly could engulf many red cells of their own size and digest them in such a short period without the phagocytosis being evident in the sections of the spleen.

Since phagocytosis was not responsible for the destruction of the injected red cells, and since the systemic blood was not hemolytic for the injected red cells, it is possible that the injected cells may have been destroyed by some substance or substances secreted by the endothelial cells of the capillaries of the liver, spleen and marrow. As the great majority of the injected red cells were destroyed in the liver capillaries, we must also consider the metabolic activities of the liver cells proper as instrumental in their destruction; also the possible hemolytic action of the fatty acids and the amino acids that might be present in the portal blood of the liver capillaries.

Effect of Splenectomy on the Destruction of Foreign Red Blood Cells.—With the data of the mechanism of destruction of foreign red cells at hand, the determination of the relative importance of the spleen in rabbits in antibody destruction was undertaken.

EXPER. 2.—Three rabbits were splenectomized and 24 hours later injected intravenously with 5 c c. of a 50% suspension of chicken washed red cells. Blood films were made at 15 minute intervals and stained with Wright's blood stain. It was found that in one rabbit the injected corpuscles disappeared from the general circulation 45 minutes after injection, in another in 1 hour, and in the third, a much smaller animal, in 1¼ hours after injection. One of the splenectomized rabbits was killed 1½ hours after injection, another 2½ hours and the third 3½ hours. The liver and marrow were sectioned:

After 1½ hours: The capillaries of the liver and marrow were filled with nucleated red cells.

After 2½ hours: Most of the injected red cells had been dissolved and many nuclei without cytoplasm were seen in the capillaries. No evidences of phagocytosis of the injected cells were found.

After 3½ hours: Only an occasional nucleated red cell and many free nuclei were found in the capillaries of the liver. Some of the nuclei were inside Kupffer cells. Almost all injected cells had disappeared from the marrow.

These results are similar to those in exper. 1 with normal rabbits and show that the removal of the spleen did not delay the disappearance of the injected cells from the general circulation, nor their destruction in the liver and marrow.

These experiments while definitely showing where foreign red blood cells intravenously injected into rabbits are destroyed still further complicate the question as to the site of hemolysin formation, placing the hemolysins in the same group with the antitoxins and precipitins. As the reticulo-endothelial apparatus of the liver, spleen, marrow and the lymph glands have been found to be concerned with the intermediary metabolism of iron, lipoids, and probably other substances, and as these same cells are highly phagocytic for certain bacteria, it seems possible that this endothelial apparatus, varying in activity in various animals, may take up from the circulation not only the iron but also the protein portion of the destroyed red cells and later produce hemolysins.

SUMMARY AND CONCLUSIONS

In rabbits, chicken blood cells injected intravenously rapidly disappear from the general circulation.

The great majority of the injected red cells accumulate within the capillaries of the liver, and the remainder in the capillaries of the spleen and marrow where they are destroyed.

The destruction of the injected cells is definitely extracellular but within the organ capillaries and not in the general circulation. Only a few Kupffer cells were found to contain remnants of ingested red cells.

Splenectomy delays neither the disappearance of the injected red cells from the general circulation, nor their destruction in the organs.

EFFECT OF SPICES ON GROWTH OF CLOSTRIDIUM BOTULINUM

Freda M. Bachmann

From the Department of Agricultural Bacteriology, University of Wisconsin, Madison

One result of the deaths from botulism that have occurred in this country in the last few years is the great interest which bacteriologists are taking in the study of the organism, especially as to its distribution and the factors which favor or inhibit its growth. Contrary to the observations of Van Ermengen,[1] who first described it, we know that it produces heat resistant spores. We know that it is not limited for its growth to meat or meat products, but that it grows and also produces its toxin in a number of vegetables and fruits when oxygen is removed. It appears also not to be limited to substances with a neutral reaction, since especially in fruits the medium is acid. Cutter [2] has reported two deaths from the consumption of tomato-onion chili sauce—a food product which usually contains a large amount of vinegar and spices, a combination of substances which I [3] found to have considerable inhibiting effect. The growth of the organism in such a medium suggests the need of again extending our knowledge of the conditions under which it may grow. Such foods as mince meat are seldom sterilized in canning in the home, and although frequently there is no attempt to seal the material, the layer of fat formed on the surface makes quite an effective seal. As mince meat is often eaten without reheating, it was thought there might be a considerable element of danger in such foods.

No investigations of the relation of Cl. botulinum to spices have thus far come to my attention, hence it seemed desirable to make such a study. A few years ago, in a study of the inhibiting effect of spices on the growth of micro-organisms, I [4] found that there was considerable difference in the effect of any one spice on different organisms, and also considerable difference in the effect of different spices. In general, cinnamon, cloves and all-spice are most effective in inhibiting the growth of micro-organisms. I also found that in general, molds are more sensitive to spices than bacteria. Later [2] I showed that there is

Received for publication, June 8, 1923.

[1] Arch. internat. de pharmacal et therap., 1896, 2, p. 355.
[2] Jour. Am. Med. Assn., 1922, 79, p. 825.
[3] Jour. Indust. and Engin. Chem., 1918, 10, p. 121.
[4] Ibid., 1916, 8, p. 619.

considerable difference in the preservative value of different brands of the same spice. In these papers my study was limited to aerobes. In the present study I used a brand of spices which I had found quite effective in inhibiting growth of such spore-forming aerobes as Bacillus subtilis, although it was not the most effective of the different brands used at that time.

In my first experiments I tried to find whether the organism would grow in mince meat. Standard recipes were consulted, and the material which I used was then prepared as follows:

1 chopped apple	1 teaspoonful cinnamon
1 cup raisins	1 teaspoonful cloves
¼ cup butter	1 teaspoonful nutmeg
1 tablespoonful vinegar	1 teaspoonful mace
1 cup sugar	1 teaspoonful salt
½ lb. Hamburger steak	

Enough water was added to make the amount 900 c c. This was cooked in a steamer for 30 minutes, then introduced in test tubes and sterilized in the autoclave. In order to have much depth of the material so that conditions would approach anaerobiosis, 6 inch test tubes were used and these were filled nearly half full. There was considerable fat on the surface. In the repetition of the experiment, the raisins were omitted and beef suet replaced the butter. The material was inoculated as soon as it was sufficiently cool after sterilization. Eight strains of C. botulinum obtained from different sources were used for inoculation. Two of the strains were known to be type A and 2 others known to be type B. The tubes were incubated at 35 C. In the first experiment the organisms, with the exception of 2 strains which I have numbered 14 and 15 and which represented type A and type B respectively, grew readily so that the mince meat was much spoiled after 1 week. In the second experiment growth was somewhat slower, but after a period of 4 weeks there was abundant growth with all strains except numbers 11 and 14. With these 2 growth was questionable. When C. botulinum grows in meat, it produces changes in the fat. This becomes rather spongy in appearance, probably due to the gas which is formed. At the same time there are whitish masses formed in the meat in the lower part of the tube that look somewhat like fat. When compared with uninoculated control tubes, there appeared to be some slight change with strains 11 and 14, but this was not marked enough to justify recording it as an unquestionable growth of the organism.

Since the organism had grown in the mince meat it seemed of interest to determine the effect of a number of different spices on its growth. As it grows readily in Hamburger steak sterilized with a small amount of water, this was used as the medium and the spices added. The Hamburger steak contained a rather large amount of fat in order to insure a good fat layer in the test tube and thus obtain anaerobic conditions. Enough water was added to 32 gm. of the meat and fat mixture to make 100 c c. To this the ground spices were added in amounts of 1, 2, and 2.5 gm. Eight spices were used: cloves, cinnamon, all-spice, ginger, nutmeg, cayenne pepper, white mustard and black mustard. The spice was well mixed by stirring, and the material was then introduced into 6 inch test tubes and sterilized in the autoclave. The tubes were inoculated as soon as they had cooled sufficiently. Six different strains of Clostridium Botulinum were used. Incubation was at 35 C.

The results of these inoculations made it evident that the organism was not affected by any of the spices used in amounts up to 2%. When 2.5 gm.

of spice were introduced into 100 c c. of the meat and water mixture, the growth of the organism was sometimes retarded. This was especially true with all-spice although there was some retardation with cloves. Higher percentages of spice were not used because even 2.5% is much more spice than would ever be used in any food product.

It was reasoned then that although the organism would not be retarded in its growth by the amount of spice used in flavoring foods, there might be a possibility that toxin production was inhibited. To determine whether toxin was produced, three tubes of meat containing 2.5% of spice were inoculated with varying amounts from a meat culture of Clostridium botulinum. This was done as follows: three loops from a meat culture were first introduced into 10 c c. of sterile water (tube A); from tube A, 0.5 c c. was introduced into a second 10 c c. of sterile water (tube B): from tube B, 0.5 c c. was introduced into a third 10 c c. of sterile water (tube C). Tubes A, B and C then contained a decreasing number of organisms and likewise a decreasing amount of initial toxin which had been carried with the inoculum from the original meat culture. From each of these tubes 0.3 c c. was transferred to tubes of spiced meat, which may be designated as A', B', and C'. A' thus received the heaviest inoculation and C' the lightest. Three tubes of meat with each of the same eight spices used before were thus prepared. Two cultures of Clostridium botulinum were used for inoculation, one of type A and one type B.

As Cl. botulinum produces a potent toxin, it was necessary (in order to prove the production of toxin in the spiced meat) to determine whether enough had been carried over from the original meat culture to kill guinea-pigs. Immediately after inoculation, guinea-pigs were forcibly fed with 1 c c. of the liquid from tubes A', thus using the tubes with the heaviest inoculation and the largest amount of toxin as controls. Of the 16 guinea-pigs that were fed from these control tubes, 8 with type A and 8 with type B, 2 died after 7 days. One of these had been given type A in white mustard and the other type A in cloves. It was concluded that except in these 2 tubes not enough toxin had been introduced to make 1 c c. of the liquid a lethal dose for guinea-pigs.

The tubes of spiced meat were then incubated for 2 weeks after which 1c c. from each of tubes C', those receiving the smallest amount of inoculum, was forcibly fed to guinea-pigs. All the guinea-pigs were dead the following morning, with the exception of the one receiving the liquid from the culture containing white mustard and type B. In these tubes with white mustard the organism had not certainly grown, and it was not unexpected that the guinea-pigs receiving this did not die. The experiment thus gave no data for concluding as to toxin production either positive or negative with Cl. botulinum type B in meat containing white mustard. As to white mustard with type A and cloves with type A, it might at first be thought that we could not conclude with absolute certainty since the control tubes proved to be toxic. However, even though the control tubes (tubes A') were toxic, it is impossible that the third tubes (tubes C') could have had enough initial toxin to have produced the death of guinea-pigs within 18 hours. All of the 16 tubes A' were inoculated in exactly the same way and only 2 of the tubes contained enough toxin to produce death in 1 c c. amounts and then only after a week. There was at least a great increase in the amount of toxin, as shown by the smaller inoculum and by the shorter time, 18 hours, in which death was produced.

The conclusions from these results are that many spices as used for flavoring foods and in even larger amounts do not prevent the growth of Cl. botulinum nor the prevention of toxin formation by this organism. Unless the food is known to have been sterilized, such foods as mince meat should be heated to the boiling point before tasting them.

SUMMARY

Experiments were made with Clostridium botulinum in mince meat and also in meat containing ground cloves, cinnamon, all-spice, nutmeg, black mustard, white mustard, cayenne pepper and ginger in amounts of 1, 2, and 2.5% to determine whether such spices in these amounts inhibit the growth of Clostridium botulinum or prevent the formation of its toxin. No inhibition of growth was found in 1 and 2% of spice, but there was some retardation with all-spice and cloves when 2.5% was used. The organisms readily form toxin in the presence of this amount of spice. Spices as used in flavoring foods do not help to make the food safe if there is contamination with Clostridium botulinum. For safety such foods as mince meat should be unquestionably sterilized or else heated to the boiling point before they are tasted.

SEROLOGIC AGGLUTINATION OF BACILLUS SPOROGENES *

Ivan C. Hall and Naomi Stark

From the Department of Bacteriology and Experimental Pathology, University of California, Berkeley

The success of Meyer [1] in 1915 in differentiating Vibrion septique, B. chauvœi, and "B. oedematis maligni" (B. sporogenes), and in identifying Vibrion septique, by the agglutination test, led the senior author (I. C. H.) to hope that this reaction might be utilized in differentiating and identifying a considerable number of carefully purified but then un-named cultures in his possession, by preparing serums for those few whose identity had been determined and testing the unidentified cultures with these known serums. This procedure resulted in the segregation of 19 cultures which were later identified as B. sporogenes by their morphologic and cultural properties.[2] There were, however, marked differences in the titer of a given serum then tested on different strains of this species, and some strains of B. sporogenes failed to agglutinate even at 1 : 20. On the other hand, none of our sporogenes serums ever gave a positive test with any other species, nor did any serum prepared against another species ever agglutinate a strain of B. sporogenes.

For these reasons, one should regard serologic agglutination as a satisfactory criterion of species identity in properly controlled positive tests, but not of differentiation in negative tests.

It is the purpose of this paper to present data in support of this limited interpretation.

Historical Review

Among the first to apply the agglutination reaction to the sporulating anaerobes were Leclainche and Vallée [3] who in 1900, recognizing certain cultural resemblances between B. chauvœi and Vibrion septique, as well as clinical similarities in the diseases for which they are responsible, distinguished them on (a) morphologic differences in impression smears from infected tissues,

Received for publication, June 9, 1923.

* Acknowledgment is made to the Logan Fellowship Fund of the University of Chicago, to the National Canners Association and the California Packers' Corporation, and to the Board of Research of the University of California, under whose grants this work was completed.

1 Jour. Infect. Dis., 1915, 17, p. 458.

2 Hall: Ibid., 1922, 30, p. 445.

3 Ann. de l'Inst. Past., 1900, 14, p. 513.

(b) specific protection experiments in actively and passively immunized animals, and (c) by the agglutination reaction.

Their conclusions are still valid, being confirmed first by Foth,[4] then by Markoff,[5] and later, as already noted, by Meyer.[1] On the other hand, the results of Hillbrand[6] who differentiated "bradshot" from "malignant edema" by the agglutination test were in conflict with those of Grosso,[7] who considered these gaseos infections of animals identical with each other but distinct from "rauschbrand." Wulff[8] also found that the agglutination test distinguishes "rauschbrand" from the diseases resembling it, and most valuable work was done by Robertson[9] on the serologic groupings of Vibrion septique.

The British Medical Research Committee[10] also recommended agglutination for the differentiation of certain anaerobic bacteria, and Weinberg and Seguin[11] not only prepared serums for a number of pure strains, but also claimed in some cases to be able to diagnose specific infections by agglutination of impure suspensions from crude wound exudates. They stated, however, that it was always necessary to control these results by other procedures.

Less promising were the findings of Passini[12] that the agglutination test fails to differentiate B. putrificus from the gas phlegmon bacillus, whatever the organisms so designated by him were. But there is considerable evidence in Passini's paper that his cultures were impure or imperfectly identified, or possibly both. Rocchi's[13] results based on microscopic methods owing to spontaneous precipitation in the macroscopic tests with serums prepared against cultures labeled B. putrificus, B. oedematis maligni, B. butyricus dimorphis, and and B. botulinus, were also contradictory, perhaps for the same reasons.

And finally both Zeissler[14] and Heller[15] condemned the agglutination test for the sporulating anaerobes because of spontaneous agglutination in the controls without added serum.

There are few references to the serologic agglutination of B. sporogenes as such, although it is certain that Meyer[1] and probably others worked with this species under other names. Weinberg and Seguin[11] referred to the ease with which agglutinating serums for B. sporogenes may be prepared in the rabbit, and the British Medical Research Committee distinguished two agglutinative groups of B. sporogenes, but gave no experimental data.

EXPERIMENTS

The data presented here concern only the rigorously purified strains of B. sporogenes and other anaerobes that have been described.[2]

Our first serum was prepared with culture 10, which is the "bacillus of malignant edema" with which Meyer[1] secured his results.

[4] Ztschr. f. Infektionkr. d. Hausthiere, 1909, 6, p. 201; quoted by Markoff, ibid., 1910, 8, p. 117.

[5] Centralbl. f. Bakteriol., I, O., 1911, 60, p. 188.

[6] Hillbrand, quoted by Heller: Jour. Infect. Dis., 1915, 27, p. 385.

[7] Berl. tierärtzl. Wchnschr., 1911, 27, p. 621. (Quoted by Heller.)

[8] Deutsche tierärtzl. Wchnschr., 1911, 20, pp. 602, 625, 673 and 704 (quoted by Heller).

[9] Jour. Path. & Bacteriol., 1920, 23, p. 153.

[10] Medical Research Committee, Special Report Series No. 39, 1919.

[11] La gangrène gazeuse, 1917.

[12] München. med. Wchnschr., 1904, 51, p. 1283.

[13] Centralbl. f. Bakteriol., I, O., 1911, 60, p. 579.

[14] Berl. klin. Wchnschr., 1919, 56, p. 107.

[15] Jour. Infect. Dis., 1915, 27, p. 385.

Rabbit 6, weighing 2,800 gm., was immunized, beginning Dec. 3, 1919, by subcutaneous injections of a 48-hour glucose broth culture of B. sporogenes 10, in 6 doses of 1-3 c c. at intervals of 2-3 days during a period of 2 weeks. There was neither loss of weight nor any other adverse symptom. Following a rest of 3 weeks, 5 c c. of blood were drawn from the ear; the serum gave a slightly positive result at a dilution of 1:20 but was negative at 1:200.

During the following 2 weeks 3 more doses of 2 c c. each were injected, and blood was drawn from the ear at the end of another week. The serum from this blood was active at 1:1,000. A larger quantity of blood was therefore drawn from the heart by means of a sterile glass barreled syringe with a 16 gage needle. (The large size of needle is important.) Serum was secured from the clotted blood after standing 24-48 hours, centrifugalized to free it from corpuscles and kept in a cool dark cupboard without preservative.

The tests were made with 24- or 48-hour glucose broth cultures grown at 37 C. in constricted tubes, tested for aerobic contamination, and strained just before use through absorbent cotton or gauze to remove clumps. It was found desirable to have a moderately turbid suspension; some of the discordant results of certain earlier workers may have been caused by too thinly grown cultures. The tests were set up with 1 c c. of the dilutions (in 0.85% NaCl) with 1 c c. of the strained culture. The dilutions of serum indicated throughout this paper were the final dilutions in the tests. Control tests without serum but with culture diluted with equal parts of salt solution served as a check against spontaneous and nonspecific clumping.

No special difficulty was encountered from spontaneous clumping or settling in view of the fact that readings were made after 2 hours' incubation at 37 C. The common practice in agglutination tests with aerobes of making final observations after refrigeration overnight is not permissible with anaerobes, owing to spontaneous settling in the controls without serum. This phenomenon may be an expression of a negative chemiotactic response to air. Slight clearing usually occurred at the top of the suspension during 2-3 hours' incubation at 37 C., but this never confused the tests; sedimentation was easily distinguished from flocculation.

Not all serums required 2 hours for action; frequently the lower dilutions agglutinated within 15 minutes, but the higher dilutions often required longer, and negative tests were so considered only after a sufficient period of incubation to make the results decisive.

It should be kept in mind that most of these cultures, other than B. welchii, B. botulinus, Vibrion septique and B. tetani were as yet unidentified, although pure. At the time when the first tests were made we were still using "B. oedematis maligni" for the species now generally designated as "B. sporogenes:" In order to save space only the essential data of the protocols are summarized (table 1).

Table 1 shows that all cultures agglutinating even at 1:20 were ultimately identified as B. sporogenes. There were striking differences, however, in the agglutinability of different strains, ranging all the way from strongly positive tests (cultures 58, 84, 113, 121 and 122) in which the titer was higher even than with the homologous antigen, down through weakly postive tests at 1:80 (culture 114) and 1:20 (cultures 54 and 115), to those failing to agglutinate even at 1:20 (cultures 54 and 118).

It is evident that positive tests identify, but negative tests do not exclude. We shall return to this point, but one should notice also that none of the cultures later identified as other than B. sporogenes ever gave a positive test with sporogenes serum.

TABLE 1

AGGLUTINATION TESTS WITH SERUM OF RABBIT 6 IMMUNIZED AGAINST B. SPOROGENES 10

Date	Culture Number	Agglutination Titer		Final Identification
		Positive	Negative	
Feb. 7, 1920	2	.....	1:20	B. welchii
	8	.....	1:20	B. botulinus type A
	10	1:400	1:800	B. sporogenes (homologous culture)
	12	.....	1:20	Vibrion septique
	14	.....	1:20	Vibrion septique
	18	.....	1:20	Vibrion septique
	20	.....	1:20	B. welchii
	28	.....	1:20	Vibrion septique
	32	.....	1:20	Vibrion septique
	36	.....	1:20	B. welchii
	42	1:200	1:400	B. sporogenes
	44	1:400	1:800	B. sporogenes
	46	1:400	1:800	B. sporogenes
	48	1:400	1:800	B. sporogenes
	50	.....	1:20	B. bifermentans
	52	1:400	1:800	B. sporogenes
	54	1:20	1:200	B. sporogenes (positive test very weak)
	58	1:800	1:1600	B. sporogenes
	66	1:200	1:400	B. sporogenes
	70	.....	1:20	B. bifermentans
	72	1:400	1:800	B. sporogenes
	74	1:400	1:800	B. sporogenes
	76	.....	1:20	B. centrosporogenes
	78	.....	1:20	B. botulinus type B
	80	.....	1:20	B. botulinus type B
	84	1:800	1:1600	B. sporogenes
	106	.....	1:20	B. tyrosinogenes
Mar. 18, 1920	10	1:400	1:800	B. sporogenes (homologous culture)
	88	1:400	1:800	B. sporogenes
	90	1:400	1:800	B. sporogenes
	92	1:400	1:800	B. sporogenes
	94	1:400	1:800	B. sporogenes
	102	.....	1:20	B. bifermentans
Oct. 26, 1920	10	1:160	1:320	B. sporogenes (homologous culture)
	54	.....	1:20	B. sporogenes (see also test of Feb. 7)
	82	.....	1:20	B. centrosporogenes
	106	.....	1:20	B. tyrosinogenes
	113	1:320	1:640	B. sporogenes
	114	1:80	1:160	B. sporogenes
	115	1:20	1:40	B. sporogenes
	116	.....	1:20	B. centrosporogenes
	118	.....	1:20	B. sporogenes
	121	1:320	1:640	B. sporogenes
	122	1:320	1:640	B. sporogenes

Furthermore, none of the agglutinating serums prepared for other species ever gave a positive result when tested against various strains of B. sporogenes in a dilution of 1:20. Several instances of such tests are tabulated in table 2.

Having established, first, that all of the cultures agglutinated by a particular sporogenes serum were essentially identical in morphology and cultural reactions,[2] and second, that none of these cultures was agglutinated by serums prepared against several other species, we now addressed ourselves to the problem of the interacting agglutination reactions within the species, as defined on morphologic and cultural grounds, in order to give special attention to strains of B. sporogenes that had failed to agglutinate with the earlier serums or that had agglutinated only in the lower dilutions. The procedures were the same as those already described except where otherwise mentioned.

Six rabbits were immunized against separate cultures of B. sporogenes selected for their apparently different susceptibility to agglutination. These cultures were rechecked for purity, morphology and cultural reactions just prior to their use, and every possible effort

TABLE 2

SERUMS FOR SPECIES OTHER THAN B. SPOROGENES FAILING TO AGGLUTINATE B. SPOROGENES STRAINS AT 1:20 DILUTION

Rabbit No.	Homologous Culture	Titer Limit	Strains of B. sporogenes Tested and Failing to Agglutinate at 1:20
35	B. bifermentans 50	1:2000	10, 52, 54, 72, 84, 113, 114, 118
906	B. butyricus 125	1:3200	10, 54, 115, 118
930	B. botulinus 8A	1:1280	10
949	B. botulinus 78B	1:5120	10, 42, 44, 46, 52, 54, 58, 66, 72, 84, 88, 90, 92, 94, 115, 118, 133
970	B. centrosporogenes 82	1:640	10, 42, 44, 46, 48, 52, 58, 66, 72, 74, 84, 88, 90, 92, 94, 113, 114, 115, 118, 121, 122
1	Vibrion septique 12	1:800	10, 42, 44, 46, 48, 52, 54, 58, 60, 66, 67, 70, 72, 74
4	Vibrion septique 14	1:2000	10, 42, 44, 46, 48, 52, 58, 60, 72, 74, 84
20	B. tetani 1	1:40	10, 52, 54, 84

made to insure their freedom from accidental contamination. The immunizing antigens were glucose broth cultures, tested at 24 hours for aerobic contamination by subculture on plain agar slants, and used at 48 hours for injection. Doses of 2 c c. each were used, and all injections were made into the marginal vein of the ear.

There were no adverse symptoms during the immunization, except loss of weight when frequent injections were made. Some of the animals actually gained weight during the inoculation periods.

The serums were tested, one at a time, against suspensions prepared as already described. The titer limits of the 6 serums against 24 strains are summarized in table 3, which shows the highest dilution of serum in which a positive test was secured; the next higher, i. e., double, gave a negative result, except in those cases in which the highest dilution tested was positive. Unfortunately, the table cannot show the wide variations in the appearance of the flocculi in the graded dilutions. In general, cultures that agglutinated in high dilutions of serum gave complete reactions in lower dilutions, while those that agglutinated only in the lower dilutions gave incomplete reactions even in these.

Table 3 shows that all of the serums were highly potent toward their homologus cultures. Four of them were active in a dilution of 1 : 5120, and two were active in a dilution of 1 : 2560. One observes that the preparation of agglutinating serums of high potency for B. sporogenes is very easy.

TABLE 3

CROSS AGGLUTINATION OF B. SPOROGENES

B. sporogenes Cultures	Serums					
	Rabbit 103* anti B. sporogenes 46	Rabbit 668† anti B. sporogenes 54	Rabbit 1013† anti B. sporogenes 94	Rabbit 116† anti B. sporogenes 115	Rabbit 681† anti B. sporogenes 118	Rabbit 770* anti B. sporogenes 133
10	+(1:5120)	+(1:80)	+(1:5120)	+(1:5120)	+(1:1280)	+(1:640)
42	+(1:5120)	+(1:80)	+(1:1280)	+(1:2560)	+(1:1280)	+(1:640)
44	+(1:5120)	+(1:40)	+(1:2560)	+(1:5120)	+(1:2560)	+(1:2180)
56	+++(1:5120)	+(1:40)	+(1:5120)	+(1:5120)	+(1:1280)	+(1:1280)
48	+(1:5120)	+(1:80)	+(1:1280)	+(1:5120)	+(1:640)	—(1:20)
52	++(1:5120)	+(1:160)	+(1:5120)	+(1:5120)	+(1:1280)	+(1:1280)
54	+(1:160)	+(1:5120)	+(1:640)	+(1:640)	—(1:20)	—(1:20)
58	++(1:5120)	+(1:80)	+(1:5120)	+(1:5120)	+(1:320)	+(1:640)
66	++(1:5120)	+(1:40)	+(1:5120)	+(1:5120)	+(1:640)	+(1:320)
72	++(1:5120)	+(1:160)	+(1:5120)	+(1:5120)	+(1:160)	+(1:1280)
74	++(1:5120)	+(1:80)	+(1:5120)	+(1:1280)	+(1:320)	+(1:1280)
84	+++(1:5120)	+(1:320)	+(1:5120)	++(1:5120)	+(1:1280)	+(1:2560)
88	++(1:5120)	+(1:160)	+(1:5120)	++(1:5120)	+(1:1280)	+(1:160)
90	+++(1:5120)	+(1:80)	+(1:5120)	+(1:5120)	+(1:1280)	+(1:640)
92	+++(1:5120)	+(1:160)	+(1:5120)	+(1:2560)	+(1:640)	+(1:320)
94	+++(1:5120)	+(1:80)	++(1:5120)	+(1:2560)	+(1:1280)	+(1:2560)
133	+++(1:5120)	+(1:160)	++(1:5120)	+(1:5120)	+(1:2560)	+(1:320)
114	++(1:5120)	+(1:80)	+(1:5120)	+(1:5120)	+(1:640)	+(1:1280)
115	+(1:5120)	+(1:320)	+(1:5120)	++(1:5120)	+(1:640)	+(1:640)
118	+++(1:5120)	+(1:160)	+(1:5120)	+(1:5120)	++(1:2560)	+(1:160)
121	+++(1:5120)	+(1:80)	++(1:5120)	+(1:1280)	++(1:640)	+(1:320)
122	+++(1:5120)	+(1:160)	++(1:5120)	++(1:5120)	+(1:1280)	+(1:2560)
133	++(1:5120)	+(1:160)	+(1:2560)	+(1:5120)	+(1:640)	+(1:2560)
150	+(1:5120)	+(1:80)	+(1:5120)	+(1:5120)	+(1:2560)	+(1:640)

* Highest dilution tested, 1:5,120.
† Highest dilution tested, 1:10,240.

There were marked differences in the limits of agglutination by these serums of the various cultures. Analysis of these data gave the results shown in table 4.

It would seem, from tables 3 and 4, that certain strains of B. sporogenes, for example, 46, 94 and 115, are capable of generating agglutinin having a wide range of application in detecting members of this species, while other strains, such as 54, 118, and 133, produce serums of much more limited applicability. Note the low titers secured with serum rabbit 668 anti B. sporogenes 54 with all except its homologous antigen, and several low titers and 3 failures to agglutinate at 1:20 with the serums prepared against cultures 118 and 133. In at least 2 of these we have cross agglutination proceeding in one direction only; serum homologous for culture 54 agglutinated cultures 118 and 133 at 1:160, but serum homologous for cultures 118 and 133 failed to agglutinate culture 54 at 1:20.

One may regard the tendencies shown by these 3 cultures particularly as an indication of antigenic specialization. B. sporogenes 54 especially deserves notice in this connection. Its serum, potent as it was for the homologous culture, agglutinated all other strains but only in relatively low dilutions. Likewise this culture was the least agglutinable by all the other serums, failing to agglutinate at all with 2 of them, as already noted.

TABLE 4

DISTRIBUTION OF CULTURES WITH RESPECT TO TITER-LIMITS FOR SIX SPOROGENES SERUMS

Titer Limits	Rabbit 103 anti B. sporogenes 46	Rabbit 668 anti B. sporogenes 54	Rabbit 1013 anti B. sporogenes 94	Rabbit 116 anti B. sporogenes 115	Rabbit 681 anti B. sporogenes 118	Rabbit 770 anti B. sporogenes 133
1:5120	23*	1	19	17		
1:2560	..	..	2	3	4	4
1:1280	..	..	2	3	9	6
1:640	..	..	1	1	7	6
1:320	..	2	..	..	2	4
1:160	1	8	..	..	1	2
1:80	..	10				
1:40	..	3				
1:20						
Negative 1:20	..	..	..	..	1	2

* These numbers indicate the number of cultures agglutinated at the titers shown.

The notion occurred to us that possibly B. sporogenes 54 might be able to combine with the agglutinins of serum prepared against culture 118 without flocculating in the test but no evidence for this could be secured. The serum of rabbit 681 anti B. sporogenes 118 when treated in a dilution of 1:10 with an excess of culture 54 at 37 C. for 2 hours, refrigerated overnight, and then centrifugalized, lost none of its agglutinating power for the homologous strain (118). It was exactly as active (1:2560) as an untreated dilution of serum included in the experiment as a control. On the other hand, serum similarly treated with culture 118 no longer agglutinated this culture at 1:20.

The interesting speculations suggested as to the complex nature of the antigenic properties of B. sporogenes should be further studied by means of absorption tests.

SUMMARY

Agglutinating serums of high potency for B. sporogenes are easily prepared by intravenous or subcutaneous injection of rabbits with glucose broth cultures. Rabbits suffer no ill effects from rapid immunization except slight loss of weight.

B. sporogenes serums are specific; they do not agglutinate other species. Seven serums prepared against different strains of B. sporogenes agglutinated most of the 24 strains tested against them, but some of them failed to agglutinate certain strains of the species. There is a tendency toward strain specificity, more marked in some strains than in others. Positive tests properly controlled identify, but negative tests may not differentiate some members of this species, except antigenically.

Serums for several other species of obligate anaerobes failed to agglutinate B. sporogenes.

THE SPECIFICITY OF THE STREPTOCOCCUS OF GASTRODUODENAL ULCER AND CERTAIN FACTORS DETERMINING ITS LOCALIZATION

Edward C. Rosenow

From the Division of Experimental Bacteriology, The Mayo Foundation, Rochester, Minn.

In previous papers I have shown that ulcer of the stomach in man and in domestic animals often is associated with a streptococcus infection in the ulcerated area, that foci of infection, such as in tonsils and teeth, harbor the streptococcus and predispose to ulcer, and that the streptococcus isolated from the ulcer and from the distant focus has elective affinity for the stomach, producing hemorrhage and ulcer on intravenous injection.[1] The character of the experimentally produced ulcers, and their location, especially with regard to nonhealing, resemble those noted in the spontaneous diseases. Among the difficulties encountered in my earlier work was the inability to maintain specific infecting power and specific immunologic properties in the streptococcus isolated. Specific infecting power disappeared on successive animal passage or aerobic cultivation. It has been found since that relatively anaerobic conditions, and keeping the organisms in latent life, tend to preserve this property. Some of the strains were put aside under these conditions in the hope that they would live and maintain specific characteristics for a long time. It is my purpose here to record the results of a study of the localizing power, the mechanism involved, and the immunologic condition of several of the strains isolated years ago, of a fresh strain from a recurrent ulcer in man, and of a series of similar strains from experimental ulcers in dogs.

Technic

The technic was similar to that employed in my earlier studies on ulcer, and in other elective localization studies. It consisted essentially of making cultures in a medium affording a gradient of oxygen pressure (tall tubes of glucose-brain-broth), and of injecting the primary cultures if pure; if not, of plating on blood-agar incubated at from 33 to 35 C. for from 12 to 18 hours, when single colonies were fished, and glucose-brain-broth inoculated for the injection of animals. The usual dose injected intravenously consisted

Received for publication, June 12, 1923.

[1] Jour. Infect. Dis., 1916, 19, p. 333; 1923, 32, p. 384.

of 5 c c. of the young, actively growing cultures (from 3 to 18 hours) in this medium. In order to maintain specific localizing power, subcultures were made as soon as growth occurred, often from 5 to 8 times each day; and for future study, they were made by inoculating tall tubes of ascites-tissue-agar, ascites-tissue-fluid, meat infusion, or ascites-glucose-agar. The animals that survived the injection were usually chloroformed for immediate examination in from 2 to 3 days. To avoid the struggle which the animals make when chloroformed, they were anesthetized in a covered pail filled with chloroform vapor.

For immunization purposes, freshly isolated strains from foci of infection, or from the ulcers that developed following intravenous injection, were grown in large amounts in 0.2% glucose-broth, and the centrifuged sediment drained free from the broth was suspended in glycerol-salt solution (C. P. glycerol, 2 parts, 25% salt solution, 1 part), so that 1 c c. contained the growth from approximately 100 c c. of glucose-broth culture. These dense suspensions were preserved in the ice chest, and the antigens for agglutination and immunization purposes were prepared from them from time to time as needed.

EXPERIMENTS ON THE LOCALIZATION OF OLD ULCER STRAINS

In studying the viability and infecting power of various old strains of streptococci, 2 of 3 strains from ulcer of the stomach in sheep, preserved in the original shake cultures in ascites-glucose-agar, were not only viable, but had retained specific power to produce lesions in the stomach of animals after 7½ years. One of these strains was studied extensively. Nine of 12 animals (10 rabbits and 2 dogs) developed hemorrhage or ulcer, or both, of the stomach or duodenum following intravenous injection of glucose-brain-broth cultures (table 1, strain 419). This affinity for the gastric mucosa was retained after 22 rapidly made subcultures. Characteristic lesions developed following injection of the heat-killed streptococcus and filtrates of glucose-brain-broth cultures (table 1). The controls injected with uninoculated broth brought to the same degree of acidity as the cultures with acetic acid and with filtrates of the uninoculated broth remained free from lesions.

Because of this remarkable result, experiments with a number of old human strains were instituted. The streptococcus in 4 cultures of 2 of these strains was viable after 8½ years. Cultures had been made of 1 of each of these on the surface of Loeffler's blood-serum slants, which had been sealed with paraffined corks, and 1 each in tall tubes of emulsified brain tissue, also sealed with paraffined corks. All produced diffuse growth in glucose-brain-broth, and small grayish green nonadherent colonies on blood-agar plates. Both cultures of one of the strains were without effect on intravenous injection in rabbits, whereas both cultures of the other strain had retained the power to produce hemorrhages with or without ulceration of the stomach in rabbits on intravenous injection (table 1, strain 112). This strain was isolated originally from a subacute duodenal ulcer Aug. 18, 1914. One culture had not been passed through animals; the other, through 3 animals. When first isolated the strain had marked affinity for the stomach and duodenum, producing hemorrhage and ulceration in nearly all of 4 rabbits, 9 dogs, and 1 guinea-pig injected intravenously in the 1st, 2d, and 3rd animal passages. The mortality was 30% at that time. The old cultures, after incubation for 24 hours, were kept in the dark at room temperature without transfer for 8½ years. Two series of experiments were made with the primary transplants from the old cultures. Seven of the 8 rabbits injected intravenously with 5 c c. each of the 24-hour culture in glucose-brain-broth developed hemorrhage or ulcer of the stomach or duodenum, without lesions elsewhere. One rabbit remained free from lesions.

Sixteen other rabbits were injected intravenously. Four received 5 c c. of the glucose-brain-broth culture, 4 a dense suspension of the living organism in sodium chlorid solution, representing the growth from 15 c c. of glucose-brain-broth in the 2d to the 6th rapidly made subcultures, 4 the heat-killed organism from 25 c c. for each rabbit, and four 20 c c. each of the corresponding filtrates. The 8 rabbits in the first 2 series, and all but 1 of the 4 injected with the filtrate developed lesions of the mucous membrane of the stomach. Aside from a few embolic lesions in the medulla of the kidney in 1, and small hemorrhages in the tricuspid valve in 2, no other lesions were found (table 1, strain 112).

TABLE 1

Incidence of Lesions of the Stomach or Duodenum, and of Other Organs Following Intravenous Injection of Living Cultures, Dead Bacteria and Filtrates of Broth Cultures of the Streptococcus of Ulcer

Strain	Source	Living Cultures			Dead Bacteria			Filtrate of Culture		
			Animals with Lesions in			Animals with Lesions in			Animals with Lesions in	
		Animals Injected	Stomach or Duodenum	Other Organs	Animals Injected	Stomach or Duodenum	Other Organs	Animals Injected	Stomach or Duodenum	Other Organs
419	Ulcer of sheep 7½ years ago............	12	9	5	2	2	1	2	2	0
112	Ulcer of duodenum in man, 8½ years ago..	16	15	3	4	4	0	4	3	1
4684	Tonsil in case of recurring ulcer............	22	20	3	4	3	2	6	5	0
4676	Ulcer of stomach in dog	17	17	4	4	3	0	13	10	0
4682 4685 4689 4744	Ulcer of stomach in dog	12	11	2	..	..	..	..	..	..
	Total..............	79	72	17	14	12	3	25	20	1

Only 1 of the 24 rabbits injected died from the effects of the injection; the others were chloroformed 2 days after injection. The blood in 20 of the 24 was sterile; in the others, it yielded the streptococcus. The strain had thus lost nearly all of its general invasive power, and the lesions were not so pronounced as those produced when the strain was isolated 8½ years before, but were similar in character following injection of the living and heat-killed organisms and the corresponding filtrates (fig. 1 *a, b, c*). The streptococcus was demonstrated in some areas of hemorrhage and in the margins of ulcerations in animals in which the living and dead streptococci were injected, but no bacteria were demonstrated in the lesions in animals injected with the filtrate.

After 9 rapidly made subcultures, only 1 of 4 rabbits developed hemorrhage of the stomach and duodenum; 2 developed mild embolic lesions in the medulla of the kidneys, and 1 had no lesions.

LOCALIZATION OF A FRESHLY ISOLATED STRAIN

Through the coöperation of Dr. Eusterman of the section on gastro-enterology in the Mayo Clinic, I have had the opportunity of studying the localizing power of the streptococcus, freshly isolated, from the tonsils of a patient with recurring ulcer. The patient, a young man, had come to the clinic a year before giving a typical history of ulcer. Ulcer of the duodenum was found, a gastro-enterostomy was performed, and complete relief from symptoms of ulcer followed. No

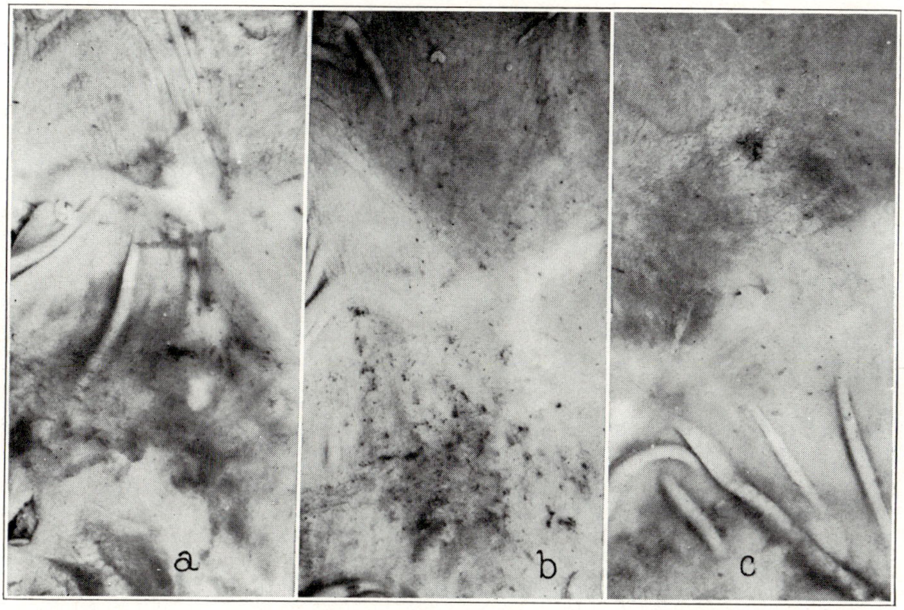

Fig. 1.—Lesions in the stomach of 3 rabbits following intravenous injection of, *a*, the living streptococcus which had been kept in latent life for 8½ years; *b*, the heat-killed organisms, and *c*, the corresponding filtrate of the glucose-brain-broth culture. Note the hemorrhages and varying degree of ulceration. (× 1.)

attention was given to foci of infection. Eleven months afterward symptoms of ulcer recurred, and the patient returned to the clinic one month later. Roentgenograms revealed an ulcer at the gastrojejunal juncture, and one along the lesser curvature of the stomach. The tonsils were large and hyperemic, and from the crypts a moderate amount of pus was expressed. A roentgenogram revealed 4 pulpless teeth, with well marked areas of rarefaction around the apexes of each. The tonsils and the infected teeth were removed in 4 sittings. Coincidental with the removal of the foci of infection, and medical management of the ulcer, the patient's symptoms subsided, and marked evidence of healing ensued.

The suspension, in sodium chlorid solution of the pus expressed from the tonsils, directly injected, produced ulcer in the 2 rabbits inoculated. The primary culture, and the 2d, 3d, 4th, 5th, and 6th rapidly made subcultures produced ulcer in nearly all animals injected. The ulcers were often situated in the lesser curvature (fig. 2*a* and *c*). Of the 12 rabbits injected with the living streptococcus soon after isolation, 10 developed lesions of the stomach, and only 3 had lesions

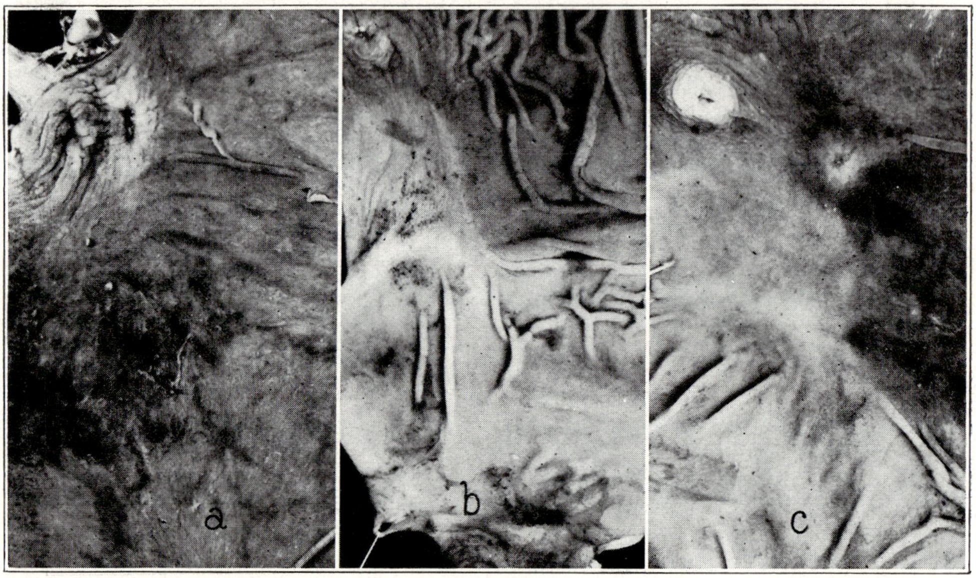

Fig. 2.—*a* and *c*, ulcer of the stomach in rabbits following intravenous inoculation of the freshly isolated culture of the streptococcus from the tonsil in the case of recurring ulcer, and *b*, the corresponding filtrate. Note the marked necrotic margins of well-formed ulcers near the cardiac orifice following injection of the living culture and the hemorrhagic ulcer near the pylorus following injection of the filtrate. (× 1.)

elsewhere, 1 of which consisted of a few hemorrhages in the appendix, 1 of hemorrhages in the tricuspid valve, and 1 of a few hemorrhagic lesions in the tendinous ends of muscles and fascia. Ten rabbits injected with this strain after 1 animal passage, and after preservation in ascites-tissue-agar stabs for from 1 to 3 months, developed ulcer with or without hemorrhages. Thus, of a total of 22 rabbits, 20 developed gastric lesions (table 1, strain 4684). Four rabbits were given the killed cultures; of these, 3 developed lesions of the stomach;

1 also developed hemorrhages in the fascia around the knee joints, and 1 hemorrhages of the tricuspid valve only. Six rabbits were injected with filtrates of actively growing cultures; of these, 5 developed hemorrhage of the stomach with or without ulceration (fig. *2b,* and table 1). Two rabbits received the filtrate after shaking with animal charcoal, and 2 the dialyzed filtrate. One of the former and both of the latter developed hemorrhage and ulcer of the stomach, with no lesions elsewhere.

Similar results were obtained by Dr. Nakamura with the living streptococcus isolated from the extirpated tonsils, and by him and Dr. Meisser with the streptococcus isolated from 3 of the infected teeth. Of the 28 rabbits injected by them, 23 developed lesions of the stomach, and a few lesions elsewhere. The washing in sodium chlorid solution of the apical end of 1 of the teeth sufficed to produce lesions of the stomach in 2 rabbits, from both of which the streptococcus was recovered, whereas the animals injected as controls with equivalent amounts of the sodium chlorid solution used in preparing the washing remained free from lesions.

ISOLATION AND LOCALIZATION OF THE STREPTOCOCCUS FROM ULCER IN THE DOG

Mann and Williamson[2] have developed a method of producing chronic ulcer in dogs. This consists essentially of transplanting the duodenum into the ileum and anastomosing the jejunum to the pyloric end of the stomach. The alkalization and other functions of the duodenum are thus circumvented. In dogs operated on in this manner, chronic ulcer develops with a good deal of regularity in the jejunum just beyond the line of anastomosis. The experimental ulcers have many of the features of chronic ulcer in man. A microscopic study of some of the experimental ulcers revealed circumscribed areas of leukocytic and round-cell infiltration far from the ulcerated area, in which gram-positive diplococci were demonstrable. On the basis of these findings, and the fact that I had previously found that spontaneous ulcer in the dog was due to a streptococcic infection, the hypothesis that these ulcers may be due to infection made possible through dysfunction induced by the operative procedure presented itself. It was thought worth while, therefore, to make a bacteriologic study of ulcers produced by the method of these investigators, and to determine the localizing power of the bacteria isolated. Moreover, since I had found that foci of infection in teeth and tonsils predispose to ulcer in man,

[2] Ann. Surg., 1923, 77, p. 409.

and apparently in the dog and the cow, a thorough search for foci of infection was made in the dogs operated on, and if found, the localizing power of the bacteria was also studied.

Cultures have been made thus far in 7 ulcers removed during exploratory operations or after death. In all cultures there have been streptococci resembling those previously isolated in spontaneous ulcer in the dog and in man. Cultures from the normal mucous membrane removed during the primary operation have not yielded the streptococcus in any of 5 instances. B. Welchii and less commonly B. coli are usually found in small numbers in both the ulcers and the normal

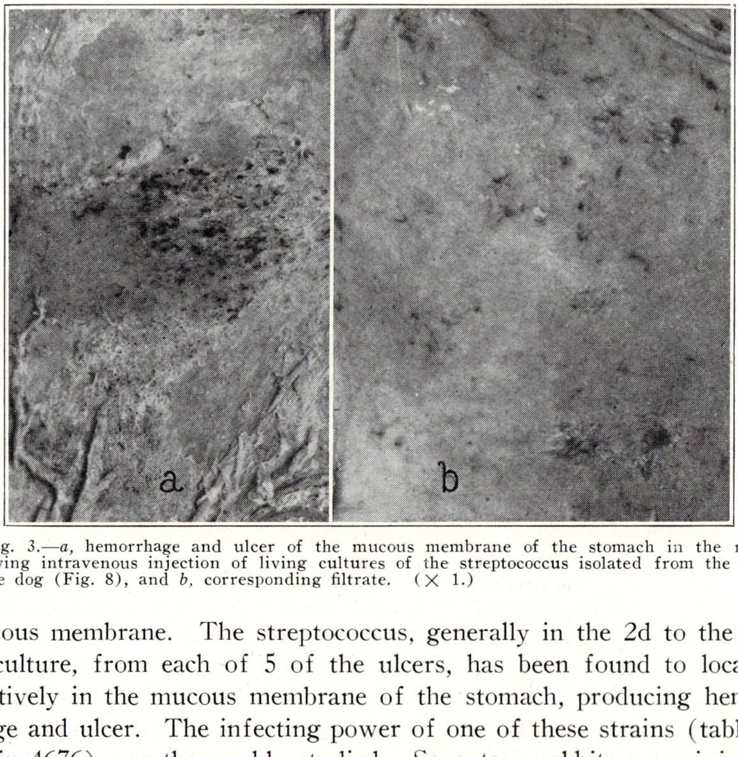

Fig. 3.—*a*, hemorrhage and ulcer of the mucous membrane of the stomach in the rabbit following intravenous injection of living cultures of the streptococcus isolated from the ulcer in the dog (Fig. 8), and *b*, corresponding filtrate. (× 1.)

mucous membrane. The streptococcus, generally in the 2d to the 3rd subculture, from each of 5 of the ulcers, has been found to localize electively in the mucous membrane of the stomach, producing hemorrhage and ulcer. The infecting power of one of these strains (table 1, strain 4676) was thoroughly studied. Seventeen rabbits were injected intravenously with the living culture (3 to 12 c c. each). Of these, all developed hemorrhage or ulcer, or both, of the stomach. Characteristic localization occurred following injection of the strain in the primary culture, in the 29th, 32d, 42d, 50th, and 53rd rapidly made subcultures (fig. 3*a*). It followed injection of the acid glucose-brain-broth culture as well as after neutralization with sodium hydroxide, and occurred in the 2 dogs injected. Only 4 animals developed lesions in other organs, and these were slight. The heat-killed organism from the 53rd rapidly made subculture, suspended in sodium chlorid solution, in amounts representing the growth of from 20 to 60 c c. of the broth culture, was injected into 4 rabbits. Of these, 3 developed lesions of the stomach, and none lesions elsewhere.

The filtrate of broth cultures in the 42d, 50th, and 53rd subcultures was injected into 13 rabbits in doses ranging from 12 to 60 c c. Of these, 10 developed lesions of the stomach, which often resembled those shown in figure *3b,* and none lesions elsewhere (table 1, strain 4676). Only 1 of 8 rabbits injected with equivalent amounts of the same batches of broth, and of the broth brought to the same degree of acidity as the culture, developed hemorrhage of the stomach.

The results following injection of the living organism of the other 4 strains were similar (table 1). Of the 12 rabbits injected, 11 developed lesions of the stomach, and only 2 had lesions elsewhere.

The findings in 1 of the dogs, which had a perforating ulcer, are noteworthy. A search for foci of infection revealed marked pyorrhea, with retraction of the gums, and absorption of the alveolar processes of 6 lower incisors. All of the teeth were loose. From the pus aspirated from the pyorrheal pockets, from the apexes of 2 of these teeth, and from the corresponding alveolar sockets, a streptococcus was isolated which resembled the one isolated from the emulsion of the ulcer, and it produced hemorrhage or ulcer of the stomach in 4 rabbits injected.

SUMMARY OF LOCALIZATION EXPERIMENTS AND THE MICROSCOPIC STUDY OF THE ULCERS

The lesions of the stomach were similar in type and location following injection of the streptococcal strains from the different species of animals. The hemorrhages were usually multiple and often widely distributed (figs. 1*b* and 3*a*). Well-formed ulcers were found most commonly along the lesser curvature, and in the pyloric third. Usually only one ulcer was found (figs. 1*c*, and 2*a* and *c*), but in some instances there were multiple ulcers (figs. 1*a*, and 3*a* and *b*). The lesions were less marked following injection of the old sheep and human strains and the recently isolated dog strains than following injection of the freshly isolated human strain.

Of the 79 animals injected with the living culture, 72 (91%) developed lesions of the stomach, and only 17 (21%) lesions in other organs. The mortality was low; only 5 of the 79 animals died from the effects of the injection. The slight general invasive power of these strains is further shown by the fact that the streptococcus was isolated from the blood in only 14 (18%) of the animals injected. Cultures were made of ulcers or hemorrhagic areas in 29 instances, and the streptococcus was isolated in 22.

Of the 14 rabbits injected with the dead bacteria, killed by heating to 60 C. for 1 hour, or with 0.2% formalin for 24 hours and then washed, 12 (85%) developed lesions of the stomach. Of the 25 injected with filtrates of actively growing cultures of the acidity of the cultures, or after neutralization, 20 (80%) developed hemorrhage or ulcer, or both, of the stomach. The lesions following injection of the dead bacteria and filtrates of cultures were usually less marked than those following injection of the living cultures; and in animals chloroformed 3 days after injection, healing was already evident. Cultures of the blood of the 39 animals injected with the dead bacteria or with the filtrate and cultures of emulsions of the mucous membrane of the stomach of 6 that developed lesions did not yield the streptococcus in a single instance.

The results with the living cultures, the dead bacteria, and the filtrates of these ulcer strains were in sharp contrast to those obtained with control freshly isolated encephalitis strains, and the corresponding dead bacteria and filtrates. Thus, of 12 rabbits injected with the live cultures of the encephalitis strains, only 2 developed lesions of the stomach, and these were relatively slight. None of 6 injected with the dead bacteria and the filtrates, respectively, developed lesions of the stomach. Moreover, as a further check, equivalent amounts of the same batches of uninoculated broth and of broth brought to the acidity of the cultures, filtered and unfiltered, were injected into 12 rabbits. Of these, only 2 developed small hemorrhages of the stomach without ulceration. Lesions of the stomach such as those observed with these ulcer strains have not been found in the examination of a large number of rabbits chloroformed for examination following intracerebral inoculation of the streptococcus from encephalitis, and in uninoculated rabbits chloroformed as controls in encephalitis experiments.

The microscopic study of sections through hemorrhagic and ulcerated areas showed, mainly, dilatation of vessels in the submucosa and mucosa, and large and small localized hemorrhages, almost always associated with a variable degree of leukocytic infiltration. The areas of hemorrhage or infiltration were usually situated near the surface of the mucous membrane, but at times were found in the deeper layers between the tubules, and in the submucosa.

The nuclei of the epithelial cells of the mucosa over the infiltrated areas before ulceration occurred and for a short distance along the margin of well-formed ulcers had lost their affinity for basic strains, and as sloughing occurred the cells became necrotic and disintegrated. Occasionally an accumulation of leukocytes in small vessels in the submucosa was found, but never well-formed thrombi. Emboli of streptococci in capillaries were never encountered. The demonstration of organisms in the lesions was not always easy, especially after marked ulceration had occurred, but it was accomplished in some ulcers that were induced with each of the strains. In this series, as in my former studies, the number of bacteria was largest in necrotic tissue just before ulceration took place (figs. 4 and 9). The amount of infiltration varied greatly, but was usually not extensive. Diffuse infiltration of mucous membrane was never found, and perforating ulcers with infiltration of the muscular and peritoneal coats were rare. The margins of the ulcers

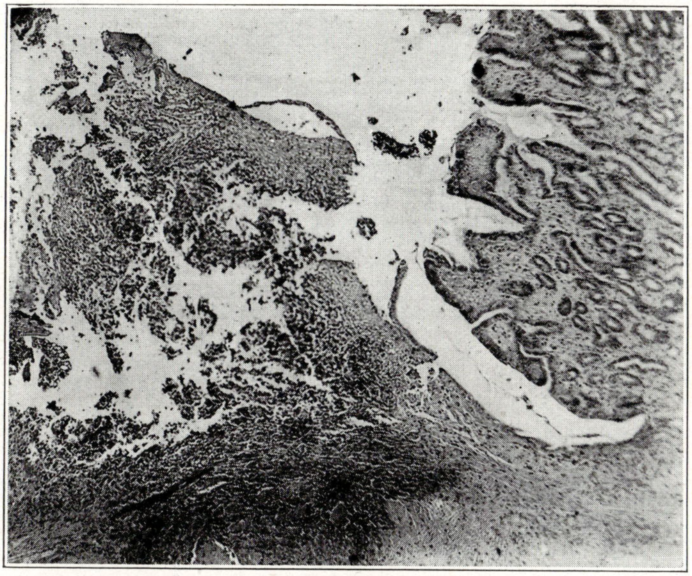

Fig. 4.—Section of ulcer in rabbit shown in figure *2a* following injection of the living culture. Note the marked leukocytic infiltration and the accompany necrosis. Hematoxylin and eosin. (× 50.)

were often undermined. The character of the ulcers following injection of the dead bacteria and the filtrates was similar to that after injection of the living cultures. The amount of leukocytic infiltration, however, was more marked in the latter. These points are well illustrated in the sections of ulcers shown in figures 4, 5, 6 and 7.

The study of sections of the ulcers induced by the operative procedure in dogs is not yet completed. In those examined, areas of

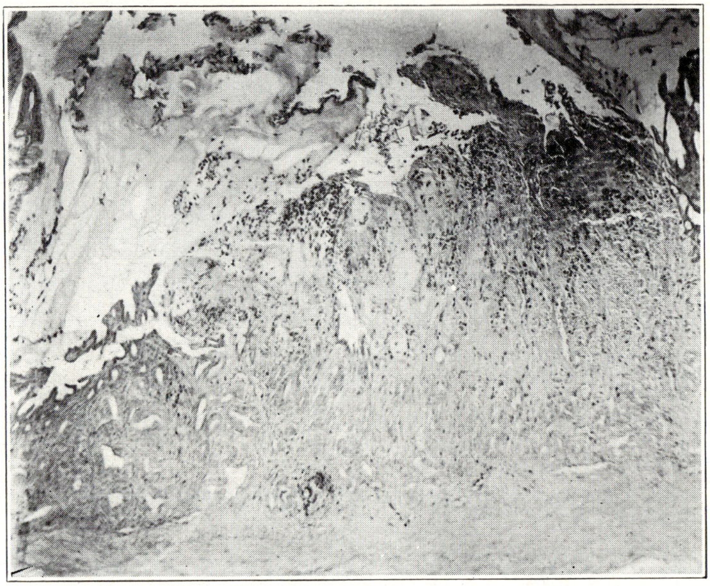

Fig. 5.—Section of ulcer near the pylorus shown in figure *2b* following injection of the filtrate of the culture injected into the rabbit that developed the ulcer shown in figures *2a* and 4. Note the relatively slight leukocytic infiltration, and the nonstaining of nuclei. Hematoxylin and eosin. (× 70.)

leukocytic and round-cell infiltration, in which the streptococcus was demonstrable, were found remote from the ulcerated surface (figs. 8, and *9a*), and in peritoneal adhesions in perforating ulcers.

IMMUNIZATION AND PROTECTIVE EXPERIMENTS

Not only was there marked similarity in the localizing power of the old strains from sheep and man and the recently isolated strains from ulcer in man and dog, but the cultural characteristics were also very similar. Since we seemed to have a method whereby specific localizing power could be maintained, it was thought worth while to immunize animals with antigens prepared from the different strains, and to ascertain whether immunity against ulcer might be induced by vaccination, and if so, to determine the immunologic similarity or dissimilarity of the streptococcus of ulcer. The ulcer and the control encephalitis antigens used for immunization purposes were prepared from cultures which produced, respectively, ulcer and encephalitis on intravenous injection into animals. In the protective experiments, the

Fig. 6.—Section of ulcer of rabbit shown in figure *3a* injected with the living culture of the streptococcus from the ulcer in the dog (fig. 8) after 29 rapidly made subcultures. Note the leukocytic infiltration in, and associated sloughing of, the mucous membrane. Hematoxylin and eosin. (× 70.)

rabbits that survived the test injections were chloroformed for immediate examination on the third day.

In the series of experiments summarized in table 2, large, normal rabbits, weighing about 2 kilograms, were selected and placed in suitable cages in groups of 4. They were fed clover, hay, oats, cabbage, and water. The immunizing injections were given intravenously during the forenoon several hours before the daily feeding. Each rabbit received 6 immunizing injections from 3 to 5 days apart, over a period of 17 days. The first 2 injections consisted of 1 and 2 c c., respectively, of the heated (60 C.) glucose-brain-broth culture inoculated from the growth in ascites-tissue-agar stabs layered with oil; the next 4 received, respectively, 3, 4, 5, and 5 c c. of the living culture. Five days after the 6th immunizing dose, 2 rabbits in each group were etherized, bled to death for serum, and examined for lesions; none was found. The others, with normal controls, were given the test injection of 5 c c. of the 18-hour cultures in glucose-brain-broth of, respectively, the old and the recently isolated strains preserved in deep stabs in ascites-tissue-agar. All animals that survived were chloroformed for immediate examination 48 hours later.

TABLE 2

SUMMARY OF IMMUNIZATION EXPERIMENTS AGAINST ULCER OF THE STOMACH IN RABBITS WITH OLD (8½ YEARS) AND RECENTLY ISOLATED STRAINS OF STREPTOCOCCI FROM HUMAN ULCER

Rabbit	Immunizing Strain	Test Strain	Lesions of the Stomach	Result
	Human Ulcer, Old Strain			
4074	112	4684	0	Appeared well; no lesions
4078	112	4684	+	Appeared well; moderate number of sharply circumscribed hemorrhages in the cardiac end of the stomach, and one small ulcer of the lesser curvature
4079	112	112	+	Appeared well; several small hemorrhages with beginning ulceration of the stomach; one hemorrhage in the tricuspid valve
4140	0	112	+	Appeared well; one deep hemorrhagic ulcer along the lesser curvature 2.5 cm. from the pyloric ring
4141	0	112	+	Appeared well; groups of small hemorrhages with slight ulceration in the stomach; small punctate hemorrhages surrounding the papilla of Vater
	Human Ulcer, New Strain			
4080	4684	112	0	Appeared well; no lesions
4081	4684	112	0	Appeared well; no lesions
4082	4684	4684	0	Appeared well; no lesions
4083	4684	4684	0	Appeared well; no lesions
4138	0	4684	+	Died in 24 hours; numerous large and small hemorrhages of the cardiac end of the stomach, associated with marked postmortem digestion
4139	0	4684	+	Died in 48 hours; numerous large and small hemorrages of cardiac end and the pyloric end of the stomach, associated with marked postmortem digestion

The results were striking. In the animals injected with the old ulcer strain, moderate immunity had developed against both the homologous organism (rabbit 4079) and the more virulent recently isolated strain (rabbits 4074 and 4078); and complete immunity against both the homologous and heterologous strain followed repeated injections of the recently isolated strain. The normal controls (rabbits 4138 and 4139) died with pronounced lesions of the stomach, whereas those immunized (rabbits 4080, 4081, 4082 and 4083) remained well and were free from lesions.

The rabbits selected in the experiment summarized in table 3 were all healthy animals, weighing about 2 kilograms each. The rabbits were injected with 5 c c. of the 18-hour cultures, at approximately the same rate, into the marginal ear vein during the forenoon several hours before they were fed. One c c. of the respective serums was given

TABLE 3

PROTECTIVE POWER OF IMMUNE RABBIT SERUM AGAINST ULCER OF THE STOMACH

Rabbit	Strain Injected	Serum Used for Treatment	Lesions of the Stomach	Results
4152	4684	0	+	Appeared well; localized hemorrhages in the pyloric ring and along the lesser curvature
4153	4684	0	+	Died in 24 hours; numerous small hemorrhages in the pyloric one third of the stomach, in the first 3 cm. of the duodenum, in the ileum, and in the appendix
4154	4684	Normal rabbit	+	Died in 24 hours; moderate number of hemorrhages along the lesser curvature of the stomach, in the first 2 cm. of the duodenum, in the descending colon, in the appendix, and in the ileum
4155	4684	Normal rabbit	+	Appeared well; small hemorrhage in the duodenum around the papilla of Vater, and one ulcer, with edematous walls, near the cardiac orifice
4156	4684	Rabbit immunized with Strain 112	0	Appeared well; no lesions of stomach, nor elsewhere
4157	4684	Rabbit immunized with Strain 112	+	Died in 24 hours; moderate number of hemorrhages in the stomach and in the descending colon, and a few in the ileum and the appendix
4158	4684	Rabbit immunized with Strain 4684	0	Appeared well; no lesions of stomach, nor elsewhere
4159	4684	Rabbit immunized with Strain 4684	0	Appeared well; no lesions of stomach, nor elsewhere
4160	112	0	+	Appeared well; 2 hemorrhagic ulcers along the lesser curvature, 1.5 cm. from the pyloric ring
4161	112	0	+	Appeared well; a few hemorrhages in the pyloric ring and in the papilla of Vater
4162	112	Normal rabbit	+	Appeared well; beginning ulceration in an area of infiltration 2.5 cm. from the pyloric ring
4163	112	Normal rabbit	+	Appeared well; 3 hemorrhagic ulcers, the largest along the lesser curvature, all 1 to 1.5 cm. from the pyloric ring
4164	112	Rabbit immunized with Strain 4684	0	Appeared well; no lesions of stomach nor elsewhere
4165	112	Rabbit immunized with Strain 4684	0	Appeared well; no lesions of stomach, nor elsewhere
4166	112	Rabbit immunized with Strain 112	+	Appeared well; two hemorrhagic ulcers 0.5 cm. from the pyloric ring
4167	112	Rabbit immunized with Strain 112	+	Appeared well; 1 hemorrhagic ulcer 2 cm. from the pyloric ring along the lesser curvature, 1 small hemorrhage in the pylorus, and a few small hemorrhages in the tricuspid valve

immediately after the injection of the culture, and repeated every 12 hours thereafter. Each lot of serum used for treatment was a mixture of the serums from 2 immunized and 2 normal rabbits, respectively.

The immune serum prepared with the recently isolated and relatively virulent ulcer strain (4684) protected completely against itself (rabbits

4158 and 4159) as well as against the one isolated $8\frac{1}{2}$ years before (rabbits 4164 and 4165). In the case of the homologous strain, both rabbits treated with this serum remained well, and no lesions of the stomach developed, whereas all of the controls, 2 without serum (rabbits 4152 and 4153) and 2 treated with normal rabbit serum (rabbits 4154 and 4155), developed lesions of the stomach. One in each group succumbed to the injection (rabbits 4153 and 4154). The serum prepared with the old ulcer strain had no protective effect against the

Fig. 7.—Section of ulcer shown in figure *3b* following injection of the filtrate of actively growing culture in the forty-second rapidly made subculture. Note the nonstaining of the nuclei, and slight infiltration beneath the sloughing area. Hematoxylin and eosin. (× 90.)

recently isolated strain in one rabbit (rabbit 4157), but appeared to afford definite protection in the other (rabbit 4156). It failed to protect against the homologous strain. The 2 rabbits injected (rabbits 4166 and 4167) developed lesions in the stomach which were about as marked as in the 4 controls, 2 untreated (rabbits 4160 and 4161) and 2 treated with the normal rabbit serum (rabbits 4162 and 4163).

The antigens used in the immunization experiments recorded in table 2 were freshly prepared, and consisted of, first, the dead, and later, the live cultures in glucose-brain-broth. Those used in the experiments summarized in table 4 were prepared by diluting dense glycerol sodium chlorid solution suspensions made from the freshly isolated strains grown in glucose-broth with sodium chlorid solution to the density of the broth culture, or 2,000,000,000 for each c c., and heating to 60 C. for 1 hour. The number and size of the immunization injections and the test inoculation were the same as in the series recorded in table 2, but in the series recorded in table 4 only dead bacteria were injected. The dense glycerol sodium chlorid solution sus-

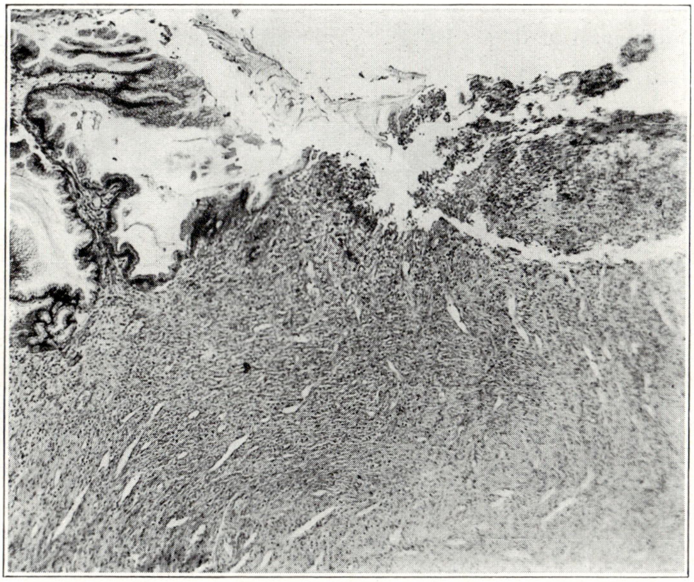

Fig. 8.—Section of ulcer in the dog yielding the streptococcus strain 4676. Note the marked leukocytic infiltration and fibrosis, extending beyond the margin of the ulcer. Hematoxylin and eosin. (× 50.)

pension of the human strain (4684) had been kept in the ice chest for 3 weeks. Antigen 4694 represented a mixture of 8 human strains from ulcer, preserved in the dense glycerol suspension for from 6 months to 1½ years; antigen 4695 consisted of a mixture of 5 dog strains which had been preserved in the glycerol suspension for from 2 to 6 weeks; and antigen 4688 represented 1 encephalitis strain preserved for 6 weeks in the glycerol suspension, and which produced encephalitis on intravenous injection when suspended in the glycerol sodium chlorid solution.

From the experiments summarized in table 4, it is seen that immunization with the heat-killed organisms from human ulcer (rabbits 4191, 4193, 4207, and 4208) afforded complete protection, and from the dog ulcers, partial protection (rabbits 4214 and 4215) against ulcer following injection of the recently isolated strain from recurrent ulcer in man, and that the encephalitis antigen was without effect (rabbits 4199 and 4200). The lesions of the stomach in these rabbits were as marked as in the unvaccinated controls (rabbits 4305 and 4306). The test human strain was in the 5th subculture. In a similar manner, protection was afforded against injection of the living streptococcus from ulcer in the dog (4676). This strain was in the 52d rapidly

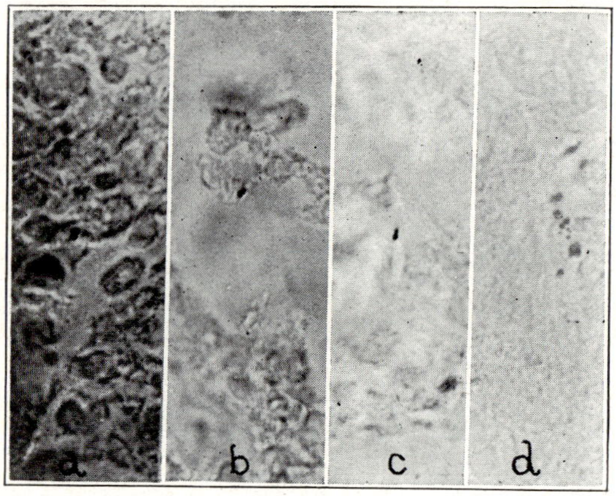

Fig. 9.—Diplococci in tissue, *a* and *b*, of ulcer shown in figure 4; *c*, of ulcer shown in figure 6, and *d*, of ulcer shown in figure 8.

made subculture. The antigens prepared from the recently isolated human strain and the dog strains protected completely (rabbits 4194, 4227, 4217, and 4218); the one representing human ulcer strains preserved for a long time in glycerol protected partially (rabbits 4209 and 4210), whereas the encephalitis strain had no protective power (rabbits 4201 and 4202), the lesions in these rabbits being as marked as in the uninoculated controls (rabbits 4307 and 4308). The results following injection of the control encephalitis streptococcus (4688) were in sharp contrast. Ulcer developed in only 1 of the 6 rabbits injected (rabbit 4335), and this one also developed encephalitis, associated with paralysis of the hind extremities, marked edema of the lungs, and severe spasms of the stomach. The other control (rabbit 4336)

TABLE 4

Summary of Immunization Experiments Against Ulcer of the Stomach in Rabbits Following Injection, Respectively, of Human and Ulcer Strains

Rabbit	Immunizing Strain of Streptococcus	Test Strain	Lesions of the Stomach	Results
		Human Ulcer		
4305	0	4684	+	Appeared well; thick layer of mucus covering the pylorus; small hemorrhages in the cardiac end of the stomach, and in the pylorus; blood and brain sterile
4306	0	4684	+	Appeared well; small hemorrhages in the cardiac end of the stomach; blood and brain sterile
	Human ulcer			
4191	4684	4684	0	Appeared well; no lesions of the stomach, nor elsewhere; blood and brain sterile
4193	4684	4684	0	Appeared well; no lesions of the stomach; a few embolic lesions in the medulla of the kidney; blood and brain sterile
4207	4694	4684	0	Appeared well; no lesions of the stomach, nor elsewhere; blood and brain sterile
4208	4694	4684	0	Appeared well; no lesions of the stomach, nor elsewhere; blood and brain sterile
	Dog ulcer			
4214	4695	4684	+	Appeared well; a few punctate hemorrhages in the cardiac end of the stomach; blood and brain sterile
4215	4695	4684	0	Appeared well; no lesions of the stomach, nor elsewhere; blood and brain sterile
	Encephalitis			
4199	4688	4684	+	Appeared well; numerous punctate hemorrhages near the cardiac end of the stomach, some with beginning ulceration
4200	4688	4684	+	Appeared well; large and small hemorrhages in the pyloric end of the stomach, and hemorrhagic infiltration of muscular layer; blood sterile
		Dog ulcer		
4307	0	4676	+	Appeared well; numerous small hemorrhages in the cardiac end of the stomach, and a few in the duodenum; blood and brain sterile; hemorrhagic mucous membrane yielded the streptococcus
4308	0	4676	+	Died in 48 hours; marked hemorrhages along the lesser curvature, and extreme postmortem digestion of the stomach; blood and brain sterile
	Human ulcer			
4194	4684	4676	0	Appeared well; no lesions of the stomach; a few embolic lesions in the medulla of the kidney; blood and brain sterile
4227	4684	4676	0	Appeared well; no lesions of the stomach nor elsewhere; blood and brain sterile
4209	4694	4676	+	Appeared well; one deep indurated ulcer with necrotic base along the lesser curvature; blood and brain sterile
4210	4694	4676	0	Appeared well; a few embolic lesions in the kidneys; no lesions of the stomach; blood sterile
	Dog ulcer			
4217	4695	4676	0	Appeared well; no lesions of the stomach, nor elsewhere; blood sterile
4218	4695	4676	0	Appeared well; no lesions of the stomach, nor elsewhere; blood sterile
	Encephalitis			
4201	4688	4676	+	Appeared well; a few hemorrhages in the pyloric end of the stomach
4202	4688	4676	+	Appeared well; one hemorrhagic ulcer 2 cm. from the pyloric ring, and a group of hemorrhages with beginning ulceration along the lesser curvature; blood sterile
		Encephalitis		
4335	0	4688	+	Complete paralysis of hind extremities; tremulous; excitable; stomach in marked spasm; necrotic ulcer along the lesser curvature; edema of lungs; cultures of blood sterile; those of the brain yielded the streptococcus injected
4336	0	4688	0	No lesions of the stomach, nor elsewhere; cultures of blood sterile; those of the brain yielded the streptococcus injected
	Human ulcer			
4248	4684	4688	0	Tremulous and excitable; no lesions of the stomach, nor elsewhere; cultures of the blood and the brain yielded the streptococcus injected
4249	4684	4688	0	No lesions of the stomach, nor elsewhere; cultures of the blood sterile; those of the brain yielded the the streptococcus injected
	Encephalitis			
4253	4688	4688	0	No lesions of the stomach, nor elsewhere; cultures of the blood and the brain sterile
4259	4688	4688	0	No lesions of the stomach, nor elsewhere; cultures of the blood and the brain sterile

remained free from symptoms, but cultures from the brain yielded the characteristic streptococcus. The human ulcer vaccine had no apparent effect in preventing localization of the encephalitis coccus in the brain, 1 of the two rabbits injected developing symptoms of encephalitis, and both yielding the organism from the brain in cultures (rabbits 4248 and 4249). The encephalitis vaccine, however, protected completely (rabbits 4253 and 4259) against invasion of the brain, the animals remaining free from symptoms, and the cultures sterile.

Other similar experiments on 2 subsequent dates gave essentially the same results. In these the immunizing effect of filtrates, of partially autolyzed organisms in the case of the human ulcer strain, and of ether-killed encephalitis organisms was tested. Repeated injection of the filtrates was without effect. The ulcer antigen, in which all of the organisms had become gram-negative from autolysis in sodium chlorid solution under ether over a period of 10 days at 37 C., had some protective action, but this was not as marked as following immunization with the gram-positive heat-killed organisms. The encephalitis antigen prepared in a similar manner, but in which the organisms had not autolyzed, protected completely against homologous, and one heterogeneous but immunologically similar, encephalitis strain.

Of the 18 rabbits injected intravenously with the freshly isolated encephalitis strain as controls, 6 were normal rabbits, and of these 2 developed marked symptoms of encephalitis, and all but 1 yielded the organism from the brain when the blood was sterile. Seven had had repeated injections of ulcer vaccines. Of these, 2 developed symptoms of encephalitis, and 4 yielded the characteristic streptococcus from the brain. Five were immunized with encephalitis vaccines. Of these, none developed symptoms, and cultures from the blood and the brain remained sterile in all. Lesions of the heart valves were found in only 2 instances, and in joints and muscles in 3. This was in sharp contrast to the results following intravenous injection of the ulcer strains. Of 55 rabbits receiving injections during the immunization experiments, none developed symptoms of encephalitis, and cultures from the brain made in 28 proved sterile in each instance (table 5). As a further check on the significance of these results, control cultures were made of the brain and the blood of 8 uninjected normal rabbits; all the cultures remained sterile.

In a later series of experiments, it was found that 2 of the encephalitis strains had largely lost the power of producing encephalitis on intravenous injection, and had acquired moderate affinity for the stomach, producing hemorrhage or ulcer in 6 of 10 rabbits injected. The agglutinating power had not changed, both strains still being agglutinated specifically by the encephalitis and the poliomyelitis serums.

Animals immunized with ulcer antigens were not protected against lesions of the stomach following the injection of the encephalitis strains that had acquired affinity for the gastric mucosa.

In summarizing all immunization experiments with the dog and the human ulcer strains and the 2 encephalitis strains (table 5), we find that the incidence of lesions in the stomach following injection of ulcer strains in normal rabbits was 82%; in rabbits immunized with the

TABLE 5
SUMMARY OF IMMUNIZATION EXPERIMENTS

Test Strains	Rabbits		Animals Injected	Localization: Stomach	Localization: Brain
Ulcer		Normal	28	23 82%	0
	Immunized	Ulcer vaccine	23	4 17%	0
	Immunized	Encephalitis vaccine	7	6 86%	0
Encephalitis		Normal	12	2 17%	9 75%
	Immunized	Ulcer vaccine	6	0	4 67%
	Immunized	Encephalitis vaccine	6	0	0

encephalitis vaccine, it was 85%, whereas in those immunized with the ulcer vaccine it was only 17%; and localization in the brain did not occur in a single instance. Following the injection of the freshly isolated encephalitis strains, localization in the stomach occurred in 2 of twelve, 17%, and in the brain in nine, 75%, of 12 normal rabbits injected. In 6 rabbits immunized with the ulcer vaccine, no lesions of the stomach were found, but in four, 67%, localization in the brain occurred, whereas following immunization with the encephalitis vaccines, localization did not occur in either the brain or the stomach.

SUMMARY AND CONCLUSIONS

The experimental studies reported here corroborate and extend my earlier results with regard to the importance of the streptococcus as a causative factor in ulcer. The maintenance of specific infecting and localizing power under relatively anaerobic conditions in latent life for as long as 8½ years, I believe, has important bearing on the question of the chronicity of ulcer and on recurring exacerbations after intervals of quiescence. The streptococcus of ulcer produces a poison within its substance and free in broth cultures, which injures selectively the mucous membrane of the stomach, producing hemorrhages, leukocytic infiltration, and ulcer. Hence, localization and growth of the living organism in the mucous membrane of the stomach may be favored by this specific poison.

The presence of the streptococcus in the ulcers in dogs, produced by the method of Mann and Williamson,[3] its elective localizing power on intravenous injection, its presence in foci of infection, and its ability to produce this poison in vitro, indicate that it is not a secondary invader, but that it plays an important part in the production of these ulcers.

The results of the immunization experiments indicate that the streptococci from ulcer, even of different species, are closely related and probably specific of this disease; that a practical method for preserving specific antigenic power has been developed, and that active and passive immunization should prove helpful in the prevention and treatment of gastroduodenal ulcer in man.

IMMUNOLOGIC ALTERATION OF BACTERIUM TYPHOSUM AND OF BACILLUS PESTIS-CAVIAE BY GROWTH IN STERILE FIXATION ABSCESSES

E. E. Ecker and Emerson Megrail

From the Departments of Pathology, and of Hygiene and Bacteriology, School of Medicine, Western Reserve University, Cleveland, Ohio.

Recently Blankenhorn, Ecker and King[1] described a serum resistant typhoid bacillus from a tibial abscess. This organism was not only poorly agglutinable by heterologous antiserums, but also by homologous antiserum. It readily stimulated the formation of agglutinins, and was capable of specific absorption. We have kept it for a period of 17 months on plain agar, and found that it has maintained its original characteristics. McIntosh and McQueen[2] isolated a similar organism from the blood stream, and in this case the homologous antiserum also failed to agglutinate but did agglutinate ordinary Bacterium typhosum. Their nonagglutinable strain absorbed the agglutinin from homologous antiserum. A similar strain is reported by Toyoda,[3] also isolated from the blood stream of the patient. Gay and Claypole[4] showed that a typhoid bacillus from the blood of suspected carrier rabbits failed to be agglutinated by strong antiserum, and that passage of a readily agglutinable culture through a rabbit reduced its agglutinability. They further found that even subcultures of typhoid bacilli on rabbit-blood agar or on bile broth led to inagglutinability. The blood and bile cultures, however, are as readily agglutinable as agar strains by the serums of rabbits immunized against blood cultures. In this respect, then, the change of Gay's organism is less profound than that of the organisms described before. The occurrence of serum resistant forms is by no means uncommon, and little is known about conditions under which these variations take place or, as just pointed out by Larson and Greenfield,[5] about the nature of the mechanism of the alteration. In view of these facts, it was thought of interest to try to produce these changes by growing an organism to which the mouse is resistant and an organism to which it is not resistant in sterile fixation abscesses.

Technic.—A 5% suspension of gum tragacanth as recommended by Benians[6] gave a too lumpy suspension for use, but a 2% suspension was free from lumps and readily passed through the needle of a syringe. The suspension was sterilized (Arnold) for 3 successive days. The hair of the mice on the dorsal region near the tail was clipped closely and the skin painted with tincture of iodin. Approximately 0.5 c c. of the gum suspension was injected subcutaneously. All experiments were made in duplicate. Twenty-four hours later material was withdrawn from the sterile abscess, plated to test the

Received for publication, June 9, 1923.

[1] Jour. Infect. Dis., 1923, 32, p. 95.
[2] Jour. Hyg., 1914, 13, p. 409.
[3] Centralbl. f. Bakteriol., I, O., 1922, 88, p. 539.
[4] Jour. Am. Med. Assn., 1913, 60, p. 1141.
[5] Proc. Soc. of Exper. Biol. & Med., 1923, 20, p. 348.
[6] Brit. Jour. Exper. Path., 1921, 2, p. 276.

sterility, and smears made for phagocytes. Injections were then made of 0.1 c c. and 0.3 c c. of a 24-hour culture of the organism used (Rawlings strain of typhoid bacillus). The organism was left in the abscess for 48 hours, plated on a modified eosin methylene-blue medium, broth cultures made from the colonies, as indicated by reaction on Russell's tubes, and the shape, and the same amount of broth culture as before injected into other mice having a like sterile abscess produced the previous day. This procedure was carried out until the Rawlings strain had been through 10 mice. The mice were apparently not affected by the organism and none died during the experiment or for several months afterward. In the case of B. pestis-caviae, the same method was carried out through 3 mice, but the bacillus was kept in the 4th and 5th mouse for 24 hours only because of the serious condition of the animals at the end of that period. The first 3 pairs of mice died 72 hours after the inoculation, and the last 2 pairs were killed immediately after the withdrawal of the material from the abscess. From the 10th mouse in the typhoid series, the organism was obtained after it had been in the mouse for 6 days, and it was obtained also after 30 days in the mouse. It could not be obtained after 40 days.

The original Rawlings strain was grown in broth plus 10% gum tragacanth for 10 days, and the abscess strain passed 10 times through mice was grown for 31 generations on glycerol agar at intervals of 1 to 2 days.

Cultural Characteristics.—When the original Rawlings strain, the 10 times transferred strains, and the gum tragacanth broth strain were compared, it was found that there was no change in general morphologic characteristics. There was no change in cultural reaction in bromcresol-purple milk, litmus milk, lead acetate agar, blood serum, gelatin, or indol production. All 4 strains fermented dextrose, galactose, maltose, levulose, mannite and glycerol in the same time. None fermented lactose, saccharose or arabinose. All showed acid production in the closed tube in xylose broth after several days' incubation, but not in the open tube. No cultural comparison was made of the B. pestis caviae strains.

TABLE 1

MAXIMAL AGGLUTINATION AT THE END OF 2, 4 AND 24 HOURS OF ABSCESS STRAINS OF BACTERIUM TYPHOSUM (RAWLINGS) AS COMPARED TO THE ORIGINAL STRAIN AND THE ORIGINAL STRAIN GROWN IN GUM TRAGACANTH BROTH

Strains	2 Hours	4 Hours	24 Hours	Controls
Original (Rawlings)	400+++	700+++	900+++	0
Abscess 1	300+	300++	300+++	0
Abscess 3	300+	400++	200+++	0
Abscess 5	50+	300++	400+++	0
Abscess 7	100+	50++	200++	0
Abscess 9	100+	300++	300+++	0
Abscess 10	300+	200+++	300+++	0
Gum broth strain	200++	600+++	900+++	0

0 indicates no agglutination; +, slight agglutination; ++, marked agglutination; +++, complete agglutination, clear supernatant fluid.

Serologic Characteristics.—All the agglutination tests were made by the macroscopic method with carefully prepared suspensions of live bacteria of the same density. Five-tenths c c. of each serum dilution, and 0.5 c c. of the bacterial suspension were mixed. Readings were made at the end of 2 and 4 hours at 37 C. and 24 hours at room temperature. The antiserums were prepared by 4 intravenous injections of rabbits with live organisms in dosages from 0.2 to 0.5 c c. The animals were bled at the end of 7 days following the last injection. The serums were heated at 56 C. for one-half hour. Controls were made by suspending 0.5 c c. of the live culture in 0.5 c c. of salt solution. Table 1 gives the results of agglutination of the original Rawlings strain as compared with that of the strains of the 1st, 3rd, 5th, 7th, 9th, and 10th transfers, and the gum tragacanth broth strain. The maximal degree of agglutination or titer of complete agglutination have been tabulated for the various periods stated.

From this experiment it is evident that all the abscess strains have a reduced agglutinability, No. 7 giving only a 2 plus agglutination at a dilution of 1:200 of the antiserum. The gum tragacanth broth strain, although slowly agglutinating in the first 2 hours, reaches the same titer as the original strain.

In a second experiment, 4 strains were again compared, namely: the original Rawlings, the 10th abscess strain, the 10th abscess strain after 30 days in the abscess, and a 10th abscess strain grown for 31 generation on glycerol agar (table 2).

TABLE 2

MAXIMAL AGGLUTINATION AT THE END OF 2, 4 AND 24 HOURS OF THE RAWLINGS STRAIN COMPARED WITH THE 10TH TRANSFERRED ABSCESS STRAIN, THE TENTH PLUS 30 DAYS' STRAIN, AND THE 10TH ABSCESS STRAIN GROWN FOR 31 GENERATIONS ON GLYCEROL AGAR

Strains	2 Hours	4 Hours	24 Hours	Controls
Original (Rawlings)	600+++	600+++	800+++	0
Abscess 10	100++	100+++	100+++	0
Abscess 10 plus 30 days	50++	100+++	100+++	0
Abscess 10 grown on glycerol	300+++	400+++	600+++	0

Again the abscess strains show reduced agglutinating capacity. Subcultures of the 10th abscess strain on glycerol agar have practically brought its agglutinating capacity back to normal, although not completely. It was found that the flakes of this strain were very finely granular, so that some tubes had the appearance of sedimentation. No such sedimentation occurred in the control tubes.

TABLE 3

AGGLUTINATION OF 3RD AND 5TH ABSCESS STRAINS OF B. PESTIS CAVIAE AS COMPARED WITH THE ORIGINAL STRAIN

Strains	2 Hours	4 Hours	24 Hours	Controls
Original B. pestis caviae	1,500+++	1,500+++	1,500+++	0
Abscess 3	100++	100+++	100+++	0
Abscess 5	50++	100+++	100+++	0

As the mouse is comparatively resistant to Bacterium typhosum, we attempted to induce the same changes in a strain of B. pestis caviae, which is shown by Webster[7] to be virulent for mice. In this series the differences were still greater. Table 3 demonstrates the relative insusceptibility of the abscess strains of this organism to agglutinins. Eight transplantations of the abscess 5 strain of B. pestis caviae on glycerol agar restored its agglutinability so that it was agglutinated in a serum dilution of 1:400.

[7] Jour. Exper. Med., 1923, 37, p. 269.

We injected rabbits with the abscess strains in order to determine the antigenic capacity of such poorly agglutinable strains. Antiserums thus obtained readily agglutinated heterologous strains, but only weakly the homologous. An antiserum produced by injection of the abscess 5 strain of B. pestis caviae completely agglutinated the original strain in a dilution of 1:1,000 while the homologous strain was agglutinated only in a dilution of 1:100. These results are in agreement with those of Blankenhorn, Ecker and King, McIntosh and McQueen and of Toyoda.

We also found that the variants completely absorb the specific agglutinins. Larson and Greenfield[5] found that staphylococci grown on glycerol broth become serum resistant and then have but little absorptive power.

Preparations from contents of the abscesses showed that on every passage phagocytosis diminished, the resistance of the bacteria to phagocytosis apparently being increased greatly. We were unable to demonstrate any capsule formation by Fontana's method and a methylene-blue capsule stain. Material from the contents of the abscess 10 mouse was inoculated into broth for 24 hours, filtered through a Berkefeld N candle and the sterile filtrate added to the original Rawlings strain and to B. dysenteriae shiga. No lysis occurred.

DISCUSSION

The problem underlying the immunologic changes of these organisms is intricate. As shown by Yanagisawa,[8] a strain of typhoid grown in 10% typhoid immune serum for 27 generations or normal serum for 21 generations becomes less agglutinable than an ordinary agar strain. The same strain grown in an immune mouse had an increased agglutinability, and cultivation on plain agar did not lower its agglutinability. Evidently, then, the tissues or fluids of the animal have contributed something toward this alteration. In our studies the changes have been a uniform lowering of agglutinability, although not as complete as in the case of the organism isolated from the human tibial abscess. The inagglutinability was greater in the case of B. pestis caviae abscess strains. Of considerable interest is the fact that the serums against the abscess strains agglutinate their antigenic strains weakly, a fact which we observed in the tibial abscess strain also, and which to a certain extent differentiates our induced alteration from that of Gay and Claypole's strains. We agree with Larson and Greenfield that Ehrlich's conception of a simple suppression of receptors does not adequately explain the phenomenon. McIntosh and McQueen believe that there is change of physical character rather than a loss of receptor which makes the organism more resistant to certain physicochemical states, and Larson and Greenfield attempt an explanation on the basis of increase of acetone-ether soluble substances by virtue of which the bacteria resist wetting and support

[8] Japan Medical World, 1923, 3, p. 19.

themselves on the surface of the medium by surface tension. Later we intend to present a study of the hydrogen-ion concentrations at which the resistant and normal strains agglutinate.

SUMMARY

It has been possible to induce relative inagglutinability of Bacterium typhosum and of B. pestis-caviae in sterile gum tragacanth fixation abscesses in mice.

The alteration was more profound in the case of B. pestis-caviae than in the case of Bacterium typhosum.

No marked changes in absorption capacity were observed.

Antiserum produced against the abscess strains only weakly agglutinates these strains, while the original strains are readily and strongly agglutinable.

No marked cultural changes occurred.

STUDIES ON THE THERMAL DEATH TIME OF SPORES OF CLOSTRIDIUM BOTULINUM *

3. DORMANCY OR SLOW GERMINATION OF SPORES UNDER OPTIMUM GROWTH CONDITIONS

GEORGINA S. BURKE

From the Laboratory of Experimental Medicine, Stanford University Medical School, San Francisco

It has long been recognized that under unfavorable conditions bacterial spores lie dormant for considerable periods of time. Usually, however, it has been assumed that it was only necessary to place them under optimum conditions in order to bring about rapid germination. The possibility that bacterial spores, like seeds of certain higher plants, may lie dormant for long periods of time under optimum growth conditions has not been generally recognized.

Evidence of such dormancy in spores of Cl. botulinum was first observed in shake agar transplants from an old meat culture. In some of the tubes no growth occurred within the usual incubation period of 24 hours at 37½ C. or 48 hours at 28 C. The first colonies did not appear until the end of the first week, and additional colonies developed at intervals during the second week. Thereafter the culture became clouded, preventing further observations. The agar was apparently favorable for growth, as shown by the behavior of transplants from other stock cultures in the same lot of medium. Barber [1] in working with single spores noticed a difference in the germination time, but attributed the lag to differences in tubes of medium from the same batch.

The slow germination in my culture, however, was apparently due to causes within the spores themselves, since individual spores within the same tube varied in their germination time. The importance of this observation in its bearing on the slow germination of heated cultures and also its similarity to the behavior of certain seeds was recognized. The following experiments were planned to determine whether dormancy under optimum growth conditions, such as occurs in seeds of plants, is characteristic of normal (unheated) spores of Cl. botulinum.

Received for publication, June 28, 1923.

* These experiments are a part of an investigation of botulism which is being made in California by the U. S. Public Health Service, Leland Stanford Junior University and the University of California, under a grant from the National Canners' Association, the Canners' League of California and the California Olive Association.

[1] Jour. Exper. Med., 1920, 32, p. 295.

The cultural method of determining germination time, with an average of one spore in each of a series of tubes, was adopted because it ensured favorable anaerobic environment and permitted observation over an indefinitely long period, neither of which was possible with the hanging drop technic. The one objection to the cultural method is the fact that actual germination of the spore cannot be observed, hence the period of dormancy recorded is the time required for the spore to germinate and for the resulting bacillus to multiply sufficiently to produce visible colonies in agar or clouding of broth. However, since growth once visible seems to increase as rapidly in a culture which develops after several months as in one that grows in 24-48 hours, it seems probable that not more than 3 days elapse between the actual germination of the spore and the appearance of visible growth in the culture.

TECHNIC OF THE EXPERIMENT

Stock Spore Culture.—The stock spore bottles were inoculated from a meat culture of strain 58, type A, of the Stanford series, originally isolated by Dr. Robert Graham from olives used in the Detroit outbreak of 1919. The spores were grown in cotton stoppered quart bottles of glucose peptic digest broth [2] and pea gelatin.[3] The column of medium in the bottles was 4 or 5 inches deep, rendering the use of an oil or petrolatum layer unnecessary for anaerobic conditions, which greatly facilitated the handling of the spores and eliminated oil as a factor in dormancy. The bottles were incubated in the dark at 37½ C. for two weeks and thereafter at room temperature, 18-26 C.

Dilution.—The number of spores and vegetative forms per c c. in the stock culture were counted in a spore counting chamber, and dilutions were made in broth in order to obtain a suspension containing 1 spore per 0.5 c c. of broth. In order to reduce as far as possible the errors in pipetting from the highly concentrated *(265 to 600 million per c c.)* stock spore culture, the dilutions were stepped down in a series of 1 : 10 dilutions, 1 c c. of the spore suspension being transferred each time to 9 c c. of broth, and care being taken to measure exactly and to rinse down spores which might cling to the glass. The method proved sufficiently accurate for practical purposes, as shown by the fact that only one colony developed in most of the agar tubes and that of the estimated number of spores in each of the 3 series, respectively, the germination of 84, 99 and 84% was recorded. Obviously, however, with this technic no conclusions can be drawn from the tubes which have remained sterile.

Inoculation of Tubes.—One half c c. of the final spore suspension, which was estimated to contain one spore for each 0.5 c c. of broth, was run into each of a series of tubes containg 3 c c. of glucose peptic digest agar (series 1 and 2)

[2] Park and Williams: Pathogenic Microorganisms, 1920, edition, p. 117. To this stock broth, 0.5% K_2HPO_4 and 1% glucose are added, and the reaction adjusted to give a post-sterilization titer of PH 7.0 to 7.5.

[3] Peas, shelled and ground, are mixed with water in the proportion of 1 pound to each liter of water. The mixture is boiled for ½ hour, strained, and 10% gelatin added. After the gelatin is entirely melted, the reaction is adjusted to give a post-sterilization titer of PH 7.0 to 7.5.

and glucose peptic digest broth, without oil stratification (series 3). All the agar was from a single lot of medium and the broth from another lot.

Soft glass tubes (3/8 inch diameter) were used. They were of uniform make, carefully washed, neutralized and sterilized before filling with the medium in order to prevent as far as possible variations in the reaction of individual culture tubes. Hydrogen-ion determinations on the contents of a series of tubes prepared in this way failed to show any appreciable variation between tubes filled from the same batch of medium.

The culture tubes were heated for 20 minutes at 100 C., chilled before inoculation, and immediately sealed in an oxygen flame after inoculation. This insured favorable anaerobic conditions and prevented the possibility of subsequent contamination. The heat of sealing produced a partial vacuum in the tubes, which probably favored growth in the broth series, since the column of broth was too shallow to permit anaerobic growth in an unsealed tube without oil stratification. Growth in the deeper levels of the agar tubes, however, was independent of the partial vacuum, and it may be noted here that the colony which appeared on the 92nd day lay below the anaerobe line level for an unsealed culture.

It was assumed that the bacilli which were carried over with the spores into the suspension would multiply rapidly when placed in fresh medium and would, therefore, not be a factor in slow germinating tubes. The number of bacilli was so small, 0.4% to 2.8% of the number of spores, as to offer little interference in observing the slower spore germination. Consequently, since it was desired to determine the occurrence of dormancy in unheated spores, no attempt was made to destroy the vegetative forms by heat. Thus heat injury is not a factor in the slow germination recorded in this experiment.

Incubation.—The agar cultures (series 1 and 2) were incubated for 6 weeks and the broth for 2 weeks at 37½ C., in the dark. Thereafter from July to November all the tubes which remained apparently sterile were kept at room or outdoor temperature in the dark. The temperature was about 20 C. during the day except for a few days in the summer, when it rose as high as 35 C. In September, just before the 144-day spore germinated, the night temperature dropped to 5 C.

Recording the Growth.—The tubes were examined daily. No cracked tubes were recorded. In some agar tubes 2 to 4 colonies appeared during the first week of incubation, and in such cases only those colonies were recorded which were isolated definitely from other growth in the tube. In the majority of agar tubes, however, only one colony appeared although the tubes were kept under observation as long as clear readings were possible. Growth in the broth tubes was necessarily recorded as growth from one spore although, judging by the distribution of spores in the agar series, some of the broth tubes certainly contained several spores. Hence the number of germinating spores recorded for series 3 during the first 2 weeks of incubation is somewhat too low, a point which has to be borne in mind in comparing the results of the 3 series.

It was obviously impossible to distinguish the growth arising from the small number of vegetative forms, transferred with the spores from the stock culture, from growth resulting from the germinated spores. Since, however, the estimated percentage of bacilli was very small (1.3% series 1, 2.8% series 2, 0.4% series 3) and it was assumed that they would multiply so rapidly in the fresh medium as not to be a factor in slow germinations, they were ignored, and all growth was recorded as spore germination.

The germination time of individual spores as indicated by the number of spores germinating from day to day is given in table 1.

A toxin-antitoxin test was made of the broth from the culture which developed after 144 days and a strong type A toxin was demonstrated by means of subcutaneous injection into guinea-pigs.

TABLE 1

LENGTH OF DORMANCY OF INDIVIDUAL SPORES AS INDICATED BY THE DAILY RECORD OF THE APPEARANCE OF GROWTH IN THE TUBES

Incubation Time in Days	No. of Spores Germinating			Incubation Time in Days	No. of Spores Germinating		
	Series 1 Agar 260 Tubes	Series 2 Agar 260 Tubes	Series 3 Broth 280 Tubes		Series 1 Agar	Series 2 Agar	Series 3 Broth
1	1	0	0	23	0	0	1
2	21	5	1*	24	1	..	2
3	41	42	8	25	..	..	1
4	51	30	12	26	..	..	2
5	29	42	13	27	..	..	1
6	20	41	11	28	..	..	1
7	9	18	13	29	..	..	1
8	14	28	19	30	..	1	2
9	13	12	20	31	..	..	1
10	7	15	16	32	..	..	1
11	4	11	11	33	..	..	1
12	3	3	16	35	..	..	1
13	1	2	26	36	..	..	1
14	2	1	12	39	..	1	1
15	1	1	4	41	..	..	1
16	..	2	8	47	..	1	1
17	..	..	7	66	..	..	1
18	..	..	3	71	1	..	..
19	1	1	4	83	..	..	1
20	..	..	6	88	..	..	1
21	..	..	2	92	..	1	..
22	..	..	2	144	..	..	1

* The number of germinations recorded for series 3 during the first month is probably too small, since each positive broth tube was necessarily recorded as growth from a single spore, whereas some of the tubes probably contained more than one spore.

DISCUSSION

The possibility of contamination was ruled out by the method of sealing the tubes. The median and temperature were favorable for growth, as shown by the fact that growth appeared in some of the tubes of each series within 24 to 48 hours, and that a majority (90%) of the spores developed within 10 to 15 days. The cultures were prepared in as uniform a manner as possible, and there is no reason for assuming that conditions were unfavorable in tubes in which slow germination occurred.

The bacilli present were few in number (approximately 1.5% of the recorded growth), and in all probability multiplied rapidly and were recorded within the first week; hence, they in no way affect the conclusions drawn and are ignored in this discussion.

The spores were not at any time heated above the incubation temperature of 37½ C. Therefore heat injury is not a factor in the experiment.

Approximately 2% of the spores (16 of the 715 recorded germinations) developed after the first month of incubation, and one produced no visible growth until the 144th day, almost 5 months after it had been placed in fresh medium under favorable growth conditions. This 144-day spore gave rise to growth which was in every way typical of Cl. botulinum and produced a strong toxin of specific type (type A), showing that the vegetative forms descended from it were normal. Ninety-two days was the longest germination observed in the agar series.

Certain normal (unheated) spores of Cl. botulinum are, therefore, capable of lying dormant under favorable growth conditions, producing no visible growth in the culture tube for as long as 92 days in agar and 144 days in broth. They may possibly lie dormant for a much longer time, for there is nothing in the present experiment indicating that either 92 or 144 days is the limit of dormancy for the species.

Within each series was a variation between the individual spores in the length of dormancy and in the relative number of spores germinating from day to day, the majority germinating within a relatively short period. These variations were in some cases observed within the same agar culture where the spores were under identical growth conditions.

Since spores placed under identical and optimum growth conditions vary in the length of time which they require to germinate and produce visible growth, their dormancy is apparently primarily dependent on factors inherent within the spore. In this discussion the primary dormancy is referred to as normal dormancy in distinction to a possible secondary dormancy due to external factors.

It is suggested in the experiment that the normal period of dormancy of the individual spore may be either prolonged or shortened by factors in the environment, such as type of medium and temperature changes. The influence of the type of medium is suggested by the fact that the spores of series 3 in broth germinated, as a whole, more slowly than spores of the same stock culture in agar, series 2. The effect of alternation of temperature is suggested by the behavior of the 144-day spore which, having remained dormant 52 days longer than any of the other spores, germinated immediately after exposure to a temperature of 5 C. for several nights, alternating with a 20 C. temperature during the day. Obviously, neither of the foregoing points is established, and one would scarcely be warranted in mentioning them were it not for their similarity to the behavior of the seeds of certain legumes.

According to Crocker[4] "dormancy in plants is common in three organs, seeds, spores and buds." Far more critical and analytic work has been done on dormancy in seeds than in either of the other forms. Because of their minute size, studies of individual bacterial spores are difficult to control and interpret; and the results of experimental work on dormancy in seeds are particularly helpful to the bacteriologist in suggesting lines of attack on the problem of dormancy.

Harrington,[5] studying the germination of "impermeable" seeds of certain leguminosae, defined impermeable seeds as those having seed coats so relatively impermeable to water at temperatures favorable for germination that they do not germinate within 10 days when placed under favorable germinating conditions. If this definition were applied to the spores of the present experiment, 22% of those germinating would be classed as impermeable. Harrington found the number of impermeable seeds varying from 11% to 97% in different lots.

Impermeable seed of certain clovers, kept between wet blotters in a germinaing chamber, lay dormant for 2 and 3 years, and some remained impermeable at the end of the third year. "It was impossible to estimate in advance what proportion of the impermeable seeds of a given lot would germinate under ordinary germinating conditions in any given length of time." Certain alternations of the temperature seemed to hasten, while others apparently retarded, germination. There are many other interesting observations in Harrington's report which cannot be revealed for lack of space, but which are pertinent to a study of bacterial spores.

The causes of dormancy in seeds are suggestive of possible conditions in bacteria, and are stated by Crocker as follows:

"1. Rudimentary embryos that must mature before germination can begin.

"2. Complete inhibition of water absorption.

"3. Mechanical resistance to the expansion of the embryo and seed contents by enclosing structures.

"4. Incasing structures interfering with oxygen absorption by the embryo and perhaps Co_2 elimination from it, resulting in the limitation of the processes dependent upon these.

"5. A state of dormancy in the embryo itself or some organ of it, in consequence of which it is unable to grow when naked and supplied with all ordinary germinative conditions.

"6. Assumption of secondary dormancy. It is rather generally recognized that some seeds capable of immediate germination can be thrown into a secondary dormancy by a period in a germinator lacking some one condition necessary for germination or involving a substance inhibiting germination or one hardening the colloids of the coat."

The structure of the bacterial spore is so little understood that it is impossible at present to speak with any certainty concerning the causes of their dormancy. Reasoning, however, from what is known

[4] Am. Jour. Botany, 1916, 3.
[5] Jour. Agric. Research, 1916, 6, No. 20.

of the resistance of spores to drying and to dye penetration and also from analogy with the results of Harrington's experiments, it would seem that the relative impermeability of the spore wall (whatever that may be) is probably one factor in dormancy. Since water is necessary for the coagulation of protein by heat, the relative impermeability of the spore wall may also determine the relative heat resistance of the individual spores. This brings us to a consideration of slow germinations as observed in series of heated cultures.

DORMANCY AND HEAT RESISTANCE

In 1918, I [6] observed slow germination in series of heated cultures of Cl. botulinum, the longest time recorded being 53 days. The germination time of the cultures in this series of tests increased regularly in direct proportion to the length of heat exposure, with two exceptions, which were however attributed to faulty technic. The conclusion was drawn, therefore, that exposure to heat retarded germination.

Dickson, Burke and Ward [7] reached similar conclusions. Weiss [8] and later Tanner [9] believed the spores were gradually injured by the heat. Dubovisky and Meyer [10] and Meyer and Esty [11] speak of germination as retarded by heat.

In recent experiments in this laboratory some 40,000 cultures, containing an average of 50,000,000 spores each, have been heated and incubated for over a year; and very long germination times have been recorded. The maximum germination times to date for the 3 types of medium, respectively, are as follows: 201 days for spores heated and incubated in sealed tubes of agar; 214 days for spores heated and incubated in sealed tubes of broth without oil; and 426 days for spores heated and incubated in sealed tubes of oil-stratified broth. The tubes of oil-stratified broth have been under observation longer than the others.

However, while the length of germination time in this series of tests, as in the 1918 series, has in general been directly proportional to the length of exposure to heat, exceptions have been the rule among cultures heated for relatively long periods of time. These irregularities were not due to faulty technic so far as could be determined, and they

6 J. A. M. A., 1918, 71, p. 518.
7 Arch. Int. Med., 1919, 24, p. 581.
8 Jour. Infect. Dis., 1921, 28, p. 70.
9 Jour. Bacteriol., 1923, 3, p. 269.
10 Jour. Infect. Dis., 1922, 31, p. 501.
11 Ibid., p. 650.

could not be explained on the hypothesis that slow germination was caused by heat injury. It became evident, therefore, that heat injury was not an adequate explanation of slow germination as observed in heated cultures, and that there must be some other factors influencing the germination of individual spores.

Recognition of slow germination or dormancy under optimum growth conditions, as a character of the normal unheated spore of Cl. botulinum, makes it necessary to review the subject and raises the question whether or not heat injury plays any part in the slow germination of heated cultures.

The factors, whatever they may be, which bring about dormancy in the unheated spore must obviously be considered the primary cause of slow germination in heated cultures; and heat, if it has any effect, must act as a secondary factor prolonging dormancy beyond the normal limit for the individual spore. Viewed primarily on the basis of normal dormancy, the direct relation between length of heat exposure and subsequent length of germination time, observed in series of heated cultures, indicates that dormancy and heat resistance are dependent on the same primary factor in the unheated spore. (As suggested above, the relative permeability of the spore wall is a possible common factor.) This conclusion seems to be in accord with all the facts, and harmonizes many things that could not be satisfactorily explained by the theory of heat inhibition.

Heat injury as a secondary factor prolonging the dormancy of the individual spores requires specific proof before it can be accepted, since the observations on which the heat injury hypothesis was originally based are more satisfactorily and simply explained on the basis of normal dormancy. The only remaining evidence in support of heat inhibition is the fact that the maximum germination time which has been observed for heated cultures is longer than that so far recorded for unheated spores in the same type of medium. (Compare 214 days for spores heated and incubated in sealed tubes of broth without oil stratification with the 144-day unheated spore culture in the same medium.) However, the number of unheated spores observed is so infinitely small in comparison to the number of heated spores that no conclusion can be drawn at present. I believe that further observations will furnish evidence of longer periods of dormancy for normal spores.

Unless definite experimental evidence can be brought forward in its favor, the heat injury hypothesis is unnecessary and, therefore, unwarranted, since all the known facts can be accounted for on the basis of normal dormancy.

DORMANCY AND FRACTIONAL STERILIZATION

Fractional sterilization during which the material is heated on 3 successive days is based on the belief that spores will germinate within 48 hours, i. e., before the 3rd period of sterilization. This method of sterilization has not always proved efficient, owing to the fact that frequently some of the spores survive the third sterilization.

Elizabeth Eckelmann [12] studied the germination time of various soil aerobes both in hanging drop preparation and on agar plates, and she found that all the spores of strains which could be destroyed by fractional sterilization germinated within 2 days (48 hours); but that the spores of strains surviving fractional sterilization required from 2 to 10 days to germinate, the majority developing between the 4th and 8th days. No record was kept beyond the 11th day.

Miss Eckelmann concluded that the ability of certain bacteria to survive fractional sterilization was due to the comparatively impermeable membrane of their spores which caused them to germinate slowly. She recommended that in order to obtain death of all spores fractional sterilization should be repeated on 7 successive days, and the material be kept at room temperature between sterilizations.

The present observations on the dormancy of normal spores of Cl. botulinum show that fractional sterilization at 100 C. for 1 hour or less on 3 successive days cannot be counted on to kill all botulinum spores. The long periods of dormancy recorded make it apparently impossible to work out any practical modification of the fractional method that will guarantee absolute sterilization for these organisms.

DORMANCY AND BACTERIOLOGIC RESEARCH

The problem of dormancy has a bearing not only on heat resistance and sterilization, but also on much of the experimental work dealing with spore-bearing bacteria.

Cultural methods of estimating the number of spore bearers in any given material, to be accurate, must take dormancy into account.

Dubovsky and Meyer [10] found that soil enrichment cultures containing less than 100 spores of Cl. botulinum rarely produced a strong toxin and often were entirely nontoxic after a 10-day incubation

[12] Centralbl. f. Bakteriol., 1917-18, 48, p. 141.

period. They state that toxin attains its maximum potency in 10 days, but they do not take into account the dormancy factor, and it is possible that a somewhat longer incubation period would have increased the number of toxic cultures.

Various investigators have experienced difficulty in obtaining growth from isolated spores. Barber, 1920,[1] attributes the negative cultures in his single spore sowings to the quality of the medium and to an apparent variation in the power of individual spores to adapt themselves to a new medium. He notes a "lag" or "tendency to latency" of from 1 to 8 days, in one experiment, which he thought in the case of two spores was due to washing in saline.

The present observations on dormancy in Cl. botulinum indicate that no conclusions can well be drawn from negative spore cultures until the limits of dormancy for the given species are established, and they emphasize the desirability of retaining negative cultures under observation for as long a time as possible in order that data concerning dormancy may be obtained.

CONCLUSIONS

The individual (unheated) spores in a given culture of Cl. botulinum vary in the time required for germination under optimum growth conditions. The majority germinate relatively quickly, but a few lie dormant for a longer time. One hundred and forty-four days is the maximum period of dormancy recorded here, but there is no evidence in these experiments to indicate that this is the limit of possible dormancy for the species.

Spores germinating after long periods of dormancy produce typical growth and strong toxin of specific type.

The behavior of dormant spores is suggestive of that of seeds of certain higher plants.

The primary factors which cause the spore to lie dormant for long periods of time under optimum growth conditions are believed to be inherent in the spore itself. It is thought that relative permeability of the spore wall is one of the factors. Environmental conditions may secondarily modify the period of dormancy.

The factors controlling dormancy in the unheated spore must be considered the primary cause of slow germination as observed in heated cultures. Heat injury, if it plays any part at all, must be a secondary factor prolonging the period of dormancy of the individaul spore beyond its normal limit.

Relative permeability of the spore wall is suggested as a possible common factor affecting both dormancy and heat resistance and accounting for the apparent relation which has been observed between length of exposure of the spores to heat and subsequent length of germination time.

Fractional sterilization as generally practiced does not insure absolute sterilization of material containing spores of Cl. botulinum because of the slow germination of many of the spores.

The problem of dormancy has a bearing on much of the experimental work dealing with spore-bearing bacteria, particularly that in which conclusions have been based on negative cultures.

THE INFLUENCE OF CHOLESTEROL ON PHAGOCYTOSIS

Ruth Tunnicliff

From the John McCormick Institute for Infectious Diseases, Chicago

Authors differ as to the effect of cholesterol on phagocytosis in vivo and in vitro. Walbum [1] concluded that it increases phagocytosis, while Stuber,[2] Dewey and Nuzum [3] found that it inhibited phagocytosis. The difference in results appears to be due to the amount of cholesterol used, Walbum's solutions of cholesterol being 20 times weaker than those used by the other investigators.

In my work Merck's pure cholesterol was used in a colloidal suspension prepared according to the method of Porges and Neubauer,[4] modified by Dewey.[5] To a solution of cholesterol dissolved in acetone warm distilled water was slowly added, the acetone removed by evaporation or boiling, and the suspension filtered. The suspensions were autoclaved for the in vivo experiments.

Normal human serum and leukocytes were used. The blood for the leukocytes was collected in 2% sodium citrate solution, centrifugated and washed twice with physiologic sodium chloride solution. A strain of Streptococcus viridans from measles was chosen which did not clump and which was not spontaneously phagocytable, yet not so virulent as not to be readily engulfed. The cocci were grown 24 hours on moist goat blood agar and the growth washed off with salt solution. Satisfactory suspensions were only slightly cloudy. The opsonic mixtures in capillary pipets were incubated 15 minutes, smeared on slides and stained with carbol thionin. One hundred polymorphonuclear leukocytes were counted and the number of cocci per leukocyte as well as the number of cells taking part in phagocytosis noted, these 2 methods giving similar results.

First, dilutions of cholesterol from 1 : 100 up were mixed with equal amounts of serum, washed leukocytes and bacterial suspensions. From these tests and the salt solution and serum controls, it was found

Received for publication, June 29, 1923.

[1] Ztschr. f. Immunitätsforsch. u. exper. Therap., 1910, 7, p. 544.

[2] Biochem. Ztschr., 1913, 51, p. 211; 53, p. 493.

[3] Jour. Infect. Dis., 1914, 15, p. 472.

[4] Biochem. Ztschr., 1908, 7, p. 152.

[5] Trans. Chicago Path. Soc., 1915, 9, p. 321.

that dilutions of cholesterol of 1 : 100 reduced phagocytosis one half, while dilutions from 1 : 500 to 1 : 2,000 promoted phagocytosis, the opsonic indexes ranging from 1.8 to 4.1. Next the cocci were sensitized with serum by suspending them in 10 times their volume of serum for 15 minutes at 37 C., washing and resuspending in salt solution. The sensitized cocci were now mixed with equal amounts of washed leukocytes and cholesterol suspensions. These mixtures, with salt solution controls, were incubated 15 minutes. Here again cholesterol diluted 1 : 500 to 1 : 2,000 gave a similar increase in the number of cocci ingested, as by the other method.

An effort was made to determine whether the action of the cholesterol was on the cocci or the leukocytes, by suspending each in cholesterol solutions 1 : 500 for 1 hour at room temperature, centrifugating, and washing twice in salt solution. Serum and leukocytes were then added to the sensitized bacteria, serum and cocci to the sensitized leukocytes. In each instance the number of cocci ingested was doubled.

Arkin [6] concluded from his experiments that cholesterol caused some phagocytosis in the absence of serum and reduced the opsonic power of normal serum probably by combining with the opsonins. I repeated his experiments, but found that cholesterol had no influence on phagocytosis in the absence of serum.

Leupold and Bogendörfer [7] found an increase in cholesterol during convalescence from infectious diseases and that cholesterol treated animals survived longer than controls. The cholesterol content of the blood rose to much above normal in these animals, but did not appear to promote phagocytosis, its protecting action lying in its faculty of binding bacterial toxins. According to these authors, cholesterol has the power to neutralize diphtheria toxin. As Wadsworth and Hoppe [8] demonstrated that diphtheria toxin had a depressing action on phagocytosis, which could not be neutralized by diphtheria antitoxin, their experiments were repeated, and other experiments were made to determine whether cholesterol could neutralize the depressing effect of diphtheria toxin on phagocytosis. Diphtheria antitoxin free from antiseptics, furnished by Dr. E. M. Houghton of Parke, Davis & Company, was used because antiseptics may inhibit phagocytosis. The results of such an experiment are illustrated in table 1. These tests were repeated 6 times, with similar results. The same results were obtained

[6] Jour. Infect. Dis., 1913, 13, p. 408.
[7] Deutsch. Arch. f. klin. Med., 1922, 140, p. 28.
[8] Jour. Immunol., 1921, 6. p. 399.

by first sensitizing the streptococci with serum. The experiments indicate that both cholesterol (1: 500) and diphtheria antitoxin can neutralize the depressing effect of diphtheria toxin on phagocytosis, normal horse serum having no such influence.

Two rabbits were injected intravenously with colloidal suspensions of cholestrol, one receiving 0.002 gm. per kilogram of weight, the other 0.016. Serum and leukocytes were collected before and one, 24 and 72 hours after the injection of cholesterol. The serum of a normal rabbit and of each cholesterinized rabbit was tested with leukocytes from both a normal and a cholesterinized rabbit, so as to determine both the opsonic and the cytophagic indexes. The cytophagic index

TABLE 1

NEUTRALIZATION BY CHOLESTEROL AND BY DIPHTHERIA ANTITOXIN OF THE DEPRESSION OF PHAGOCYTOSIS BY DIPHTHERIA TOXIN

Mixtures	Number of Cocci per Leukocyte
Equal parts of serum + leukocytes + salt solution + salt solution + streptococcus suspension	4.2
Equal parts of serum + leukocytes + cholesterol 1: 500 + salt solution + streptococcus suspension	9.7
Equal parts of serum + leukocytes + salt solution + diphtheria toxin + streptococcus suspension	1.7
Equal parts of serum + leukocytes + normal horse serum + diphtheria toxin + streptococcus suspension	2.2
Equal parts of serum + leukocytes + cholesterol 1:500 + diphtheria toxin + streptococcus suspension	4.3
Equal parts of serum + leukocytes + diphtheria antitoxin + diphtheria toxin + streptococcus suspension	3.7
Equal parts of serum + leukocytes + diphtheria antitoxin + salt solution + streptococcus suspension	4.8
Equal parts of serum + leukocytes + normal horse serum + salt solution + streptococcus suspension	4.2

in this case is the relation between normal serum and normal leukocytes, and normal serum and cholesterinized leukocytes, and indicates the relative activity of the leukocytes of the cholesterinized rabbit.

The rabbit receiving the small dose of cholesterol showed no appreciable increase in either the opsonic or the cytophagic index at the end of one hour. Twenty-four hours later the opsonic index was 2.2; the cytophagic index, 1.9. At the end of 48 hours, the opsonic index was 1.6; the cytophagic index, 2.2. Both the indexes were normal 72 hours after the injection of cholesterol.

The opsonic index of the rabbit receiving the larger dose was 0.8, the cytophagic index 0.6, one hour after injection; 24 hours later the opsonic index reached 0.44, and the cytophagic index 0.8. At the end of 48 hours the opsonic index was still low, 0.41; the cytophagic index, 0.67. Both indexes were normal 3 days later.

SUMMARY

Colloidal suspensions of cholesterol in dilutions of 1:100 inhibit, while dilutions of 1:500 to 1:2,000 appear to increase phagocytosis in vivo.

The intravenous injection of a small dose of cholesterol into rabbits has a stimulating effect on phagocytosis, while a larger dose may have a depressing influence.

The depressing effect of diphtheria toxin on phagocytosis appears to be neutralized by weak colloidal suspensions of cholesterol, as well as by diphtheria antitoxin.

TOXIN PRODUCTION AND SIGNS OF SPOILAGE IN COMMERCIALLY CANNED VEGETABLES AND FRUITS INOCULATED WITH DETOXIFIED SPORES OF B. BOTULINUS. XII *

P. Schoenholz, J. R. Esty and K. F. Meyer

From the George Williams Hooper Foundation for Medical Research, University of California, San Francisco, Calif., and the Research Laboratory of the National Canners' Association, Washington, D. C.

Epidemiologic investigations on botulism in the United States have aroused considerable discussion among public health workers, food packers, dealers and consumers concerning the liability of certain foods to favor the growth and toxin production of B. botulinus. It is now recognized that certain articles of food are more frequently implicated in outbreaks than others, but the reasons are obscure and still remain to be worked out. Early in the course of an analysis of the published and unpublished data dealing with the botulism problem, it was realized that the occurrence of B. botulinus toxin in containers was not only dependent on the presence of heat resisting spores of the anaerobe on the raw products and their survival, but also on the existence of certain physical and chemical conditions or factors essential to their germination and proliferation. Accurate information relative to the complex metabolism of this organism is gradually accumulating in one of the laboratories (G. W. H. F.) through a systematic study of the optimum condition of growth, the nutrition and the biochemical activities of B. botulinus in simple mediums. A number of important practical questions, however, made it necessary to publish the experiments reported in this paper before the chemical work had been completed.

It is deemed profitable to review, briefly, some of the questions as they appeared to those who approached the problem from an epidemiologic point of view. For the sake of discussion, the various canned food products involved in human and animal botulism outbreaks are summarized in table 1.[1]

Received for publication, July 2, 1923

* This study was aided by grants from the National Canners' Association, the Canners' League of California and the California Olive Association.

[1] Geiger, J. C.; Dickson, E. C., and Meyer, K. F.: The Epidemiology of Botulism, Public Health Bulletin, 1922, No. 127.

It will be noted from table 1 that in 77 instances plant products preserved by heat have caused outbreaks, while in 18 reports animal products incompletely preserved by curing or pickling are mentioned as the toxin containing foods. Canned products provide anaerobic conditions favorable for the growth of B. botulinus spores that have survived the heating process. Since toxin production in canned vegetables follows the failure to destroy the resistant spores, it is not surprising that a relatively high proportion of botulism outbreaks have been traced to food canned in a household where facilities for maintaining cooking temperatures considerably above the boiling point are not always readily available. However, commercially canned foods are by no means exempt, and 27 instances are now on record in which products canned on a large scale have given rise to botulism. On further analysis, it is noted that certain types of vegetables are more liable to contain the toxin of B. botulinus than others. In fact, the impres-

TABLE 1

HOME AND COMMERCIALLY PRESERVED PLANT AND ANIMAL PRODUCTS RESPONSIBLE FOR HUMAN AND ANIMAL BOTULISM OUTBREAKS

Food	Number of Out-breaks	Bacterio-logically Proved	Spoilage			No Spoilage	Number of Chicken Out-breaks
			Visible and Odor	Taste	Unknown		
Home Preserved:							
String beans	21	6	9	6	3	3	25
Corn	12	6	9	2	..	1	13
Asparagus	5	3	3	1	..	1	3
Spinach	2	0	1	..	..	1	..
Apricots	3	1	1	2	..	..	1
Peas	..	..	..	..	..	..	3
Pears	2	..	1	1 (2) (not abnormal)			
Chili sauce	1	1					
Beets	1						
Beets and turnip tops	1	..	..	..	..	1	
Pickled fish	1	..	1	..	..	..	1
Commercially Packed:							
Spinach	8	6	2	1	1	4	2
Ripe pickled olives	7	6	4	1	1	1	
Minced olive relish	3	1	1	..	..	2	
Beets	2	0	..	1	.	1	
String beans	3	0	..	1	2	0	
Beans and pork	1						
Corn	1	..	..	1			
Tuna fish	1	..	1				
Pumpkin	1						
Evaporated milk	1	..	1				
Totals	77	30	34	17	7	15	48
	18 outbreaks due to animal products 10 instances of botulism, causative food unknown						
Total	105 reports of botulism outbreaks in the United States by the end of June, 1922						

sion is being disseminated by the daily press that ripe olives and spinach particularly are frequently contaminated with this anaerobe. The data in table 1 refute these statements decisively, but seriously implicate home canned string beans and corn. The question naturally arises, Why are these two vegetables so frequently the source of intoxications? A careful study of published and unpublished reports indicates that frequently only one jar or container of an underprocessed lot is toxic; in fact, only a relatively small percentage of the entire pack is contaminated with B. botulinus. Unfortunately, the actual number of containers which are toxic or which harbor viable spores of B. botulinus has never been determined, but the recent observations made on some lots of commercially packed spinach have created a feeling of uneasiness.[2] It has been proved that nearly 70% of the cases of one spinach pack had to be discarded on account of spoilage. Over 45% of the cans examined contained viable bacteria, and the liquor of 27% of the swelled cans was toxic for guinea-pigs. Unquestionably, underprocessing of spinach, string beans, and corn carries grave consequences, but it is by no means clear whether the composition of the canned products, the rate of heat penetration or the reaction of the food stuff is responsible for this fact. The data available at the time this study was undertaken favored the view that the composition and heat penetration were more important than the reaction, but actual experiments alone could settle the uncertainty. Intimately associated with the solution of this problem is the question: Given an actual, massive infection, is B. botulinus able to multiply regularly and produce its characteristic toxin in every jar or can, or do the spores remain quiescent, and is their development correspondingly retarded or even completely suspended? The occurrence of the latter condition was anticipated on account of the fact, repeatedly noted by several investigators, that retarded germination is a property peculiar to heated spores of B. botulinus. Most of the observations on retarded germination have, however, been made on culture mediums of optimum reaction and composition, but nothing is known with regard to the conditions in canned foods. Moreover, the food packer is obviously anxious to know whether the toxin of B. botulinus develops soon after the packing, whether it increases in potency, or whether it deteriorates on storage. The available epidemiologic data are not sufficiently complete to answer these questions, but it

[2] The temperature employed in processing was about 100 or 101 C., and the time also was inadequate. This process has been recognized in the industry as insufficient.

is known that in 2 instances the canned products (string beans and pickled fish) were less than 2 weeks old. According to the history of one chicken outbreak (Report 17 [1]), sufficient toxin was produced in a period of 3 days in a half gallon jar of string beans, canned by the cold pack method, to be fatal when fed to chickens. On the other hand, it is established that in the majority of outbreaks, food products were involved which had been preserved for from 2 to 26 months previous to consumption.

The various problems outlined in the preceding paragraph are, however, overshadowed by the important question: Is the toxin production in canned foods regularly associated with the development of metabolic products which would enable the dealer or consumer to judge the food as unfit for consumption? Essentially this becomes a question of whether the growth of B. botulinus in every canned food is accompanied by gas production with the resultant occurrence of leaking jars or bulging cans, by the production of a peculiar, offensive odor, or by the distinct disintegration of the vegetable or meat fibers. It has been pointed out in a recent paper [1] that the association of physical signs of spoilage with toxicity has been overemphasized. The prevalent idea that the food must always be visibly spoiled in order to be toxic is not entirely supported by the available epidemiologic observations, although there is no doubt that in the majority of instances the canned product is so spoiled as to attract readily the attention of the one who opens the container. Numerous reports on botulism caused by home canned string beans definitely indicate the amount of gas, odor, turbidity of liquor or disintegration of the contents of a jar was so slight that the housewife was prompted to confirm her impression by tasting it. In fact, spoilage was, in several cases, not noticed by the intelligent consumer until the food became heated, during the process of cooking. These facts naturally prompted the question: Why are certain products more liable to spoilage than others, and why is toxin production not regularly accompanied by visible disintegration or odor? As these questions are of the greatest importance to the food packer, dealer and consumer, it is self-evident that the inoculation experiments with canned vegetables and fruits considered this aspect carefully, in accordance with the epidemiologic observations already reported. It was noted that string beans, spinach and asparagus may occasionally reach the dangerous toxic stage before the signs of spoilage are readily recognizable. Products rich in proteins and carbohydrates as a rule show relatively rapid and marked decomposition.

A number of workers (van Ermengem,[3] Gaffky[3] and others) have noted that B. botulinus grows in infusions prepared from vegetables, such as peas, beans, etc., but to Dickson[4] belongs the credit of having demonstrated conclusively the relationship of canned, underprocessed vegetables to human and animal botulism. This investigator artificially inoculated 8 cans of string beans with an unheated culture of B. bolutinus. He kept the cans at room temperature for from 2 to 12 months. As a rule, weak toxins were demonstrated; the beans exhibited no signs of spoilage and had a good odor. In a later paper, Dickson, Burke and Ward[5] report on studies made on cans of commercially canned peaches, apricots and pears, artificially infected with thoroughly washed spores, resealed and incubated at 26 C. After a lapse of 3 months, sufficient toxin had been generated in the container to kill guinea-pigs within 48 hours, when subcutaneously inoculated. In another series of tests, the same workers inoculated jars of fresh prunes and peaches with washed spores of B. botulinus, and then subjected the products to the processing procedures customary in the household. After 2 months at room temperature the jars were opened. A pure culture of B. botulinus was obtained, although in none of the jars was the juice sufficiently toxic that 1 c c. would cause any symptoms when injected into a guinea-pig. Thom, Edmondson and Giltner[6] inoculated canned corn, peas, deviled ham, tongue, canned Swiss cheese and sausages with B. botulinus, and placed these foods in an icebox at an average temperature of 12 C. After a week, the Swiss cheese and the peas showed some signs of putrefaction. The organism was recovered from the two foods, but no toxicity was recorded. Armstrong, Story and Scott[7] prepared a medium consisting of chopped ripe unspoiled olives and brine, which was sterilized at 15 pounds' pressure for 30 minutes. The substratum was inoculated with B. botulinus and, after an incubation of 9 days at 37 C., contained abundant spores and a potent toxin. In an interesting paper by Koser, Edmondson and Giltner,[8] it is shown that the development of B. botulinus in canned spinach is somewhat irregular. In some instances, there was evidence of a rapid multiplication, while in others there was apparently neither growth nor toxin formation. These workers state that the growth of B. botulinus in canned spinach is accompanied by the evolution of gas as well as by the elaboration of the specific toxin. In one instance, however, the toxin production had advanced to such a stage as to produce a fatal result, while at the same time gas production either had not occurred or was insufficient to cause bulging of the can. This publication is unquestionably the best study on the development of B. botulinus in a canned food product, and the technical principles employed should be followed by those interested in similar problems. In a recent communication, Bengtson[9] reports on some work done on cans of string beans, peas, spinach, olives, corn and beets, artificially inoculated with a month old, unheated culture of B. botulinus. The liquors of the inoculated cans were tested for toxins on the 7th, 8th, 9th, and 10th day of incubation at 37 C. The string beans, spinach, peas, and corn were found to be toxic. The mice inoculated with the samples from the canned beets and olives survived. Since the cans of spinach, olives, beets, and

[3] Handbuch. d. pathog. Microorganism, Kolle u. Wassermann, 1912, 4, p. 921.

[4] Monograph Rockefeller Inst. Med. Res., 1918, No. 8.

[5] Arch. Int. Med., 1919, 24, p. 581.

[6] Jour. Am. Med. Assn., 1919, 73, p. 907.

[7] Public Health Rept., 1919, 34, Pt. 2, p. 2877.

[8] Jour. Am. Med. Assn., 1921, 77, p. 1250.

[9] Public Health Rept., 1921, 36, p. 1665.

string beans exhibited no offensive odor, nor any swelling of the cans, Bengtson expressed some doubts as to the validity of her results. She considered it possible that the small amount of inoculum may have contained sufficient toxin to account for the development of symptoms in the experimental animals. This may be true, but this interpretation does not explain the absence of toxin in the beets and olives which had been inoculated and incubated for the same period. The series is unquestionably too small to permit any general conclusions.

This brief review dealing with the reports on artificially inoculated canned food products indicates that only one or two foods were carefully studied; the number of cans selected for analysis was, as a rule, too small, or the period of observation was too short. It appeared to us that the artificial inoculation of a large series of cans of different food products, kept at room and incubator temperatures, and examined at varying periods of time for over 12 months, should furnish information of practical value. With this plan in mind, the following products have been studied: Asparagus, corn, peas, sweet potatoes, salmon, beets, pickled ripe olives, green and red peppers, spinach, string beans, evaporated and sweetened condensed milk, pumpkin, tomatoes, sauerkraut, apricots, cherries, peaches, pears, plums, raspberries and strawberries.

General Technic of Inoculating Cans and Methods of Recording Growth, Toxin Production and Spoilage

The cans of commercially packed food products were secured from a grocery store and represented either first or second grade goods. One end was carefully cleaned with soap and water, flamed with a Bunsen burner and punctured in two places with the sharp point of a "radial" can opener, previously sterilized. One c c. of a spore suspension was introduced by means of a graduated pipet, and the openings were immediately soldered. In this connection, it should be emphasized that this mode of inoculation released the vacuum and a certain amount of air entered the can. Proper consideration should be given to this condition in the interpretation of the results.

As a rule, the spore suspensions were prepared from 10 day old peptic digest veal infusion gelatin cultures, incubated at 37.5 C. The spores were suspended in salt solution and repeatedly washed in the same fluid; they were heated at 80 C. for one hour, or at a higher temperature for a shorter period of time. The concentration of the spore suspensions was determined by counts in a Halber chamber. Table 2 shows the number of spores inoculated in each series, the strains used in preparing the suspension and the manner of heating the preparation.

In a number of instances, soil suspensions heated for one hour in the Arnold sterilizer were mixed with the spores and added to the contents of the cans. The infected cans were kept either in the working room of the laboratory at an average temperature of 18 to 20 C., or in an incubator room of an average temperature of 35 C. Hhey were examined daily, and after 10 to 14 days' incubation, they were opened aseptically by puncture, and a small sample removed for toxin determinations and cultures. Whenever possible, the cans were resoldered, reincubated, and tested at a later date. The final tests in series 1 and 2 were made at the end of 10 months to one year of incubation. These methods of examination were chosen to determine the shortest period of toxin production and spoilage. Furthermore, it was of interest to know whether toxic products would increase or decrease in potency on standing. It is evident that the procedure chosen possesses several sources of error: 1. The opening of a "swell" releases the accumulated gases, thus reducing the pressure, which may have an influence on the growth of B. botulinus. 2. The escape of the gases may also prevent detection of spoilage on subsequent examination. 3. The repeated introduction of air and resoldering of the cans without previous exhaustion may seriously impair the growth vigor of B. botulinus. As the intervals between several examinations in most cases were from 2 to 6 months, the objection mentioned under "2" played a subordinate rôle; in fact, the data to be presented definitely show that flat cans repeatedly opened may finally develop into "swells." On the other hand, "hard swells" sometimes remained flat when resealed and incubated. It has been

TABLE 2

PREPARATION OF SPORE SUSPENSION USED FOR EXPERIMENTAL INOCULATION OF THE CANNED FOODS

Suspension No.	Strains	Number	Heated at	Inoculum	Used in Series
1	54 Type A 38 Type A 62 Type A	3	95 C. for 10 minutes	100 million	I
2	54 Type A	1	95 C. for 10 minutes	100 million	II
3	38 Type A	1	80 C. for 1 hour	50 million	II
4	19 Type A 38 Type A 58 Type A 62 Type A 87 Type A 40 Type B	6	80 C. for 1 hour	10 billion	III
5	38 Type A 97 Type A	2 (dried spores)	80 C. for 1 hour	17 billion	IV

customary to designate these cans as "spoiled." B. botulinus is not a strict anaerobe, and comparative tests have shown that the introduction of air on repeated examination will not influence the growth of the organism, provided the conditions are otherwise favorable. Nothing is known with regard to the influence of gas pressure on B. botulinus, but it is felt that in these comparative tests the factor is probably insignificant and can be overlooked.

Spoilage was judged according to the following outline:

A. Visible Spoilage.—(a) Appearance of container, whether bulging of lids, "swell," leaking of imperfect seam, improperly sealed rubber ring, or streaks of leaking contents on jar, can or label.

(b) Presence of gas, under light or marked pressure, odor of gas, test for hydrogen.

(c) Physical appearance, such as turbidity of liquor, sediment, disintegration of stalks, pods, etc., and general consistency of the contents.

(d) Odor of the content, such as sour, rancid, musty, repulsive.

B. Chemical Changes.—Change in the reaction as estimated by comparative P_H determinations. Toxin tests were invariably made on guinea-pigs weighing from 250 to 300 gm. As a rule, subcutaneous inoculations were chosen for the preliminary tests. Doubtful results were verified by feeding, or toxin—antitoxin neutralization tests with heated and unheated liquors, emulsions, or extracts of the food. Whenever practical the MLD for each toxic product was determined by serial dilutions. One MLD was represented by the amount of brine, juice or syrup which killed a guinea-pig of the weight stated, in 96 hours. Cultures were made in beef heart peptic digest broth, and tested by shake cultures or toxin tests on mice. All P_H determinations were made electrometrically in Clark's shaking electrode by Miss E. Brink.

EXPERIMENTAL DATA

The observations on the cans artifically inoculated with detoxified spores of B. botulinus are arranged according to the products; the group of very acid foods is summarized in one paragraph.

Toxin Production in Canned Asparagus.—The tins of asparagus, inoculated with heated spores of B. botulinus by the methods just described, furnished a number of interesting facts. The experiments are briefly summarized in the following paragraph, while the results from one series of experiments are shown in table 3 and in greater detail in table 4.

TABLE 3

TOXIN PRODUCTION IN CANNED ASPARAGUS INOCULATED WITH HEATED SPORES OF B. BOTULINUS

No. 2 Cans "Tall"

Series Number	Incubation Period		Number of Cans				Total Number of Cans	Total Content Spoiled	Total Number Toxic	Cultural Test	P_H
	Temperature	Duration	Flat	Toxic	Sp.-H.S.†	Toxic					
III	35 C.	10-14 da.	6	5	6	3	12	0	8: 3 W* 3 S 2 VT	++	3.7-5.2
	35 C.	30 da.	0	0	1	0	1	1	1 VT		
	35 C.	67 da.	5	2	0	0	5	0	2 W	++	
	35 C.	5½ mo.	6‡	4	3	2	9	3	6: 5 W 1 S	++	

No. 2 Cans "Short"

Series Number	Temperature	Duration	Flat	Toxic	Sp.-H.S.†	Toxic	Total Number of Cans	Total Content Spoiled	Total Number Toxic	Cultural Test	P_H
III	35 C.	10-14 da.	9	9	1	1	10	0	10: 4 W 4 S 2 VT	....	4.7-5.5
	35 C.	30 da.	0	0	4	4	4	0	4: 1 S 3 VT		
	35 C.	67 da.	3	3	0	0	3	0	3: 1 W 2 VT		
	35 C.	5½ mo.	5	5	5	5	10	6	10: 2 W 4 S 4 VT		

† Sp.-H.S. indicates springer-hard swell.

* In this and all following tables toxicity is expressed as follows: VW = very weeak (2 c c. inoculated subcutaneously fatal to 250-300 gm. guinea-pig in more than 6 days); W = weak toxin (2 c c. inoculated subcutaneously fatal to 250-300 gm. guinea-pig in about 4 days); S = strong toxin (0.01 c c. inoculated subcutaneously fatal to 250-300 gm. guinea-pig in about 4 days); VT = very toxic (0.001 c c., or less, inoculated subcutaneously fatal to 250–300 gm. guinea-pig in about 4 days).

‡ Two of these cans were previously soft swells.

Four cans of asparagus inoculated with suspension No. 1 (100,000,000 spores) were held at room temperature for from 60 days to 12 months, and tested at varying intervals. The cans remained flat, and the contents appeared normal even after 12 months. After 60, 90 and 129 days, toxin could not be demonstrated in the liquor. Two cans opened on the 129th day were resoldered and, when tested again after 12 months' incubation, proved to be toxic. One-tenth c c. of liquor from one of the cans was fatal to a guinea-pig in 24 hours,

TABLE 4

THE COURSE OF TOXIN PRODUCTION AND SIGNS OF SPOILAGE IN CANNED ASPARAGUS INOCULATED WITH HEATED SPORES OF B. BOTULINUS

Can No.	Incubation Period	Appearance of Container	Condition of Contents	PH	Cultural Test	Toxin Determinations 2 c c.	1 c c.	0.1 c c.	0.01 c c.	0.001 c c.	0.0001 c c.
					Series III. 35 C. No. 2 Cans "Tall"						
1	14 d. 35 C. 3 d. R.T.	Flat	OK	5.2	....	......	......	4 da.	9 da.		
1	5½ mo.	Flat	Musty odor	4.85	....	90 hr.	......	Neg.			
3	10 da.	Flat	OK	4.75	++	......	Neg.	60 hr.			
3	67 da.	Flat	OK	4.71	....	......	......	Neg.			
3	5½ mo.	Springer	OK	4.36	++	25 hr. 2 pigs					
5	10 da.	Flat	OK	5.26	++	......	90 hr.	19 da.			
5	67 da.	Flat	OK	4.8	....	Symptoms 36 hr., recov. 72 hr.					
5	5½ mo.	Flat	OK	4.41	++						
6	14 d. 35 C. 3 d. R.T.	Flat	OK	3.78	....	......	......	Neg.	Neg.		
6	5½ mo.	Flat	OK	3.32	++	Neg.					
7	10 da.	S. swell	OK	3.95	++	......	Neg.	Neg.			
7	67 da.	Flat	OK	4.03	....	Neg.					
7	5½ mo.	Flat	OK	3.79	++	Neg.					
12	10 da.	Flat	OK	4.75	++	......	16 hr.	......	......	14 da.	11 da.
12	67 da.	Flat	OK	4.67	....	24 hr.	......	30 hr.	6 da.		
12	5½ mo.	Flat	OK	4.51	....	40 hr.	......	108 hr.	Neg.		
					No. 2 Cans "Short"						
1	10 da.	Flat	OK	5.46	++	......	16 hr.	20 hr.	......	Neg.	
1	30 da.	Springer	OK	....	....	......	16 hr.	16 hr.	......	30 hr.	6 da.
1	67 da.	Flat	OK	5.05	....	......	14 hr.	14 hr.	20 hr.	30 hr.	Neg.
1	5½ mo.	H. swell	Sour	4.9	....	18 hr.	......	24 hr.	40 hr.	72 hr.	22 da.
3	10 da.	Flat	OK	5.46	++	......	16 hr.	20 hr.	......	Neg.	
3	30 da.	Springer	OK	....	....	......	16 hr.	16 hr.	......	30 hr.	6 da.
3	67 da.	Flat	OK	5.63	....	......	14 hr.	18 hr.	18 hr.	......	Neg.
3	5½ mo.	H. swell	OK	4.4	....	18 hr.	......	18 hr.	40 hr.	7 da.	
4	10 da.	Flat	OK	5.41	++	......	16 hr.	40 hr.	......	5 da.	13 da.
4	30 da.	Springer	OK	....	....	......	16 hr.	40 hr.	48 hr.	......	Neg.
4	5½ mo.	Flat	OK	4.36	....	......	......	7½ da.	Neg.	10 da.	
11	10 da.	Flat	OK	4.74	++	......	16 hr.	......	......	6 da.	6 da.
11	30 da.	Springer	OK	5.0	....	......	16 hr.	16 hr.	......	16 hr.	
11	5½ mo.	Flat	OK	4.55	....	......	......	60 hr.	Neg.	Neg.	

while 2 c c. of the other had the same effect in 20 hours. The H-ion concentration of the brine of the nontoxic cans varied from P_H 4.02 to 5.01, while those of the toxic tins were P_H 4.78 and 4.75. The nontoxin containing tins showed the presense of viable B. botulinus spores, as evidenced by enrichment cultures in beef heart and deep liver agar. Four additional cans treated similarly, but incubated at 35 C., remained flat, and, when tested at different intervals, revealed a normal content. One weak toxin could be demonstrated in a container incubated for 10 days. Three of the 4 cans were tested for B. botulinus, and they gave positive cultures. The toxic liquor had a P_H of 5.24, while one nontoxic can gave a reading of P_H 4.96.

In a second series consisting of 5 No. 1 cans of asparagus, inoculated with suspension No. 3 (50,000,000 spores), and held at 35 C. for from 10 days to 10 months, the cans remained flat; and, when examined, exhibited a normal appearance. One weakly toxic brine was demonstrated after 10 days' incubation.

A third series, consisting of 2 different lots of asparagus, namely, 12 cans of No. 2 tall and 10 cans of No. 2 short, were inoculated with suspension No. 4 (10,000,000,000 spores, mixed strains).

For the sake of clearness, the observations recorded from each set of cans are discussed separately.

(*a*) *Tall Cans.*—Six of the 12 cans, incubated at 35 C. for from 10 to 14 days, remained flat. The contents presented a normal appearance, but the liquor from 5 cans was toxic. The MLD varied from 0.1 c c. to 0.001 c c. on subcutaneous inoculation of guinea-pigs. Six containers were abnormal, either "springers," "soft" or "hard swells." In these cans, the contents appeared normal, although the brine of 3 was toxic. The H-ion concentration varied from P_H 3.7 to P_H 5.2. The normal and abnormal cans were resealed and repeatedly tested. The following observations were made on these tins: 1 can (no. 6, table 4)[10] remained nontoxic during the period of 5½ months, although B. botulinus could be demonstrated in subcultures. One showed an abnormal appearance and emanated a sour odor, while 2 cans (nos. 5 and 12, table 4) remained flat during the period of incubation; the contents showed no spoilage, but proved toxic to guinea-pigs on subcutaneous inoculation. Three of the 8 "springers" and "swells" showed an apparently sound content and were nontoxic during the incubation period of 5½ months. One of the 3 tins (No. 2) had to be discarded after 10 days on account of spoilage; it was nontoxic. The remaining 5 cans of this series of 8 were all toxic and spoiled. The other 2 (nos. 3 and 4) were toxic, but the contents appeared normal.

(*b*) *Short Cans.*—Ten small tins of asparagus were treated in exactly the same manner as those just reported. After from 10 to 14 days' incubation at 35 C., all but one can (table 3) remained flat. The

[10] For the sake of brevity all of the tests are not represented in detail.

apparently normal contents were toxic in amounts varying from 0.1 c c. to 0.001 c c. During the 5½ months' incubation period, three cans, namely, nos. 2, 6 and 7, remained flat, while 7 developed "springers" to "hard swells." The contents of one of the flat and 4 of the 7 abnormal cans exhibited no signs of spoilage. They remained, however, toxic during the entire period. The other 3 "swells" were distinctly spoiled. Some of the experimental results are shown in table 4.

In analyzing the findings in table 4 more carefully, it was noted that an interesting relationship existed between the reaction and the toxicity of the brine. The data in table 5 illustrate this point.

TABLE 5

EFFECT OF VARIATIONS IN H-ION CONCENTRATION IN CANNED ASPARAGUS ON TOXIN PRODUCTION

No. 2 Cans "Tall." Series III					No. 2 Can "Short." Series III				
Can Number	P_H 10 Days	M L D 10 Days,	P_H 5½ mos.	M L D 5½ mos.,	Can Number	P_H 10 Days	M L D 10 Days,	P_H 5½ mos.	M L D 5½ mos.,
		c c.		c c.			c c.		c c.
6	3.7	Neg.	3.32	Neg.	11	4.7	0.001	4.55	0.1
7	3.9	Neg.	3.79	Neg.	12	5.0	0.01	5.0	0.001
2	4.5	Neg.	....	.....	7	5.1	0.001	4.9	0.001
11	4.67	0.1 neg.	4.41	Neg.	9	5.2	0.1	4.6	0.01
4	4.5	1.0	....	.....	6	5.3	0.01	4.8	0.01
3	4.7	0.1 ?	4.36	2.0	4	5.4	0.001	4.36	0.01
9	4.7	0.01	4.47	1.0	5	5.4	0.01	5.0	0.1
10	4.7	0.001	....	...	1	5.4	0.1	4.9	0.001
12	4.7	0.01	4.51	0.1	3	5.4	0.1	4.4	0.001
8	5.0	0.1	4.35	0.01	2	5.1	0.1	4.8	0.01
5	5.2	0.1	4.41	2.0					
1	5.2	0.1	4.85	2.0					

It will be noted from table 5 that the nontoxic liquors from cans 6 and 7 had a P_H value of 3.7 and 3.9, respectively, when tested after 10 days' incubation. After 5½ months, the acidity had dropped to P_H 3.32 and 3.79, respectively. The brine from can 2, giving a reading of P_H 4.5, was nontoxic after 10 days' incubation, and had to be discarded at this time on account of the condition of the container. It is not unlikely that, on prolonged incubation, this can might have produced a toxin similar in strength to that found in container 4. Another nontoxic can (no. 11), inoculated with soil in addition to the spore suspension of B. botulinus, had a P_H value of 4.67. As other tins similarly inoculated furnished nearly identical P_H values and potent toxins, it is difficult to explain the exception of can 11. In all probability, the composition of the food product sometimes, irrespective of the P_H, controls the germination and toxin production of B. botulinus.

Summary.—Eighteen of 35 tins of commercially packed first or second grade asparagus inoculated with heated spores of B. botulinus and held at incubator or room temperature for periods of time ranging from 10 days to 12 months developed "swells" or showed distinct spoilage. The contents of 15 were highly toxic for guinea-pigs; 3 of the 18 cans just mentioned were flat, but contained a spoiled and toxic food product. The contents of 7 of 17 flat cans proved highly toxic, although no signs of spoilage could be detected by several observers. Eight cans incubated for relatively short periods proved nontoxic and exhibited no spoilage. The same findings were even made on 2 cans incubated for 10 months. The experiments observed indicate that toxin production by B. botulinus in canned asparagus is not always accompanied by spoilage of sufficient intensity to warn the dealer or consumer.

Toxin Production in Canned Corn, Peas, Sweet Potatoes and Salmon.—Canned corn: Five no. 2 cans of corn, inoculated with suspension no. 1 (100,000,000 spores) were incubated at room temperature for from 10 days to 12 months. In addition, 3 were held at 35 C. for 24 hours, after which they were kept at room temperature for 9, 60, and 90 days. At 35 C. all cans developed "hard swells" after 24 hours' incubation, and at room temperature the appearance was abnormal within 3 days. The contents showed at times slight blackening, marked disintegration, and an offensive odor was given off. One c c. of a 1:10,000 dilution of the juice proved fatal to a guinea-pig in approximately 4 days. One tin held at room temperature for 10 days was less toxic, i. e., 1 c c. of a 1:100 dilution killed a guinea-pig in 24 hours (1:1,000 negative). This may be attributed to the slower growth and the correspondingly slower toxin production at a temperature of about 18 to 20 C.

Canned Peas: Observations similar to those made on canned corn were recorded on 8 cans of peas. The infected cans were held at 35 C. for 3 days instead of one day, and then placed at room temperature. The strong butyric acid odor and the marked disintegration of the peas indicated pronounced spoilage. On prolonged incubation, the toxicity of the liquor increased: no deterioration was ever noticed.

Canned Sweet Potatoes: Eighteen cans of mashed sweet potatoes were inoculated with heated spores of B. botulinus and incubated at 35 C. Within 10 days, the tins had developed "hard swells." On examination, the contents appeared firm, but gave off a strong butyric odor. On account of the solid nature of the sweet potatoes, the toxicity was determined by emulsifying a portion of the contents in saline. The supernatant fluid of the centrifugalized suspension was tested as customary in 2 c c. amounts on guinea-pigs. Invariably such a dose proved fatal in from 16 to 36 hours. At room temperature, spoilage and toxin production were slower. In fact, one can was still "flat" after 60 days' incubation, and was nontoxic. Another, receiving similar treatment, but held for 10 months, developed a "hard swell," exhibited distinct spoilage, and was toxic.

Canned Salmon: Six cans of red Alaska salmon were inoculated with suspension No. 2 (50,000,000 spores). Three, held at 35 C. for 4 days, followed by incubation at room temperature for from 6 to 90 days, developed "hard swells" in 96 hours. The partially liquefied contents gave off a pungent, putrid, butyric odor, and, when tested on guinea-pigs in 1:5,000 to 1:10,000 dilutions, proved fatal in from 2 to 4 days. Again, spoilage and toxin production were slower at room temperature. Even after 60 and 90 days, the cans remained flat. The salmon was firm, and the slight butyric acid odor could have been readily overlooked by the less scrupulous consumer. The MLD of these 2 cans was 1:10 and 1:100, respectively. When held for 12 months, spoilage was pronounced, and 1 c c. of a 1:10,000 dilution of the centrifugalized liquid was fatal to a guinea-pig in 40 hours.

Toxin Production in Canned Beets.—Observations on three series of canned beets inoculated with heated spores of B. botulinus and held at room and at incubator temperatures are summarized:

In the first series, 4 No. 2 cans, inoculated with suspension No. 1 (100,000,000 spores) and incubated at room temperature for from 60 days to 12 months, remained flat and the contents appeared normal. Toxin was demonstrated in the liquor from 2 tins, one after 90 days' incubation, another after 129 days. A 1:100 dilution of the liquor from the former container killed a guinea-pig in 20 hours, while a 1:10 dilution of the latter was fatal to a guinea-pig in 80 hours. However, the liquor from this tin, when retested after 12 months' incubation, was nontoxic in 0.1 c c. dilution. The acidity of the one nontoxic liquor was P_H 5.2, that of a toxic one P_H 5.5. One of 5 cans, similarly inoculated, but held at 35 C. for 10 days, became a "hard swell." On examination, the contents appeared normal, but 0.1 c c. of the fluid proved fatal to a guinea-pig in 48 hours. The other tins remained "flat," and the contents were nontoxic; however, on subculturing in beef heart medium, B. botulinus was demonstrated. The H-ion concentration of the liquor from 2 cans was P_H 5.37 and P_H 4.82.

In a second series, four of 5 No. 2 cans, inoculated with suspension No. 3, and incubated at 35 C. for a period of time ranging from 10 days to 10 months, remained "flat," and the contents revealed a normal appearance. The liquor from one tin was slightly toxic. One container held for 10 months developed a "springer." Toxin could not be demonstrated in 1c c. of the fluid, but on subculturing, viable B. botulinus organisms were demonstrated.

A third series, consisting of 12 No. 2 cans of beets, was inoculated with suspension No. 4 (10,000,000,000 spores) and held at 35 C. for from 10 days to 5½ months. After from 10 to 14 days' incubation, the contents from 3 of 7 "flat" cans gave off a suspicious, musty or slightly rancid odor, although the consistency of the beets remained firm and the color normal. The acidity varied from P_H 5.45 to 5.76. Three of the 5 "swells" that developed during the same incubation period presented a similar appearance and odor. The acidity varied from P_H 4.85 to P_H 6.27 with an average of P_H 5.43. The MLD of the liquor from both normal and abnormal containers varied from 0.1 c c. to 0.0001 c c. The "flat" cans on further incubation developed "swells," the contents were distinctly spoiled and highly toxic to guinea-pigs. Table 6 presents a few typical observations made on individual cans repeatedly tested. It is at once obvious that: (1) the contents of the nontoxic tins may become toxic; (2) the toxicity of the liquor increases on prolonged incubation; (3) prolonged incubation increases the number of "swells."

The results from series 1 and 2 conflict with those secured in series 3, but fortunately another group of tins inoculated with 17,000,000,000 heated, dried spores of strains 38 and 97, incubated at 35 C. and tested after 27 days and again after 3½ months, furnished results similar to those in series 1 and 2. Irregular spoilage and toxin production were observed. It was noted that the liquor of the 3 "swells" developing in 27 to 112 days was toxic, while that from only one the 3 "flat" tins proved fatal to a guinea-pig on subcutaneous inoculation. In spite of the

TABLE 6

THE COURSE OF TOXIN PRODUCTION AND SIGNS OF SPOILAGE IN CANNED BEETS INOCULATED WITH HEATED SPORES OF B. BOTULINUS

Series III 35 C.

Can No.	Incubation Period	Appearance of Container	Condition of Contents	P_H	Cultural Test	Toxin Determinations: 2 c c.	1 c c.	0.1 c c.	0 01 c c.	0.001 c c.	0.0001 c c.
3	14 d. 35 C. 3 d. R.T.	Flat	OK	5.56	....	......	......	30 hr.	40 hr.	11 da.±	
3	5½ mo.	H. swell	Spoiled, bad	5.71	....	......	......	18 hr.	20 hr.	24 hr.	7 da. 1:5000
4	14 d. 35 C. 3 d. R.T.	Flat	OK	5.45	....	......	......	4 da.	17 da.		
4	5½ mo.	S. swell	Bad	5.28	....	18 hr.	......	18 hr.	.....	40 hr.	72 hr. 1:5000
5	10 da.	Flat	Musty	5.13	++	......	5½ da.	17 da.			
5	67 da.	H. swell	OK	5.47	....	14 hr.	......	14 hr.	16 hr.	20 hr.	Neg.
5	5½ mo.	S. swell	Bad	5.16	....	......	......	......	18 hr.	20 hr.	24 hr. 1:50 000
6	10 da.	Springer	OK	5.76	++	......	30 hr.	48 hr.	13 da.	15 da ±	
6	30 da.	H. swell	Very sour	....	....	......	16 hr.	16 hr.	16 hr.	20 hr.	60 hr.
7	10 da.	Flat	Suspicious odor	5.50	++	......	20 hr.	30 hr.			
7	30 da.	Springer	OK	....	....	......	16 hr.	16 hr.	......	20 hr.	90 hr.
7	67 da.	Springer	OK	5.87	....	......	14 hr.	14 hr.	14 hr.	14 hr.	Neg.
7	5½ mo.	Flat	Off	5.04	....	......	......	......	54 hr.	100 hr.	Neg.
9	10 da.	Flat	Off	5.36	++	......	16 hr.	16 hr.	......	Neg.	16 da.
9	67 da.	H. swell	OK	5.39	++	......	14 hr.	18 hr.	14 hr.	20 hr.	Neg.
9	5½ mo.	H. swell	Bad	4.96	....	......	......	......	18 hr.	30 hr.	30 hr.
10	14 d. 35 C. 3 d. R.T.	Flat	OK	5.6	....	......	......	16 hr.	40 hr.	6 da.	Neg.
10	5½ mo.	H. swell	Bad	5.28	....	......	......	18 hr.	18 hr.	30 hr.	20 hr. 1:5000

large number of spores introduced into each container, the liquor from 2 remained nontoxic for a period of 3½ months. The acidity of the nontoxic liquors was P_H 3.75 to P_H 4, while that of the toxic ones varied from P_H 4.45 to P_H 5.05.

Summary.—Seventeen of 31 cans of beets inoculated with heated spores of B. botulinus and incubated in the manner previously described developed "swells." The toxic content of 15 abnormal tins gave off a suspicious, musty or slightly rancid odor. Fourteen tins remained "flat." The contents of 4 "flat" cans was normal in appearance and odor, but proved highly poisonous to guinea-pigs. The MLD of the liquor from both normal and abnormal tins varied from 2 c c. (1 tin) to 0.0001 c c. No deterioration of toxin was noted. Prolonged incubation of canned beets increases the number of "swells."

Toxin Production in Ripe Olives.—The experimental data recorded from 2 series of experiments on ripe olives inoculated with heated spores of B. botulinus are summarized in table 7.

TABLE 7

TOXIN PRODUCTION IN CANNED RIPE OLIVES INOCULATED WITH HEATED SPORES OF B. BOTULINUS

Series Number	Incubation Period		Number of Cans		Total Number of Cans	Total Content Spoiled	Total Number Toxic	Cultural Test	PH
	Temperature	Duration	Flat	Toxic					
II	R. T.	30 days	1	0	1	0	0	++	6.89
	R. T.	129 days	1	0	1	0	0		
	35 C.	10 days	1	0	1	0	0	++	
	35 C.	17 days	1	1	1	0	1W	++	
	35 C.	22 days	1	0	1	0	0	++	
	35 C.	10 mos.	3	3	3	0	3W	++	
III	35 C.	10 days	4	1VW	4	0	1VW*	....	6.6-7.0
	35 C.	67 days	4	1W	4	0	1W*		
	35 C.	5½ mos.	6	0	6	0	0	++	5.1-5.7

* Same can tested.

In the first series, 2 glass jars inoculated with suspension No. 3 (50,000,000 spores), held at room temperature, and tested after 30 and 129 days, showed no bulging of the lids or leakage. The contents appeared normal, and the brine was nontoxic. The brine from 6 jars similarly inoculated, but held at 35 C. for a period of time ranging from 10 days to 10 months, was weakly toxic, 2 c.c. of the liquor being fatal to a guinea-pig in from 4 to 7 days. The physical appearance and odor of the toxic and nontoxic olives remained normal, but the subcultures of the brine of the nontoxic jars were positive for B. botulinus.

In a second series, 6 No. 2 tall cans of ripe olives were inoculated with suspension No. 4 (10,000,000,000 spores), and incubated at 35 C. for from 10 days to 5½ months. The cans remained "flat" throughout the entire period, and the contents appeared normal in odor and in physical appearance. A very weak toxin was demonstrated in one tin tested after 10 days' and again after 67 days' incubation. When first examined, 2 c c. of the brine killed a guinea-pig in 14 days, but after 67 days' incubation, the same amount proved fatal to a guinea-pig in 4 days. The toxicity of the brine had increased slightly in the interval elapsing between the 2 tests. Subcultures from the nontoxic liquors were positive for B. botulinus.

It must be emphasized that growth and toxin production, irrespective of the suitable reaction, are very irregular in sound, unbroken, ripe olives. Potent toxins have not been demonstrated in any of the experimentally inoculated containers.

Toxin Production in Green and Red Peppers.—Table 8 presents the results obtained by inoculating green and red peppers with heated spores of B. botulinus, followed by incubation at room and incubator temperature.

1. Green Peppers: In series 1, 10 cans (no. 2 short) of green peppers were inoculated with suspension No. 3 (50,000,000 organisms). Five were held at room temperature for 10 months. The contents appeared normal, but 2 c c. of the juice, inoculated subcutaneously, was fatal to guinea-pigs in from 24 to 90 hours. The contents of the 5 cans, incubated at 35 C. for a period of time ranging from 10 days to 10 months, remained normal and nontoxic. However, subcultures in beef heart medium demonstrated the presence of viable B. botulinus organisms.

After 5½ months' incubation at 35 C., the liquor of 4 cans (No. 2 short) of green peppers inoculated with suspension no. 4 (10,000,000,000 spores) was weakly toxic to guinea-pigs, i. e., 2 c c. proved fatal in 15 days. Subcultures from the contents of 3 tins were positive for B. botulinus.

TABLE 8

TOXIN PRODUCTION IN CANNED GREEN AND RED PEPPERS INOCULATED WITH HEATED SPORES OF B. BOTULINUS

Series Number	Incubation Period		Number of Cans				Total Number Cans	Total Contents Spoiled	Total Number Toxic	Cultural Test	P_H
	Temperature	Duration	Flat	Toxic	Sp.-H.S.	Toxic					
II	R. T.	10 mo.	5	5	...	...	5	0	5	++	
Green	35 C.	10 da.	1	0	...	...	1	0	0	++	
pep-	35 C.	22 da.	1	0	...	...	1	0	0	++	
pers	35 C.	10 mo.	3	0	...	...	3	0	0	++	4.6
III	35 C.	5½ mo.	4	1 VW	...	...	4	0	1VW	3 ++	
II	R. T.	10 mo.	6	3 W	...	...	6	0	3W	5 ++	
Red	35 C.	10 da.	1	0	...	...	1	0	0	1 —	
pep-	35 C.	22 da.	1	0	...	...	1	0	0	++	
pers	35 C.	10 mo.	1	0	3	1 VW	4	4 pale	1VW, 1 ?	++	
III	35 C.	5½ mo.	4	0	...	...	4	0	0	++	

2. Red Peppers: Six cans (no. 2 short) of red peppers, inoculated with suspension No. 3 (50,000,000 spores), and held at room temperature for 10 months, remained "flat," and the contents presented a normal appearance. Two c c. of the liquor from 2 containers killed guinea-pigs in 56 hours, while a guinea-pig receiving the same amount from a 3rd tin died in 5 days. Viable organisms were demonstrated in subcultures of the liquor. Six additional tins were inoculated in the same manner, but held at 35 C. Two incubated for 10 and 22 days were normal in appearance and were nontoxic, but B. botulinus was demonstrated in subcultures. After 10 months' incubation, 3 of the remaining 4 containers developed "hard swells." The contents were pale in color. Whether this change was the result of prolonged incubation or due to other factors has not been determined. Only one of the tins was slightly toxic.

In series 2, four of the cans of red peppers, inoculated with suspension no. 4 (10,000,000,000 spores) and incubated at 35 C. for 5½ months, remained "flat," the contents had a normal appearance and were nontoxic for guinea-pigs. Cultures, however, revealed the presence of B. botulinus.

Summary.—The liquor removed from 6 of the 14 cans of green peppers artificially inoculated with heated spores of B. botulinus and incubated for varing periods of time at room temperature and at 35 C. was weakly toxic for guinea-pigs. No visible signs of spoilage could be detected. Three of 16 cans of red peppers treated in a similar manner developed "hard swells;" the contents of one abnormal container was slightly toxic.

Toxin Production in Canned Spinach.—Three series of experiments conducted with canned spinach revealed several interesting facts. The data dealing with these studies are summarized in table 9.

TABLE 9

TOXIN PRODUCTION IN CANNED SPINACH INOCULATED WITH HEATED SPORES OF B. BOTULINUS

Series Number	Incubation Period		Number of Cans				Total Number Cans	Total Contents Spoiled	Total Number Toxic	Cultural Test	PH
	Temperature	Duration	Flat	Toxic	Sp.-H.S.	Toxic					
I	R. T.	60 da.	1	1	...	...	1	1	1VW	++	5.27
	R. T.	90 da.	..	...	1	1	1	0	1S	++	4.88
	R. T.	129 da.	2	0	...	...	2	0	0	1 —* 1 ++	
	R. T.	12 mo.	2	2	...	...	2	...	2W	++	5.15-5.29
	35 C.	10 da.	..	...	1	1	1	1	1W	++	5.8
	35 C.	40 da.	..	...	1	1	1	1	1VW	....	5.1
	35 C.	60-65 d.	..	...	2	0	2	0	0	1±, 1+	5.0
II	35 C.	10 da.	1	1	...	...	1	0	1W	++	
	35 C.	17 da.	..	...	1	1	1	0	1W	++	
	35 C.	22 da.	1	0	...	...	1	0	0	++	
	35 C.	10 mo.	..	...	1	...	1	0	0	—	3.68
III	35 C.	10-14 d.	9	6	2	2	11	3	8 {1VW 1W 3S 3VT	++	5.33-5.60
	35 C.	30 da.	1	1	...	...	1	0	1W		
	35 C.	67 da.	2	2	1	1	3	0	3 {2W 1S		
	35 C.	5½ mo.	3	2	6	6	9	1	8 {1W 2S 5VT		

* Became ++ when retested after 12 months' incubation.

In series 1, four no. 2½ cans of spinach, inoculated with suspension no. 1 (100,000,000 spores), were held at room temperature and tested at intervals ranging from 60 days to 12 months. The following observations were made. One "flat" can, tested after 60 days, presented a normal content, but a very weak toxin had been formed. Another container, held for 90 days, had developed a "springer." The apparently normal contents, when tested on guinea-pigs, was found to be very toxic. Two other cans, tested after 129 days, remained "flat," the contents were also normal in appearance, and they were nontoxic. A subculture of the liquor from one container was negative for B. botulinus. This result may be attributed to the fact that the sample of spinach chosen for the culture was too small. It was shown that the contents of this can was toxic when retested at the end of 12 months. B. botulinus was then readily demonstrated in the liquor. The H-ion concentration of the normal and abnormal tins varied from P_H 4.88 to P_H 5.29.

Two of the 4 remaining cans of series no. 1, incubated at 35 C., and examined after 10 and 40 days, developed "springers." The spoiled contents gave off a putrid odor, but the liquor was weakly toxic. A 3rd container held for 60 days and another for 65 days had developed the condition of a "springer" and a "swell," respectively. The contents were normal in odor and appearance. Toxin could not be demonstrated in either tin. The acidity of the toxic and nontoxic liquors varied from P_H 5.0 to P_H 5.8.

In a second series of experiments, 4 no. 10 cans of spinach were inoculated with suspension no. 3 (50,000,000 spores) and incubated at 35 C. A weak toxin was demonstrated in one "flat" can after 10 days' incubation. Another container incubated for 17 days developed a "swell." The liquor from this tin was slightly toxic. On the other hand, the contents of 2 other tins incubated for 22 days and 10 months were nontoxic. Both the toxic and nontoxic contents were normal.

In series 3, nine of 11 no. 2½ cans of spinach, inoculated with suspension no. 4 (10,000,000,000 spores) and incubated at 35 C. for from 10 to 14 days, remained "flat." The MLD of the liquors removed from 6 toxic tins varied from 1 c c. to 0.001 c c. The contents of one was decidedly spoiled, but the others appeared normal. The acidity varied from P_H 5.33 to P_H 5.6. The contents of the 2 "swells" (P_H 6.13 and P_H 6.98) presented an excessive gas production, was distinctly spoiled and proved very toxic; 0.001 c c. of one liquor proved fatal to a guinea-pig in 60 hours, the same dose of the other in 8 days. The 2 "swells" could not be resoldered, and had to be discarded. Nine "flat" tins were resealed, and repeatedly tested. Two cans, tested after 67 days, remained "flat," and the toxic contents appeared normal; the 3rd one had developed into a "springer" and contained a toxic liquor. After 5½ months' incubation, 3 cans remained "flat." The liquor from 2 was still weakly toxic, while the 3rd had become nontoxic. The remaining 6 tins had all developed into "swells" and were very highly poisonous, but only one appeared distinctly spoiled.

The effect of prolonged incubation on the production of toxin deserves further consideration.

It will be noted in table 10 that: (1) nontoxic liquors (cans no. 2 and no. 12) may on prolonged incubation become highly poisonous; (2) in case weak toxins are produced in the first 10 days, only a trace may remain after a longer period (cans no. 3 and no. 6); (3) a strong toxin once formed does not deteriorate during 5½ months of incubation; in fact, it may increase in strength (can no. 4 and no. 7). In this connection, it should be stated that no tests have been conducted during the period from 14 days to 5½ months. It is naturally possible that the period of highest potency has not been recognized in cans 3 and 6.

The reaction of the spinach in its relation to the generation of toxin is shown in table 11.

It will be noted that the reaction of spinach processed under pressure is, as a whole, favorable for the development of B. botulinus and its toxin. The most potent poisons were formed in the liquor which was less acid. Since

TABLE 10

THE COURSE OF TOXIN PRODUCTION AND SIGNS OF SPOILAGE IN CANNED SPINACH INOCULATED WITH HEATED SPORES OF B. BOTULINUS

Series III. 35 C.

Can No.	Incubation Period	Appearance of Container	Condition of Contents	PH	Cultural Test	Toxin Determinations 2 c c.	1 c c.	0.1 c c.	0.01 c c.	0.001 c c.	0.0001 c c.
2	14 d. 35 C. 3 d. R.T.	Flat	OK	5.53	....	......	......	Neg.	Neg.		
2	5½ mo.	Springer	....	4.8	....	......	......	......	40 hr.	96 hr.	
3	14 d. 35 C. 3 d. R.T.	Flat	OK	5.33	....	......	2 da.	5 da.			
3	5½ mo.	Flat	OK	4.6	....	60 hr.	......	Neg.			
4	10 da.	Flat	Sour	5.42	++	......	48 hr.	90 hr.	96 hr.		
4	67 da.	Flipper	OK	5.40	....	21 hr.	......	36 hr.	42 hr.	Neg.	
4	5½ mo.	S. swell	Off butyric	5.1	....	18 hr.	......	8 hr.	18 hr.	30 hr.	11 da.
6	14 d. 35 C. 3 d. R.T.	Flat	OK	5.36	....	......	......	3 da.	20 da.±		
6	5½ mo.	Flat	OK	5.1	....	Neg.	......	Neg.			
7	14 d. 35 C. 3 d. R.T.	Flat	OK	5.49	....	......	......	20 hr.	40 hr.	4 da.	19 da.±
7	5½ mo.	Springer	OK	5.2	....	......	......	18 hr.	40 hr.	50 hr.	7 da.
9	10 da.	Flat	OK	5.4	++	......	40 hr.	56 hr.	11 da.	14 da.	
9	30 da.	Flat	OK	....	....	......	36 hr.	48 hr.	Neg.	Neg.	
9	67 da.	Flat	OK	4.53	....	30 hr.	......	42 hr.	Neg.		
9	5½ mo.	Flat	OK	4.45	....	40 hr.	......	108 hr.			
10	10 da.	H. swell	Gas	6.13	++	......	20 hr.	......	60 hr.	60 hr.	
12	14 d. 35 C. 3 d. R.T.	Flat	OK	5.60	....	......	......	Neg.	Neg.		
12	5½ mo.	H. swell	OK	5.0	....	......	......	18 hr.	18 hr.	80 hr.	13 da. 1:50,000

TABLE 11

EFFECT OF PH ON TOXIN PRODUCTION IN CANNED SPINACH

Can Number	PH 10-14 Days	M L D 10-14 Days	PH 5½ Months	M L D 5½ Months
		c c.		c c.
1	5.33	Negative		
3	5.33	0.01	4.6	2.0
6	5.36	0.1	5.1	Negative
5	5.37	1.0	5.0	0.01
9	5.40	0.1	4.45	0.1
4	5.42	0.01	5.1	0.0002
7	5.49	0.001	5.20	0.0002
2	5.53	Negative	4.8	0.001
12	5.60	Negative	5.0	0.0001
10	6.13	0.001		
11	6.98	0.001		

the H-ion concentration was determined simultaneously with the toxicity tests, it is obviously impossible to surmise the effect of variations in the initial H-ion concentration on the toxin production. From the available data, however, it appears that an increased acidity has a marked influence on growth and toxin production.

Summary.—Fifteen of the 24 cans of spinach (nos. 2½ and 10) inoculated with heated spores of B. botulinus and held at room or incubator temperature for from 10 days to 12 months developed "swells." The toxic contents of 5 of the abnormal containers gave off a sour, butyric and sometimes cheesy odor. It is, however, important to state that 4 no. 2½ cans and one no. 10 can, with a decidedly toxic content, were "flat." They presented a normal appearance and odor even after 5½ months' incubation at 35 C. (1 can) or 12 months at room temperature (2 cans). Under ordinary circumstances, these cans would unquestionably have reached the consumer, and, when only warmed up, might have caused cases of botulism.

Toxin Production in Canned String Beans.—The data obtained by inoculating canned string beans with heated spores of B. botulinus may be summarized as follows:

In series 1, four no. 2 cans of string beans, inoculated with suspension no. 1 (100,000,000 spores), and held at room temperature, remained "flat." The contents were neither spoiled nor toxic, although cultural tests showed the presence of B. botulinus. The liquors gave average electrometric readings of P_H 5.1. The 4 tins similarly inoculated, but held at 35 C. remained "flat," and the contents were normal. One c c. of a 1:10 dilution of the liquor from one tin killed a guinea-pig in 12 days. B. botulinus was demonstrated in subcultures from the toxic and nontoxic tins. The acidity varied from P_H 4.8 to P_H 5.1.

A second series, consisting of 5 no. 2 cans of string beans, inoculated with suspension no. 3 (50,000,000 spores) and incubated at 35 C., remained "flat" during a period of 10 months, and the contents appeared normal. After 22 days' incubation, one very weak toxin was produced; 2 c c. of this toxic liquor was fatal to a guinea-pig in 9 days. The P_H of an uninoculated tin was 5.1.

In series 3, eleven no. 2 cans of string beans were inoculated with suspension no. 4 (10,000,000,000 spores) and incubated at 35 C. After from 10 to 14 days, the liquors of 6 of the 9 "flat" and otherwise normal appearing cans were toxic; the MLD varied from 1 c c. to 0.001 c c. The acidity fluctuated from P_H 4.5 to 5.39. Subcultures of the nontoxic juices were positive for B. botulinus. The contents of the 2 "swells" was normal in appearance and odor, but toxins in 0.1 c c. and 0.001 cc. amounts were demonstrated. The acidity of these 2 tins was P_H 5.78 and P_H 5.54, respectively. After 5½ months, 2 of the 3 previously nontoxic liquors became toxic. The 3rd was slightly toxic after 67 days, as evidenced by typical symptoms in a guinea-pig 40 hours after the injection of the juice, followed, however, by complete recovery. Two cc. of the contents from the same tin was nontoxic after 5½ months' incubation. During the same time, 2 of the previously "flat" containers developed "swells." Some of the detailed results are shown in table 12.

It is again obvious that no prolonged incubation a nontoxic liquor may become toxic. A weakly toxic one may remain the same or may increase in toxicity. As a rule, a highly poisonous product retains its original potency. There is certainly very little evidence of toxin deterioration.

It will be noted in table 13 that toxin, although produced irregularly in string beans, is capable of being formed throughout a wide acid range. Within certain limits there seems to be little relation between acidity and toxin production.

TABLE 12

THE COURSE OF TOXIN PRODUCTION AND SIGNS OF SPOILAGE IN CANNED STRING BEANS INOCULATED WITH HEATED SPORES OF B. BOTULINUS

Series III. 35 C.

Can No.	Incubation Period	Appearance of Container	Condition of Contents	P_H	Cultural Test	Toxin Determinations 2 c c.	1 c c.	0.1 c c.	0.01 c c.	0.001 c c.	0.0001 c c.
1	10 da.	Flat	OK	5.29	++	Neg. symptoms					
1	67 da.	Flat	OK	4.96	....	40 hr. survived					
1	5½ mo.	Flat	OK	5.0	++	Neg.					
2	14 d. 35 C. 3 d. R.T.	Flat	OK	5.21	....	Neg.					
2	5½ mo.	Flat	OK	4.94	++	6 da.					
4	10 da.	Springer	OK	5.78	++	......	40 hr.	96 hr.			
4	67 da.	H. swell	OK	5.20	....	14 hr.	......	14 hr.			
4	5½ mo.	Springer	OK	5.0	....	18 hr.	......	26 hr.	40 hr.	7 da.	
5	10 da.	Flipper	OK	4.50	++	......	15 da.				
5	67 da.	Springer	OK	4.51	++	14 da.					
5	5½ mo.	Flat*	OK	4.3	++	13 da.					
6	14 d. 35 C. 3 d. R.T.	Flat	OK	5.06	....	......	......	30 hr.	5 da.		
6	5½ mo.	Springer	slightly off	5.0	....	18 hr.	......	18 hr.	30 hr.	48 hr.	
7	10 da.	Flat	OK	5.39	++	34 da.	......	Neg.	Neg.		
7	67 da.	Flat	OK	5.09	....	14 hr.	......	Neg.	Neg.		
7	5½ mo.	Springer	OK	5.2	....	18 hr.	......	18 hr.			
8	10 da.	Flat	OK	5.20	++	......	30 hr.	......	15 da.	11 da.	
8	67 da.	Flat	OK	5.45	....	24 hr.	......	48 hr.	Neg.		
8	5½ mo.	Flat	OK	4.8	....	40 hr.	......	60 hr.			
12	14 d. 35 C. 3 d. R.T.	Flat	OK	5.05	....	......	......	30 hr.	48 hr.	4 da.	
12	5½ mo.	Flat	.....	4.8	....	......	......	40 hr.	56 hr.	5½ da.	

* Can did not develop a springer after resealing on 67th day.

Summary.—Only 5 of 24 cans of string beans inoculated with heated spores of B. botulinus and kept under observation in the usual manner developed "swells." The pods were firm, and a slightly objectionable odor was detected in only one tin, although all of the liquors proved toxic to guinea-pigs. Seven flat cans gave similar results.

Further studies on the growth and toxin production of B. botulinus in home canned string beans are necessary in order to explain the frequent occurrence of botulism due to this vegetable.

Toxin Production in Evaporated Milk.—In series 1, the following observations were made on 5 cans (baby size, pin hole filler) of evaporated milk,

TABLE 13

EFFECT OF PH ON TOXIN PRODUCTION IN CANNED STRING BEANS

Can Number	PH 10 Days	M L D 10 Days	PH 5½ Months	M L D 5½ Months
		c c.		c c.
5	4.5	2.0	4.3	2.0
12	5.05	0.001	4.8	0.001
6	5.06	0.01	5.0	0.001+
9	5.10	0.1+	6.0	0.1+
3	5.11	0.001	5.0	0.1 neg.
8	5.20	0.1	4.8	0.1
2	5.21	0.1 neg.	4.9	2.0
1	5.29	Negative	5.0	Negative
7	5.39	Negative	5.2	0.01
11	5.54	0.001+		
4	5.78	0.1	5.0	0.001

TABLE 14

TOXIN PRODUCTION IN CANNED EVAPORATED MILK INOCULATED WITH HEATED SPORES OF B. BOTULINUS

Series Number	Temperature	Incubation Period	Number of Spores Inoculated	Number of Cans: Flat	Number of Cans: Toxic	Number of Cans: Sp. H.S.	Number of Cans: Toxic	Total Number Cans	Total Content Spoiled	Total Number Toxic	Cultural Tests
1	R. T.	10 da.	1 billion	1	1	0	0	1	0	1VW	++
	R. T.	122 da.	100 thousand 50 million 1 billion	3	3	0	0	3	3	3 {1S {2VT	
	R. T.	129 da.	50 million	1	1	0	0	1	0	1W	++
	35 C.	10 da.	50 million	1	1	0	0	1	0	1VW	++
	35 C.	17 da.	25 million	1	0	0	0	1	0	0	++
	35 C.	22 da.	50 million	1	0	0	0	1	0	0	++
	35 C.	10 mo.	50 million	2	1	0	0	2	2	1VW	++
II	35 C.	10 da.	10 billion	2	0	0	0	2	0	0	++
	35 C.	14 da.	10 billion	1	1	0	0	1	0	1W*	++
	35 C.	67 da.	10 billion	2	1	0	0	2	0	1W*	++
	35 C.	5½ mo.	10 billion	4	0	1	0	5	3	0†	++
	35 C.	10 da.	Soil suspension + 10 billion spores	2	1	0	0	2	2	1S	++
	35 C.	5½ mo.	Soil suspension + 10 billion spores	4	3	0	0	4	4	3W	++

* Same cans.
† One nontoxic can had been weakly toxic after 14 and 67 days.

inoculated with varying numbers of spores of suspension no. 3 and held at room temperature. The contents of one container, tested after 10 days, presented a normal appearance, but was weakly toxic to guinea-pigs; that of 3 other cans held for 122 days was coagulated, gave off a strong butyric acid odor and was very toxic when tested on guinea-pigs. The contents of the 5th tin opened on the 129th day was not spoiled, but was weakly toxic. Three cans similarly inoculated, but held at 35 C. for 10, 17 and 22 days, did not show any visible signs of spoilage, but the contents of one tin tested after 10 days was very weakly toxic. Two other tins of the same series held for 10 months appeared slightly thickened, but no objectionable odor could be detected. A very weak toxin was demonstrated in the contents of one tin.

In series 2, twelve cans (baby size, pin hole filler) were inoculated with suspension no. 4 (10,000,000,000 spores). Six received, in addition, a small amount of heated (Arnold 1 hour) soil, which, on previous tests had been found to contain spores of B. botulinus. A weak toxin was demonstrated in one container tested after 14 days' and again after 67 days' incubation at 35 C. After 5½ months, the contents of the same tin and 3 others were nontoxic, although the contents of 2 were slightly curdled. The cheesy contents of 2 of the 6 cans inoculated with soil and tested after 10 days' incubation at 35 C. gave off a marked butyric acid odor. One contained a strong toxin (1 c c. of a 1:1,000 dilution was fatal to a guinea-pig in 13 days). The other 4 cans remained "flat" for a period of 5½ months, but when examined the milk was found to be coagulated and gave off an acid odor. The whey of 3 tins was toxic; 1 c c. of a 1:5 dilution killed a guinea-pig in from 3 to 5 days.

It will be seen that: (1) spoilage in evaporated milk is irregular; (2) apparently the number of organisms inoculated does not play an important rôle in spoilage; (3) milk appearing normal may be weakly toxic; (4) the addition of soil increases spoilage but does not materially increase the production of toxin.

Numerous cans of sweetened condensed milk inoculated with spore suspension no. 4 remained normal. The contents were always nontoxic, but viable B. botulinus was demonstrated in cultures made from the cans which had been incubated for 5½ months.

Summary.—It is obvious from the data presented that the toxin production and degree of spoilage noted in evaporated milk inoculated with spores of B. botulinus are very irregular. The contents of 4 cans were spoiled and toxic, 4 others presented a normal but toxic content; 2 were coagulated and nontoxic, while 6 were neither toxic nor spoiled. In 6 cans, inoculated with a mixture of soil and heated spores of B. botulinus, distinct spoilage was noted, although only 4 strong and one weak toxin could be demonstrated. The addition of soil obviously increases spoilage, but does not influence the toxin production. There are definite indications that the toxin once formed in evaporated milk may deteriorate on prolonged incubation.

Toxin Production in Very Acid Foods.—When heated spores of B. botulinus were inoculated into canned tomatoes, sauerkraut, apricots, cherries, peaches, pears, plums, raspberries, and strawberries, visible spoilage of the contents could not be detected at any time, although a few "swells" developed after prolonged incubation. No relationship could be established between the bulging of the container and the toxicity of the contents. In the majority of cases, subcultures prepared in beef heart with samples of the contents gave a luxuriant growth of B. botulinus. In a number of instances, however, these cultures remained sterile. It is impossible to offer a satisfactory explanation of these results, but in future tests the following factors deserve careful consideration: (1) the size of the sample to be chosen for the culture; (2) the retarded germination of the spores; (3) the possibility of an injury or even the destruction of the spores incubated for months in an acid food.

In no case were toxins demonstrated previous to 5½ months' incubation at 35 C., or 10 months at room temperature. After this period very weak toxins were formed in a small number of cans of the products enumerated in table 15.

TABLE 15

TOXINS FORMED IN CANS OF VARIOUS FOODS

Food	Total Number Tested	Suspension Number	Number of Spores	Number Toxic	Incubation Period
Tomatoes......	10	(3)	50,000,000	2 very weak toxins	10 mo. R. T.
Apricots.......	22	(1)	100,000,000	2 very weak toxins	12 mo. R. T.
Cherries........	14	(1)	100,000,000	6 (4 weak toxins)	12 mo. R. T.
		(4)	10,000,000,000	(2 weak toxins)	5½ mo. 35 C.
Peaches........	17	(4)	10,000,000,000	2 weak toxins	5½ mo. 35 C.
Pears..........	21	(1)	100,000,000	2 weak toxins	12 mo. R. T.
Plums.........	17	(4)	10,000,000,000	6 (4 very weak toxins)	5½ mo. 35 C.
		(1)	100,000,000	(2 very weak)	12 mo. R. T.
Strawberries...	7	(1)	100,000,000	2 weak toxins	12 mo. R. T.

It will be noted that the majority of products which became toxic had been held at room temperature. A few samples were found to be weakly toxic after an incubation of 5½ months at 35 C. It is not unlikely that an increase in the dissociation of the H-ions at the higher temperature was responsible for the differences in toxin formation. Preliminary toxin tests were carried out in the usual manner. As a control a number of the toxic syrups were forcibly fed and some tested by a toxin-antitoxin neutralization test. It was not surprising to find that a few liquors which were fatal to guinea-pigs were not neutralized by the antitoxin. In fact, it was found that the toxic substances were heat resistant, and were harmless on feeding. These observations indicate that the presence of botulinus toxin in acid foods must be determined by feeding and not by inoculation tests. Cans containing soil, in addition to the spores, showed no increased toxicity. The toxin content of the liquors was, as a rule, very low, and it is most unlikely that their consumption would have caused human botulism. The experiments should be repeated and the cans kept under observation for several years. In this connection, it should be stated that the spores used for the infection experiments were not heated in the fruit juice; in fact, the spores were introduced into the containers in enormous numbers and not subjected to the severe injury of processing. It is most unlikely that they would have survived the commercial processing procedures without serious injury and consequent retarded germination. The latter factor is an important one in food with an acidity below P_H 4.5, and is mainly responsible for the weak toxins produced in a few cans after prolonged incubation.

From a practical standpoint it may be stated that no outbreak of botulism from commercially canned fruits has been reported. Furthermore, it is believed that there is no danger of botulism from this source unless the raw product contains bruised or rotting portions not removed by trimming.

DISCUSSION

The data presented in the preceding paragraphs definitely indicate that sterile canned food products artificially contaminated with detoxified spores of B. botulinus, but not processed after the inoculation, may present varying degrees of spoilage, and may contain the specific toxin, when incubated at 35 C. or at room temperature for at least one year. For the sake of discussion, the canned foods are conveniently divided into 3 groups: (1) foods which exhibit marked physical and chemical changes and become regularly toxic; (2) very acid products, which rarely, if ever, show signs of botulinus spoilage, and (3) certain vegetables which spoil and become toxic irregularly. The products of the last group may be highly poisonous, but may present little or no visible sign of spoilage.

Corn, peas, sweet potatoes, and salmon, for example, belong to the first group. Growth of B. botulinus spores is quite regular in these foods, and little or no retarded toxin production has been noted. It is well known that the first 3 products are rich in carbohydrates, while salmon consists mostly of protein. On account of this composition and favorable reaction, these products form a suitable medium for the growth of B. botulinus. Spoilage occurs in all the tins held both at 35 C. and at room temperature; invariably the content is highly toxic. However, in 2 cans of salmon held at room temperature for 60 and 90 days, the visible spoilage of the toxic contents was doubtful or exceedingly slight.

Very acid vegetables, such as sauerkraut and tomatoes, and acid fruits, including apricots, cherries, peaches, pears, plums, raspberries, and strawberries, compose the second group. The only sign of spoilage may consist of a slight bulging of the containers; invariably the contents have appeared normal. In all probability, these "swells" are due to the liberation of hydrogen caused by the action of the acids on the tin plate, and are not due to bacterial activity.

The observations recorded in this paper indicate that toxins are rarely, if at all, generated in acid fruits inoculated with pure, detoxified spore suspensions and not processed subsequently. However, Dickson, Burke and Ward,[5] who inoculated canned peaches, pears, and apricots with thoroughly washed spores of B. botulinus, report that after 3 months' incubation at 26 C., 1 c c. of the syrup proved fatal to guinea-pigs within 48 hours. The production of toxins in this short period of time seems, in the light of the data mentioned in this paper, rather doubtful. It is not stated by the investigators whether the spores were heated to destroy the vegetative forms, nor did they consider the possibility that toxins might cling to the washed organisms. Thom, Edmondson and Giltner[6] have demonstrated that B. botulinus suspensions must be washed about 14 times before they are entirely free from toxin. Furthermore, it is still an open question whether the organism is capable of generating toxins by mere disintegration of its washed vegetative forms, or unheated spores.[11] It is quite possible that toxin production in acid fruits inoculated with a large number of unheated spores is mainly due to the action of ferments and by no means indicative of growth. As the spores are always subjected to heat in the course of the usual canning procedures, it is impossible to draw far-reaching conclusions from the inoculation experiments conduced with unheated spore suspensions. The data presented in this paper, however, indicate that detoxified spores of B. botulinus do not find in acid products a favorable medium for their growth.

The third group includes a variety of food products, such as asparagus, beets, olives, peppers, spinach, string beans, and evaporated milk. It has been noted that the products (1) may at times be spoiled, but nontoxic; (2) that they may be spoiled and toxic, and (3) most important of all, they may present no visible signs of spoilage, although they are poisonous. Spoilage without toxin production is rare, although several such instances have been recorded in the course of the numerous tests. With but one exception, this phenomenon has been noted in tins incubated for a long period. The following expla-

[11] Coleman and Meyer: Some Observations on the Pathogenicity of B. botulinus, Paper X of this series: Jour. Infect. Dis., 1922, 31, p. 622.

nations can be offered for this condition: (1) The contents of a few tins may have been nonsterile originally; or (2) B. botulinus may have grown and produced a weak toxin, which, however, deteriorated on prolonged incubation. The following observation deserves some consideration in this connection. Two tins of asparagus to which soil had been added produced "swells" in less than 14 days. The liquors were nontoxic, but beef heart cultures prepared from the contents gave positive findings for B. botulinus. It is not unlikely that (1) the composition and reaction of the contents in the 2 containers favored primarily the soil organisms, and the accumulation of metabolites rendered the environment unsuitable for the germination of the B. botulinus spores; or (2) the toxic products of B. botulinus have been destroyed by the growth of the soil bacteria. These points are being investigated, and the results will be reported at a later date.

Contrary to the repeated observations made on veal infusion or beef heart peptone cultures, the data presented in this paper indicate that the toxin once formed in canned food products kept at 35 C. or room temperature rarely deteriorates. In fact, it is known that it increased on standing at 20 C., and it is therefore possible that underprocessed foods, which have been preserved for several months are far more dangerous than those which have been preserved quite recently, not only on account of the behavior of the toxin in vegetables, but also as a result of the peculiar retarded germination of the spores. Careful attention should be given to these points in the investigation of future outbreaks of botulism.

In the past, too much emphasis has been placed on the simultaneous occurrence of spoilage and toxin production. It is quite true that, as a rule, products which are toxic show the more common signs of spoilage. It should, however, be kept in mind that when B. botulinus spores survive the process because of understerilization, other spores may survive the treatment and cause spoilage. It is quite possible that in some regions other spores, for example those of B. sporogenes, are likely to occur in vastly greater numbers than those of B. botulinus, and for that reason survive processing even though in the same number they are less resistant to heat. Visible spoilage of certain vegetables is therefore frequently enhanced by bacteria which are associated with B. botulinus in nature. That this type of association does not, however, always occur, and that in some instances containers reach the consumer in which B. botulinus is the only organism present, has already been reported.[12] In the inoculation series with pure cultures of detoxified spores, it has been noted that certain cans of vegetables have remained normal in appearance, although they have been very poisonous. These observations are quite in harmony with the histories dealing with outbreaks of human or animal botulism. The incriminated food, such as string beans, spinach, ripe olives, and potted meat (Loch Maree, Scotland) is stated to have appeared normal in texture, taste and odor; in others, the disintegration of the product is reported to have been so slight that the housewife was prompted to confirm her doubts by tasting the suspected food. At times the taste was abnormal; in several instances spoilage was not noted until the food had been heated. The data of interest are summarized in table 16.

TABLE 16

OBSERVATIONS RECORDED IN THE HISTORIES OF AMERICAN OUTBREAKS OF BOTULISM *

Report No.	Description of Odor or Taste
	Home Canned String Beans
1	"Odor unpleasant"
2	"Taste not right"
9, 11	Jar leaking, sharp, biting taste on cooking, diagreeable odor
12	Peculiar taste, attributed to lemon juice
13	On boiling, disagreeable odor, peculiar irritating taste
15	Beans hard, but supposedly not spoiled
17	No evidence of spoilage, no bad odor or taste
	Commercially Canned Vegetables and Fruits
3	Spinach. Visible spoilage and repulsive odor on heating
4	Spinach. Neither spoiled in appearance or taste, or odor on boiling
7	Minced olives. No odor when opened, no bad taste when consumed, but a definits odor emanated from the tin when removed from garbage pail 2 days later
19	Minced olives. Bitter, or of unusual taste
21	Minced olives. No evident signs of spoilage

* For details consult reference 1.

It will be noted from table 16, that the string beans involved in 3 of 8 outbreaks were apparently normal in appearance and odor, while in 2 other instances, they were so slightly spoiled that the housewife tasted the suspicious food in order to confirm her distrust. In the other 3 instances, the string beans gave off a bad odor which, however, did not prevent the consumer from sampling the food.

It has already been stated that the toxin production in string beans and sound ripe olives is irregular. Visible spoilage of the contents is frequently not demonstrable. Many tins have been inoculated, and when examined by several workers have been declared normal and fit for consumption, although toxins have subsequently been demon-

[12] Jour. Infect Dis., 1922, 31, p. 501.

strated by feeding experiments on guinea-pigs. It must also be emphasized that this laboratory has encountered great difficulty in producing potent toxins in sound and sterile commercially or home canned ripe olives and string beans. In fact, it has been noted that a mash of the fruits or vegetables makes a much more suitable culture medium than the whole product. The cellular casing enclosing the olives and string bean pods apparently renders the food material inaccessible for the bacteria. This may explain why sometimes bruised, partially decomposed, vegetables and fruits may undergo botulinus spoilage more readily than sound raw products.

DeBord, Edmondson and Thom[13] made cultures from 500 glass or tin containers of commercially packed olives. Satisfactory odor and appearance were so uniformly accompanied by sterility that they limited their studies to material which did not pass physical examination. They, furthermore, found that in all of the material infected with B. botulinus the odor detected when the container was opened or the odor of the olives when secured separately from the original container was distinctly offensive. It was, however, impossible to select toxin containing samples from other spoiled samples without tests on animals. Koser[14] found that 9.5% of apparently sound ripe olives revealed the presence of living micro-organisms. B. botulinus, however, was only demonstrated in containers which appeared spoiled. On the other hand, the data presented in this paper reveal the possibility of toxin production in tins of pickled ripe olives which present no signs of spoilage, provided B. botulinus is the only organism surviving the process of sterilization.

It has been noted repeatedly that asparagus, beets, and spinach may appear perfectly normal and still contain the potent toxin of B. botulinus. There are several instances on record in which spinach apparently normal was the causative food in outbreaks of botulism (San Diego and Kendallville). Thom[15] points out that the toxicity, particularly in spinach, from which either pure or mixed cultures have been obtained, is generally associated with definite signs of spoilage, but that the product may sometimes reach the dangerous stage before spoilage is recognizable. He emphasizes the fact, however, that in the toxic samples the evidence of spoilage is rarely, if ever, absent.

[13] Jour. Am. Med. Assn., 1920, 74, p. 1220.
[14] Jour. Agric. Res., 1920, 20, p. 375.
[15] Am. Jour. Pub. Health, 1922, 12, p. 49.

In another communication,[16] he says, "In dealing with products that have been canned for several weeks to several months, the results of physical examination have so consistently coincided with those of cultural and animal experiment that we have regularly 'eaten our judgment' in various canned foods." It is unquestionably true that in nearly 99% of the instances, the poisonous food product is visibly spoiled and has therefore been discarded. However, the observations made by this laboratory in the course of numerous epidemiologic investigations, and more recently on the artificially infected tins, emphasize the fact that contaminated food may pass through a stage when signs of spoilage are not noticeable, but potent toxins may be demonstrated. This phenomenon is particularly noticeable in contaminated cans of asparagus, beets, olives, spinach, and string beans held at room temperature for from 60 days to 12 months, or for 10 days at 35 C. Table 17 illustrates this statement.

TABLE 17

THE TOXICITY OF INFECTED CANS AT VARYING PERIODS OF INCUBATION

Products Artificially Infected	Held at Room Temperature (20 C.) for From 60 Days to 12 Months		Incubated at 35 C. for 10 Days	
	Spoilage as Judged by Appearance of Containers, Odor and Contents, Per cent of Cans	Toxicity for Guinea-Pigs, Per cent of Cans	Spoilage, Per cent of Cans	Toxicity, Per cent of Cans
Asparagus	0	50	31	81
Beets	0	50	42	100
Ripe pickled olives	0	0	0	20
Spinach	25	100	23	77
String beans	0	0	15	69

Incubation at body temperature tends to increase spoilage. The commercial packer who keeps his products in relatively warm storehouses, or who ships his goods during the summer months, favors the growth of the bacteria which have survived the processing procedures. The "swelled" cans are eliminated from the pack in the course of the ordinary trade procedures, as unmerchantable, and it is not unlikely that numerous toxic cans have as a result of these occurrences never reached the consumer. Incubation of a definite percentage of cans in order to detect defects in sterilization can, therefore, be highly recommended.

It is most regrettable that, in spite of the numerous tests conducted by Weinzirl[17] and Cheney,[18] no laboratory has conducted

[16] Address before Home Canners Association of America, May 3, 1922.
[17] Jour. Med. Res., 1919, 39, p. 349.
[18] Ibid., 40, p. 177.

thorough bacteriologic or toxicologic tests on spoiled commercially canned food, except on pickled olives and spinach. The actual percentage of toxic and spoiled cans of string beans, asparagus, beets, etc., which as "swells" never reach the consumer, is not known. It is, therefore, suggested that in the future spoiled cans of a lot of spinach, olives, etc., be retained by the packer or distributor and, in case it is proved that the spoilage is due to understerilization, it should be referred to a laboratory properly equipped for toxicologic examinations. In this manner, the toxin incidence of spoiled canned food could be determined, and its relationship to a product or to a lot of canned goods could be based on facts and not on mere conjectures.

The recent literature on botulism presents a tendency to attribute all outbreaks of this intoxication to commercially canned food, although detailed epidemiologic studies indicate that 62 of the known 97 human and practically all the fatalities among chickens are directly traceable to home preserved vegetable and animal products. There seems to be no reason for supposing that the usual signs of warning to the consumer are less evident in the case of foods prepared in the household than those purchased in the market. It appears profitable to analyze briefly this supposition. Sterilization of vegetables or fruits by some of the methods commonly employed in the household is practically impossible. Facilities for maintaining cooking temperatures considerable above the boiling point are not always available. The major portion of home preserved foods are packed in glass jars. The bacterial activity in underprocessed products causes the evolution of gases and subsequently a bulging of the lid indicating spoilage. Frequently, however, the gases escape through a leaky rubber ring, and very little outside evidence of fermentation is noticeable on the container. It can be stated without any fear of contradiction that the testing for the existence of a vacuum is not in the province of an ordinary housewife. Furthermore, strains of B. botulinus have been isolated which produce a potent poison and relatively little gas. It is, therefore, quite conceivable that food products may undergo botulinus spoilage with little or no gas production, leaving no trace on the lids and presenting even a fair vacuum, although they are highly toxic. This condition is not infrequently noted in home canned string beans. It has been stated that the odor which emanates from a jar on opening may be used as a criterion to detect spoiled home canned food products. Sufficient evidence has been presented in this paper to indicate that asparagus, string beans, beets, and even spinach may be toxic, although the odor may be either only slightly "off" or considered by several experienced workers as typical for the food product. Most of the odors are due to volatile substances, and their detection is sometimes difficult when the jar or its contents is cold. Moreover, home canned foods are consumed mostly during the winter months, and the jars removed from the cold pantry or cellar are rarely warmed up before they are opened or examined. Under these circumstances, it sometimes happens that spoilage is only noted when the product is warmed up or boiled. The presence of spoilage is not always indicated by a readily detected odor and failure to recognize unusual odors is rather common among many people. Equally unreliable as a criterion of spoilage is the appearance of the liquor or the color and the texture of the product. The average consumers of home canned foods lack the necessary experience to make a competent examination of the products from the foregoing point of view. This statement is borne out in this laboratory by the fact that string beans and spinach were designated by the consumer as normal in texture, taste, etc., although they proved to be definitely desintegrated, discolored and highly toxic.

The prevention of human botulism will, therefore, remain a difficult problem until safe processing procedures are employed in the household for the preservation of certain vegetables; it is advisable to keep in mind that the judgment of such products is difficult, and their consumption may involve some risk. It must, therefore, be recommended that such food be recooked before serving it. In this connection, attention is called to the fact that housewives frequently preserve fruits or vegetables which are not fresh. The spores of B. botulinus, if present, may rapidly increase in numbers whenever spoilage of the raw products occurs to any extent. The use of fresh and sound raw products preferably obtained directly from the home garden and packed with the least delay is one of the greatest means of protection against botulism. When once this prerequisite is appreciated by the home canner and processing procedures are employed which destroy the spores of this anaerobe in products with a P_H above 4.5, the uncertainty and uneasiness which is felt by the consumer in judging or in deciding the ultimate disposal of an apparently sound or slightly spoiled can or jar of preserved food will be completely eliminated .

The question, "Why are certain products more liable to botulinus spoilage than others?" deserves some consideration. The subject is best discussed under three headings: (1) the degree of contamination; (2) the composition and the reaction of the product, and (3) retarded germination.

(1) The results recorded in the 3 experimental series show some discrepancy. Spoilage and toxin production, both as to frequency and potency, were much lower in the first 2 series than in the 3rd. Several explanations may be offered for these variations. The suspensions used in the 3 series were not identical. The number of strains and the size of the inoculum varied. Most of the strains used in the suspension employed in the last series of experiments were isolated from foods responsible for human and animal cases of botulism. In the first series, 100,000,000, in the second 50,000,000 and in the third 10,000,000,000 spores were used for the infection of each can. The highest percentages of spoilage and toxicity were noted in the third series. These and similar observations indicate that the degree of contamination has a considerable influence on the course and extent of the botulinus spoilage in canned foods. It is unnecessary to dwell on this point. Numerous observations indicate that underprocessed lots of spinach, asparagus, etc., which have been poorly blanched, or, as a report definitely states, could not be freed from soil and fertilizer adherent to the raw product, may show a high percentage of spoilage and B. botulinus containing toxic or nontoxic cans. Cleanliness, soundness, and careful blanching of the raw material have probably prevented the occurrence of toxic cans in lots which have in the past been underprocessed. It must be kept in mind that B. botulinus as a soil anaerobe is usually accompanied by other spoilage bacteria, which may assist its growth and toxin production. Cans of spinach artificially contaminated with B. botulinus and soil bacteria were slightly more toxic than those infected with pure cultures of the toxicogenic anaerobe. String beans regularly became poisonous when contaminated with soil and B. botulinus mixtures. Infections of this vegetable with pure cultures produced irregularly toxic liquors of average or low potency. No differences between the cans of asparagus and beets inoculated with or without soil were recorded. On the other hand, spoilage in milk was more regular when soil was added, although no difference could be noted in the potency of the poison. As a whole, the results indicate that the percentage of spoiled cans was increased when the food was artificially contaminated with soil together with B. botulinus spores, but the percentage of toxic tins remained approximately the same in the series infected with pure or mixed cultures.

These laboratory observations are in part confirmed by epidemiologic observations, that is, any lot of food showing an appreciable percentage of spoilage due to understerilization is potentially dangerous. Extensive spoilage is, however, not only clear evidence of a radical failure in sterilization, but also of a high degree of contamination of the raw material. Lots of canned foods showing this condition should be removed from sale and inspected by a competent person to determine the cause of spoilage. If it is not shown definitely that spoilage is due to some other cause than underprocessing the spoiled cans should be destroyed, and the normal cans reprocessed.

(2) The two most important factors which influence the germination and growth of B. botulinus spores in canned food are the composition and the reaction of the product. Studies conducted by C. Ç. Dozier in this laboratory have shown that B. botulinus has, in peptone solution, a growth range from P_H 4.5 to 9.0. In vegetable infusions as, for example, peas, corn, beans and spinach, in which the acidity has been partially neutralized, the growth of the spores is just as good in spinach with a P_H of 5.94 as in peas with a P_H of 7.05, while in the foods with a natural reaction, the growth is better in corn with a P_H of 6.4 than in spinach with a P_H of 5.0. These and similar tests which will be reported more in detail elsewhere indicate that the composition of the food, the protein and carbohydrate and salt content are probably just as important as the reactions in governing the liability of certain vegetables to B. botulinus spoilage. Variations in the reaction are probably responsible for the differences in spoilage and toxicity in one and the same or in different products. The influence of the hydrogen-ion concentration on the production of B. botulinus toxin in artificially infected tins is shown in table 18.

TABLE 18

AVERAGE PH OF TINS BEFORE INOCULATION, AFTER INOCULATION (TOXIC AND NONTOXIC)

Products	P_H Before Inoculation. Series 1 and 2	P_H after Inoculation and Incubation	
		Toxic Liquors Average	Nontoxic Liquors Average
Asparagus	5.5; 5.4; (average 5.65)*	4.9	4.5
Beets	5.0; 4.95; 4.86; (average 5.21)	5.4	4.8
Spinach	5.3; 5.17; (average 5.43)	5.25	5.04 (3.68)
String beans	5.56; 5.39; 5.08; (average 5.97); home canned 5.97.	5.06	4.9

* Averages calculated from figures given in National Canners' Association Bull. 17 L, 1921.

Unfortunately, determinations of the reaction were not made on all the containers before the inoculation, and it is, therefore, impossible to draw final conclusions; but the few comparative tests indicate that the hydrogen-ion concentration of the nontoxic liquor and of normal, but inoculated and incubated cans, showed a higher hydrogen-ion concentration than that of the toxic ones. In certain containers and some products, as for example string beans, a reaction close to a P_H of 5.0 is apparently of greater consequence for the germination of the B. botulinus spores than the same reaction in spinach or asparagus. In food products which furnish little extractives and food material in the liquors or brine and those which have a P_H close to 5.0 or below 5.0, B. botulinus grows apparently with considerable difficulty, or not at all. This fact may explain, in part, why B. botulinus develops better in home, than in commercially, canned string beans. In the former, the hydrogen-ion concentration is always lower, probably due to the shorter and less vigorous sterilizing procedures.

Seasonal variations in the raw material bring about differences in the composition of the finished product. Furthermore, Bigelow and Cathcart[19] have pointed out that the time and temperature applied in the course of sterilization have a marked influence on the acidity of the contents of a can. It is, therefore, not at all surprising to record a striking difference in the liability of certain vegetables, either as individual cans or lots, to undergo botulinus spoilage. The fundamental chemical factors which are responsible for these conditions deserve careful study. They will be considered in the papers dealing with the biochemical activities of B. botulinus.

(3) The data presented in this and subsequent papers leave no doubt that the irregular growth of B. botulinus in underprocessed vegetables even in test tubes is in part due to the peculiar retarded germination of its spores. The repeated examination of numerous containers has shown that even slightly heated spores may remain quiescent for weeks, and toxin production may be delayed for 12 months or even longer. This behavior of the B. botulinus spores should be carefully considered in connection with the sterility tests of canned goods. Observations made in the course of experiments dealing with the processing of spinach suggest that containers to be tested for sterility from B. botulinus should be incubated for at least 6 to 12 months. These points have been discussed in a recent paper by one of the writers,[12] and will also be considered in a communication on experimental packing tests.

[19] National Canners' Association, Bull 17 L, 1921.

RECOMMENDATIONS

Based on the facts presented in this paper, it is considered advisable to make certain recommendations regarding the handling of the raw products, preparing them for canning, and the procedures other than adequate sterilization which will safeguard against botulism. These recommendations are briefly summarized under the following 5 heads: (1) sanitation, (2) processing, (3) coding, (4) incubation, and (5) storage.

1. *Sanitation.*—It has been shown that B. botulinus occurs naturally in the soil and is widely distributed throughout the world. It has also been shown that with B. botulinus, as with other bacteria, the number of organisms present in food has a profound influence on the amount of heat necessary to sterilize—the greater the number of organisms, the longer the process must be made. It is obvious from this that the first step in preventing B. botulinus from existing in canned foods is to cleanse the raw product thoroughly. From a practical standpoint it can be said that the thorough removal of dirt is one of the essential features in safeguarding against botulism. It has also been shown that B. botulinus thrives and multiplies when present in decaying vegetation. Whenever spoilage of the raw product occurs to any extent, spores of B. botulinus, if present, may increase rapidly in numbers. From this it is evident that raw material which has been improperly stored so that it heats, permits the growth of mold, or shows some evidence of decomposition, is far more liable to contain large numbers of resistant spores of B. botulinus than sound and fresh material. The use of fresh and sound raw products packed with the least delay is one of the greatest means of protection against botulism. Those products which from their nature must be stored before being canned (for instance, sweet potatoes, apples, pears and dried beans) should be stored under conditions that will prevent molding and excessive deterioration. The statements above apply particularly to nonacid products. The more acid products, such as fruit, tomatoes, kraut and rhubarb, are not suitable mediums for the growth of B. botulinus; but even in fruit it has been shown that bruises, worm holes, decay and other defects may make possible the growth of B. botulinus, and such portions should be removed before canning, or fruit containing such imperfections discarded. All practical measures should be adopted to secure the highest degree of sanitation with all products.

2. *Processing.*—Products with a P_H value below 4.5 are not subject to botulinus spoilage when packed under proper sanitary conditions. All products with a higher P_H value than 4.5 should be processed so that all portions of the can will be heated sufficinetly to destroy the most resistant strains of B. botulinus. The time and temperature of processing necessary with each canned product under the usual canning conditions are being determined by means of the data already presented in Paper XI of this series.[20]

3. *Coding.*—A system should be adopted in every plant by which each can is so marked that it may be identified with the batch with which it was processed, with the block in the warehouse in which it was stored, or with a lot of cans no larger than a day's run on a single line. There are many reasons why such a system of coding should be adopted. Among these reasons are the following:

(a) It sometimes happens that some imperfection in the raw product, indiscernible until after canning, results in an abnormal appearance, odor or taste in the finished product.

(b) A mistake is sometimes made in the strength of brine or syrup.

(c) Imperfections in the can and improper double-seaming are usually limited to relatively small lots.

(d) Because of some peculiarity of the raw product, it is discolored by the process more at some times than others. In such cases coding sometimes makes it possible to grade the canned product according to color or to separate out a quantity of goods whose color is not up to the average.

(e) A mistake in the operation of the filler or miscalculation of the extent to which goods will swell or shrink sometimes causes the improper filling of canned foods which is only detected after the goods are stored.

(f) A mistake in either time or temperature of processing may result in a single batch of cans being understerilized or overcooked.

(g) On incubating samples as suggested below, it may be found that the process employed is insufficient. In such cases it is of the utmost importance to be able to separate all goods shown to be underprocessed.

4. *Incubation.*—It is believed that the recommendations given above, if followed without variation, will yield a safe product with respect to

[20] Esty, J. R., and Meyer, K. F.: Jour. Infect. Dis., 1922, 31, p. 65.

botulism. The uncertainty of the human factor must always be considered and guarded against. With this in view, it is strongly recommended that cans be withdrawn systematically from all products (except molasses and syrups) having a P_H value greater than 4.5, and incubated for at least 10 days at a temperature not higher than 37 C. If such incubation shows more than 5% spoilage, every effort should be made to ascertain the cause of the spoilage. Unless it is found to be due to some other cause than underprocessing, the swelled cans should be destroyed and the flat ones resterilized by safe processing procedures.

5. *Storage.*—If, on storage, the spoilage in products with a P_H value above 4.5 due to understerilization is found to be material, the swelled cans should be destroyed, and the cans which appear normal should be reprocessed as directed under "incubation." Before such action can be taken, however, the cause of the spoilage should be accurately determined. Resterilization is obviously of no value if a considerable amount of spoilage in any lot of goods is found to be due to some other cause than understerilization.

SUMMARY AND CONCLUSIONS

Systematic bacteriologic and toxicologic studies made on 346 cans of commercially packed food products of both plant and animal origin, artificially inoculated with washed and heated spores of B. botulinus, but not processed after the inoculation, and incubated at room temperature, at 35 C., or both, for periods extending from 10 days to 12 months, suggest the following conclusions:

Corn, peas, salmon, sweet potatoes, and pumpkin undergo spoilage regularly after relatively short periods of incubation; the decomposed products are very toxic.

Spoilage and toxin production in asparagus and beets are irregular, and growth at room temperature is frequently retarded. The cans may remain flat, although the contents are spoiled and toxic. The toxin production of B. botulinus in asparagus and beets is not always accompanied by spoilage of sufficient intensity to warn the consumer.

Toxin production, irrespective of the suitable reaction, is irregular in sound, unbroken ripe "mission" olives. Potent toxins are rarely obtained in experimentally infected cans.

Red and green peppers (pimentoes) rarely exhibit visible signs of spoilage. The contents of the abnormal containers is weakly toxic.

The multiplication of B. botulinus in spinach is irregular and is not always accompanied by the evolution of gas. In a series of 24 cans, five (4 no. 2½ and 1 no. 10) cans with toxic contents remained "flat." Even after an incubation at 35 C. for 5½ months and at room temperature for 12 months, the toxic spinach was judged to be normal in appearance and odor. Spoiled and toxic spinach may give off a sour butyric acid, or sometimes a cheesy odor.

Growth of B. botulinus is irregular in string beans. Bulging of the cans occurs in about 50% of the inoculated tins, but spoilage of the contents is rare. Toxins are frequently found in cans which have a normal odor and present firm pods of a natural color.

Spoilage and toxin production are irregular in evaporated milk. The toxins once formed may deteriorate on prolonged incubation. The available evidence indicates that spores of B. botulinus cannot grow in sweetened condensed milk.

Moderate toxin production in acid fruits and vegetables, as, for example, apricots, cherries, peaches, plums, raspberries, strawberries, tomatoes, and sauerkraut, may occur after prolonged incubation, and then in exceptional instances only.

NEW METHOD FOR INCREASING YIELD OF THERAPEUTIC AND DIAGNOSTIC SERUM

JULES FREUND

From Antitoxin and Vaccine Laboratory, Department of Public Health of the Commonwealth of Massachusetts, Boston

The existing methods for obtaining serum for therapeutic and diagnostic purposes, especially from the horse, are open to two main objections, namely, a low yield of serum compared to the theoretical possibility and the presence of hemoglobin from destruction of red cells. The principle of the methods commonly used is the same, although the practice varies in essential details: usually the blood is allowed to clot and the serum withdrawn once or many times during contraction of the clot; or the clot is compressed by weights in order to squeeze out the serum; or the blood may be allowed to clot on some meshed material suspended to secure a better separation of the serum. According to experience, the largest yield is obtained by pressure on the clot by a weight, but any of the methods in use in which the blood clot is subjected to pressure or other manipulations results in the destruction of some of the red cells. In addition, when pressure is used, the choice of the proper weight is difficult; too light a weight defeats the purpose of the method; too heavy a weight causes lysis of so many red cells that the serum becomes unfit for use.

The method now described is an application of pressure by weight without destruction of red cells. The cells are separated before clotting, and the clotted plasma subjected to pressure to yield the maximum of serum. A sufficient pressure can be applied to the clotted plasma to cause almost complete separation of the fibrin and serum with no danger of hemolysis. There are two methods for obtaining plasma free from hemoglobin, namely, (1) the addition of chemicals, such as sodium citrate and oxalate, to the freshly drawn blood, and (2) cooling the blood and maintaining it at a low temperature. In both cases the plasma can be syphoned off after the cells have settled and before clotting.

TECHNIC

Forty c c. of a 25% solution of sodium citrate is put in a jar and 3,000 c c. of blood drawn in the same receptacle, the mixture allowed to stand for 12 to 24 hours, preferably at room temperature, because the blood cells separate

Received for publication, July 2, 1923.

more quickly at room than at icebox temperature. The plasma is then drawn off into a second jar containing 20 c c. of a 25% solution of calcium chloride. The clot is formed in 30 to 40 minutes. Three or four hours later, the clot is cut in 4 or 5 places and the proper weight, to be described, placed thereon. The serum which is squeezed out is drawn off the following day. The percentage of the serum procured by this method is shown in the table.

The second method prevents clotting by means of cooling: the blood is drawn into a jar and placed in ice water of a temperature from 0 to 1 C. (not higher) for 24 hours. The plasma is syphoned into a second jar and allowed to clot at room temperature, 30 to 40 minutes being sufficient. The remainder of the procedure is carried out as described for the citrated blood method.

In both methods, the size of the jar for collecting the blood is 55 x 15 cm.; for squeezing out the serum, 22 x 18 cm.; and a weight of 15 pounds is used. The weight was prepared as follows: Melted paraffin was poured into the jar and strings placed in it while it was liquid. After the paraffin solidified, the jar was put in a water bath and heated until the paraffin began to melt. When the outside began to soften, the paraffin block was taken out. In order to obtain a negative mold for the weight, a plaster paris form was cast. It was found practical in making the form to use 5% acetic acid instead of water. After removing the paraffin, 15 to 16 pounds of lead were poured into the form, and copper wire to serve as a handle was fixed in the lead before solidification. The weight was then copper plated.

As can be seen from the table, a comparison of the two methods and another in which the serum is drawn off from the usual clot at 2-day intervals during an 8-day period has been made. It is apparent that the new method, whether the plasma is obtained by use of citrate or by means of cooling, gives a greater yield of serum than the method in which the serum is collected from the whole blood clot. The relative increase in serum depends on the bleeding history of the horse. The animal at its first bleeding gives a blood which produces a firm clot which does not contract easily, and consequently the amount of serum obtained is lower than that obtained by the method now described, the percentage of increase in a horse which had been bled but once ranging from 43 to 95%. This difference was not noted in horses bled many times. However, in the experiments with blood from horses which had been bled often, an increase in yield was obtained amounting to 8 to 40%. Since the methods are convenient, require no elaborate apparatus, shorten the time necessary for collecting serum, give a yield of 10 to 95% greater than that obtained from the whole blood, and the serum being free from hemoglobin, it is obvious that either method is applicable to the collection of serum for therapeutic and diagnostic purposes.

As a possible additional method, it seems that the preliminary separation of the cells from the plasma by the methods described would permit the use of defibrination to obtain a large quantity of hemoglobin-free serum. The main reason that defibrinated blood is not generally used for serum production is because defibrination by means of shaking with glass beads yields a serum which contains a considerable quantity of hemoglobin. The hemolysis caused by defibrination of whole blood is obviated by the separation method, and we find that defibrination of recalcified citrate plasma or cooled plasma gives a rather high yield of serum.

TABLE 1

SERUM YIELD IN HORSE BLED MANY TIMES AND IN ONE NOT BLED PREVIOUSLY

Horse Blood	Quantity of Blood in C c.	Serum Yield in C c.	Serum Yield in Per Cent.	Gain in in Per Cent.
1. Horse injected with pneumococci and bled many times				
Separation method with cooling	2,000	1,210	60.5	+40
Separation method with citrate	2,000	1,150	57.5	+33
Usual method—collection of serum at 2-day intervals for a period of 8 days	2.000	860	43.0	....
Separation method with citrate	3 000	1,680	56	+10
Separation method with cooling	3,000	1,650	55	+ 8
Usual method	3,000	1,560	51	....
2. Horse not bled previously				
Separation method with citrate	3,000	1,581	52.7	+43
Usual method	3,000 (2 jars, 1,500)	1,089	36.6	....
Separation method with citrate	3 000	1,550	51.7	95
Separation method with cooling	3,000	1,390	46 3	76
Usual method	3,000 (2 jars, 1,500)	780	26.0	....

SUMMARY AND CONCLUSIONS

By separating the blood cells before the plasma clots a large amount of serum free from hemoglobin can be obtained. In comparison with the method in which repeated withdrawals of serum are made over a period of 8 days, it has been found possible to obtain from 10 to 95% greater yield of serum free from hemoglobin. The variation in the yield depends on whether the animal has been bled before or not. In the case of animals which have been bled but once, the difference is great, as much as 95%.

RELATION OF BACTERIUM PULLORUM TO HATCHABILITY OF EGGS

F. R. Beaudette, L. D. Bushnell and L. F. Payne

From the Bacteriological Laboratories, Kansas Agricultural Experiment Station, Manhattan, Kan.

In 1922, Beaudette, Bushnell and Payne [1] reported on an organism isolated from the unabsorbed yolk of chicks "dead in the shell." Cultivation of this organism would not permit differentiation from Bact. pullorum. In a few instances, different eggs from the same hen yielded pure cultures of this organism. This was taken as evidence of an ovarian infection. In order to determine whether this might be the case, blood was drawn from 3 hens whose eggs had been found to contain the organism. The serum thus obtained was used in agglutination tests on various strains of the organism. The serum of a rooster was also included as a control. The antigen for the test was prepared by suspending agar slant cultures of various strains in salt solution and killing at 60 C. (table 1).

TABLE 1

Agglutination by Serum of Three Hens and One Rooster of Organism from Unabsorbed Yolk of Chicks "Dead in the Shell"

Antigen	Fowls	Agglutinin Titers
30	30	1:640, complete
40	41	1:640, partial
41	41	1:640, partial
29	41	1:640, partial
37	41	1:640, partial
34	25	1:640, complete
32	25	1:640, complete
25	25	1:640, complete
37	25	1:640, complete
27	25	1:640, complete
29	25	1:640, complete
2	(Rooster) 438 (control)	Trace in 1:40
3	438	Trace in 1:40
48	438	Trace in 1:40
4	438	Trace in 1:40
39	438	Trace in 1:40

The result showed that the organism was Bact. pullorum, and it was found later that these fowls had infected ovaries. The serum of

Received for publication, July 3, 1923.

[1] Jour. Infect. Dis., 1923, 32, p. 124.

the rooster failed to agglutinate, although it is known that roosters occasionally react positively to the test. The results seemed to justify testing the entire flock. Accordingly, all fowls were bled, and the macroscopic agglutination test was made. The antigen used was a mixture of several strains of the organism isolated from the unabsorbed yolk of chicks "dead in the shell," and was prepared as described.

In all, 259 fowls were tested; of these 41, or 15.8%, reacted positively.

In order to determine whether the presence of the organism in the egg influenced hatchability, a comparison was made between the percentage of fertile eggs that were hatched from infected and noninfected hens. Fortunately, most of the individual hatching records were available for this purpose, and the comparison is made in table 2.

TABLE 2

A COMPARISON OF THE HATCHABILITY OF EGGS FROM INFECTED AND NONINFECTED HENS (1922)

Reaction	No. of Hens	Eggs Incubated	% Fertile	% Fertile Hatched
Infected	41	861	69.57	53.58
Noninfected	218	6,387	77.10	65.10
Total	259	7,248	76.21	63.86

The results show that 53.58% of the fertile eggs from infected hens hatched, whereas 65.10% of the fertile eggs from noninfected hens hatched. This represents a difference of 11.52% in hatchability. While this is a signficant difference, there is only a difference of 1.24% between the flock average and the average for noninfected hens; that is to say, if in this particular flock all reacting fowls were eliminated, the hatchability of fertile eggs would have been increased only 1.24%. Obviously, this percentage will vary in every flock, depending on the percentage of the flock infected and the percentage of infected eggs used for incubation.

Thirty-four of the 41 hens found to be infected were known to have been in the breeding flock for more than one year. Assuming the infection to have been present throughout this time, it was thought advisable to examine their previous records. The results are presented in table 3. In a few instances, bacteriologic examinations had been made of the unabsorbed yolk of chicks "dead in the shell" produced by these hens.

It was found that 1,462 fertile eggs were obtained from the infected hens and 553, or 37.8%, hatched. Of the 25 eggs which contained dead embryos, 12, or 48%, yielded a culture of Bact. pullorum. The 12 infected eggs were produced by 8 of the hens.

Table 4 is included to show the percentage of fertile eggs from the flock under study that hatched during the 4-year period from 1919 to 1922 inclusive. This, of course, includes both infected and non-infected hens.

TABLE 3

SUMMARY OF DATA ON THE HATCHING RECORD OF HENS KNOWN TO BE INFECTED WITH BACT. PULLORUM

No. of Hens	Eggs Incubated	Fertile	Percentage of Fertile Eggs Hatched	Eggs Examined	Bacterium pullorum Found
34	2,073	1,462	37.8	25	12

TABLE 4

LOSSES IN ARTIFICIAL INCUBATION

Year	Fertile Eggs	Percentage of Fertile Eggs Hatched
1919	5,384	30.3
1920	7,687	32.0
1921	3,832	53.9
1922	5,694	63.9
Total	22,597	43.3

TABLE 5

COMPARING HATCHABILITY OF FERTILE EGGS FROM INFECTED HENS WITH THE FLOCK AVERAGE

Year	Infected Hens			Percentage Hatched by Entire Flock
	No. of Hens	Fertile Eggs	Percentage Hatched	
1919	3	123	18.9	30.3
1920	13	569	23.3	32.0
1921	15	278	46.4	53.9
1922	28	492	54.4	63.9

The percentage of fertile eggs hatched from the entire flock for the 4 years was 43.3 as compared to 37.8% hatchability of the fertile eggs from the infected hens during this period. Referring to table 4, it will be seen that there is considerable variation in the hatchability of the fertile eggs for the different years. The hatch for the years 1919 and 1920 was unusually low, and perhaps may be accounted for, in part, by faulty incubation. The records for the next 2 years, however, are what might be expected from an average establishment.

In view of the fact that there is considerable variation in the percentage hatched for different years, a more nearly correct comparison should be obtained by calculating the percentage of fertile eggs from infected hens by years, and comparing these with the average hatched by the entire flock for the corresponding years.

The results show clearly that for every year the percentage of fertile eggs from infected hens hatched is far below the average of that of the entire flock for the corresponding year.

There was considerable variation in hatchability of the fertile eggs from different hens. In some cases the percentage hatched was unusually high, while in other instances the percentage hatched was very low. If we were to judge infectivity from the percentage hatched, some of these fowls certainly would not be classed as diseased. On the other hand, certain fowls hatched a much lower percentage of their fertile eggs than the average hatched by the flock. In other fowls the percentage of fertile eggs hatched increased each year from below the average hatch of the flock to a point considerably above the flock average. In one case, a high percentage hatched is interposed between two low records.

No definite explanation, based on known facts, can be given for this variation. In those cases in which the hatchability of fertile eggs from infected hens was below the average hatched, it might be assumed that the organism was present in a large percentage of the eggs used for hatching purposes. Yet this does not seem to be an adequate explanation, because it is known positively that the organism may be present, the egg may hatch, and the chick suffer from white diarrhea after hatching. Just why the organism exerts its influence before rather than after hatching, might possibly be correlated with virulence of the strain or number of organisms present. Our experiments show, as has been reported elsewhere, that 0.1 c c. of a 24-hour broth culture of Bact. pullorum will produce 100% mortality in developing embryos. It is quite likely, however, that this number of organisms would not be present under natural conditions. That virulence is a factor in this connection seems rather doubtful, because inoculation of eggs with old laboratory strains of the organism produced as high mortality as did freshly isolated strains. The resistance of the developing embryo might exert some influence, but this hardly seems possible in view of the fact that Sherman [2] was unable to demonstrate hemolysin in the blood of chicks during incubation until they had started to pip the shell. The presence of complement could not be demonstrated until several hours later. It seems logical to suppose that faulty incubation would intensify the low percentage hatched, but this does not account for the variations in every case.

One hen presents what appears to be an interesting case. The percentage hatched for this bird in 1920 was 25.3, which was below the average hatched by the entire flock for the year, but in 1921 and 1922 the average was considerably above the flock average. The agglutination test was first made on June 2, 1921, and at this time complete agglutination was observed in a 1:640 dilution, indicating a strongly positive reaction. The next determination was made on Jan. 25, 1922, and at this time the titer was found to have dropped to complete clumping in a serum dilution of 1:80 and marked clumping in a 1:160 dilution. No agglutination occurred in the higher dilutions. The results of the Jan. 25 test still indicated a positive reaction, although a marked increase in hatchability over the previous year was noted. Because the percentage hatched for 1922 was so high, the owner disliked to discard this fowl and suggested that another test be made. Accordingly, a third test was made on April 13, 1922, and it was found that a marked clumping occurred in the 1:40 dilution of serum only and no visible clumping in higher dilutions. This could not be considered as a positive reaction.

It is impossible to explain this decrease in agglutinins and increase in hatchability until further investigation can be made.

We have attempted to determine the influence of the males on hatchability and fertility in this flock. Our records show that in the case of most males the hatchability of fertile eggs from noninfected hens is 10% higher than the hatchability of fertile eggs from infected hens. It has also been found that the fertility of eggs from noninfected hens is 10.4% higher than the fertility of eggs from infected hens when used with the same male.

The correlation between infection and low hatchability, as indicated by the records for 1922 seemed to justify the application of the test the following year. In 1923, 183 fowls were tested and 19, or 10.3%, of the flock were found to be infected. The percentage of fertile eggs that were hatched from infected and noninfected hens is given in table 6, which shows that 18.2% more of the fertile eggs

[2] Ibid., 1919, 25, p. 256.

from the noninfected hens hatched than from the infected hens. It will also be noted that the fertility of eggs from noninfected hens is 33.4% more than from infected hens. The difference in hatchability of fertile eggs from infected and noninfected hens was greater in 1923 than in 1922, yet the removal of infected birds from this flock would only have increased the hatchability by 0.8%.

That low hatchability, due to infection by this organism exists in flocks other than the one reported, was shown by a large number of inquiries regarding losses in the shell.

As an illustration, we mention the hatching record of a flock of 26 fowls, of which 11, or 42.3%, were found to be infected in 1922; the infected fowls were eliminated and the flock replenished with new hens, and prior to the 1923 hatching season the flock was again tested and found to be free from the infection. A comparison of the hatching record shows that the percentage of fertile eggs hatched was increased from 35.18% to 97.14%, or a difference of 61.96%. This difference cannot be attributed to better management because both hatches received the same attention. It might be added that hens were always used for hatching in this flock. Two dead embryos were produced during this year, due to chilling. Of the 68 chicks produced, none died of white diarrhea.

TABLE 6

HATCHABILITY OF FERTILE EGGS FROM INFECTED AND NONINFECTED HENS OF 1923

	No. of Hens	Eggs Incubated	% Fertile	% Fertile Hatch	% Total Incubated Hatch
Infected	19	387	57.0	45.2	25.8
Noninfected	164	5,066	90.4	63.4	57.4
Total	183	5,453	88.0	62.6	55.1

DISCUSSION

From our study of Bact. pullorum in relation to poor hatchability, it appears that this organism is at least one factor to be taken into consideration. While the eggs from all infected hens do not show a uniformly low hatchability, the average hatchability of fertile eggs from infected hens is below the average for noninfected hens. The fertility of eggs from infected hens appears to be considerably lower than the fertility of eggs from noninfected hens. From this it might be supposed that the organism may exert its influence at different stages of the incubation period. In the first place, the egg may be rendered infertile. If this does not occur, and an embryo is produced, death of the embryo may take place at any stage in the incubation period. Usually the largest mortality takes place about the nineteenth day of incubation. If the egg should hatch and produce a chick, it may suffer from white diarrhea. Bact. pullorum infection of the chick from the egg has long been known, but in view of our experiments it appears that we must recognize another loss due to this organism.

From the material presented in this paper it is apparent that Rettger's cycle of infection might be enlarged as shown in table 7:

TABLE 7

ENLARGEMENT OF RETTGER'S CYCLE OF INFECTION

Eggs of Infected Hen	Possible Outcome
A. Not infected	Healthy chick
B. Infected	Infertility
C. Infected	Dead embryo
D. Infected	Chick lives but suffers from white diarrhea
E. Not infected	Healthy chick, but soon contracts infection of white diarrhea from D.

CONCLUSIONS

The agglutination test applied to a flock in which poor hatching was reported showed that 15.8% of the fowls were infected with Bact. pullorum.

The fertile eggs from infected hens gave a 53.58% hatch, whereas the fertile eggs from noninfected hens gave a 65.10% hatch.

Fertile eggs from all infected hens do not give a uniformly low hatch. This suggests the possibility that other factors are necessary to bring about death of the embryo during the incubation period.

Infection by Bact. pullorum has been found to cause a marked reduction in fertility. For one flock the fertility of eggs from infected hens was 57% as compared to 90.4% fertility for noninfected hens.

CLASMATOCYTES AND RESISTANCE TO STREPTOCOCCUS INFECTION

STUDIES IN STREPTOCOCCUS INFECTION AND IMMUNITY. V *

Frederick P. Gay and L. F. Morrison

This particular study began logically in our consideration of the existence and nature of a local form of immunity as outlined in our two most recent papers.[1] The particular phase of the investigation that we wish here to present, however, deals rather with natural resistance than with acquired active immunity as dealt with in our work on experimental erysipelas. This work on erysipelas, together with a survey of the literature, led us to believe that there is actually a form of resistance which may be artificially produced by immunization which is local rather than general; that is to say, which is most effectively brought about by administration of the immunizing doses in a locality or tissue which is subsequently infected. In brief, our results, both with experimental erysipelas and subsequently our unpublished findings in experimental empyema, show that when given doses of streptococcus administered at definitely spaced intervals are administered intradermally, better protection results against intradermal infection than when the immunizing doses are given intravenously or intrapleurally. In the same way, immunization in the pleura protects better against experimental pleurisy than precisely the same doses at the same intervals and with the same total amount given intradermally or intravenously. As we have previously indicated, it is extremely difficult to make these results, which are frequently indicated, fully convincing owing to the fact that precisely the right grade of immunity must be produced and no more, else the local form of protection will

Received for publication, June 28, 1923.

* Preceding Studies in this series are: Gay, F. P., and Stone, R. L.: Jour. Infect. Dis., 1920, 26, p. 265. Gay, F. P., and Morrison, L. F.: Ibid., 1921, 28, p. 1. Gay, F. P., and Rhodes, B.: Ibid., 29, p. 217. Gay, F. P., and Rhodes, B.: Ibid., 1922, 31, p. 101. Gay, F. P.: Jour. Immunol., 1923, 8, p. 1.

Of correlative interest are the following articles by our associates: Cook, M. W.; Mix, V., and Culvyhouse, E. O.: Jour. Infect. Dis., 1921, 28, p. 93. Foster, L. F., and Randall, S. B.: Jour. Bacteriol., 1921, 6, p. 143. Foster, L. F.: Ibid., p. 161. Foster, L. F.: Ibid., p. 211.

* This study, begun in the University of California, was largely carried out in the United States Hygienic Laboratory, Washington, D. C., through the courtesy of the Surgeon-General of the United States Public Health Service, and with the constant cooperation of Dr. G. W. McCoy, Director of the Laboratory, for whose interest and aid we wish here to express our great appreciation.

[1] Gay, F. P., and Rhodes, B.: Jour. Infect. Dis., 1922, 31, p. 101. Gay, F. P.: Jour. Immunol., 1923, 8, p. 1.

flow over into a more general protection which is everywhere manifest, and precisely the correct multiple of lethal doses must be administered to these "locally" but not generally immunized animals or the protection is not evident. But we wish to leave this phase of our problem to further consideration.

In our continued studies on experimental empyema in the rabbit, we have frequently noted a predominance of large mononuclear cells in the exudate of successfully immunized animals on reinoculation of multiples of the fatal dose in contrast to the predominance of polymorphonuclear cells which are invariably found in animals that are in the course of a fatal infection.

Our first idea, which we find has been a common one, was that these cells were derived from the serosa of the cavity. We find they have been described as endothelial cells by Nagao,[2] Wallgren,[3] Dumarest and Parodi,[4] and Durham.[5]

Here let us recall again the literary evidence that we have previously assembled [6] which associates streptococcus infections, particularly healing streptococcus infections, with the presence of cells of a similar appearance but usually designated as macrophages.

Recent work by histologists in particular has led to a clear definition and identification of a group of cells occurring primarily in connective tissue but also elsewhere in the body, to which various names have been given: "Clasmatocytes" by Ranvier,[7] "ruhende Wanderzellen" by Maximow,[8] and "tissue macrophages" by Evans and Scott.[9] The interest of histologists in this group of cells has been primarily to throw light on the origin and relationship of "cell stems" (Sabin [10]). Certain characteristic properties of the clasmatocytes or macrophages have been pointed out and have given the criteria of their differentiation. Clasmatocytes may be differentiated from the fibroblasts of connective tissue by their properties of taking up and retaining in their vacuoles certain dye stuffs, particularly those of the acid azo group (Evans and Scott [9]). The clasmatocytes as they occur in connective tissue usually have definite pseudopodial processes and have been referred to as "trailers" (Buxton and Torrey [11]). When they occur in exudates in serous cavities they are usually ovoid in appearance, with a large excentric and often indented nucleus, which latter form resembles the transitional cells of the circulating blood.

We have already referred to the fact that these clasmatocytes as they occur in serous exudates have often been regarded as endothelial or serosal cells, and

[2] Jour. Infect. Dis., 1920, 27, p. 327.
[3] Beitr. z. path. Anat. u. z. allg. Path., 1899, 25, p. 206.
[4] Rev. de la tuberculose, 1921, 2, p. 44-50.
[5] Jour. Path. & Bacteriol., 1897, 4, p. 338.
[6] Gay, F. P.: Jour. Immunol., 1923, 8, p. 1.
[7] Compt. rend. Acad. d. sc., 1890, 110, p. 165.
[8] Arch. f. micr. Anat., 1906, 67, p. 680.
[9] Pub. Carnegie Inst. of Wash., 1921, 10, p. 48.
[10] Physiol. Rev., 1922, 2, p. 38.
[11] Jour. Med. Research, 1906, 15, p. 55.

yet Ranvier[12] states clearly that they are probably the same as connective tissue clasmatocytes. Buxton and Torrey[11] also insist that these cells, free in the cavity, are not endothelial in origin but derived from the connective tissue, a fact which has now been conclusively proved with proper differential staining by the work of Schott,[13] and of Cunningham.[14]

The precise origin of clasmatocytes or "histiocytes," as they are also called, has been a matter of much consideration but of no final decision by histologists. Sabin,[10] who has made a most careful review of the subject, tells us that clasmatocytes are at least allied to the large mononuclear cells and the transitionals of the circulating blood. They are certainly of a common origin with these cells from the embryonic endothelium, and may be derived from the adult endothelium, as Mallory[15] and Foot[16] have insisted. It is quite possible that they may also be derived in part from the circulating blood as McJunkin[17] has urged. But at all events, clasmatocytes may be differentiated from adult endothelium by means of the specific stains we have mentioned.

Endothelial cells have undoubted phagocytic properties, but clasmatocytes have even superior ability in this respect in taking up both particles of pigment and bacteria. The original assertion of Metchnikoff[18] that the macrophages (clasmatocytes) which occur in the lesions of erysipelas have nothing to do with the destruction of the cocci has been denied by a series of investigators. Without going into the details of the evidence afforded, it is perfectly clear that Buxton and Torrey,[11, 19] Zangemeister and Gans,[20] Wallgren,[3] Foot,[21] Cunningham,[14, 22] Durham,[5] MacCallum,[23] and Smith, Willis and Lewis[24] attribute a significant and at times a supreme importance to these macrophages or clasmatocytes in disposing of the agents both of chronic (e. g., B. tuberculosis) and of acute infections. An important rôle in phagocytosis is further suggested for these cells by their undoubted properties of migration, as evidenced by their pseudopodial processes in connective tissue, by their ameboid motion in exudates (Ranvier[12]), and further by their superior property of resistance to extraneous influences, as for example, when their vitality is tested outside the body (Lewis and McCoy[25]).

Clasmatocytes may be identified wherever they occur in the body by the vital staining of the animal with trypan blue. Four or more injections at daily intervals of 3 to 5 c c. of a 1% trypan blue solution in saline intravenously in rabbits leads to a general blue coloration, and on examination the dyestuff is found collected in considerable masses in the "vacuolar apparatus" of the clasmatocytes and elsewhere

[12] Compt. rend Acad. d. sc., 1890, 110, p. 768.
[13] Arch. f. mikr. Anat. u. Entwick, 1909, 74, p. 143.
[14] Am. J. Physiol., 1922, 59, p. 1; Johns Hopkins Hosp. Bull., 1922, 33, p. 257.
[15] Jour. Exper. Med., 1898, 3, p. 611.
[16] Jour. Med. Res., 1919, 40, p. 353.
[17] Am. Jour. Anat., 1919, 25, p. 27.
[18] Virchows Arch. f. path. Anat. u. Physiol., 1887, 107, p. 209.
[19] Jour. Med. Res., 1906, 15, p. 73.
[20] München. med. Wchnschr., 1909, 56, p. 793.
[21] Jour. Exper. Med., 1920, 32, p. 513; 1922, 36, p. 607.
[22] Am. Jour. Anat., 1922, 30, p. 399; Am. Jour. Physiol., 1922, 62, p. 248.
[23] Johns Hopkins Hosp. Bull., 1903, 14, p. 105.
[24] Am. Rev. Tuberc., 1922, 6, p. 21.
[25] Johns Hopkins Hosp. Bull., 1922, 33, p. 284.

only diffusely throughout the tissues. The contrast in staining reaction between serosal cells and clasmocytes is well evidenced on examining the omentum of one of these vitally stained rabbits. Such a preparation spread over a glass slide and fixed my methyl alcohol shows the clasmatocytes with their elongated processes and larger and smaller masses of pigment, which group characteristically away from the nucleus. Serosal cells are diffusely stained a pale blue, and such fine granules of pigment as occur are characteristically perinuclear in position.

In such a vitally stained animal, nearly all the free cells in the peritoneal and pleural cavities are clasmatocytes and not serosal cells as they may appear to be in an ordinary fixed and stained specimen. Another method of identifying clasmatocytes which is of particular advantage in the study of exudates lies in the use of a dilute solution (1:400 or more) of neutral red. This dye is taken up by the vacuoles in living clasmatocytes instantaneously, and no such pigment accumulations are found in other cells. A further advantage of neutral red in these studies of ours which deal with the resistance of clasmatocytes to the streptococcus, is the fact that these cells take up the dyestuff only when living, although they may stain perfectly well to all appearance with other staining methods. Our first results were obtained with a contrast stain of hematoxylin and eosin, and although under normal conditions this method checks closely with the neutral red stain in estimating the percentage of clasmatocytes present, it will be found to vary markedly and to be higher than the neutral red count when the clasmatocytes have been subjected to unfavorable conditions, such as the presence of many bacteria.

We shall report in this article a study of the relationship which seems to exist between the number of clasmatocytes present in the pleural cavity of rabbits and the resistance of that cavity to an otherwise fatal infection with many multiples of the fatal dose of our hemolytic streptococcus "H". We shall touch on the similiar relationship which apparently exists also in the much more powerful acquired resistance which can be produced by immunization. But a full consideration of the latter and more important phase must be left for future consideration. We have repeatedly described the form of experimental empyema in rabbits which has been so useful to us in studying the course of streptococcus infection. For several years we have employed a passage strain of the hemolytic Streptococcus pyogenes (Holman) originally derived from an instance of fatal human empyema.

This strain, designated "H", under the perfected conditions of our experimentataion, produces with absolute regularity and in a very small dose a fatal syndrome in rabbits, which resembles human empyema. The most important factor in our success depends on the fact that the virulence of our passage strain has remained fixed by conservation of the source material in the pleural field of an animal that has succumbed to this infection. Such a pleural fluid kept in the icebox for weeks yields, when inoculated in broth, a culture of undiminished virulence. According to routine, we do not use a fluid more than one month old. Subcultures from 0.1 c c. of this pleural fluid into beef infusion broth of a P_H of from 7.4 to 7.6 gives in 24 hours a growth which usually kills rabbits in a dose of 0.00001 c c. diluted in broth to a volume of 1 c c. To still further standardize our technic

TABLE 1

THE MIMIMAL LETHAL DOSE OF THE PASSAGE CULTURE OF S. PYOGENES "H" AS DETERMINED AT INTERVALS BETWEEN OCTOBER, 1922, AND MAY, 1923, WHEN INJECTED INTRAPLEURALLY INTO ADULT RABBITS

Amount of 24-Hour Broth Culture	Average Number of Streptococci	Number of Rabbits	Dead	Recovered
0.001 c c.	222,666+	19	19	None
0.0001 c c.	14,550	4	3	1*
0.00001 c c.	1,344	5	4	1
0.000001 c c.	210	11	0	All
0.0000001 c c.	11	2	0	All

* This animal was, through error, not examined, and the recovery may have been due to a faulty inoculation.

we have determined during the current year our minimum lethal dose of culture with more precision, as is evident in the appended table 1 which summarizes all the results obtained at different periods during the past 8 months.

It is evident from this table that the majority of animals with a dose of 0.00001 c c. die of a fatal infection, whereas animals with a tenth of that dose, namely, 0.000001 c c., invariably recover. It is evident, then, that in our previous work we have used an excessive amount of culture (0.1 : 0.2) when we wished to demonstrate delicate degrees of protection. We have usually employed, in other words, from 10,000 to 20,000 minimum lethal doses. It is probable that our previous estimate of the minimum lethal dose as 0.001 c c. was less accurately determined, since our results previously with greater dilutions than this amount were variable; or else our culture may have increased slightly in virulence; or the particular stock of animals employed in Washington may have been less resistant. At all events, we feel certain that in dilutions of 0.001 c c., as the usual infecting dose, we are employing many multiples (approximately 100) of the minimum lethal dose.

It seemed, further, important to estimate rather carefully the approximate number of bacteria that were present in a fatal dose and multiples of it. Our results in attempts to estimate bacteria in a given culture by the plating method have until this year been rather unsuccessful, but we have now a technic which we believe to be extremely accurate for this purpose, and which briefly summarized is as follows:

Method of Estimating Viable Streptococci in a Broth Culture or Pleural Fluid.—A series of dilutions is made in broth from the original culture beginning with a dilution of 1: 100, using 0.1 c c. of the culture to 9.9 c c. of infusion broth, and extending in multiples of 10 to the expected necessary end point, as determined by previous experience. A fresh sterile pipet is employed for each successive dilution.

TABLE 2

Number of 24-Hour Broth Cultures Plated	Average Number of Streptococci per C c.	Actual Counts Obtained in Millions			
		100-200	200-300	300-400	400-500
38	266,140,350	15	14	5	4

2. 0.5 c c. of fresh defibrinated sterile rabbit blood is added to each of a series of sterile tubes marked to correspond to the culture-dilution series. One c c. from each broth dilution from the greatest to the least is added to respective blood tubes. The same pipet may be used in ascending dilutions.

3. 15 c c. of melted and cooled fluid agar is added to each tube of blood-broth dilution, and the tube is rolled and poured in Petri dishes as usual.

The accuracy and consistency of this method of estimation of streptococci is best evidenced by the totality of our results over a period of 8 months with different 24-hour broth cultures both from the same and from different pleural fluids, as shown in the following table 2. This table further comprises results obtained by 4 different persons. The successive dilutions, moreover, show surprisingly accurate diminution of colonies in accordance with the dilution factor. The original broth dilutions when incubated with the plates show sterile cultures at the same vanishing point.

CELL CONTENT OF THE NORMAL PLEURAL CAVITY OF THE RABBIT

The normal pleural cavity of a rabbit free from ascites contains on an average about 0.1 c c. of fluid. In some cases the fluid is in so small an amount as not to be measurable in an ordinary pipet, but in instances of this sort we have obtained consistent estimates of the cells present in such a cavity by introducing 1 c c. of broth at the apex of the cavity, allowing it to flow over the surface of the lungs and pleura repeatedly, and finally withdrawing it. Our earlier estimates of cell content were unfortunately only differential, that is to say, the percentage proportion of clasmatocytes to polymorphonuclear and other cells was estimated in smears from such a cavity which were stained by hematoxylin and eosin.

Technic of Hematoxylin and Eosin Stain.—Smears air dried and fixed 3 to 5 minutes with methyl alcohol. Stain in 0.5% alcoholic eosin about 6 seconds; wash in distilled water, and stain in Delafield's alum hematoxylin 1 to 1½ minutes. Wash and dry.

We still use this method as a check to the neural red stain for a differential count, and they check perfectly in a normal cavity; but, as we have already indicated, under abnormal conditions of infection and even following the injection of various relatively harmless substances, it is found that the clasmatocytes as determined by the hematoxylin and eosin stain are more numerous than the living clasmatocytes as evidenced by staining with neutral red.

Technic of Staining Clasmatocytes in Exudates with Neutral Red.—Clasmatocytes retain their normal living properties of absorbing neural red better when the final dilution of the dye to be added to the pleural exudate is made by the addition of equal parts of rabbit serum to 1% aqueous solution rather than when made with broth or saline. This serum dye dilution (1:200) may be kept indefinitely if sterile, and is added in approximately equal parts to the cellular fluid to be examined. In ordinary inactivated rabbit serum the dye becomes brownish, but may be restored to a permanent cherry red by acidulating the mixture with dilute (1:1,000) HCl to a P_H of from 6.2 to 6.4.

The differential count of pleural cavity cells, although of interest and significant in all phases of our work, is not so important as the actual number of cells of each of the different types that are present in the cavity. We have, therefore, in all our later experiments supplemented the differential count by a total white blood cell determination and thereby determined the actual number of cells of each type that are present in a cavity under varying conditions. We have been surprised to find usually a close correspondence in the total number of cells of each variety in the different animals whose cavities were examined under any one particular set of conditions. It should be stated that the total cell counts given under the different headings which we shall take up represent an average usually of from 3 to 10 animals. These animals have, with a few rare exceptions, agreed so closely and one set of conditions has given results so far different from another set of conditions that we feel certain our results represent truly average findings.

The cells which we designate as clasmatocytes in the various pleural exudates studied are cells which are found when stained in neutral red to have taken up the dye within a few seconds. The red stain appears in the form of larger and smaller globoid masses, the larger of which show refractile margins. The nucleus of the cell remains unstained, is often indented, and is excentrically placed. A control stain of such an exudate by hematoxylin and eosin shows the nucleus more clearly; it is frequently indented, and at times two or more nuclei are present and always peripherally placed. Under certain conditions, as already noted, the hematoxylin and eosin count of clasmatocytes is larger than the neutral red count, but the percentage we have taken in estimating the total number of clasmatocytes present when there was a difference has been the neutral red count as representing the living clasmatocytes.

TABLE 3

CELL CONTENT OF THE PLEURAL CAVITY OF NORMAL RABBITS

Rabbits	Clasmatocytes Neutral Red, %	Clasmatocytes Hematoxylin and Eosin, %	Total Number of Leuko-cytes	Total Number of Clasmato-cytes	Total Number of Polymorpho-nuclears
62/88	91	92	327,500	298,025	29,475
64/88	89	84.6	285,000	253,650	31,350
60/88	74	..	280,000	207,200	72,800
61/88	81	..	340.000	275,400	64,600
65/88	90	..	517,500	268,338	49,162
Average	85.1	..	350,000	300,522	49,478

The clasmatocytes are also usually distinguishable in size from polymorphonuclear and other cells. They vary markedly but on the average are slightly though distinctly larger than polymorphonuclears, and from a minimal size actually less than polymorphonuclears, they may range to as much as three times the diameter of that cell.[26]

In table 3 we present determinations of the total number of clasmatocytes and other cells present in the normal right pleural cavity of 5 different rabbits, together with a check differential count of the neutral red stain by the hematoxylin and eosin stain in 2 instances. It should be stated that the cells listed as others are predominantly polymorphonuclears. In 2 instances the number of lymphocytes present in the total count was ⅓ of 1%, respectively. For our purposes here we shall classify all cells other than clasmatocytes as polymorphonuclears. As

[26] Measurements of rabbit cells have given us diameters as follows: Erythrocytes about 6 microns; polymorphonuclears 9.25 microns and clasmatocytes on the average 11.6 microns, with picked cells that ran as high as 23 microns.

is evident from this table, the average number of clasmatocytes present in a normal rabbit's pleural cavity is a little over 300,000 and the polymorphonuclear cells slightly under 50,000.

It has long been recognized that various substances injected into the cavities or tissues of the animal body produce exudates which vary somewhat in their nature. These exudates vary first of all in time relation, the polymorphonuclear cells appearing first followed by mononuclear cells. If an early stage is chosen for comparison, say 24 hours, the majority of substances will have produced a polymorphonuclear exudate. Such an exudate follows the injection of practically all bacteria. Wells [27] has carefully reviewed the chemotactic effect of various substances on leukocytes, and it does not concern us at this point to go more fully into the extensive literature on this subject, except to say that apart from the varying power of different substances to attract cells it would seem that the cells most usually attracted are polymorphonuclear in type, as might be expected from their facility in migration. Indeed, there is some doubt from the literature as to whether there are specific attracting substances for other types of leukocytes. Harvey [28] has claimed that pilocarpine, muscarine, and barium chloride produce a true general lymphocytosis. Recently Bergel [29] claims to have obtained a preponderating number of these cells in the pleural or peritoneal cavities by the injection of oils and lecithin. There is not, so far as we are aware, any definite reference to a specific attraction of well differentiated clasmatocytes in any of this work.

PLEURAL EXUDATES FOLLOWING THE INJECTION OF VARIOUS SUBSTANCES

Having determined by a chance observation that the injection of a small amount of plain infusion broth into the pleural cavity of rabbits produces at the end of 24 hours a relatively large number of clasmatocytes, and having observed the relation of these cells to the destruction of streptococci in such a cavity, we have tried in a preliminary fashion to test the effect of several different substances in relation to the type of exudate produced. With the knowledge of the actual number of cells of clasmatocytic or polymorphonuclear type present in the normal cavity, we are in a position to compare these average normal counts with those in animals that have received 24 hours previously any

[27] Chemical Pathology, 1918, p. 256.
[28] Jour. Physiol., 1906, 35, p. 115.
[29] Ztschr. f. exper. Path. u. Therap., 1920, 21, p. 216.

given substance. It is already well known that an exudate follows a well defined course, irrespective of the substance inroduced, which in its most characteristic features may include a diminution of cells already present, followed by a polymorphonuclear increase, and subsequently—usually in from 2 to 4 days—by a mononuclear increase. It is important, therefore, that a fixed period of time be chosen in comparing exudates produced by different substances, for even in those exudates which show a predominance of clasmatocytes at the end of 24 hours—for example, infusion broth—there is an earlier stage—say, 18 hours—in which the polymorphonuclear cells predominate, as we have also determined.

TABLE 4

THE LOCAL CELLULAR RESPONSE FOLLOWING THE INJECTION OF VARIOUS SUBSTANCES INTO THE PLEURAL CAVITY OF RABBITS AND THE RESULTANT PROTECTION AFFORDED AGAINST THE INJECTION OF 100 M L D OF STREPTOCOCCUS "H" 24 HOURS LATER

Substance	Clasmatocytes in Millions	Polymorphonuclears in Millions	Protection
(Normal) (5)*	0.3	0.05	None (19+)
NaCl 0.5% sol. (1)	0.9	0.2	
1% peptone in water	...	...	None (4)
1% peptone in NaCl, 0.5% (4)	1.5	1.1	None (2)
1% gelatin in NaCl, 0.5% (3)	1.7	1.5	None (2)
Whole egg white (3)	0.7	5.9	None (2)
5% aleuronat in NaCl, 0.5% (3)	3.8	58.9	None (3)
1% aleuronat in NaCl, 0.5% (3)	2.0	15.0	
5% Higgins ink in NaCl, 0.5% (3)	1.6	1.7	None (2)
1% "Norit" in NaCl, 0.5% (1) (vegetable charcoal)	0.6	0.2	
1% $BaSO_4$ in NaCl, 0.5% (2)	2.4	2.6	
Infusion broth (6) (1% peptone + 0.5% NaCl)	4.3	1.9	Complete (12)
Infusion broth, without peptone or salt (concentrated × 10) (3)	18.7	47.9	Complete (3)
1% egg white in NaCl, 0.5% (3)	4.7	2.9	Complete (5)
5% diatomaceous earth in NaCl, 0.5% (3)	6.8	86.3	None (3)

* The figures in parenthesis give the number of animals on which the average of cell counts was based; or, in case of protection, the animals tested.

In table 4 are presented the results, in most cases an average of determinations from 3 to 6 animals in respect to millions of clasmatocytes and of polymorphonuclear cells which are present in the pleural cavity of rabbits which have received 24 hours previously the particular substance enumerated, each in a volume of 3 c c. In the last column there is listed, so far as fully determined, the protection of similarly prepared animals when infected with 100 M. L. D. of streptococcus "H" (24-hour broth culture in a volume of 1 c c.; actual dosage 0.001 c c.).

A careful inspection of this table brings out several interesting facts, which, although significant of a relation between the number of clasmatocytes present and protection, cannot properly be regarded as conclusive. It will be seen that the substances vary markedly both in the total number of cells produced and, particularly, in the relative numbers of the two types of cells, clasmatocytes and polymorphonuclears, which are provoked by the respective materials. The normal number of clasmatocytes present is increased from 0.3 of a million all the way up to over 18,000,000 or actually to over 62 times. Furthermore, it appears from the materials tested so far that, with a single exception, when over 4,000,000 clasmatocytes are present in the cavity the animal is protected against large multiples of the fatal dose of our streptococcus.

Preparation with 5% diatomaceous earth affords an apparent exception to this finding. In this case, nearly 8,000,000 clasmatocytes were present, but no protection ensued. The clasmatocytes from these animals when stained with neutral red took the stain but were strikingly abnormal in appearance, even when contrasted with the cells of the opposite pleural cavity (not inoculated) of the same animal; the stain appeared in much more diffuse form and never in large vacuoles. A similar finding was obtained following aleuronat, but there the total count did not reach 4,000,000. We believe that in these instances the clasmatocytes, though apparently living, may have lost their capacity for further phagocytosis through having been filled with particles of the first injected materials.

And again there is evidence both from our own results and from those of others, that large numbers of polymorphonuclears actually lower resistance. This condition is fulfilled both in aleuronat and diatomaceous earth animals.

In spite of the general acceptance of polymorphonuclears as furnishing the chief cellular protective mechanism of the body (Metchnikoff), we find a few statements which would indicate that they are of little or actually of negative value under conditions such as we are describing. Thus, Buxton and Torrey, [11, 19] attribute little significance to polymorphonuclears in disposing of bacteria in the peritoneum. Simon [30] found that bacteria increase in an exudate produced by aleuronat (polymorphonuclear) as well as in a normal cavity, and Kracht [31] states that such an exudate actually furnishes food material

[30] Centralbl. f. Bakteriol., I, O., 1901, 29, p. 113.
[31] Inaug. Dissert., Greifswald, 1888.

for bacterial increase. At all events, the number of polymorphonuclears in the exudate produced by subsances which gave rise to protection in our experience has seemed of little significance. We find nearly 59,000,000 after injections of 5% aleuronat and over 86,000,000 after diatomaceous earth, both of which fail to protect. There are less than 2,000,000 polymorphonuclears after infusion broth, which protects completely. Another interesting comparison lies in the results produced by whole egg white, and by 1% egg white, respectively. The whole

TABLE 5

NORMAL ADULT RABBITS INOCULATED WITH 100 M L D STREPTOCOCCUS "H" INTRAPLEURALLY AND KILLED OR DEAD AT SUBSEQUENT INTERVALS

Interval	Rabbits	Amount of Fluid in C c.	Total Leuko-cytes	Per Cent. Clas-mato-cytes	Total Number of Clas-mato-cytes	Total Number of Poly-morpho-nuclears	Bacteria in Cavity	Blood Culture
1 Hour	130	1.6	5,680,000	10.0	568.000	5,112,000	×2	00
	142	1.0	2,600,000	7.0	182,000	2,418,000	×50	0+
	137	0.8	1,520,000	0.0	0	1,520,000	×2.5	0+
Average	...	...	....	...	250,000	3,016.666		
3 Hours	38/88	1.0	3,450,000	1.6	55,200	3,394,800	×100	0+
	133	1.2	132,000	0.0	0	132,000	×12	0+
	144	1.0	8,550,000	1.0	85,500	8,464,500	×10	0+
	145	1.0	8,050,000	0.0	0	8,050,000	×1.5	00
Average	...	...	....	...	35,175	5,010,325		
6 Hours	39/88	1.5	20,400,000	0.0	0	20,400,000	×250	00
	160	1.0	22,450,000	3.0	673,500	21,776,500	×100	0+
Average	...	...	....	...	336,750	21,088,250		
24 Hours	45/88	4.0	315,800,000	7.0	22,106.000	293,694,000	×15	+
	161	6.0	15,600,000	4.7	733,200	14,866,800	×1000	0+
	162	9.0	76,950,000	1.9	1,462,050	75,487,950	×10	00
	152	13.0	1,027,000	7.0	71,890	955,110	×1500	0+
Average	...	...	....	...	6,093.285	71,250,965		
48 Hours	200	12.0	51,900,000	0	0	51,900,000	×1000	+
96 Hours	215	5.0	8,250,000	0	0	8.250,000	×100	+
	187	15.0	?	0	0	?	×250	+
	216	20.0	?	0	0	?	×1400	+

? = Impossible to count owing to the disintegration of the cells.

egg white produces less than 1,000,000 clasmatocytes, whereas 1% egg white produces nearly 5,000,000. Whole egg white produces nearly 6,000,000 polymorphonuclears, but 1% egg white less than 3,000,000. The first fluid gives no protection; the second complete. It may be said in this connection that there is no great variation in the actual numbers of clasmatocytes and polymorphonuclear cells produced by solutions varying from 1 to 50% of egg white, but 75% egg white produces a count similar to whole egg white. The most successful material in producing a large classmatocyte count and an apparently related protection to streptococcus infection, so far determined, is ordinary infusion broth. If such broth, even without peptone and salt, is concentrated 10 times, its protective value is enormously increased. It is evident, further, that the extractives from beef are responsible, since the same amount of peptone and salt solution produces little effect. It is evident that an extended investigation of the clasmatocye producing properties of a number of other substances will will yield results of interest, but our present inquiry has extended rather to the aspect of the exact mechanism of the protection afforded by one of the substances, namely, infusion broth.

THE COURSE OF STREPTOCOCCUS INFECTION IN NORMAL AND IN BROTH PREPARED (CLASMATOCYTE) ANIMALS

In tables 5 and 6 are presented the results from the examination at different intervals following the inoculation of 100 or more fatal doses of passage streptococcus "H" in the pleural cavities, on the one hand, of the normal, and on the other, of broth prepared animals. A great many other animals have been employed in addition to those listed, but are not included because the data on them are incomplete; notably, they do not contain total as well as differential counts. It should be said, however, that these additional data are corroborative so far as they go, to the general results obtained with the more completely studied animals. The significant facts determined in these two tables comprise the actual number of clasmatocytes and of polymorphonuclear cells present in the cavity; the diminution or increase at successive intervals in the number of bacteria injected and the presence or absence of streptococci in the general circulating blood of the animal. Data on each and all of these conditions have yielded results of interest, some of which we may explain before commenting on the tables more fully.

BLOOD CULTURES IN NORMAL AND PROTECTED ANIMALS

We have made the statement several times in our publications on experimental empyema that the rabbit syndrome resembles its human analogue so far as we understand it, and among other facts resembles it in that it is never in the form of a septicemia. This statement, which we find subsequently has been corroborated in somewhat similar experiments by Noetzel,[32] requires further definition. It is perfectly

[32] Arch. f. klin. Chir., 1906, 80, p. 679.

true that normal animals when infected intrapleurally with a fatal dose of the streptococcus usually yield sterile cultures from the blood even when the local process has extended into both cavities, and at times when it has reached a fatal termination, even when cultures of even as much as 1 c c. of blood are made in 10 c c. of broth. This certainly

TABLE 6

EFFECT OF INJECTING 100 M L D OF STREPTOCOCCUS "H" IN RABBITS PREPARED BY BROTH INJECTION 24 HOURS PREVIOUSLY

Interval	Rabbits	Amount of Fluid in C c.	Total Leuko-cytes	Per Cent. Clas-mato-cytes	Total Number of Clas-mato-cytes	Total Number of Poly-morpho-nuclears	Bacteria in Cavity	Blood Culture
Prepared cavity before infection. Average of six animals	...	0.2	6,252,500	70.1	4,321,250	1,931,250	—	—
1 Hour	126	2.0	21,900,000	36.0	7,884,000	....	×1	00
	139	Trace	6,550,000	52.0	3,406,000	....	×10	0+
	138	0.8	26,520,000	52.0	13,790,400	....	×0.1	0+
	135	0.85	21,887,500	50.4	11,031,300	....	×7.5	0+
	136	1.5	6,450,000	40.0	2,580 000	....	×10	0+
Average	...	...	16,661,500	46.08	7,738,340	8,923,160		
3 Hours	34/88	0.3	192,300,000	12.0	22,076,000	....	×0	0+
	132	1.5	86,100,000	7.0	6,027,000	....	×30	0+
	140	Trace	15,400,000	17.6	2,710,400	....	×0.1	00
	143	0.5	31,175,000	27.0	8,417,250	....	×8	0+
Average	...	...	81,243,750	15.9	9,807,662	71,436,088		
6 Hours	35/88	Trace	5,250,000	51.2	2,688,000	....	×0	0+
	154	Trace	8,750,000	42.6	3,727,500	....	×0	00
	155	Trace	1,135,000	21.2	240,620	....	×7	00
	156	Trace	10,500,000	12.2	1,281,000	....	×0.01	00
Average	...	...	6,408,750	31.8	1,984,280	4,424,470		
12 Hours	36/88	Trace	2,850,000	100.0	2,850,000	0	×0	0+
24 Hours	19/89	0.5	2,035,000	14.3	291,005	....	×0	00
	94/89	Trace	260,000	18.0	46,800	....	×0	00
	157	0.2	990,000	55.7	551.430	....	×0	00
	158	Trace	1,450,000	73.0	1,058,500	....	×0	00
Average	...	...	1,183,250	40.3	486,684	696,566		

indicates that not many organisms are present in the circulating blood, and this particular series of experiments corroborates our previous findings in this regard. In the latter experiments, however, the animals were all exsanguinated before being chloroformed for examination, and the blood obtained from them, which would often total 50 to 60 c c. was defibrinated in a sterile flask and kept in the icebox. Cultures made from this blood (1 c c.) at once were frequently sterile, but cultures made 10 days or 2 weeks later often gave positive cultures in a dilution of 1 c c. or even 0.1 c c., which would indicate, in our opinion, not only that the blood of such animals possesses little bactericidal power for the streptococcus, but further that small numbers of streptococci are actually present in the blood, which subsequently increase to sufficient numbers to be detectable in ordinary cultures. The two notations under the blood culture, for example O +, indicate that the blood, at first perfectly sterile (in 1 c c.), was subsequently positive. This only emphasizes the contrast obtained in those instances where both cultures are sterile.

Bacteria Present in the Cavity.—Owing to our new method of estimating the number of streptococci present in a culture or a fluid which we have already described, we place considerable significance on the actual numbers of bacteria estimated to be present in a given pleural cavity as compared with the initial number of bacteria injected, which was in all instances carefully determined. The figure in the column "Bacteria in Cavity" represents the number of multiples of those injected.

An inspection of tables 5 and 6 and of the accompanying explanatory figures 1 and 2 shows the striking differences that occur following infection of the pleural cavity of normal, unprotected rabbits as compared with broth prepared perfectly protected animals. The complete set of observations we have made, which are extensive, include those made at intervals subsequent to 96 hours in the case of the normal infected animals, and will be referred to, although not represented in the table. In the first place, the protected animal never shows any considerable amount of fluid even one hour after the inoculation of the culture, which process in itself introduces 1 c c. of broth into the cavity. This fluid rapidly decreases until at the end of 24 hours the usual amount present in a normal cavity alone remains. In fact, the cavity of the prepared animal is essentially restored to normal at this period; the clasmatocytes are slightly above the normal count, and the polymorphonuclears still remain increased something over 10 times, but the cavity is sterile, as also is the blood. There is never infection of the left cavity, which begins regularly at the end of 24 hours in the normal unprotected animal. The cells in the cavity of the broth prepared animal show the following course following first the broth injection and the subsequent injection 24 hours later of culture. The clasmatocytes gradually rise following the broth inoculation from the normal of 300,000 to 4,000,000 and immediately following infection shoot upward until they reach, at the end of 3 hours, a maximum of nearly 10,000,000. The polymorphonuclear cells, which are slightly although not remarkably increased by the broth injection, also shoot up to a corresponding maximum of 71,000,000 at the 3-hour period. Both cells fall sharply between 3 and 6 hours so that the clasmatocytes reach a count of 2,000,000 and the polymorphonuclears 4,000,000 at this period.

The course following infection in an unprepared normal animal is quite different from that in the broth prepared animal, particularly as to the period at which the maximum is reached by both types of

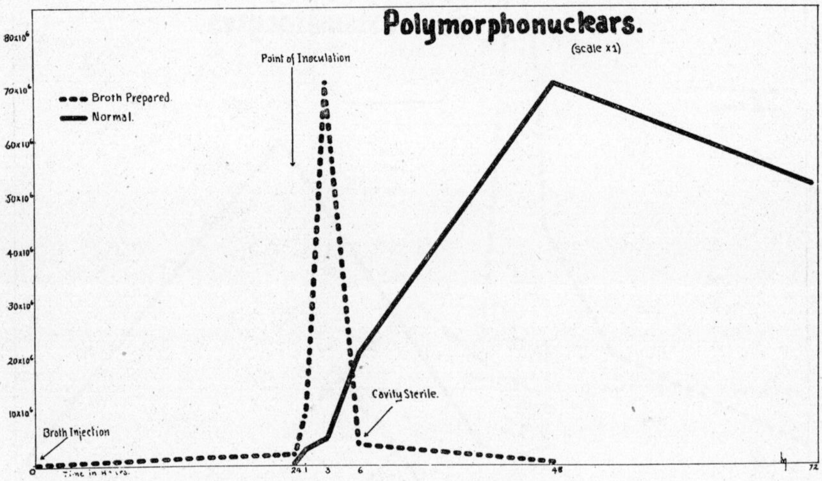

Fig. 1.—Graph indicating numbers of polymorphonuclear cells in normal and broth protected animals at intervals following streptococcus infection.

cells. The clasmatocytes in the normal animal reach a maximum of only two-thirds the number (6,000,000) attained in the broth animal, and that only 24 hours after infection. The polymorphonuclears rise as high in the normal as in the protected animal, but again at the delayed period of 24 hours. Subsequent observations, indicated in the table and extended by further observations on animals dying or killed at a period later than 2 days, show that beginning with 48 hours there are no longer any living clasmatocytes in the normal animal, and the bacteria steadily increase until death. The polymorphonuclears may remain fairly high in the normal animal in spite of the advance of the infection, but it should be remarked that we have used no criterion for the vitality of these polymorphonuclear cells as we have in the case of the clasmatocytes stained with neutral red. At all events, counts beyond the 3- or 4-day period counts of either type of cells are impossible, nothing but débris being found in the fluid, which is swarming with streptococci. It should further be noted that there is a steady increase in the fluid in a normal animal following infection until at the point of death, as we have frequently mentioned, as much as 20 to 25 c c. may be found in one or both cavities. These last remarks both as to

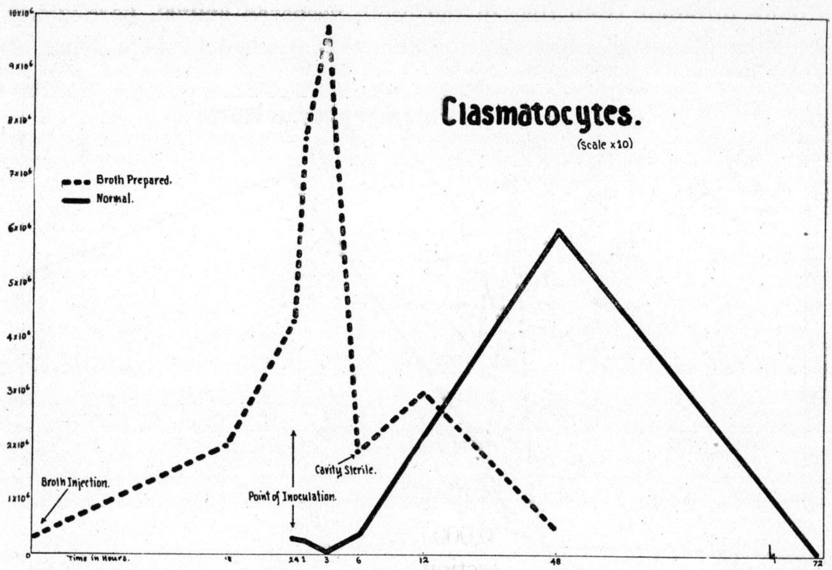

Fig. 2.—Graph indicating numbers of clasmatocytes in normal and broth protected animals at intervals following streptococcus infection.

cell appearance and bacteria should be contrasted with the essentially normal appearance of the protected animal, which is reached in 24 hours.

Cultures from the pleural cavity of protected animals show a sharp decrease in the number of bacteria even at the 3-hour period, and in 6 hours most cavities are already sterile. In 24 hours, as before mentioned, both cavity and blood culture are uniformly sterile. It is evident from the blood cultures that a certain number of bacteria reach the blood stream up to, and including, the 12-hour period; in fact, they seem to do so up to this period as frequently as they do in normal animals, but there is a sharp difference in the cultures from the 2 series in 24 hours. Whereas in the protected animals the blood has apparently succeeded in killing off the few cocci that have strayed into it so that all cultures are permanently sterile, in the unprotected animal, in 3 out of 5 cases in the table, in 24 hours the blood cultures were positive at once or eventually.

It might well be questioned on the basis of this comparative study of the course of infection between broth protected and normal animals, why we assume that the clasmatocytes alone are responsible for the protection in the first set. As indicated by the graphs, there is an acute crisis both of polymorphonuclear cells and of clasmatocytes, and at first glance it might appear that one set of cells is as responsible as the other. The peaks in the two lines coincide and are rapidly followed by sterilization of the cavity. It may be pointed out that just as many polymorphonuclears are eventually present in the cavity of the normal as of the protected animals, but it may be argued that they arrive too late to destroy the bacteria, as they might be thought to do between 3 and 6 hours, because the bacteria have increased to such a number that the task is impossible. Again, the polymorphonuclear cells in the normal animal in 24 hours may not be living cells, and so incapable of phagocytosis, whereas we might assume that the polymorphonuclears in 3 hours in the broth prepared animal are active. It is evident that we could not maintain our thesis on the superiority of clasmatocytes in protecting against streptococci on the basis of this part of the study alone. We refer again to the results in protection which occur in accordance with the respective numbers of polymorphonuclear cells and clasmatocytes as produced by the injection of various substances. Here the indication seems clear that in spite of enormous numbers of polymorphonuclears no considerable protection is afforded—for example, when 5% aleuronat is used—whereas the rise of clasmatocytes above a certain level usually seems to insure protection.

We have not so far made extended efforts to study the inner mechanism of the destruction of streptococci by the two categories of cells. It is, of course, well known that polymorphonuclears show marked phagocytosis even in fatally infected animals. We also have numerous observations that a true phagocytosis of streptococci by clasmatocytes takes place, as has been mentioned by many observers. We have not as yet struck on the most determinative conditions to show pure clasmatocyte phagocytosis, because when many clasmatocytes are present in a fluid following infection, few cocci can be found either in or out of the cells. We have so far failed also to demonstrate a destruction of cocci when mixed with exudates outside the body, whether these exudates be composed largely of clasmatocytes or of polymorphonuclear cells. Here, again, we believe the demonstration merely awaits the choice of suitable conditions.

RELATION OF CLASMATOCYTES TO ACQUIRED IMMUNITY

It has been suggested both by Buxton [33] and by Kanai [34] that acquired streptococcus immunity might in some way be related to clasmatocytes. Our observations on this more interesting and important phase of the question are still far from conclusive. They do, however, present in an undoubted fashion certain rather surprising results, which we believe should be presented at this time. Our first interest in the clasmatocytes as related to protection against the streptococcus was aroused by our observations that at the end of 24 hours after infection with multiple lethal doses, immunized animals show a higher percentage of clasmatocytes than normal, fatally infected animals. The mass of data we collected at that time is nearly valueless owing to the fact that no estimate was made of the total numbers of each of these cells present in the cavity or of the bacterial content of these cavities in any but a general way.

We have only recently returned to this phase of the question and present in table 7 the rather striking results obtained on the examination of a series of actively immunized animals both before and following the injection of 100 lethal doses of streptococcus "H" and both with and without preparation by broth. This experiment shows several things of interest. These animals were all immunized by means of sublethal doses of living stock "H" streptococcus culture which, as we have previously stated, has little pathogenic effect. The injections were given in one set of animals intravenously and in another intradermally, and the animals then were tested both intradermally and intraveously with erysipelas producing and fatal doses, respectively, and found to be protected fully. After a period of about 6 weeks, they were used for this experiment. It should be emphasized that none of these animals had ever received a dose of streptococcus intrapleurally, and they were as nearly similar in resistance as could well be brought about. The pleural fluids of 4 of these animals were examined without any further treatment, both right and left cavities in most of them being employed, and the resultant average of 7 separate determinations gives a total clasmatocyte count of over one and one-half million, which is more than

[33] Jour. Med. Res., 1907, 16, p. 251.
[34] Verhandl. d. japan. path. Gesellsch., 1919, 9, p. 126.

5 times the number present in the normal animal, and a polymorphonuclear count of somewhat over 200,000, which is about 4 times the normal count. The pleural cavities of all these animals were perfectly normal in appearance. It would appear, then, that immunization followed by successful recovery from infection leads to an increase

TABLE 7

CELL RESPONSE IN ACTIVELY IMMUNIZED ANIMALS, WITH AND WITHOUT BROTH PREPARATION, AND WITH AND WITHOUT INFECTION BY 100 M L D PASSAGE "H" STREPTOCOCCUS

I. Animals examined without preparation. Seven pleural cavities in 4 different immune animals. Cavities normal

	Total Number of Leukocytes	Per Cent. Clasmatocytes	Total Number of Clasmatocytes	Total Number of Polymorphonuclears
Average	1,772,356	86.7	1,536,953	235,403

II. Four animals given 3 c.c. infusion broth and examined 24 hours later

	Total Number of Leukocytes	Per Cent. Clasmatocytes	Total Number of Clasmatocytes	Total Number of Polymorphonuclears
Average	13,806,225	45.75	6,427,275	7,378,950

III. Immune animals infected with 100 M L D without preparation, and killed at different periods subsequently

Rabbit No.	Killed	Amount of Fluid in C c.	Total No. of Leukocytes	Per Cent. Clasmatocytes	Total No. of Clasmatocytes	Total No. of Polymorphonuclears	Bacteria in Cavity	Blood Culture
115	3 hours	0.8	6,112,500	0	0	6,112,500	×840	00
115	6 hours	0.35	15,207,500	0	0	15,207,500	×1900	0+
113	24 hours	Trace	600,000	82.0	492,000	108,000	0	00

IV. Immune animals, broth prepared, and then infected with 100 M L D

Rabbit No.	Killed	Amount of Fluid in C c.	Total No. of Leukocytes	Per Cent. Clasmatocytes	Total No. of Clasmatocytes	Total No. of Polymorphonuclears	Bacteria in Cavity	Blood Culture
239	3 hours	3.7	229,400,000	6.7	15,300,980	214,099,020	×1/150	00
240	6 hours	Trace	19,550,000	67.4	13,164,920	6,385,080	0	00
24/89	24 hours	0.1	4,650,000	33.7	1,567,050	3,082,950	0	00

of the clasmatocytes and also, to some extent, of the polymorphonuclears in the pleural cavity and possibly elsewhere in the body.

When animals of this type are prepared by broth, the usual response follows; in this case, however, indicated by a greater relative increase of the polymorphonuclear cells than occurs in the normal animal. The clasmatocyte count in broth prepared immune animals was one and one-half times that produced in the normal animal and the polymorphonuclear count about 3 times the normal. The result on infection of animals in this series which is given in detail, and observation of their pleural cavities at subsequent intervals of 3, 6 and 24 hours, give most interesting results. So far as one can judge from this small series, the injection of a multiple of fatal doses of bacteria in an actively immunized animal in which, as we have just stated, clasmatocytes are present in large numbers, causes a sharp diminution in the clasmatocytes for a period of about 6 hours, during which period the bacteria actually increased to larger numbers than they do in the normal animal, in spite of the presence of rapidly increasing numbers of polymorphonuclear cells. At the end of 24 hours, however, the animal has fully recovered, the cavity is sterile and the cells have nearly reached their normal counts. The broth prepared immune series shows a striking contrast to this; there is apparently no diminution, but, on the other hand, a sharp increase in the number of clasmatocytes, which reaches 15 times the number originally present in the cavity before infection and 75 times the number present in the normal rabbit cavity. Coincident with this, the cavity is almost sterile at the end of 3 hours and completely so in 6 hours. There is also, to be sure, an enormous increase of polymorphonuclear cells in an early animal of this series, but we believe that this experiment pleads on the whole for the superiority of the clasmatocytes rather than that of the polymorphonuclears.

As bearing on the origin of clasmatocytes found in the serous cavities, we would say that their increase in immunized animals following infection is not, in our experience, directly from the circulating blood. In a series of animals we found no increase in the large mononuclear-transitional ratio in the blood until from 3 to 5 days following infection.

PASSIVE IMMUNITY

Although the evidence we have so far adduced in respect to active acquired immunity would indicate that the clasmatocytes may well play the important rôle, or at least an accessory rôle in protection, our evidence for the nature of passive immunity in respect to clasmatocytes is not yet quite clear. One thing, however, seems definite. The injection of the serum of a rabbit highly immunized against the streptococcus and subsequently inactivated by heating to 56 C. produces a cellular output very similar, when injected into the pleural cavity of a normal rabbit, to that induced by normal inactivated rabbit serum. The average total clasmatocyte count in 5 animals treated with immune serum was 2,100,530 cells, whereas in 4 animals given the same dose (3 c c.) of normal rabbit serum the clasmatocytes totaled on an average 2,446,450 cells; polymorphonuclears following immune serum 1,153,470 cells; polymorphonuclears following normal serum 2,053,553 cells. Here, if anything, the number of clasmatocytes is slightly in favor of the normal serum treated animals. There are suggestive results in the continuation of these experiments, so far as we have gone. Unfortunately, through a series of accidents, the normal control animals that were allowed to progress after infection without examination were found to have been faultily inoculated, that is, the bacteria were not injected into the cavity but into the muscles. We know from previous experience * that normal serum given before infection does not protect,

TABLE 8

COMPARISON OF FINDINGS IN ANIMALS PREPARED BY IMMUNE RABBIT SERUM AND NORMAL RABBIT SERUM INFECTED WITH 100 M L D AND KILLED 3 HOURS LATER

Prep.	Rabbits	Amount of Fluid in C c.	Total Leuko-cytes	Per Cent. Clas-mato-cytes	Total No. of Clas-mato-cytes	Total No. of Poly-morpho-nuclears	Bacteria in Cavity	Blood Culture
I. S.	252	0.9	10,980,000	7.6	827,640	10,062,360	0	00
N. S.	246	Trace	3,550,000	2.0	71,000	3,479,000	×1/40	00
N. S.	247	1.0	19,000,000	0	0	19,000,000	×1/6	++

whereas immune serum does; but it would have been reassuring to have had a series of controls in connection with these particular experiments. At all events, our series of controls with immune serum correspond to our previous findings. Three animals given 3 c c. of immune serum 24 hours before the inoculation of 100 M. L. D. when killed 24 hours later showed little fluid in the pleural cavity and sterile cultures; blood cultures were also sterile. Two more animals that were left unmolested recovered perfectly. The one striking finding that we adduce as suggestive rests in an experiment in which 2 animals given normal serum and one animal given immune serum were killed 3 hours after the inoculation of the usual test dose. It will be seen (table 8) that while the bacteria are somewhat reduced in the 2 normal animals the cultures are sterile in the immune animal, and whereas in one normal animal there were no clasmatocytes found with neutral red, and in the other only 71,000, there were over 827,000 in the immune serum

* Gay and Stone: Jour. Infect. Dis., 1920, 26, p. 265.

prepared animal. The polymorphonuclears were nearly double the number in one of the normal serum controls that were found in the immune serum animal.

COMPARISON OF EXPERIMENTAL PLEURITIS WITH EXPERIMENTAL PERITONITIS

There has been much interest both on the part of bacteriologists and of surgeons in the difference in susceptibility to bacterial infections between the pleural and peritoneal cavities. It is generally recognized (Noetzel,[32, 35] Yates [36]) that the peritoneum is less susceptible than the pleura. In our experiments, this difference is striking. We have found, for instance, that the peritoneal cavity is over 1,000 times more resistant to our particular strain of streptococcus than is the pleural cavity as evidenced in table 9.

TABLE 9

DETERMINATION OF THE M L D OF PASSAGE STREPTOCOCCUS "H" INTRAPERITONEALLY IN RABBITS

Dosage	Number of Animals	Dead	Recovered
10 c c.	2	2	0
1 c c.	2	2	0
0.1 c c.	17	4	13 (76%)
0.001 c c.	4	0	4

Here the M L D was not exactly determined, but more than three fourths of the animals that were given 0.1, which is 1,000 times the minimum lethal dose in the pleura (0.00001), recovered. Many explanations have been offered by those who have investigated this question to account for the differences in resistance of these two adjacent cavities lined with the same cells. Extensive studies have described the rates of disappearance of bacteria injected into the peritoneal cavity, but not so minute attention has been paid to the pleural cavity. It is recognized that the organisms injected into the peritoneum invade the circulating blood with great rapidity (Buxton,[37] Durham,[5] and Noetzel [32, 35]). Many authors who have studied this problem are inclined to attribute the greatest importance to the resorption of bacteria by the blood stream from the peritoneum as accounting for the relatively great resistance of this cavity (Jensen,[38] Grober,[39] and Landsberg [40]).

[35] Arch. f. klin. Chir., 1898, 57, p. 311.
[36] Trans. Am. Surg. Assn., 1919.
[37] Jour. Med. Res., 1907, 16, p. 41.
[38] Ueber pneumokokken Peritonitis, 1903, 69, p. 1134; 70, p. 91.
[39] Die Resorptionskraft der Pleura, Habitatumschrift, 1901.
[40] Wien Arch. f. inn. Med., 1921, 2, p. 467.

Other authors would attribute as great or greater importance to the local destructive effect of the exudate (Buxton and Torrey,[41] Jensen,[38] and Noetzel [32]). There are other factors also which would account in part for the differences between the pleura and peritoneum: a positive pressure in the peritoneum aiding in resorption as against the negative pressure in the pleura; a greater surface in the peritoneal area both for localized resorption and for the production of an exudate which is normally greater in amount than in the pleural cavity. In more chronic conditions of inflammation of these cavities such complicating factors as pneumothorax are of course of great importance, and there is general agreement that inflammation at least of the fibrinous type prevents resorption.

Our own experience shows not only that bacteria injected into the peritoneum are rapidly absorbed into the circulating blood but are present in the mediastinal lymph nodes within a few minutes. Similar results both as regards blood and lymph nodes are also obtained following intrapleural injection, but it is likewise certain that although the blood may be invaded, many organisms are disposed of locally, as evidenced for instance in our broth prepared animals when eventual recovery from the process occurs in spite of positive blood cultures in the early hours following infection. Ultimate recovery of the animal therefore depends on the success in local destruction of the bacteria which if allowed to increase lead finally to increasing numbers in the blood, and the eventual death of the animal from both local and general causes.

We attribute the superiority of the peritoneal cavity in resisting streptococcus infection to the presence normally of greater numbers of clasmatocytes than are at hand in the pleural cavity. The average total peritoneal clasmatocyte count in 4 animals was 1,689,613, that is to say, nearly 6 times as many as are present in the pleural cavity. When 0.1 c c. of our passage culture, which is on the borderline of tolerance, and from which two-thirds of the animals recover, is injected into the peritoneum, cultures usually do not become negative locally until the 3rd or 4th day, although a sharp diminution is evident as early as in from 6 to 12 hours. The 3 to 5% of polymorphonuclear cells that are present normally increases in from 3 to 4 hours to over 90%, but by the 12th hour there is a restoration to nearly the normal relationship, which continues undiminished until the sterilization of the cavity, that is to say, clasmatocytes in large numbers are constantly present. The

[41] Jour. Med. Research, 1906, 15, p. 5.

blood may contain a few cocci, as shown by a negative first culture (1 c c.) and an eventual positive culture even after the peritoneal cavity has become sterile.

Invasion of the pleura on either or both sides seems invariable when 0.1 c c. is given intraperitoneally, but the cavity finally clears at about the same time or even slightly before the peritoneal cavity becomes sterile; that is, in 2 or 3 days. Here the interesting point is that the differential count of cells in the pleural cavity shows consistently a high clasmatocyte proportion which, although it may be slightly below normal, that is, 70 to 75%, never descends very low except in 3 animals in which the estimated number of bacteria in the cavity reached the maxima recorded, namely, 30,000, 40,000 and 360,000 cocci. Here, again, we regret the absence of total leukocyte counts, but certainly the indications all are that such pleural cavities become eventually sterile and become sterile without the intervention of any considerable numbers of polymorphonuclear cells, but with a constantly increasing number of clasmatocytes, as indicated by the fixed differential count and the increasing amount of fluid in the cavity. The bacterial counts recorded in the pleural cavity after intraperitoneal infection actually exceed markedly the sublethal dose of cocci that can be tolerated when injected in a single dose, but this may be readily explained by the certainty that the invasion of the cavity by small numbers of cocci is continuous rather than explosive which would give the cells opportunity for disposal of the bacteria.

Although it is true that the currents of bacterial resorption are doubtless anteriad draining from the peritoneum toward the pleura, rather than the reverse, it is not yet quite clear why the invasion of the mediastinal lymphatics after peritoneal infection should of necessity lead to the involvement of the pleural cavity, and here again the striking contrast is that the peritoneal cavity is rarely invaded after fatal pleural infection. Peritoneal cultures are invariably sterile for 2 or 3 days, even when both pleural cavities are filled with pus; it is only in the last stages of infection that the peritoneal cultures are positive, and then the organisms are present only in small numbers. This also is explained, in addition to the direction of the current, by the presence of greater numbers of clasmatocytes in the peritoneum.

SPREAD OF STREPTOCOCCI FROM OTHER LOCI OF INFECTION

In connection with our work on experimental erysipelas, and incidental to the study of intraperitoneal and intrapleural routes of infection with our passage culture, we have made a number of preliminary observations on the areas involved in the rabbit following inoculation in different parts of the body. Animals have been killed at intervals following inoculation of 0.1 c c. of passage culture "H", or 10,000 times the fatal intrapleural dose. This dose, to repeat, produces erysipelas when injected intradermally with regularity but does not kill,[42] and the infection never extends beyond the adjacent lymph nodes. Other lymph nodes, peritoneum, and pleura remain uniformly sterile when the animals are killed all the way from 1 to 12 days, although the local lesion gives a positive culture for an even longer period.

Subcutaneous Infection.—Three animals examined on the 4th day showed an involvement of the adjacent lymph nodes, but in 2 of these animals the pleura, peritoneum and blood were all sterile.

Intramuscular Injections.—Four animals killed from 18 hours to 6 days gave sterile cultures everywhere except from the adjacent lymph nodes.

Intradural Injections.—Four of the 6 animals died in 24 hours, with general involvement of the entire body. The 2 additional animals killed on the second day showed positive blood culture in only one, and the organism was not present in the body in either elsewhere than in the brain.

It is evident from these casual observations that there is in muscle, connective tissue and skin a mechanism for locally disposing of many fatal intrapleural doses of our streptococcus, whereas injections into a serous cavity—meninges, pleura and to a less extent, peritoneum—lead to a more or less rapid fatal infection. It is evident that these comparisons not only are not incompatible with a protection for which clasmatocytes may be responsible, but actually suggest its probability.

RESPONSE FOLLOWING INJECTION OF A SUBLETHAL DOSE OF STREPTOCOCCI INTRAPLEURALLY

A series of animals were infected at different times with the standard sublethal dose of streptococcus "H" as given in table 1, namely, 0.000001 c c. of culture. They are presented in table 10. It should be recalled in connection with this table that all animals with this dose allowed to go without intervention have recovered perfectly. Here it is evident that in some animals the cavity inoculated is found sterile on the 1st and 2d days, although positive cultures may be obtained for

[42] Gay, F. P., and Rhodes, B.: Jour. Infect. Dis., 1922, 31, p. 101.

as long as 3 days. The sterility of the pleural culture, moreover, does not assure a sterile blood culture at that particular time which corresponds to the results with a nonfatal dose in the peritoneum. What we believe is striking, however, in this series, is that although the organisms may have increased markedly, with the exception of those in the first 2 animals, there is a constantly high clasmatocyte percentage throughout the series, which is sharply in contrast with the disappearance of any but débris of cells after the second day in normal animals infected with a fatal dose of streptococci. In other words, although bacteria are still present, they are probably being slowly destroyed; or,

TABLE 10

EFFECT OF INJECTING A SUBLETHAL DOSE OF STREPTOCOCCUS "H" IN NORMAL RABBITS

Rabbits	Killed	Amount of Fluid in C c.	Total Leukocytes	Per Cent. Clasmatocytes	Total No. of Clasmatocytes	Total No. of Polymorphonuclears	Bacteria in Cavity	Blood Culture
131	1 hour	1.9	3,400,000	12.0	408,000	2,992,000	×1	0+
134	3 hours	1.5	75,520,000	0.0	0	75,520,000	×65	0+
45/89	6 hours	2.0	....	98.6	......	....	×24	0+
82/82	1 day	0.5	....	47.3	......	....	×640	0+
93/89	1 day	2.6	....	65.5	......	....	×0	00
57/89	1 day	Trace	....	31.0	......	....	×0	0+
38/89	2 days	0.1	....	66.2	......	....	×0	0+
43/87	2 days	1.5	....	0.5	......	....	×200	0+
97/89	3 days	Trace	....	60.0	......	....	×0	00
83/89	3 days	1.0	....	94.0	......	....	×1000	0+
58/89	3 days	8.6	....	89.6	......	....	×650000	0+
33/89	5 days	0.2	....	93.0	......	....	×0	00
82/89	7 days	Trace	....	Recovered	......	....	.....	00

at all events, there is evidence that a margin of safety is present in the presence of living clasmatocytes, which results in eventual sterilization of the cavity and recovery of the animal.

SUMMARY AND CONCLUSIONS

Our main thesis here is that the "clasmatocytes" or "tissue macrophages" are in large part, if not entirely, responsible for the natural resistance of rabbits to experimental streptococcus infection; this, in spite of the obvious presence of polymorphonuclear cells, which have so long been held entirely responsible for the cellular protective mechanism in acute infections (Metchnikoff). Clasmatocytes seem likewise implicated in both the active and passive forms of acquired streptococcus immunity, but here our evidence as to the exact mechanism is as yet incomplete.

Clasmatocytes are now identified by modern vital staining methods and can be readily differentiated from fibroblasts, serosal cells and adult endothelium. Their identity with or relationship to the large mononuclears of the blood do not concern us here. We have confirmed and extended the observations that the cells normally present in both pleural and peritoneal exudates are nearly all clasmatocytes. We have estimated the actual number of clasmatocytes present in the pleural cavity of the rabbit.

Various relatively harmless substances when injected into the pleural cavity of normal rabbits produce exudates which, at a fixed interval of time (24 hours), vary in the relative numbers of clasmatocytes and polymorphonuclear cells present. Substances like aleuronat, diatomaceous earth and whole egg white produce large numbers of polymorphonuclear cells but relatively and usually absolutely small numbers of clasmatocytes; plain infusion broth even without peptone and salt, and 1% egg white produce relatively and actually large numbers of clasmatocytes and few polymorphonuclear cells. We believe this increase of clasmatocytes is from the adjacent connective tissue and not from the circulating blood.

Animals in which the rich polymorphonuclear exudate has been produced die as readily of experimental streptococcus pleurisy as do normal animals; indeed, there is evidence that excessive numbers of polymorphonuclear cells actually render rabbits less resistant. A high clasmatocyte exudate (e. g., about 4,000,000 cells in the cavity) insures the animal against many multiples of the fatal infecting dose of streptococcus. There is at least one exception to this last statement when there are likewise enormous numbers of poymorphonuclears present (with diatomaceous earth), but we do not regard this exception as invalidating the essential relationship of clasmatocytes to protection.

In continuing our studies on experimental empyema, we have described certain perfected methods which standardize the virulence of the culture we use, the accuracy of dosage, and which render possible the close estimation of the actual numbers of bacteria present in broth cultures used for inoculation and in pleural fluids resulting from such infection.

A detailed comparison of the occurrences in the pleural cavity following infection in normal rabbits and in broth protected rabbits is given. In the normal animal the injected streptococci steadily increase until death, which occurs in from 5 to 7 days. The amount of pleural fluid likewise steadily increases, and the opposite cavity is soon involved. In the broth protected animal there is no increase in fluid, and the bacteria steadily decrease, and the cultures from the cavity are sterile in from 3 to 24 hours.

An acute crisis both of the clasmatocytes and of the polymorphonuclear cells occurs in broth prepared animals at about the third hour following infection. After 24 hours the pleural cavity in such animals has returned to a normal condition. In the normal, unprotected animal the polymorphonuclears steadily increase to a maximum that is reached in 24 hours, and which is as great as that reached in 3 hours in the protected animal. The recognizable polymorphonuclears thereafter decrease gradually until on the 3rd or 4th day they have all disintegrated. The living clasmatocytes in the normal animal increase slowly up to 24 hours, and then decrease rapidly until at 48 hours they have entirely disappeared. They never reach the maximum attained at 3 hours in the broth protected animals.

When normal animals are given a sublethal dose of streptococcus, the sterilization of the cavity is delayed for 3 or 4 days, but there is evidence that the proportion of clasmatocytes, with the exception of an initial diminution, remains high thoroughout the diminishing infection.

The peritoneal cavity under our conditions of experimentation is at least a thousand times as resistant as the pleural cavity to streptococcus infection. Although complete sterilization may not occur for several days as with the sublethal dose in the pleura, the bacteria never increase excessively owing to the larger numbers of clasmatocytes normally present. A greater resorption from the peritoneum may be another reason for its greater resistance.

One or both pleural cavities are regularly invaded following nonfatal intraperitoneal infection; the actual number of bacteria in the pleura in the early stages exceeds many times the fatal dose when direct infection into the pleura is practiced, and yet these animals recover. Throughout this process the pleural differential count of clasmatocytes remains high in contrast to what occurs in the course of a fatal intrapleural infection.

Infection of areas in the body in which clasmatocytes are normally present in large numbers, skin, subcutaneous connective tissue and muscle, is self limited, never extending beyond the adjacent lymph node. Infection of serous cavities, subdural, intrapleural and intraperitoneal in which only a few clasmatocytes are normally present is followed by a fatal infection of varying degree, depending on the amount of exudate (clasmatocytes) present.

Active immunization against the streptococcus is followed by a definite increase of clasmatocytes and to less extent of polymorphonuclear cells in the pleural cavity. We do not know how general this increase may be. When broth is injected in such immune animals, the clasmatocytes are still further increased. Infection of both plain immune and broth prepared immune rabbits is followed by more or less rapid sterilization of the cavity. In the broth prepared immune series the sterilization proceeded much more rapidly, and here the clasmatocytes rapidly increased during the early hours after infection.

The injection of rabbit antistreptococcus serum into the pleural cavity produces no greater clasmatocyte response than does normal rabbit serum. In a preliminary experiment the clasmatocyte count at 3 hours after infection was high in the immune serum prepared animal, and the cavity was sterile, but in the normal serum prepared animals the clasmatocytes were markedly lowered, and there was only a slight decrease in bacteria.

The suggestion is further made that local immunity to streptococcus infection, such as we have previously described, is best explained on the supposition that clasmatocytes are responsible for it. The association of undifferentiated "macrophages," since the early work of Metchnikoff, with local streptococcus infection, and particularly with healing streptococcus wounds, is also recalled in this connection.

INTESTINAL SPIROCHETES

Leland W. Parr

From the Department of Hygiene and Bacteriology, University of Chicago

Intestinal spirochetes have been reported almost from the beginning of the bacteriologic era. They have been found frequently in cases of Asiatic Cholera.[1] The earliest of these references is a paper by Escherich[2] reporting cholera cases, in which he states that he found "teeth spirilla" in cholera stools. These spirochetes could not be cultivated. Klein[3] published a note on a new method for staining the flagella of cholera vibrios. It seems almost certain now that what he called vibrio flagella were really intestinal spirochetes. Kuisl[4] studied intestinal spirochetes, making use of the regular evacuations of 2 healthy subjects and of the intestinal tract from necropsies of 6 victims of suicide and murder. Kuisl found that spirochetes were present in some cases and not in others. He noticed in the healthy subjects that a diet rich in meat and eggs increased the spirochete content of the feces, whereas a diet of starchy foods caused the spirochetes to disappear in part or entirely.

In the literature there are many references to the occurrence of intestinal spirochetes in diseased conditions, notably infant diarrhea,[5] choleriform enteritis[6] appendicitis,[7] carcinoma ventriculi[8] ulcerative colitis,[9] pernicious anemia,[10] rheumatoid arthritis,[11] ulcerating tumors,[12] and three types of dysentery, i. e., pure spirochetal dysentery,[13] pure fusopirochetal dysentery,[14] and protozoal

Received for publication, July 4, 1923.

[1] Escherich: Aerzt. Intelligenzbl., 1884, 31, p. 561; Lustig and Giaxa: Wien. med. Wchnschr., 1886, 36, pp. 342, 383, 423; Fürbringer: Deutsch. med. Wchnschr., 1892, 18, p. 768; Netter: Bull. et mém. Soc. méd. d. hôp., 1892, 9, pp. 543, 573; Kowalski: Wien. klin. Wchnschr., 1893, 6, p. 888; Abel: Centralbl. f. Bakteriol., 1894, 15, p. 212; Aufrecht: Ibid., 1894, 15, p. 405; Escherich: Ibid., 1894, 15, p, 408; Lustig and Giaxa: Ibid., 1894, 15, p. 721; Rechtsamer: Ibid., 1894, 15, p. 795; Kowalski: Ibid., 1894, 16, p. 321; Grassberger: Wien. klin. Wchnschr., 1894, 7, p. 942; Mühlens: Ztschr. f. Hyg. u. Infektionskrankh., 1907, 57, p. 405; Hassenforder: Thesis, Lyon, 1914.

[2] Aerzt. Intelligenzbl., 1884, 31, p. 561.

[3] Centralbl. f. Bakteriol., 1893, 14, p. 818.

[4] Aerzt. Intelligenzbl., 1885, 32, p. 433.

[5] Escherich: München. med. Wchnschr., 1886, 33, p. 315; Teissier and Ch. Richet fils: Bull. et mem. Soc. méd. d. hôp., 1911, 31, p. 775; Hassenforder: Thesis, Lyon, 1914.

[6] Fürbringer: Deutsch. med. Wchnschr., 1892, 18, p. 768; Aufrecht: Centralbl. f. Bakteriol., 1894, 15, p. 405; Courmont and Lesieur: Lyon méd., 1911, 116, p. 359; Hassenforder: Thesis, Lyon, 1914.

[7] Thiroloix and Durand: Bull. et mém. Soc. méd. d. hôp., 1911, 31, p. 658; Kreinitz: Deutsch. med. Wchnschr., 1906, 32, p. 872.

[8] Luger and Neuberger: Ztschr. f. klin. Med., 1921, 92, p. 54.

[9] Thiroloix and Durand: Bull. et mem. Soc. méd. d. hôp., 1911, 31, p. 653; Hassenforder: Thesis, Lyon, 1914.

[10] Thomson and Thomson: Proc. Roy. Soc. Med., 1913-14, 7, Marcus Beck Reports, p. 47.

[11] Ibid. Stühmer: München. med. Wchnschr., 1921, 66, p. 768.

[12] Loewenthal: Berl. klin. Wchnschr., 1906, 43, p. 283.

[13] Le Dantec: Compt. rend. Biol., 1903, 55, p. 617; Mühlens: Cited by Hassenforder: Thesis, Lyon, 1914; Werner: Centralbl. f. Bakteriol., I, O., 1909, 52, p. 241; Doreau: Cited by Hassenforder: Thesis, Lyon, 1914; Rispal: Ibid. Langendörfer and Peters: München. med. Wchnschr., 1921, 68, p. 12; Pecker: Thesis, Paris, 1921, Unavailable, reviewed by deLavergne: Paris méd., 1922, 12, p. 467.

[14] Luger: Wien. klin. Wchnschr., 1917, 30, p. 1643; Ibid. Arch. f. Verdauungskr., 1921, 29, p. 59; Bouchet and Leroux: Progres méd., 1921, 28, p. 437; deLavergne: Paris méd., 1922, 12, p. 467; Ibid. Bull. et mém. Soc. méd. d. hôp., 1922, 38, p. 620.

dysenteries in which the spirochetes alone or with fusiform bacilli, have produced secondary complications and a condition of chronicity.[15]

Intestinal spirochetes have also been noticed in most animals.[16] This raises a question as to the identity of the animal and human intestinal spirochetes and the mode of infestation of man. A further point of interest in spirochetes is the resemblance of those of the mouth and the intestine and the possibility that the buccal and enteric spirochetes are the same.

Bienstock[17] early declared that spiral forms could not exist in the intestine, because not having spores they could not survive passage through the stomach from the mouth. Kuisl[4] however, established the presence of spirochetes in the normal intestine, in some cases, at least.

Miller[18] was one of the first to sugest that intestinal spirochetes might be derived from the mouth. Macfie[19] found that the intestinal spirochetes which he encountered on the Gold Coast of Africa readily withstood the action of artificial gastric juice. Hence intestinal spirochetes are to be studied as well as the organisms of diphtheria,[20] of tuberculosis,[21] and hemolytic streptococci[22] in the attempt to discover the relationship of the organisms of the upper cavities to those of the intestine proper.

This paper is concerned only with the intestinal spirochetes of man and common laboratory animals.

Morphology and Characteristics of Intestinal Spirochetes

Various writers have described intestinal spirochetes and some have reported elaborate measurements and descriptions of four or five types. Castellani has described a highly pleomorphic form.[23] The cultures which Hogue[24] obtained showed a variety of morphology equal to that seen in fecal emulsions from different persons and animals. Fantham[25] claims that the curves which spirochetes show are functions of the condition of motion at the time of fixation and cannot be a proper basis for classification. The most typical spirochetes of the intestine resemble the short mouth forms, but there are others like relapsing fever spirochetes in appearance. Sometimes heavy, long forms are seen with much flatter curves than the usual spirochetes exhibit. Cultural and serologic reactions for these intestinal organisms are very desirable to facilitate classification. In the absence of reliable methods for obtaining these reactions morphologic differences should not be emphasized, especially in view of variations noted above.

[15] Dumont: Paris méd., 1922, 12, p. 161; deLavergne: Thesis, Paris méd., 1922, 12, p. 467; Hassenforder: Thesis, Lyon, 1914.

[16] Escherich: München. med. Wchnschr., 1896, 33, p. 759; Smith: Centralbl. f. Bakteriol., 1891, 10, p. 179, and 1894, 16, p. 324; Bizzozero: Ibid., 1893, 13, p. 623; Salomon: Ibid., 1896, 19, p. 433; Regaud: Compt. rénd. Soc. biol., 1909, 46, pp. 229, 617; Hassenforder: Thesis, Lyon, 1914; Macfie: Lancet, 1917, 1, p. 336; Hollande: Compt. rénd. Acad., 1921, 172, p. 1693.

[17] Cited by Kuisl: Aerzt. Intelligenbl., 1885, 32, p. 433.

[18] Microorganisms of the Human Mouth, E. E. White Co., 1890.

[19] Lancet, 1917, 1, p. 336.

[20] Günther: Centralbl. f. Bakteriol., 1, O., 1907, 43, p. 648; Everall: Jour. Am. Med. Assn., 1911, 56, p. 199; Cargin: Lancet, 1913, 1, p. 23; Rolleston: Ibid., 1913, 1, p. 129; Schroedel: München. med. Wchnschr., 1900, 47, p. 395; Susswein: Wien. klin. Wchnschr., 1902, 15, p. 148; Bosse: Centralbl. f. Bakteriol, 1, O., 1903, 33, p. 478.

[21] Brown and Sampson: N. Y. State Med. Jour., 1921, 21, p. 260; Redman: Jour. Path. & Bacteriol., 1922, 25, p. 433.

[22] Davis: Jour. Infect. Dis., 1920, 26, p. 171; Moody and Irons: Ibid., 1920, 27, p. 363; Wordley: Lancet, 1922, 2, p. 610.

[23] Cited by Vaughan: Epidemiology and Public Health, 1923, 2, p. 424.

[24] Jour. Exper. Med., 1922, 36, p. 617.

[25] Brit. Med. Jour., 1916, 2, p. 815.

FILTRABILITY OF INTESTINAL SPIROCHETES

Wolbach[26] reported that he was able to pass a certain intestinal spirochete through Berkefeld filters. He demonstrated the organism in the filtrate and also cut sections of the filters and showed by appropriate staining that spirochetes were present in the filter pores in the vegetative form. Wolbach also reported cultivating the filtered spirochetes. In my efforts to cultivate the spirochetes I have filtered about 40 different fecal and cecal emulsions obtained from necropsies, healthy persons, sick persons, and animals and have used 36 different Mandler, Berkefeld N and Berkefeld V filters. The filtrates have been incubated with acid, neutral and alkaline broths, aerobically and anaerobically. Use has been made of such enriching materials as dextrose, blood, serum, and ascites fluid. I have never been able to obtain a satisfactory growth in over 900 tubes so incubated and carried 2 months before discarding. In at least 6 cases, however, I have been able to demonstrate spirochetes in the filtrate. In one case examination was made at once on completion of filtering, and smears made from centrifuged portions of the filtrate showed many typical spirochetes in every field of vision. This filtration work was carried out using an apparatus described elsewhere[27] which allows easy and aseptic fractional filtration. Gravity filtration was used following the method of Wolbach.

CULTIVABILITY OF INTESTINAL SPIROCHETES

As noted above, Wolbach grew the spirochetes found in the intestine by filtering them away from the accompanying contamination and incubating the filtrate aerobically in slightly acid broth. Hogue[24] has also reported growing the spirochetes by methods she had previously found useful in work with certain intestinal protozoa. Her cultures were grown in serum saline and were admittedly not free from contamination, though she felt she was working with spirochetes derived from single parent cells. Her work was all aerobic, and it was noted that Noguchi sterile tissue anaerobic methods were not successful. I have tried to confirm the cultivations of both of these workers, but with only indifferent success. I have had tubes in both series in which I could find intestinal spirochetes many days after the initial filtration or inoculation, but in each case the number of such forms was small, and I could not obtain growth in subcultures. Several other methods were tried, but without success.

DISTRIBUTION OF INTESTINAL SPIROCHETES IN THE HEALTHY

A survey of the literature with regard to the distribution of intestinal spirochetes in healthy persons reveals conflicting data. Kuisl[4] found spirochetes regularly present in the feces of 2 healthy persons and in 4 of 6 necropsies of victims of suicide and murder. Wolbach[26] stated that the intestinal spirochete was almost constant in human feces. Macfie[19] never failed to find spirochetes in examinations of natives or of Europeans at Accra, Gold Coast. Carter[28] found spirochetes in 41% of the healthy soldiers he examined during the World War. Porter[29] examined 60 Europeans and Colonials in South Africa and found that 28% excreted spirochetes. Macfie and Carter[30] stated that Spirochaeta eurygyrata might be found in more than half the people from temperate climates. Crowell and Haughwout,[31] who studied the

[26] Am. Jour. Trop. Dis. and Prev. Med., 1918, 2, p. 494.
[27] Parr: Jour. Am. Med. Assn., 1923, 80, p. 1775.
[28] Ann Trop. Med. & Parasitol., 1917, 10, p. 391.
[29] Pub. South African Inst. Med. Res., 1918, No. 11.
[30] Ann. Trop. Med. & Parasitol., 1917, 11, p. 75.
[31] Jour. Infect. Dis., 1918, 22, p. 189.

intestintal parasites in 46 adult Philippinos, found spirochetes in 73% of the cases. On the other hand, Hegner[32] made a like survey in Porto Rico and found intestinal spirochetes in only 1 of 83 cases.

My first work was to determine what percentage of normal persons living in the Chicago region harbored intestinal spirochetes. Adult stool samples were mostly obtained from students, and baby stool samples from the nursery of the obstetric ward of a neighboring hospital. The samples were emulsified in saline so that in opacity they matched tube 8 of the McFarland nephalometer scale.[33] The emulsions so made were thoroughly agitated, and smears were prepared and stained with Sterling's gentian violet. Intestinal spirochetes are gram-negative and take the counterstain weakly. This quality and the fact that they cannot be readily cultivated explain why so many workers have overlooked the presence of intestinal spirochetes in many subjects. When gram stains were made use of, as was the case several times, gentian violet stains

TABLE 1

PRESENCE OF INTESTINAL SPIROCHETES IN HEALTHY HUMAN SUBJECTS

	Number Examined	Positive	Percentage Positive
All subjects	173	48	27.7
Men	95	37	38.9
Women	28	8	28.5
Children under 14 years, over 14 days	17	3	17.6
Babies under 14 days	33	0	0

were also made. The dark field was little used in this survey. It is of great value in the study of numbers of living spirochetes, but in any effort to ascertain the abundance of intestinal spirochetes in the feces, where many other forms also occur, a fixed stain gives better results. The smears made and stained, as mentioned, were carefully examined microscopically, and the number of spirochetes noted. If none were seen in 50 fields of vision, the specimen was recorded as negative; but if every field showed several spirochetes, approximately 2% or more of all forms seen, the specimen was reckoned as a distinct positive. In no case was a significant number of spirochetes found. In a number of cases there was a trace only of spirochetes, perhaps 10 forms in the entire 50 fields. Such cases were considered positive, although their significance was less than if there were 500 times as many spirochetes present. In most of the cases more than one stool was examined. The findings are tabulated in table 1.

[32] Jour. Am. Med. Assn., 1921, 77, p. 1439.
[33] Ibid., 1907, 49, p. 1176.

Turning from human to animal subjects, I have to report the results of a similar survey conducted on animals. In this animal work, the cecum contents were examined instead of the excreted feces because other work indicated that the cecum was the true home of the spirochetes. Because of this fact, the material was limited, as the animal had to be killed in order to get the material. Only healthy animals were studied. I examined 1 dog, 55 wild rats, 27 wild mice, 37 guinea-pigs, 61 white mice, 63 white rats and 37 rabbits. In all species examined I found a certain percentage of positives, except for the 1 dog and the 37 rabbits. All white rats examined, with one exception, showed intestinal spirochetes. Of guinea-pigs examined, all but 2 gave positive findings. The white mice were 88% spirochete positive, while the wild rats were only 21% positive and the wild mice 22% positive. Dogs frequently show spirochetes,[6] and one negative case only is not sufficient for any conclusion. But the fact that there was not a trace of intestinal spirochetes in any one of 37 rabbits of a variety of sizes killed at different times during the last 3 years, and in some cases housed for weeks in the same cages with guinea-pigs, 94% positive for spirochetes, seems to have some significance.

DISTRIBUTION OF INTESTINAL SPIROCHETES IN THE SICK

In a review of the literature on this subject, two or three points stand out. Intestinal spirochetes have been found in many cases of cholera. Hassenforder[34] examined 868 suspected cholera samples. He found spirochetes in 51% of the 533 cholera positive samples, but in only 8% of the 335 cholera negative samples. Capellani[35] even went so far as to state that all grave cases of cholera were characterized by the presence of spirochetes in the stools. On the other hand, Kowalski[36] found no spirochetes in more than 100 cases of cholera in an outbreak at Trieste.

Another point of interest is the absence of spirochetes in cases of bacillary dysentery or typhoid fever. Thus deLavergne[37] reported that intestinal spirochetes had never been pointed out in the course of bacillary dysentery, and his study of 7 cases confirmed this statement. Torrey[38] reported on the examination of 103 stools from 22 typhoid patients finding all samples spirochete-free. This absence of spirochetes has been noticed in other conditions. Thus Hogue[24] found no spirochetes in 180 stools from 105 unclassified patients in the Johns Hopkins Hospital. Faust and Wassell[39] examined stools from 359 routine patients at the Church General Hospital, Wuchang, China, and found only 2 patients with intestinal spirochetes. But Porter[29] dealing with 93 patients in the native wards of the General Hospital of Johannesburg, South

[34] Thesis, Lyon, 1913-1914.
[35] Cited by Hassenforder, Thesis, Lyon, 1913-1914.
[36] Centralbl. f. Bakteriol., 1894, 15, p. 408.
[37] Paris méd., 1922, 12, p. 467; Bull. et mém. Soc. méd. d. hôp., 1922, 38, p. 620.
[38] Jour. Infect. Dis., 1915, 16, p. 72.
[39] China Med. Jour., 1921, 35, p. 532.

Africa, encountered 29 patients spirochete positive. And Haughwout and Horrilleno[40] found 61% of 100 sick Philippino children spirochete positive. In my work I have examined material from 130 hospital cases, 14 baby feeding cases and 49 food poisoning cases, finding spirochetes in 31% of the samples submitted, which is not greatly different from the average found for healthy persons in this region. I also had material from 4 cases of typhoid, and in all samples examined spirochetes were absent.

In reading the literature, one is impressed by the emphasis placed on the assumption that spirochetal enteritis is secondary to some protozoal infestation, usually amebic dysentery. Hogue's case[24] was a chronic diarrhea of 13 years' standing, which yielded Chilomastix mesnili and Trichomonas hominis, as well as the spirochetes. Porter[29] reported many cases of double infestation and several cases in which 3 forms were harbored within the intestine. Luger[41] reported a case in which the fusospirochetal symbiosis and Giardia intestinalis were both concerned, and he cited like cases from Mayer, Assmy, Prowazek and Werner. Macfie[42] reported a case of monkey dysentery in which ameba and spirochetes were found. Carter[28] found spirochetes in 56% of a large number of soldiers from the Near East in the World War. Fantham[43] made 3,325 examinations of stools from 1,291 patients and found spirochetes in only 42; but his record states that many of the men had had many doses of emetin before he had had occasion to examine them. Among others who have noted the relationship of intestinal spirochetes to amebic dysentery, particularly chronic amebic dysentery, one may note Teissier, Ch. Richet fils and Tanon; Roux and Tribondeau; Marotte; Tournade; Dernier and Huet; Leger, Ravaut; Muhlens; Werner; deLavergne; and Dumont[44] I have had no opportunity to study intestinal spirochetes in connection with amebic dysentery, either acute or chronic.

CONSTANCY OF APPEARANCE OF INTESTINAL SPIROCHETES IN STOOLS

There are those who believe that spirochetes form coccoid bodies which can account for a relatively invisible and filter-passing stage of the organisms.[45] I have made some observations recorded in table 2 which bear on this point. A number of different persons submitted stool specimens 3 or more times. These stools were examined for the presence or absence of spirochetes. Table 2 shows that in most of the cases spirochetes either were constantly present or were not to be found. Between these two extremes, however, I found subjects such as S. W. T., in whom the findings were at times positive and at times negative.

[40] Philippine Jour. Sc., 1920, 16, p. 1.
[41] Wien. klin. Wchnschr., 1917, 30, p. 1643.
[42] Ann. Trop. Med. and Parasitol., 1915, 9, p. 507.
[43] Lancet, 1916, 1, p. 1165.
[44] Cited by deLavergne: Paris méd., 1922, 12, p. 467; and Dumont: Paris méd., 1922, 12, p. 161.
[45] Fantham: Brit. Med. Jour., 1916, 2, p. 815; Ibid: Ann. Trop. Med. & Parasitol., 1915, 9, p. 391; Balfour: Jour. Trop. Med., 1911, 14, p. 113; Gleitsmann: Centralbl. f. Bakteriol., 1913, 1, O., 68, pp. 31, 493.

TABLE 2

CONSTANCY OF FINDINGS IN REPEATED EXAMINATIONS OF SUBJECTS

Subject	Times Examined	Positive	Negative
L. W. P.	140	132	8*
T. E. B.	26	26	0†
P. P. P.	8	0	8†
R. A. C.	8	0	8†
S. E. B.	6	6	0†
A. F. R.	6	6	0†
S. W. T.	6	3	3
E. I. M.	6	4	2
R. R. M.	5	0	5†
R. G. P.	4	0	4†
G. B. P.	4	0	4†
O. L. W.	3	1	2

* All the 8 negatives in this case came during an experiment involving special diet and perhaps should not be included in this table.

† Constant findings, i. e., all negative or all positive.

PERSISTENCY OF INTESTINAL SPIROCHETES IN STORED FECES

An interesting observation is that made by Thomson and Thomson,[10] in which they described a spirochete found in an obscure bottle of stored feces. It has been shown that significant chances go on in stored fecal material. Jordan [46] reported a large increase of B. coli during the first few days of storage. I made an attempt to find out how long after the storage of feces I could detect spirochetes and also whether fecal samples reported spirochete-free would subsequently show the presence of spirochetes. Fecal emulsions were made from 22 stool samples and stored in the dark at room temperature. From time to time distilled water was added to compensate for evaporation. In 19 cases, the storage with occasional examination was continued for more than 7 months. Spirochetes were found in one positive sample after 279 days of storage. Three other positive samples were found to contain spirochetes after 237, 219, and 217 days, respectively. Nine originally negative samples were included in the lot studied, and in two cases positive results were obtained after storage. This might be taken to indicate that reproductive granules had been present originally and had during storage developed into vegetative forms. It seems more likely, however, that a few forms were present the first time, but were not detected, since in these samples the number present at any of the observations was small. The spirochetes observed in the stored emulsions seemed in every way typical.

[46] Abstracts, Bacteriol., 1921, 5, p. 12.

LOCALIZATION OF THE INTESTINAL SPIROCHETES IN THE CECUM

Some of the early work on spirochetes suggested a localization for these forms in a particular part of the intestinal tract. Kuisl [4] noted that spirochetes were most common in the cecum and ascending colon of his necropsy cases. Escherich [47] found that in 17 cases of infant diarrhea terminating fatally spirochetes were found in the upper colon in 16 cases, but in only 2 cases in the ileum. In table 3 is recorded the findings from 7 necropsies conducted by the department of pathology. This table shows that in my examination of the human material I found some cases which were free from spirochetes; others in which there were spirochetes at the higher levels only; and a third group in which

TABLE 3

Intestinal Spirochete Survey in Human Autopsies

Age	Sex	Diagnosis	Percentage Spirochetes Found			
			Ileum	Cecum	Rectum*	Cecum Colon Ratio†
68	Male	Lung gangrene...........	0	0	0	0
50	Male	Acute nephritis...........	0	10.7	0	∞
12	Female	Bronchopneumonia.......	0	2.9	0.1	29
59	Male	Syphilis aneurysm.........	0	?	0	?
58	Female	Bronchopneumonia.......	0	3.1	0	∞
0	.....	Syphilitic, baby about 2 weeks..................	0	0	0	0
70	Female	Carcinoma...............	0	0	0	0

* The rectum of man was used here, but in animal work I have spoken of the lower colon instead.

† The cecum colon ratio is the whole or decimal number expressing the ratio of the cecum percentage of spirochetes to the lower colon percentage.

there were spirochetes in the rectum, but relatively fewer than at higher levels. I should not group 7 cases into 3 groups were it not for the fact that animal experiments justify that grouping. I made a thorough study of spirochete content of the cecum and colon in 41 white rats, white mice and guinea-pigs, and found in 38 that the ratio of the percentage of microbial forms in the cecum occurring as spirochetes to the ratio of microbial forms in the lower colon appearing as spirochetes was greater than 1. In 4 cases there were many cecum spirochetes and not any colon spirochetes. There were only 3 instances in which there were relatively more spirochetes in the colon than in the cecum, and here the excess was very small. In this series of animals there were none which were spirochete-free, but in other work I have encountered such animals, though not frequently. None of these 41 animals was receiving special

[47] München. med. Wchnschr., 1886, 33, p. 315.

diets. Just what the significance of this cecum-colon spirochete ratio is remains to be seen. At least it seems that intestinal spirochetes localize in the cecum.

DISTRIBUTION OF INTESTINAL SPIROCHETES IN HUMAN SUBJECTS ON DIET

In the minds of many, the saprophytic spirochetes have been associated with putrefactive processes. This belief may date back to the observations of Kuisl,[4] who stated that a diet rich in meat and eggs

TABLE 4

THE EFFECT OF LACTOSE DIET ON THE ABUNDANCE OF INTESTINAL SPIROCHETES

Stool, L. W. P.	Lactose Taken Previous 24 Hours	Percentage Spirochetes Found	Stool, T. E. B.	Lactose Taken Previous 24 Hours	Percentage Spirochetes Found
1	0	2	1	0	2
2	0	3	2	0	2
3	0	4	3	0	2
4	0	3	4	0	2
5	200 gm.	8	5	50 gm.	1.5
6	—*	10	6	150 gm.	3.8
7	300 gm.	1.7	7	150 gm.	1.6†
8	—	0.025	8	150 gm.	1.3
9	300 gm.	0.3	9	—	0.7
10	300 gm.	0	10	150 gm.	0.4
11	300 gm.	0	11	—	0.1
12	—	0	12	—	0.2
13	—	0	13	150 gm.	0.2
14	—	0	14	150 gm.	0.02
15	—	0	15	—	0.05
16	300 gm.	0	16	225 gm.	0.3
17	0	0.025	17	—	1.0
18	—	0.2	18	300 gm.	1.0
19	100 gm.	0.02	19	0	1.0
20	50 gm.	0.045	20	0	0.25
21	0	0.4			
22	0	1.5			
23	0	4.5			

* The dash means that the stool in question came on the same day as the one next above.
† On this day there were 6 bowel movements, but unfortunately only this one, No. 7, was submitted for examination.

increased the number of spirochetes whereas a diet of starchy foods decreased or eliminated them. It seems to be well established that a diet rich in lactose favors and eventually give rise to an aciduric flora in which fermentation rather than putrefaction is the predominating activity.[48] In my work, lactose was fed to 2 men. Both kept on a general diet but consciously restricted animal protein and increased the consumption of white bread, milk and toast. The lactose was taken between meals suspended in cold water. In both cases, on the third or

[48] Herter: Brit. Med. Jour., 1897, 2, p. 1847; Herter and Kendall: Jour. Biol. Chem., 1908, 5, p. 298; Rettger and Horton: Centralbl. f. Bakteriol., 1914, 1, O., 73, p. 362, and 75, p. 219; Torrey: Jour. Med. Res., 1919, 39, p. 415; Rettger and Cheplin: Transformation of the Intestinal Flora, 1921; Cannon: Jour. Infect. Dis., 1921, 29, p. 369; et al.

fourth day of lactose feeding there was a period of diarrhea which, which however, did not persist. Table 4 records the findings.

More recently, the effect of the consumption of acidophilus milk on the presence of the intestinal spirochetes was tried. There have been many references in the literature concerning the use of acidophilus milk.[49] Acidolphilus milk was prepared fresh each day and administered without lactose reinforcement. The milk was checked several times and was shown to be a pure culture of the organism each time examined. Eight liters of the preparation were administered to the subject in 10 days. The subject was examined before, during and after the milk ingestion for the urinary indican reaction, for the presence or absence of spirochetes in the feces, and for the C/A ratio of Cannon.[50] It was found that the originally indican-positive reaction persisted throughout the experiment, but the degree of the reaction varied. The reaction did not vary, however, in any relationship to the milk eaten. One of the strongest reactions for indican, Obermayer test, came on the 12th day. The spirochetes were not eliminated from the feces, but it seemed conclusive that they were decreased in number. The ratio of colon bacilli present to those of the acidophilus type decreased, but could be reduced no lower than 16 to 73. Both in the lactose feeding work and in this milk feeding, the spirochetes reappeared in the original concentration very soon after stopping the lactose or the milk.

DISTRIBUTION OF INTESTINAL SPIROCHETES IN ANIMALS ON DIET

Some studies were made on the effect of diet on the presence of spirochetes in animals.

In a typical experiment, 16 healthy adult rats from the same lot were used. They were fed in sub-lots. Rats 70 to 73 received water and 3 parts of roasted beef to 1 part of lactose. Rats 75 to 78 were fed roasted beef and water only. Rats 80 to 83 received water, carrots, oats and bread. Rats 85 to 88 were fed no water, but had all the milk they could drink containing bread sprinkled heavily with lactose. The animals were kept on these diets for a week and were then killed and examined. Material was taken from the cecum and lower colon in each rat, and the spirochete content and hydrogen ion reaction determined for each specimen. The findings are recorded in table 5, from which it will be seen that the acid-producing carbohydrate diet had the greatest

[49] Cheplin and Wiseman: Bost. Med. & Surg. Jour., 1921, 185, p. 627; Rettger and Cheplin: Arch. Int. Med., 1922, 29, p. 357; Bassler and Lutz: Jour. Am. Med. Assn., 1922, 79, p. 607; Kopeloff and Cheney: ibid., 1922, 79, p. 609; Bass: Southern Med. Jour., 1923, 16, p. 1; Gompertz and Vorhaus: Jour. Am. Med. Assn., 1923, 80, p. 90; Kopeloff and Beerman: Abst., Bacteriol., 1923, 7, p. 28; Cheplin, Fulmer and Barney: Jour. Am. Med. Assn., 1923, 80, p. 1896.

[50] Jour. Infect. Dis., 1921, 29, p. 369.

effect on the spirochete content. The determination of the hydrogen-ion concentration was made on emulsions of fecal material which had been centrifuged at high speed for an hour. The supernatant liquid was tested with colorimetric indicators against standards freshly prepared from buffer solutions checked electrometrically. Methyl red, brom cresol purple, brom thymol blue, and phenol red were used as indicators. Each sample was run twice, using a different indicator each time. If the two results could not be checked, the reading was taken using the dye most appropriate for the range in question. In other animal work the fecal emulsions were cleared by filtration, but it was found that filtrates so obtained had been altered by passage through the filter, and so the method was abandoned.[51]

Some work was done, making use of fasting animals. Kendall[52] made bacteriologic examinations of the colon contents of a man who had taken no

TABLE 5

THE EFFECT OF DIET IN WHITE RATS ON THE PH AND ABUNDANCE OF SPIROCHETES AT DIFFERENT LEVELS

Rat Number	Spirochetes %			PH	
	Cecum	Colon	Cecum Colon Ratio	Cecum	Colon
70	0	0	0	6.6	7.0
71	?	3	<1	6.0	—*
72	5	5	1	6.8	6.6
73	0.5	0	∞	6.4	7.0
75	0	0.1	<1	7.0	7.0
76	0	0	0	7.0	7.0
77	10	0	∞	7.0	6.8
78	0.5	0	∞	7.0	6.8
80	2	0.8	2.5	6.7	6.3
81	1.5	0.8	1.8	6.6	5.9
82	0.1	0	∞	7.0	6.6
83	2	—*	—	6.6	—*
85	0	0.1	<1	4.6	5.6
86	0	0	0	5.0	6.6
87	0	0	0	4.8	5.5
88	0	0	0	5.0	5.6

* Tube broken in centrifuge.

food for more than 30 days and found 3 types of organisms only, viz., B. mesentericus, B. coli and M. ovalis. The colon type was in great predominance. This persistence of the colon type is significant. In other work, such as intestinal obstruction,[53] it has been found that no matter what the diet or the original flora, the colon type predominates just before the animal with obstruction dies. The effect of fasting on the presence of intestinal spirochetes was tested on guinea-pigs. Seven healthy guinea-pigs, spirochete-positive by fecal tests, were taken and placed in a clean cage with plenty of water, but no food. On the 6th day, 1 of the animals died. There was no evidence of infection in the dead pig; the other 6 seemed healthy and they had not eaten any of the body of their dead companion, so the 6 remaining guina-pigs were killed and studied. The cecal p_H varied from 6.6 to 7.2. No spirochetes were found in the lower colon or in the ileum, but in 4 out of 6 a few spirochetes were found in the cecum. Fasting, then, seems to reduce the number of spirochetes present.

51 Hudson and Parr: to be published.

52 Publication 203, Carnegie Institution, Washington, 1915, p. 232.

53 Cannon, Dragstedt and Dragstedt: Jour. Infect. Dis., 1920, 27, p. 138.

THE EFFECT OF CALOMEL ON THE PRESENCE OF INTESTINAL SPIROCHETES IN MAN

Hassenforder and others[54] have suggested that calomel rids the intestine of spirochetes. Calomel was twice tried in the case of L. W. P. Both times careful examinations were made for several days before and after taking the drug, so that proper judgment could be had as to the results obtained. The first time 8 quarter grain tablets of calomel were given, not followed by any other treatment. The second time, 3 weeks later, 12 quarter grain tablets of calomel were taken, followed 6 hours later by a mildly cathartic dose of Epsom salts. For the first experiment, 9 preliminary stools were studied. In these the spirochete content ranged from 2.6 to 8% of all organisms seen in smears, with an average for the 9 of 3.6. Four stools were the result of the calomel ingestion, and they had a spirochete content ranging from 0.3 to 7.5% with an average of 2.4. Four stools were taken following the calomel stools and for the 4 a range of from 1.2 to 7.5% was obtained with an average of 3.8. For the second run 6 stools were taken for a preliminary with a content range of from 0.9 to 5.5% and an average of 3.5. The calomel and salts effect for the second experiment gave 4 stools ranging in spirochete content from 3.6 to 9.3% with an average of 5.7. Five stools were taken during the next 5 days and it was found that their spirochete content varied from 2.4 to 5.9% with an average of 3.8%. Thus, while there was some increase in the spirochete content excreted immediately following a large dose of calomel, there was no elimination of the spirochetes.

Animal Inoculation with Intestinal Spirochete Material

LeDantec[55] reported that spirochetal dysentery was perhaps transmissible to dogs, as one of his patients recounted how his dog had eaten part of the mucus of an evacuation and had been attacked by spirochetal dysentery some days later. Vaughan[56] feels, however, that LeDantec has never been confirmed in his primary conclusions concerning spirochetal dysentery as an entity among diseases, hence his indirect testimony might even more be discounted. Blanchard[55] introduced the exudate from the false membrane of a case of Vincent's angina into the digestive tube of a dog and determined a dysenteriform state in the dog in which both spirochetes and fusiform bacilli were recovered from the stools. Tanon[55] tried the effects of subcutaneous, intravenous and intestinal injections of spirochetal material into guinea-pigs, rabbits and monkeys but with negative results. Teissier and Ch. Richet fils[57]

[54] Roos: Cited by Luger: Wien. klin. Wchnschr., 1917, 30, p. 1643; Hassenforder: Thesis, Lyons, 1914.

[55] Cited by Hassenforder: Thesis, Lyons, 1914.

[56] Epidemiology and Public Health, 1923, 2, p. 424.

[57] Bull. et. mém. Soc. méd. d hôp., 1911, 31, p. 775.

irritated the digestive tract of rabbits and guinea-pigs by the use of sodium sulphate, magnesium sulphate, and in some cases castor oil, and fed the animals fecal emulsions rich in spirochetes. They also fed the same material to animals in which the gastric contents had been neutralized. All feeding results were negative. They injected the material into animals subcutaneously and found that abscesses were formed, but examination of the abscesses showed that they were spirochete-free. When intraperitoneal injections were made into guinea-pigs, 2 cases gave exudates in the peritoneum which were rich in spirochetes. But this material failed to produce spirochetes when injected into a second series of pigs. Hassenforder[34] reported that intrarectal injections of the fecal emulsions containing spirochetes had no effect on young cats unless the material also contained virulent ameba. I repeated some of this work, especially intraperitoneal injections into guinea-pigs. In a series of 6 animals injected, there was none showing an exudate containing spirochetes. Intratesticular injections in rabbits were also negative.

THE FUSOSPIROCHETAL SYMBIOSIS IN THE INTESTINE

As indicated elsewhere in this paper, the fusospirochetal symbiosis is being emphasized in Europe in a number of obscure dysenteries which appear to be secondary to a primary amebic dysentery or other protozoal affliction. These fusospirochetal dysenteries resist emetin, but yield to treatment with the arsenicals used in work with syphilis. In such cases the stools show large numbers of spirochetes and fusiform bacilli, and these microbes disappear from the stools with the amelioration of the condition. In this work I have not dealt with any cases of spirochetal dysentery but I have found 6 times from 20 to 50% of spirochetes in the cecum of guinea-pigs and white rats apparently healthy. In none of the work has the presence of fusiform bacilli been noticeable, although it is obvious that in the dark field or in stained smears it is difficult to say that any given bacillary form is not present. It is significant that the person from whom most of the fecal specimens used were obtained suffered from Vincent's angina in 1914. It is not known whether his stools contained spirochetes before that time or not. Such a history was not obtained from any of the others from whom specimens were secured. The pathogenicity of the intestinal spirochete is not a settled matter. Many feel that it is purely a saprophyte, but that, like the mouth and preputial forms, it may on occasion give rise to secondary manifestations of considerable importance and tenacity. At least we are not dealing with pseudospirochetes such as have been described for the blood and for certain cultures.[58] Further work on obscure and chronic diarrheas will doubtless shed more light on the question.

[58] Schultz: Jour. Lab. & Clin. Med., 1923, 8, p. 375; Florence: Jour. Bacteriol., 1921, 6, p. 371; Koga and Otsubo: Jour. Infect. Dis., 1919, 24, p. 56.

SUMMARY

Intestinal spirochetes are widespread among healthy persons of the Chicago region, being found in approximately a third of all such persons examined.

The exact degree of spirochete infestation is probably much greater than this and would be difficult to ascertain; for it seems that intestinal spirochetes localize in the cecum and ascending colon, and that there are persons so infested who rarely if ever show the organisms in the feces.

It has been found that most of the laboratory animals also harbor intestinal spirochetes, the rabbit being the only exception thus far encountered.

Neither in human necropsy cases nor in killed animals have intestinal spirochetes been found in the ileum.

Intestinal spirochetes seem to enter into severe intestinal disorders in a secondary rôle in occasional cases, nearly a score of which have been reported from Germany and France. One case has thus far been described in the United States. In this matter, as in spirochetal bronchitis described by Castellani, information on the subject will probably bring more cases to notice. In the common infectious diseases of this country, it seems that intestinal spirochetes play no part.

While the degree of infestation of healthy persons is slight, amounting usually to less than a twentieth of the entire microbial flora, there appear to be those who always excrete some spirochetes in every stool. On the other hand, there appear to be those who never harbor the intestinal spirochete.

Intestinal spirochetes may be found in feces 7 months, or longer, after storage.

A carbohydrate diet appears to discourage the presence of intestinal spirochetes and may even cause them to disappear temporarily. The ingestion of acidophilis milk has the same effect. Protein feeding may favor the presence of spirochetes if it does not produce a condition of such metabolic unbalance as to suppress the spirochetes. Fasting tends to diminish the number of intestinal spirochetes found in the stools.

The administration of calomel failed to drive out the intestinal spirochetes or in any signficant way to affect their abundance.

All animal inoculation work has been uniformly negative.

Under favorable conditions, spirochetes may pass Berkefeld N filters, probably in a vegetative form. I have found no evidence to show that intestinal spirochetes have a granule phase.

Satisfactory serial culture of the spirochetes found in the feces cannot be reported at this time.

It is suggested that classification of intestinal spirochetes by morphology into several types be discouraged and that pending accurate cultural and serologic data the spirochetes found in the intestine be known simply as Spirochaeta eurygyrata.

The relationship of the spirochetes of the intestine to those of the buccal cavity and the possibility of the localization of the fusospirochetal symbiosis in the intestine are two propositions worthy of further study.

GERMINATION OF SPORES OF B. BOTULINUS IN COLLODION SACS IN ABDOMEN OF GUINEA-PIGS AND RABBITS

George E. Coleman

Santa Barbara, Calif.

Within the past two years as a result of the intensive study of botulism in America, various suggestions have been made for the protection of those who use canned foods. As these foods, without showing visible evidence of spoilage, sometimes contain potent toxins of B. botulinus, the precautions suggested are usually confined to the heating of the product for a period and at a temperature sufficient to destroy such toxin. It has been shown by Esty and Meyer [1] and other workers that the spores of many strains of B. botulinus are highly resistant to heat; consequently, a temperature which will destroy the toxin does not always destroy the spores of this organism.

It has also been shown by Orr,[2] Thom, Edmonson and Giltner,[3] and Coleman and Meyer [4] that enormous numbers of the detoxified spores of B. botulinus may be ingested by animals without producing symptoms of botulism. The latter were unable to produce the disease unless the spores were fed in amounts greatly in excess of those used by other investigators.

Whatever may be the possible sources of toxin production from these ingested spores, it is of considerable interest to know whether they actually germinate and multiply in the animal body and produce toxin there. Some investigators of the pathogenicity of spores of B. botulinus have assumed that the spores germinate when fed or injected, but it remained for Coleman and Meyer [4] to prove by direct evidence that such germination does take place. They injected the detoxified spores into a closed loop in the jugular vein of guinea-pigs and into the anterior chamber of the eyes of rabbits, and the germination of the spores under these conditions was unmistakable. Moreover, the emulsions of the excised vein and the liquid withdrawn from it as well as the liquid withdrawn from the eyes of the injected rabbits were invariably highly toxic when injected into other animals.

Received for publication, July 5, 1923.

1 Jour. Infect. Dis., 1922, 31, p. 650.
2 Ibid., 1922, 30, p. 118.
3 Arch. Int. Med., 1920, 26, p. 356.
4 Jour. Infect. Dis., 1922, 31, p. 622.

In an effort to give further evidence of this germination, it occurred to me to enclose the detoxified spores in collodion sacs and to introduce these sacs into the abdomen of guinea-pigs and rabbits.

In 1896, Metchnikoff, Roux and Salimbeni [5] used collodion sacs in the study of the toxic effects on guinea-pigs from the dialysis of cholera toxin through the walls of sacs containing cultures of the vibrio and introduced into the peritoneal cavity. Two years later Vincent [6] studied the enhancement of the virulence of saprophytic species by collodion sac passage through rabbits. Nocard and Roux [7] showed changes in the contents of collodion sacs introduced intraperitoneally into animals which appeared to give evidence of multiplication of inoculated material from pleuropneumonia in cattle. Nocard [8] studied the relation of human to avian tuberculosis by the growth of the human type in collodion sacs placed in chickens. None of these authors describe their method of making collodion sacs.

Most writers give as a characteristic of true toxins their inability to dialyze through collodion or parchment, though it has been stated by Rodet and Guéchoff [9] that certain toxins dialyze slowly and with difficulty. Crediropoulo and Ruffer [9] believe that immunizing substances pass through the dialyzers first. Miller,[10] who minutely describes his method for making collodion sacs, while unable to dialyze diphtheria toxin through sacs placed in the incubator, introduced them into the peritoneal cavity of guinea-pigs for the purpose of studying the rate of toxin absorption by the animal body. The toxin under these conditions dialyzed more or less freely. He also stated that the diphtheria toxin in these sacs while in the body of guinea-pigs undergoes some change which makes it more toxic, but that sacs taken from a guinea-pig containing the original toxin are not more permeable than the control sac which had never been in the guinea-pig. Gates,[11] who has standardized a method for making collodion sacs and for their use [12] in bacterial cultivation in vitro, made an exhaustive study of their permeability with salts and inorganic compounds and states[11] the following interesting facts: "Oxygen in solution rapidly diffuses through the sac wall. . . . This fact probably explains the consistent

[5] Ann. de l'Inst. Pasteur, 1896, 10, p. 257.
[6] Ibid., 1898, 12, p. 785.
[7] Ibid., p. 240.
[8] Ibid., p. 561.
[9] Cited by Besson: Technique Microbiologique, 1908, p. 207.
[10] Jour. Infect. Dis., 1911, 8, p. 50.
[11] Jour. Exper. Med., 1921, 33, p, 25.
[12] Ibid., 1922, 35, p. 635.

failure of representative strict anaerobes to grow in permeable sacs intraperitoneally implanted." He cites Haggard and Henderson [13] as estimating the oxygen tension of the peritoneal cavity to be about 45 mm. In the experiments of Vincent,[6] oxygen was injected into the abdomen of his animals in an effort to promote the growth of aerobic species, although the lack of this element did not subsequently prove to be the cause of his early failure to secure growth in the sacs.

Gates [11] further states that the hydrogen-ion concentration of the sac contents tends to come into an equilibrium with that of the peritoneal fluid. He also remarks that the sacs are permeable to the diffusible products of bacterial metabolism as shown by the tissue reactions which occur around actively growing cultures. This I have repeatedly noted during the course of my experiments. Bronfenbrenner and Schlessinger [14] have stated that filtered cultures of B. botulinus contain large quantities of ammonia salts and that these filtered cultures are toxic to animals in massive doses without an incubation period. As the toxin of B. botulinus does not appear to dialyze, it is possible that the intense tissue reaction surrounding the sacs containing a growth of B. botulinus spores may be due to these or other salts which are probably dialyzable.

After testing the permeability of sacs to salt solution, I made numerous preliminary tests with the filtered toxin of B. botulinus, using sacs of various thicknesses having a capacity of 0.5 c c., 15 c c. and allowed it to dialyze into salt solution or water at room and incubator temperatures during different periods of time up to two weeks. The results were somewhat irregular, but from the fact that the dialysate in large amounts from most of the largest and thinnest sacs from which the dialysis continued for 10 days proved absolutely inocuous to guinea-pigs or mice, I believe that those few sacs from which the dialysate proved toxic could not have been intact and that B. botulinus toxin does not dialyze in vitro or in vivo through collodion sacs, as our experiments to be enumerated below will show.

Technic.—The methods of Gates [11] who made his collodion sacs on a gelatine capsule foundation which was then dissolved with hot water is minutely described in his paper, and the reason for its various stages fully discussed. As my experiments originally were undertaken in a tentative way, and as I was already familiar with the method in use some years ago at the Pasteur Institute in Paris which seemed simpler, I used that method in the preparation of sacs which is as follows: A small bulb was blown in a piece of glass tubing

[13] Jour. Biol. Chem., 1919, 38, p. 71.
[14] Jour. Am. Med. Assn., 1922, 78, p. 1519.

having an exterior diameter of 7 mm. about 5 cm. from its sealed and rounded end. This tubing was dipped twice to a point half way up the bulb in commercial collodion (U.S.P.) care being taken that the collodion contained no air bubbles. After dipping, the collodion was allowed to drain and dry slightly. A cut was then made through the collodion around the center of the bulb, and after a slight flicking with the thumb nail around the edge of the incision the collodion could be easily peeled off. A piece of glass tubing having a constriction about 3 cm. from its end was then inserted in the open end of the sac, the edges of the sac were welded to the tube with a hot knife, tied with silk thread and the whole covered with fresh collodion. The sacs were filled with water by means of a capillary pipet, placed in a large tube of water and immediately sterilized. The water was then withdrawn and the sac filled with toxin or a spore suspension and the glass tube sealed in the flame at its constricted point. Aseptic precautions were observed throughout these manipulations, and tubes made in this way remained intact. These sacs averaged about 2 cm. to 3 cm. in length or with attached glass tube about 5 cm. to 6 cm., and had a capacity of about 0.3 c c. to 1.0 c c.

The spores used were several months old and were from cultures in veal peptic digest gelatine. They contained rare vegetative forms, all of which failed to stain by the Gram method. They were washed 3 times and suspended in salt solution. Immediately before using they were invariably heated in a sealed tube for one hour at 80 C. Toxicity tests of the heated suspension were always negative for guinea-pigs. After heating the spores, control cultures were made in beef heart medium as described by Dubovsky and Meyer,[15] and the toxicity of the cultures verified. They were also grown in deep agar for verification of their purity. Controls from the heated suspension were allowed to remain in the incubator for the same length of time as the sacs remained in the animal body. the resulting growth, if any, noted in both cases, and the purity of these organisms again verified by cultures. Tubes of beef heart and agar mediums were also heated for about 2 minutes at 100 C. after inoculation of a very minute amount of suspension from sacs and controls, in order to note the relative numbers of spores and vegetative forms, especially those developing in the agar medium. Toxicity tests on guinea-pigs were also made in each instance, the amount inoculated from the control often being larger than that from the sac.

The growth of B. botulinus spores in collodion sacs placed in the animal body was very heavy, resembling a 48 hour nonsporulating culture in beef heart medium. Morphologically, the bacilli were frequently somewhat thinner than is usual for B. botulinus. No spore formation was ever noted even after 22 days in rabbits. In this case (exper. 8, sac 2) practically all the spores developed, for none was seen in the microscopic preparation, and there was no growth in the heated agar tubes after 7 days' incubation. The toxin produced by the growth of the spores in the sacs was very potent and did not seem to dialyze through the membrane, for the animals remained in excellent condition until killed.

[15] Jour. Infect. Dis., 1922, 31, p. 501.

TABLE 1

COLLODION SACS IN ABDOMEN OF GUINEA-PIGS

Experiment	Spores per C c.	Days in Abdomen	Microscopic Examination of Sacs	Toxicity of Contents of Sacs for Guinea-Pigs	Toxicity Control for Guinea-Pigs	Cultures from Sacs	Cultures from Controls
Guinea-Pig 1	Strains 62-23	2 and 20½ hours	Growth doubtful, contamination	....	No toxin	B. botulinus	
Guinea-Pig 2	Strains 62-23	6	A little growth contamination	Botulism, died in 6 hours	Lost weight recovered	B. botulinus	
Guinea-Pig 3	Strain 23	6	Heavy growth of pure B. botulinus, no spores seen	Botulism, died in 18 hours	Botulism, 8 days	Pure B. botulinus	
Guinea-Pig 4	Strain 23 300 million per c c.	7	Very heavy growth of B. botulinus	Botulism, died in 6 hours	No symptoms; no growth apparent	Heated agar + unheated agar ++++, heated beef heart slight growth in 18 hours; unheated beef heart heavy growth in 18 hours	Heated agar ++++, unheated agar ++++
Guinea-Pig 5	Strain 23; Sac 1 very small, 100 million per c c.; spores only	7	No growth; small dialysing surface	No symptoms	No growth, 1½ c c. injected; no symptoms	B. botulinus, pure	
	Sac 2 same guinea-pig same time 100 million spores + leukocytes	7	Fair growth, contaminated, leukocytes dead phagocytosis	Botulism, died in 19 hours	....	B. botulinus, cocci	
Rabbit 1	Strain 23 200 million per c c.	7	No growth	No symptoms	No symptoms		
Rabbit 2	Strain 23 200 million sac 1	13	Heavy growth, pure; no spores seen	Botulism, died in 7 hours, ½ sac contents	Double dose botulism in 33 hours, rare gram + forms	Heated agar, after 72 hours 2 colonies; unheated agar after 18 hours heavy growth B. botulinus	
	Sac 2, same animal, same time	22	No spores seen; heavy growth	Botulism, died in 7 hours	....	Heated agar, after 7 days negative; unheated agar, after 18 hours ++++; B. botulinus	

During the course of these experiments we were studying the action in vitro of leukocytes on the toxin of B. botulinus, the results of which are soon to be published, and we thought it would be of interest to add leukocytes to some of the spore suspensions and place them in the sacs. The results of some of these experiments are given in table 1.

DISCUSSION

Owing to the variability in the size and consequently of the dialyzing surface of the sacs used in these experiments, no conclusions can be drawn as to the time required for the penetration of the body fluids into the sacs, but it would appear that several days are necessary for sufficient nutrient medium to penetrate to enable the spores to germinate.

I made no attempt to cause the germination of the spores of other anaerobes under the conditions of the foregoing experiments; however, the fact of an anaerobic contamination luxuriantly growing in one of our sacs should be noted. The consistent failure of strict anaerobes to grow in permeable sacs intraperitoneally implanted as mentioned by Gates and my success with B. botulinus may be explained possibly by the fact that in my experiments some of the oxygen was driven out of the salt solution containing spores by heating for one hour at 80 C. immediately before placing in the sacs.

TABLE 2

NEUTRALIZATION TESTS OF SERUM FROM RABBIT 2 KILLED 22 DAYS AFTER PLACING SACS IN ABDOMEN

Guinea-Pig 1, 368 gm., 1 c c. 0.0038 toxin + 0.7 c c. normal rabbit serum	Died in 84 hours
Guinea-Pig 2, 365 gm., 1 c c. 0.0038 toxin + 0.7 c c. normal rabbit serum	Died in 16 hours
Guinea-Pig 3, 228 gm., 1 c c. 0.0038 toxin + 0.8 c c. normal rabbit serum	Died in 84 hours
Guinea-Pig 4, 382 gm., 1 c c. 0.0038 toxin + 0.7 c c. serum from rabbit 2	Died in 27½ hours
Guinea-Pig 5, 375 gm., 1 c c. 0.0038 toxin + 0.7 c c. serum from rabbit 2	Died in 34 hours
Guinea-Pig 6, 227 gm., 1 c c. 0.0038 toxin + 0.8 c c. serum from rabbit 2	Died in 96 hours

In the one experiment undertaken to ascertain whether the serum of a rabbit (sac withdrawn after 22 days, in which potent toxin remained in the sac for probably at least 12 days) would neutralize B. botulinus toxin (same strain), the results were negative.

The addition of fresh guinea-pig leukocytes to the spore suspensions in the few experiments recorded appeared neither to prevent the germination of the spores in the sac nor in any way to neutralize the toxin produced. It is more than probable that, though they englobed some of the spores, the leukocytes died before the body fluids dialyzed into the sac, and even under these conditions their survival for any length of time is problematic.

SUMMARY

The results of these experiments taken in conjunction with those previously reported by Coleman and Meyer [4] should leave no doubt as to the ability of the spores of B. botulinus to germinate in the animal body.

As spoiled foods are sometimes veritable cultures of B. botulinus and may contain enormous numbers of the spores of this organism, it is of the utmost importance to know the possible effect of the ingestion of viable spores. Since they are able under unknown conditions to germinate in the animal body, the necessity for discarding spoiled foods is apparent, and no attempts to make them safe by heating should ever be attempted.

CONCLUSION

The heated spores of B. botulinus germinate freely, and the resulting bacilli multiply and produce toxin when enclosed in collodion sacs introduced into the abdomen of guinea-pigs and rabbits.

B. botulinus toxin does not dialyze in vitro nor does the toxin produced in sacs from the germination of spores dialyze into the body fluids of guinea-pigs and rabbits.

STUDIES ON BACILLUS PESTIS

I. OPTIMUM AND LIMITING HYDROGEN-ION CONCENTRATION FOR THE GROWTH OF BACILLUS PESTIS

RIGNEY D'AUNOY

From the Department of Pathology, Tulane University, and the Rathbone Memorial Laboratories of the Charity Hospital, New Orleans, La.

Bacillus pestis is said to require a neutral or slightly alkaline medium for best cultural results. In terms of titrimetry, a medium 0.2% alkaline using phenolphthalein as an indicator usually answers all the requirements for profuse growth of the organisms. Within recent years, due principally to the contributions of Sörenson, Michaelis, Clark and Lubs, our knowledge of the adjustment of laboratory food stuffs has been fairly revolutionized by the introduction of the newer physicochemical concept of hydrogen-ion concentration. These workers have shown that not only must the total value of acid or alkali present in culture mediums be considered, but that in addition the ionized portion of such acid or alkali, exerting tremendous influence as it does on various physiologic activities, must be carefully adjusted and controlled. Since that time numerous workers in the application of these methods to the field of bacteriology have shown that various bacterial forms have definite optimum hydrogen-ion concentrations at which their functional activities are at a height, and limiting hydrogen-ion concentrations beyond which their life cycles are arrested. In this study a determination of the range of growth and the optimum requirements of B. pestis on the basis of this newer concept have been undertaken.

Mediums.—Veal infusion broth was the substrate used throughout the experiments. It was prepared by allowing 1,000 gm. of finely minced lean veal to infuse in 1,000 c c. of tap water over night in the icebox. After boiling for one-half hour and straining through cloth, 1% proteose peptone was added, and the reaction adjusted to P_H 7. After stabilization in the autoclave at one atmosphere for 20 minutes, the broth was filtered and finally sterilized by exposure to live steam for 30 minutes on each of 3 successive days. The same lot of medium was used throughout the experiments. The desired reaction was obtained by adding N/10 sodium hydroxide or hydrochloric acid solutions. As it was necessary to keep the hydrogen-ion concentration constant throughout the experiments, buffering of the broth by means of 0.5 molecular Na_2HPO_4 and KH_2PO_4 solutions was resorted to. By the addition of appropriate com-

Received for publication, July 5, 1923.

binations of these solutions, a series of mediums ranging from P_H 4 to P_H 9 was readily obtained. Table 1 illustrates the preparation of this series.

Determination of Hydrogen-Ion Concentration.—Of the two methods of determining hydrogen-ion concentration, the colorimetric method is generally employed when the solutions under test are of a more or less complex nature, and when from the nature of the experiments a large number of determinations over a broad range and of relative accuracy are desired. In this study, colorimetric comparisons of mediums and of cultures were made with standard buffer solutions prepared according to Clark and Lubs, and checked by means of a hydrogen electrode. Brom thymol blue, methyl red, thymol blue and cresol red were the indicators used.

TABLE 1

COMPOSITION OF BUFFERED MEDIUMS

50 Cc. Broth + 10 C c. 5 M Phosphate Solutions + 0.1 N NaOH or HCl as Indicated

P_H Value of Mixture	KH_2PO_4 C c.	Na_2HPO_4 C c.	NaOH C c.	HCl C c.
		P_H of medium basic = 6.4		
4.0	...	...	...	9.4
4.2	10.0	...	...	8.6
4.4	10.0	...	...	7.5
4.6	9.6	0.4	...	6.8
4.8	9.0	1.0	...	6.0
5.0	8.5	1.5	...	5.2
5.2	7.4	2.6	...	4.3
5.4	7.2	2.8	...	3.5
5.6	7.0	3.0	...	2.4
5.8	6.3	3.7	...	2.0
		P_H of medium basic = 7.4		
6.0	8.5	1.5	...	2.3
6.2	8.0	2.0	...	2.1
6.4	6.4	3.6	...	1.8
6.6	5.8	4.2	...	1.2
6.8	5.0	5.0	...	0.8
7.0	4.0	6.0	...	0.6
7.2	2.5	7.5	1.0	
7.4	2.0	8.0	2.4	
7.6	1.0	9.0	3.8	
7.8	0.9	9.1	4.6	
8.0	0.65	9.35	5.0	
8.2	0.55	9.45	6.8	
8.4	0.4	9.6	7.4	
8.6	0.2	9.8	8.2	
8:8	...	10.0	9.4	
9.0	...	10.0	10.0	

Cultures.—The following cultures were used in the experiments.

I. P. 137, N. Y.—Secured from Dr. McCoy, Director of Hygienic laboratories. No information available as to date of isolation.

II. Manila, Philippine strain secured from Dr. H. W. Wade—probably a pneumonic strain. Artificially cultivated in these laboratories since 1913.

III. New Orleans, U. S. P. H. Service, 474, isolated from rat. Secured from Dr. Williams of Public Health Service.

IV. New Orleans, Human case, J, 1920, isolated in the laboratories of the Charity Hospital by means of blood culture 18 hours before death of patient.

V. Beaumont, Texas—Human case, E. B., 1920, subsequently fatal. Secured from Dr. Paul Eaton.

VI. B. 127 Jedda. Secured from Dr. McCoy, Director of Hygienic laboratories.

Actively growing 48-hour cultures on plain nutrient agar adjusted to a P_H of 7 were used as the starting point. As it appeared desirable to study coincidentally the behavior of organisms recently isolated from animal hosts and prolonged artificially cultured isolations, in all the experiments 2 cultures of the same strain were used. The one (designated "A") was an isolation from a fatal case of experimental white rat bubonic plague, the culture being in its first generation on artificial medium. The other (designated "B") was of the same organism, grown for at least 10 generations and for periods varying from 1 to 10 years on artificial medium.

TABLE 2

EFFECTS OF SALT CONCENTRATION ON GROWTH OF B. PESTIS

Molal Concentration	NaCl Cultures						KCl Cultures					
	1	2	3	4	5	6	1	2	3	4	5	6
1.00	±	++	++	±	±	++	—	+	+	±	—	+
0.75	++	+++	+++	++	+++	+++	++	+++	+++	+	+	++
0.50, 0.25, 0.10, 0.05, 0.025, salt free	+++	+++	+++	+++	+++	+++	+++	+++	+++	+++	+++	+++

Since it was necessary to use potassium and sodium salts in buffering, it became essential to determine the concentration in which these various salts would inhibit the growth of B. pestis. Accordingly, experiments as shown in tables 2 and 3 were made. In the main experiments, the concentration of phosphates was kept far below that which caused inhibition in the preliminary experiments.

Optimum Growth of Bacillus Pestis in Buffered Veal Infusion Broth.—200 c c. portions of medium of various hydrogen-ion concentrations were inoculated with 0.1 c c. of a 1 : 2 dilution of an actively growing 48-hour culture

TABLE 3

EFFECTS OF 5 MOLECULAR $Na_2HPO_4 + KH_2PO_4$ ON B. PESTIS

Molal Concentration	Series A Cultures						Series B Cultures					
	1	2	3	4	5	6	1	2	3	4	5	6
1.00	±	+	+	±	++	+	0	±	+	±	+	+
0.75	++	++	+++	++	+++	+++	++	+++	+++	+++	++	++
0.50, 0.40, 0.30, 0.20, 0.10, salt-free	+++	+++	+++	+++	+++	+++	+++	+++	+++	+++	+++	+++

of B. pestis in salt-free broth P_H 7. Immediately after inoculation P_H determinations of subinoculations were made. Incubation for 80 hours at 28 to 30 C. was accomplished, after which time growth was determined by plating methods, triplicate plates (agar Ph $_H$.8 to 7.4) being poured and the results averaged. Hydrogen-ion determinations of cultures were made at time of plating. Table 4 deals with recent isolation from fatal experimental white rat infection (series A) and table 5 with stock cultures of the same isolation (series B). The results of all experiments have been averaged and expressed graphically in chart 1, in which logarithms of number of organisms per c c. were plated as ordinates

TABLE 4

OPTIMUM GROWTH B. PESTIS BUFFERED BROTH, SERIES A, FIRST GENERATION CULTURES RECOVERED FROM WHITE RAT INFECTION

PH after Inoculation						PH after 80 Hours' Incubation						Growth Expressed as Number of Organisms per C c.					
Culture No.						Culture No.						Culture No.					
1	2	3	4	5	6	1	2	3	4	5	6	1	2	3	4	5	6
4.0	4.0	4.0	4.0	4.0	4.1	4.0	4.0	4.0	4.1	4.0	4.1	....	....	....	....	....	....
4.2	4.2	4.2	4.2	4.3	4.2	4.2	4.2	4.2	4.2	4.3	4.2	....	....	....	....	....	....
4.4	4.4	4.4	4.4	4.4	4.4	4.4	4.4	4.4	4.4	4.4	4.4	....	....	....	....	....	....
4.6	4.6	4.6	4.6	4.6	4.6	4.6	4.6	4.6	4.6	4.6	4.6	....	....	....	....	....	....
4.8	4.8	4.8	4.8	4.8	4.8	4.8	4.6	4.8	4.7	4.8	4.8	420	....	600	....	....	....
5.0	5.0	5.0	5.0	5.0	5.0	5.0	5.0	5.0	5.0	5.0	5.0	25,000	11,000	9,000	5,000	4,000	6,000
5.2	5.2	5.2	5.2	5.2	5.2	5.2	5.2	5.2	4.9	4.9	5.2	38,000	21,000	11,000	4,000	3,000	11,000
5.4	5.4	5.4	5.4	5.4	5.5	5.4	5.4	5.4	5.4	5.3	5.4	650,000	240,000	110,000	110,000	86,000	220,000
5.6	5.6	5.6	5.6	5.6	5.6	5.6	5.6	5.6	5.6	5.6	5.6	40,000,000	30,000,000	45,000,000	60,000,000	29,000,000	45,000,000
5.8	5.8	5.8	5.8	5.8	5.8	5.8	5.8	5.8	5.8	5.8	5.8	280,000,000	180,000,000	260,000,000	210,000,000	195,000,000	205,000,000
6.0	6.0	6.0	6.0	6.0	6.0	6.0	6.0	6.0	6.0	6.0	6.0	450,000,000	425,000,000	390,000,000	310,000,000	325,000,000	340,000,000
6.2	6.2	6.2	6.2	6.2	6.2	6.2	6.2	6.2	6.2	6.2	6.2	780,000,000	698,000,000	720,000,000	780,000,000	765,000,000	790,000,000
6.4	6.4	6.4	6.4	6.4	6.4	6.4	6.4	6.4	6.4	6.4	6.4	640,000,000	590,000,000	610,000,000	610,000,000	625,000,000	635,000,000
6.6	6.6	6.6	6.6	6.6	6.6	6.6	6.6	6.6	6.6	6.6	6.6	400,000,000	390,000,000	410,000,000	380,000,000	375,000,000	385,000,000
6.8	6.8	6.8	6.8	6.8	6.8	6.8	6.8	6.8	6.8	6.8	6.8	340,000,000	260,000,000	280,000,000	310,000,000	300,000,000	180,000,000
7.0	7.0	7.0	7.0	7.1	7.0	7.0	7.0	7.0	7.0	7.0	7.0	110,000,000	90,000,000	85,000,000	110,000,000	85,000,000	90,000,000
7.2	7.2	7.2	7.2	7.2	7.2	7.2	7.2	7.2	7.2	7.2	7.2	40,000,000	20,000,000	19,000,000	16,000,000	14,000,000	9,000,000
7.4	7.4	7.4	7.4	7.4	7.4	7.4	7.4	7.4	7.4	7.4	7.4	1,000,000	950,000	890,000	750,000	865,000	875,000
7.6	7.6	7.6	7.6	7.6	7.6	7.6	7.6	7.6	7.6	7.6	7.7	600,000	400,000	485,000	515,000	560,000	510,000
7.8	7.8	7.8	7.8	7.8	7.8	7.8	7.8	7.9	7.8	7.8	7.8	50,000	35,000	19,000	17,000	6,000	9,000
8.0	8.0	8.0	8.0	8.0	8.0	8.0	8.1	8.0	8.0	8.0	8.0	19,000	9,000	11,000	15,000	6,000	8,500
8.2	8.2	8.2	8.3	8.2	8.2	8.2	8.2	8.2	8.2	8.2	8.2	11,000	6,000	4,000	3,000	2,500	900
8.4	8.5	8.4	8.4	8.4	8.4	8.4	8.4	8.4	8.4	8.4	8.5	4,000	1,000	600	900	700	....
8.6	8.6	8.6	8.6	8.7	8.6	8.6	8.7	8.6	8.6	8.6	8.6	....	....	....	....	....	....
8.8	8.8	8.9	8.8	8.9	8.8	8.8	8.8	8.8	8.8	8.8	8.8	....	....	....	....	....	....
9.0	9.0	9.0	9.0	9.0	9.0	9.0	9.0	9.0	8.9	9.0	9.0	....	....	....	....	....	....

TABLE 5

Optimum Growth B. Pestis Buffered Broth, Series B, Stock Cultures

PH after Inoculation						PH after 80 Hours' Incubation						Growth Expressed as Number of Organisms per C c.					
Culture No.						Culture No.						Culture No.					
1	2	3	4	5	6	1	2	3	4	5	6	1	2	3	4	5	6
4.0	4.1	4.0	4.0	4.0	4.1	4.0	4.0	4.0	4.1	4.0	4.1	....	....	....	....	....	....
4.2	4.2	4.2	4.2	4.1	4.2	4.2	4.2	4.2	4.2	4.2	4.2	300	....	600	100	200	....
4.4	4.4	4.4	4.4	4.4	4.3	4.4	4.4	4.4	4.4	4.4	4.4	600	....	900	650	900	600
4.6	4.6	4.5	4.6	4.6	4.6	4.6	4.6	4.5	4.6	4.6	4.6	1,400	2,250	1,100	950	1,100	1,100
4.8	4.8	4.7	4.8	4.8	4.8	4.8	4.8	4.8	4.8	4.8	4.8	4,900	4,100	2,700	5,100	6,500	10,500
5.0	5.1	5.0	5.0	5.0	5.0	5.0	5.1	5.0	5.0	5.0	5.0	11,300	83,500	49,250	65,500	73,500	82,500
5.2	5.2	5.2	5.2	5.2	5.2	5.2	5.2	5.2	5.2	5.2	5.2	650,000	880,000	657,000	450,000	560,000	610,000
5.4	5.4	5.4	5.4	5.4	5.4	5.4	5.4	5.4	5.4	5.4	5.4	53,000,000	47,000,000	21,000,000	26,000,000	39,500,000	27,000,000
5.6	5.6	5.6	5.6	5.6	5.6	5.6	5.6	5.6	5.6	5.6	5.6	281,000,000	410,000,000	365,000,000	397,000,000	199,000,000	101,000,000
5.8	5.8	5.8	5.8	5.8	5.8	5.8	5.8	5.8	5.8	5.8	5.8	365,000,000	550,000,000	470,000,000	461,000,000	380,000,000	298,000,000
6.0	6.0	6.0	6.0	6.0	6.0	6.0	6.0	6.0	6.0	6.0	6.0	498,000,000	610,000,000	510,000,000	680,000,000	465,000,000	485,000,000
6.2	6.2	6.2	6.2	6.2	6.2	6.2	6.2	6.2	6.2	6.2	6.0	679,000,000	800,000,000	691,000,000	810,000,000	690,000,000	690,000,000
6.4	6.4	6.4	6.4	6.4	6.4	6.4	6.4	6.4	6.4	6.4	6.4	782,000,000	750,000,000	690,000,000	710,000,000	760,000,000	782,000,000
6.6	6.6	6.5	6.6	6.6	6.6	6.6	6.6	6.6	6.6	6.6	6.6	790,000,000	750,000,000	610,000,000	605,000,000	760,000,000	754,000,000
6.8	6.8	6.8	6.8	6.8	6.8	6.8	6.8	6.8	6.8	6.8	6.8	684,000,000	700,000,000	484,000,000	651,000,000	600,000,000	585,000,000
7.0	7.1	7.0	7.0	7.0	7.0	7.0	7.0	7.0	7.0	7.0	7.1	585,000,000	640,000,000	361,000,000	528,000,000	510,000,000	461,000,000
7.2	7.2	7.2	7.2	7.2	7.2	7.2	7.2	7.2	7.2	7.2	7.2	208,000,000	110,000,000	180,000,000	197,000,000	201,000,000	101,000,000
7.4	7.4	7.4	7.4	7.4	7.4	7.4	7.4	7.4	7.4	7.4	7.4	88,000,000	90,000,000	64,000,000	29,000,000	81,000,000	61,000,000
7.6	7.6	7.6	7.6	7.6	7.6	7.6	7.6	7.6	7.6	7.6	7.6	11,000,000	27,000,000	19,000,000	19,000,000	20,000,000	11,000,000
7.8	7.8	7.8	7.8	7.8	7.8	7.8	7.8	7.8	7.8	7.8	7.8	1,300,000	1,640,000	950,000	698,000	987,000	265,000
8.0	8.0	8.0	8.0	8.0	8.0	8.0	8.0	8.0	8.0	8.0	8.0	495,000	680,000	200,000	320,000	265,000	110,000
8.2	8.2	8.1	8.2	8.2	8.2	8.2	8.2	8.2	8.2	8.2	8.2	210,000	480,000	89,000	87,000	110,000	86,000
8.4	8.4	8.4	8.4	8.4	8.4	8.4	8.4	8.4	8.4	8.4	8.4	19,500	26,000	7,000	14,600	14,800	9,000
8.6	8.6	8.6	8.6	8.6	8.6	8.6	8.6	8.6	8.6	8.6	8.6	3,600	14,000	3,500	3,500	9,200	600
8.8	8.8	8.8	8.8	8.8	8.8	8.8	8.8	8.8	8.8	8.8	8.8	900	....	....	....	....	....
9.0	9.0	9.0	9.0	9.0	9.0	9.0	9.0	9.0	9.0	9.0	9.0	....	....	....	....	....	....

with hydrogen-ion concentration of medium as abscissae, organisms of series A being represented by dotted lines, those of series B by solid lines.

DISCUSSION

Consideration of the tables and chart embodying the results of the experiments shows that B. pestis has a fairly large range of growth as expressed on the basis of requirements of hydrogen-ion concentration. Of the 6 stock cultures studied, the limiting values lay between P_H 5.0 and P_H 8.2, with optimum growth occurring at P_H 6.2 to P_H 7.0, or slightly on the acid side. Variations naturally occurred, but the results on the whole for the different isolations were quite constant.

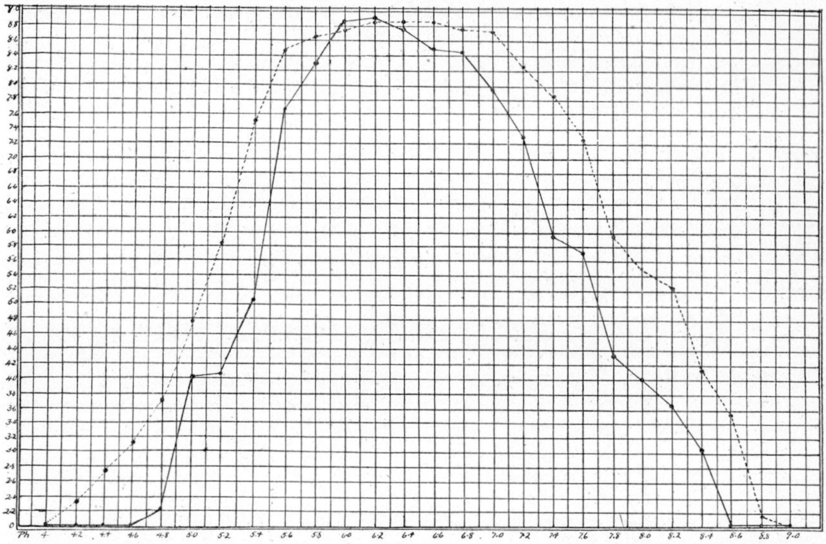

Chart 1.—Growth curve of B. pestis. The broken line indicates stock cultures; the continuous line, first generation cultures. The numbers at the left indicate the logarithins of the number of organisms per c c.

With the first generation of artificially cultivated strains, the limiting P_H values were 5.4 and 7.6, with maximum growth occurring between the points P_H 6.0 and P_H 6.6. Here again the results were quite constant for the different isolations.

With both stock cultures and recent isolations it appears that the rise in the growth curve is greater on the acid than on the alkaline side, indicating that even though the organism grows best in an acid medium, it is more tolerant to alkalis than to acids.

It is of interest to note that the stock cultures had an optimal zone of growth somewhat more marked than that displayed by the recent isolations. The latter seemed to have more of a tendency toward a definite optimum point of growth in contradistinction to the plateau-like tendency of the stock cultures. The range of growth of the stock strains was far greater than that of the recent isolations, with considerable more tolerance for alkali on their part.

II. THE FINAL HYDROGEN-ION CONCENTRATION OF BACILLUS PESTIS UNDER VARYING CULTURAL CONDITIONS IN DEXTROSE MEDIUM

The recent introduction in bacteriologic technic of the concept of hydrogen-ion concentration has opened a fruitful field of investigation into the metabolic activities of various organisms. Clark and Lubs [1] best express the importance of hydrogen-ion concentration in the study of bacterial life cycles in the following quotation: "Hydrogen-ion concentration influences the condition in solution of every substance with acidic or basic properties—native proteins and their hydrolytic products, amines and amides, carboxyl, sulphonic and phenolic compounds, even alcoholic compounds as well as many inorganic compounds. It has a large effect on the effective solubilities and dispersion of colloids, upon determining tautomeric equilibria, and in one way or another of governing the activity of catalysts, such as hydrolytic enzymes and oxidases. One or the other of these effects, induced directly or indirectly by the hydrogen-ion concentration, must impress bacterial life." It appears that a method of such far reaching influence should be applied to the study of pathogenic organisms with an ultimate view of attempting clearer elucidation of their behavior when in the body fluids and tissues of man and animal.

In part 1, definite optimum and final hydrogen-ion concentration limits for the growth of B. pestis in plain buffered broth have been established. At the present phase of a proposed systematic investigation into various aspects of the biologic and immunologic activities of B. pestis it appears desirable to study the final hydrogen-ion concentration of this organism in dextrose broth, and the influence of varying proportions of the sugar with mediums of varying initial reactions on this final limit.

That the glucose content of the medium employed influences the final limit of acid production of an organism has been established. Thus Avery and Cullen [2] have noted differences in final acidity in dextrose cultures of pneumococci by varying the carbohydrate content of the medium between 0.4% and 4%. Foster,[3] working with streptococci, established 0.2% dextrose as the minimum requirement for optimum acid production. Clark and Lubs,[4] with members of the colon group, varied the dextrose content of broth from 0 to 0.5%, and showed that with increased dextrose concentration up to a certain point greater final acidity resulted.

Numerous investigators have suggested the use of various substances which are able to neutralize by their buffer action some of the acid produced in actively growing cultures. Thus Clark,[5] working with B. coli, showed that this organism produced somewhat lower P_H limits when grown in highly buffered mediums. Bronfenbrenner and Schlesinger [6] showed that the amount of free acid produced by B. coli with any given percentage of carbohydrate depends upon the proportion of buffer salts present in the medium. Kligler,[7] studying the same organism, recorded the buffer action of peptone. He showed the buffer keeps the hydrogen-ion concentration below the lethal point allowing the organism to continue metabolism over longer periods. It thus seems to be

[1] The Determination of Hydrogen-Ions, 1916. J. Bact. 2, 1.
[2] Jour. Exper. Med., 1919, 30, 359.
[3] Jour. Bacteriol., 1921, 6, p. 2.
[4] Jour. Infect. Dis., 1915, 17, p. 160.
[5] Jour. Biol. Chem., 1915, 22, p. 87.
[6] Proc. Soc. Exper. Biol .and Med., 1918, 16, p. 44.
[7] Jour. Bacteriol., 1916, 1, 663.

well established that an organism requires a definite concentration of carbohydrate to produce its characteristic final hydrogen-ion concentration, and that this minimum carbohydrate concentration is closely dependent on the amount of buffer salts present, the latter in increasing amounts delaying the final limiting acidity.

Mediums.—One per cent. Difco peptone water served as a base for all mediums. Dextrose solution in triple distilled water and sterilized by filtration through Berkefeld candles was added in the desired proportions. Preliminary experiments with mediums prepared this way, but containing no carbohydrate, failed to reveal under conditions identical with the main tests any increase in hydrogen-ion concentration, after active growth of B. pestis, eliminating the possibility of any carbohydrate substance which Foster[3] found in Parke-Davis peptone, and which Pick[8] has shown is present in Witte's peptone. Adjustment of mediums to the desired hydrogen-ion concentration was made by colorimetric methods according to the technic of Clark and Lubs, all lots being finally checked by electrometric measurements.

Cultures.—Five cultures of B. pestis were employed in this study: B. 125, Bombay, Hygienic Laboratories, Washington, D. C. (McCoy, 1920); Philippine 1, Manila Bureau of Science (Wade, 1915); human case 6, Charity Hospital (D'Aunoy, 1920); rat 465, U. S. P. H. S., New Orleans (Williams, 1921); and human case 2, Charity Hospital (Duval, 1914). These were stock cultures of B. pestis, ranging from the 5th to the 50th generation. In addition, first generation cultivations of the same organisms recovered from fatal animal infections were used as indicated.

Hydrogen-Ion Concentrations.—Hydrogen-ion determinations at appropriate stages of the experiments were made by using the comparator superposition method of Walpole[9] in order to eliminate as far as possible errors due to color and turbidity. One c c. portions of cultures diluted with 3 c c. of freshly boiled triple distilled water were place in Pyrex glass tubes and compared with the standards, Clark and Lubs solutions being used. Final check electrometric determinations were always made.

Final Hydrogen-Ion Concentration of B. Pestis in 1% Dextrose Broth Initial P_H 6.8.—Two loopfuls from 60-hour agar slants of B. pestis grown at temperatures of 28 C. to 32 C. were inoculated in 10 c c. portions of 1% dextrose broth P_H 6.8. After 48 hours' incubation at temperatures of 30 C., transplants were made into similar mediums. This was repeated for 4 generations. Of such fourth generation cultures, 0.2 c c. portions were inoculated in flasks containing 200 c c. of 1% dextrose broth P_H 6.8. Immediately after inoculation of the 200 c c. portions of mediums P_H determinations were made, and regularly thereafter every 24 hours for a period of 6 days, incubation in the meantime being at temperatures of 28 C. to 30 C (table 6).

The data secured were fairly uniform for the various isolations studied. The final limits noted after 144 hours' incubation of the cultures were 4.8 and 5.0, the latter figure being secured with one isolation. Of the 2nd generation cultures, changes between their final limit and that of the same isolation artificially cultivated over longer periods were noted in one instance. It appears as a result of this experiment that the final hydrogen-ion concentration of B. pestis when grown in 1% dextrose broth of an initial reaction of P_H 6.8 is 4.8, and

8 Ztschr. f. phynk. Chem., 1898, 24, 246.

9 Biol. Chem. Jour., 1911, 5, p. 207.

that prolonged artificial cultivation of the organism has nó influence on the establishment of this final limit.

Influence of Varying Proportions of Dextrose and Varying Initial Reactions on Final Hydrogen-Ion Concentration of B. Pestis.—One hundred cubic centimeter portions of broth P_H 6.8 containing from 0.1 to 1.0% of dextrose were inoculated with 0.2 c c. of fourth generation 60-hour cultures of B. pestis grown in 1.0 % dextrose broth and incubated for 6 days. At the end of this time P_H readings were made (table 7).

TABLE 6

FINAL HYDROGEN-ION CONCENTRATION OF B. PESTIS IN 1% DEXTROSE BROTH

Culture	On Inoculation	Hydrogen-ion Concentration Determinations					
		24 Hrs.	48 Hrs.	72 Hrs.	96 Hrs.	120 Hrs.	144 Hrs.
B. 125, Bombay Hygienic Lab., (?) generation	6.8	5.9	5.2	4.9	4.9	4.9	4.8
Philippine 1, Manila Bureau of Science, (?) generation	6.7	5.8	5.8	5.0	4.9	4.8	4.8
Human Case 6, Charity Hospital N. O. 1921, 40th generation	6.8	5.9	5.9	4.9	4.9	4.8	4 8
Rat 465, N. O., U. S. P. H. S., 50th generation	6.8	6.1	6.1	5.0	5.0	4.8	4.8
Human Case 2, Charity Hospital N. O. 1914, 53d (?) generation	6.7	6.5	6.5	5.1	4.9	4.8	4.8
Philippine 1, 3d generation	6.8	6.6	6.6	5.8	4.9	4.8	4.8
Human Case 6, 2d generation	6.8	6.7	6.7	5.1	4.9	4.8	4.8
Rat 465, 3d generation	6.8	6.8	6.8	5.2	5.1	4.9	4.8
Human Case 2, 2d generation	6.8	6.6	6.6	5.2	5.0	5.0	5.0

TABLE 7

FINAL HYDROGEN-ION CONCENTRATION OF B. PESTIS IN DEXTROSE BROTH OF VARYING CONCENTRATIONS

Culture	P_H Initial	P_H Final in Percentage Dextrose Broth 144 Hours Incubation					
		0.1	0.2	0.3	0.5	0.8	1.0
B. 125, Bombay Hygienic Laboratory, (?) generation	6.8	5.8	5.8	5.2	4.8	4.8	4.8
Philippine 1, Manila Bureau of Science, (?) generation	6.8	5.9	5.8	5.2	4.8	4.8	4.8
Human Case 6, Charity Hospital N. O. 1921, 40th generation	6.8	5.9	5.8	5.3	4.8	4.8	4.8
Rat 465, N. O., U. S. P. H. S., 50th generation	6.8	6.0	5.7	5.3	4.8	4.9	4.8
Human Case 2, Charity Hospital N. O. 1914, 53d (?) generation	6.8	5.9	5.8	5.2	4.8	4.8	4.8
Philippine 1, 3d generation	6.8	5.9	5.7	5.2	4.8	4.8	4.8
Human Case 6, 2d generation	6.8	5.9	5.7	5.2	4.8	4.8	4.8
Rat 465, 3d generation	6.8	5.8	5.8	5.3	4.8	4.8	4.8
Human Case 2, 2d generation	6.8	5.8	5.7	5.2	5.0	5.0	4.9

None of the cultures grown in mediums containing less than 0.5% dextrose resulted in the production of the characteristic final hydrogen-ion concentration previously noted for mediums of this particular initial reaction. Here again no differences were noted between recent isolations from fatal experimental infections and cultures artificially grown for varying periods of time. From the data obtained it is possible to state state that B. pestis requires a minimum concentration of 0.5% dextrose to produce its characteristic acid production in broth adjusted to the initial reaction of P_H 6.8.

Four lots of veal infusion broth adjusted to P_H 6.8, P_H 7.2 and P_H 7.4, respectively, with dextrose in concentrations varying from 0 to 1% were used. Inoculation into 100 c c. portions of such mediums with 0.2 c c. portions from 48-hour fourth generation cultures of B. pestis grown in 1% dextrose broth, P_H 6.8, was made. Incubation was allowed from 28 C. to 32 C. for 6 days, in order to insure completion of carbohydrate changes. After this time final P_H readings were made (table 8).

For the 5 isolations of B. pestis studied the final hydrogen-ion concentration was uniformly obtained with a dextrose concentration of

TABLE 8

RELATION BETWEEN INITIAL REACTION AND DEXTROSE CONCENTRATION OF MEDIUM TO FINAL HYDROGEN-ION CONCENTRATION OF B. PESTIS

P_H Initial	P_H Final in Percentage Dextrose-Broth, 144 Hours Incubation						Culture
	0.1	0.2	0.3	0.5	0.8	1.0	
6.8	5.8	5.8	5.2	4.8	4.8	4.8	B 125, Bombay
7.2	6.2	6.2	5.9	4.8	4.8	4.8	Hygienic Laboratory,
7.4	6.8	6.6	6.5	5.5	5.5	5.5	(?) generation
7.6	6.9	6.5	6.2	6.0	5.8	5.8	
6.8	5.9	5.8	5.3	4.8	4.8	4.8	Human Case 6,
7.2	6.0	5.9	5.4	4.8	4.8	4.8	Charity Hospital
7.4	6.9	6.6	6.3	5.9	5.5	5.5	N. O. 1921,
7.6	6.9	6.6	6.3	6.1	6.0	5.9	40th generation
o.8	5.9	5.7	5.2	4.8	4.8	4.8	Human Case 6,
7.2	6.0	5.8	5.1	4.8	4.8	4.8	Charity Hospital
7.4	6.9	6.6	6.2	5.9	5.5	5.5	N. O. 1921,
7.6	6.9	6.5	6.3	6.0	5.9	5.9	2d generation
6.8	6.0	5.7	5.3	4.8	4.8	4.8	Rat 465, N. O.,
7.2	6.1	5.8	5.4	4.8	4.8	4.8	U. S. P. H. S.,
7.4	6.9	6.6	6.1	5.8	5.5	5.5	50th generation
7.6	6.9	6.5	6.0	6.0	5.9	5.9	
6.8	5.9	5.8	5.2	4.8	4.8	4.8	Human Case 2,
7.2	6.0	5.9	5.1	4.8	4.8	4.8	Charity Hospital
7.4	6.9	6.4	6.2	5.9	5.5	5.5	N. O. 1914,
7.6	6.8	6.4	6.0	6.0	5.9	5.8	53d (?) generation

0.5% only with such cultures as were grown in mediums of an initial reaction of P_H 7.2 or of higher acidic value. Of the cultures grown in mediums of less initial acidic values, a greater concentration of dextrose was required to reach or even approximate the previously noted final limit. This experiment shows, as would be expected, that the minimum concentration of dextrose needed to produce a characteristic final P_H stands in intimate relationship to the initial hydrogen-ion concentration of the medium employed. It also stresses the point previously noted for other organisms that limiting values should be expressed only as in relationship to initial medium reaction and carbohydrate concentration.

III. THE FERMENTATION REACTIONS OF BACILLUS PESTIS

The extensive literature on the bacteriology of plague contains comparatively little relative to the reactions of B. pestis on carbohydrates. Gioso and Biginelli[10] record the production of lactic acid as a result of the growth of B. pestis in dextrose mediums. The Indian Plague commission[11] found that acid was formed in dextrose, galactose, levulose and mannite, but not in dulcite or lactose. Calvert[12] records acid production in litmus glucose agar. Herzog[13] says that the organism does not "ferment" dextrose, lactose, levulose or mannite. He probably does not refer to acid production, but simply to gas production by the term "fermenting." MacConkey,[14] using bile salt medium as a base, records acidification without gas in dextrose, dextrin, galactose, levulose, maltose and mannite, but no changes in dulcite, lactose, raffinose, saccharose and sorbite. Wherry,[15] studying human strains and squirrel strains, found acid production, without gas, in dextrose, galactose, levulose, maltose and mannite, with no changes in inulin, lactose or saccharose. Vorland[16] records acidification of arabinose, dextrose, dextrin, levulose, galactose, maltose, mannit, glycerine, glycerol, xylose, salicin, saccharose, by a single human strain culture. The Advistory Committee,[17] using MacConkey's medium, records acid production with dextrose, galactose, levulose and mannite, with no changes in dulcite and lactose. McCoy[18] reported that he could find no differences between old laboratory strains and new highly virulent isolations from San Francisco as regards carbohydrate fermentation. They all gave acidity with dextrose, levulose, galactose, mannite and maltose, with no changes noted with inulin, lactose or saccharose. Berlin[19] studied 55 strains. He reports acidification with arabinose, dextrose, galactose, levulose, maltose and mannite, with no changes in adonite, dextrin, dulcite, inulin, lactose, raffinose and saccharose. He concluded that age and virulence of cultures does not influence acid production. Wade,[20] working with 10 strains, reports regular and strong fermentation with dextrose, levulose and mannite, with irregular fermentation of arabinose, galactose, glycerinol, maltose and salicin. Adonite, dextrin, dulcite, inulin, lactose, raffinose, saccharose and sorbite he claims are not affected.

In this study there is recorded the fermentative action of B. pestis on various carbohydrates and carbohydrate-like substances. Acid production is here considered on the basis of total acidity, as shown by the titration of cultures with standard alkali solutions and on the basis of ionized acid as measured by the final hydrogen-ion concentration of cultures.

Mediums.—One per cent. Difco peptone solution was the substrate used, because previous experience showed that it did not contain any carbohydate-like reacting fraction so often encountered in other peptones. The appropriate

[10] Riv. d'igiene, 1898.

[11] Dieudonne, A., and Otto, R.: Kolle u. Wassermann's Handbuch der pathogenen Mikroorganismen, J. 1912, 4, p. 173.

[12] Circular Trop. Dis., Manila, 1901, No. 3.

[13] Publications Bureau Govt. Lab., Manila, 1907, No. 23.

[14] Jour. Hygiene, 1905, 5, p. 333.

[15] Jour. Infect. Dis., 1905, 2, p. 577.

[16] Centralbl. f. Bakteriol., I, O., 1908, 45, p. 193.

[17] Report on plague investigation in India, Jour. Hygiene, 1909, 8, p. 302.

[18] Jour. Infect. Dis., 1909, 6, p. 170.

[19] Centralbl. f. Bakteriol., Ref., 1915, 63, p. 70.

[20] Philippine Jour. Sc., 1916, 11, p. 159.

TABLE 9

FERMENTATION REACTIONS OF B. PESTIS

Culture Number	Source	Adonite		Arabinose		Dextrin		Dextrose		Dulcit		Galactose		Glycerol		Inulin		Lactose		Levulose		Maltose	
		Final P_H	C c. per 100 N-NaOH	Final P_H	C c. per 100 N-NaOH	Final P_H	C c. per 100 N-NaOH	Final P_H	C c. per 100 N-NaOH	Final P_H	C c. per 100 N-NaOH	Final P_H	C c. per 100 N-NaOH	Final P_H	C c. per 100 N-NaOH	Final P_H	C c. per 100 N-NaOH	Final P_H	C c. per 100 N-NaOH	Final P_H	C c. per 100 N-NaOH	Final P_H	C c. per 100 N-NaOH
	Hygenic Laboratory																						
1	B140-7007	6.6	0	5.8	1.2	6.6	0	4.8	2.50	6.4	0	5.3	1.50	6.4	0	6.4	0	6.2	0	5.0	1.9	5.2	1.1
2	B128-Hopkins	6.6	0	5.6	1.4	6.6	0	4.8	2.50	6.3	0	5.0	1.80	6.5	0	6.2	0	6.3	0	5.1	1.6	5.2	1.2
3	B132-Wayson 5	6.6	0	5.4	1.6	6.4	0	4.7	1.95	6.2	0	5.0	1.80	6.3	0	6.3	0	6.4	0	5.1	1.5	5.1	1.0
4	B123-Manila	6.4	0	5.1	1.8	6.3	0	4.8	2.50	6.2	0	5.0	1.75	6.2	0	6.3	0	6.2	0	5.0	1.6	5.2	1.0
5	B126-P. R. Pig	6.4	0	5.8	1.2	6.2	0	4.8	2.60	6.3	0	5.0	1.75	6.1	0.05	6.2	0	6.2	0	5.0	1.7	5.3	0.9
6	B122-Frisco	6.4	0	6.4	0.1	6.2	0	4.9	2.50	6.4	0	5.0	2.00	6.6	0	6.2	0	6.2	0	5.1	1.8	5.3	0.9
7	B127-Jedda	6.6	0	6.4	0.2	6.3	0	4.9	2.35	6.5	0.1	5.0	1.90	6.5	0	6.2	0	6.3	0	5.2	1.9	6.2	0
8	B129-R. I.	6.6	0	6.2	0.3	6.4	0	4.8	2.35	6.2	0	5.0	1.75	5.2	0.9	6.3	0	6.2	0	5.1	1.8	5.3	1.0
9	B139-P. R. Pig 73	6.4	0	5.3	1.5	6.5	0	4.8	2.60	6.3	0	5.0	1.50	6.4	0	6.4	0	6.2	0	5.1	1.7	5.2	1.0
10	B125-Bombay	6.3	0	5.2	1.7	6.6	0	4.8	2.60	6.3	0	5.0	1.45	6.4	0	6.5	0	6.2	0	5.0	1.7	6.2	0
11	B123-Wayson S-50	6.4	0	5.2	1.9	6.6	0	4.8	2.50	6.4	0	5.0	1.40	6.5	0	6.6	0	6.2	0	5.1	1.6	5.3	1.1
12	B134-N. O. 1900	6.4	0	5.2	1.8	6.4	0	4.7	2.40	6.3	0	5.0	1.50	6.6	0	6.2	0	6.2	0	5.1	1.6	5.2	1.2
13	B135-"14"	6.5	0	5.6	1.2	6.4	0	4.8	2.35	6.2	0	5.0	1.80	6.4	0	6.2	0	6.3	0	5.0	1.6	5.2	1.1
14	B138-P. R. Pig 118	6.5	0	5.6	1.3	6.3	0	4.8	2.40	6.2	0	5.0	1.80	6.2	0	6.2	0	6.1	0	5.0	1.9	5.2	1.1
15	B136-Rat 66	6.4	0	5.6	1.4	6.2	0	4.8	2.45	6.2	0	5.2	1.50	6.3	0	6.1	0	6.0	0	5.0	1.9	6.3	0
16	B130-Squirrel	6.3	0.05	6.4	0.1	6.1	0	4.8	2.50	6.2	0	5.2	1.40	6.4	0	6.2	0	6.1	0	5.1	1.8	5.3	1.2
17	B124-P. I.	6.4	0	5.9	0.6	6.0	0	4.8	2.50	6.1	0	5.2	1.40	5.2	1.0	6.2	0	6.2	0	5.1	1.7	6.3	0
18	B137-N. Y.	6.6	0	5.8	1.2	6.1	0	4.7	2.45	6.2	0	5.1	1.40	6.6	0	6.2	0	6.2	0	5.0	1.7	5.3	1.0
	U. S. P. H. Service																						
19	N. O. Rat 472	6.5	0	5.8	1.3	6.3	0	4.9	2.40	6.3	0.1	5.2	1.50	6.4	0	6.3	0	6.2	0	5.1	1.6	5.3	1.0
20	465	6.4	0	5.6	1.5	6.4	0	4.9	2.50	6.4	0.1	5.0	1.50	6.5	0	6.3	0	6.2	0	5.1	1.6	5.3	0.9
21	474	6.4	0	5.6	1.4	6.3	0	4.9	2.50	6.3	0	5.0	1.40	6.4	0	6.0	0	6.2	0	5.1	1.5	6.4	0
22	473	6.5	0	5.9	0.3	6.3	0	4.8	2.50	6.2	0	5.0	1.60	6.4	0	6.2	0	6.2	0	5.0	1.7	6.4	0
23	487	6.4	0	5.9	0.9	6.2	0	4.7	2.40	6.2	0	5.0	1.40	6.3	0	6.2	0	6.3	0	5.0	1.8	5.3	1.1
	Beaumont, Tex.																						
24	Case "Pat"	6.3	0	5.4	1.7	6.2	0	4.8	2.40	6.2	0	5.2	1.50	5.1	1.0	6.2	0	6.3	0	5.0	1.9	5.3	0.9
25	"Buxom"	6.3	0	5.2	1.6	6.3	0	4.8	2.40	6.2	0	5.2	1.45	6.4	0	6.3	0	6.3	0	5.0	1.6	5.2	0.8
26	Rat, Pumping Stat	6.6	0	5.2	1.5	6.1	0	4.8	2.45	6.2	0	5.1	1.45	6.6	0	6.4	0	6.2	0	5.0	1.7	6.4	0
27	Rat, Buford St.	6.5	0	5.2	1.4	6.1	0	4.8	2.45	6.2	0	5.3	1.50	6.4	0	6.4	0	6.2	0	5.0	1.7	6.4	0
28	Rat "A. B."	6.5	0	5.2	1.2	6.2	0	4.9	2.40	6.3	0	5.0	1.50	6.6	0	6.4	0	6.2	0	5.1	1.7	5.2	1.1
29	Human Case "E. B."	6.4	0	5.6	1.3	6.3	0	4.7	2.40	6.2	0	5.0	1.45	6.6	0	6.4	0	6.3	0	5.1	1.7	6.2	0
	Port Arthur, Tex.																						
30	Rat 1	6.4	0	5.6	1.3	6.3	0	4.8	2.40	6.2	0	5.0	1.40	6.5	0	6.4	0	6.3	0	5.1	1.6	5.2	1.1
31	Rat 2	6.3	0	5.6	1.1	6.2	0	4.8	2.40	6.2	0	5.0	1.40	6.4	0	6.3	0	6.3	0	5.1	1.6	5.3	1.2
	Pensacola, Fla.																						
32	"Bun" Rat	6.3	0	5.6	1.2	6.2	0	4.8	2.40	6.2	0	5.0	1.45	6.4	0	6.3	0	6.4	0	5.1	1.7	5.2	1.2
33	2 Rat	6.5	0	6.4	0.1	6.1	0	4.7	2.50	6.2	0	5.2	1.50	6.4	0	6.4	0	6.2	0	5.1	1.8	5.3	1.1
34	3 Rat	6.4	0	6.6	0.05	6.2	0	4.7	2.50	6.2	0	5.2	1.45	6.4	0	6.4	0	6.2	0	5.1	1.7	5.3	1.0
	Philippine Bureau Sc.																						
35	1	6.4	0	5.8	1.2	6.3	0	4.8	2.45	6.3	0	5.2	1.45	5.0	1.1	6.2	0	6.2	0	5.0	1.6	6.2	0
36	Manila Case 1	6.5	0	5.8	1.3	6.4	0	4.8	2.45	6.2	0	5.2	1.50	6.2	0	6.2	0	6.2	0	5.0	1.5	5.3	1.0
37	Manila Case 2	6.3	0	5.6	1.4	6.4	0	4.8	2.45	6.2	0	5.2	1.50	6.3	0	6.2	0	6.2	0	5.1	1.7	5.3	1.1
38	Manila Case 3	6.3	0	5.6	1.6	6.5	0	4.8	2.50	6.2	0	5.0	1.60	5.0	1.0	6.2	0	6.3	0	5.0	1.6	5.3	1.0
39	Manila Case 6	6.2	0.1	5.6	1.5	6.5	0	4.8	2.45	6.3	0	5.0	1.50	6.3	0	6.2	0	6.2	0	5.0	1.6	5.2	1.1
	New Orleans, La.																						
40	Rat 1912, Duval	6.1	0.1	5.6	1.4	6.4	0	4.9	2.45	6.3	0	5.0	1.45	5.0	1.2	6.2	0	6.2	0	5.1	1.6	5.2	1.1
41	Human Case 1, 1914	6.1	0.1	6.0	0.3	6.5	0	4.9	2.45	6.4	0.1	5.0	1.50	6.2	0.05	6.3	0	6.2	0	5.0	1.7	6.6	0
42	Case 2, 1914	6.2	0	5.6	1.4	6.5	0	4.9	2.40	6.2	0	5.2	1.40	6.4	0	6.3	0	6.2	0	5.0	1.7	5.2	1.2
43	Case 4, 1914	6.3	0	5.6	1.8	6.5	0	4.8	2.50	6.2	0	5.2	1.45	6.5	0	6.3	0	6.3	0	5.1	1.7	5.2	1.2
44	Rat A, 1914	6.4	0	5.8	1.3	6.4	0	4.8	2.45	6.2	0	5.2	1.50	6.4	0	6.3	0	6.2	0	5.1	1.8	5.2	1.2
45	Human Case 1, 1920	6.4	0	5.6	1.2	6.5	0	4.8	2.50	6.2	0	5.1	1.50	6.5	0	6.2	0	6.2	0	5.0	1.6	5.2	1.2
46	Human Case 2, 1920	6.4	0	5.6	1.4	6.5	0	4.8	2.40	6.2	0	5.0	1.50	5.0	1.1	6.2	0	6.2	0	5.0	1.7	6.2	0
47	Human Case 6, 1920	6.5	0	5.6	1.5	6.4	0	4.8	2.40	6.1	0	5.0	1.45	6.4	0	6.2	0	6.3	0	5.1	1.7	6.3	0
	Lister Institute																						
48	331, Manchuria	6.3	0	5.9	0.2	6.5	0	4.7	2.45	6.2	0	5.0	1.40	6.5	0	6.2	0	6.2	0	5.0	1.6	6.2	0
49	332, Alepo Maru	6.4	0	5.6	1.5	6.4	0	4.8	2.45	6.2	0	5.0	1.45	6.4	0	6.2	0	6.2	0	5.0	1.7	5.3	1.2
50	148, K120 Aviru	6.5	0	5.4	1.8	6.4	0	4.8	2.40	6.2	0	5.0	1.45	6.4	0	6.2	0	6.2	0	5.0	1.6	5.2	1.2

TABLE 9—*Continued*

Fermentation Reactions of B. Pestis

Culture Number	Source	Mannite Final P_H	Mannite C c. per 100 N-NaOH	Melizitose Final P_H	Melizitose C c. per 100 N-NaOH	Perseitol Final P_H	Perseitol C c. per 100 N-NaOH	Quercite Final P_H	Quercite C c. per 100 N-NaOH	Raffinose Final P_H	Raffinose C c. per 100 N-NaOH	Rhamnose Final P_H	Rhamnose C c. per 100 N-NaOH	Saccharose Final P_H	Saccharose C c. per 100 N-NaOH	Salicin Final P_H	Salicin C c. per 100 N-NaOH	Sorbite Final P_H	Sorbite C c. per 100 N-NaOH	Trehalose Final P_H	Trehalose C c. per 100 N-NaOH	Xylose Final P_H	Xylose C c. per 100 N-NaOH
	Hygenic Laboratory																						
1	B140-7007	5.0	1.9	6.1	0	6.2	0	6.6	0	6.6	0	6.5	0	6.6	0	5.2	0.9	6.7	0	6.7	0	6.7	0
2	B128-Hopkins	5.0	1.8	6.2	0	6.3	0	6.8	0	6.6	0	6.4	0	6.5	0	6.4	0	6.7	0	6.7	0	6.5	0
3	B132-Wayson 5	5.0	1.9	6.2	0	6.4	0	6.8	0	6.5	0	6.3	0	6.4	0	6.3	0	6.7	0	6.6	0	6.4	0
4	B123-Manila	4.9	2.0	6.3	0	6.4	0	6.9	0	6.5	0	6.5	0	6.3	0	6.2	0	6.6	0	6.8	0	6.6	0
5	B126-P. R. Pig	5.0	1.9	6.4	0	6.4	0	6.9	0	6.4	0	6.5	0	6.3	0	5.1	1.1	6.7	0	6.6	0	6.6	0
6	B122-Frisco	5.1	1.8	6.3	0	6.4	0	6.8	0	6.6	0	6.5	0	6.3	0	6.2	0	6.7	0	6.6	0	6.5	0
7	B127-Jedda	5.0	1.8	6.2	0	6.3	0	6.8	0	6.5	0	6.4	0	6.3	0	6.2	0	6.8	0	6.6	0	6.4	0
8	B129-R. I.	5.0	1.9	6.1	0	6.2	0	6.6	0	6.4	0	6.3	0	6.2	0	6.2	0	6.7	0	6.5	0	6.6	0
9	B139-P. R. Pig 73	5.1	1.8	6.2	0	6.3	0	6.6	0	6.7	0	6.3	0	6.3	0	6.3	0	6.6	0	6.4	0	6.6	0
10	B125-Bombay	5.1	1.7	6.1	0	6.3	0	6.6	0	6.7	0	6.3	0	6.4	0	6.4	0	6.6	0	6.3	0	6.5	0
11	B123-Wayson S-50	5.0	1.7	6.1	0	6.3	0	6.6	0	6.7	0	6.3	0	6.4	0	6.5	0	6.6	0	6.3	0	6.4	0
12	B134-N. O. 1900	4.9	1.9	6.2	0	6.3	0	6.6	0	6.7	0	6.6	0	6.5	0	5.1	0.9	6.5	0	6.3	0	6.4	0
13	B135-"14"	5.0	1.8	6.2	0	6.4	0	6.6	0	6.5	0	6.7	0	6.4	0	6.6	0	6.5	0	6.3	0	6.5	0
14	B138-P. R. Pig 118	5.0	1.8	6.3	0	6.4	0	6.8	0	6.5	0	6.5	0	6.5	0	6.6	0	6.6	0	6.3	0	6.6	0
15	B136-Rat 66	5.0	1.8	6.4	0	6.4	0	6.8	0	6.6	0	6.4	0	6.6	0	6.5	0	6.7	0	6.4	0	6.6	0
16	B130-Squirrel	5.0	1.9	6.5	0	6.3	0	6.6	0	6.6	0	6.3	0	6.7	0	6.5	0	6.7	0	6.4	0	6.6	0
17	B124-P. I.	5.1	1.9	6.4	0	6.3	0	6.8	0	6.6	0	6.2	0	6.5	0	6.4	0	6.6	0	6.4	0	6.7	0
18	B137-N. Y.	5.0	1.8	6.4	0	6.2	0	6.8	0	6.5	0	6.3	0	6.4	0	5.1	1.1	6.5	0	6.4	0	6.7	0
	U. S. P. H. Service																						
19	N. O. Rat 472	5.0	1.9	6.3	0	6.3	0	6.9	0	6.5	0	6.3	0	6.4	0	6.3	0	6.6	0	6.4	0	6.7	0
20	465	5.0	1.9	6.2	0	6.4	0	6.6	0	6.6	0	6.4	0	6.4	0	6.3	0	6.6	0	6.3	0	6.6	0
21	474	5.0	1.9	6.5	0	6.4	0	6.6	0	6.6	0	6.4	0	6.3	0	6.3	0	6.6	0	6.5	0	6.6	0
22	473	5.1	1.8	6.4	0	6.4	0	6.6	0	6.6	0	6.4	0	6.3	0	6.3	0	6.5	0	6.5	0	6.6	0
23	487	5.1	1.7	6.4	0	6.4	0	6.6	0	6.6	0	6.4	0	6.3	0	5.0	1.1	6.5	0	6.6	0	6.7	0
	Beaumont, Tex.																						
24	Case "Pat"	5.1	1.7	6.3	0	6.3	0	6.6	0	6.5	0	6.3	0	6.4	0	6.3	0	6.6	0	6.7	0	6.5	0
25	"Buxom"	5.1	1.8	6.2	0	6.3	0	6.8	0	6.6	0	6.6	0	6.4	0	6.2	0	6.4	0	6.7	0	6.5	0
26	Rat, Pumping Stat.	5.3	1.7	6.2	0	6.3	0	6.8	0	6.7	0	6.7	0	6.5	0	6.2	0	6.5	0	6.7	0	6.4	0
27	Rat; Buford St.	5.2	1.7	6.3	0	6.3	0	6.6	0	6.7	0	6.5	0	6.5	0	6.2	0	6.5	0	6.7	0	6.4	0
28	Rat "A. B."	5.0	1.8	6.3	0	6.3	0	6.6	0	6.6	0	6.4	0	6.5	0	6.2	0	6.6	0	6.7	0	6.4	0
29	Human Case "E. B."	5.0	1.7	6.3	0	6.3	0	6.6	0	6.5	0	6.4	0	6.6	0	6.3	0	6.6	0	6.7	0	6.5	0
	Port Arthur, Tex.																						
30	Rat 1	5.2	1.8	6.3	0	6.3	0	6.8	0	6.5	0	6.4	0	6.6	0	5.1	1.1	6.6	0	6.6	0	6.6	0
31	Rat 2	5.0	1.8	6.4	0	6.3	0	6.6	0	6.5	0	6.5	0	6.4	0	6.2	0	6.7	0	6.6	0	6.7	0
	Pensacola, Fla.																						
32	"Bun" Rat	5.1	1.7	6.5	0	6.3	0	6.8	0	6.6	0	6.5	0	6.4	0	6.2	0	6.7	0	6.6	0	6.5	0
33	2 Rat	5.1	1.6	6.3	0	6.4	0	6.8	0	6.7	0	6.5	0	6.3	0	6.2	0	6.7	0	6.6	0	6.4	0
34	3 Rat	5.1	1.5	6.3	0	6.4	0	6.6	0	6.8	0	6.6	0	6.3	0	6.3	0	6.6	0	6.6	0	6.6	0
	Philippine Bureau Sc.																						
35	1	5.1	1.6	6.3	0	6.4	0	6.6	0	6.7	0	6.5	0	6.5	0	6.2	0	6.6	0	6.6	0	6.4	0
36	Manila Case 1	5.0	1.7	6.2	0	6.4	0	6.8	0	6.6	0	6.6	0	6.6	0	6.4	0	6.6	0	6.6	0	6.5	0
37	Manila Case 2	5.0	1.8	6.3	0	6.3	0	6.9	0	6.6	0	6.4	0	6.6	0	6.4	0	6.5	0	6.7	0	6.5	0
38	Manila Case 3	5.0	1.9	6.2	0	6.4	0	6.6	0	6.7	0	6.3	0	6.6	0	6.3	0	6.4	0	6.7	0	6.5	0
39	Manila Case 6	5.0	2.0	6.2	0	6.4	0	6.6	0	6.5	0	6.4	0	6.7	0	6.3	0	6.4	0	6.5	0	6.5	0
	New Orleans, La.																						
40	Rat 1912, Duval	5.3	1.4	6.2	0	6.4	0	6.7	0	6.4	0	6.4	0	6.5	0	6.3	0	6.4	0	6.5	0	6.5	0
41	Human Case 1, 1914	5.2	1.5	6.3	0	6.4	0	6.7	0	6.5	0	6.5	0	6.5	0	6.4	0	6.5	0	6.7	0	6.4	0
42	Case 2, 1914	5.1	1.7	6.3	0	6.3	0	6.7	0	6.4	0	6.5	0	6.3	0	6.3	0	6.6	0	6.7	0	6.5	0
43	Case 4, 1914	5.0	1.6	6.2	0	6.5	0	6.7	0	6.6	0	6.6	0	6.4	0	6.4	0	6.5	0	6.7	0	6.6	0
44	Rat A, 1914	5.0	1.9	6.2	0	6.5	0	6.7	0	6.5	0	6.5	0	6.4	0	6.3	0	6.4	0	6.6	0	6.5	0
45	Human Case 1, 1920	5.0	1.8	6.2	0	6.4	0	6.7	0	6.6	0	6.5	0	6.3	0	5.1	0.8	6.4	0	6.6	0	6.5	0
46	Human Case 2, 1920	5.0	1.7	6.2	0	6.4	0	6.8	0	6.7	0	6.5	0	6.5	0	6.4	0	6.4	0	6.6	0	6.5	0
47	Human Case 6, 1920	5.2	1.5	6.2	0	6.4	0	6.6	0	6.5	0	6.5	0	6.5	0	6.3	0	6.5	0	6.7	0	6.6	0
	Lister Institute																						
48	331, Manchuria	5.0	1.8	6.3	0	6.4	0	6.6	0	6.6	0	6.4	0	6.7	0	5.1	0.9	6.6	0	6.6	0	6.5	0
49	332, Alepo Maru	5.0	1.9	6.2	0	6.3	0	6.6	0	6.7	0	6.6	0	6.4	0	6.4	0	6.6	0	6.5	0	6.5	0
50	148, K120 Aviru	5.0	1.9	6.3	0	6.5	0	6.6	0	6.7	0	6.5	0	6.6	0	6.4	0	6.7	0	6.4	0	6.5	0

fermentable substances were added to this base in the form of Berkefeld filtered distilled water solutions to be concentration of 1% in all cases. Medium was adjusted to a final reaction of P_H 6.6. Twenty-two fermentable substances were used as follows: adonite, arabinose, dextrose, dextrin, dulcite, galactose, glycerol, inulin, lactose, levulose, maltose, mannite, melizitose, perseitol, quercite, raffinose, rhamnose, saccharose, salicin, sorbite, trehalose and xylose.

Hydrogen-Ion Concentration.—As in other studies of this series, hydrogen-ion determinations were carried out principally by the colorimetric method, comparison being made with buffer solutions standardized electrometrically. Occasional check electrometric determinations were made on batches of mediums and on cultures.

Cultures.—In this study, 50 strains of B. pestis were used, their sources being tabulated in table 9.

In numerous instances first and second generations of B. pestis recovered from experimental white rat infections were studied with the idea of determining the effects of prolonged growth on their fermentative power. This was accomplished by comparing the reactions of these recent isolations with those by the same strains that had been artificially cultivated on plain agar for a number of years. As no comparative changes could be noted with the recent isolations, their use was soon discarded, and the bulk of the work carried out with old stock cultures.

All the cultures were planted in peptone water P_H 7 and allowed to grow for 36 hours at 28 to 32 C. At the end of this time 0.1 c c. portions of cultures were planted in 25 c.c. portions of carbohydrate containing peptone water (P_H 6.6), and incubated for 1 week at 30-32 C. At the end of this time the cultures were titrated with N/20 NaOH using phenolphthalein as an indicator, and there was recorded the number of cubic centimeters of N/NaOH required to bring the reaction to the same point as that of similarly titrated uninoculated mediums which had been kept under the same conditions. Coincidentally, hydrogen-ion concentration determinations were made. In a number of instances the titrations and P_H determinations were repeated after 12 to 20 days of growth with no difference in results. Titrations were made of choice with heated cultures; P_H determinations with culture dilutions kept at temperatures of 30 to 32 C.

DISCUSSION

The results obtained (table 9) were striking in their uniformity. All the isolations strongly fermented dextrose, galactose, levulose and mannite; arabinose and maltose were affected by a number; glycerol and salicin by a few; with none of the strains were changes noted with adonite, dextrin, dulcite, inulin, lactose, melezitose, perseitol, quercite, raffinose, rhamnose, saccharose, sorbite, trehablose or xylose.

As a number of the isolations were those used previously by McCoy and Wade, it was interesting to compare the present results with those previously recorded by them. Thus, Wade's cultures A, B, G, H and I corresponded to cultures 40, 41, 38, 35, 36 of the ones I studied and McCoy's cultures, Manila, Bombay, Jedda, N. Y., Frisco and Reddy Island, corresponded with cultures 4, 10, 7, 18, 6 and 17.

The results with cultures representing the Wade series were in accord except with glycerol and salicin. Here cultures 41 and 36 (B and I Wade) did not attack salcin, although so reported by Wade. As he mentioned that salicin was peculiarly nonfermentable in peptone water, these cultures were studied with salicin agar, salicin beef broth, veal broth with no fermentation in early transplants, but slight acidification after repeated cultivation in such mediums. By adopting the same plan it was possible to cause slight acidification eventually with salicin peptone water cultures. With glycerol only cultures 40, 38 and 35 (Wade's A, G, N) showed any fermentation activity. Many of the other cultures, however, when repeatedly cultivated in glycerol containing mediums eventually produced acidification, although slight.

Compared with McCoy's series, discrepancies were noted with cultures 10 and 7, which did not ferment maltose. Here again after adaptation of these organisms to maltose mediums by frequent transplanting, attack of the carbohydrate with resulting acidification occurred.

IV. THE PRODUCTION OF HIGH TITER AGGLUTINATING SERUM FOR BACILLUS PESTIS

A review of the literature shows that considerable divergence of opinion exists as to the practicability of producing high titer agglutinating serums for B. pestis. Wyssokowitz and Zabolotny [21] report the examination for agglutinins of 4 antipest serums produced by horses. The reaction of agglutination was demonstrated in dilutions as high as 1:20 in only one case. No mention is made whether homologous or heterologous organisms were used in the tests. Paltauf [22] records similar conclusions. Kolle and Martini,[23] using practically avirulent cultures, were able to produce serums agglutinating in titers as high as 1:6,000. Strong [24] concludes that agglutinins for B. pestis are formed slowly, and in small amounts, becoming demonstrable only in highly immunized animals. All investigators agree that considerable technical difficulties are encountered in attempts at demonstrating agglutinins for B. pestis, these difficulties being due principally to the tendency to spontaneous clumping. Thus, Kossell and Overback,[25] agreeing with the German Plague Commission, stressed the practical impossibility of securing suspensions microscopically free from clumps, and recommended that macroscopic agglutination reactions only be made with B. pestis. Klein [26] pointed out that on agar the sticky viscid growth so commonly encountered in such cultures of B. pestis is due to the production of gelatinous interstitial substances which are not soluble in broth. He therefore recommended that the organisms be suspended in normal salt solution for use in the agglutination reaction. Gauthier and Raybawd [27] found spontaneous flocculation with gelatin grown plague cultures even when the organisms were suspended in salt solutions. They could not differentiate such spontaneous flocculations from true agglutination. Strong [24] experienced considerable difficulty in making proper suspensions. He emulsified small portions from agar slants in normal salt solution, but even after all his precautions he noted spontaneous precipitation after 2-3 hours, especially so when dealing with the more attenuated cultures. Following Shibayama's [28] suggestion, he grew his cultures at 5 to 8 C. in order to keep mucoid production at a minimum, and while he found that such cultures when grown for a number of generations were

21 Ann. de Inst. Pasteur, 1897, 11, p. 662.

22 Wien. klin Wchnschr., 1897, 10, p. 537.

23 Deutsch. med. Wcnschr., 1902, 28, p. 46.

24 Philippine Jour. Sc., 1907, 2, p. 2.

25 Lancet, 1901, 1, pp. 456 and 1535.

26 Ibid., 1901, I, p. 1535.

27 Comp. rend. Soc. de biol., 1904, 56, p. 391.

28 Centralbl. f. Bakteriol., I, O., 1905, 38, p. 482.

less viscid, still they became spontaneously agglutinated from suspensions in salt solutions in much shorter time than did those grown at 30 C.

As a further step in a proposed comparative investigation of various isolations of B. pestis, it seemed desirable to undertake the production of agglutinating serums by various methods, having especially in mind the future use of these serums in immunologic experiments.

After various attempts at devising a suitable culture medium as a sub-strate for growing the organisms for animal inoculation, and for later agglutination tests, veal infusion 1% proteose peptone agar buffered with fifth molecular Na_2PHO_4 and KH_2PO_4 solutions and adjusted to a P_H of 6.6 was finally decided on as best suited. The addition to the agar of serum, either human or animal, as suggested by Rowland,[29] was tried and early discarded, as it seemed that organisms then invariably showed a far greater tendency to early spontaneous clumping than when grown on any other type of medium.

Two liter Erlenmeyer flasks containing a layer of agar prepared as indicated were inoculated by means of sterile pipettes with actively growing 60-hour cultures in veal infusion peptone broth buffered and adjusted to a P_H of 6.6. Enough of such inoculum was used to cover the whole surface of the agar with a thin film. Cultures were grown at temperatures of 18 to 20 C. as suggested by Martini[30] as a means of keeping mucoid production at a minimum.

Experience showed that 24-hour growths were never sufficient to allow good suspensions, as B. pestis at best grows fairly slowly, especially when recently isolated. Accordingly, no attempts were made to secure suspensions from cultures less than 50 hours old; the best suspensions resulted from organisms grown for periods of 60-70 hours. After appropriate incubation, the cultures were placed in the icebox and kept at 10 C. for a period of one half to one hour. This thoroughly solidified the agar and rendered the subsequent washing off process much simpler. Chilled salt solution adjusted to a P_H of 6.8 was used in washing off bacterial growths; by a rotary motion of the flask most of the growth could be brought into coarse suspension in a short time. In a few instances a sterile glass L tube was used to scrape off bacterial growth from the agar surfaces. The resultant coarse suspensions were transferred to 250 c c. Florence flasks containing about 100 gm. of sterile, carefully washed white sand, and by a rotary motion for periods ranging from 15 minutes to an hour intimate contact affected between bacterial aggregates and sand, with the result that most of the clumps were broken up. Early use was made of a pestle and mortar containing sand in an attempt to break up clumps, but as disintegration of the bacterial bodies invariably took place the method was discarded. After breaking up of most of the larger bacterial clumps as outlined, the suspensions were filtered through improvised sand filters made from 25 mm. diameter Pyrex glass test tubes drawn at one end to a fairly fine point, plugged with cotton and filled with a column of washed white sand 10 cm. in length, a head of 4 cm, over the top of the sand being allowed for the fluid to be filtered. The resultant suspensions were invariably homogeneous and have not presented between 37.5 an 2 C. any tendency to spontaneous agglutination over periods as long as 2 years. The bacterial suspensions were standardized to a concentration of ten thousand million per c c. dilution being made to this concentration by means of salt solution adjusted to a P_H of 6.8. The finished suspensions were placed in securely plugged sterile bottles, rubber stoppered and paraffin capped, and stored in the dark at temperatures of 10 to 15 C. for future use. Before use, cultures

29 Jour. Hygiene, Plague Suppl. III, 1913-14.
30 International Plague Conference XIII, Mukden, 1911.

were made from these suspensions, and, as indicated in the protocols, virulence determinations made whenever required.

In addition to the suspensions of organisms of full virulence prepared as indicated, suspensions of attenuated organisms of all strains were prepared. Here, buffered alcoholic veal infusion broth P_H 7. was used, growth being allowed for 3 weeks at 41 to 43 C. according to the observations of Hetsch.[31] At the end of that time reinoculation of each strain was made in a similar medium, and growth continued for 2 weeks longer, after which transplants were made to flasks of veal infusion peptone agar P_H 6.6. After incubation for 60-70 hours at 18 to 20 C., the growths were washed off and suspensions made and adjusted as previously outlined for the isolations of full virulence.

Production of Immune Serum.—Numerous methods for the production of immune serums were used. For sake of completeness a brief survey of these methods is included. At the beginning bacterial suspensions of full virulence were killed by heat or by chloroform and injected intravenously at 3-day intervals into full grown, healthy rabbits, the initial dose being 1,000,000,000 organisms increased to 4,000,000,000 for the fourth and subsequent doses. Even though as many as 25 injections were given a number of the rabbits, the strongest serum obtained in 15 attempts was one clumping the homologous strains in dilution of 1 : 160. The combined intraperitoneal intravenous method of killed organisms and the injection of attenuated organisms even over long periods of time gave results not even as satisfactory. Finally, based on Strong's observations, the method of injecting massive doses of living organisms, attenuated at first and finally of full virulence over long periods of time, was adopted with results uniformly satisfactory. By following this method, serums of an agglutinating titer of 1 : 6,000 were produced for all of the 10 strains studied with agglutination as high as 1 : 15,000 in a number of instances. The following records selected from typical experiments give details of injections with the ultimate results. It must be emphasized here that all agglutinations reported are those observed for the homologous strains used in producing antiserum. No cross agglutinations are reported.

Exper. 19.—Two full grown male rabbits were injected intravenously on 34 occasions with strain C. H. I. isolated by blood culture methods from a fatal case of human bubonic plague in the Charity Hospital laboratories, and artificially cultivated for over 4 years. The suspension regularly caused death in full grown white rats within 48 hours after intraperitoneal injection of 100,000 organisms. Attenuation of organisms was accomplished as previously indicated. After such attenuation, 100,000,000 organisms failed to produce fatality in full grown white rats within 120 hours. An initial dose of 50,000,000 attenuated organisms was injected in the marginal ear vein of the rabbits, increased to 500,000,000 for the second and 1,000,000,000 for the subsequent injections. Six such injections were given at intervals of 3 days. Organisms of full virulence were now injected at 3-day intervals on 28 occasions, the initial dose being 50,000,000 organisms rapidly increased to 4,000,000,000 for the seventh and subsequent injections. The rabbits at the end of the injection period had lost 100 and 300 gm., respectively. Agglutination was complete in serum dilutions of 1: 9,500 and 1: 9,000 six days after the last injection.

Exper 35.—Here culture C. H. 6 recovered by blood culture methods from a fatal case of human bubonic plague was used. The organisms in suspensions were in their third generation or artificial cultivation. One thousand organisms when injected intraperitoneally in full grown white rats cause fatality in 16 hours. Attenuation as indicated so altered virulence that 1,000,000 organisms when introduced intraperitoneally in full grown white rats did not cause fatality within 100 hours. An initial dose of 50,000 attenuated organisms was introduced into the blood stream of 3 full grown rabbits. One died within 24 hours. The remaining 2 were reinjected at 3-day intervals on 8 occasions with attenuated organisms, the dose being doubled after each inoculation. Four days after the 8th injection, full virulence organisms were injected in an initial dose of 100,000 rapidly increasing with each subsequent

[31] Ztschr. f. Hyg. u. Infectionskrankh., 1904, 48, p. 442.

injection to 4,000,000,000 organisms. Thirty-one injections of full virulence organisms were given at 3-day intervals. Six days after the last injection full agglutination took place in a dilution of 1: 14,500 with the serum of both animals.

The macroscopic agglutination technic was used throughout. Antiserum dilutions were made with salt solution adjusted to a P_H of 6.8, equal portions of live virulent bacterial suspensions being added, and the mixtures allowed to remain at room temperature for 2 hours, after which time readings were made. In all series, controls in all diluations with rabbit and human serums were made, as well as controls with simple suspension dilutions. In a number of instances, reactions were read as a check after standing over night either at laboratory or icebox temperatures, with no differences in final results. As stated, intravenous injections of live organisms attenuated at first by growth in alcohol broth and finally of full virulence resulted in the uniform production of serums with agglutinating titers of 1:6,000 to 1:15,000.

V. EFFECTS OF PLAGUE SERUM, SERUM FROM PLAGUE CONVALESCENTS, PLAGUE ANTISERUMS, AND NORMAL SERUM OF VARIOUS MAMMALS ON THE VIABILITY AND DEVELOPMENT OF B. PESTIS

The immunity against B. pestis under natural and artificial conditions of certain mammals presents a problem of great interest. As a preliminary to the study of some of the factors which may influence this immunity, it was considered desirable to record the effects of plague serums, serums derived from plague convalescents, plague antiserums secured from various sources, (including those prepared in these laboratories) and normal serums from different animals on the visability and development of B. pestis.

It was only because a wide diversity of conclusions exists as to the possible bacteriolytic action of various plague immune serums and serums derived from cases of human plague, that it was deemed necessary to repeat in a measure numerous experiments previously performed by various workers. The German Plague Commission concluded that pest immune serums contain specific bactericidal substances, but recorded no experiments which would substantiate such conclusions. Kolle and Martini[32] demonstrated some bactericidal action of plague serum by eliciting Pfeiffer's phenomenon in guinea-pigs and rats following the injection of comparatively large doses of pest immune serum. Markl[33] found that phagocytosis was the principal if not only factor concerned in freeing previously immunized animals from injected pest bacilli. Kolle[34] later agreed with this last view. He was unable to demonstrate bactericidal action in pest immune serums even after varying the type of serum used to supply the alexin

[32] Deutsch. med. Wchnschr., 1902, 28, p. 45.
[33] Ztschr. f. Hyg. u. Infectionskrankh., 1903, 42, p. 244.
[34] Ibid., 1904, 48, p. 371.

required to complete the reaction. Skschivan[35] obtained Pfeiffer's phenomenon in guinea-pigs previously inoculated with Paris antipest serum. Row[36] concluded that the serum of plague convalescents is highly bactericidal to the specific micro-organism, that the serum of patients in the early stage of plague is somewhat inhibitory to the growth of bacillus pestis, and finally that normal human serum exerts no bactericidal action. In a later communication,[37] he claimed that the lysogenic power of serums derived from plague convalescents is due to the combined action of two substances; the one stable at a temperation of 56 C., the other destroyed at this temperature. His study of various samples of Roux's antiplague serum lead him to conclude that this serum does not exert much bacteriolytic action, but that its lysogenic properties are greatly enhanced by the addition of fresh serum derived from man, rabbit and rat. Wright and Windsor[38] showed that normal human serum exerts no bactericidal action on B. pestis. Lamb and Forster[39] studied the effects of normal human, horse, ox, sheep, goat, monkey, rat, and guinea-pig serums, and could find in such serums no appreciable bactericidal or bacteriolytic action for B. pestis. Schouroupoff[40] concluded that antipest serum is partly bactericidal. Strong[41] after carefully conducted experiments could find no bactericidal action in a number of specimens of antipest serums studied.

Throughout these experiments a highly virulent strain of B. pestis recovered by blood culture from a subsequently fatal case of human bubonic plague, and in its second degeneration on artificial medium, was principally used. In addition, other strains obtained from various sources, as indicated in the records of experiments, were used. All cultures were grown in veal infusion broth (P_H 6.6) for 48 hours between 28 and 32 C. Serum from plague patients and plague convalescents was secured by venipuncture; serum from lower animals by cardiopuncture or venipuncture. Plague antiserums prepared in the Pasteur Institute of Paris by the Beaumont Board of Health and lots produced in these laboratories in rabbits were studied. Wright's procedure slightly modified[42] was used in the early part of the experiments in studying bactericidal and bacteriolytic action of the various serums. This method was early discarded for the simpler one outlined later. A series of dilutions of 48-hour broth plague cultures grown in buffered veal infusion broth P_H 6.6 was prepared in sterile test tubes, using as the diluent sterile salt solution. Equal quantities of such dilutions of the serum to be tested, and of normal serum of various types to supply alexin, were brought together and thoroughly mixed. At the same time a series of controls consisting of equal portions of sterile normal serum and culture dilutions was similarly prepared. After incubation for 36 hours at 30 to 32 C., determinations of bactericidal and bacteriolytic properties of the tested serums were made by morphologic and cultural comparison with the serum dilution controls. Viability determinations were carried out by plating on agar (P_H 6.8—7.0).

I. Effects of Human Plague Serum on Bacillus Pestis.—For these experiments serum obtained by venipuncture from 4 human cases of bubonic plague at the height of the disease was used. The first patient, an adult male, had

35 Centralbl. f. Bakteriol., 1903, 33, 271.
36 British Med. Jour., 1902, 2, p. 1895; Bombay Med. & Phys. Soc. Jour., 1902, No. IV.
37 Brit. Med. Jour., 1903, 3, p. 1077.
38 Jour. Hyg., 1902, No. 10.
39 Lancet, 1906, 2, p. 9.
40 Arch. d. Sc. Biol., 1905, 11, p. 196.
41 Philippine Jour. Sc., 1907, 2, p. 155.
42 Proc. Roy Soc., 1902, 71, p. 54.

TABLE 10

BACTERIOLYTIC ACTION OF SERUM OF PLAGUE PATIENTS

Plague Culture Dilutions	Mixture Unheated Serum and Plague Culture Dilution		Mixture Heated Serum 56 C. and Plague Culture Dilution		Mixture Heated Serum 68 C. and Plague Culture Dilution		Mixture Serum 28–30 C. and Plague Culture Dilution		Mixture Serum 2 C. and Plague Culture Dilution		Control Mixture Normal Serum and Plague Culture Dilution	
	Growth	Morphology	Growth	Morphology	Growth	Morphology	Growth	Morphology	Growth	Morphology	Growth	Morphology
1,000,000 500,000 100,000 50,000 10,000 5,000 1,000 500 200 100 50	0	No organisms on smear	+++	No change	+++	No change	+++	No change	0	No organisms on smear	+++	No change
25	0	Few vacuolated rods	+++	No change	+++	No change	+++	No change	0	Few rods	+++	No change
10	Occasional colony	Many rods markedly vacuolated	+++	No change	+++	No change	+++	No change	Few colonies	Many rods markedly vacuolated	+++	No change
2	Occasional colony	Many rods markedly vacuolated	+++	No change	+++	No change	+++	No change	Occasional colony	Many rods markedly vacuolated	+++	No change

a unilateral inguinal bubo, a temperature of 104 F., and was irrational at the time of securing the blood. He died 36 hours later. The second patient at the time of bleeding was well advanced in the disease, and subsequently recovered. One portion of serum was heated to 56 C. for 15 minutes in a water bath; another to 68 C. for 15 minutes; one untreated and used immediately; one allowed to remain at laboratory temperature (25—36C.) for 4 days, and one stored in the icebox at a temperature of 2 C. for 10 days. All portions were subsequently tested as previously outlined, with the results illustrated in tables 10. Table 10 shows that serum from plague patients may exert a strong bacteriolytic action on B. pestis. This lytic action when present is destroyed by treating at 56 C. and above; exposure to light and temperatures averaging 32 C. for a period of 4 days has a similar effect. On the other hand, no loss of bacteriolytic power was shown in serum stored in the dark at 2 C. for 10 days. Two other serums obtained at the height of disease, one from a subsequently fatal case of plague and one from a case which later recovered, were tested, the former with negative, the latter with positive results as regards bacteriolytic power. Here 6 strains of B. pestis were used, one being homologous for the specific serum in each instance. From these experiments it appears that the bacteriolytic action of serum derived from human plague cases is inconstant. The factors concerned when lysis does take place can be altered or rendered inert by heating at 35 C. for 4 days, at 55 C. or above for 15 minutes, but are not affected by temperature as low as 2 C.

TABLE 11

REACTIVATION OF PLAGUE SERUM

Plague Culture Dilution	Serum Heated 56 C. + Equal Part Guinea-Pig Serum + Plague Culture Dilution		Serum Heated 68 C. + Equal Part Guinea-Pig Serum + Plague Culture Dilution		Normal Serum + Equal Part Guinea-Pig Serum + Plague Culture Dilution; Control	
	Growth	Morphology	Growth	Morphology	Growth	Morphology
1,000,000 500,000 100,000 50,000 10,000 5,000 1,000 500 200 100 50	0	No organisms	+++	No change	+++	No change
25	0	Few vacuolated forms	+++	No change	+++	No change
10	Occasional colony	Many vacuolated rods	+++	No change	+++	No change
2	Few colonies	Many vacuolated rods	+++	No change	+++	No change

That alexin plays an important part in this lysis is demonstrated by the fact that reactivation and subsequent lytic action of previously active plague serum heated to 56 C. readily takes place on the addition of normal guinea-pig serum. Table 11 gives the details of a typical experiment on which the foregoing statement is based. These results on the whole agree closely with these of Row. Bearing in mind the importance of having an alexin with receptors suitable to unite with the amboceptors in the immune serum in experiments of this kind, serum of pigeon, ox, horse, chicken, rabbit and rat in addition to guinea-pig serum were used for supplying alexin to active and inactivated serums. At no phase could it be shown that alteration in the type of complement used produced differing results. In an attempt at determining the nature of the serum constituent which contains one of the factors concerned in the production of lysis, precipitation of the globulins from the lytic plague serums by CO_2 was resorted to. The resultant globulin when dissolved in various solvents failed to show bacteriolytic properties for B. pestis.

Effect of Serum From Plague Convalescents on Bacillus Pestis.—Serum from two recovered human cases of bubonic plague was secured. Serum 1 was obtained from a man who had recovered after bilateral inguinal involvement. The material was secured 10 months after full recovery. Serum 2 came from an adult colored man who had suffered from a unilateral inguinal lesion. Fourteen months had elapsed since his recovery. Each of these serums was treated with 12 strains of B. pestis. No bacteriolytic action could be demonstrated with these portions of plague convalescent serum. These results are in contradiction to those by Row.

Effect of Plague Antiserums on B. Pestis.—Here antiserums from 3 sources were used: Antiserum "Beaumont H." produced in horses by the injection in increasing doses of killed organisms. Its titer in agglutinins and precipitins had not been determined; it was highly protective for animals in that 3 c.c. protected a 15 gm. white rat against 10 lethal doses of virulent B. pestis (homologous culture). Serum P. 1028 was prepared in the Pasteur Institute of Paris. Its precipitin titer was high, but it had practically no agglutinating value for 7 organisms studied; protective experiments were not made; serums R. 1017, R. 1018, R. 1019, R. 1020, R. 1021, R. 1922 and R. 1923 were from immunized rabbits. Serums R. 1017 and R. 1018 were produced entirely by killed micro-organisms; their agglutinating titers were 1:110 for the homologous organism. Their precipitin titers were practically negligible. Serums R. 1019 and R. 1020 were produced by injection of increasing doses of plague proteotoxin prepared according to the method outlined by Eberson;[43] the agglutinating titer in each case was 1:65 for the organism from which the proteotoxin had been prepared. Serums R. 1021, R. 1022 and R. 1023 were produced by the injection of live organisms according to a method previously outlined; the agglutinating titers of these serums were 1:8,120, 1:6,500 and 1:6,300, respectively. Portions of all serums were tested as outlined, untreated serum, serum heated to 56 C. and serum heated to 68 C. being used. Twelve strains of B. pestis were used in nearly all instances, the homologous organisms being always included. Reactivation by means of the addition of fresh serum (generally guinea-pig serum) was done in all cases of heated antiserums, and further tests carried out.

Exper. 1: Equal parts of antiserum Beaumont H. unheated, heated to 56 C. and heated to 68 C. were mixed with increasing dilutions of plague suspensions (1:2 to 1:1,000,000) and various alexin containing serums; contact was allowed for 48 hours. After this time plating was used to determine viablity of organisms. With the unheated serum there was inhibition of growth as compared with the controls in the mixture of organism dilution in the 1:1,000,000 series. There were no differences between the heated to 56 C. and the heated to 68 C. series and the controls. Ten strains of B. pestis were used.

Exper. 2: Here antiserum P. 1428 was employed. The results were similar to those in exper. 1. Complete inhibition of growth of the organisms in the 1:1,000,000 dilution took place regularly. Heated serums showed no inhibition. Twelve strains of B. pestis were employed.

Exper. 3: In all the tests of this series (Serums R. 1017, R. 1018, R. 1019 and R. 1020) there was no difference between the serum mixtures and the control

[43] Jour. Infect Dis., 1917, 20, p. 180.

mixtures as to viability of organisms. Here in numbers of series alexin in the form of guinea-pig, human and sheep serums was added to the antiserums with no differences in ultimate results. Twelve strains of B. pestis were used.

Exper. 4: All the serums of the series (R. 1021, R. 1022 and R. 1023) showed inhibition of growth in the unheated antiserum-organism mixtures in varying degrees. In some instances (R. 1022) complete inhibition of growth took place in the 1:5 mixture with the homologous organism. No lytic action was noted with heated serums, but was present with serums stored at 2 C. for 3 weeks. Reactivation of serums heated to 56 C. with complete resumption of lytic action was always noted on the addition of native complement to such heated serums; such additions did not influence the action of serums heated to 68 C.

From these experiments it will be seen that antiserum Beaumont H. exerted slight bacteriolytic action; that antiserum Pasteur 1028 reacted in a similar manner; that no appreciable bacteriolytic action in serums R. 1017, R. 1018, R. 1019 and R. 1020 could be noted, and finally that serums R. 1021, R. 1022 and R. 1023 were greatly highly bacteriolytic for cultures of B. pestis. The bacteriolytic power of the latter serums was destroyed by heat at 56 C., but reactivation of their lost lytic powers was readily accomplished by the addition of alexin in the form of various normal serums to such heated antiserums.

Effect of Normal Serum of Various Mammals on B. Pestis.—Serum was obtained from the following animals and tested as outlined: man, horse, ox, sheep, rabbit, guinea-pig, rat, chicken, pigeon, sparrow and goose. Contrary to expectations, the serum of mammals naturally immune even under artificial conditions to B. Pestis did not exert a higher bactericidal or bacteriolytic action than did serums from animals highly susceptible to plague infection. Here again native complement was supplied by the addition of serum from various animals, in an attempt to eliminate as a source of error use of a serum containing complement with receptors not suitable to unite with the natural amboceptors contained in the tested serum.

DISCUSSION

Due to their diversity, the results of the experiments herein reported do not clear up the question of bacteriolysis of plague organisms by antiserums and serums from human plague cases. Of the 4 human plague serums studied, bacteriolysis was secured with 2, and not secured with a similar number. It so happened that lysis was obtained with serum from a case in which there was subsequent recovery and with serum from a subsequently fatal case, with no lysis noted in serums from a series of cases with similar ultimate results. All cases were at the height of the disease when serum was secured, and the homologous organism was generally included in the number used in the tests. In these experiments the question of host resistance and various other factors of somatic cell response over which we have no control must be considered. It does however, appear to be definitely established that when lysis takes place with such serums two factors are concerned; one is alexin; the other, a body destroyed by temperatures of 68 C. and above, but not affected by freezing. These observations are in line with the still generally prevailing ideas of modes and methods of action of lytic antibodies.

Of the two serums from plague convalescents studied, neither showed lysis. Here a number of strains of the organism were employed. Acquired immunity, if such exists following recovery from the disease, must depend on some little understood anti-infectious power of the host serum and not on any demonstrable substance which per se can cause lysis of the bacterial body, or even inhibit its development.

The results obtained with rabbit antiserums are interesting. In those produced by means of killed organisms and plague proteotoxin no bacteriolytic action could be demonstrated. In the majority of cases, however, with those animals in which virulent living organisms were principally used as the inoculating agent, serums of high agglutinating titer and of strong lytic values were produced.

It is felt justifiable to conclude that lysis of plague cultures, be they homologous or heterologous, may be produced by various natural and artificial plague serums, although such lysis is extremely variable. The reasons for such irregularity in lysis are not evident. It is believed, however, that an explanation is to be sought along far different lines from those customarily investigated. As a result of experiments now being conducted, it appears possible that specific iso-electric points exist for lysis of various organisms. In experiments of this nature, electrolytes present in diluent fluid, various constituents of the serums themselves, and even alterations in surface tension are all possible factors involved in the production of these definite iso-electric points; these iso-electric points, in addition to other influences, may be fairly selective determinants of precipitation, agglutination and lysis of various bacterial forms.

CONCLUSIONS

Six strains of B. pestis artificially cultivated for periods varying from 1 to 10 years showed a growth range from P_H 5.0—P_H 8.2 in salt-free veal broth, optimum growth occurring at P_H 6.2—P_H 7.0. The same strains recovered from fatal experimental white rat infection showed a growth range from P_H 5.4—P_H 7.6, with optimum growth at P_H 6.0—P_H 6.6. Above or below these limits growth was slight.

Recently isolated cultures showed a more decided optimum point of growth in contradistinction to the more marked optimum zone displayed by stock cultures.

The final hydrogen-ion concentration of B. pestis when grown in 1.0% dextrose broth of an initial reaction P_H 6.8 is P_H 4.80. This final limit is uninfluenced by prolonged artificial cultivation.

With medium adjusted to a P_H 6.8, a dextrose concentration of at least 0.5% is necessary for the establishment of the final characteristic hydrogen-ion concentration of B. pestis.

The minimum concentration of dextrose needed by B. pestis to give its characteristic final hydrogen-ion concentration is intimately dependent on the initial reaction of the medium employed.

Fifty strains of B. pestis from various parts of the world caused regular and strong acidification with dextrose, galactose, levulose and mannite. Most of the cultures produced acid with arabinose and maltose; a number with glycer and salicin. No changes were noted with adonite, dextrin, dulcite, inulin, lactose, melizitose, persertol, quertzite, raffinose, rhamnose, saccharose, sorbite, trehalose, and xyclose.

Organisms which on first cultivations would not attack arabinose, maltose, glycerol, and salicin, caused weak acid production after repeated cultivation in medium containing these substances. For none of the other carbohydrates was this noted.

Carbohydrate fermentation as a basis for classifying B. pestis is of no value.

The production of agglutinating serums for B. pestis by rabbits is recorded. Cultures were grown in veal infusion agar P_H 6.6 for 50 to 60 hours; growth was washed off, and the suspensions filtered through sand. Final suspensions to a concentration of 10,000,000,000 organisms per c c. were made in salt solution P_H 6.8. Such suspensions have shown no tendency to spontaneous agglutination for as long as two years at from 10 to 38 C. Injections of killed organisms, either intravenous, intraperitoneal or combined, even over long periods of time, gave indifferent results. Intravenous injections of live organisms attenuated at first by growth in alcohol broth and finally of full virulence resulted in the uniform production of serums with agglutinating titers of 1:6,000 to 1:15,000.

Serums obtained from cases of plague showed irregular bacteriolytic action on B. pestis. Heating to 56 C. and above for 15 minutes, and temperatures of 25-36 C. over periods of 4 days destroyed such action when present. Freezing did not alter it.

Two different bodies are concerned with bacteriolysis of plague cultures by such serums. One is alexin; the other is destroyed by heat at 68 C. and is not demonstrable in the CO_2 precipitable globulin.

No appreciable bacteriolytic action could be demonstrated in plague convalescent serums from human cases 10 and 14 months after recovery.

Protective antiplague serums of various types showed practically no bacteriolytic action. High titer agglutinating serums produced through rabbits generally showed marked lytic acid.

No bactericidal or bacteriolytic action for B. pestis could be demonstrated in normal serum from man, horse, ox, sheep, rabbit, guinea-pig, rat, chicken, pigeon, sparrow and goose.

It is suggested that variations in specific iso-electric limits account in a great measure for the varying results obtained with the lytic experiments.

THE COMMON COLD *

INFLUENZA STUDIES, XIV

EDWIN O. JORDAN, JOHN F. NORTON
AND
WILLIAM B. SHARP

From the Department of Hygiene and Bacteriology of the University of Chicago

Clinically, the common cold may be considered as essentially characterized by hyperemia, excessive secretion, or both, of the mucous membranes lining the nose, throat, or bronchi. Extension from one part of the upper respiratory tract to another is frequent. The familiar symptoms are irritation, dryness, or swelling of the part involved, sometimes with excessive secretion, all leading to a loose or dry cough, obstruction to nasal breathing, hoarseness, or sore throat. Often there are more general symptoms, such as fever, aching, or constipation; headache is not infrequent.

A cold should not be arbitrarily assumed to be an infection of the respiratory membrane. The clinical resemblance between some colds and any known infective process is not a close one. There is often no demarcated area of infection to correspond with that produced by such known parasites of the membrane as those of diphtheria or Vincent's angina. Purulent discharges or lymph node inflammation may occur, but are not common and when present may represent complicating or concomitant infection, such as sinusitis.

The popular conceptions of the causes of colds vary, and undoubtedly include factors which are of great importance. In devising a comprehensive program for the study of colds, it seemed desirable to include definite data concerning these popular ideas. Data were furnished us by over 1,200 students at the University of Chicago, 200 at the California Institute of Technology at Pasadena, and 200 at the University of Texas Medical School, Galveston, Texas. About one third of the University of Chicago group were women. All the members of the other groups were men. Cooperation was entirely voluntary and unrestricted, except that the students at the California

Received for publication, July 15, 1923.

* This is one of a series of studies carried out in connection with the Influenza Commission established and financially aided by the Metropolitan Life Insurance Company of New York. Part of the expense of these studies has been met by a grant from the University of Chicago.

Institute of Technology included in our records were limited to those that had resided in Southern California for at least five years.

The term "cold," as used in this inquiry, was limited to those conditions characterized by a diffuse congestion or excessive mucous discharge from the respiratory membranes, and therefore did not include tonsillitis or sinusitis, but only those conditions often termed "coryza," "catarrhal rhinitis" or "bronchitis." A questionnaire (appended herewith) was filled out by each subject and coupons* also furnished for reporting current colds. The reports for the Chicago series covered a period of seven months, beginning Nov. 1. 1919.

QUESTIONNAIRE A
CONDITION OF RESPIRATORY ORGANS

Name .... Address...................... Telephone.......
Please fill out briefly ("yes" or "no" where possible), but carefully throughout, as even the apparently minor details help to show what factors influence these diseases.
Occupation or position?.. Age?.................
How long have you lived in Chicago?.............. Previous address?......................
Last came to Chicago? (date) ....
Do you live in house?.................. Apartment?.............. Single room?............
Do you spend most of your time in a room kept hot?........ Moderate?........ Cold?........
Are the other rooms you sit in kept hot?.............. Moderate?........... Cold?.........
When asleep, do you have windows wide open?...... Open a few inches?...... Closed?......
How many sleep in your bed-room?........ How many live in your house or rooms?........
How many of the latter have frequent colds?...
How many have had Influenza?............ Pneumonia?.............. When?.............

PERSONAL CONDITIONS

In winter, do you wear light clothing?............ Heavy?.......... Medium?...........
Do you exercise regularly?.............. Indoors?............. Outdoors?.............
What form of exercise?.......... How much?.......... Daily?.......... Weekly?.........
Are you subject to Hay Fever?...... "Rose Cold?"...... Asthma?...... Constipation?......
At what time of the year do these occur chiefly?...
Have you ever had Influenza?............ Pneumonia?............. Dates?...............
Have you any obstruction to your left nostril?.......... Right?.......... Both?..........
Have you a chronic nasal discharge?.................. Sinus Disease?.....................
Do you often have sore throat?............ Hoarseness?.......... Chronic Cough?..........
Do you regularly use antiseptic mouth wash?.......... Nasal Spray or Douche?..........
Gargle?..................... What antiseptic, if any?.................................
Have you had any operation on Nose?....... Throat?....... Ears?....... Sinuses?.......
Do you have colds frequently?....... Twice yearly?....... Yearly?....... Less often?.......
At what time of year usually?............ How long do they last?.......................
Do they begin in Nose?............... Throat?................ Chest?.................
Do they then extend to Nose?...... Sinuses?...... Throat?...... Larynx?...... Chest........
Are they usually mild?............... Moderate?............... Severe?..................
Do you think your colds are caused by: Chilling after exercising or overheating?...........
Draughts?................ Wet Shoes?................ Wet Clothing?..................
Crowded rooms or cars?................ Constipation?................ Nearness to others with colds?............ Exposure to cold?.............. Sudden chilling?.............
What other causes do you suspect?................

An attempt was made to classify clinically the types of colds most frequently experienced by students at the University of Chicago. The

* Symptoms: (a) irritation or dryness of nose; (b) same of throat; (c) same of chest; (d) secretion from nose; (e) same from eyes; (f) chilly sensations; (g) headache; (h) backache; (i) general aching; (j) fever; (k) sick all over (l) pains (state where); (m) dry cough; (n) loose cough; (o) difficulty in breathing through nose; (p) tightness of chest in breathing; (q) hoarseness; (r) sore throat; (s) constipation; (t) other symptoms (state what). Apparent Cause: (1) due to draughts; (2) to chilling; (3) to wet shoes; (4) to wet clothing; (5) to fatigue; (6) to constipation; (7) to hot crowded room or car; (8) to chilling after exercise; (9 to use of common towel with others; (10) to direct contact with person with cold; (11) if so, when and how often? (12) How many in family had colds recently? when? duration? (13) What other cause is suspected?

data were obtained by individual questioning by one of us and are necessarily limited in accuracy by the exactness of memory of the subjects. Some light on the validity of these data was obtained later. Table 1 shows that in 61% of the subjects in this series the usual colds were limited to the nose, in 33% the cold extended to the chest, in 4% it was limited to the chest and in 2% extended from chest to nose. Table 2 lists the sequence of local symptoms in a series of 51

TABLE 1
TYPES OF COLDS
Chicago Series

	Total	Usually Nose	Usually Nose to Chest	Usually Chest	Usually Chest to Nose
Number of Students	502	306	165	20	11
Percentage	...	61	33	4	2

TABLE 2
SEQUENCE OF LOCAL SYMPTOMS IN COLDS PERSONALLY EXAMINED

	Number
Colds beginning in nose	24
Limited, bilateral	5
Limited, unilateral	2
Extending to throat	5
Extending to chest	7
Extending to throat then chest	3
Extending to chest then throat	1
Extending to throat then larynx	1
Colds beginning in throat	16
Limited	6
Extending to nose	2
Extending to nose then chest	4
Extending to chest	4
Colds beginning in chest	11
Limited	2
Extending to throat	1
Extending to throat then nose	1
Extending to nose	7

persons personally examined by us while the colds were in progress. Of this number, 24 (or 47%) started in the nose, 16 (32%) in the throat, and 11 (21%) in the chest. Of the last 11, nearly all were reported by the subjects as unusual, so that it is probably true that the most frequent form of cold does not begin in the chest. This series of 51 colds also demonstrated to us the difficulty of classifying colds according to symptoms. No one sequence of local symptoms is followed by more than a few of these cases.

In table 3, the type of cold is correlated with duration, severity and frequency, and in table 4 duration and severity are compared.

It seemed possible that some help might be obtained in studying the factors concerned in the causes of colds if these factors were compared with individual susceptibility. The only basis for a grouping according to susceptibility is frequency. Tables 5, 6 and 7 show the frequency

TABLE 3

RELATION OF TYPE OF COLD TO DURATION, SEVERITY AND FREQUENCY

Chicago Series

	Students whose Type of Cold was			
	Nose, No.	Nose to Chest, No.	Chest, No.	Chest to Nose, No.
Total colds	306	165	20	11
Duration of Colds:				
Usually under 1 week	72	33	4	4
Usually 1 to 3 weeks	203	112	15	5
Usually over 3 weeks	31	20	1	2
Severity of Colds:				
Usually mild	93	31	6	1
Usually moderate	184	106	10	9
Usually severe	29	28	4	1
Yearly Frequency of Colds:				
Usually more than 2	89	64	3	5
Usually 2	144	82	5	4
Usually 1	49	9	6	1
Usually less than 1	24	10	6	1

TABLE 4

COMPARISON OF DURATION WITH SEVERITY OF COLDS

Chicago Series

Cold Considered as	Where the Average Cold Persists					
	Under 1 Week		1 to 3 Weeks		Over 3 Weeks	
	No.	Percent	No.	Percent	No.	Percent
Mild	51	45	70	21	10	19
Moderate	57	51	221	66	31	57
Severe	6	5	44	13	13	24
Total No.	113	..	335	..	54	..

of colds among the groups of students questioned at the University of Chicago, at the California Institute of Technology (Pasadena), and at the University of Texas Medical School (Galveston). The frequency is correlated with duration, severity and sequence of symptoms. The statements of the students, though based on memory, probably give approximately the average attack rates for the past few years. Three hundred forty-seven students at the University of Chicago agreed to report, and we believe did report all their colds from Nov. 1, 1919, to June 1, 1920. Although the number of attacks might be somewhat different (usually less) than the yearly average, the data serve to control the statements based on recollection. Of those who reported, 24% proved to have more than their stated average, 33% less and 43% the same number. We feel that the control is sufficiently close to warrant accepting the averages recorded in the tables as approximately correct. If we assume that

TABLE 5
FREQUENCY OF COLDS
Chicago Series

Age Group	All Colds	Yearly Frequency: More Than Two	Two	One	Less Than One
1 to 15	2	1	1	0	0
16 to 20	213	75	94	29	15
21 to 25	203	64	96	25	18
26 to 30	55	14	28	7	6
Over 30 or unknown	29	7	16	4	2
All ages	502	161	235	65	41
Percentage	100	32	47	13	8

	Students Whose Yearly Frequency of Colds Was: More Than Two		Two		One		Less Than One	
	No.	%	No.	%	No.	%	No.	%
Total colds	161	..	235	..	65	..	41	..
Duration: usually								
Under 1 week	39	24	48	21	14	22	12	29
1 to 3 weeks	102	63	163	69	43	66	27	66
Over 3 weeks	20	13	24	10	8	12	2	5
Severity: usually								
Mild	33	21	48	20	25	39	25	61
Moderate	107	66	157	67	32	49	13	32
Severe	21	13	30	13	8	12	3	7
Type: usually								
Nose	89	55	144	61	49	75	24	59
Nose to chest	64	40	82	35	9	14	10	25
Chest	3	2	5	2	6	9	6	14
Chest to nose	5	3	4	2	1	2	1	2

there is sufficient intermingling of students so as generally to expose all to whatever virus may be concerned in colds, then the difference in rate of attack depends on the factors involved in personal resistance. The variously susceptible groups show about the same average sequence of symptoms except for a slight tendency in the Chicago group toward the chest as a starting place among those having infrequent colds. When colds are infrequent they apparently tend to run a milder course, and in the California and Galveston series were of shorter duration.

TABLE 6

FREQUENCY OF COLDS

Pasadena Series

	Total	Yearly Frequency				
		More Than Two	Two	One	Less Than One	Never Attacked
Number of students......	200	49	83	44	19	5
Percentage...............	100	24	41	22	10	3

	Students Whose Yearly Frequency of Colds Was							
	More Than Two		Two		One		Less Than One	
	No.	%	No.	%	No.	%	No.	%
Total colds..................	49	..	83	..	44	..	19	..
Duration: usually								
Under 1 week.............	17	34	17	20	17	39	15	79
1 to 3 weeks..............	21	43	62	75	20	45	4	21
Over 3 weeks..............	7	14	0	..	5	11	0	..
Not specified.............	4	9	4	5	2	5	0	..
Severity: usually								
Mild......................	18	37	51	61	31	71	14	73
Moderate.................	26	53	32	39	12	27	4	21
Severe....................	5	10	0	..	0	..	0	..
Not specified.............	0	..	0	..	1	2	1	6
Type: usually								
Nose......................	40	82	71	85	39	88	13	69
Nose to chest............	9	18	11	14	2	5	1	5
Chest.....................	0	..	0	..	1	2	0	..
Chest to nose............	0	..	1	1	0	..	1	5
Not specified.............	0	..	0	..	2	5	4	21

TABLE 7

FREQUENCY OF COLDS

Galveston Series

	Total	Yearly Frequency			
		More Than Two	Two	One	Less Than One
Number of students.................	201	36	79	40	46
Percentage............................	100	18	39	20	23

	Students Whose Yearly Frequency of Colds Was							
	More Than Two		Two		One		Less Than One	
	No.	%	No.	%	No.	%	No.	%
Total colds..................	36	..	79	..	40	..	46	..
Duration: usually								
Under 1 week.............	14	39	29	37	16	40	13	28
1 to 3 weeks..............	17	47	37	47	22	55	13	28
Over 3 weeks..............	1	3	7	9	0	0	2	4
Not specified.............	4	11	6	7	2	5	18	40
Severity: usually								
Mild......................	10	28	34	43	21	52	30	65
Moderate.................	22	61	40	51	17	43	9	20
Severe....................	4	11	5	6	2	5	0	0
Not specified.............	0	0	0	0	0	0	7	15
Type: usually								
Nose......................	28	78	52	66	32	80	26	57
Nose to chest............	7	19	20	25	6	15	6	13
Chest or not specified.....	1	3	7	9	2	5	14	30

The students were asked to specify the factors which appeared to them to bring on their colds. The replies are undoubtedly somewhat influenced by local and family traditions and prejudice. In table 8 we have listed the specified "causes" of the colds which occurred during the observation period at the University of Chicago, together with those reported as most frequently responsible for the colds among the students questioned at the University of Chicago, at the California Institute of Technology and at the University of Texas Medical School. In the first group the stated factors ranked the same regardless of

TABLE 8

FACTORS MOST FREQUENTLY THOUGHT RESPONSIBLE FOR COLDS

	Chicago				Pasadena		Galveston	
	Among All Students		Among Students under Observation		Among All Students		Among All Students	
	No.	%	No.	%	No.	%	No.	%
Total suggestions	1,261	..	336	..	338	..	453	..
Heart Function Strains:								
Chilling after exercise	200	16	42	12	96	28	75	16
Sudden chilling	134	11	76	23	30	9	60	13
Exposure to cold	118	9	..	..	30	9	52	11
Draughts	176	14	42	12	41	12	76	17
Poor ventilation	6	1	..	..	..	..	..	..
Wet shoes	106	8	23	7	19	6	29	6
Wet clothing or hair	42	3	4	1	11	3	20	5
Swimming	5	1	..	..	..	..	..	..
Change of climate, clothing or temperature	17	2	..	..	..	..	..	..
Contagion:								
Nearness to other cases	196	15	32	10	42	12	80	18
Recent colds in family	...	..	19	6	..	..	..	..
Crowded rooms or cars	99	8	31	9	15	4	27	6
Towels used also by others	...	..	8	2	..	..	..	..
Other Factors:								
Fatigue	45	3	36	11	..	..	8*	2
Constipation	97	7	23	7	40	12	26	6
Nasal trouble	13	1	..	..	2	1	..	..
Tonsil trouble	7	1	..	..	3	1	..	..
Overeating	...	..	..	..	9	3	..	..

* Includes other scattered factors.

whether there were general or local symptoms and were independent of the sequence of symptoms and of the season. All chest colds were ascribed to chilling or draughts, but the number was too small to be significant. Associated factors are grouped together; the first group contains those which might throw excessive strain on the heat regulating mechanism of the body. Exposure to cold, draughts or sudden chills, chilling after overeating, wet shoes, clothes, hair or exposure after swimming with resultant tendency to chill, all strain the heat regulating function. These factors were by far the most popular of those given as "the cause" of colds. The second group bore on the possibility of contagion. Proximity to other persons having colds, either in the family or classroom, crowded rooms or cars, and the use of common towels are examples of this group. Some students thought they were infected while swimming. The third group includes other factors such as fatigue and constipation, which it was thought might predispose to colds. Chronic ailments of the nose and throat would presumably increase the frequency of colds.

It is noteworthy that few of those answering the questions attributed their colds to mechanical irritation of the mucous membrane, although it is generally believed that autogenous infection not infrequently follows such irritation. The "infection" ascribed to swimming pool water may conceivably be fundamentally due to increased susceptibility caused by action of the water on the mucous surfaces. Dust is also regarded as probably a factor of importance. These factors were rarely considered important in the self-observative opinions of these college students.

TABLE 9

CHICAGO RESIDENCE IN CHICAGO GROUP

Residence	Number
Five years or more	168
One to four years	141
Less than one year	192

The most prevalent view among the subjects questioned is that colds result from factors which strain the heat regulating functions of the body. The four groups of students in Chicago, Pasadena and Galveston, reported, respectively, 55%, 65%, 67% and 68% of their colds as connected with these factors. Two-fifths of these listed also contact with other cases of colds.

We have encountered the popular conviction that the prevention of colds lies essentially in building up a resistance against strains on the heat regulating mechanism. The general assumption is that those who sleep with windows wide open and wear light clothing all winter, and who exercise regularly, especially out of doors, throw greater than the average work on this mechanism, and, judging from the amount of exposure possible without discomfort, acquire greater resistance, thereby preventing colds. We find that these practices are carried out by the same proportion of those with frequent as by those with infrequent colds (table 9).

The seasonal distribution of colds for the Chicago, Pasadena, and Galveston groups is given in table 10. The Pasadena group includes only those who have resided in California for 5 or more years, while the Chicago group contains many who had recently arrived in that city.

The proportionate frequency of colds is slightly less in the Southern California group. Among this group we also find a higher percentage of colds in the winter months as compared with the other seasons than in the Chicago group. In California, January and February are the months in which the weather is most likely to be damp and chilly, while in Chicago it may be disagreeable and changeable from October to April, and we should therefore expect a more even distribution of

TABLE 10

"RESISTANCE BUILDING" PRACTICES. CHICAGO GROUP

	Yearly Frequency of Colds			
	More Than Two, Percentage	Two, Percentage	One, Percentage	Less Than One, Percentage
Students Who Throughout the Winter Keep:				
Windows wide open	70	75	66	83
Windows open a few inches	30	24.5	34	15
Windows closed	..	0.5	..	2
Students Who Throughout the Winter wear:				
Light clothing	16	17	21	27
Medium weight clothing	70	72	70	61
Heavy clothing	14	11	9	12
Students Who Exercise Regularly by:				
Games, hikes, etc.	10	12	16	12
Outdoor walking	33	35	30	37
Swimming	24	17	15	13
Gymnastics	33	36	39	38

colds in the latter climate. The seasonal occurrence bears no relation to the duration or type of cold. Seasonal distribution may be accounted for to some degree by excessive strains on the heat regulating mechanism of the body during certain seasons.

Concerning the physiologic mechanics involved in strain on the heat regulating function, we know but little. Mudd and Grant [1] have shown that external chilling reduces the temperature and causes vasoconstriction in the respiratory mucous membranes. The latter was observed also in the skin of the head and neck. Recovery is not accompanied by a marked vasodilation. In one case of chronic pharyngitis and another of acute throat inflammation, chilling caused no depression

[1] Jour Med. Researh, 1919, 40, p. 53.

of the aropharyngeal curve—the reflexes being presumably interrupted by the inflammatory processes. Lermoyez [2] has suggested that chilling initiates metabolic alterations which result in protein shock, which is manifested as a cold. Further investigation along these lines is needed.

The effect of climatic conditions is illustrated in connection with data obtained from medical students in Galveston. This city is reputed to be a city of colds—the high incidence being frequently a matter of comment, both by natives and visitors. We found that students when in Galveston were more liable to colds than when elsewhere. This is shown by the incidence of colds among a group of medical students who were native Texans, but who had done their premedical work in another Texas city. Of these students, 46% reported that they were more liable to colds in Galveston, whereas 15% stated that they had more colds in the other city. The remaining 39% could distinguish no difference in the two localities. Galveston is a seaport city with a comparatively high humidity, and a cold wave is keenly felt. The winters are usually mild, but this mildness is at times interrupted by northerly winds which bring a sudden but usually short cold wave. Chilly and disagreeable rainy spells are not infrequent. "Dust storms" may be a factor.

TABLE 11

RELATIVE FREQUENCY AND SEASONAL OCCURRENCE OF COLDS

	Chicago, Percentage	Pasadena, Percentage	Galveston, Percentage
Yearly Frequency:			
More than two	32	24	18
Two	47	42	39
One	13	22	20
Less than one	8	12	23
Seasonal Occurrence:			
Autumn	25	14	20
Winter	44	63	61
Spring	26	15	12
Summer	2	8	7

"Contagion" is the second general factor thought to be concerned with the development of colds (table 8). The possibility of prejudice exists here to almost the same extent as with other factors. If we regard as "susceptibles" those who have frequent colds, and as "resistants" those who are infrequently attacked, our statistics show the probability of home contact in about the same proportion in each group. The number of instances of reported home contact is small,

[2] Bull. et mém. soc. méd. d. hôp. de Paris, 1921, 45, p. 1183.

however, in comparison with the number who were not aware of any direct contact. The intermingling of students is so general that it is rarely possible to trace a definite contact with other cases. At the present time, however, the only data pointing to the contagiousness of colds are epidemiologic.

Constipation was reported by some students as a definite cause for colds. It is possible that when this appears among the early symptoms it might be thought to be the cause. In our series of 230 observed colds, 42 patients reported constipation as one of the symptoms, and in a few subjects of the same series it definitely preceded other symptoms. Our data do not suggest any causal relationship.

Nose and throat defects are not infrequently reported as causative factors in colds. It is also believed that colds become less frequent following nose or throat operations. Our data, given in table 12 do not confirm such observations.

TABLE 12

EFFECT OF SURGICAL OPERATIONS ON THE FREQUENCY OF COLDS

Chicago Series

Yearly Frequency	History of			
	Nose Operation		Throat Operation	
	Number	Percentage	Number	Percentage
More than two	40	34	53	35
Two	57	48	73	49
One	9	8	13	9
Less than one	12	10	11	7
Total	118	100	150	100

Many studies have been made on the bacteriology of colds. Our studies taken in conjunction with those already reported from this and other laboratories show either that colds may be caused by a number of different micro-organisms, or that the cold virus has so far eluded laboratory workers. In connection with this investigation, two series of cultural studies were made. The first consisted in following the throat flora of 13 subjects for a number of weeks during the season when colds are more likely to occur. In the second, single examinations were made and the flora of those with colds compared with those without.

1st Series.—Daily examinations were made in 10 subjects from the middle of Nov., 1920, to Dec. 10, and on 13 subjects from Jan. 5 to Jan. 26, 1921, according to the following method: Nasopharyngeal swabs were streaked on blood-agar plates. After 24 and 48 hours' incubation the plates were examined, and the approximate percentage of each colony type determined. Four groups were recognized: (1) organisms presenting a green zone whether streptococci or pneumococci; (2) staphylococci; (3) organisms producing colonies resembling the gram-negative cocci, diptheroids, etc.; (4) other conspicuous organisms, such as the Pfeiffer bacilli or the hemolytic streptococci. The classification by plate inspection was controlled by frequent complete bacteriologic studies.

The subjects of these operations (assuming that the operations were all justified) may have been more susceptible to infections, and while the operations may have not resulted in making them as a class more resistant than the average, it cannot be concluded that individuals may not have been better off after operations than they would otherwise have been.

Of the 13 subjects, 5 developed colds while under our observation. Two had 2 colds each, making a total of 7 colds. Table 13 records the findings in a typical subject. No one group of organisms continually predominates in the nasal pharynx of a healthy person; one group prevails one day, another the next, or one group may persist for several days in the largest proportion and then the relative numbers suddenly change. The same is true during colds. While recognizing the crudeness of methods from a quantitative standpoint, these studies furnish evidence of the variety of bacteria existing in the nasal pharynx during a cold. If any one of these groups was alone concerned in causing colds, we should expect such a group to be continually predominant.

2nd Series.—The same methods were employed in studying the flora of 251 students at the California Institute of Technology, of whom 69 had colds at the time of examination. Only one swab was made from each subject. The results are shown in table 13. Again, no one group of organisms was found to be characteristic of a cold.

Our more complete bacterial analyses confirmed the results obtained by inspection of plates. For example, a type IV pneumococcus was the predominating organism in 3 of the 7 colds studied in series I—but we failed to find it in 2 of these subjects during other attacks. Furthermore, it was frequently the most prevalent bacterium in the nasal pharynx of healthy persons. In the California series, the only organism to appear much more frequently in colds than in health was Friedländer's bacillus, which was found in 1/10th of the colds but only in 1/25th of the normal subjects.

On account of the interest in the group of Pfeiffer bacilli our findings are given. In the series reported in table 13 these organisms were found at least once in 11 of the 13 subjects. From 255 swabs taken from this group when the throat appeared to be normal, Pfeiffer bacilli were isolated 29 times (12.8%). From 25 swabs of the same subjects during a cold, Pfeiffer bacilli were isolated once (4%). Among 116 students at the University of Chicago, these organisms were isolated twice from 9 normal throats (22.2%) and 10 times from

TABLE 13

COMPARATIVE PREVALENCE OF CERTAIN GROUPS OF BACTERIA IN THE THROAT IN HEALTH AND IN COLDS

Subject 3

Date	Findings on Blood-Agar Plate	Date	Findings on Blood-Agar Plate
1920		1921	
Nov. 16	C. G.	Jan. 5	C. G.
17	G. S. C.	6	S. C.
18	C.	7	C. S. G.
19	C. G. S.	10	G. S.
22	C. S.	11	C. S. G.
23	C. S. G.	12	C. G.
		13	C. G.
24	C. G. S.	14	G. S.
26	G. C.	17	C. G.
29	C.	18	C. S. G.
30	C. G.		
Dec. 1	C.	20	C. G.
2	C. G. S.	21	G. S.
3	G. S.	24	G. C.
6	G. S. C.	25	G. S.
7	G. C.	26	G. S.
8	S. G. C.		
10	G. S.		

In this table and in table 14, G. indicates organisms whose colonies produce a green zone on blood-agar plates; S., organisms whose colonies resemble those of the Staphylococcus; C., organisms whose colonies resemble those of the catarrhalis group. The order in which the letters appear corresponds to the order of prevalence on the plate; thus, G. S. C. indicates green producers in largest numbers, staphylococcus-like colonies next; and third, catarrhalis-like colonies. The periods during which the subject had a cold are indicated by the heavy black line.

98 throats during colds (9.8%). In Pasadena, Pfeiffer bacilli were found 5 times in 182 normal throats (2.7%) and 4 times from the throats of 69 persons with colds (5.7%). These results do not indicate that the Pfeiffer bacilli are of great etiologic importance in colds.

Many workers have searched for an organism which could be established as the etiologic factor in colds. Since an excellent discussion and summary are to be found in a paper by Mudd, Grant and Goldman,[3] we shall cite only a few of the more important investigations. Osborne,[4]

[3] Ann. Otol., Rhinol. & Laryngol., 1921, 30, p. 1.
[4] New York Med. Jour., 1919, 109, p. 529.

in a discussion of the etiology and treatment of colds, regards them as definitely contagious and suggests that many germs may produce colds. Mudd, Grant and Goldman also mention this possibility. MacCallum [5] states that chilling of the skin in some way favors infection by organisms present in the throat during health. Bloomfield [6] found a similarity in the throat flora in normal subjects and in persons with colds. He thinks that none of the usual throat inhabitants, such as the streptococci, staphylococci, pneumococci or Pfeiffer bacilli cause colds, but that during a cold these organisms find favorable conditions for multiplication and may produce complications. Williams, Nevin and Gurley [7] also found the throat flora to be similar in colds and in health. Our investigations confirm this view.

Specific organisms have been suspected of being the exciting agent by a number of investigators. The epidemiologic studies by Overton [8] at Camp Upton suggest the pneumococcus. Floyd [9] found this organism frequently in colds. Gordon,[10] working with our Chicago students, found pneumococci in 35% of cold cases, but in only 21% of the healthy subjects. Williams, Nevin and Gurley report 39% and 26% respectively. Gordon also studied the presence of pneumococci in the subjects on whom we have reported (table 13). Pneumococci were found continuously in only 3 cases of severe cold, and in only 2 of these had the pneumococcus been uniformly absent prior to the development of the cold. Gordon concluded that the pneumococcus complicated, rather than caused, colds. Cooper, Mishulow and Blanc [11] found no serologic relationship between type IV pneumococci isolated from colds. This is further evidence that this organism is not the etiologic agent.

There is no evidence that the streptococci, staphylcocci or the gram-negative cocci [12] are the inciting agents. That the Pfeiffer bacilli are directly concerned, is likewise improbable. Jordan and Sharp [13] found no serologic identity among strains from colds, and reported unsuccessful attempts to prevent colds by the use of a vaccine which contained these organisms, together with pneumococci and streptococci.

5 Textbook of Pathology, 1918, p. 370.
6 Bull. Johns Hopkins Hosp., 1921, 32, p. 121.
7 Jour. Immunol., 1921, 6, p. 5.
8 Am. Jour. Public Health, 1920, 10, p. 431.
9 Boston Med. & Surg. Jour., 1920, 182, p. 389.
10 Jour. Infect. Dis., 1921, 29, p. 437.
11 Jour. Immunol., 1921, 6, p. 25.
12 Gordon: Jour. Infect. Dis., 1921, 29, p. 462.
13 Ibid., 1922, 31, p. 198.

Tunnicliff[14] isolated an anaerobic bacillus which appeared responsible for colds, and Howell[15] partially confirmed her work. On the other hand, Hall[16] was unable to find this organism in colds of our Chicago series. Kruse[17] and Foster[18] have attributed certain types of cold to a filterable virus, but Schmidt[19] thinks the evidence is insufficient. Foster described coccoid bodies in filtrate cultures, but Branham and Hall[20] were unable to find them in our Chicago cases. It is true, however, that our cases presented a different clinical picture from those described by Foster.

TABLE 14

PLATE READINGS OF PREDOMINANT THROAT FLORA OF COLD CASES AND NORMAL SUBJECTS IN PASADENA

Flora	Normal		Colds	
	No.	%	No.	%
G. S.	28	16	11	16
G. S. C.	24	13	13	19
G. C. S.	18	10	10	14
S.	5	3	2	3
S. G.	19	10	8	12
S. G. C.	35	19	7	10
S. C. G.	15	8	7	10
C. G. S.	17	9	4	6
C. S. G.	10	6	4	6
Not read*	11	6	3	4

Occasionally other organisms, such as Friedländer's bacillus, were found. Findings for the Pfeiffer bacilli are noted in the text.

* Usually contaminated plates. Scattering groupings are also included here.

SUMMARY

The statistical and laboratory data here presented indicate that the common cold is not a simple type of infection, perhaps in some instances not even an infectious process at all. Numerous factors are undoubtedly concerned in the production of a cold. Our evidence does not support the view that a cold is always due primarily to the entrance of some virus from without the body. On the contrary, it appears that internal body changes may be the more important factors. These changes in turn are closely associated with outside influences. Of 2388 students questioned at the University of Chicago, the California Institute of Technology and the University of Texas Medical School

[14] Ibid., 1915, 16, p. 493.
[15] Ibid., 1915, 16, p. 456.
[16] Ibid., 1921, 28, p. 127.
[17] München. med. Wchnschr., 1914, 61, p. 1547.
[18] Jour. Infect. Dis., 1917, 21, p. 451.
[19] Deusch. med. Wchnschr., 1920, 46, p. 1181.
[20] Jour. Infect. Dis., 1921, 28, p. 143.

1530 (64%) cited some factor influencing the heat regulating mechanism of the body as in their opinion the most common "cause" of their colds. The variation among the three groups was insignificant. While the statements of these students should be regarded rather as popular impressions than as scientific facts, it is difficult to avoid the conclusion that chilling of the body is really an important predisposing factor. Some scientific basis for this is found in the experiments of Mudd and his associates, to which reference has already been made.

Exposure to persons having colds was listed as the presumable cause of colds by 22% of the students in these same groups. It is obviously impossible to exclude absolutely the possibility of contact with colds in any group of persons more or less intimately associated with one another. The variation among the geographic groups in this respect was slight. The observation has not infrequently been made that colds run through a family or school,[21] but in such cases it is difficult to distinguish between actual contagion and simultaneous exposure to predisposing environmental influences.

The remaining 14% constituting our groups mention other factors, such as fatigue, constipation and nose or throat troubles. Our data on the latter, although limited, tend to show that while nose or throat operations may reduce the number of colds in individual instances, the effect of such operations was not statistically measurable.

Climatic conditions might naturally be supposed to influence the degree of strain on the heat regulating mechanism of the body. Tables 5, 6, 7 and 11, which deal with the frequency and seasonal occurrence of colds in the Chicago, Pasadena and Galveston groups, should give some indications concerning these climatic conditions. The yearly frequency of colds is surprisingly close in the 3 groups, considering the great differences in climate. The number of students having more than 2 colds a year is slightly higher in the Chicago and is lowest in the Galveston group, but this may be accounted for by the longer winter season in Chicago, a fact which makes the seasonal distribution of colds in Chicago also somewhat more uniform than in the other 2 cities. On account of the relatively even and mild climate of California, it is surprising that we should find a lower frequency of colds in Galveston than in Pasadena. It is possible, however, that this may be due partly to the migration of naturally susceptible persons to California. The colds in these 2 groups were of somewhat shorter duration and of

[21] For example, Osborne, New York Med. Jour., 1919, 109, p. 529.

slightly less severity than of those in the Chicago group. In general, however, our statistics do not show such a marked difference in frequency, severity or duration of colds among students in Chicago, Pasadena and Galveston as might have been anticipated on the basis of climatic conditions.

It is popularly supposed that those persons who keep themselves in excellent physical condition, who exercise regularly and who sleep with wide open windows, are less liable to respiratory disorders than those not following these practices. Our statistics indicate that this may not always be true, (table 10). Exposure to cold air as a preventive of colds may not always be as successful as sometimes supposed.

The results of our laboratory investigations (tables 13 and 14) correspond in the main with those obtained by other investigators. No one organism or group of organisms has been shown to predominate during colds. The question of a specific infectious virus is therefore still an open one.

CONCLUSIONS

The common cold generally starts in the nose. About one third of these colds extend to the chest.

The sequence of the local symptoms in colds is not uniform.

There is no definite correlation between type, duration, severity and frequency of colds, except that infrequent colds tend to run a milder course.

In our California and Galveston groups, colds, while of about the same yearly frequency as in the Chicago group, tended to be concentrated into a shorter period, were of somewhat less severity and of somewhat shorter duration. In general, however, the differences in the three groups were less than might be expected on the basis of climatic conditions alone.

Of the persons from whom data were gathered, 64% believed that their colds were induced by some strain on the heat regulating mechanism of the body.

Possible contact with others having colds was stated by 22% of persons questioned to have preceded their own colds.

"Resistance building" practices apparently had little effect on the frequency of colds.

Our data do not show that nose or throat operations result in a marked reduction of the frequency of colds.

Among the bacteria cultivable on blood-agar plates, no one bacterium or group of bacteria has been found to predominate in the upper respiratory tract during a cold.

Whether or not a cold is the result of a specific infectious process is unknown. It is clear, however, that outside influences, particularly those involving chilling of the body, may serve to induce a cold, even if these influences cannot be regarded as the most important etiologic factors.

THE EFFECT OF KAOLIN ON THE INTESTINAL FLORA IN NORMAL AND PATHOLOGIC CONDITIONS

ONE PLATE

Louis Henry Braafladt

From the John McCormick Institute for Infectious Diseases, Chicago

This study was begun in August, 1919,[1] when the epidemic of Asiatic cholera which swept over China that year reached Tsinan. Kaolin was used with success on a fairly representative number of cases treated at the University Hospital at that time, as well as on a few sporadic cases in 1920. Its effect on acute amebic dysentery, acute bacillary dysentery, and chronic ulcerative colitis was also noted.

Very little work has been done which throws any light on how it affects pathogenic intestinal micro-organisms and their toxins and toxic products. So far is I know, no observations have been recorded dealing with its effect on the normal flora of the intestine.

History of Kaolin.—The etymology of the word "kaolin" is simple, yet interesting. It is a transliteration of two Chinese character which mean high mountain range. When Chinese pronounce these characters, it sounds to a foreigner like kao-ling or gao-ling.

According to Keenan,[2] who has written an interesting history on kaolin, the first appearance of the word in Europe was in a letter from a Jesuit missionary to China, Father Dentrecolle, to the procureur of the order of Paris, in 1712. In this letter, as well as in one written in 1722, he describes in a fascinating way the large porcelain industry about the city King-te-chen, where as many as a half a million people were employed in it. The 3,000 kilns at night so illuminated the hills surrounding the city that it seemed like a vast city abandoned to the flames. Both letters are to be found in the appendix to Bushnell's[3] translation of the classical work on pottery and porcelain, the "T'ao Shuo."

Following the publication of these letters, a contemporary chemist, R. A. F. de Reamur, analyzed specimens of kaolin which had been sent him from China and found them to be the chief ingredient of porcelain or chinaware of the Orient. This seems to have stimulated the search for deposits in France, England, and America.

William Cookworthy discovered deposits at Tregonnin Hill, Cornwall, in 1750. In 1768, he procured a patent for the making of porcelain. Keenan says: "In France the kaolin quarries that made Limoges famous were the accidental

Received for publication, July 25, 1923.

[1] Editorial, China Med. Jour., 33, p. 574.

[2] American Druggist, 1914, 62, p. 55.

[3] Clarendon Press, Oxford, 1910.

discovery, in 1765, of Madame Darnet, the wife of a surgeon at St. Yrieix, near Limoges. Coming upon a white unctuous earth in a ravine, she thought of using it for washing linen. Having showed it to her husband, he suspected that this might be the clay that all were looking for. He took it to a pharmacist at Bordeaux, named Villaris, who recognized it to be kaolin. This discovery led to the establishment of the remarkable works of Limoges, . . . the principle factory being a purely American concern, The Haviland, and to this day the United States is chiefly supplied with porcelain from the American works of Haviland and of Straus in Limoges."

In this country, the Cherokee Indians are believed to have mined a crude kaolin in North Carolina for export to England more than two centuries ago. "The Indians are said to have carried the clay from the Smoky Mountains to the coast under the name of *Unakah*, which was their name for the Smokies (meaning white), still called Unakah in Mitchell County and Unakoi in Cherokee. A patent was applied for in England in 1744 for the production of porcelain from an earth mixture called Unaker, referred to as ' the produce of the Cherokee nation of America', the name being derived in a manner analogous to that of kaolin in China, from the place of origin of the clay—the mountains bounding North Carolina on the northwest, called Unaker." Watts[4] does not believe that pure kaolin was produced in America as early as this but that it was a mixture of kaolin, feldspar and quartz. It is now mined in Pennsylvania, Delaware, Virginia, Georgia, Florida and North and South Carolina. The total yield in the United States in 1912 was only 27,000 tons. The deposits in Cornwall and Devon, England, are still being worked on a large scale. In 1912, 237,366 tons of English clay valued at $1,541,105 were imported by this country.

Its Composition.—Feldspar of granitic rock is a double silicate of aluminum and alkali. When exposed to the prolonged action of water charged with carbon dioxide, weathering takes place, that is, the feldspar breaks down. The alkali is eliminated and water is taken up, the resulting substance being hydrous aluminum silicate. Keenan represents this action as follows:

Feldspar................	K_2O	Al_2O_3	6 $Si\ O_2$	
Removal of............	K_2O		4 $Si\ O_2$	
Addition of............				2 H_2O
		Al_2O_3	2 $Si\ O_2$	2 H_2O

Rains and floods have washed this decomposition product to places where it has become mixed with quartz, sand and various minerals. Some of the purest deposits of kaolin in America are the result of sedimentation during times of floods.

The crude kaolin when dug from its bed or washed out hydraulically is usually purified, that is, freed from gritty particles, such as sand and mica, by repeated washing and decantation (elutriation). It is then run into filter presses where the water, at a pressure of 100 to 120 pounds per square inch, escapes. The moist cakes are left to dry by exposing them to the air or steam heat. This product contains more or less impurities, depending on the thoroughness of the washing and the efficiency of the method used to remove the water. For pharmaceutical purposes, the alkali which it may contain is removed by treating with 5% hydrochloric acid. After that it is treated with dilute sulphuric acid to remove other impurities, and then washed thoroughly with water to remove the chlorides and sulphates. A pure kaolin contains approximately 47% of silica, 40% of aluminia, and 13% of water.[5]

[4] Bull. 53, Dept. of Interior, Bureau of Mines, 1913, p. 37.
[5] U. S. Dispensatory, Ed. 20, p. 605.

Its Properties.—The British Pharmacopoeia[6] describes it as "a soft whitish powder, insoluble in water, or in dilute acids." It was introduced into the U. S. P. VIII, for the purpose of forming the basis of the preparation of Cataplasma Kaolini, which was dropped from the U. S. P. IX, but introduced into the National Formulary, Ed. IV.[7] Here it is described as "a soft, white, or yellowish white powder or in lumps, insoluble in water and in cold dilute acids and in solutions of the alkali hydroxides. It has an earthy or clay-like odor when moistened with water." Tests for its purity are found in the U. S. P. VIII, the B. P., and other pharmacopeias.

Flack,[8] experimenting on several samples of kaolin from reliable sources, found that they did not possess similar amounts of adsorptive power. Scoville[9] showed that alkaloids present in solutions filtered through a layer of kaolin are removed by it. Fantus,[10] correctly, I think, maintains that Fuller's earth should not be given as a synonym for kaolin because of differences in their adsorptive action.

The pharmacopeias of Britain,[11] Norway,[12] and the United States (VIII[13]) describe kaolin under its proper name. Those of Germany,[14] Austria,[15] Belgium,[16] The Netherlands,[17] Japan,[18] and Italy[19] fail to distinguish kaolin from the argillaceus earths which have been known for ages as "bolus," "bolus alba" being the term under which they describe it.

Its Uses.—These are manifold. It is used in the manufacture of porcelain, pottery and false teeth; in certain toilet powders and face cleansing clays (popular today, and selling at high prices; when a thick suspension of kaolin in water, costing about 30 cents a pound would probably be just as effective). It is used as filtering medium to clear syrup, beer and cloudy solutions of volatile oils. In pharmacy and medicine its chief use has been as a basis of a cleanly form of poultice, "cataplasma kaolini," N. F.; as an excipient in making pills which are readily oxidized or reduced when in contact with organic matter, especially pills of potassium permanganate, silver nitrate, silver oxide and the like. It has been used as a dusting powder in wounds on ulcerated surfaces and diphtheritic sore throats. Hemmeter, many years ago, advised its use in hyperacidity of the stomach.

The success with which it has been used during the last few years in gastrointestinal disorders produced by bacteria that liberate soluble toxic products in the intestine, would seem to justify amply the time spent on this study.

Owing to differences observed by Scoville and Fantus in particular, in the adsorptive action of various specimens on the market, the necessity for using a standardized, pure product in internal disorders and in experimental work to obtain uniform and reliable results, is apparent. That used throughout this work was Merck & Company's: Kaolin Merck, U. S. P. VIII.

[6] The British Pharmocopoeia, 1914, p. 199.
[7] The National Formulary, Ed. 4, 1916, p. 309.
[8] Am. Jour. Pharm., 1906, 78, p. 419.
[9] Ibid., 1916, 88, p. 506.
[10] Jour. Am. Med. Assn., 1915, 64, p. 1838.
[11] The British Pharmaceutical Codex, 1911, p. 556.
[12] Den Norske Pharmacopø, Ed. IV, 1913, p. 183.
[13] U. S. P. VIII Revision, 1905, p. 252.
[14] Pharmacopeia Germanica, Ed. Altera, 1882, p. 42.
[15] Pharmocopeia Austria, Edito Octava, 1906, p. 60.
[16] Pharmacopeia Belgica, Ed. II, 1885, p. 40.
[17] Nederlandsche Pharmacopoe, IV, 1915, p. 67.
[18] The Pharmacopoeia of Japan, III, 1907, p. 60.
[19] Pharmacopeia Ufficiale del Regno D'Italia, IV, 1920, p. 71.

EXPERIMENTAL WORK

This was conducted on rats, rabbits, guinea-pigs, dogs, and on 4 healthy men volunteers. It was hoped that it would throw some light on:

(*a*) The effect that kaolin has on pathogenic organisms that invade the intestine of man, such as the dysentery bacillus, typhoid and paratyphoid bacilli, B. enteritidis, B. botulinus, and Vib. cholerae.

(*b*) Its effect on the toxins and toxic products produced by these organisms.

(*c*) Its effect on the normal flora of the intestine.

The Effect of Kaolin on Bacteria Growing in Artificial Mediums.— One gram of sterile kaolin was added to 24-hour cultures (about 8 c c. of favorable medium in each tube) of B. dysenteriae (Shiga), *B.* typhosus and B. paratyphosus, B. botulinus, B. enteritidis. The cultures were left at room temperature for two hours, being shaken up well every half hour. In subcultures growth was obtained from all of them.

Although it is evident from this that kaolin is not strongly bactericidal, in agreement with Walker [20] and others, still there is a possibility that it might inhibit the growth of bacteria or accelerate it.

Culver and Novrogordato [21] found that certain insoluble and chemically inert dusts, such as quartzite and wood charcoal, added to culture medium augmented the growth of B. pyocyaneous, streptococcus, and B. tuberculosis (human).

Two experiments were made to ascertain whether kaolin has a similar effect:

1. One c c. of a suspension of B. coli was added to 5 c c. of sterile salt solution; further dilutions were made from this into other 5 c c. amounts. Agar tubes, each containing exactly 5 c c. of medium, were melted. To each of half the number of agar tubes, 10 mg. of sterile kaolin were added, also 0.1 c c. of B. coli dilution. They were shaken well and plated. After 24 hour's incubation, the number of colonies on the kaolinized plates that could be counted with accuracy, using the low power lens, were compared with the numbers on the corresponding control plates. The difference between the average number obtained from 3 plates and their controls were negligible.

2. In the second experiment, 1 gm. of kaolin was added to a tube containing 8 c c. of broth. This was inoculated with 0.1 c c. of a 24-hour broth culture of B. coli. A control tube containing a similar amount of broth was inoculated with 0.1 c c. of the same culture. The tubes were incubated for 3 hours, being shaken up thoroughly every 5 minutes. Then 0.1 c c. from each tube was added to 2 tubes containing 5 c c. of sterile salt solution; further dilutions were made

[20] Proc. Royal Soc. of Med., 1921, 14, p. 23.

[21] Med. Jour. of South Africa, 17, No. 2, p. 209.

from these. (The kaolinized culture, as well as the control, were now left undisturbed in the incubator for 48 hours.) One tenth c c. from each dilution was mixed with 8 c c. melted agar and poured into plates. After 24 hours' incubation the colonies were carefully counted, using a microscope with low power lens. The average number from a standard square in the center and from 2 squares at opposite sides of the plate was used in computing the total number of colonies on the plate. This method of counting was followed in all our subsequent work.

After 48 hours' dilutions, plates and counts were made from the supernatant fluid in the kaolinized culture, and from the control as described above. The results of these two experiments are recorded in table 1.

TABLE 1

EFFECT OF KAOLIN ON GROWTH OF B. COLI

	Colonies on Kaolin Plate	Colonies on Control Plate	Approximate Ratio Between Them
High dilution plate 3-hour culture..........	28,000	103,000	1 : 4
Low dilution plate 3-hour culture...........	55,200	149,280	1 : 3
High dilution plate 48-hour culture.........	64,800	79,200	4 : 5
Low dilution plate 48-hour culture..........	130,200	149,200	4 : 5

The first experiment indicates that kaolin has no effect on the growth of bacteria in solid mediums. Perhaps an average from a larger number of such plates would have been different.

The second experiment shows that when added to fluid mediums incubated at about body temperature and kept in motion—a condition somewhat analogous to that of a large amount of the substance in the intestine—it carries down with it a large number of bacteria. There were from 3 to 4 times as many colonies on the control plates as on the ones made from the kaolinized culture.

Whether or not there is a definite union between the bacteria and the particles of kaolin, as is the case between it and toxin molecules, is not clear.

Further, when the kaolinized culture as well as the control are left undisturbed for 48 hours, and the plates are inoculated from dilution made from the supernatant fluid, there are almost as many bacteria in 0.1 c c. of this fluid as in an equal amount from the control.

THE EFFECT OF KAOLIN ON BACTERIAL TOXINS AND TOXIC PRODUCTS

To increase their virulence, two animal passages were made of strains of B. typhosus and paratyphosus, B. dysenteriae (Shiga), and B. enteritidis.

They were grown in 500 c c. flasks containing 250 c c. dextrose broth each, for 4 days. They were killed by heating in a water bath at 60 C. for 20 minutes, then filtered through porcelain filters. Five c c. doses of these toxic filtrates were injected into rabbits intravenously. One was injected with 5 c c. dextrose broth as a control.

Five c c. of each toxic filtrate were placed in tubes containing 1 gm. of kaolin each. These were well mixed, incubated for 20 minutes, being shaken every 5 minutes, then centrifuged, and the supernatant fluids injected into rabbits intravenously. In the case of B. botulinus A, 0.5 c c. of a fluid culture, 14 days old, obtained from Dr. Geiger, Chicago University, was used. The exact lethal dose for a rabbit was not determined, but the amount used surely contained several lethal doses. It was diluted with 5 c c. of salt solution and injected subcutaneously. A similar amount of the culture, also diluted with salt solution, was mixed with 4 gm. of kaolin, centrifuged and injected. This experiment was repeated with similar results as recorded in table 2.

TABLE 2

THE EFFECT OF KAOLIN ON BACTERIAL TOXINS AND TOXIC PRODUCTS

Rabbit	Toxin or Toxic Product from	Intravenous Injection of	Result
1	B. typhosus	5 c c. toxic filtrate	Quiet for 24 hours
2	B. paratyphosus B	5 c c. toxic filtrate	Quiet for 28 hours
3	B. enteritidis	5 c c. toxic filtrate	Died after 24 hours
4	B. dysenteriae (Shiga)	5 c c. toxic filtrate	Died after 12 hours
5	B. botulinus A	0.5 c c. fluid culture (subcutaneously)	Died after 10 hours
6	B. typhosus	5 c c. toxic filtrate treated with kaolin	Eating after 6 to 7 hours
7	B. paratyphosus B	5 c c. toxic filtrate treated with kaolin	Eating after 8 hours
8	B. enteritidis	5 c c. toxic filtrate treated with kaolin	Eating after 8 hours
9	B. dysenteriae (Shiga)	5 c c. toxic filtrate treated with kaolin	Eating after 7 hours
10	B. botulinus A	0.5 c c. fluid culture treated with kaolin	Eating after 6 hours
11	(Control)	5 c c. dextrose broth	Eating after 6 to 7 hours

The effect of kaolin on diphtheria toxin was also determined. No. 2a toxin, prepared by Dr. George H. Weaver, was used. The MLD of this toxin was found to be 0.012 c c.. Throughout the experiment the amount taken as one MLD was 0.015 c c., so as to be sure that it would be fatal. In the first experiment single MLD doses were added to 1 c c. of sterile salt solution, shaken up with various amounts of kaolin for 15 to 20 minutes, centrifuged, and the clear, supernatant fluid injected hypodermically into young guinea-pigs weighing about 250 gm.

TABLE 3

THE EFFECT OF KAOLIN ON DIPHTHERIA TOXIN

Guinea-Pig	One c c. Salt Solution Containing 1 MLD Treated with	Result
1	10 mg. kaolin	Died in 88 hours
2	10 mg. kaolin	Died in 66 hours
3	25 mg. kaolin	Lived
4	25 mg. kaolin	Lived
5	50 mg. kaolin	Lived
6	50 mg. kaolin	Lived
7	100 mg. kaolin	Lived
8	100 mg. kaolin	Lived
9	(Control—1 MLD)	Died in 92 hours

The second experiment was made in the same manner as the first, except that a 20% suspension of kaolin was used in place of the powder. The same amount of toxin and kaolin was used as before (0.05 c c. of a 20% suspension = 10 mg. of the powder).

In the second part of this experiment, 5 MLD doses were used, and 5 times as much kaolin suspension as in the first. Each dose was made up to 2.5 c c. with salt solution (table 4).

Hektoen and Rappaport[22] found that frequent insufflations of kaolin powder into the throats of diphtheria patients, in which large numbers of bacilli were present, removed these completely and apparently permanently in from 2 to 4 days. It was discontinued because of the inconvenience it caused the patients. A thick suspension would probably have been more convenient, and perhaps more effective, as the particles of kaolin would have been more completely separated from one another.

TABLE 4

THE EFFECT OF KAOLIN ON DIPHTHERIA TOXIN, CONTINUED

Guinea-Pig	One MLD + Salt Solution q.s. to Make 1 c c. Treated with	Result
10	0.05 c c. kaolin suspension	Died in 42 hours
11	0.125 c c. kaolin suspension	Lived
12	0.25 c c. kaolin suspension	Lived
13	0.63 c c. kaolin suspension	Lived
14	Control (1 MLD)	Died in 48 hours
	Five MLD + Salt Solution q.s. to Make 2.5 c c. Treated with	
15	0.25 c c. kaolin suspension	Died in 48 hours
16	0.63 c c. kaolin suspension	Lived
17	1.25 c c. kaolin suspension	Lived
18	2.5 c c. kaolin suspension	Lived
19	Control (5 MLD)	Died in 16 hours

The Effect of Kaolin on the Normal Intestinal Flora.—Much time was spent in trying out various mediums and methods in becoming familiar with the types of bacteria normally present in the intestines of rats, dogs, and human beings. Kaolin appeared to decrease the number of gram-negative bacteria in feces and to increase the gram-positive. I then decided to concentrate the attention on its effect on the proteolytic and aciduric groups and on B. welchii.

For this purpose, the 5% acid liver agar medium recommended by Torrey,[23] and that described by Ayers and Rupp,[24] were found most suitable. B. acidophilus does not grow on Ayers-Rupp medium, and gram-negative bacilli, as well as most cocci, do not as a rule grow on highly acid liver agar medium. However, this selective action by the latter is not absolute. A plate inoculated from a suspension of a stool predominantly putrefactive produces a number of colonies of gram-negative bacilli. A plate from the same batch of medium, with the same amount of medium poured into it, and incubated along with

[22] Jour. Am. Med. Assn., 1915, 64, p. 1985.
[23] Jour. of Bacteriol., 1917, 2, p. 435.
[24] Ibid., 1918, 3, p. 433.

the former, but inoculated with a suspension from a predominantly aciduric stool, developed only colonies of gram-positive bacilli, yeasts, and a few cocci. This was observed several times. If as much as 10 c c. of the acid medium were poured into the plate, it would not be as inhibitory as if only 6 or 7 c c. were used. The thinner the plate, the more easily could the morphology of the colony be established clearly.

Technic.—A small amount of stool was put directly into a sterile test tube; about 0.5 gm. was mixed thoroughly with 10 c c. of sterile salt solution. Further dilutions were made from this. Exactly 0.05 c c. of the highest dilution was spread over an Ayers-Rupp plate with a sterile glass rod. and a similar amount over one half of a liver-agar plate; 0.05 c c. of an appropriate dilution of B. acidophilus was spread over the other half for comparison. Another set of plates was inoculated in a similar manner from the next lower dilution. The stool was usually plated within half an hour after it had been passed. The Ayers-Rupp plates were incubated for 24 hours, and the liver-agar plates for 72. The set of plates having a representative number of colonies on them were selected for counting. The number of types of colonies found on the plate was first determined with the aid of the microscope; then one of each stained by Gram's method. Only colonies of gram-negative bacilli were counted on Ayers-Rupp plates, and those of gram-positive bacilli, and which looked like the control colonies on the same plate, were counted on the liver agar plates. Doubtful colonies on the latter were inoculated into dextrose broth, and later into blood agar, litmus milk, gelatine and the sugars for further study.

The advantage of having a pure culture of B. acidophilus as a control on the same liver-agar plate as colonies growing from the stool is obvious. The age of the plate, its thickness, the slight difference in reaction of plates made from different batches of medium, all affect the morphology of the B. acidophilus colonies.

Feeding Experiments on White Rats.—All were young, almost grown-up rats. Fifteen were divided into 3 groups of 5 each. To each of the first group, 5 gm. of ground boiled meat were given per day; to each of the second, 5 gm. of bread moistened in water and sprinkled over with 2 gm. of lactose; to each of the third group, 5 gm. of bread moistened in water and sprinkled with 2 gm. of kaolin. Water was given to all.

It was thought possible that the bread had something to do with the results in those given bread and kaolin. To each of another group of 4 rats 5 gm. of boiled, ground meat mixed with 2 gm. of kaolin were given over a period of 40 days. The results are given in table 6.

Feeding Experiment on Dogs.—Three healthy dogs were used. To each of Nos. 1 and 2, weighing 15 and 18 pounds, 200 gm. of boiled, ground beef mixed

TABLE 5

THE EFFECT OF MEAT, BREAD AND LACTOSE, AND BREAD AND KAOLIN ON THE INTESTINAL FLORA

Rats	Diet	Day of Feeding	Percentage of Aciduric-Proteolytic (A–P) Ratio	Remarks
1	....	0	4 - 96	Before feeding was begun
6	....	0	1 - 99	
11	....	0	1 - 99	
2	5 gm. meat	8	2 - 98	
3	5 gm. meat	12	3 - 97	
4	5 gm. meat	16	1 - 99	
5	5 gm. meat	20	5 - 95	
7	5 gm. bread + 2 gm. lactose	8	85 - 15	
8	5 gm. bread + 2 gm. lactose	12	60 - 40	
9	5 gm. bread + 2 gm. lactose	16	99 - 1	
10	5 gm. bread + 2 gm. lactose	20	92 - 8	
12	5 gm. bread + 2 gm. kaolin	8	97 - 3	
13	5 gm. bread + 2 gm. kaolin	12	80 - 20	
14	5 gm. bread + 2 gm. kaolin	16	99 - 1	
15	5 gm. bread + 2 gm. kaolin	20	92 - 8	
1	5 gm. bread + 2 gm. kaolin	6	92 - 8	Meat group changed to bread and kaolin
3	2 gm. bread + 2 gm. kaolin	10	96 - 4	
12	5 gm. meat	6	50 - 50	Bread and kaolin group changed to meat
15	5 gm. meat	10	1 - 99	
7	5 gm. meat	6	88 - 12	Bread and lactose group changed to meat
8	5 gm. meat	10	80 - 20	
9	5 gm. meat	14	15 - 85	

TABLE 6

EFFECT OF BOILED GROUND MEAT AND KAOLIN ON INTESTINAL FLORA

Rat	Diet	Day of Feeding	Percentage of A–P Ratio
16...........................	5 gm. meat, 2 gm. koalin	10	95 - 1
17...........................	5 gm. meat, 2 gm. kaolin	16	99 - 1
18...........................	5 gm. meat, 2 gm. kaolin	30	88 - 12
19...........................	5 gm. meat, 2 gm. kaolin	34	98 - 2
16...........................	5 gm. meat, 2 gm. kaolin	35	99 - 1
17...........................	5 gm. meat, 2 gm. kaolin	36	98 - 2
18...........................	5 gm. meat, 2 gm. kaolin	37	95 - 5
19...........................	5 gm. meat, 2 gm. kaolin	38	96 - 4
16...........................	5 gm. meat, 2 gm. kaolin	39	98 - 2
17...........................	5 gm. meat, 2 gm. kaolin	40	95 - 5

with 30 gm. kaolin were given per day. No. 3, that weighed 35 pounds, received 300 gm. of meat and 60 gm. of kaolin.

One c c. from each dilution of 1 : 100, 1 : 500, 1 : 2500 and 1 : 12500 were inoculated into tubes containing about 8 c c. of fresh, whole, sterile milk. The tubes were heated to 80 C. for 20 minutes in a water bath, to kill all vegetative forms, then cooled quickly in cold running water to bring the cream to the surface, thus forming a relatively anaerobic medium for spores of B. welchii to develop in. These were incubated for 72 hours. When there was evidence of the "stormy fermentation" described by Simonds,[25] odor of butyric acid, and large gram-positive bacilli present, the culture was counted positive for B. welchii.

TABLE 7

THE EFFECT OF KAOLIN ON THE INTESTINAL FLORA OF DOGS

Day of Feeding	Percentage of Aciduric-Proteolytic Ratio			Remarks
	Dog 1	Dog 2	Dog 3	
	3 - 97	1 - 99	4 - 96	Before feeding was commenced
5	60 - 40	66 - 44	70 - 30	
8	50 - 50	70 - 30	50 - 50	
11	....	94 - 6	50 - 50	No. 1 plates spoiled
15	58*- 42	75*- 25	67 - 33	
22	80*- 20	70*- 30	86*- 14	
25	60*- 40	50 - 50	60*- 40	
27	32 - 68	57*- 43	54*- 46	
29	45*- 55	80*- 20	70*- 30	Kaolin stopped
4	50 - 50	70*- 30	50*- 50	
8	20 - 80	25 - 75	90*- 10	

* In these the larger, flat, light brown, and the fuzzy colonies made up of somewhat longer, thinner, gram-positive bacilli, predominated. In the others, the regular edged, smaller, dark brown, heaped-up colonies, just like the control colonies, were most numerous. These types will be described later.

As the flora became predominantly aciduric, spores of B. welchii diminished in number; at times they were absent in all dilutions. They were present in all dilutions before feeding was commenced.

Feeding Experiment in Men.—Three vigorous, healthy men volunteered, together with myself, to take 30 gm. of kaolin per day for one month. Three of us took 60 gm. per day for a while. All continued their usual diet. The kaolin was usually taken in about 2 ounces of water just before retiring, or in the middle of the forenoon.

C and D, while taking 2 ounces a day, had to take a cathartic once or twice, but it was not uncommon for them to have to do so ordinarily. B did not become constipated even while taking that amount. The stools were more copious than usual, and the first part passed was drier than the rest, but there was no diarrhea. Three reported a gain

[25] Monographs of the Rockefeller Institute of Med. Research, 1915, No. 5.

in appetite; two, who weighed themselves before and after the experiment, gained 5 and 3 pounds; two, who had been troubled with flatulency, reported improvement.

In one, the flora remained predominantly aciduric for 8 days after kaolin was stopped and in another for 12 days.

TABLE 8

THE EFFECT OF KAOLIN ON THE INTESTINAL FLORA OF MAN

Day of Feeding	Percentage of Aciduric-Proteolytic Ratio				Remarks
	A	B	C	D	
	2 - 98	1 - 99	1 - 99	3 - 97	Before feeding was commenced.
8	5 - 95	20 - 80	96 - 4	65*- 35	C and D took 60 gm. per day the first 8 days, B took 60 gm. per day from the 8th to 17th day
12	2 - 98	95 - 5	50 - 50	70*- 30	
16	20 - 80	98 - 2	98*- 2	68*- 32	
20	30 - 70	90*- 10	99*- 1	discontinued	
26	55 - 45	**89*- 11**	93*- 7		
30	**61*- 39**	95*- 5	**40*- 60**		
34	50 - 50	90 - 10	50*- 50		
38	10 - 90	5 - 95	60 - 40		
42	....	....	55 - 45		
46	....	....	15 - 85		

Bold faced figures = date on which kaolin was stopped

TABLE 9

THE EFFECT OF KAOLIN ON THE DEVELOPMENT OF B. WELCHII SPORES IN THE INTESTINE OF MAN

Day of Feeding	B. welchii Spores in 1 c c. of Serial Dilutions Made from Suspensions of the Stools of															
	A				B				C				D			
	1: 100	1: 500	1: 2500	1: 12500	1: 100	1: 500	1: 2500	1: 12500	1: 100	1: 500	1: 2500	1: 12500	1: 100	1: 500	1: 2500	1: 12500
Before feeding	+	+	+	0	+	+	+	+	+	0	+	+	+	+	+	+
8	+	+	0	0	0	+	0	0	0	0	0	0	0	0	0	0
12	0	0	0	0	0	0	0	0	0	0	0	0	0	0	0	0
16	+	0	0	0	0	0	0	0	0	0	0	0	+	0	0	0
20	0	0	0	0	0	0	0	0	0	0	0	0	discontinued			
26	0	0	0	0	**0**	**0**	**0**	**0**	0	0	0	0				
30	**0**	**0**	**0**	**0**	0	0	0	0	**0**	**0**	**0**	**0**				
34	0	0	0	0	+	0	0	0	0	0	0	0				
38	0	+	0	0	0	0	0	0	0	0	0	0				
42	..	..	..	..	0	0	0	0	0	0	0	0				

+ = culture positive for B. welchii spores.
0 = culture negative for B. welchii spores.
Bold faced figures = kaolin stoped on that date.

Rettger and Cheplin,[26] found that they could change the flora in rats and in man by feeding lactose or dextrin. This has been repeated by Cannon and McNease,[27] and others. Barker,[28] procured favorable results in typhoid patients by feeding them lactose and milk, and

[26] Intestinal Flora, 1920.

[27] Jour. Infect. Dis., 1921, 29, p. 369.

[28] Jour. Am. Med. Assn., 1914, 63, p. 929.

Torrey,[29] observed that feeding a high carbohydrate diet (lactose) to such patients tended to reduce the number of putrefactive bacteria and to increase the aciduric.

In three of the men fed kaolin in this experiment, the flora became predominantly aciduric in 8 to 10 days, in the fourth more slowly. Much smaller amounts of it was taken than is necessary with lactose. It does not cause the patient so much discomfort, nor upset the digestion as lactose frequently does. It also has a protective action on the intestinal mucosa that is of value when this is irritated and damaged by bacteria or their products.

The disappearance of flatulency, when one takes kaolin over a long period of time, is not strange, since the proteolytic bacteria are gradually replaced by aciduric organisms. The fact that the gas bacillus also almost disappears may be a potent factor in the same direction.

Hines,[30] and others have observed that B. welchii spores disappear from the stool when it becomes aciduric.

Klein,[31] Tissier,[32] and Kendall [33] hold that B. welchii are frequently the cause of diarrhea. Shamberg,[34] believes that it is an important factor in poisoning from eating sausages.

Characteristics of Typical Colonies, and Organisms Comprising Them Which Develop from an Aciduric Stool on Acid Liver Agar.— When the flora is beginning to change to one chiefly aciduric, especially in man, the type of B. acidophilus colony found on the liver-agar medium is round, dark brown to light brown (amber) at the edges, coarsely granular (fig. 2), very much like the control colony on the other half of the plate (fig. 1).

Stained by Gram's method, the organism is a small gram-positive bacillus, tapering at the ends, frequently arranged end to end much like a lanceolated diplococcus but having no capsule. Some longer bacilli are also seen. Two or three lying parallel is characteristic (fig. 4). They look very much like those from the control colonies (fig. 3).

When the flora has remained aciduric for some days, another type of colony appears in increasing numbers; one that is larger than the former, flatter, a lighter brown, not so round and with less regular

[29] Jour. Infect. Dis., 1915, 16, p. 72.
[30] Jour. Infect. Dis., 1923, 32, p. 280.
[31] Report of Med. Officer to Loc. Govt., 1896, Vol. 25 supplement, p. 173.
[32] Ann. de l'Inst. Pasteur, 1905, 19, p. 273.
[33] Jour. Med. Res., 1911, 25, p. 117.
[34] Ztschr. f. Hyg. u. Infektionskrankh., 1902, 41, p. 183.

edges (fig. 5, b). These are also composed of gram-positive bacilli much like the control, but a trifle thinner (fig. 6). A third type of colony is also found, especially in specimens from dogs, which is fuzzy, dark brown at the center, lighter toward the edges; at times the whole colony is quite light. It has numerous strandlike outgrowths at the edges making it appear much like a bunch of cotton (fig. 5, c). It is composed of gram-positive bacilli which in the original colonies (direct from the stool) are thinner and longer than the first two described; they grow in long threads lying parallel. This arrangement disappears soon when transferred to other mediums. Fewer long forms, too, are then found (fig. 7).

As the flora begins to revert back to the proteolytic type, the B and C types of colonies disappear first, leaving sometimes almost a pure culture of type A colony in the liver agar medium. This is most pronounced in stools from man.

The question arises: Do these different-looking colonies represent different types of a group of aciduric bacilli whose biologic reaction in various culture mediums are much alike, or are they different manifestations of a pleomorphic organism which appears in different shapes, depending on whether its environment is favorable or not?

It was noticed that the larger, light brown colonies, as well as the fuzzy ones, lost much of their original appearance after having been transferred into dextrose broth, incubated for 24 hours, and again seeded on acid liver agar. This process was therefore repeated 5 times. It was then found that type *B* colony was producing a large number of colnies similar to type *A* and the control colonies (fig. 8). Likewise type *C* colony had lost its fuzziness, and was now producing colonies which for the most part resembled the large light brown colony (type *B*); a few round, dark brown colonies were also seen, much like the control colonies (fig. 9). In stained preparations, the bacilli of both types were now more like the control than before.

Subcultures of the three types of colonies and of the control were carried through dextrose broth, litmus milk, gelatine, blood agar and the sugars. In dextrose broth, after 24 hours' incubation, the growth from types *B* and *C* were more scanty than that from type *A* and the control. After making subcultures a few times, it became more abundant. In all types the broth tubes remained quite clear, except near the bottom where they were a trifle cloudy, and the bacteria seemed to adhere to the sides of the tubes. On the bottom of all there was a white sediment of bacteria. All turned litmus milk acid. After from

3 to 4 days, a white coagulum began to form at the bottom of the tubes, extending gradually upward, without separation of serum. This was repeated a number of times. The coagulum did not commence forming at the same time in all tubes, but it eventually appeared. The growth of all types in gelatine was uncertain. After 5 days' incubation an almost imperceptible growth of each was obtained on blood agar; there was no hemolysis and no green discoloration of the medium. After 48 hours' incubation, all types had fermented dextrose, maltose and saccharose. After 72 hours, lactose and mannite would usually be slightly acid. Salicin, dulcite and inulin were never fermented. No gas appeared in any of the tubes.

Streptococcus fecalis, with which the bacillus from type *A* colony might be confused, makes dextrose broth uniformly cloudy; it grows well on blood agar; it ferments salicin, and in dextrose broth it develops long chains. Its colonies are finely granular and of a dirty grayish brown at the center to gray at the edges, in contrast to the amber brown edges of colonies of this bacillus growing on acid liver agar.

There is a possibility that the 3 types of colonies, *A, B,* and *C,* represent different forms of growth of the same organism. When the pabulum in the intestine begins to become favorable for the growth of aciduric organisms, the B. acidophilus forms colonies such as type *A,* just like those produced by it when it has grown on artificial mediums for a long time. When the environment becomes more favorable for its development, it produces colonies of the *B* and *C* type as well.

The other possibility is that these three types of colonies represent different organisms belonging to the same group, which culturally behave very much alike. If this is so, better results should be obtained when B. acidophilus is fed to patients if a mixed culture is used.

CLINICAL OBSERVATIONS

Asiatic Cholera.—A study of 100 consecutive cases was made during the epidemic referred to, and reported to the Conference of the China Medical Missionary Association, Peking, in February, 1920 (Braafladt [35]).

Microscopic preparations stained with one tenth strength carbol fuchsin were made from small, white flakes taken from the thin, watery stools of a large number of cases. These contained almost a pure culture of gram-negative bacilli. Some were slightly bent,

[35] China Med. Jour., 1920, 34, p. 243.

tapering at the end much like cholera vibrio. Judging from the smears, it was not possible to be sure that the organisms were not colon bacilli, although they were very small. When grown on artificial mediums, they could not be thus mistaken. For lack of time, not many strains were studied. One was observed over a long period of time. In the original smear this strain did not seem different from the others. The patient from whom it was taken recovered.

One c c. of a 24-hour broth culture of this strain caused the death of a guinea-pig in 24 hours, injected intraperitoneally. The vibrio was recovered in pure culture from the serous peritoneal fluid at necropsy. A slant agar culture, one week old, contained numerous involution forms; it liquefied gelatine; growth was much augmented by incubating for 24 hours in salt peptone solution; it agglutinated very well with serum from convalescing patients.

There is probably no other disease amenable to treatment the death rate of which can be reduced so markedly by beginning treatment early as cholera. This seems especially true when kaolin is used. Of the 17 deaths in this series, only 1 occurred among the 42 patients that entered on the first day of illness; 4 of the 24 that entered on the second day died, and 12 of the 34 that entered on the third day or later.

It seems that the copious watery evacuations and vomiting are due primarily to the local irritative action on the intestinal mucosa of the toxins liberated by the rapidly multiplying bacteria. Those symptoms which come on after the diarrhea and vomiting have persisted for some time, such as cramps, hoarseness, failing vision and deafness—the syndrome of collapse—may be considered as secondary and, in part at least, due to the effect of the toxins entering the blood stream. If this interpretation is correct, it is not difficult to understand why kaolin taken in large quantities early in the disease checks it so effectually.

To facilitate study, the patients were placed in two groups according to the severity of the symptoms at the time of admission. Those severely ill were placed in group A, those moderately ill in group B; there were 67 in the first group and 33 in the second. Table 10 shows the relative frequency of the symptoms observed in this series, and the number of patients that died in each group.

As soon as the patient was admitted the pulse rate, respiratory rate, and the axillary and rectal temperatures were recorded. The low axillary temperature and elevated rectal temperature recorded by

Manson,[36] was not commonly observed by us. The greatest difference recorded was 5 F. If we had taken the temperatures of the fatal cases shortly before death, the difference would undoubtedly have been greater.

White cell counts were taken in only 5 cases. All had a leukocytosis. The increase in number of white blood cells is undoubtedly a relative one, owing to the marked anhydremia. MacCallum [37] states that the red cells are far above 5,000,000 per c. mm. The increase in specific gravity of the blood is most likely due to the same cause. The frequency of oliguria and the development of toxic symptoms induced us to try the phenolsulphonephthalein renal function test in a few patients, one of whom had developed toxic symptoms. All the 10 patients tested had sustained injuries of the kidneys. The tardy appearance

TABLE 10

GROUPING OF PATIENTS BASED ON SYMPTOMS PRESENT ON ADMISSION TO THE HOSPITAL

	Of the Total 100 Cases	Group A (67)		Group B (33)	
		Number	Percentage	Number	Percentage
Copious watery stools	100	67	100	33	100
Vomiting	100	67	100	33	100
Cramps	66	58	86	8	24
Hoarseness	54	48	72	6	18
Deafness	19	18	27	1	3
Failing vision	6	6	9	0	0
Died	17	15	22	2	6

of the drug in the urine, and the small amount excreted during the first hour as compared with the large amount excreted during the second hour indicated that the renal cells had not lost their power of excreting, but that the process was slowed up due to the swelling of the cells and the lowered blood pressure.

Treatment.—The wards on the ground floor were given over to cholera patients; ordinary patients were cared for on the second and third floors. Cheap Chinese beds covered with straw matting and hospital bedding consisting of a sheet and one or two blankets were used. The straw mats were usually burned when the patient left the hospital; the bedding was soaked in 5% phenol for some hours and dried in the sun before being given to the next patient. The floors were mopped with antiseptics once or more a day. The food for the cholera patients came from the general kitchen, but all dishes were boiled before returning. Almost all the physicians, interns, nurses

[36] Tropical Diseases, Ed. 5, p. 462.

[37] Text Book of Pathology, 1918, p. 449.

and coolies working in the cholera wards were vaccinated against cholera. None of these contracted the disease, nor did a single case develop among the ordinary patients on the floors above.

On admission the patients received 1 c c. of brandy and ether, half and half, subcutaneously; if restless, an eighth or a sixth of a grain of morphine. If the radial pulse was very weak or could no longer be felt and there was danger the patient would die in a short time, he was given hypertonic salt solution intravenously at once. It was introduced by gravitation at an average rate of 1 liter per half hour. The formula used was that recommended by Rogers: sodium chloride 120 grains, potassium chloride 6 grains, calcium chloride 4 grains, to one pint of water; then sterilized. From 1 to 3 liters were introduced at a time. Frequently after some hours a second injection was necessary, and sometimes a third.

In the beginning all patients were given salt solution. Some, however, who were not in severe collapse became very uncomfortable after the injection.

Having read an abstract of an article written by Kuhne,[38] wherein he reports that he had given up all other forms of treatment, including hypertonic salt solution, for kaolin, reducing his mortality from 60 to 3% among soldiers suffering with cholera during the Balkan war in 1910, we decided to try it for those moderately ill. Since it proved satisfactory, we later used it also for those severely ill. Table 11 shows that 15 in Group A (severely ill) received this treatment, as compared with 20 in group B (moderately ill). It was given by mouth in a heavy suspension, about as thick as a thin gruel: 800 gm. stirred up in 1,000 c c. of water. The vomiting ceased more quickly when a thick suspension was used than when a thin one was used. If the vomiting was severe, 3 ounces of the suspension were given every half hour. After from 6 to 8 hours, the vomiting abated and the diarrhea decreased. It was then given only once every hour, and finally every 2 hours. As a rule, it was not necessary to give kaolin over a period of more than 12 to 15 hours, and frequently 6 to 7 hours sufficed. No food was given during the time kaolin was being administered.

Only one of the 35 patients who received kaolin died; this patient was unconscious at the time of admission, and had complete suppression of the urine, so that it is a quesion whether any form of treatment would have helped her.

[38] Rev. Suisse Romande, 1918, 38, p. 555.

The average number of days spent in the hospital by each patient, the total number of patients receiving salt solution treatment only, salt solution and kaolin, or kaolin only, as well as the number that died in each of these groups are given in table 11.

In the autumn of 1920, three middle-aged men suffering with cholera were admitted to the hospital. All were in collapse when admited, the radial pulse could no longer be felt at the wrist in two of them, and it was very weak in the third. Two of them were given kaolin, one hypertonic salt solution. The two given kaolin recovered and the third, who received salt solution, died.

Wylie [39] reported good results with kaolin during the 1919 epidemic at Paotingfu, but gives no details. Walker [40] used it at Foochow and

TABLE 11

THE RELATION OF THE VARIOUS FORMS OF TREATMENT TO THE LENGTH OF STAY IN THE HOSPITAL AND TO THE DEATH RATE

Treatment Received	Of the Total 100 Patients	Average Number of Days in Hospital	Number that Died
Salt solution only	41	8	9
Salt solution plus kaolin	24	6	7
Kaolin only	35	4	1

TABLE 12

AVERAGE AMOUNT OF HYPERTONIC SALT SOLUTION, KAOLIN, OR BOTH GIVEN TO PATIENTS

	Hypertonic Salt Solution, C c.	Salt Solution, and Kaolin, C c.	Salt Solution, and Kaolin, Gm.	Koalin, Gm.
To those that recovered	4,130	4.300	800	1,078
To those that died	5,059	3,570	913	2,150 (1 case)

Hinghua the same summer, in 75 cases at the latter place, without any deaths. There is a possibility that some of these were not genuine cholera cases, as the diagnosis was based only on clinical manifestations. Some of the patients were in extreme collapse when treatment was begun. Crawford [41] used kaolin during the epidemic of 1921 at Tzeluitsing, and had a mortality of 20%. He says: "Undoubtedly kaolin is of great value, but it is an absolute failure if not taken EARLY in the disease." The explanation of his rather high death rate, as well as of his conclusion, probably lies in the fact which he records earlier in his communication, that he telegraphed for kaolin but

[39] China Med. Jour., 1920, 34, p. 252.
[40] Proc. Royal Med. Soc., 1921, 14, p. 23.
[41] China Med. Jour., 1921, 35, p. 417.

did not receive it until after the epidemic was over. In the meantime, he secured some earth locally from the Luchow porcelain works, and used it on the cases he reports. The uncertainty of the adsorptive power of impure and unstandardized clays may create impressions that are erroneous. It is a question just how much value to place on results obtained with them.

When my series of cases was reported at the Conference in Peking, February, 1920, I made the following comment:

A great deal of work on the chemistry of colloids has been done during the last few years, but the field is as yet largely unexplored, It has been fairly well established that there is an adsorptive interaction between colloids and crystalloids, and according to Young,[42] it has been found that a similar interaction takes place between two opposite electrically charged colloids when in proper concentration.

It is highly probable that when kaolin is taken in large quantities by mouth by a patient suffering with cholera, it quickly combines with the toxins liberated in the intestine rendering them harmless. It is also probable that it makes a rather unfavorable medium for the bacteria to multiply in. Those of our patients who received kaolin only made a much quicker recovery than the others. None of them developed the distressing and dangerous toxic symptoms which many of the others did.

In 1921, while at home on furlough in England, Dr. Walker showed experimentally that, so far as the effect of kaolin on cholera vibrio and its toxins is concerned, this interpretation, based largely on clinical evidence, was essentially correct. Some of his results are:

(1) In a rabbit fed 20 c c. of a 50% kaolin suspension, and a similar amount given per rectum, when chloroformed 42 hours later, traces of kaolin were found adhering to the wall of the small intestine high up, and this increased in amount to the cecum, while the colon was filled with kaolin and feces.

(2) Filtrates from alkaline peptone cultures—the organism being passed through 3 to 5 guinea-pigs first to increase its virulence—as well as filtrates from the killed, ground-up and washed vibrios, killed rabbits when injected intravenously in 2 c c. doses. These toxic filtrates lost their toxicity when shaken up with kaolin.

(3) Growths on subculture were obtained in all cases in which different amounts of kaolin had been added to broth cultures of the vibrios, showing that it had no bactericidal effect.

He concludes that the effect of kaolin on the vibrio in the intestine is a purely mechanical one, and on the toxin liberated by them, one of adsorption.

Dysentery.—CASE 1.—A child, 5 years old, had been suffering for 7 days from tenesmus and frequent loose bowel movements which contained mucus and

[42] Zinsser: Infection and Resistance, 1919, p. 556.

blood. He was anemic, weak, fretful, and did not care for food. No amebas were found, and 3 injections of emetine had no effect. Shiga's dysentery bacillus, common in north China, did not grow. Clinically, the condition was like bacillary dysentery and it was treated as such, but with poor results. On the 11th day, the child was still having 20 to 30 stools in 24 hours. A suspension of 3 ounces of kaolin in water and simple syrup was given in 5 doses, one each hour. The following day he had 3 bowel movements, which were formed. He was kept on a light diet for some days, and recovery was complete.

CASE 2.—A child, 14 months old, developed small, loose, greenish bowel movements about every half hour. They contained blood and mucus. The temperature ranged from 100 F. to 104 F. He was fretful and losing strength rapidly. No amebas were found, but a growth of Shiga's dysentery bacillus was obtained. The usual forms of treatment were of no avail. On the 7th day, he was given 2 ounces of kaolin in water and syrup. The following day, he had 3 bowel movements and on the next, 2; these were formed. He had no more trouble.

CASE 3.—There was mucus in the stools of a man who had repeated attacks of "dyspepsia" every summer for a number of years. Several examinations failed to reveal amebas or dysentery bacilli. He had 5 to 8 bowel movements per day, and a dull pain in the lower part of the abdomen. He was not given any food for 24 hours, and treated with bismuth and salol. Only milk was given the second day. On the third day he was in pain as before, and the diarrhea continued. He was then given 300 gm. of kaolin in water, divided into 5 hourly doses. The pain disappeared the next day and the stools became formed. On the fourth day after the kaolin had been taken, the pain and diarrhea reappeared. The stool was again examined, and a few amebas were found. After a thorough course of oil of chenopodium and emetine the condition cleared up.

In the first two cases of bacillary dysentery, the beneficial action of kaolin can be accounted for by the adsorptive effect it has on the toxin liberated by this organism, as well as by its protection of the inflamed mucosa. In the case of chronic amebic dysentery, we see that its effect was only temporary, owing largely to its protective action on the mucosa.

Chronic Ulcerative Colitis.—An elderly man who had had several attacks of amebic dysentery for which he had been treated, complained of recurring dull pain in the lower epigastrium and inability to eat anything but light food. The stools contained mucus, slight traces of blood, and pus. Proctoscopic examination revealed small shallow ulcers on an inflamed and thickened mucosa. No amebas or cysts were found. He was given one ounce of kaolin in water per day for a month. The pain disappeared after the second or third day, the bowel movements were reduced to 2 or 3 per day. The pus, blood, and most of the mucus disappeared from the stools. He was able to eat a more varied diet than before. As he was lost from observation, it is not known whether improvement was permanent.

Here, too, the protective action of the kaolin on the inflamed and ulcerated mucosa is probably its most important action, but the tendency it has to change the intestinal flora from a proteolytic to an aciduric type when taken over a long period of time may also have a beneficial effect in these cases. It may also adsorb some of the toxic products resulting from the extensive putrefaction which takes place in a bowel that is ulcerated. (This will be discussed later.)

Acute and Chronic Enteritis.—Through the permission of Dr. W. J. Quigly, attending physician at Cook County Hospital, and with the co-operation of Dr. L. E. Hines, three patients with pulmonary tuberculosis, one with acute enteritis and two with chronic enteritis, were treated with kaolin over a period ranging from 1 to 6 weeks. In all, the pain disappeared after a few days, so did most of the mucus, and the number of bowel movements were reduced, while the appetite increased. One gained 5 pounds in 2 weeks, and one 21 pounds in 6 weeks. In the last named, the flora became predominantly aciduric. Gas bacillus spores, too, diminished in number in the stools.

Hess [43] used kaolin in infant diarrhea without much success. He does not state the amount given. He says only that it was given by the "teaspoon." He probably did not give enough to obtain results.

DISCUSSION

That kaolin taken over a long time tends to change the intestinal flora to an aciduric type indicates that such a change does not depend wholly on the presence in the intestine of utilizable carbohydrate (lactose or dextrine). Meat, kaolin, and water fed to rats and dogs over a period of from 10 to 30 days produces a similar effect. Just how kaolin produces this effect is difficult to say; it may be by absorbing the toxic products of proteolysis, thus making the pabulum in the intestine unfavorable for the development of proteolytic bacteria.

Dragstedt [44] found that thyroparathyroidectomized dogs can be kept alive for at least a year by feeding large amounts of lactose, thus changing the intestinal flora and ridding the intestine of the toxic products of proteolysis. He believes that the tetany, or depression, from which those dogs that have not been fed lactose die in a few days is due to the absorption of these products.

[43] Jour. Am. Med. Assn., 1916, 66, p. 106.
[44] Am. Jour. Physiol., 1923, 64, p. 424.

He consented to try kaolin instead of lactose on some of the dogs, and he has given me permission to state that in preliminary experiments the results are that kaolin in 100 gm. doses per day prevents the onset of tetany in much the same manner as does lactose.

This points to an adsorption of toxic products of proteolysis by kaolin just as it adsorbs the toxins and toxic products of pathogenic bacteria multiplying in the intestine. Or, it may be due largely to the fact that it changes the type of bacteria in the intestine, and that the toxic effect of the products of proteolysis is for that reason diminished —the proteolytic bacteria being practically eliminated.

The exact nature of the reaction that takes place between kaolin and toxins, or toxic products, is not fully understood, but it is probably an electrical one. Bayliss,[45] Macleod [46] and others hold that kaolin carries an electronegative charge. This may change to a positive charge when in an acid suspension.

The prompt neutralizing effect that kaolin has on toxins and toxic products of pathogenic intestinal organisms when these are treated with it, centrifuged, and the supernatant fluid injected into animals, largely explains the favorable results obtained with it in the patients suffering with Asiatic cholera, bacillary dysentery, and acute enteritis reported in this paper. It would also seem to indicate that it might be beneficial in typhoid, meat poisoning due to the enteriditis-parathyphoid group, and in botulism, especially if given early in the disease.

SUMMARY AND CONCLUSIONS

Kaolin does not act as an antiseptic, but it "carries down with it" large numbers of bacteria in fluid mediums when mixed with them and kept in motion for 2 to 3 hours. Whether this is a purely mechanical action, or whether kaolin has some specific attraction for bacteria, is not clear. When not kept in motion it does not reduce the number of bacteria to any extent.

It combines with toxins and toxic products of Vib. cholerae, B. dysenteriae (Shiga), B. enteritidis, B. diphtheriae, B. botulinus, B. typhosus, B. paratyphosus B., and, perhaps, of putrefactive and proteolytic bacteria, rendering them harmless.

When taken by mouth over a period of from 10 to 30 days in sufficient quantities (1 to 2 ounces per day for a man), it changes the

[45] Quoted by Walker, Proc. Royal med. Soc., 1921, 14, p. 23.
[46] Physiol. and Biochem. in Modern Medicine, 1918, p. 55.

intestinal flora of rats, dogs and men from a predominantly proteolytic type to an aciduric one.

It practically eliminates B. welchii from the stool; it does not upset digestion.

It has been used with success in Asiatic cholera, bacillary dysentery, chronic ulcerative colitis and acute enteritis.

Plate 1

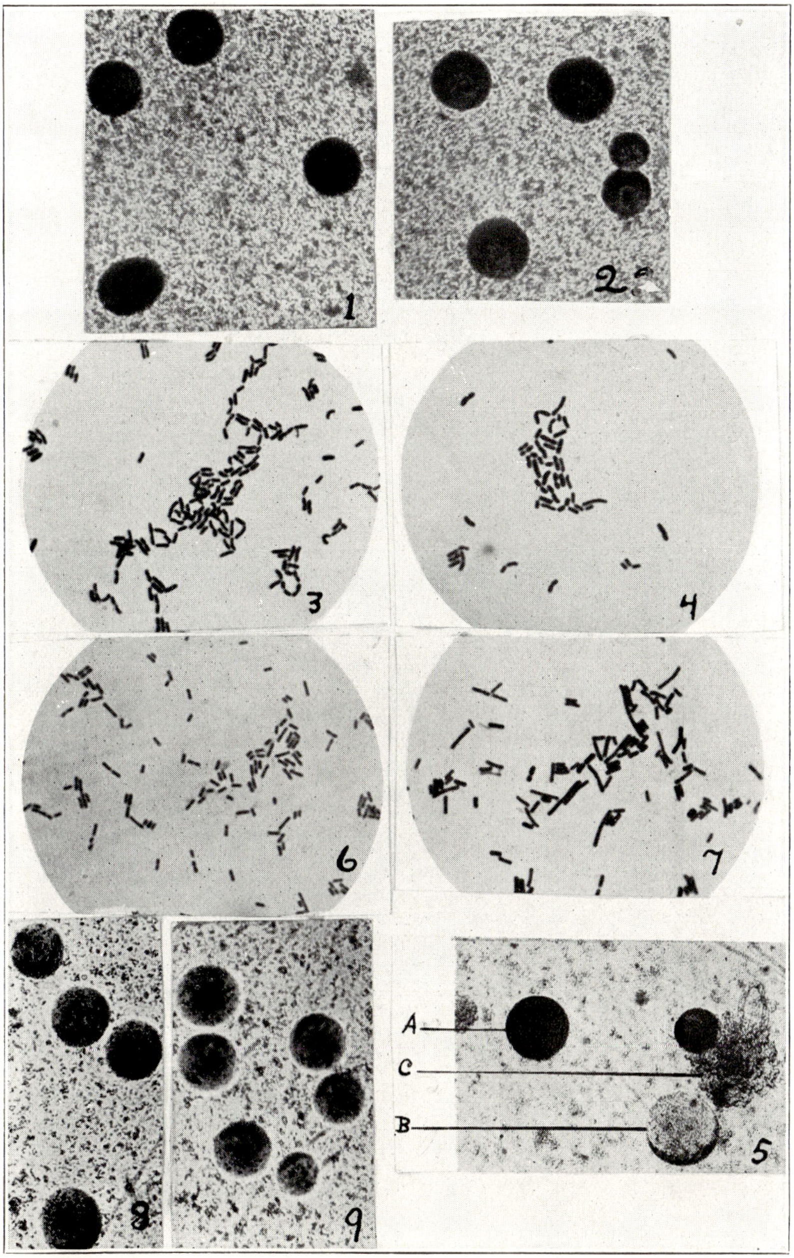

Fig. 1.—Five day old colonies of B. acidophilus (control) growing on 5% acid liver agar. X 41.

Fig. 2.—Five day old colonies of gram-positive bacilli growing on the other half of same plate as that in Fig. 1. From C's stool on 10th day of feeding. X 41.

Fig. 3.—B. acidophilus from control colonies in Fig. 1. X 1200.

Fig. 4.—Gram-positive bacillus from colonies in Fig. 2. X 1200.

Fig. 5.—Five day old colonies of gram-positive bacilli on 5% acid liver agar. From aciduric stool of dog fed on kaolin. *A* indicates a dark brown, round colony, just like the control colonies; *B*, a large, flat, light brown colony; *C*, a fuzzy colony. X 41.

Fig. 6.—Gram-positive bacillus from B colonies in Fig. 5. X 1200.

Fig. 7.—Gram-positive bacillus from C colonies in Fig. 5. X 1200.

Fig. 8.—Five day old colonies of type B (large, flat, light brown) colony in pure culture after making subcultures five times from dextrose broth into acid liver agar.

Fig. 9.—Five day old pure culture of fuzzy colony after making subcultures five times from dextrose broth into acid liver gar.

II. CHEMOTHERAPY OF EXPERIMENTAL TYPHOID CARRIER CONDITION

T. D. Beckwith

From the Department of Bacteriology and Experimental Pathology, University of California, Berkeley

Numerous attempts both clinical and experimental have been made to sterilize the focus of infection in the typhoid carrier. Results have not been satisfactory (Beckwith [1] gives resumé). The possibility of application of chemotherapy to the treatment of infections is limited by a variety of factors which include not only the comparative susceptibility of host and infecting agent to the therapeutic agent, and the period during which the material added to the circulation remains active as a germicide (Jacobs,[2] Gay and Morrison [3]), but also the site of the infection. It is evident that it is much easier to treat a surface lesion as a wound or to combat a septicemia than it is to reach effectively a deeper site, such as the gallbladder wall or the bile in a chronic carrier of B. typhosus or of V. cholerae. In the latter instance, not only are the tissues difficult of access under normal conditions but in the pathologic state these difficulties are increased greatly. Circulation is impeded by emboli and thrombi, tissues are much thickened as a result of the inflammatory process, epithelium is destroyed (Bindseil,[4] Goebel,[5] Messerschmidt,[6] Meyer, Neilson and Feusier,[7] Beckwith [8]). The fact that one may find substances secreted through the liver in the bile with germicidal coefficient unimpaired does not guarantee their effectiveness in a condition of infection. The vast amount of research carried out on hepatic function testing has proved conclusively that excretion in the pathologic liver and gallbladder is vastly different both in volume and in mechanism from that in the normal. The problem therefore is a most complicated one. The author has shown in a previous article [1] that a dyestuff of the triphenylmethane series, new fast green 3 B, has a certain value for clearing up rabbits experi-

Received for publication, July 15, 1923.

* Aided by grant from University Board of Research.

[1] Jour. Infect. Dis., 1921, 29, p. 495.
[2] Jour. Exper. Med., 1916, 23, p. 563.
[3] Jour. Infect. Dis., 1921, 28, p. 1.
[4] Ztschr. f. Hyg. u. Infektionskrankh., 1913, 74, p. 369.
[5] Ibid., 1914, 78, p. 555.
[6] Ibid., 1913, 75, p. 411.
[7] Jour. Infect. Dis., 1921, 38, p. 70.
[8] Ibid., 1922, 31, p. 468.

mentally infected with B. typhosus. On the other hand, it was demonstrated that by means of such injections of the dyestuff emboli may be produced resulting in sudden death of the animal. Reasons for this change from sol to gel are indicated in an article by Gay and Beckwith.[9] This dye stuff therefore is unsafe for use.

Further attempts to sterilize gallbladders of experimental animals were then made and are described in the following discussion.

ARSPHENAMIN AND NEO-ARSPHENAMIN

Although arsphenamin and neo-arsphenamin are efficacious in the treatment of spirochetal and of certain protozoan diseases, attempts to adopt them for infections of bacterial origin have not been so successful. Allison,[10] using arsphenamin in experimentally produced streptococcic septicemia, reports favorable results with this compound in watery solution. Schöbl[11] included it in an extensive series of compounds while making a survey in an attempt to find some substance of value for the purpose of sterilizing experimentally produced carriers of cholera, and states that it is worthless. A number of workers have endeavored to treat typhoid carriers with it. From the experimental side, Uhlenhuth and Messerschmidt,[12] Hailer and Wolf[13] and Haibe[14] have reported unfavorable results with infections of B. typhosus, while Leitner[15] using neo-arsphenamin on human carriers of B. paratyphosus B. states that out of 12 cases, 3 cleared after one injection, 7 after two treatments, while 2 were not affected. Of this series of cases, 10 were feces carriers, while 2 showed the organisms both in the feces and urine. Incidentally also it should be noted that Tsuzuki and Ishida[16] find arsenic acid of value in the treatment of human carriers.

It thus appears that while the preponderant weight of opinion is against these compounds for use with carriers of B. typhosus, nevertheless the number of observers is not large, and neither is there entire harmony if we are to consider paratyphoid as a portion of the entity. Therefore it was decided to experiment both with arsphenamin and with neo-arsphenamin on prepared rabbit carriers. Experiments were carried out as follows:

Arsphenamin, Exper. 1.—A 0.6 gm. ampule of arsphenamin (Metz) was placed on 30 c c. of freshly redistilled water, and to this was added sufficient normal NaOH to cause the precipitate to go into solution. Hydrogen-ion concentration of this injection fluid was 8.2. The dosage used in the animals was at the rate of 0.02 gm. per kilo. Rabbit 876, of 3,500 gm. weight, received intravenously 3 injections of the dosage noted above, the first interval being 4 days and the second 3 days. Forty-eight hours after the third treatment, the animal was killed by chloroform. Necropsy revealed a somewhat enlarged gallbladder containing 2 c c. of very light, nearly colorless bile. Inoculation of this bile into beef bouillon, followed by culture and agglutination with anti-typhoid serum, proved the presence of B. typhosus.

[9] Am. Jour. Hyg., 1922, 2, p. 467.
[10] Jour. Med. Research, 1918, 38, p. 55.
[11] Philippine Jour. Sc., Sec. B., 1917, 12, p. 215
[12] Deutsch. med. Wchnscher., 1912, 38, p. 2397; 1920, 46, p. 1293.
[13] Arb. a. d. k. Gsndhtsamte, 1915, 48, p. 80.
[14] Acad. roy. de méd. de Belg., 1921, 22, p. 1.
[15] Wien. klin. Wchnschr., 1918, 31, p. 731.
[16] Deutsch. med. Wchnschr., 1910, 36, p. 1605.

Exper. 2.—Rabbit 898, weighing 3,800 gm., received into the ear vein a like series of injection of arsphenamin of the same dosages and at the same intervals. Four days following the last treatment the animal was killed by chloroform. Necropsy revealed a much enlarged gallbladder containing 2.5 c c. of light and almost colorless bile, together with a quantity of mucoid material. By broth culture followed by agglutination with antityphoid serum, this bile was proved to contain B. typhosus.

Neo-Arsphenamin, Exper. 3.—Rabbit 307, weighing 2,200 gm., received intravenously a watery solution of neo-arsphenamin at the rate of 0.04 gm. per kilo. This solution was made up in freshly redistilled water each time. The salt was the Metz brand. Three injections were made at intervals of 9 and 10 days, respectively. At the time of necropsy, 3 days following the final treatment, the gallbladder was found to have very much thickened walls and to contain 0.75 c c. of thick, nearly milk white bile. B. typhosus was proved to be present in this bile by culture followed by agglutination with antityphoid serum. It is thus evident that neither arsphenamin nor neo-arsphenamin is of value for the purpose of ridding experimental rabbit gallbladder carriers of B. typhosus of the infecting agent.

IODINE

Sollman[17] finds that iodine administered intravenously is bound at once through the protein rather than by the alkali. The resulting combination is firm, and liberation of the iodin does not take place readily at the hydrogen-ion concentration of the body. Moreover, only approximately 1% of such iodine is excreted through the bile. Magee[18] studied the diffusability of a large series of antiseptics by placing the compound to be tested in a U tube in contact with 10% egg white. Iodine did not spread through such a system within a 7 day period. The results of these two investigators do not indicate strong probabilities that iodine may be found to be efficient in treatment of the typhoid carrier, as it is bound quickly and diffuses slowly.

Nevertheless, the possibility of use of iodine both by mouth and by direct injection has been given much attention during the past decade since Kraus called attention to its application in Bulgaria as an intestinal antiseptic. Löwy,[19] Bourdreau,[20] and Kalberlah[21] have reported favorable results clinically with human carriers of typhoid and the first included certain experimental pathologic observations which likewise appeared to lend proof of favorable action. Tsuzuki and Ishida[16] find potassium iodide of value for the treatment of the typhoid carrier state. None of these authors used intravenous injection. For cholera, Löwy[22] and Bourdreau[23] found tincture of iodine of value if taken by mouth, and Strisower[24] has a similar report for iodide of potassium. Tincture of iodine through the mouth has drawn favorable comment from Baillie,[25] Doufour,[26] Bourdeau,[20] St. Aubyn-Farrer,[27] Bird,[28] Bhattacharjee,[29]

17 Jour. Pharm. & Exper. Med., 1916-17, 9, p. 269.
18 Edin. Med. Jour., 1917, 18, p. 86.
19 Med. klin., 1915, 11, p. 729.
20 Jour. de méd. de Bourdeaux, 1916, 87, p. 39.
21 Med. klin., 1915, p. 581.
22 Wien. klin. Wchnschr., 1914, 27, p. 467.
23 Jour. de méd. de Bourdeaux, 1920, 91, p. 495.
24 Wien. klin. Wchnschr., 1913, 26, p. 2078.
25 Lancet, 1919, 1, p. 423.
26 Bull. et mém. la Soc. méd. d. hôp. de Paris, 1920, 44, p. 693.
27 Lancet, 1920, 198, p. 679.
28 Ibid., 1920, 198, p. 546.
29 Ind. Med. Gaz., 1921, 56, p. 49.

Jansen and Maher[30] and Nobécourt[31] for a great variety of infections, including bronchopneumonia, tuberculosis, rheumatism, malaria, puerperal infection, etc. The work of certain of these will be found summarized editorially in the Presse médical.[32] On the other hand, Hailer and Rimpau,[33] using iodiform and methyl iodide intrarectally on rabbits experimentally infected with B. typhosus, were unable to obtain a favorable outcome. It thus appears that there has not been complete accord between theory and practice.

It was decided to include tincture of iodine in this series on account of the clinical observations previously noted and also because it was desired to note the possible effects of the intravenous injection of a preparation ordinarily used for external application only. Following was the procedure:

Exper. 4.—Rabbit 368, a normal male, weighing approximately 3,000 gm., was given intravenously 0.3 c c. of tincture of iodine, diluted to 1.5 c c. with sterile distilled water. Injection was intravenous into the posterior vein of the ear. There were no effects noticeable other than a comparatively small amount of inflammation 24 hours afterward at the point of injection.

Exper. 5.—Two rabbits previously subjected to laparotomy with direct injection of B. typhosus into the gall-bladder were treated with tincture of iodine as follows: Feb. 17, 0.4 c c.; Feb. 20, 0.5 c c.; Feb. 23, 0.5 c c.; Feb. 25, 0.5 c c.; Feb. 28, 0.75 c c. All these dosages were diluted to at least 2 c c. with distilled water. The rabbits were killed on March 1 by exsanguination. No effects due to the intravenous application of the iodine other than inflammation at the point of injection were to be noted. Histologic sections were not prepared. The bile from each of these animals developed B. typhosus as proved by culture and agglutination. It thus appears that tincture of iodine applied intravenously to experimental rabbit carriers of B. typhosus is not efficacious for the purpose of clearing up the focus in the gallbladder.

Acid Dyestuffs

The acid dyestuffs have been given comparatively little attention as it has been the feeling on the part of scientific workers that basic materials are more effective sterilizing agents. Simon and Wood,[34] and Uhlenhuth and Messerschmidt[12] have shown that in the test tube, basic coloring matters are more active than those of acid reaction; of the latter group they have utilized such dyes as acid fuchsin, acid violet and acid green 3 B in order to demonstrate comparative effects. In spite of these observations Chreinisse[35] states that he feels that acid dyestuffs may be found to be active in the body.

Attention has recently been vigorously redirected to these acid dye materials by Churchman,[36] who states that acid fuchsin is bacteriostatic to gram-negative micro-organisms of which B. typhosus is one. His work[37] indicates likewise that possibly it may be the sulphonic acid content of the molecular structure that produces this effect. In order to learn additional facts concerning the possible effects of certain acid dyes in the body of the experimental animal, a series of such coloring matters was selected: acid blue, acid brown, acid green G,

30 München. med. Wchnschr., 1922, 69, p. 1004.
31 Bull. de l'Acad. de méd., 1922, 88, p. 179.
32 Presse méd., 1920, 28, p. 678.
33 Arb. a. d. k. Gesndhtsamte., 1911, 36, p. 409.
34 Am. Jour. Med. Sc., 1914, 147, p. 247.
35 Presse méd., 1921, p. 805.
36 Proc. Soc. Exper. Biol. & Med., 1922, 19, p. 288; Jour. Exper. Med., 1923, 37, p. 1.
37 Proc. Soc. Exper. Biol. & Med., 1922, 19, p. 317.

acid magenta, acid orange, acid violet, acid yellow, Coleman and Bell formyl violet, British Dyestuffs Corp. Ltd.

The last was used by Fairbrother and Renshaw,[38] and the stain was furnished through the courtesy of the British Dyestuffs Corporation.

Hydrogen-Ion Concentration of Solutions of Acid Stains.—Since it is desirable for purposes of intravenous injection to use materials as near to the point of neutrality as possible, the reaction of a series of 0.5% solutions of these stains in distilled water was determined electrometrically by Mr. Greenberg of the department of biochemistry of this University. The results are shown in table 1.

Effect of Body Cells on Acid Dyestuffs.—It is of interest and of value to learn whether a compound injected intravenously into the circulation is removed promptly or not. Although it is to be expected that extraneous substances will be broken down or excreted or both, this change should not take place too promptly if we are to obtain a maximum effect. An endeavor was made, therefore, to learn which body cells and fluids may be expected to act on these materials when within the circulating blood in contact with the various tissues. Methods described by the author[39] were therefore followed. A rabbit was

TABLE 1

REACTIONS OF 0.5% SOLUTIONS OF CERTAIN STAINS IN DISTILLED WATER

Name	PH
Acid blue	4.00
Acid brown	2.45
Acid fuchsin	4.45
Acid green G	3.30
Acid magenta	4.30
Acid orange	2.70
Acid violet	5.30
Acid yellow	7.65
Formyl violet	6.85
Distilled water	5.00

exsanguinated with care, and certain of its tissues were macerated in sterile salt solution as soon as possible after death. To some of the resultant cell suspensions were added sufficient of the 0.5% solutions of the dyestuffs so that the concentration of the stain might lie between 1:5,000 and 1:15,000. The higher concentration was used for yellowish compounds, while the lower limits were approached by bluish compounds, which were thus more easily distinguishable from the natural tint of the cells. These tubes were then placed in the 37 C. incubator and observed at the end of 1, 3 and 24 hours to determine the degree of decolorization occurring in the supernatants. Results are shown in table 2. The plus sign indicates decolorization of the supernatant fluid in the tube by the tissue; no effect of cells on dyestuffs is shown by the minus sign, while ± denotes lessening of intensity of color but not its entire loss.

Fat Solubility.—It is stated by certain workers that the solubility of a substance in lipoid material determines within large degree the reciprocal activity between the body cells and itself. To learn the fat solubility of these acid stains, the following experiment was tried:

Exper. 6.—One c c. of olive oil was placed in each of a series of agglutination tubes. In each of a second series of these tubes was pipetted 1 c c. of

38 Jour. Path. & Bacteriol., 1922, 35, p. 145.

39 Jour. Infect. Dis., 1921, 28, p. 170.

paraffin oil. These tubes of oil were then tinted with the foregoing series of acid stains in 0.5 % solution in distilled water. The mixtures of aqueous stain solution and oil were then shaken thoroughly, and the tubes placed in the incubator at 37 C. At the end of 24 hours, no tube of oil had taken up any color, thus indicating that these acid dyestuffs are not lipoid soluble.

Chemotherapeutic Attemps with Acid Dyestuffs. Acid Blue. This dye is soluble in distilled water, and its presence in bile may be demonstrated by the addition of amyl alcohol which gives a blue zone. At least 3 c c. of a 0.5% solution may be administered to a 3,000 gm. rabbit intravenously, without apparent ill effects. Necropsy of a normal animal exsanguinated one and a quarter hours after injection revealed the coloring matter in the bile and in the duodenal contents but not elsewhere. The coloring matter is thus excreted through the bile.

TABLE 2

EFFECT OF VARIOUS TISSUES ON CERTAIN ACID DYESTUFFS

	Liver	Spleen	Lung	Kidney	Brain	Serum	Red Blood Cells	Check
Acid violet								
1 hour.......	—	—	—	—	±	—	—	—
3 hours......	—	—	—	—	±	..	..	—
21 hours......	—	±	—	—	—	—	—	—
Acid fuchsin								
1 hour.......	—	—	—	—	—	±	—	—
3 hours......	—	—	—	—	±	..	..	—
21 hours......	—	—	—	—	±	±	—	—
Acid yellow								
1 hour.......	—	—	—	—	—	—	—	—
3 hours......	—	±	—	±	—	..	..	—
21 hours......	—	+*	+	+*	—	—	—	—
Acid blue								
1 hour.......	±	±	±	+	+	±	±	—
3 hours......	+	+	±	+	+	..	..	—
21 hours......	+	+	+	+	+	+	+	—
Acid green								
1 hour.......	+	±	—	+	±	±	—	—
3 hours......	+	±	—	+	±	..	..	—
21 hours......	+	+	±	+	±	±	+	—
Acid magenta								
1 hour.......	±	—	±	±	±	±	—	—
3 hours......	±	—	±	±	±	..	..	—
21 hours......	±	±	—	+	+	—	—	—
Acid orange								
1 hour.......	—	—	—	—	—	—	—	—
3 hours......	±	—	—	±	—	..	..	—
21 hours......	±	—	—	±	—	—	—	—
Acid brown								
1 hour.......	+	—	—	—	—	—	—	—
3 hours......	+	—	—	+	—	..	..	—
21 hours......	+	—	—	+	—	—	—	—

* = Color restored by addition of H_2O_2.

Exper. 7.—To rabbit 620, which had received 1/20 of a 24-hour blood-agar slant of B. typhosus of strain No. 3, was administered 9 c c. of the solution of this dye over a period of 6 days. Injections were made every other day with 1 c c. for the initial and 3 c c. for the final amount. Fifty minutes after the final injection, this animal was bled to death and necropsy performed at once. No trace of the stain was to be found anywhere, including the urine and the bile. As the bile of a normal animal was found to be heavily tinted, it appears possible that absence of coloring matter in this animal may be accounted for by the suggestion of the interruption of the hepatic function. Bile from this animal added to beef broth and then incubated yielded B. typhosus, thus proving that the focus of infection had not been cleared up by this dye material.

Acid Brown.—This compound does not seem to form a stable solution in distilled water, as a precipitate forms within 24 hours. When present in bile, it may be detected by amyl alcohol, which produces a yellowish layer. Amounts as high as 3 c c. of a fresh aqueous solution may be injected intravenously into rabbits weighing 3,000 gm. No unfavorable symptoms arise.

Exper. 8.—Rabbit 633 had received by intracystic injection 1/20 of a 24-hour blood-agar slant of B. typhosus. To it was given intravenously a total of 8 c c. of 0.5% solution of this stain in distilled water. Injections extended over a period of 6 days, were made every other day, began with 1 c c. and concluded with 3 c c. Fifty minutes after the final treatment, the animal was killed by exsanguination and an immediate necropsy performed. No trace of the coloring matter was to be noted in any tissue. Amyl alcohol indicated a very small amount in the bile, but none in the urine. One quarter c c. of this bile was added to beef bouillon, and after incubation B. typhosus developed. It was thus shown that acid brown is valueless for the purpose sought in this experiment.

Acid Green G.—This stain is soluble in water, and such solution is permanent. Its presence in bile may be detected by the addition of amyl alcohol. Rabbits withstand without any evident ill effect intravenous injections of 3 c c. of a 0.5% distilled water solution of dye. On necropsy shortly after final injection into the normal animal a trace of the dyestuff was discernible in the fascia over the abdomen. Amyl alcohol indicated a large amount in the bile but none in the urine.

Exper. 9.—Rabbit 804 had received 1/20 of a 24-hour blood-agar slant of B. typhosus by direct injection into the gallbladder. Intravenous applications totaling 6 c c. were given over a period of 5 days, beginning with 1 c c. and finishing with 3 c c. Twenty hours after the last of these the animal was exsanguinated. When bile from the gallgladder had been added to beef broth and incubated, growth appeared slowly and was attended by pellicle formation. It thus was decidedly atypical for typhoid, but was proved to be such by sugar fermentations and by agglutination with antityphoid serum. Evidently the focus of infection within the gallbladder had not been sterilized by the action of the dyestuff, although the resultant growth from bile broth culture did not fulfil the usual criteria for B. typhosus in all respects.

Exper. 10.—Rabbit 353 likewise had received 1/20 tube of a 24-hour blood-agar slant of B. typhosus. To it was given intravenously an aggregate amount of 15 c c. of 0.5% aqueous solution of the acid green over a period of 11 days and consisting of 1 c c. on the first day, 2 c c. on the third, with 3 c c. on the fifth, seventh, ninth and eleventh days. Twenty-four hours following the final injection, the animal was killed by exsanguination, when aspirated bile was added to broth tubes and incubated. B. typhosus was demonstrated by culture followed by confirmatory agglutination.

It thus appears that acid green is ineffective for the purpose in view.

Acid Magenta.—This material may be injected intravenously into the rabbit in large amounts in 0.5% solution, 3 c c. being given with no sign of discomfort to the animal. When an animal is necropsied shortly after admission of this dye to the circulation, traces of the stain are found occasionally in the cortex of the kidney, and amyl alcohol reveals the fact that comparatively small amounts are in the urine. It is not present in the bile, although amyl alcohol serves to differentiate it when artificial mixtures of the stain in bile are prepared. Although it appears that this compound is not excreted by way of the bile, it seemed advisable to incorporate an experiment with it in this series.

Exper. 11.—Rabbit 870 had been prepared as an artificial typhoid carrier by intracystic injection of 1/10 of a 24-hour slant of blood-agar culture of B. typhosus. A total of 6 c c. of the 0.5% aqueous solution of this dyestuff was administered by the intravenous route over a period of 5 days, and with dosages of 1 c c. the first, 2 c c. the third and 3 c c. the fifth day. On the day following the final dose, the animal was killed and necropsied. Inoculums of the bile placed in beef bouillon gave a pure culture of B. typhosus, as proved by agglutination with antityphoid serum. Acid magenta therefore is inefficient for our purpose.

Acid Orange.—This compound is highly soluble in water, and by addition of amyl alcohol may be recognized when present in bile. It is nontoxic when used for intravenous injection, since 3 c c. of a 0.5% solution produces no ill effects. It is excreted rapidly through the urine, and the kidney cortex of an animal recently treated with it shows heavy yellow mottling.

Exper. 12.—Rabbit 680 had been prepared as a typhoid carrier by gallbladder injection of 1/20 of a 24-hour blood-agar slant of B. typhosus. Later, it received an aggregate amount of 10 c c. of a 0.5% solution of the dye. Dosages included 1 c c. the first, 3 c c. the third, 3 c c. the fifth and 3 c c. the seevnth day, after which within one-half hour the animal was exsanguinated. The kidney and urine were heavily colored, but there was no stain in the bile. A pure culture of B. typhosus developed from this bile when placed in broth culture tubes. Growth was slow but was positive. Acid orange therefore is useless for sterilizing an infected typhoid gallbladder.

Acid Violet.—This anilin derivative dissolves readily in water, and its presence is readily indicated in bile by amyl alcohol. The injection of amounts as high as 4 c c. of 0.5% solution in distilled water produces no seeming discomfort to a 3,000 gm. rabbit. It is excreted both by the urine and by way of the bile and may be seen in quantity in the duodenal contents.

Exper. 13.—Rabbit 829, a known carrier which had received 1/10 of a 24-hour slant of B. typhosus grown on blood agar, was used for this test. A total of 14 c c. of a 0.5% solution of the coloring matter in distilled water was introduced intravenously over 12 days. The amounts began with 0.5 c c. and finished with 4 c c. Necropsy performed one-half hour after the final treatment revealed a heavily tinted gallbladder and bile, but the B. typhosus had not been killed, as was proved by subsequent culture in beef bouillon followed by agglutination. Acid violet therefore is an unsatisfactory material for the purpose of sterilizing gallbladders infected with B. typhosus.

Acid Yellow.—This coloring matter is highly soluble in distilled water, may be separated out from bile by the addition of amyl alcohol, and as much as 3.5 c c. of a 0.5% solution may be injected intravenously into a 3,000 gm. rabbit without apparent signs of distress. It is excreted by the urine rather than by the bile.

Exper. 14.—Rabbit 684, a carrier produced by laparotomy, received a total amount of 6 c c. of the dyestuff, the dosage being given on alternate days. On exsanguination, B. typhosus was recovered from the bile by culture. No trace of the stain was discernible in the tissues. Acid yellow therefore did not clear up the infected gallbladder.

Formyl Violet.—This compound is also soluble in water, and amyl alcohol removes it moderately well from bile when in solution in that liquid. Moreover, rabbits tolerate it easily following intravenous injection. It is excreted rapidly through the bile and causes intense color in that medium. Bile colored with this stain is not germicidal to B. typhosus.

Exper. 15.—Rabbit 374 was the known animal carrier utilized in this experiment. After receiving an aggregate amount of 15 c c. of a 0.5% solution running over a series of alternate days and commencing with 2 c c. and finishing with 4 c c., it was exsanguinated. Necropsy showed the bile to be moderately tinted, but there was no stain elsewhere. B. typhosus on culture was proved to be still present in the gallbladder, thus showing that formyl violet is inefficient for the purpose sought.

Acid Green G and Acid Orange Combined in Solution.—It will be recalled that B. typhosus isolated from animal 804 after treatment with acid green G showed a tendency toward formation of a marked pellicle. That which developed from 680, to which had been administered acid orange, grew slowly. Each was atypical in character. Subsequent subculture after two or three transplants in beef broth gave B. typhosus, which was entirely normal. As these interesting deviations are differences which might indicate that a slight inhibiting effect had been produced, it was decided to treat a known prepared carrier with each one at the same time. Results appear in the following test.

Exper. 16.—Carrier 312 received a series of 6 injections, given on alternate days. The solutions of the 2 dyes were mixed together at the moment of injection, equal portions being used. The volume inserted into the circulation commenced with 1 c c., and finished with 3 c c., the concentration of the dye materials being 0.5%. At necropsy immediately following bleeding, bile was cultivated into broth, and after incubation B. typhosus developed in pure culture, but it showed the same tendency toward formation of a heavy pellicle as had been observed on the previous occasion. Thus again, although the gallbladder wall had not been sterilized by the treatment, the growth habit of the organism had been altered.

CONCLUSIONS

A series of experiments was carried out for the purpose of determining the possible effectiveness of certain compounds for clearing up experimentally produced rabbit carriers of B. typhosus. In these were included: (1) arsphenamine and neo-arsphenamine, (2) iodine, (3) acid dyestuffs. None of these was effective for the purpose sought. Certain temporary changes in the growth habit of B. typhosus may be encountered as a result of intravenous injection of particular dyestuffs.

MODIFICATION OF KLEIN MEDIUM FOR ISOLATION OF THE DIPHTHERIA BACILLUS

Emerson Megrail

From the Department of Hygiene and Bacteriology, School of Medicine, Western Reserve University, Cleveland, Ohio

The preparation and use of Loeffler's blood serum plates for routine isolation of the diphtheria bacillus have certain disadvantages which are well known. An easily prepared, clear, liquefiable medium for this purpose would be desirable in laboratories where isolations are made routinely for virulence tests.

Klein [1] devised a medium with these qualifications and found that the diphtheria bacillus grew as well on it as on Loeffler's blood serum. He used as a basis for his medium, horse or mule serum treated with 15% sodium hydroxide in the proportion of 1 part of the hydroxide to 9 parts of the serum. This mixture was kept in the incubator at 37 C. for 48 hours and was then neutralized with 25% hydrochloric acid. This neutralized serum was added to 4 parts of nutrient agar and sterilized in the autoclave at 105 C. for ½ hour.

Zurukzoglu [2] experimented with pure cultures of B. diphtheriae on this medium, finding that the morphology of the organisms differed and that granule production was not as marked as seen on blood serum. He also states that the medium permits the growth of large numbers of other organisms.

In a former article [3] I noted that a medium made after the manner of Klein, using either fresh or chloroform-preserved beef serum gave as good growth of the diphtheria bacillus as that on blood serum. The organisms, however, are smaller, but the granule production is about the same when a differential stain such as Albert's is used. In later experiments with the medium it was found that 8 parts of the beef serum and 2 parts of normal sodium hydroxide kept for the same period and at the same temperature as in the original method and neutralized with normal hydrochloric acid could be boiled without causing coagulation. This, when added to 4 parts of nutrient agar, could

Received for publication, July 26, 1923.

[1] Deutsch. med. Wchnschr., 1920, 46, p. 297.
[2] Centralbl. f. Bakteriol., I, O., 1921, 86, p. 440.
[3] Jour. Infect. Dis., 1922, 31, p. 393.

be sterilized in the autoclave at 15 pounds' pressure. Due probably to the buffer action of the serum, the amount of the hydrochloric acid necessary for neutralization could not be estimated. The resulting medium is clear and light brown. It gave the same results in regard to growth and morphology as the older formula. The reaction of the medium used in this work varied from P_H 7.1 to 7.5.

When attempts were made to use the medium for isolation of the diphtheria bacillus from routine throat cultures, the heavy growth of other organisms, particularly the staphylococcus, obscured the growth of the diphtheria bacilli so much that attempts were made to modify the medium so that the staphylococcus could be eliminated.

Rosolic acid used according to the method of Bronfenbrenner, Schellenger and Solitsky [4] was found to inhibit the diphtheria bacillus as well as the staphylococcus. Since the staphylococcus ferments lactose and the diphtheria bacillus does not, an attempt was made to make use of this by adding lactose and Andrade indicator or eosin-methylene blue to the medium. It was found that the staphylococcus did not produce enough acid, to make isolation easy, except where the growth was heavy.

A number of investigators have used telluric acid or a salt of telluric acid for enrichment or as an indicator in medium for the diphtheria bacillus. As the mediums used by these investigators does not offer any clear advantage in preparation over ordinary blood serum mediums, it was decided to use potassium tellurite, but in connection with the modified Klein medium: 2 c c. of a 1% aqueous solution of potassium tellurite was added to each flask of 100 c c. of the medium. It was found that the tellurite produced a distinct blackening of the medium when it was sterilized, even a temperature of 100 C. for 10 minutes caused a slight darkening. This darkening of the medium had no apparent effect on the morphology or growth of diphtheria organisms. Accordingly, to have a clear colorless medium it was found necessary to add the tellurite after melting the agar and before plates were poured. The appearance of colonies on tellurite medium, which has been described by several investigators, was found to be the same on the modified Klein medium. Colonies of diphtheria bacilli have a grayish black center and a grayish white periphery. B. hofmanni give the same appearance. Staphylococcus colonies are entirely black.

[4] Jour. Bacteriol., 1920, 5, p. 79.

In order to compare this medium with Loeffler's blood serum for isolation of B. diphtheriae, 49 routine throat or nasal cultures, positive according to the morphologic picture, were streaked on the two mediums, using one plate only of each medium for each culture. From each plate 6 colonies most suggesting B. diphtheriae were picked for morphologic study. It was found that the diphtheria colonies on the Klein tellurite medium were much larger and of more typical appearance after 40 hours' incubation. Studies were therefore made after this time from the modified Klein medium plates, but after 20 hours' incubation from the blood serum plates. All morphologic studies were made after staining by Albert's method. Of these 49 cultures 6 had to be discarded for comparative purposes, as the blood serum plates were overgrown with spreaders. The results obtained in the 43 isolations showed that of the 258 possible diphtheria colonies picked from each medium, 41% of those taken from Loeffler's medium and 76% from the new medium had the morphology of diphtheria. In 3 specimens, diphtheria organisms were found on Loeffler's medium and not on the new medium, while there were 6 specimens in which the organisms were found on the modified Klein medium and not on Loeffler's medium. In one specimen, organisms with the morphology of diphtheria were found in the original mixed culture but were not isolated on either of the 2 mediums.

When dilutions of 1:10,000 and 1:20,000 of potassium tellurite were used in comparison with 1:5,000, it was found that 1:20,000 potassium tellurite allowed the staphylococcus to grow and that their colonies appeared more like that of the diphtheria colonies. The 1:10,000 dilution gave equally good results as the 1:5,000 dilution.

It was also noted that plates of the tellurite Klein medium left at room temperature for several days were not overgrown with spreaders, while plates of Loeffler's and Klein medium without tellurite were frequently overgrown.

Control cultures of staphylococci, streptococci and diphtheria bacilli were plated on the modified Klein medium without tellurite and on the same medium with 1:5,000 and 1:10,000 of potassium tellurite, to compare relative inhibitory powers of the tellurite toward diphtheria and other organisms. Colony counts showed that there was almost a complete inhibition of staphylococcus cultures, only a few colonies developing in 64 hours. There was also a reduction in the number of diphtheria colonies, averaging probably 25%. There was a reduction in the number of colonies of two Hofmann cultures, but no marked reduction in two streptococcus cultures.

SUMMARY

A liquefiable blood serum medium made according to the method of Klein with the addition of from 1: 5,000 to 1: 10,000 dilution of potassium tellurite gives good results in the isolation of the diphtheria bacillus.

Potassium tellurite will inhibit the diphtheria bacillus to some extent, but this disadvantage is overbalanced by the typical appearance of the colony and the marked inhibition of staphylococcus and B. subtilis.

HYDROGEN-ION STUDIES

IX. THE PREPARATION OF SPECIFIC PRECIPITIN AS DRY POWDER

Edwin F. Hirsch

From the Pathological Laboratory of St. Luke's Hospital, Chicago. Aided by the Winfield Peck Memorial Fund

It is known generally that immune substances such as diphtheria antitoxin may be separated from serums by chemicals which precipitate the globulin portion. Pfeiffer and Proskauer[1] separated the globulin and albumin fractions of cholera immune serum and found in the globulin fraction the immune substances concerned with the Pfeiffer reaction. Brodie[2] was among the first to observe diphtheria antitoxin in the globulin precipitate of immune serum. Dieudonne[3] about the same time found that the globulin precipitated with carbon dioxide (carbonic acid) contains no diphtheria antitoxin. Belfanti and Carboni[4] confirmed this observation, and extended it to include the precipitate obtained with acetic acid. They found, as Brodie[2] had, that diphtheria antitoxin is precipitated by magnesium and ammonium sulphates when these salts are added in amounts prescribed for precipitating globulins from serum. His and Atkinson,[5] from a comparative study of the amount of globulin in normal and antitoxic serums, concluded that the amount of globulins in immune serums is greatly increased, and that the diphtheria antitoxin power of both normal and immune serum is contained in the globulin fraction. Pick,[6] by classic experiments, demonstrated in the globulin fraction of horse, goat, rabbit, and guinea-pig serums substances with immune properties for diphtheria toxin, tetanus toxin, the cholera lysin (Pfeiffer's phenomenon), as well as the typhoid agglutinin and the cholera agglutinin. In these experiments a division of the globulins was made; one portion soluble in saturated sodium chloride solution (pseudoglobulin), the other insoluble (euglobulin). Rodhain[7] found the opsonins and agglutinins for streptococci in the euglobulin fraction of immune rabbit serum. Moll[8] observed in rabbit blood an increase of the globulin fraction after foreign serum injections. These observations concerning the association of substances possessing immune properties with the globulin fraction of blood serum have been extended by Kapsenberg[9] and others to include the substance in human blood serum responsible for a positive Wassermann reaction. Recently, Herrold[9a] reports that almost all of the syphilitic antibody is contained in the euglobulin fraction of spinal fluids and serums, and suggests a procedure for concentrating this fraction.

Received for publication, July 30, 1923.

1 Centralbl. f. Bakteriol., I. O., 1896, 19, p. 191.
2 Jour. Path. & Bacteriol., 1896-97, 4, p. 460.
3 Arb. a. d. k. Gsndhtsamte, 1897, 13, p. 293.
4 Centralbl. f. Bakteriol., Ref., 1898, 23, p. 906.
5 Jour. Exper. Med., 1900-01, 5, p. 47.
6 Beitr. z. Chem. Physiol. u. Path., 1901, 1, p. 351.
7 Ibid., 1902-03, 3, p. 451.
8 Ibid., 1904, 4, p. 578.
9 Ann. de l'Inst. Pasteur., 1921, 35, p. 648.
9a Jour. Am. Med. Assn., 1923, 81, p. 203.

Although there is this unanimity regarding the precipitation of the immune substances by globulin precipitants and that with the establishment of immunity there is a definite increase of the serum globulins, Hurwitz and Meyer [10] observed an increase of the globulins long before immune substances reach an appreciable concentration, and when the globulin and antibody curves seem to be parallel there is a definite lack of correspondence between them in various stages of an experimental immunization. The rise in globulins according to these investigators may be a manifestation of an upset in the delicate protein balance because of the disturbed metabolism following the inoculation of toxins.

However, it may be that in the establishment of immunity, the substances with immune properties arise through chemical changes of proteins having globulin characteristics, which with the inception of immunization appear in the blood plasma without specific immune properties, these being acquired as the substances become chemically complete.

All of these observations regarding the presence of immune substances in the serum globulins naturally have suggested to those interested, methods for separating these substances (antitoxin) from serum. The advantages accruing from such purification and concentration obviously are great. The first practical method for concentrating diphtheria antitoxin was suggested by Gibson.[11] According to this method the globulins are precipitated by half saturation with ammonium sulphate, and the pseudoglobulin (horse serum), which contains the antitoxin, is dissolved in a saturated sodium chloride solution. From the saturated salt solution the antitoxin is precipitated by acetic acid or by half saturation with ammonium sulphate. The precipitate obtained with acid is dialyzed, neutralized with sodium carbonate, and then is sterilized; that obtained by second precipitation with ammonium sulphate is dialyzed and then sterilized. Other methods have been suggested by Banzhaf,[12] and more recently by Heineman,[13] these depending on fractional precipitation of the globulins with ammonium sulphate, combined with heating to certain temperatures of the precipitating mixtures.

These refining methods concern the concentration of antitoxins for commercial purposes. Certain studies with precipitin serums suggested the possibility of concentrating the precipitins in the hope of affording better opportunity to study the chemical behavior of these substances. Experiments with precipitin serums stored in the laboratory for several months demonstrated that in rabbit serum the precipitins are contained largely in the euglobulin fraction, and that an aqueous solution of this fraction gives strong precipitin reactions when mixed with homologous antigenic serum. In discussing these observations with Dr. E. R. LeCount, he suggested the possibility of reducing to solid form the substances in solution responsible for the precipitin reaction.

10 Jour. Infect. Dis., 1918, 22, p. 1.

11 Jour. Biol. Chem., 1905-06, 1, p. 161.

12 Collected Studies from the Research Laboratory, Dept. of Health, City of New York, 1912-13, 7, p. 114.

13 Jour. Infect. Dis., 1916, 19, p. 433.

Many antigenic substances are prepared as solids and are preserved indefinitely in this form, but there seem to be no similar antibody preparations, such as precipitins, or antitoxins.

The precipitation of globulin from serum by dilute acids has been known for some time. According to Dieudonne [3] and others, this portion contains no substance with immune properties. In previous experiments with the hydrogen-ion range of the precipitin reaction,[14] this globulin fraction was precipated with N/100 HNO_3 from sheep serum, washed thoroughly with distilled water, and dissolved in water alkalinized with a few drops of N/100 NaOH. This globulin solution reacts with homologous immune serum within a hydrogen-ion range the same as that observed for mixtures of native serum and immune serum. It seems, then, from these experiments that the globulin portion precipitated with acid has antigenic properties, and in the concentration or purification of immune serum this fraction may be removed without loss of the immune substances except as these may be occluded mechanically in the precipitate. As was mentioned above, the precipitin substance is contained largely in that portion of the globulin fraction insoluble in a saturated solution of sodium chloride.

These results, based on observations already mentioned, suggested the following procedure for recovering the precipitin from immune serum, and after solution of the euglobulin fraction in water other experiments demonstrated procedures by which the substances with precipitin properties may be reduced to solid form. Blood from immune rabbits is drawn into a small amount of an aqueous 2% sodium citrate solution, centrifuged, and the plasma carefully transferred into sterile containers. Before any manipulation of the blood plasma is begun, there should elapse a period of time during which the liquid undergoes a process known commercially as "ripening." Unless this period elapses, which preferably should be not less than a month and if possible longer, the precipitin substances are unstable, and a product is obtained which resembles closely in chemical behavior, the euglobulin of normal serum and is without precipitin properties or loses them very soon. To a given volume of immune plasma N/100 HNO_3 is added until the maximum opacity due to the precipitating globulin is obtained. Usually this is about 3 to 4 c c. for each c c. of rabbit plasma. The dilute acid not only precipitates the globulin, but also coagulates in the plasma a substance that separates out like a fibrin

[14] Ibid., 1923, 32, p. 439.

clot. When the maximum turbidity has been obtained with the N/100 acid, the turbid liquid is allowed to stand about an hour, during which time coarse flocculi form and settle out. These and the clotted substance are filtered off, and to the clear filtrate is added an equal volume of a saturated aqueous ammonium sulphate solution. After complete precipitation the mixture is filtered, the white precipitate is washed with a half saturated aqueous solution of ammonium sulphate and then with a saturated aqueous solution of sodium chloride. The gummy precipitate on the filter paper is extracted with distilled water equal to twice the original volume of the plasma. This slightly opalescent and viscid liquid gives typical specific precipitin reactions. In attempting to reduce directly this liquid by simply drying, a residue was obtained insoluble in water or dilute acid or alkali. This suggested attempts to convert the substances into acid or alkali salts. When the liquid was made alkaline and then evaporated, a similar insoluble substance was obtained; the acidified solution, however, gave a product which dissolved. Finally, other experiments demonstrated that the addition of N/10 HCl drop by drop to the aqueous extract of the euglobulin fraction (containing also a little salt) caused a white, finely flocculent precipitate to form. This could be dried slowly and when dry was soluble in distilled water. Accordingly, the aqueous globulin solution is placed in 15 c c. centrifuge tubes and to approximately 10 c c. volume 0.5 to 1 c c. N/10 HCl is added drop by drop. A finely flocculent white precipitate forms. This is centrifuged to the bottom of the tube, and the supernatant liquid is poured into another centrifuge tube where, on standing, more of the precipitate settles out.[15]

The tube containing the centrifuged precipitate is inverted, the small amount of liquid present is drained off, and the protein precipitate dried in a vacuum desiccator until it becomes of brittle putty-like consistency. It is removed then, divided into small particles, spread out on a watch crystal, thoroughly dried and stored in a desiccator. When dried there remains a white starchlike powder or mass, soluble in water-like gelatin, forming a clear or slightly opalescent liquid.

It is likely that further work may demonstrate revisions of the procedure outlined, these being necessary because some antibodies may be found chiefly in the pseudoglobulin fraction of rabbit or other animal plasma. With some antisubstances it may be necessary to com-

[15] The chemical processes concerned in this precipitation are probably explained by the forcing out of solution of the protein chloride by the acid in the presence of inorganic salts according to the Donnan membrane equilibrium. J. Loeb: Proteins and the Theory of Colloidal Behavior, 1922, p. 273.)

bine the protein with a weak acid or other substance in order that dissociation products may not interfere with the completion of the immune reaction.

The solution obtained by dissolving the protein powder in distilled water is weakly acid, and does not give specific precipitin reactions when mixed with homologous antigenic serum. However, when this acid solution has been made neutral to litmus by N/100 NaOH added drop by drop, the liquid forms a precipitate even with high dilutions of the homologous antigenic serum. In a typical experiment an anti-human serum powder dissolved in water and neutralized gave precipitin reactions in dilutions as high as 1:12,800.[16] The amount of powder dissolved was very small, and, although not accurately weighed, did not exceed 10:20 mg. per c c. of the solute.

The gradual neutralization of the immune protein solution by N/100 NaOH causes an increasing turbidity of the liquid until a certain reaction is reached when the protein solution breaks, and small flocculi precipitate. The addition of more alkali dissolves these flocculi, the liquid becomes opalescent, until finally sufficient alkali has been added, and the liquid again becomes clear or slightly opalescent. This behavior of the immune protein solution is like that of a protein dissolved and ionized as an acid salt. The solution of such a protein brought to a certain hydrogen-ion concentration by alkali becomes turbid, and at this critical point, specific for the protein and known as its isolectric point, the solution breaks and flocculi of protein separate out. More alkali forces the protein flocculi into solution again. In testing the precipitin properties of an immune protein solution the greatest and most rapid precipitation occurs with homologous antigenic serum when the reaction of the solute is near the flocculation point of the immune protein substance. This agrees with observations [17] on the agglutination of bacteria by immune serum near their iso-electric point.

The moist precipitate obtained by adding N/10 HCl to the aqueous extract of the immune serum euglobulin fraction (containing also a small amount of salt) is easily and readily soluble in distilled water. That obtained in a similar way from nonimmune rabbit serum is only slightly and slowly soluble in water, and may be washed repeatedly with water, only small amounts dissolving. These differences in solu-

[16] Because of the low viscosity of the immune protein powder solution and the diluted antigenic serum and the consequent rapid diffusion of the one liquid into the other, the usual ring method for conducting the precipitin test is not always satisfactory. The clouding of the entire tube content indicates the progress of precipitation of the contained colloids. Approximately equal volumes of the two liquids should be used.

[17] Ztschr. f. Immuntätsf., 1903, 16, p. 517.

bility are marked. The slightly soluble precipitate also dissolves readily in N/100 NaOH, or N/100 HNO_3, solubility tests resembling those of a protein at its iso-electric point. When immune plasma is used soon after being taken from a rabbit, the precipitate obtained with the addition of N/10 HCI to the aqueous solution of the euglobulin fraction manifests solubility reactions like those of a nonimmune serum precipitate. No precipitin reactions have been observed with such preparations. The final drying of the moist immune serum precipitate may not be made too quickly because of a change into a similar relatively insoluble protein substance. The protein substance prepared from immune plasma and having specific immune properties, then, differs sharply in its solubility reactions from that prepared from the nonimmune, a characteristic dependent probably on its salt-like composition.

The importance of the hydrogen-ion concentration in the precipitin test has been observed in previous experiments with mixtures of sheep serum and homologous immune rabbit serum.[14] With those experiments the precipitin reaction occurred in a hydrogen-ion concentration range expressed by P_H 6.0 to P_H 9.4. Other experiments not published have determined the range for mixtures of human serum and homologous immune rabbit serum to be from P_H 5.6 to P_H 9.9; with guinea-pig serum and homologous immune rabbit serum from P_H 5.5 to P_H 10.0. These results suggest that the chemical activity of the precipitin and antigen in combining to form a precipitate is dependent on the hydrogen-ion concentration of the medium, and that the reaction of the medium is within a definite range in order that a precipitate may form. This seems to be the reason why the acid solutions of immune protein powder form no precipitate when mixed with homologous antigenic serum.

The protein salt probably dissociates like other ampholytes, in a way such as Levene and Simms [18] pointed out recently. Within a certain hydrogen-ion range in which the basic dissociation predominates it combines with acid substances to form acid salts; above and below this P_H range the basic dissociation is suppressed. Similar relations probably exist for antigenic substances, and the mutual concurrence of optimum relationships for both the antigen and the immune substance in a certain hydrogen-ion range permits completion of the chemical phenomena characterizing an immune reaction. In discussing the iso-

[18] Jour. Biol. Chem., 1923, 55, p. 801.

electric range of an ampholyte, Levene and Simms say that with aspartic acid, glutamic acid and many proteins, the iso-electric point may be a sharp boundary marking a definite change in chemical behavior because of the proximity of the acid and basic dissociation constants to the iso-electric point.

DISCUSSION

The preparation of a solid substance which in solution possesses immune properties affords many possibilities as regards further chemical study of such a substance. From the work done so far has come the understanding that to have immune reactions completed a certain hydrogen-ion range of the medium is necessary. This probably is true for many, if not all, immune substances. For the precipitin test in particular there is an optimum P_H near the iso-electric point of the immune protein, of the antigenic protein, or both, where the maximum precipitate is formed. This suggests also that certain serums which have in the usual tests little antibody content may be demonstrated to have a large amount when the reaction of the serum is brought to the proper and optimum hydrogen-ion concentration. It is not unlikely that many other substances with immune properties can be prepared in solid form, according to the method mentioned here or slightly modified, and kept as such indefinitely without loss of potency and without danger of deterioration by bacterial contamination. Commercially this may be advantageous.

SUMMARY

According to the method described, specific precipitins may be prepared as dry powders.

The powder so prepared is a protein-acid salt, soluble in water forming a liquid with an acid reaction. Neutralized with N/100 NaOH to within a certain P_H range this solution gives specific precipitin reactions on mixing with homologous antigenic serum.

Probably other antisubstances may be prepared in solid form by this method, or by slight modification of the essentials described.

EFFECT OF BENZYL BENZOATE ON ANTIBODY FORMATION IN RABBIT

Ludwig A. Emge

From the Division of Obstetrics and Gynecology, Stanford University School of Medicine, San Francisco

In a previous article [1] on the effect of benzyl benzoate on the leukocytes of the rabbit, I stated that larger subcutaneous doses caused latent or quiescent infections to become active; also that changes occurred in the leukocytic picture which suggested that benzyl benzoate has a mildly depressant influence on the number and grouping of the leukocytes of rabbits. These results led me to think that benzyl benzoate may inhibit antibody formation, and I undertook to investigate this question as here recorded.

By careful observation I tried to select animals free from infection. It was the intention to study the changes in the blood picture with the effects on antibody production at the same time. Since the blood picture is greatly influenced by the process of immunization as well as by the frequent bleeding, I refrain from recording the leukocytic curves at this time as they are misleading and in no way express the influence of benzyl benzoate when used as in the previous study. Neither are weight curves given as the weight was not influenced by either the immunization or the injection of benzyl benzoate.

The antibody the formation of which I chose to study was the lysin for sheep corpuscles. Benzyl benzoate injections were given subcutaneously in sterile olive oil in doses and at times varying with each experiment.

The hemolytic amboceptor was produced by injecting rabbits intravenously with 2, 3 and 4 c c. of a fresh 50% suspension of goat corpuscles, carefully washed in salt solution. The injections were given at 2 day intervals so that the actual process of immunization covered 7 days. In exper. 4, the third dose was increased to 5 c c. The intravenous immunization is relatively reliable, uniform, and advantageous on account of the brief period required to obtain a good response. The loss of animals from anaphylaxis was 3 of 14. The determination of the

Received for publication, July 31, 1923.

[1] Jour. Pharm. & Exper. Therap., 1921, 17, p. 415.

amboceptor titer was begun 48 hours after the first injection of goat corpuscles.

Guinea-pig serum freshly collected was used as complement, and titrated against a known amboceptor. The titer thus found was then doubled in amount for the titration of the amboceptor in my experiments. Each rabbit was bled from the ear veins every second or third day, varying with each experiment, regularly 6 hours after the morning feeding. In several experiments the animals were bled on consecutive days when the peak of antibody production was expected to be reached. The blood was collected in heat dried test tubes, the serum obtained by centrifugating, and heated in the water bath at 56 C. for one hour. Serum containing hemoglobin was discarded.

Gradually decreasing amounts of immune serum in 1 c c. of salt solution were added to 1 c c. of a 50% suspension of washed goat blood.

Control tests were made with goat blood and amboceptor or complement or salt solution only.

The first reading for hemolysis was made after one hour's incubation at 37 C. It was repeated after one hour in the icebox. Doubtful tubes were centrifugated. In order to eliminate the personal element as much as possible all results here recorded are based on complete hemolysis only, partial hemolysis being disregarded entirely.

It was found that in the type of immunization here studied, the height of amboceptor production occurred quite regularly between the 16th and 17th day after the first injection. There are variations in the normal height of the amboceptor curve which are somewhat dependent on the age and weight of the animals (exper. 1). There is much less variation in the time at which the peak of greatest amboceptor formation is reached, and this seldom varied more than 48 hours in animals not injected with benzyl benzoate.

EXPER. 1.—Rabbits 1, 2, and 10 (controls): This experiment was carried out in order to obtain a normal amboceptor curve for comparison later. Rabbits 1 and 2, of different sex and breed, were of about the same age and weight. Rabbit 10 was a younger and lighter animal. There was great similarity in the amboceptor titrations of 1 and 2; in rabbit 10 the amboceptor formation was less vigorous and its acme brief. The peak of all curves was reached between 16 and 17 days after the first injection. In all 3 animals, the final base line was reached after between 28 and 30 days (table 1).

EXPER. 2.—Rabbits 3 and 4: Two large rabbits of the same litter but opposite sex were immunized as stated. Assuming that antibody production was still on the increase on the 13th day, they now were given daily subcutaneous injections of 0.3 c c. and 0.4 c c. of benzyl benzoate in sterile olive oil corresponding to 0.1 c c. and 0.15 c c. of the benzoate per kg. body-weight. The expected further rise in antibody production failed to take place and a low level was reached on the 20th and 22nd days, respectively, all amboceptor having disappeared completely on the 25th day. Disregarding the peak of the curve, it appeared that antibody formation was shortened approximately 7 days (table 2).

TABLE 1

INJECTION OF 2, 3, 4 CC. OF 50% SUSPENSION OF GOAT CORPUSCLES ON 1ST, 4TH AND 7TH DAYS, RESPECTIVELY

Days After First Injection of Goat Corpuscles	Rabbit 1	Rabbit 2	Rabbit 10
7	100	100	100
8	.....	.....	300
9	800	500	.....
11	.....	900	500
12	1,400	.....	.....
13	.....	1,100	.....
14	2,000	1,600	1,000
16	.....	.....	1,700
17	2,400	2,300	.....
18	.....	.....	1,250
19	.....	2,100	.....
20	2,000	.....	.....
21	2,100	2,000	.....
22	.....	1,600	1,000
24	.....	1,400	.....
26	400	600	500
28	.....	300	100
30	200	150	100
34	200	150	50

TABLE 2

INJECTION OF 2, 3, 4 CC. OF 50% SUSPENSION OF GOAT CORPUSCLES ON 1ST, 4TH AND 7TH DAYS, RESPECTIVELY, AND DAILY INJECTIONS OF BENZYL BENZOATE BEGINNING ON THE THIRTEENTH DAY

Days After First Injection of Goat Corpuscles	Rabbit 3	Rabbit 5
12	2,500	2,450
16	1,875	1,000
20	1,100	100
23	100	50
25	50	50
27	0	0

EXPER. 3.—Rabbits 5 and 6: In this experiment the process of immunization preceded the administration of benzyl benzoate by 5 days. The dosage of benzyl benzoate used was 0.1065 and 0.2 c c., respectively, corresponding to 0.05 c c. and 0.1 c c. per kg. of body weight. The peak of antibody formation in rabbits 5 and 6 was fairly high, due perhaps to the goat blood used. But the high point in antibody formation did not last as long as expected, and there was a rapid drop to the base line. It is of interest to note that after the discontinuance of benzyl benzoate injections a slight rise in antibody production took place (table 3).

TABLE 3

INJECTION OF 2, 3, 4 CC. OF 50% SUSPENSION OF GOAT CORPUSCLES ON 1ST, 4TH AND 7TH DAYS, RESPECTIVELY, AND DAILY INJECTIONS OF BENZYL BENZOATE BEGINNING 5 DAYS PRIOR TO IMMUNIZATION

Days After First Injection of Goat Corpuscles	Rabbit 5	Rabbit 6
2	0	0
4	50	50
7	700	700
9	1,900	1,900
10	2,500	2,450
12	2,000	2,800
14	2,000	2,475
16	1,800	1,600
17	1,600	1,300
19	1,000	1,000
21	900	950
23	800	100
25	300	50
28	400	150
33	100	100

EXPER. 4.—Rabbits 7 and 8: Immunization and benzyl benzoate administration were begun simultaneously in 2 female rabbits of the same litter but of unequal weight. The dosage of benzyl benzoate was increased to 0.756 c c. and 0.4575 c c., corresponding to 0.28 c c. and 0.25 c c. per kg. body weight. It was found that the peak of antibody production was reached sooner and that the return to a lower level was more rapid than in the average normal curve; in other words, the shifting of the curve is to the left, being both lowered and foreshortened (table 4).

TABLE 4

INJECTION OF 2, 3, 5 CC. OF 50% SUSPENSION OF GOAT CORPUSCLES ON 1ST, 4TH AND 7TH DAYS, RESPECTIVELY, AND DAILY INJECTIONS OF BENZYL BENZOATE

Days After First Injection of Goat Corpuscles	Rabbit 7	Rabbit 8
5	50	50
7	750	600
9	1,600	1,100
11	1,000	1,800
13	900	1,000
15	1,000	900
16	800	750
18	1,000	900
20	850	500
22	300	200
24	100	100
26	100	100
28	100	100
30	100	100
32	100	100
34	50	50

EXPER. 5.—Rabbits 11 and 12: This experiment was essentially like the previous one, except that the dosage of benzyl benzoate injected was increased to 1.2 c c. and 1.5 c c. corresponding to 1 c c. per kg. body weight, as the animals were of lesser weight than in the preceding experiment. Here the high level is broken early but the base line was reached at a later period than theoretically expected (table 5).

TABLE 5

INJECTION OF 2, 3, 4 CC. OF 50% SUSPENSION OF GOAT CORPUSCLES ON 1ST, 4TH AND 7TH DAYS, RESPECTIVELY, AND DAILY INJECTIONS OF BENZYL BENZOATE

Days After First Injection of Goat Corpuscles	Rabbit 11	Rabbit 12
6	700	100
8	1,000	500
10	1,250	800
13	1,450	1,200
15	1,425	1,100
17	1,000	550
19	1,000	900
21	1,000	900
23	700	700
25	500	550
27	300	450
29	.....	450
31	300	.....
33	100	300
34	.....	150

While the dosage of benzyl benzoate in these experiments is higher than that in man it may be pointed out that herbivorous animals possess a greater resistance to this drug.

CONCLUSIONS

The results indicate that in rabbits the subcutaneous administration of benzyl benzoate exerts a mildly depressing influence on the production of hemolytic amboceptor. If this may be taken as an indicator for antibody formation in general, the results are of interest in connection with previous observations on the depressing influence of benzyl benzoate on the white blood cells of the rabbit during which period of depression quiescent infections may become active.

THE INHIBITION OF PUTREFACTIVE SPORE-BEARING ANAEROBES BY BACTERIUM ACIDOPHILUS

John C. Torrey and Morton C. Kahn

From the Department of Hygiene, Cornell University Medical College, New York City

Within recent years it has been demonstrated that B. acidophilus and also B. bifidus are capable under certain conditions of diet of overgrowing and markedly suppressing the types of bacteria usually dominant both in the intestinal tract of the human adult and also in that of certain lower mammals.[1-6]

There is available, however, no definite information in regard to the biologic or chemical factors which permit these aciduric organisms to become predominant. The investigations of Kendall,[2] Torrey,[3] Rettger and his co-workers [4] and others have established the fact that diets containing liberal amounts of lactose are particularly effective in stimulating the overgrowth of B. acidophilus in the intestine, and one of us [3] has also recently demonstrated that dextrin is equally efficacious. Further, through the studies of Hull and Rettger [4] and Rettger and Cheplin,[5] it has been shown that lactose and dextrin are so slowly absorbed from the digestive tract that a part of the amount fed reaches the lower bowel, the normal habitat of these bacilli. This, as Rettger has emphasized, provides a favorable pabulum for B. acidophilus and permits the rapid development of this organism. It would seem, however, that these conditions might be equally favorable for the growth of such fermentative organisms as B. coli and streptococci and that the predominance of B. acidophilus is probably attained through factors other than or additional to more mechanical overgrowth. Kopeloff [7] in an inquiry into the cause for the improvement in obstinate cases of constipation following the ingestion of large amounts of B. acidophilus milk cultures with a consequent simplification of the intestinal flora,

Received for publication, July 27, 1923.

1 Distaso and Schiller: Compt. rend. Soc. biol., 1914, 76, p. 243.

2 Kendall, A. I.: Jour. Med. Res., 1911, 25, p. 117; Am. Jour. Med. Sc., 1918, 156, p. 157.

3 Torrey, J. C.: Jour. Infect. Dis., 1915, 16, p. 72; Jour. Med. Res., 1919, 39, p. 415.

4 Hull and Rettger: Jour. Bacteriol., 1917, 2, p. 47.

5 Rettger and Cheplin: Transformation of the Intestinal Flora, 1921.

6 Cannon, P. R.: Jour. Infect. Dis., 1920, 27, p. 139; 1921, 29, p. 369.

7 Jour. Am. Med. Assn., 1923, 80, p. 602.

has submitted evidence which he believes indicates that the phenomenon is due to biologic rather than chemical or physical factors, but he did not carry the analysis further.

This study is limited to an effort to determine the mode of action whereby the B. acidophilus is able to inhibit the growth and activity of one group of proteolytic organisms native to the intestinal tract, namely, the putrefactive anaerobes; for it has been observed by one of us that the overgrowth of the B. acidophilus in the intestines of both dogs and humans causes a practically complete elimination of these organisms from this locality. It must be admitted, however, that it is not feasible to attempt the reproduction in the test tube of the complex conditions within the intestines. Our experimental methods, nevertheless, have permitted a close analysis of the relation of acidity to proteolysis by putrefactive spore bearing anaerobes, and our results in this direction constitute the principal contribution of this study.

EXPERIMENTS WITH COMBINED STRAINS OF B. ACIDOPHILUS AND VARIOUS TYPES OF ANAEROBIC SPORE BEARING PUTREFACTIVE BACTERIA

The following experiments illustrate the inhibitory effect on proteolysis which is exercised by B. acidophilus when grown in association with putrefactive anaerobes in a medium favorable to both types of organisms. These anaerobes were strains with definite histories which had been purified by one of us [8] by the Barber single cell technic. In most of these tests the rate and degree of proteolysis was gaged by observing the degree of disintegration of a cube of coagulated egg albumin. These cubes, about one-fourth inch square, were placed in sterile test tubes and covered with 10 c c. of casein digest broth [8] to which, in most of the experiments, a fraction of 1% of glucose had been added. These tubes were then autoclaved at 15 lbs. of pressure. Complete anaerobiosis was obtained by boiling the medium just prior to inoculation and then covering with a vaseline cap. This provided conditions which were favorable alike for the anaerobes and the aciduric organisms. When seeded together, digestion and disintegration of the egg cubes occurred with greater or less rapidity or was entirely inhibited according to the experimental condtions.

Exper. 1.—Medium: Casein digest meat infusion peptone broth with 0.5% glucose, P_H 6.6; tubed in 10 c c. amounts and egg cubes added. Proteolytic

[8] Kahn, M. C.: Jour. Med. Res., 1922, 43, p. 155.

anaerobes: B. histolyticus, B. sporogenes, B. botulinus, B. bellonensis, and B. bifermentans. These cultures were generally about 1 week old, but it was found that whether old, spore stage or young, vegetating cultures were used, made no difference in the time of onset and rapidity of proteolysis. B. acidophilus. mixture of strains B, F, and G, 24-hour growth in 2% glucose, meat infusion, peptone broth, unneutralized.

Control Series 1.—Six tubes were inoculated with 0.5 c c. of each of the anaerobe cultures to serve as control for the rate of proteolysis.

Control Series 2.—Two tubes were inoculated with 0.5 c c. of B. acidophilus and incubated with and without vaseline caps, and 2 tubes of uninoculated medium with and without vaseline caps for sterility tests.

Test Series.—Six tubes of medium were inoculated respectively with 0.5 c c. of an anaerobe culture and 0.5 c c. of the B. acidophilus culture; incubation at 37 C.

Results

Mixture of anaerobes and B. acidophilus.	Control, anaerobes alone.
1 day. Heavy growth; no digestion in any tube.	Heavy growth; traces of digestion with B. sporogenes, B. botulinus; others, no change.
3 days. No digestion in any tube.	Digestion: B. sporogenes, nearly complete. B. botulinus, marked. B. bifermentans, marked. B. histolyticus, slight. B. bellonensis, slight.
8 days. No digestion in any tube.	Digestion in all tubes, nearly complete.
13 days. Marked digestion of egg cubes in all except B. bellonensis.	Complete digestion in all tubes.

B. acidophilus controls showed a heavy growth with a stringy, mucoid deposit overlaying the egg cubes. Microscopic examination after 24 hours' incubation showed that in every instance B. acidophilus had markedly overgrown the anaerobes. Tests for viability after 13 days indicated that B. acidophilus had died out except in the tubes seeded with B. bellonensis and B. bifermentans, thus indicating that the more actively proteolytic organisms had overgrown and destroyed B. acidophilus.

This experiment, of which the essential features were repeatedly confirmed by other tests, indicates that in the presence of slightly over 0.5% glucose B. acidophilus is able to overgrow the 6 varieties of spore-bearing proteolytic anaerobes to such an extent that their digestive powers for coagulated egg albumin are completely inhibited for 10 days, but after that the proteolytic organisms gain the upper hand and soon effect the complete digestion of the egg cubes.

As both these anaerobes and B. acidophilus grow well in milk, an experiment similar to that described above was carried out in this medium.

Exper. 2.—Medium: Skimmed milk tubed in about 15 c c. amounts and autoclaved. Proteolytic anaerboes: as in experiment 1. B. acidophilus: Milk clotting strain, M.

Control Series 1.—Milk tubes seeded with equal dosages of each of the 5 test anaerobes.

Control Series 2.—Milk tubes seeded with B. acidophilus and incubated with and without vaseline.

Test Series.—Milk tubes seeded with uniform amounts of each of the test anaerobes together with 0.5 c c. of a 24-hour growth of B. acidophilus in milk. The medium was boiled just before seeding and then sealed with vaseline.

Results.—After 28 hours' incubation digestion of the casein was markedly advanced in all the tubes seeded with the anaerobes alone. The tubes seeded with the mixtures of B. acidophilus and the anaerobes exhibited no digestion and in most instances an acid clot.

After 7 days, the clots in the control tubes for anaerobes were from two-thirds to three-fourths digested. B. acidophilus controls and the tubes seeded with mixtures of anaerobes and B. acidophilus showed no digestion.

After 14 days there was practically complete digestion in the anaerobe control tubes but none in the tubes seeded with mixtures of B. acidophilus and the anaerobes.

The H-ion concentrations in the latter tubes were much below 5.6.

Viability tests after 13 days showed that B. acidophilus was alive in all the tubes seeded with the mixtures of B. acidophilus and the various anaerobes.

The foregoing experiment with milk medium demonstrated that in this medium B. acidophilus is able to overgrow these proteolytic organisms and hold in check indefinitely their casein digesting propensities. The experiment also indicated that the acidity of the clotted milk was the important factor in the inhibition.

The following tests were carried out with single strains of B. acidophilus and B. bifidus to determine whether there exist any marked differences among the various representatives of these aciduric bacteria as regards their antiproteolytic propensities. B. acidophilus strains tested included those which did not clot milk and also gas-producing types. The medium and procedure were similar to that described under exper. 1, except that the casein broth was slightly enriched with a 20% addition of whey broth in order to obtain a luxuriant growth of all strains of B. acidophilus; this modification also permitted a strong growth of the anaerobes.

Exper. 3.—Test medium: Casein digest, 0.5% glucose broth plus egg cubes (exper. 1) plus 20% of whey broth, reaction p_H 6.9. Proteolytic anaerobes: B. histolyticus, B. sporogenes, B. acidophilus strains: A, B, J (gas producing), M. (gas producing and milk clotting, R (milk clotting). Procedure: As in exper. 1. The anaerobes grew up strongly in combined seeding with the B. acidophilus strains as was evidenced by the marked production of gas in all tubes.

Results.—After 4 days, anaerobe controls showed practically complete proteolysis. B. acidophilus J plus B. sporogenes showed a slight trace of proteolysis; all others were negative.

After 7 days, anaerobe controls showed practically complete proteolysis. B. acidophilus J plus anaerobes showed marked proteolysis in all tubes. B. acidophilus M tubes showed fairly marked proteolysis with B. sporogenes; B. acidophilus A and R, the same result with B. oedematis. B. acidophilus B plus anaerobes showed no proteolysis in any tube.

After 14 days, anaerobe controls showed complete digestion of the egg cubes in all tubes; B. acidophilus J plus anaerobes, complete in all tubes. B. acidophilus M. showed no digestion with B. histolyticus and nearly complete with B. sporogenes; A and R, nearly complete with B. sporogenes and negative with the others; B. moderate proteolysis with B. sporogenes and negative with the others.

II. B. bifidus: strain isolated from stool of human adult. Proteolytic anaerobes: as in exper. 1. Test medium: Liver peptone broth, 1% gelatin, 0.5% glucose, egg cubes, p_H 6.8. Procedure: Medium seeded as in exper. 1. Both the spore-bearing anaerobes and B. bfidus grew luxuriantly.

After 2 days, anaerobe controls showed beginning of digestion of egg cubes; no proteolysis in tubes in which B. bifidus also seeded.

After 7 days, anaerobe controls showed nearly complete or complete digestion of egg cubes; none in tubes in which B. bifidus also seeded.

After 23 days, same result as for 7 days. Reaction of all tubes to which B. bifidus had been added was p_H 5.8; control tubes, 7.2.

The results reported in exper. 3 indicate that strains of B. acidophilus differ considerably in their antiproteolytic properties. As will be demonstrated presently, however, these differences are quite definitely correlated with the degree of acid production. The two strains of B. bifidus tested seemed to be fully as efficient inhibitors of proteolysis as any of the strains of B. acidophilus; in fact, the anaerobes did not grow up again after 2 to 3 weeks' incubation as occurred in the B. acidophilus experiments after 1 to 2 weeks. The differences in the mediums employed in these two tests, however, probably account for the apparently greater inhibitory action of B. bifidus.

In connection with exper. 1 the question arose whether with the simultaneous seeding of the proteolytic anaerobes and the B. acidophilus the former were able to come to full development. Accordingly, in other tests the mediums were first seeded with the anaerobes and incubated for about 18 hours before B. acidophilus was added, as is described in the following proctol.

Exper. 4, Test A.—Medium: Partially skimmed milk. Cultures: The same strains of B. acidophilus and spore-bearing anaerobes as employed in expers. 1 and 2. Procedure: Duplicate cultures of these anaerobes were made in the foregoing medium. They were incubated 18 hours, a luxuriant growth resulting. One set of cultures was then seeded with 0.5 c c. of a 24-hour milk culture of B. acidophilus and the other kept as a control.

Results.—Proteolysis occurred in the control tubes in a typical manner, but in the tubes to which B. acidophilus had been added it was completely checked; even after one month's incubation there was no proteolysis observable, whereas the casein in the control tubes was completely digested.

Test B.—Medium: Casein digest broth with egg cubes, but without glucose. Procedure: Duplicate seedings of the anaerobe strains specified in exper. 1 were made into the foregoing medium and incubated 18 hours. A vigorous growth resulted. Sufficient glucose in sterile solution was then added to each tube to bring the amount to 0.5%; 0.5 c c. of a washed suspension of B. acidophilus (24 hour growth) in salt solution (approximately 4 billion per c c.) was then added to each tube of one set and the other was kept as a control. Both sets were then incubated at 37 C.

Results.—Digestion in the control tubes proceeded rapidly and was practically complete in all within 4 or 5 days. In the tubes to which washed B. acidophilus had been added, proteolysis was completely checked up to 10 days.

By exper. 4 it was demonstrated that even when these proteolytic anaerobes had been given an opportunity to establish themselves strongly in the fluid culture mediums employed, B. acidophilus succeeded in outgrowing them and holding them in check in the presence of 0.5% or more of a suitable carbohydrate.

Further tests were conducted to determine whether B. acidophilus could inhibit these anaerobes in a medium favorable to both but to which no carbohydrate had been added; also whether actively growing cultures of B. acidophilus produced a substance in the medium, other than acidity, which acted in a bacteriostatic manner on these anaerobes. All of these experiments resulted negatively and forced us to the conclusion that in vitro, at least, inhibition was due entirely to the acid produced. This conclusion was further substantiated by the finding, described above, that the strains of B. acidophilus most effective as antiproteolytic agents were those producing the greater amounts of acid. The following series of experiments were carried out to analyze further this acidity factor.

THE INFLUENCE OF THE H-ION CONCENTRATION ON THE INHIBITION OF PROTEOLYSIS BY SPORE-BEARING ANAEROBES GROWN IN ASSOCIATION WITH B. ACIDOPHILUS AND B. COLI

Many years ago Bienstock[8a] reported that milk medium to which fibrin had been added is not digested by B. putrificus (probably B. sporogenes) if it is seeded also with B. coli or B. aerogenes. Later Tissier and Gaschung[9] observed that the digestive ferments of the proteolytic bacteria (B. subtilis, B. mesentericus, B. putrificus) are checked by

8a Ann. de l'Inst. Pasteur, 1899, 13, p. 854.

9 Ibid., 1903, 17, p. 540.

the acid produced by lactic acid organisms (B. paralacticus) in milk and that the former tend to disappear and go into the spore stage. This suggested sparing effect of fermentation on proteolysis has found subsequent confirmation by the work of Kendall and others, but the part played by the acid factor in such experiments has not been fully evaluated heretofore. The following tests were conducted to correlate accurately the degree of inhibition of proteolysis with the amount of acid present, and also to determine just what amounts of the carbohydrates employed, glucose or lactose, are necessary to permit B. acidophilus to check the growth and activity of these anaerobes.

In these experiments, graded amounts of glucose or lactose (from 0.1 to 1.0%) were added to the casein digest egg cube medium, and these tubes were seeded with B. sporogenes and with one or the other of the two selected strains of B. acidophilus (strain B which produced considerable amounts of acid but does not clot milk, and strain M which forms less acid and is a milk clotter). A third series was seeded with B. coli and B. sporogenes, and a fourth with B. sporogenes alone. The acidity factor was controlled by other series of tubes seeded with B. acidophilus B and M, and B. coli. B. sporogenes was selected as the proteolytic organism because of its exceptionally potent digestive properties for coagulated egg albumin.

Exper. 5.—Test Medium: Casein digest sugar-free broth plus coagulated egg albumin cubes P_H 7. Series of tubes were prepared containing the following percentages of glucose: 0.1, 0.2, 0.3, 0.4, 0.5, 0.75, and 1.0; other series were prepared with the same amounts of lactose. Inoculation cultures: B. sporogenes, 0.5 c c. of a 6-day growth in casein digest broth; B. acidophilus, 0.5 c c. of a normal salt solution suspension prepared by centrifuging 18-hour glucose broth cultures and using the sediment for the suspension; B. coli, 0.5 c c. of a suspension prepared as for B. acidophilus. Procedure: A series of these egg cube broth tubes with graded amounts of glucose were inoculated with B. acidophilus, strains B or M, and with B. sporogenes. The surface of the medium in each tube was covered with about 1 cm. of soft vaseline which permitted the escape of gas but yet maintained anaerobiosis.

A similar series was prepared employing lactose instead of glucose. Controls consisted of: (a) A series of the glucose and also the lactose tubes seeded with B. acidophilus strains alone, and also with B. coli alone; (b) a series of glucose tubes and also a 1.0% lactose[10] tube planted with B. sporogenes; and (c) an unseeded tube of the medium to serve as a control of sterility and reaction.

All these tubes were incubated at 37 C. and examined each day for 7 consecutive days for degree of growth, proteolysis and H-ion concentration. In determining the latter, approximately 1.0 c c. of the fluid was removed from a tube by means of a Pasteur capillary pipet—the tip of which was sealed and broken after plunging through the vaseline cap—and adding it to 4 c c. of a dye indicator solution. These dye indicator solutions in neutral water were prepared

[10] As B. sporogenes does not split lactose, it was not necessary to run a full series with this sugar.

TABLE 1

INHIBITION OF PROTEOLYSIS OF CUBES OF COAGULATED EGG ALBUMIN BY B. SPOROGENES WHEN GROWN IN ASSOCIATION WITH B. ACIDOPHILUS OR B. COLI IN PRESENCE OF GRADED AMOUNTS OF GLUCOSE OR LACTOSE

Strains	Per Cent. Sugar	Glucose								Lactose							
		1st Day		3d Day		5th Day		14th Day		1st Day		3d Day		5th Day		14th Day	
		Proteolysis*	P_H	Proteolysis	P_H	Proteolysis	P_H	Proteolysis	P_H	Proteolysis	P_H	Proteolysis	P_H	Proteolysis	P_H	Proteolysis	P_H
B. acidophilus B.	0.1	—	6.6	+++	6.4	++++	6.4	compl	6.7	—	6.6	+++	6.3	++++	6.4	compl.	6.6
B. acidophilus M.		+—	6.6	compl.	6.5	compl.	6.4	compl	6.6	—	6.5	compl.	6.5	compl.	6.6	compl.	6.6
B. coli..........		—	6.4	compl.	6.4	compl.	6.4	compl.	6.9	—	6.4	++++	6.4	compl.	6.4	compl.	6.7
B. sporogenes....		+	6.6	++++	6.5	++++	6.4	compl.	6.8								
B. acidophilus B.	0.2	—	6.2	+++	6.3	++++	6.4	compl.	6.6	—	6.6	+++	6.3	++++	6.4	compl.	6.6
B. acidophilus M.		+—	6.3	compl.	6.4	compl	6.4	compl.	6.5	—	6.5	compl.	6.5	compl.	6.4	compl.	6.5
B. coli..........		—	6.2	compl.	6.3	compl.	6.4	compl.	6.9	—	6.2	++++	6.4	compl.	6.4	compl.	6.7
B. sporogenes....		+	6.6	++++	6.4	++++	6.4	compl.	6.8								
B. acidophilus B.	0.3	—	5.7	++	6.1	+++	6.4	compl.	6.7	—	6.4	+—	5.8	+++	6.4	compl.	6.6
B. acidophilus M.		—	5.8	++++	6.4	compl.	6.4	compl.	6.4	—	5.8	compl.	6.3	compl.	6.2	compl.	6.5
B. coli..........		—	5.9	++	6.1	compl.	6.4	compl.	6.9	—	5.8	+—	6.0	compl.	6.4	compl.	6.7
B. sporogenes....		+	6.2	++++	6.4	++++	6.4	compl.	6.8								
B. acidophilus B.	0.4	—	5.4	—	5.6	—	5.6	compl.	6.6	—	5.1	—	5.8	—	5.8	compl.	6.4
B. acidophilus M.		—	5.8	++	6.4	compl.	6.4	compl.	6.5	—	5.4	++	5.7	compl.	6.2	compl.	6.3
B. coli..........		—	5.6	—	5.9	compl.	6.3	compl.	6.8	—	5.6	—	5.8	compl.	6.3	compl.	6.6
B. sporogenes....		+—	6.2	++++	6.4	++++	6.4	compl.	6.8								
B. acidophilus B.	0.5	—	5.2	—	5.4	—	5.4	—	5.3	—	5.1	—	5.1	—	5.4	compl.	6.4
B. acidophilus M.		—	5.6	+	6.1	++++	6.3	compl.	6.4	—	5.4	—	5.3	++	6.0	compl.	6.4
B. coli..........		—	5.3	—	5.6	—	5.5	compl.	6.5	—	5.4	—	5.7	+	6.0	compl.	6.6
B. sporogenes....		+—	5.6	+	5.8	++++	6.4	compl.	6.5								
B. acidophilus B.	0.75	—	5.0	—	4.8	—	4.8	—	4.6	—	5.0	—	5.0	—	5.2	—	5.0
B. acidophilus M.		—	5.4	—	5.4	—	5.6	—	5.3	—	5.0	—	5.1	—	5.2	—	5.0
B. coli..........		—	5.2	—	5.4	—	5.3	—	5.3	—	5.0	—	5.4	—	5.2	—	5.2
B. sporogenes....		—	5.4	—	5.4	+—	5.8	compl.	6.5								
B. acidophilus B.	1.0	—	5.0	—	4.4	—	4.4	—	4.4	—	5.0	—	4.4	—	4.4	..	...
B. acidophilus M.		—	5.0	—	5.2	—	5.0	—	4.6	—	4.8	—	4.8	—	4.8	—	4.8
B. coli..........		—	4.8	—	4.8	—	4.8	—	4.7	—	4.8	—	4.6	—	4.6	—	4.7
B. sporogenes....		—	4.8	—	4.8	—	4.8	—	4.7	—	6.3	++	6.4	++++	6.5	compl.	6.5

* Degrees of proteolysis indicated as follows: +—, trace; +, slight; ++, moderate; +++, marked; ++++, nearly complete; compl., complete.

with brom-thymol blue, brom-cresol purple or methyl red, as called for. In reading the H-ion concentrations, comparisons were made with a LaMotte series of buffered standards prepared with these color indicators. The essential accuracy of this method was substantiated by the consistency of the readings from day to day. In the following tables the findings on selected days only are given by way of illustration.

The figures in the tables indicate clearly that inhibition of proteolysis under the conditions of this experiment is directly correlated with the degree of acidity at a given time. Irrespective of the type of acid

TABLE 2

CONTROLS FOR ACID PRODUCTION BY B. ACIDOPHILUS STRAINS AND B. COLI FOR TABLE 1a

	Per Cent. Sugar	1st Day		3d Day		5th Day		7th Day		14th Day	
		Glucose P_H	Lactose P_H	Glucose P_H	Lactose P_H	Glucose P_H	Lactose P_H	Glucose P_H	Lactose P_H	Glucose P_H	Lactose P_H
B. acidophilus B......	0.1	6.1	6.2	6.2	6.6	6.6	6.6	6.6	6.3	6.6	6.4
B. acidophilus M......		6.6	6.6	6.6	6.5	6.6	6.5	6.6	6.6	6.5	6.5
B. coli................		6.2	6.3	6.4	6.3	6.4	6.3	6.5	6.5	...	6.5
B. acidophilus B......	0.2	5.8	6.8	5.6	5.8	5.6	6.0	5.8	5.9	5.5	5.9
B. acidophilus M......		6.1	6.2	6.3	6.3	6.3	6.2	6.3	6.2	6.4	6.2
B. coli................		6.0	6.0	6.3	6.2	6.3	6.2	6.4	6.4	...	6.5
B. acidophilus B......	0.3	5.4	6.8	5.4	5.6	5.2	5.4	5.1	5.2	5.2	5.4
B. acidophilus M......		5.6	5.5	5.6	5.8	5.8	5.6	5.8	5.7	5.8	5.6
B. coli................		5.7	5.7	5.8	5.7	6.0	5.8	6.2	6.2	...	6.4
B. acidophilus B......	0.4	5.0	6.8	5.0	5.0	5.0	4.6	4.8	4.8	4.9	5.1
B. acidophilus M......		5.4	5.4	5.5	5.6	5.6	5.6	5.7	5.5	5.5	5.5
B. coli................		5.5	5.6	5.5	5.6	5.6	5.7	5.6	6.0	...	5.7
B. acidophilus B......	0.5	5.0	6.8	4.6	4.6	4.6	4.6	4.6	4.6	4.8	4.7
B. acidophilus M......		5.0	5.5	5.2	5.4	5.2	5.3	5.0	5.3	4.9	5.3
B. coli................		5.4	5.5	5.5	5.4	5.6	5.4	5.6	5.3	...	5.7
B. acidophilus B......	0.75	5.2	6.8	4.4	4.6	4.4	4.6	4.4	4.4	4.4	4.4
B. acidophilus M......		5.2	5.2	4.6	5.0	4.6	4.8	4.6	4.9	4.6	4.7
B. coli................		5.2	5.5	5.0	5.2	4.9	5.3	5.0	4.8	...	5.0
B. acidophilus B......	1.0	5.4	6.8	4.4	4.4	...	4.4	...	4.4	...	4.4
B. acidophilus M......		4.8	4.8	4.4	4.4	4.4	4.4	4.4	4.5	4.4	4.4
B. coli................		5.2	5.4	4.9	5.2	4.9	5.3	5.0	4.8	...	5.0

producing organism grown in association with B. sporogenes, visible proteolysis, as evidenced by the digestion of the egg cube, starts at P_H 5.8 and becomes rapid when the reaction reaches points between 6.0 to 6.4. A comparison of table 1 with table 2 also indicates that B. sporogenes can initiate its proteolytic action at as high a degree of acidity as P_H 5.2, but at this point the digestion affects only the nitrogenous substances in solution. This proteolysis is evidenced by a gradual and progressive trend toward neutrality and probably occurs only after the available carbohydrate in the medium has been greatly reduced or exhausted through fermentation. As stated above, however, it is only when the H-ion concentration reaches P_H 5.8 or above that the digestion of the native protein (coagulated egg albumin) is first apparent. If sufficient sugar is present (0.75% or more) to permit the maintenance of an acidity of P_H 5.6 or more, the egg cubes remain intact.

The titration figures given in the control tabulations indicate that the production of alkalinity is due to the B. sporogenes and to a less degree to B. coli. With B. coli, however, nitrogenous material is not attacked actively in the presence of available carbohydrates, whereas this factor affects the proteolytic activity of B. sporogenes in less degree. B. acidophilus makes slight demand on the nitrogenous substances in the medium as is evidenced by the marked stability of reaction in the control tubes for this organism containing only 0.1% of glucose or

TABLE 3

COMPARATIVE TESTS OF LACTIC AND HYDROCHLORIC ACIDS IN THE INHIBITION OF PROTEOLYSIS OF COAGULATED EGG ALBUMEN BY B. SPOROGENES

Initial P_H	Growth		1st Day Proteolysis		2d Day Proteolysis		5th Day Proteolysis		10th Day Proteolysis		Final P_H 10th Day	
	HCl	Lactic	HCl	Lactic	HCl	Lactic	HCl	Lactic	HCl	Lactic	HCl	Lactic
6.2	++++	++++	++	—	++++	+	compl.	++++	compl.	compl.	6.5	6.5
5.8	++++	+++	+	—	+++	—	compl.	+++	compl.	compl.	6.5	6.3
5.4	+++	++	—	—	++	—	++++	+	compl.	+++	6.4	6.3
5.0	+—	+—	—	—	—	—	—	—	—	—	5.6	5.4
Control 7.2	++++	++++	++++	++++	++++	++++	compl.	compl.	compl.	compl.	6.8	6.8

lactose; the sugars are apparently exhausted after 24 hours' growth, but the H-ion concentration with strain M remained practically constant for 14 days, although with strain B there occurred a slight trend toward neutrality.

These tabulations also bring out the point that the variety of sugar incorporated in the medium was a factor of some slight importance in determining the degree of inhibition of B. sporogenes when grown in association with B. acidophilus or B. coli. Lactose was rather more effective than glucose up to 5 days. With glucose as well as lactose, however, as much as 0.75% was necessary to permit the 2 strains of B. acidophilus and the B. coli strain to check proteolysis completely for 14 days. With smaller amounts of these sugars B. acidophilus strain B proved much more effective in this inhibition than did strain M or B. coli. In the experiments with the lactose medium a somewhat longer period of inhibition was obtained with the milk clotting B.

acidophilus strain M than with the glucose medium. B. acidophilus B splits lactose slowly, and at the end of 24 hours' incubation had produced little acid, but in 3 days its acidity production exceeded that of strain M and also of B. coli and in the end, as with glucose, it proved a more effective inhibitor of proteolysis than did the two latter organisms.

As is well known, B. acidophilus and also B. coli belong in the group of lactic acid producing organisms. The question arose, accordingly, whether the efficiency of these organisms in checking proteolysis might be ascribed, in part at least, to the larger amounts of this acid produced. Lactic acid has been given credit by numerous investigators [11] as an effective antiputrefactive agent, especially in reference to the intestinal tract, but their conclusions have been almost entirely unsupported by experimental evidence. It seemed desirable, accordingly, to carry out the following experiment in which a comparative test was made of lactic and hydrochloric acids as regards their relative efficiency in the inhibition of the decomposition of coagulated egg albumin by B. sporogenes.

Exper. 6.—Medium: Casein digest, meat infusion, peptone broth with egg cubes added as explained under exper. 1. The control tubes contained this medium with a reaction of P_H 7.2. Other tubes of medium were given the following H-ion concentrations through the addition of lactic or hydrochloric acid: 5.0, 5.4, 5.8, and 6.2. Test organism: B. sporogenes. Procedures: The tubes of culture medium, prepared as above, were seeded with sporogenes and sealed with petrolatum. They were incubated and the degree of digestion of the egg cubes and the change in the reactions were noted from day to day for 6 days and on the 10th day.

The foregoing experiment, the results of which were confirmed, indicated that at a given H-ion concentration between 5.0 and 6.2, lactic acid exercised a distinctly greater inhibitory action on proteolysis by B. sporogenes than did hydrochloric acid. This was particularly obvious after 2 days' incubation and distinguishable after 6 days. At the end of the period of observation, 10 days, there was, however, little difference in the degree of digestion in the two sets of tubes. It should be observed, also, that at this time all tubes showing marked proteolysis exhibited reactions between P_H 6.3 and 6.5. The lactic acid also seemed to inhibit the growth of B. sporogenes to a greater degree than did hydrochloric acid, and this factor probably accounts largely for the differences in proteolysis noted above.

[11] For bibliography and discussion the reader is referred to Rettger and Cheplin, Intestinal Flora, 1921.

Belonovsky,[12] many years ago, suggested that there may be other antiputrefactive substances produced by lactic acid bacillli which are quite as important as the lactic acid in curtailing putrefaction. As stated above, our efforts to detect any such products developed during the growth of B. acidophilus have proved fruitless. In one of these experiments the egg cube casein digest broth medium was employed without the addition of any sugar, and B. acidophilous was added in the form of a washed 18-hour growth suspended in salt solution. Although B. acidophilus grew well in this medium, no inhibition of proteolysis by the spore-bearing anaerobes seeded simultaneously was observable. The same result was obtained when only 0.1% of lactose was added to this medium. In another experiment minced beef heart medium [13] with a reaction of P_H 6.8 was employed. The anaerobes used were B. histolyticus, B. putrificus, and B. sporogenes; B. acidophilus strains were B. and M. All of these strains grew up strongly in the medium. Because of the absence of sufficient carbohydrates, however, B. acidophilus strains were able to produce an acidity no greater than P_H 6.2 to 6.4. Daily observations failed to reveal any inhibition of the digestion of the meat when B. acidophilus and the proteolytic anaerobes grew up together under these conditions. Thus the two experiments detailed above and certain others of a similar nature disclosed no inhibitory product of B. acidophilus other than acidity which was effective on these spore-bearing anaerobes.

DISCUSSION

As Cannon and McNease [14] have observed, changes and transformations in the intestinal flora may be dependent on a considerable number of different factors, but for our present purposes the predominance of B. acidophilus, with a consequent simplification of the flora, which follows the ingestion of diets containing liberal amounts of lactose or dextrin, might be considered to be due to one or more of the following three causes: (a) to the production in situ of sufficient acid to inhibit the growth of certain other intestinal bacteria; (b) to the elaboration of inhibitory metabolic products other than acids; (c) to the mechanical crowding out and starvation of other bacterial types through the overgrowth of B. acidophilus by virtue of the fact that diets of that

[12] Ibid., 1907, 21, p. 1001.

[13] Minced beef heart, 500 gm.; peptone, 10 gm., water, 1000 c c. This mixture was cooked slowly for 2 hours in a double boiler and tubed by placing the minced meat in tubes to the depth of about 1 inch and the fluid to a total of about 2 inches.

[14] Jour. Infect. Dis., 1923, 32, p. 175.

character produce conditions in the lower bowel which are particularly favorable for this organism. It is probable, however, that as regards the principal native types of intestinal bacteria one factor may be operative principally in the suppression of one bacterial group and another for a different group. In this study we are concerned alone with the determination of the cause of the inhibition of the spore-bearing putrefactive anaerobes and, as a result of these experiments, we are convinced that certainly in vitro and probably in vivo this inhibition is due to the increased acidity produced by B. acidophilus.

The inhibitory effect of acidity, especially of lactic acid, on proteolysis has been suggested in the past by a number of investigators [11] as a reasonable explanation for the apparent antiputrefactive effect on intestinal floras of such agents as milk soured with B. bulgaricus. Certain of these advocates of sour milk therapy have placed the emphasis on the acid proformed, whereas, on the other hand, Wegele [15] claimed that the acid produced by B. bulgaricus when growing in the intestine is the more important factor in checking putrefaction in that locality. In view of the fact, however, that the inability of B. bulgaricus to become acclimatized to the intestinal tract of man and white rats has recently been demonstrated by Rahe,[16] Hull and Rettger [4] and Rettger and Cheplin,[5] the theory of Wegele as applied to this bacillus is hardly tenable. B. acidophilus, on the other hand, apparently adapts itself more readily to intestinal conditions (Rettger and Cheplin,[5] Kopeloff [7]), and the possible effect of its acid production in situ is deserving of more serious consideration.

Rettger and Cheplin,[5] as a result of their experiments with white rats and human subjects, reached the conclusion that the acidity factor is of little or no importance in permitting the predominance of B. acidophilus within the intestinal tract. In the case of rats they found that the H-ion concentrations within the cecum and colon of animals harboring a simplified flora, strongly dominated by B. acidophilus, ran almost parallel with those of animals harboring the usual complex floras, the hydrogen-ion readings for material from each of these localities ranging in the two sets of animals from 5.6 to 6.2. In view of our results, however, it should be noted that this degree of acidity is sufficient to inhibit at least the active production of proteolytic ferments if these spore-bearing putrefactive anaerobes were prone to develop in the intestines of these rodents. In a recent article by Cannon and

[15] Deutsch. med. Wchnschr., 1908, 34, p. 11.
[16] Jour. Infect. Dis., 1915, 16, p. 210.

McNease [14] on the influence of H-ion concentration on bacterial types prevailing in the intestinal tract the conclusion was reached that the acidity factor is an important one in bringing about the simplification of the intestinal flora in white rats when fed on diets containing lactose. Their findings in regard to the reaction of material in the cecum, at least, showed a much higher acidity than the figures reported by Rettger and Cheplin, as the acidity in this locality reached at times an H-ion concentration of 4.4 to 4.6, and in the colon of 5.0 to 6.2. This former acidity, in itself, is not only sufficient to check absolutely growth of B. sporogenes according to our findings, but also, as they point out, that of the colon group.

Rettger and Cheplin carried out similar acid titration experiments with human subjects, except that the acidity of the intestinal content could be estimated only from determinations made with the stool specimens. With two of these subjects on an ordinary diet the hydrogen-ion readings ranged from 6.0 to 6.4, and no increase in acidity occurred when B. acidophilus was brought to predominance through feeding lactose, or cultures and lactose. With two other individuals, however, under similar treatment the acidity reached a considerably higher point, namely 5.0 to 5.5. In each of these cases, too, it is reasonable to suppose that the acidity at higher levels of the large intestine would be greater than that shown by stool specimens. These several findings, in fact, would seem to be quite compatible with the theory that the enhanced acidity developed within the intestinal tract as the result of the predominance of B. acidophilus or related organisms is the important factor in the suppression of the spore-bearing putrefactive anaerobes. Further, it has been our experience as the result of bacterial analyses of many fecal specimens from normal and abnormal human subjects that the specimens in which these anaerobes were present in largest numbers showed H-ion concentrations ranging from 6.4 to 7.4 —the zone for their optimal growth in culture mediums—whereas in more acid specimens the group was practically unrepresented.

Dernby and Blanc [17] in a recent study reported that the B. sporogenes was capable of growing in a fluid medium giving H-ion concentrations within the range of 4.0 to 8.0, although only a trace of growth was noted in acidities greater than 4.9. Working with sterile ferments prepared by filtering 3-day broth cultures of this organism, these investigators also found that gelatin and peptone were digested within the

[17] Jour. Bacteriol., 1921, 6, p. 419.

same H-ion concentration zone, with the maximal degree of digestion between 5.5 and 6.3. No tests, however, were carried out in which the relation of the H-ion concentrations of the substrate to the production of tryptic ferments by the growing organism was determined. Our experiments cover this point and show that, although ferments capable of digesting some nitrogenous substance in the medium—probably peptone—may be formed at reactions between 5.0 and 5.8 (tables 1 and 3) a tryptic ferment of such a nature or in sufficient amount as to proteolyse native proteins does not manifest itself unless the H-ion concentration rises above 5.8 to 6.0. We are in practical agreement with these investigators as regards the zone for optimal growth of B. sporogenes, namely, 6.3 to 7.5.

SUMMARY

It has been determined that when B. acidophilus is grown in association with each of several varieties of proteolytic spore-bearing anaerobes, including B. sporogenes, B. histolyticus and B. botulinus, in a medium favorable to both, proteolysis of solidified egg albumin cubes is prevented for a period of 10 days or more in the presence of 0.5% of glucose. The control tubes showed advanced digestion in 3 or 4 days. Further, if these organisms are grown in association in milk, digestion of the casein is inhibited indefinitely, whereas in the control cultures it is marked in 2 or 3 days. Strains of B. acidophilus were found to differ considerably in their antiputrefactive properties, and these differences were correlated with the amount of acid produced.

In other experiments with the same medium the proteolytic anaerobes were given an 18-hour start and established themselves fully before B acidophilus was seeded into the tubes, but even under these conditions the aciduric bacteria were able to overgrow the proteolytic organisms and inhibit their digestive functions for the periods specified.

The inhibition of the proteolytic anaerobes by B. acidophilus seemed to be dependent entirely on the acid produced by the latter. Comparative tests of B. acidophilus and B. coli as proteolytic inhibitors showed that in general no great difference existed between them, although one strain of B. acidophilus employed caused greater inhibition than the B. coli strain used, but this was clearly related to the greater amount of acid produced by the former.

Irrespective of the type of acid producing organism grown in association with B. sporogenes, visible proteolysis, as evidenced by the digestion and disintegration of the egg cubes, started at about P_H 5.8 and became rapid when the reaction reached points between 6.0 and 6.4, although proteolytic action on the nitrogenous substances in solution was initiated at as high a degree of acidity as P_H 5. If sufficient sugar was present, either glucose or lactose (0.75% or more), to permit the maintenance of an acidity of P_H 5.6 or higher, the egg cubes remained intact indefinitely.

Lactic acid was found to exercise a somewhat greater inhibitory effect on proteolysis by B. sporogenes than did hydrchloric acid.

No inhibitory product, other than acidity, for these spore-bearing putrefactive anaerobes could be detected in the fluid cultures of B. acidophilus.

EXPERIMENTS IN PRODUCTION OF TYPHOID AGGLUTININS IN SUCCESSIVE GENERATIONS OF RABBITS

M. F. Guyer and E. A. Smith

From the Zoological Laboratory, University of Wisconsin, Madison

Two different opinions have been advanced to account for the fact that some races of men and some strains of animals are more immune than others to certain germ diseases. According to the one view, when the germs of such a disease are first introduced into a population, all susceptible persons—and this probably means most of the population—are likely to become infected. Some persons, however, will usually prove to be wholly or partially immune from the first. Those of the population unable to successfully combat the infection die. Since the next generation springs from the survivors, it tends to inherit the natural immunity possessed by its parents. Succeeding generations suffer from the same infection until mainly persons who can in some degree resist it are left. In other words, the population ultimately comes to consist of the descendants of those who originally possessed a complete or partial natural immunity; susceptible strains have been eliminated through exposure generation after generation to the disease in question. In this explanation, the hereditary resistance which finally prevails is not attributed in any degree to the immunity acquired by those persons that had the disease and recovered.

According to the other view, when the disease is first introduced into the population many persons contract it. Those who recover do so because they probably receive a less severe infection to begin with and are therefore able to build up a resistance through the reactions of their own living tissues. This acquired immunity not only persists and protects the recovered person against further attacks of the disease, but also is transmitted in some degree to the offspring. When the latter, in turn, contract the disease they develop a still greater immunity. This continues generation after generation, and thus a racial immunity is gradually established.

This second view obviously carries with it not only the implication that such immunity is transmitted to the young, but also that it becomes

Received for publication, July 15, 1923.

hereditary. The theory that such acquirements can become truly heritable, most present-day geneticists and embryologists and many students of evolution regard as probably untenable in the light of our modern knowledge of the origin of germ cells, the behavior of hereditary traits, and the apparent lack of relation between such mutations as do occur and any discernible external causative agent. It is clear that the matter can be settled only by further experimentation.

Encouraged by the results of earlier experiments [1] in which inheritable eye defects were produced in fetal young by the injection of pulped crystalline lens or of lens antibodies into pregnant rabbits and guinea-pigs, the writers have undertaken experiments the ultimate goal of which is to determine whether or not hereditary immunity can be induced. While that goal has not yet been attained, the results are encouraging, and it has seemed advisable as a report of progress to publish certain of the facts accumulated so far.

Bacillus typhosus was chosen as a test organism for several reasons: in the first place, standardized strains of it can be easily obtained; secondly, rabbits will readily build up antibodies against it although they do not develop typhoid fever; and lastly, the agglutination test affords a ready means of determining the degree of immunization which has been attained. Our experiments have been in progress over three years, during which time four generations of rabbits have been secured.

It is a well-known fact that rabbits and other animals untreated experimentally in any way may give positive typhoid-agglutinin reactions in low dilutions; any rabbit the blood of which showed positive reactions in a dilution of 1:40 was rejected. In our first experiments, pregnant females were used. On the day the animal was bred or the the day after, each female was given an injection of 0.5 c c. vaccine intravenously. At first so-called strain 1, which contained only dead typhoid bacilli, was employed, but for the majority of our experiments a vaccine designated as strain 2 was used. Besides typhoid bacilli, this vaccine contained paratyphoid A and B. Several injections of vaccine given at intervals of a week were followed by doses of 0.5 c c. of living bacilli suspended in salt solution. For injections of living typhoid bacilli, 24-hour agar slant cultures washed down with 2 c c. of normal salt solution were used. One half c c. of such a suspension was injected

[1] Guyer and Smith: Jour. Exper. Zoöl., 1918, 26, p. 65, 1920, 31, p. 171.

intravenously. When, as happened occasionally, 40 and 48 hour cultures of typhoid were employed as antigen, either more salt solution was added or a smaller dose was administered. It is obvious that our suspensions of typhoid bacilli were only approximately the same, but for producing antibodies accurately measured doses of antigen are not necessary. Sooner or later, however, we expect to check our results by using the method devised by Gates [2] for standardizing suspensions. After some experimentation, we found that we were giving an unnecessarily large number of doses to secure a maximum result, so we reduced the number; but still, for some months, we kept a week as the interval of time between doses. During the last year and a half, the interval between injections has been cut to one day.

The agglutination test—both microscopic and macroscopic—was employed at intervals to determine the degree of immunization which had been developed. To obtain blood for the microscopic agglutination test the fur is clipped from the ear of the rabbit and, after wiping the ear with alcohol, a drop of blood is drawn from the marginal vein. This blood is allowed to clot and dry on a slide. Normal salt solution is mixed with the dried blood until the solution becomes "strawberry" red. This color is supposed to indicate a dilution of 1 part blood to 10 parts salt solution. To a platinum loop of this 1:10 dilution placed on a cover slip, a loop of salt solution is added to make a 1:20 dilution; to a loop of the 1:20 dilution placed on another cover slip, a loop of salt solution is added to make a 1:40 dilution. Similarly from a 1:40 dilution a 1:80 is made and so on up to a 1:320 dilution or higher. Then to the first cover slip containing a 1:10 dilution of blood a loop of typhoid suspension in salt solution is added, thus making a final dilution of 1:20. Likewise the 1:20 becomes a 1:40 dilution when an equal amount of typhoid suspension is added to it, and the 1:320 becomes a 1:640 dilution when similarly mixed with typhoid suspension. Next, over a hollow ground slide previously ringed with petrolatum, each cover slip is inverted and pressed down to prevent the admission of air. After standing an hour at room temperature the preparations are examined under the microscope. If the typhoid bacilli that were added are clumped, the blood has developed the type of antibodies known as agglutinins. The larger the amount of agglutinins there is, the higher will be the dilution in which clumping or agglutination occurs, and the

[2] Jour. Exper. Med., 1918, 27, p. 725.

greatest dilution that will still produce the reaction is supposed to indicate the degree of immunity the animal has acquired. The microscopic test, although obviously inexact as regards the amount of real dilution in the "strawberry red" serum, with which the scale is started, nevertheless has certain advantages: blood can be drawn and kept for days before the test is made, and, what is of great importance in the case of very young animals, only a small amount of blood is required.

The more accurate macroscopic test was used in all the later experiments whenever sufficient blood could be drawn. The procedure for this test is different. A 24-hour agar slant culture of typhoid bacilli is washed down with a small amount of normal salt solution, and the suspension is then made up to 10 c c. by the addition of more normal salt solution. The blood to be tested is drawn from the artery of the rabbit's ear into a glass syringe and then put into centrifuge tubes. The antiserum secured by centrifuging is made into a 1:5 dilution with salt solution. In each of a series of tubes 0.5 c c. of salt solution is placed; to the first tube containing 0.5 c c. of salt solution an equal amount of the 1:5 dilution of antiserum is added, producing 1 c c. of a 1:10 dilution of the antiserum; 0.5 c c. of this 1:10 dilution is then carried over into the second tube containing 0.5 c c. of salt solution, leaving 0.5 c c. of the 1:10 dilution in the first tube and 1 c c. of a 1:20 dilution the second tube; 0.5 c c. of the 1:20 dilution is carried over into a third tube to make a 1:40 dilution. This procedure is repeated in successive dilutions until one of 1:40,960 is secured. Five c c. from the last tube are discarded. Thus each tube contains 0.5 c c. of liquid, and the scale of antiseral dilutions ranges from 10 to 40,960. To each tube, 0.5 c c. of the thyroid suspension is added. This again dilutes the contents of each by half, so that the final dilutions range from 20 to 81,920. The tubes are incubated at 37.5 C. for 2 hours before readings are made. For controls one tube containing 0.5 c c. typhoid suspension (antigen), one containing 0.5 c c. of the 1:10 dilution of antiserum, and one containing 0.5 c c. of salt solution were incubated along with the other series of tubes.

In our later experiments each kind of test was employed, but the macroscopic is preferable because of the greater accuracy possible in the initial dilution. In very young animals, however, only a drop or two of blood can be taken; hence one is dependent on the microscopic test. As the animals grew older, both microscopic and macroscopic tests were applied. Theoretically the results from the two tests should be the same, but as a matter of fact they rarely coincided. The macroscopic test almost invariably yielded a higher titer, indicating that our initial dilutions for the microscopic test, based on judgment of color, were too great.

Our first intention was to immunize the females to typhoid during pregnancy, but we soon found that because of the high intrauterine mortality this procedure was not feasible. Of twenty-seven females injected during pregnancy, for example, only 4 produced young. Of 15 young carried through the gestation period, 13 were born alive, but only 5 were cared for by the mother. The other 8 were partially eaten. The 23 females that did not give birth to young were known to have mated, hence we concluded that in most cases, at least, their young died in utero from the effects of toxic substances that passed through the placenta.

Young, however, were easily secured when the females were bred after the immunization was completed. A total of 18 females bred after receiving the doses of typhoid vaccine and bacilli produced 68 young. At intervals of a month, the blood of the mothers and young was tested for agglutinating power. In all cases the blood of the young agglutinated typhoid bacilli, and in the majority of cases the titer was equal to that of the mother at the first test. Individual young in the same litter sometimes showed differences in titer.

As shown in the accompanying tables, titers gradually dropped in succeeding months in both mother and offspring. The rate of this drop varied in different families. The titer of the young in one family, for example, dropped from 320 to 160 in 4 months, while that of the mother remained at 320. At the end of 5 months, the titer of the young was 80. The same titer was maintained for 9 months, when the tests were discontinued. The detailed evidence for the foregoing statement is set forth in the following tables:

Table 1 shows the record of a female that was immunized during pregnancy.

Table 1 is a record of female 23A3 and her young; the details of immunization of the animal are recorded in part 1 of the table. Five young (55A series) in utero during the immunization were born on May 22. On the day of birth, all gave the microscopic agglutination test in blood dilutions of 320 with a slight clumping in a dilution of 640. By Oct. 9, the titer of the young and that of the mother had dropped to 80. During the next 2 months, the 5th and 6th months after birth, the blood of the young increased in agglutinating power. On Nov. 17, for example, one of these young, 55A5, had a titer of 320. In January, the titer had returned to 80, where it remained through March.

Tables 2 to 6 inclusive show records of females and young which were obtained through matings made after immunization was completed.

TABLE 1

I. TREATMENT OF FEMALE 23A3

Remarks	Date of Inoculation, 1919	Dosage in C c.	Agglutination (Microscopic)	
			Date	Dilution
April 22, 23A3	....	....	April 22	0
bred to 23A2..............	April 22	1.0 vaccine		
	May 1	1.0 vaccine		
	May 8	1.0 vaccine		
	May 15	0.5 living germs		
Five young born May 22... (55A series)	....	....	May 22	640

II. AGGLUTINATION TESTS (MICROSCOPIC) OF MOTHER 23A3 AND YOUNG (55A SERIES)

1919–20	Rabbit	Titers	Remarks
May 22......................	23A3	640	
	55A1 to 55A5	320	
June 12.....................	23A3	320	
	55A1 to 55A5	640	55A1, 55A3 were males; 55A2, 55A4, 55A5, females
June 27.....................	23A3	320	
	55A1 to 55A5	320	
July 29......................	23A3	320	
	55A1 to 55A5	320	
Aug. 14......................	23A3	320	
	55A1 to 55A4	160	
	55A5	320	
Oct. 9........................	23A3	80	
	55A1 to 55A5	80	
Nov. 17......................	23A3	80	
	55A1 to 55A4	160	
	55A5	320	
Dec. 8........................	55A1	160	
	55A4	160	
Jan. 21.......................	55A4	80	
March 12.....................	55A1	80	
	55A4	80	

Tables 2 to 6, inclusive, show records of females and young which were obtained through matings made after immunization was completed.

Table 2 is the record of female 4B2. She was first bred on Feb. 13, 1919. On Feb. 14, her blood when tested was negative in all dilutions. She was given doses of vaccine intravenously on Feb. 14, 15, 20, 21 and 22. These were followed by living bacilli on Feb. 27, March 6, April 24, May 1, and May 8. Her highest titer (microscopic test) was reached on May 16, when blood diluted 640 times agglutinated typhoid bacilli.

As no young resulted from the first mating, 4B2 was rebred on April 24. This mating also proving sterile, another mating was made on June 15, without further injections. On July 16, six young (51A series) were born. These were first

TABLE 2

I. TREATMENT OF FEMALE 4B2

Remarks	Date of Inoculation, 1919	Dosage in C c.	Agglutination (Microscopic)	
			Date	Dilution
Feb. 13, 4B2 bred to 4A8; no young born	Feb. 14	0.5 vaccine	Feb. 14	0
	Feb. 15	0.5 vaccine		
	Feb. 20	0.5 vaccine		
	Feb. 21	0.5 vaccine		
	Feb. 22	0.5 vaccine		
			Feb. 27	80
	Feb. 27	0.5 living germs		
	Mar. 6	0.5 living germs		
			Apr. 22	160
Apr. 24, rebred to 4A8; no young born	Apr. 24	0.5 living germs		
	May 1	0.5 living germs		
	May 8	0.5 living germs		
			May 16	640
June 15, rebred to 4A8				
July 16, six young born (numbered 51A)				
			Aug. 14	320

II. AGGLUTINATION TESTS (MICROSCOPIC) OF MOTHER (4B2) AND YOUNG (51A SERIES)

1919	Rabbit	Titers	Remarks
Aug. 14	4B2	320	
	51A1	320	
	51A2	320	
	51A3	320	
	51A4	320	
	51A5	320	
	51A6	320	
Sept. 12	4B2	160	
	51A1	160	
	51A2	80	
	51A3	80	
	51A4	160	51A5 and 51A6 died of slobbers
Oct. 9	4B2	320	
	51A1	160	
	51A2	80	
	51A3	80	51A4 died
Nov. 17	4B2	160	
	51A1	160	
	51A2	160	51A3 died

tested on Aug. 14. The blood of the mother and that of each of the young gave positive microscopic agglutinating reactions in dilutions of 320. By Sept. 12, when the young were next tested, the titer of 51A2 and 51A3 had dropped to 160, while the blood of the mother and that of the other 2 young gave faint positive tests in dilutions of 320. On Oct. 9, the date of the next test, the mother's blood still gave a positive reaction in a dilution of 320, but of the 3 young still alive, 51A2 and 51A3 had a titer of 80, while 51A1 still reacted positively in a dilution of 160. At the time of the last test, Nov. 17, the blood of the mother reacted positively in a dilution of 320, but 51A1 and 51A2, the only survivors of the litter, had a titer of 160.

Table 3 is the record of 21A2 and her young (52A series). The details of immunization are set forth in the table. The young when first tested 5 weeks

TABLE 3

I. TREATMENT OF FEMALE 21A2

Remarks	Date of Inoculation, 1919	Dosage in C c.	Agglutination (Microscopic)	
			Date	Dilution
Feb. 13, 21A2 bred to 12B2; no young born	....	....	....	20
	Feb. 14	0.5 vaccine		
	Feb. 15	0.5 vaccine		
	Feb. 20	0.5 vaccine		
	Feb. 21	0.5 vaccine		
	Feb. 22	0.5 vaccine		
			Feb. 27	80
	Feb. 27	0.5 living germs		
	Mar. 6	0.5 living germs		
			Apr. 21	160
	Apr. 24	0.5 living germs		
	May 8	0:5 living germs		
			May 16	640
May 21, remated to 12B2				
June 22, six young born (numbered 52A); one with paralyzed hind legs was killed			July 9	160

II. AGGLUTINATION TESTS (MICROSCOPIC) OF MOTHER (21A2) AND YOUNG (52A SERIES)

1919-20	Rabbit	Titers
July 29	21A2	320
	52A1 to 52A5, all	320
Aug. 13	21A2	320
	52A1 to 52A5, all	160
Sept. 12	21A2	320
	52A1	320
	52A2 to 52A5, all	80
Oct. 9	21A2	160
	52A1	80
	52A2 to 52A5, all	80
Nov. 17	21A2	320
	52A1	160
	52A2 to 52A5, all	160
Dec. 8	21A2	160
	52A1	80
	52A2 to 52A5, all	80
Jan. 21	52A1 to 52A5, all	80
March 12	21A2	80
	52A1 to 52A5, all	80

after birth gave positive agglutinating reactions by the microscopic test in dilutions of 320. After 4 months the highest titer was 160, and the blood of some of the young gave positive reactions in dilutions of only 80. By the end of March, the highest titer was 80. During the period from July to March, the titer of the mother fell from 640 to 80.

Table 4 records the treatment of female 11. There is nothing in the data concerning her litter (53A series) that needs especial mention. The titer of one of the young 5 months after birth had dropped to 80. The titer of the mother fell from 320 in June to 160 in November.

Table 5 is the record of 23B3 and her young (54A series). There is a fluctuation in the titer of the young. At the first testing of the blood, July 29, the

TABLE 4

I. TREATMENT OF FEMALE 11

Remarks	Date of Inoculation, 1919	Dosage in C c.	Agglutination (Microscopic)	
			Date	Dilution
Feb. 12, No. 11 mated to 4A7; no young born	....	....	....	0
	Feb. 14	0.5 vaccine		
	Feb. 15	0.5 vaccine		
	Feb. 20	0.5 vaccine		
	Feb. 21	0.5 vaccine		
	Feb. 22	0.5 vaccine		
			Feb. 27	80
	Feb. 27	0.5 living germs		
	Mar. 6	0.5 living germs		
			Apr. 22	160
	Apr. 24	0.5 living germs		
	May 1	0.5 living germs		
	May 8	0.5 living germs		
			May 16	320
Mated to 3A1; June 16, two young born (numbered 53A)			June 27	320

II. AGGLUTINATION TESTS (MICROSCOPIC) OF MOTHER (11) AND YOUNG (53A SERIES)

1919	Rabbit	Titers	Remarks
June 27	11	320	
	53A1 and 53A2	320	
July 29	11	320	
	53A1 and 53A2	160	
Aug. 14	11	160	
	53A1 and 53A2	80	
Sept. 12	11	320	
	53A1	80	
	53A2	80	
Oct. 9	11	160	For further tests on 11 and a second litter see table 7
	53A1	80	
	53A2	80	
Nov. 17	11	160	
	53A1	80	
	53A2	80	For tests on the offspring of female 53A2 see table 8

reaction was positive in dilutions up to 320, but on Aug. 14 and Sept. 12 the blood had lost most of its agglutinating power, as it gave a positive reaction in a dilution of only 20. In the next two tests made on Oct. 9 and Nov. 17 the blood showed a gain in agglutinating ability as it reacted positively in a dilution of 80.

Table 6 gives the history of female 4A6 and her young (56A series). The young began with a titer of 320 on Aug. 14 and 8 months later still retained a titer of 160.

TABLE 5

I. TREATMENT OF FEMALE 23B3

Remarks	Date of Inoculation, 1919	Dosage in C c.	Agglutination (Microscopic)	
			Date	Dilution
Feb. 14, 23B3 bred to 21A3; no young born	....	....	Feb. 14	0
	Feb. 14	0.5 vaccine		
	Feb. 15	0.5 vaccine		
	Feb. 20	0.5 vaccine		
	Feb. 21	0.5 vaccine		
	Feb. 22	0.5 vaccine		
			Feb. 27	80
	Feb. 27	0.5 living germs		
	Mar. 6	0.5 living germs		
			Apr. 22	160
	Apr. 24	0.5 living germs		
	May 1	0.5 living germs		
	May 8	0.5 living germs		
			May 16	640
Remated to 21A3; eight young born (54A series) June 19				
			July 29	640

II. AGGLUTINATION TESTS (MICROSCOPIC) OF MOTHER 23B3 AND YOUNG (54A SERIES)

1919	Rabbit	Titers	Remarks
July 29......................	23B3	640	
	54A1 to 54A8	320	
Aug. 14......................	23B3	320	
	54A1 to 54A7	20	54A8 died
Sept. 12......................	23B3	160	
	54A1 to 54A7	20	
Oct. 9........................	23B3	80	
	54A1 to 54A5	40	54A6 and 54A7 died
Nov. 17......................	23B3	160	
	54A1 to 54A4	80	
	54A5	40	

TABLE 6

I. TREATMENT OF FEMALE 4A6

Remarks	Date of Inoculation, 1919	Dosage in C c.	Agglutination (Microscopic)	
			Date	Dilution
			Apr. 22	0
	Apr. 22	1.0 vaccine		
Apr. 24, 4A6 bred to 4A7, rebred Apr. 30; no young born	May 1	1.0 vaccine		
	May 8	1.0 vaccine		
	May 15	0.5 living germs		
	May 23	0.5 living germs		
Bred to 4A7 July 1; seven young born (56A series)			Aug. 14	640

II. AGGLUTINATION TESTS (MICROSCOPIC) OF MOTHER 4A6 AND YOUNG (56A SERIES)

1919–20	Rabbit	Titers	Remarks
Aug. 14......................	4A6	320	
	56A1 to 56A7	320	
Sept. 13......................	4A6	320	
	56A1 to 56A7	160	Two young died
Oct. 9........................	4A6	320	
	56A1 to 56A5	160	
Nov. 17......................	4A6	160	
	56A1	160	
	56A2 to 56A5	320	

Certain females, without further immunization, were tested for their ability to transmit immunity to a second litter. Table 7 shows that such a second litter (53B series) from female 11, for instance, gave a faint positive reaction in a dilution of 160, which was the titer of the mother. Two months later the titer in both mother and young had dropped to 80.

TABLE 7

AGGLUTINATION TESTS (MICROSCOPIC) OF FEMALE 11 AND HER SECOND LITTER (53B SERIES)

1919–20	Rabbit	Titers	Remarks
Nov. 17	11	160	Mated to male 25 Oct. 16; six young born Nov. 16 (numbered 53B)
Dec. 8	11	80	
	All young but 53B5	80	
	53B5	80	
Jan. 21	11	80	
	53B1 to 53B4	80	53B5 and 53B6 died

Since a mother could evidently pass on immunity to more than one litter, it became of interest to know whether individuals which had acquired immunity from their mothers could transmit it to their offspring. Young females with a titer of 120 or 160 which had been obtained from their immunized mothers were bred. The offspring of such second generation animals had a titer as high, and in some instances even higher, than the mothers. The details of this are shown in tables 8 and 9.

Table 8 is a record of female 53A2 and her young (90A series). This female, one of the offspring of a mother whose record is given in table 4, was bred to male 25. Six young were born on Dec. 12. When tested on Jan. 21, the mother gave a faint positive agglutination in a dilution of 160. Three of the young gave better agglutination in 160 than the mother; one gave the same reaction as the mother; 2 were negative in dilutions of 160 but positive in 80. This family was not tested again until March 12. The mother and 2 of the young gave positive reactions in a dilution of 80; 3 of the litter reacted in a dilution of 60, and 1 had dropped to a titer of 40. On July 11 this same female bore 2 young (90B series). When on Oct. 4 these young were first tested, 90B1 had a titer of 160, while that of the mother was only 80. The other individual of this litter, 90B2, gave a reaction in a dilution of only 40.

Table 9 also shows tests made on second generation young, whose parents were untreated, but whose maternal grandmother had been immunized to typhoid bacilli. One of the litter, 53A1, whose record is given in table 4, was bred to male 55A1, the pedigree of which is given in table 1. Five young (91 A series) were born on May 2. When first tested on May 22, the mother and three of the young gave positive reactions in a dilution of 80. Two of the young, however, had the ability to agglutinate typhoid bacilli in dilution of 120. On July 3, two of the young gave a faint positive reaction in a dilution of 120; one had a titer of 160; the mother and the other 2 still reacted in a dilution of 80. By Aug. 7, 91A4, the animal which had a titer of 160 on July 3 was again tested, but this time the reaction in a dilution of 120 was faint. By Oct. only 3 of the litter reacted in a dilution of 80, while the titer of the mother and the remaining 2 was 60.

TABLE 8

AGGLUTINATION TESTS (MICROSCOPIC) OF FEMALE 53A2 AND HER YOUNG (90A SERIES)

1919–20	Rabbit	Titers	Remarks
Nov. 17	53A2	80	53A2, daughter of an inoculated mother (see table 4), bore six young (90A series) on Dec. 12, by male 25
Jan. 21	53A2	80	
	90A1	160	
	90A2	80	
	90A3	80	
	90A4	160	
	90A5	80	
	90A6	160	
March 12	53A2	80	
	90A1	80	
	90A2	60	
	90A3	40	
	90A4	60	
	90A5	60	
	90A6	80	
			July 11, 53A2 bore 90B1 and 90B2, fathered by 55A1
Oct. 4	53A2	80	
	90B1	160	
	90B2	40	

TABLE 9

AGGLUTINATION TESTS (MICROSCOPIC) ON SECOND GENERATION YOUNG; GRANDMOTHERS IMMUNIZED, PARENTS UNTREATED

1920	Rabbit	Titers	Remarks
March 12	53A1	80	53A1 (see table 4), bred to 55A1 (see table 1) April 2; five young born (91A series)
	55A1	60	
May 22	53A1	80	
	91A1	120	
	91A2	80	
	91A3	80	
	91A4	120	
	91A5	80	
July 3	53A1	80	
	91A1	80	
	91A2	80	
	91A3	120	
	91A4	160	
	91A5	80	
Aug. 7	53A1	60	
	91A4	120	
Oct. 4	53A1	60	
	91A1	80	
	91A2	60	
	91A3	60	
	91A4	80	
	91A5	60	

We next experimented on the second and third generation animals to determine whether or not such animals could be made to develop still higher titers than had been acquired by their immunized ancestors. If this were so, then it became of much importance to learn whether a high titer is prolonged in their offspring, and whether their offspring will acquire a still higher titer on immunization. Children and grandchildren from such second and third generation animals, with titers of 80 to 160, were immunized by repeated doses of vaccine and typhoid bacilli. Of 10 second generation females treated during pregnancy, none reared young. Two (53A2, 90A1), however, as set forth in tables 10 and 11, gave birth to full term young which, although dead, were found in time to make blood tests. The blood of these young showed positive titers (160 and 320, respectively).

TABLE 10

TREATMENT OF FEMALE 53A2

Remarks	Date of Injection, 1921	Dosage in C c.	Agglutination	
			Date	Dilution
53A2 previously used in an experiment had a titer of 2,560 on Sept. 26; 5 young born Oct. 25; all this litter but one eaten by mother; one discovered at 12, shortly after birth with heart intact and leukocytes active; blood tested	Oct. 6	0.5 vaccine	Sept. 26	2,560 (macrosc.)
	Oct. 8	1.0 vaccine	Oct. 19	2,560
	Oct. 11	0.5 living germs		
	Oct. 13	1.0 living germs		
			One young Oct. 25	160 (microsc.)

Table 10 records the treatment of female 53A2, a second generation animal. Her titer was unusually high when the experiment was begun, for only a short time before, along with a number of other females, she had been immunized, but no young were secured. On Sept. 26, her blood by the macroscopic test agglutinated typhoid bacilli in a dilution of 2,560. Although repeatedly injected during pregnancy from Oct. 6 to Oct. 13, her titer did not rise above this. As young were expected on the morning of Oct. 25, several inspections of the cage were made. At 12 o'clock the remains of 5 young were found, all but one badly chewed by the mother. The uninjured one had the heart intact and the leukocytes still active. A microscopic blood test showed that the blood of the young had an agglutinating titer of 160.

Table 11 describes the treatment of female 90A1, a daughter of 53A2 (see table 8). As a result of a previous immunization, she had a titer of 2,560 when the experiment began. With treatment during pregnancy from Oct. 6 to 13, the titer of her blood was increased to 5,120. On the morning of Oct. 25, three dead young were found in her cage, but only one of them had not been mutilated. How long they had been dead could not be determined. The blood from the heart of the intact animal when tested was found to agglutinate in a dilution of 320. However, in such a case acid agglutination might account for the titer.

Third generation typhoid animals immunized before breeding produced young readily. Of the 12 animals experimented on, the tabulated records of only 3 are given. The tests on 91A5 and her family were carried through a period of 8 months, while those on 91A4 and 91A1 were continued for 5 months.

Table 12 is a record of female 91A5 (table 9) and her offspring (98B series). On May 4, the day after breeding, this female, previously immunized, had a titer of 10,240 when tested by the macroscopic test but only 2,560 by the microscopic test. Of the 9 young born on June 3, only 6 were alive July 1, when the first test was made. The blood of the mother on this date, by the microscopic test, had a titer faintly positive in a dilution of 1,280. One of the 6 young showed a positive reaction in a dilution of 240; one, a faint reaction in 160; the remaining 4 yielded titers of 120.

TABLE 11

TREATMENT OF FEMALE 90A1

Remarks	Date of Injection, 1921	Dosage in C c.	Agglutination	
			Date	Dilution
90A1 bred to male 57A4 on Sept. 26			Sept. 26	2,560 (macrosc.)
	Oct. 6	0.5 vaccine		
	Oct. 8	1.0 vaccine		
	Oct. 11	0.5 living germs		
	Oct. 13	1.0 living germs	Oct. 19	5,120 (macrosc.)
Oct. 25, three young found dead; 2 of these were partly eaten; third one intact was opened up and blood from the heart tested; just how long these had been dead could not be accurately determined and the high titer may be due to acid agglutination	....	....	1 young Oct. 25	320 (microsc.)

At the time of the second test, July 28, the titer of the mother by the microscopic test was 320. Only 3 of the young were alive and these all had a titer of 80. The result of a similar test on Aug. 25 was the same. In order to make sure that no mistake in technic was made on Aug. 25, a second test was run from the same blood samples with the same results.

The test on Sept. 22 showed that the mother by the microscopic test still had a titer of 320 (but 640 by the macroscopic test). Microscopic tests on the young showed that the titer of 2 had risen; one from 80 to 160, a second from 80 to 240. A macroscopic test on the young corroborated these results.

The macroscopic tests in October and November showed a decrease in titer of the young, only one of which retained a titer of 80. In December, however, all 3 of the young had titers of 80, while in February one, 98B2, had a titer of 160. The titer of the mother remained constant throughout the period.

Table 13 records the tests on 91A4 (table 9) and her offspring (97B series). Aug. 19, this female showed after immunization a titer of 10,240. This dropped to 640 by Oct. 6, at which point it was maintained until February. The February monthly test, however, showed that it had risen to 1,280. The young, beginning with a titer of 160 three weeks after birth, maintained that titer with slight fluctuations until January. In that month there was a drop to 80 in all but one individual which still maintained the higher titer. One of the litter showed a rise to 320 on Feb. 3.

TABLE 12

I. TREATMENT OF FEMALE 91A5

Remarks	Date of Inoculation, 1921	Dosage in C c.	Agglutination	
			Date	Dilution
91A5 bred to 71A3 on May 3, 1921	Apr. 16	0.5 vaccine	Apr. 16	80
	Apr. 18	1.0 vaccine		
	Apr. 20	2.0 vaccine	May 4	
	Apr. 23	0.5 living germs	....	2,560 (microsc.) 10,240 (macrosc.)
	Apr. 25	1.5 living germs		
9 young born June 3; three died before tests were made				

II. AGGLUTINATION TESTS OF MOTHER (91A5) AND YOUNG (98B SERIES

Date	Rabbit	Titers
July 1	91A5	640 (microsc.)
	Young 1	80 (microsc.)
	Young 2	240 (microsc.)
	Young 3	120 (microsc.)
	Young 4	120 (microsc.)
	Young 5	120 (microsc.)
	Young 6	120 (microsc.)
July 28	91A5	320 (microsc.)
		640 (macrosc.)
	Young 1	80 (microsc.)
	Young 2	80 (microsc.)
	Young 3	40 (microsc.)
Aug. 25	91A5	640 (macrosc.)
		240 (microsc.)
	Young 1	80 (microsc.)
	Young 2	80 (microsc.)
	Young 3	40 (microsc.)
Aug. 25	91A5	160 (microsc.)
	Young 1	80 (microsc.)
	Young 2	80 (microsc.)
	Young 3	80 (microsc.)
Sept. 22	91A5	640 (macrosc.)
	Young 1	80 (macrosc.)
	Young 2	160 (macrosc.)
	Young 3	240 (macrosc.)
	91A5	320 (microsc.)
	Young 1	80 (microsc.)
	Young 2	160 (microsc.)
	Young 3	160 (microsc.)
Oct. 20	91A5	640 (macrosc.)
	Young 1	80 (macrosc.)
	Young 2	40 (macrosc.)
	Young 3	20 (macrosc.)
	91A5	160 (microsc.)
	Young 1	80 (microsc.)
	Young 2	80 (microsc.)
	Young 3	40 (microsc.)
Nov. 17	91A5	640 (macrosc.)
	98B1	80 (macrosc.)
	98B2	40 (macrosc.)
	98B3	20 (macrosc.)
Dec. 15	91A5	640 (macrosc.)
	98B1	80 (macrosc.)
	98B2	80 (macrosc.)
	98B3	80 (macrosc.)
Feb. 14	91A5	640 (macrosc.)
	98B1	80 (macrosc.)
	98B2	160 (macrosc.)
	98B3	40 (macrosc.)

Table 14 contains the record of 91A1 (table 9) and her young (110A series). All the young were tested each month. A glance through the table shows a striking uniformity in the reactions of the young to the agglutination test. Two months after birth, in November, the titers of 3 dropped to 80; one remained at 160. In December, all had a titer of 160, while in January all dropped to 40. The test in February showed a rise to 80 in 110A1 and 110A4; the other two, 110A2 and 110A3, each had a titer of 160.

TABLE 13

I. TREATMENT OF FEMALE 91A4

Remarks	Date of Injection, 1921	Dosage in C c.	Agglutination	
			Date	Dilution
All injections made intraperitoneally	Aug. 4	0.5 vaccine		
	Aug. 6	1.0 vaccine		
	Aug. 8	1.5 vaccine		
Bred to 49A1	Aug. 11	0.5 living germs		
	Aug. 13	1.0 living germs	Aug. 19	10,240 (macrosc.)
Five young born Sept. 16				

II. AGGLUTINATION TESTS OF 91A4 AND YOUNG 97B SERIES

Date	Rabbit	Titers
Oct. 6	91A4	640 (macrosc.)
		320 (microsc.)
	Young 1	160 (microsc.)
	Young 2	160 (microsc.)
	Young 3	160 (microsc.)
	Young 4	160 (microsc.)
	Young 5	160 (microsc.)
Nov. 10	91A4	640 (macrosc.)
		320 (microsc.)
	Young 1	80 (microsc.)
	Young 2	80 (microsc.)
	Young 3	80 (microsc.)
	Young 4	160 (microsc.)
	Young 5	160 (microsc.)
Dec. 8	91A4	640 (macrosc.)
		640 (microsc.)
	Young 1	160 (microsc.)
	Young 2	320 (microsc.)
	Young 3	160 (microsc.)
	Young 4	320 (microsc.)
	Young 5	320 (microsc.)
Jan. 9	91A4	640 (macrosc.)
		320 (microsc.)
	Young 1, white	160 (macrosc.)
		160 (microsc.)
	Young 2, white	80 (macrosc.)
		80 (microsc.)
	Young 1, pigmented	80 (macrosc.)
		80 (microsc.)
	Young 4, pigmented	80 (macrosc.)
		80 (microsc.)
	Young 5, pigmented	40 (macrosc.)
		40 (microsc.)
Feb. 3	91A4	1280 (macrosc.)
	97B1, pigmented	40 (macrosc.)
	97B2, pigmented	40 (macrosc.)
	97B4, white	320 (macrosc.)
	97B5, white	80 (macrosc.)

An individual, 98A3, four generations removed from the ancestor (female 11) first immunized was treated with vaccine and later with living typhoid bacilli as set forth in table 15. The animal attained the unusual titer of 40,960 after immunization. This record of 98A3

TABLE 14

I. TREATMENT OF FEMALE 91A1

Remarks	Date of Inoculation	Dosage in C c.	Agglutination	
			Date	Dilution
Bred to 71A3 on May 5, 1921	Apr. 23	0.5 vaccine	Apr. 23	160 (microsc.)
	Apr. 25	1.0 vaccine	May 14	640 (microsc.)
				1,280 (macrosc.)
	Apr. 27	2.0 vaccine	July 13	1,280 (macrosc.)
	Apr. 30	0.5 living germs	July 22	640 (microsc.)
	May 2	2.0 living germs	....	1,280 (macrosc.)
	July 13	3.0 milk		
	July 23	0.5 vaccine	July 23	1,280 (macrosc.)
	July 25	1.0 vaccine		
	July 27	1.5 vaccine		
	July 30	0.5 living germs		
	Aug. 2	1.0 living germs	Aug. 9	10,240 (macrosc.)
Bred to 92B3 on Aug. 11; Sept. 12, 6 young born				

II. AGGLUTINATION TESTS OF MOTHER 91A1 AND YOUNG (110A SERIES)

Date	Rabbit	Titers
Oct. 6	91A1	640 (macrosc.)
		320 (microsc.)
	Young 1	160 (microsc.)
	Young 2	160 (microsc.)
	Young 3	160 (microsc.)
	Young 4	160 (microsc.)
	Young 5	160 (microsc.)
	Young 6	160 (microsc.)
Nov. 10	91A1	640 (macrosc.)
		320 (microsc.)
	Young 1	80 (microsc.)
	Young 2	80 (microsc.)
	Young 3	80 (microsc.)
	Young 4	160 (microsc.)
Dec. 8	91A1	1280 (macrosc.)
		640 (microsc.)
	Young 1	160 (microsc.)
	Young 2	160 (microsc.)
	Young 3	160 (microsc.)
	Young 4	160 (microsc.)
Jan. 12	Young 1	40 (macrosc.)
		40 (microsc.)
	Young 2	40 (macrosc.)
		40 (microsc.)
	Young 3	40 (macrosc.)
		40 (microsc.)
	Young 4	40 (macrosc.)
		40 (microsc.)
Feb. 8	110A1	80 (macrosc.)
	110A2	160 (macrosc.)
	110A3	160 (macrosc.)
	110A4	80 (macrosc.)

(table 15) and of her young (111A series) discloses further that individual fluctuations in the titers of the young occurred during the 2d, 3rd, and 4th months after birth. In February, 5 months after birth, the 2 young still alive each had a titer of 320.

TABLE 15

I. TREATMENT OF FEMALE 98A3

Remarks	Date of Injection	Dosage in C c.	Agglutination (Macroscopic)	
			Date	Dilution
Bred to male 97A2	July 23	0.5 vaccine	July 23	20
	July 25	1.0 vaccine		
	July 27	1.5 vaccine		
	July 30	0.5 living germs		
	Aug. 2	1.5 living germs		
Sept. 10, 4 young born			Aug. 9	40,960

II. AGGLUTINATION TESTS OF MOTHER 98A3 AND YOUNG 111A1 SERIES

Date	Rabbit	Titers
Oct. 5	98A3	1280 (macrosc.)
		640 (microsc.)
	Young 1	320 (microsc.)
	Young 2	320 (microsc.)
	Young 3	160 (microsc.)
	Young 4	160 (microsc.)
Nov. 10	98A3	1280 (macrosc.)
		320 (microsc.)
	Young 1	160 (microsc.)
	Young 2	160 (microsc.)
	Young 3	160 (microsc.)
	Young 4	160 (microsc.)
Dec. 8	98A3	1280 (macrosc.)
		640 (microsc.)
	Young 1	320 (microsc.)
	Young 2	160 (microsc.)
	Young 3	160 (microsc.)
	Young 4	160 (microsc.)
Jan. 5	98A3	1280 (macrosc.)
		640 (microsc.)
	Young 1, pigmented	80 (macrosc.)
		40 (microsc.)
	Young 2, white	20 (macrosc.)
		20 (microsc.)
	Other 2 died	
Feb. 2	98A3	640 (macrosc.)
	111A1	320 (macrosc.)
	111A2	320 (macrosc.)

A brother, 98A4, of female 98A3 was immunized to typhoid about a year later and gave the same high titer of 40,960 as she did. After this showing of high titers in fourth generation animals various individuals from other strains which had been under immunization for 3 or 4 generations were tested, and it was found that a considerably higher titer could be developed in them than could be engendered in previously untreated first generation animals. Thus, male 92A2 and female 92A3, offspring of 51A2 by 51A1 (table 2), each developed a titer of 20,480, and of their 2 young (107A series), one developed a titer of 20,480 on immunization, the other a titer of 40,960. Another female, 113A2, four generations removed from her ancestor which was first treated (23A3 of table 1), on immunization yielded a titer of 40,960.

For our purposes it was clearly necessary to know more about the maximum titer obtainable as the result of typhoid immunization in the first generation. Because of the lack of precision in the microscopic agglutinin reaction, and for purposes of control and comparison, an additional series of tests were made macroscopically on a group of 4 rabbits taken at random from our untreated stock supply. Great care was taken to have all measurements accurate. As a further precaution all titrations were done in duplicate. On this group, after immunization the serum of male N1A4 ran 3 plus in all dilutions from 40 to 5,120 inclusive; that of female N4A1 did likewise; that of female N5A4 gave 3 plus in all dilutions up to and including 2,560 and 2 plus in a dilution of 5,120; and male N7A4 gave 3 plus in dilutions up to 1,280, 2 plus in dilution 2,560 and 1 plus in dilution 5,120. Without giving space to the formal tabulation of these results, then, it may be said that in each of the 4 rabbits immunized the highest dilution in which positive results were secured was 1 to 5,120. We regard this as the standard maximum titer for typhoid agglutinins in our strains of rabbits in the first generation, according to the macroscopic test, using our materials and methods of immunization.

It is an interesting fact that young of immunized mothers, as shown in tables 1, 8, 12, 13, 14 and 15, not only fluctuated in titer during the 2d, 3d and 4th months, but almost invariably gained in titer the 5th or 6th month after birth. This variation in antibody formation was shown by a few individuals produced by the first immunized mothers. In 55A5 (table 1), for instance, 6 months after birth the titer rose from 80 to 320, and the other 4 young in this litter showed titers higher than that of the mother. Another example of this occurs in table 8.

This rise in titer would seem to indicate that the body of the young animal is constructing antibodies to supplement those derived from the mother. Possibly in the process of development some organ important in the production of agglutinins, inactive at first, commence to function.

Since rabbits begin to breed when from 5 to 8 months old, it may be at the time of sexual maturity some secretion is liberated into the blood which stimulates increased antibody formation or causes a general speeding up of metabolism. Solution of this phenomenon may throw additional light on the problem of agglutinin production.

There has been much discussion recently of protein therapy and nonspecific immunization (for literature see Petersen[3]). Some of our own experiments show how other antigens may augment the production of typhoid agglutinins. We found that animals which had been immunized to any one of various foreign proteins would, when later immunized to typhoid, give the typhoid-agglutinin reaction in higher dilution than would animals which had not first received a protein treatment; also, that the titer of animals immunized to typhoid could be raised by injections of other proteins. For example, rabbit 28C2, descendant of a female which had received large injections of an anti-lens fowl serum, was immunized to typhoid and developed a titer of 20,480. This is higher than we ever secured from immunizations of rabbits which had never been used in any kind of serologic experiment. It is clear from this that the history of animals used in such experiments should be known. On the other hand, 2 rabbits 90A2 and 93A3, previously immunized to typhoid bacilli, showed an increased ability to agglutinate such bacilli after 3 intravenous injections of cow's milk given on successive days in quantities of 2, 4 and 6 c c., respectively.

After establishing the fact that the young rabbits receive immunity from the mother, the question arises as to how the antibodies pass from mother to young. Does the fetus receive the antibodies from the blood of the mother before birth? Or, as has been suggested by some investigators, do the antibodies accumulate in the milk, especially the colostrum, and get into the young animal after birth?

Our first attempt to solve this question was by exchanging young from an immunized mother with the young from a normal mother. As shown in table 16, we found that when nursed by a normal mother, young born of an immunized mother retained a fairly high titer for several months. On the other hand, the young of the normal mother nursed by the immunized mother, acquired a titer from the milk of the foster mother, but lost it rapidly after weaning time.

3 Protein Therapy and Nonspecific Resistance, 1922.

Table 16 gives the detailed results of this exchange. On May 22 a female, 23B, that gave negative reactions in all dilutions was bred to male 16A2. There resulted from this mating 3 young born June 23, 1920. One June 21, an immunized mother, 52A2 (see table 3), had given birth to 3 young (93A series). The litters were exchanged so that the immunized mother nursed the young from the negative female and vice versa.

The first test of the young was made on July 3. The young of the immunized mother of 52A2 nursed by 23B2 gave positive agglutinating reactions in dilutions through 120, although the foster mother herself remained negative in all dilutions. The young of 23B2, however, nursed by the immunized female, 52A2, gave positive reactions in dilutions of 80, while 52A2 herself gave a positive reaction in a dilution of 160.

TABLE 16

EXCHANGE OF YOUNG; MOTHER 52A2 IMMUNIZED; MOTHER 23B2 UNTREATED

1920	Rabbit	Titers (Microscopic)	Remarks
May 22	23B2	0	23B2 bred to a normal male (16A2), May 22; had 3 young (94A series) June 23
June 24	23B2	0	
	Young of 23B2	0	June 24, these young exchanged for the 3 young (93A series) of immunized mother 52A2 born June 21, fathered by 55A1
July 3	52A2	120	
	23B2	0	
	Young of 52A2 nursed by 23B2	120	
	Young of 23B3 nursed by 52A2	80	
Aug. 7	52A2	160	
	23B2	0	
	Of young of 52A2 nursed by 23B2		
	Two gave	120	
	One gave	120	
	Of young of 23B2 nursed by 52A2		
	Two gave	0	
	One gave	80	
Oct. 4	52A2	120	
	23B2	0	
	Of young of 52A2 nursed by 23B2		
	93A2 gave	120	93A1 died
	93A3 gave	120	
	Of young of 23B2 nursed by 52A2		
	94A1 gave	40	
	94A2 gave	0	
	94A3 gave	20	

The next test was made on Aug. 7. Two of the young of 52A2 nursed by 23B2 whose reaction still remained negative had a positive titer in dilutions of 120. One gave a faint reaction in a dilution of 160. Of the young of 23B2 nursed by 52A2, 2 gave negative reactions while one was still positive in a dilution of 80. The female 52A2 still gave a positive reaction in dilutions through 160.

On Oct. 4, the tests were as follows: 93A2 and 93A3, young of 52A2 reared by 23B2, still retained agglutinating power; 93A2 gave a faint positive reaction in a dilution of 160 while 93A3 was positive in a dilution of 120. The reactions of the foster mother continued to be negative. The young of 23B2 reared by 52A2 gave reactions as follows: 94A1 positive in a dilution of 40; 94A2 negative; 94A3 a faint positive reaction in 20. The immunity which the 3 young acquired after birth through the milk of 52A2 lasted about 3 months. The immunity possessed by the young of 52A2, gained during development within the mother and partly through 2 days of suckling before the exchange was made, persisted undiminished during the 3 months the tests were made.

To determine certainly that antibodies pass from the mother to the offspring through the placenta as well as through the milk, rabbits immunized to sheep serum were killed just before the young were due. The fetuses removed from the uterus were washed in warm sterile salt solution before the membranes were ruptured. Their blood was drawn from the end of the umbilical cord into a glass tube, A precipitin test made with the serum obtained from the fetal blood showed that the fetal blood gave positive reactions in dilutions of 10 to 2,560.

Other females immunized to typhoid bacilli were also killed a few days before their young were to be born. In these experiments amniotic fluid as well as blood was collected and tested for agglutination. In all cases the blood of the unborn young gave positive tests in dilutions similar to or very near those of the mother's blood. The amniotic fluid likewise gave positive agglutination reactions but in dilutions slightly lower than the embryonic blood. The details of these experiments will be published separately.

REVIEW OF LITERATURE

Several investigators have established the fact that offspring born of mothers previously rendered immune to a disease are immune for weeks or months after birth. As early as 1888, Chauveau [4] observed that lambs from anthrax-immune ewes were more resistant to anthrax than lambs from normal ewes. Ehrlich [5] showed that mice could transmit to their offspring an immunity against the vegetable poisons ricin and abrin. From the fact that immunized males when mated to normal females did not produce immune offspring, and from the absence of immunity in the grandchildren of immunized females, Ehrlich concluded that the antibodies were transmitted from mother to offspring through the blood during gestation or through the milk after birth.

As Famulener [6] gives an extensive review of the various papers prior to 1912 that deal with the transmission of immunity from mother to offspring, we will discuss chiefly papers that deal with typhoid agglutinins, and with such others as throw light on the problems undertaken by us.

[4] Ann. de l'Inst. Pasteur, 1888, 11, p. 66.
[5] Ztschr. f. Hyg. u. Infektionskrankh., 1892, 12, p. 183.
[6] Jour. Infect. Dis., 1912, 10, p. 332.

Some of the clinical cases reported show that mothers who have typhoid while pregnant usually abort. Schumacher,[7] Staübli,[8] Mosse and Daunic [9] state that blood taken from the end of the cord when full-term children are born to mothers who have suffered from typhoid during pregnancy gave positive agglutinating reactions. Scholtz [10] found that the blood from a 7 months' infant was also positive. On the other hand, Etienne,[11] Charrier and Apert [12] and Dogliotte [13] found that under similar circumstances the body fluids from fetuses (three to 6 months old) were negative to the agglutinin test.

Experiments with typhoid on animals by various investigators substantiate the positive clinical findings. Young rabbits born from a mother inoculated with typhoid bacilli 6 days before parturition when tested for agglutinating power of blood were found positive by Widal and Sicard.[14] The blood of the young, however, was weaker in agglutinating power than that of the mother. The experiments of Remlinger,[15] Jurewitsch [16] and Staübli [17] indicate that guinea-pigs immunized during pregnancy in the majority of cases transmit agglutinins to the young.

Howell and Eby [18] in their experiments immunized one rabbit against B. typhosus. Agglutinins persisted in the blood of the young 4 weeks after parturition. They found that antisheep and antihuman hemolysins were transmitted to the young but gradually diminished until at the end of 11 weeks none were detectable.

In the experiments cited so far no attempt was made to find out whether the agglutinins were transmitted to the young in utero or through the milk of the mother. Castaigne,[19] Courmont and Cade [20] report cases of infants nursing from mothers who had typhoid after parturition gave positive reactions against typhoid bacilli. Mothers who had suffered from typhoid from 2 to 21 years before parturition had milk positive in dilutions of 1 : 25 and blood positive in dilutions of

[7] Ztschr. f. Hyg. u. Infektionskrankh., 1901, 37, p. 323.
[8] München. med. Wchnschr., 1906, 53, p. 768.
[9] Compt. rend. Soc. de biol., 1897, 49, p. 238.
[10] Hyg. Rundschau., 1898, 8, p. 417.
[11] Presse méd., 1896, 4, p. 465.
[12] Compt. rend. Soc. de biol., 1896, 48, p. 1103.
[13] Gior. d. r. Accad. di med. di Torino, 1897, 60, p. 419.
[14] Ann. de l'Inst. Pasteur, 1897, 11, p. 353.
[15] Ibid., 1899, 13, p. 129.
[16] Centralbl. f. Bakteriol., I. O., 1903, 33, p. 76.
[17] Ibid., p. 458.
[18] Jour. Infect. Dis., 1920, 27, p. 550.
[19] Semaine med., 1897, 17, p. 429.
[20] Compt. rend. Soc. de biol., 1899, 51, p. 619.

1:50, but the nursing children remained negative. Achard and Bensuade [21] describe the case of a mother who contracted typhoid while nursing a child. In this case the milk of the mother became positive only in dilutions of 1:10 and the child remained negative.

Schumacher [7] immunized a goat late in pregnancy and tested the blood of the kid before it had suckled. No agglutinins were found. McArthur [22] states that pigs of mothers immunized to hog cholera are rendered passively immune, and second litters were as highly immune as the first litters or even more so. He infers that the antibodies are transferred through the milk from the fact that the immunity lasts only a few weeks after weaning. He also found that nursing pigs sicken as soon as the mother becomes infected with the disease.

Famulener [6] as a result of his experiments with hemolysins, concludes that goats actively immunized against sheep blood corpuscles during gestation transmit the specific hemolysin to the young, not through the placenta, but through the colostrum. He found that colostrum from goats immunized during gestation contains more hemolysin than the blood serum. That the suckling kids obtain the hemolysin from the colostrum is indicated by the fact that young kids not permitted to nurse show no hemolysin. The placenta, he concludes, plays a minor rôle in the passage of hemolysins. When, however, mothers were not immunized until after the birth of the young, the milk failed to transmit any demonstrable immunity to the nursing kids. Young kids 10 to 18 days old were given injections of sheep blood cells, and a slight but definite hemolysis was produced at the end of 12 days. Famulener claims that the blood of the kid has only a slight capacity for antibody formation. He believes that the young animal soon after birth receives colostrum containing hemolysins and is thus rendered immune by way of the alimentary tract. This supposed permeability of the alimentary tract to antibodies is believed to last only a few days.

In experimenting with agglutinins against Bacillus abortus, Little and Orcut [23] found that while the colostrum and milk of the mother was high in agglutinins, the serum of the calf was negative until after its first meal. After a few days the titer of the calf's serum increased. In 2 calves the titer went above that of the mother. These investigators, like Famulener, believe that the antibodies pass from mother to offspring in the colostrum and are absorbed through the walls of the digestive tract.

[21] Bull. et mém. Soc. méd. d. hôp. de Paris, 1896, 13, p. 697.
[22] Jour. Infect. Dis., 1918, 22, p. 541.
[23] Jour. Exper. Med., 1922, 35, p. 161.

Recently Bourgnin,[24] on the other hand, finds that the placentae of rabbits and guinea-pigs are permeable to antibodies and enzymes. Agglutinins produced when the mother was injected with Bacillus paratyphosus A and B, with B. typhosus or with B. coli passed the placenta. Diphtheria antitoxin passed through more slowly than the agglutinins. She concludes that the relative concentrations which substances reach on the two sides of the placenta depend on whether they are indifferent substances, or whether they are substances, the concencentration of which in the serum, the maternal or fetal organism can regulate.

DISCUSSION

Before taking up any discussion of our own results, it seems wisest to point out several things that may have led to the great confusion of opinion as to how antibodies pass from mother to offspring. In the first place, several different types of antibodies have been employed by the numerous workers in this field. Precipitins, agglutinins, and cytolysins, such as bacteriolysins and hemolysins, are antibodies of different orders. In agglutinins, for example, so far as we know, only one thing is involved in producing the reaction, whereas cytolysins require alexin plus something else.

Perhaps of more importance in bringing about confusion than the different kinds of antibodies, is the fact that different kinds of animals have been used. Goats, cows, pigs, man, sheep, rabbits, and guinea-pigs have all served for such investigations. May not the fact that these animals have different placental relationships to the mother account for the different results? Goats, cows, and sheep have a cotyledonary type of placentation in which the chorion comes in contact with the uterine mucosa in a number of separate places. The developing pig with its diffuse placentation can be easily separated from the uterus, as the chorion develops small villi which simply touch the maternal wall. The rabbit and guinea-pig, on the other hand, with discoidal placentae, have a more intimate connection with the mother. While in the cotlyedonary and diffuse types of placentation the embryonic blood vessels are separated from the blood of the mother by epithelial cells of the chorion and mucosa, in the rabbit, the blood capillaries of the embryo are bathed directly in maternal blood. However this may be, we feel that in any event so far as rabbits are concerned, we have demonstrated the passage of precipitins and agglutinins to the fetus both by way of the milk and

[24] Am. Jour. Physiol., 1922, 59, p. 122.

through the placenta. Moreover, Bourquin [24] found that in rabbits and guinea-pigs agglutinins of B. coli, B. typhosus, and B. paratyphosus passed the placenta. Since the conclusion that antibodies pass to young only through milk is based largely on investigations made on goats, cows and pigs, the evidence taken all together indicates that the manner in which the young are connected to the uterus may be an important factor in deciding what can pass by way of the placenta from mother to offspring.

The fact that young of a normal mother nursed by an immunized mother lose their acquired titer rapidly after weaning time, whereas young of immunized mothers, even when nursed by normal mothers with negative reactions, maintain their titer for some months and may even transmit it to their own offspring, leads one to believe that in the latter, which have acquired their immunity reactions through placental transmission, some mechanism concerned with the production of antibodies has been influenced in the young rabbit which was left untouched by such passive transfers as occur through milk.

Our demonstration that injections of milk into rabbits immunized to typhoid will increase the ability of the animal to agglutinate typhoid bacilli merely corroborates the work of various other investigators, of course, who have found that the introduction of an alien antigen into the blood stream may enhance the output of antibodies for a different antigen used at an earlier time. Our finding that a rabbit first immunized to serum-proteins responds to the introduction of typhoid bacilli by a more generous production of agglutinins than does an untreated rabbit is in line with recent work on the production of non-specific immunity. It would seem that a given antigen renders the organ concerned with antibody production more responsive to any subsequent antigen. It is clear from this fact that for the sake of accuracy investigators should know whether the animals they are using in an immunologic experiment have ever been previously used in serologic work.

The spontaneous rise in titer which is likely to occur in placentally immunized young in from 3 to 5 months after birth is difficult to explain unless it be that some organ or organs in the young concerned with the production of immunity begins to function at that time. It may possibly be related to the onset of sexual maturity, at which period there seems to be an increased activity in the lymphoid tissues of the body.

It is of interest to learn that uterine young may not only acquire immunity reactions from their mothers but may retain them sufficiently to transmit them in a measurable degree, without further immunization, to their own offspring. Even if this is nothing more than placental transmission, it may be of practical importance since, in placental mammals, a large percentage of a population might, in time, through such transmission come to exhibit some degree of immunity to a widely prevalent disease.

Lastly, it would seem from our experiments so far that when succeeding generations of rabbits are immunized to typhoid baciili some modification is made in the immunity mechanism whereby individuals of later generations are capable of developing higher titers against these germs than were the individuals of the first generation treated. Whether the new condition is merely congenital or whether it is truly hereditary —that is, due to factors present in the germ cell at the time of conception—remains yet to be established. Our ultimate goal is the solution of this problem, but we expect to carry our experiments through several further generations before trying to decide. We are endeavoring in every way to avoid selection, since it is obvious that if we selected for breeding purposes in each generation only those individuals that showed the highest titers, we might merely be taking the place of a "natural selection" which might operate on an original natural immunity or, conceivably, concentrate various multiple or supplementary factors in successive generations. As a matter of fact, any selection that we may have done so far has been in a negative direction, since at the outset we rejected every rabbit that showed even the low positive "group" reactions up to 1 to 40 that may legitimately be expected to exist in ordinary untreated rabbits.

If a truly hereditary immunity can be established by immunization generation after generation against germs of disease, we should eventually not only secure generations which exhibit increased immunity, but this new acquisition should be capable also of transmission by means of the immune males of such stock into nonimmune strains. At the present stage of our experiments, it is probably not yet worth while to make this final test.

SUMMARY

In subjecting successive generations of rabbits to typhoid innoculations it was found that considerably higher agglutination titers could be developed in individuals of strains which had been under immunization for 3 or 4 generations than in first generation animals of untreated stock.

While in successive months there was, with more or less fluctuation, a gradual lowering in the titer of the offspring of immunized mothers, almost invariably a decided, spontaneous increase in titer occurred in such young during the fifth or sixth month after birth.

Animals immunized to typhoid bacilli had their titers heightened by the subsequent injection of foreign proteins. Also, animals first immunized to foreign proteins developed higher titers when immunized to typhoid than did the controls.

That antibodies pass from mother to offspring through the placenta and not merely by way of the milk was determined: (1) by immunizing pregnant females to typhoid bacilli, killing them a few days before term, and testing the blood and the amniotic fluids of their fetuses for agglutinins; (2) by immunizing pregnant females to sheep serum and then making precipitin tests on the fetal blood. It is suggested that the conflicting evidence regarding the passage of antibodies through the placenta may be due in part not only to the type of antibody concerned, but also to the fact that structurally the placental relations between mother and young are different in different kinds of animals.

The young of immunized mothers can, without further immunization, transmit agglutinating ability to their own offspring. Even if this is merely a placental rather than a truly hereditary transmission, it may be of practical importance, since by such means a general population might in time become more or less immune to a disease.

COMPARATIVE RESISTANCE OF BACTERIA FROM NATIVE HABITATS AND FROM ARTIFICIAL CULTURES

E. G. Hastings

From the Department of Agricultural Bacteriology, University of Wisconsin

The resistance of bacteria and their spores to various physical and chemical agents is of much importance in various relations. It has been the subject of many investigations, most of which, for obvious reasons, have been made with disease-producing bacteria and with those obtained from artificial cultures rather than with organisms derived directly from their native environment. The observations to be reported in this paper would seem to indicate that many of the conclusions drawn from such work may have little, if any, value in indicating the resistance of the organism under natural conditions.

In the summer of 1900 an outbreak of anthrax occurred in the northern part of Wisconsin. The source of the outbreak was a tannery which had been using imported hides, some of which were infected with anthrax spores. The flooding of the river into which the tannery refuse was passed caused grazing lands to become contaminated with the organism. When the flood water receded, it left stagnant pools in the pastures. A veterinarian forwarded to us for examination a sample of water which he had collected from one of these ponds in a pasture in which the disease had occurred.

Plate cultures prepared from the water yielded such numbers of anthrax colonies that it was certain that growth of the organism had taken place in the water. A more complete history of the sample was not obtained at the time of its receipt, and owing to the loss of the records of the sender, it was impossible to obtain such a history later. It would seem from what is known concerning the source of the sample that the pond had become polluted and that growth and sporulation had taken place in the water.

Since I was interested in the viability of bacteria and bacterial spores in water, a portion of the sample was placed in a glass stoppered bottle and was subjected to the varying temperature changes that normally occur in the laboratory. It was examined at intervals for

Received for publication, Aug. 1, 1923.

the presence of viable and virulent anthrax spores by preparing plate cultures and by the inoculation of animals with cultures thus isolated. All such examinations up to and including the one made after 18.5 years yielded positive results. Examinations made thereafter gave negative results. The number of anthrax spores diminished as the period of storage lengthened until it was necessary to use 2-3 c.c. to obtain an anthrax colony where 0.01 c.c. had originally supplied numerous colonies. The germination of the spores was apparently as rapid at the end of the period as at first, since well developed colonies were obtained in 24 hours' incubation at 37 C.

A survey of the observations made by others showed that the maximum period of viability of anthrax spores noted in raw water had been 5 months. In sterile distilled water the spores had been found alive after 30 months. In this instance the anthrax spores have persisted in raw water for 42 times as long as had been noted by any previous worker. They have persisted 7 times as long as any one has noted when the spores were in sterile distilled water.

Morris [1] reports the persistence of virulent spores of anthrax for a period of 12 years in water taken from a lake. The records of the experiment were destroyed by fire, and it is now impossible to determine whether the water was raw or sterilized or anything concerning the source of the spores. Morris also reports the persistence of virulent anthrax during a period of 10 years in milk taken from the udder of a cow that had died of the disease.

The cause of the marked increase in persistence in the present instance as compared with the period of persistence noted by others may possibly find its explanation in the fact that the other observers used the spores formed in artificial cultures for the seeding of the water on which observations were to be made, while in my case the water had become contaminated in the pasture with an organism fresh from its native habitat. This supposition is supported by the observations of Morris on naturally infected milk.

For a long time I have had the idea that cultures of any organism grown in the laboratory might vary widely in their resistance to an unfavorable environment from the same organism which had not been exposed to the weakening effects of its own by-products. This idea was partially confirmed by work done some years ago when organisms of the colon group, isolated from water, were transferred from agar slopes inoculated from the original plate cultures into

[1] Thirty-Third Annual Report of the Louisiana Agric. Exper. Station, 1921.

sterile tap water. These suspensions were protected from evaporation. Nine out of the 22 cultures used remained viable for 3 years. The maximum period of resistance noted was approximately 5 years.

In order to test the idea still further, some observations have been made on the persistence of a nonspore-forming organism which constantly occurs on the corn plant. This organism is one of the colon-aerogenes group. Pure cultures of this organism were isolated from corn stover which had been air dried for two years. The cultures were transferred every three days during a period of one month. Suspensions of the 24-hour growth from agar were made in sterile distilled water. Strips of filter paper were moistened with this suspension and were then placed in a dry incubator at 37° C. Strips of paper were also moistened with milk cultures of the organism.

On the paper infected from the agar culture the organism remained alive for 31 days; on the paper infected with milk cultures it was viable for 96 days. After the corn stover had been in the incubator for 17 months, it still contained large numbers of the organism in question. This dry corn stover has, for the past three and one-half years, been kept at room temperature. The organisms are still alive and can be easily isolated by moistening the corn stover with sterile water, thus using the stover as an enrichment culture medium.

This nonspore-forming organism fresh from its native habitat has resisted drying for over 7 years in comparison with a period of 1 to 3 months when artificial cultures were used. The organism in question is one which produces chiefly volatile acids and alcohol, and these only in small amounts. These products could not be present on the paper to lessen the period of viability of organisms from the artificial culture, as might be true if nonvolatile acids were formed.

The most apparent explanation of the marked difference in viability between the organisms from a native habitat and an artificial one seems to rest on the weakening effects of its environment in the artificial cultures. These observations are indicative of the fact, which has been made use of by some, that if one wishes to keep a pure culture alive for the maximum period of time, it is desirable to grow it upon a medium that will permit only a limited development and thus the formation of a minimum amount of by-products. This can be attained by using a medium containing small quantities of nutrient material, or by using a medium that is somewhat unfavorable for the organism.

If B. tuberculosis is seeded on a medium containing only purified casein and glycerol, the growth is slow and meager in comparison with that obtained in the ordinary beef infusion peptone phosphate glycerol medium. The viability is inverse to the profuseness of growth, transfers from the casein medium showing prompt development after approximately 2 years' incubation at 37 C., while cultures on the usual medium are not viable after a few weeks.

There are many things that indicate that organisms growing in their native habitat have marked powers of vitality both as to persistence and rapidity of growth. An instance of this is in the case of the persistence of certain organisms of the Bact. bulgaricum or Bact. casei group on the dried stomach of the calf. The rennet used in the manufacture of Swiss cheese is made by placing a small amount of the dried stomach in whey and incubating at high temperatures. There results a culture consisting largely of the acid-forming bacilli of the Bact. bulgaricum group. Under normal conditions, the stomachs are collected from farms in certain European countries. They are assembled by the exporter, sold to the wholesaler on this side of the water, passed on to the retailer, and hence to the cheese maker. It is certain that frequently the rennets have been dried for long periods of time and yet the acid-forming bacteria thereon develop quickly in the warm whey. The number of living cells introduced into the whey cannot be large, yet the progress of the fermentation is as rapid as when a much greater initial seeding from a culture grown under artificial conditions is used.

The number of organisms of the colon-aerogenes group on dried corn tissue is not large. Their development is rapid when the tissue is moistened with water and incubated at 20 C. Within 24 hours gas will be produced in large quantities. It would seem that this is evidence of the increased vitality of these cells over those from our cultures. The initial stationary phase and the lag phase of cultures described by Buchannan [2] are here either absent or short. It has been shown by numerous workers in references collected by Salter [3] that the previous history of the culture determines the length of these phases. Such conditions as those to which artificial cultures are exposed have a marked influence in prolonging the length of these periods. This is shown in a marked degree by B. tuberculosis. During the past decade tuberculin has been prepared in our laboratories. It has been noted often that the condition of the cultures from which the inoculations are made are responsible for the rapidity of the growth. Fresh cultures

[2] Jour. Infect. Dis., 1918, 23, p. 109.
[3] Ibid., 1919, 24, p. 260.

showed no stationary or lag period, while with older cultures these phases were marked.

Bacteriologists are accustomed to use, in determining the resistance of organisms to chemical and physical agents, cells which have been grown under artificial conditions. It may well be that the cells in such cultures are weakened before they are exposed to the agent in question and that the conclusions drawn from such work with reference to the resistance of the organism are wholly erroneous. If such variations in resistance between bacterial cells from their native habitat and those grown under laboratory conditions do exist, as seems possible from the data presented, they may be of great practical importance, especially in the case of disease-producing organisms.

SUMMARY

Anthrax spores have remained viable and virulent in naturally contaminated water for much longer periods than have been noted by previous investigators who presumably used spores from artificial cultures. The maximum period of persistence noted by us was 18.5 years, as compared with 5 months in previous observations.

A member of the B. coli-aerogenes group found on the corn plant remained viable on the naturally contaminated tissue for 7 years. The maximum period of resistance of cells from cultures isolated from the same tissue was 3 months.

It is believed that these marked differences in resistance of organisms from their native environment and from artificial cultures is due to the weakening effect of the environment in the artificial cultures.

It seems probable that observations as to the resistance of an organism to physical and chemical agents made on cells from artificial cultures may have little or no value in indicating the resistance of cells of the same organism as it occurs in nature.

CHANGES IN STREPTOCOCCUS FROM ENCEPHALITIS, INDUCED EXPERIMENTALLY, AND THEIR SIGNIFICANCE IN PATHOGENESIS OF EPIDEMIC ENCEPHALITIS AND INFLUENZA

Edward C. Rosenow

From the Division of Experimental Bacteriology, the Mayo Foundation, Rochester, Minn.

Instances of disease resembling the condition we now designate "encephalitis lethargica" have appeared at various times during past centuries. A well-nigh constant relationship has existed between cases of disease with lethargy as a prominent symptom and the occurrence of epidemics of fevers now generally recognized as influenzal in character. During the seventeenth century, influenza occurred repeatedly in epidemic proportions in both the old world and the new, and Crookshank, according to Garrison,[1] "believes that the lethargic encephalitis at Copenhagen (1657), described by Bartholin, the English febrile epidemic of 1661 described by Willis as affecting 'brains and nervous stocks,' the 'comatose fever' of Sydenham (1673-1675), and a case of encephalitis lethargica described by Albrecht of Hildesheim (1695), were all manifestations of influenza." It followed the epidemic of influenza of 1889-1890. The unprecedented presence of encephalitis during the past few years following the pandemic of influenza of 1918-1919 is probably only another, although an extreme, example indicating relationship between influenza and encephalitis.

The occurrence of influenza in cases of encephalitis, usually some time previous to the onset of the encephalitic attack, has been noted so commonly in the recent epidemic that most clinicians have come to believe that causal relationship between these two diseases must exist.

Many investigators have directed their efforts toward the isolation of the etiologic agent in epidemic encephalitis during its recent widespread prevalence. In my own studies in this field, I have produced characteristic symptoms and lesions in animals with a somewhat peculiar streptococcus isolated from typical cases of lethargic encephalitis and from a series of cases of epidemic hiccup, and we have demonstrated the streptococcus in the lesions of a series of typical cases of encephalitis.[2]

Impressed by the frequency of a history of influenza in patients with encephalitis who have come under my observation and by the similarity

Received for publication, Aug. 7, 1923.

[1] History of Medicine, 1921, p. 311.

[2] Rosenow, E. C.: Jour. Am. Med. Assn., 1922, 79, p. 433; Jour. Infect. Dis., 1923, 32, p. 41, 72. Rosenow, E. C., and Jackson, G. H., Jr.: Ibid., p. 144.

of the streptococcus in certain respects to the one isolated so commonly during the pandemic of influenza, experiments were undertaken which I thought might throw light on the nature of the supposed etiologic relationship between these diseases. I shall now report the results of a study of a typical case of encephalitis, with a history of influenza.

HISTORY OF CASE

J. K., a farmer, aged 46, came to the Mayo Clinic on June 2, 1920. In January, the patient's entire family had become ill with severe attacks of influenza shortly after a son was brought home from college ill with the disease. The patient was the last to be taken ill; he had a moderately severe attack which kept him in bed for a week, and from which he never fully recovered. He had continuous pressure in his head, and repeated attacks of headache, and felt weak, but was able to do most of his spring work. About 2 months before coming to the Clinic, the patient complained of pain in his legs, which was aching in character, more or less constant, and associated with similar pains in his arms and other parts of his body. At the same time he began to have difficulty in walking, which progressed steadily until, about 10 days before I saw him, he became unable to walk because of inability to maintain his balance, and weakness. About a month previously, difficulty in swallowing had developed; speech had become difficult and incoherent, and the patient had been unmanageable at intervals.

Three weeks after the onset of his symptoms of encephalitis, his 8-year old daughter developed poliomyelitis. Her temperature rose to 106 F. during the 3 days of illness. Ascending paralysis of the extremities developed, followed by inability to talk and difficulty in breathing, and death occurred from respiratory paralysis.

When the patient was examined in the Neurological Section, after coming to the Clinic, his expression was that of mental apathy. His mind was disoriented most of the time. During lucid intervals, he answered questions intelligently, but was unable to carry on a coherent conversation. He was restless, tossed about in bed, and made repeated efforts to get up. He had sufficient strength to sit up on the side of the bed, but was unsteady, and was unable to stand on account of ataxia and weakness of the lower extremities. His legs were spastic, and patellar and ankle clonus and a marked Babinski sign were noted. The grasping power of his hands was noticeably reduced. Movements of the tongue were slow, and there was some difficulty in swallowing. There was diminution of strength and moderate decrease in speed on the right side, and the muscle tonus was greatly increased. Abdominal and cremasteric reflexes were absent, but bladder and rectal control was retained. The right pupil was somewhat larger than the left, and the reaction of both pupils was slightly diminished. The muscles of the forehead and those around the mouth and eyes were weak, and closure of both eyes could be easily overcome with the fingers.

The urine contained a small amount of albumin; the hemoglobin was 70, erythrocytes 4,480,000, leukocytes 6,800; Wassermann tests of the blood and spinal fluid were negative. The spinal fluid obtained June 4 was clear, and contained 31 lymphocytes for each cubic millimeter; the Nonne reaction was positive. The patient's temperature, pulse and respirations, were normal during a period of 11 days in the hospital.

The streptococcus isolated from the brain of rabbits that developed encephalitis following injections of the washings of the swabs from the throat of the patient was found to be agglutinated markedly and specifically by my antipoliomyelitis serum. For this reason, after there had been no material change in the patient's condition for 7 days, he was given 22 c c. of the serum intravenously on June 9, and 20 c c. of blood were withdrawn for agglutinating purposes. His face became flushed immediately after giving the serum, and he was unusually restless for a few hours after the injection. After that he became quiet, and slept most of the night, whereas he had been extremely noisy and restless on previous nights. The following day he was more oriented, and answered questions more quickly and more intelligently. The incoordination, the spasticity, and the increase in reflexes were less marked. He was given 48 c c. of the serum at 11 a. m., and 60 c c. at 5 p. m. without untoward immediate effects. Improvement was again noted the next day and continued for 2 days, when the patient was taken home. After exhaustion incident to the journey home, he grew worse, and died 2 weeks later. Coincidental with the improvement following injection of the antipoliomyelitis serum, the patient's own serum developed the power to agglutinate his own and 2 other strains of streptococci from encephalitis.

Experiments on Intracerebral Injection of the Streptococcus According to Animal Passage

The washings from the patient's throat, obtained on 3 occasions, 2 and 6 days apart, were injected intracerebrally (first animal passage) into 5 rabbits (table 1). One of the rabbits remained well. Four developed symptoms of encephalitis similar to those described in the following protocol:

TABLE 1

Incidence of the More Important Symptoms Following Intracerebral Inoculation, According to Animal Passage

Animal Passage	Number of Animals Injected	Mortality Percentage	Spasms of		Tremor	Ataxia	Nystagmus	Hyperpnea	Paralysis	Lethargy		Meningitis	
			Diaphragm	Other Muscles						Number	Percentage	Number	Percentage
First.....	5	60	1	2	4	2	2	1	3	0	..	1	20
Second...	17	89	0	2	8	5	1	2	12	3	18	2	12
Third....	9	100	1	1	6	3	1	2	2	5	56	2	22
Fourth...	8	50	1	2	4	1	2	0	5	2	25	4	50
Fifth.....	6	100	0	0	4	1	0	3	4	1	17	4	67
Total..	45	...	3	7	26	12	6	8	26	11	24	13	29
4th and 5th 1 yr. later....	8	12.5	0	0	2	1	0	1	1	0	..	0	..

Rabbit 1, weighing 2,000 gm., was injected June 2, 1920, with 0.1 c c. of the nasopharyngeal washings. On June 3, the animal was tremulous and ataxic. On June 4, there were marked tremor and twitching of the muscles, spasms of the hind extremities, rhythmic spasms of the diaphragm, and inconstant horizontal nystagmus, all of which became worse on exertion, and spastic weakness of the hind extremities. On June 5, the animal was found dead. Necropsy revealed moderate congestion of the vessels of the pia, edema and infiltration of the pia over the anterior aspect of the medulla and over the posterior portion of the cerebellum at the junction of the medulla, and moderately turbid cerebrospinal fluid. There was no lesion at the point of inoculation.

Cultures from the blood and the brain contained a large number of moist, green-producing streptococci and a few staphylococci. Microscopic sections of the brain, medulla, and cerebellum showed leukocytic infiltration of the meninges, most marked on the anterior aspect of the medulla, and parenchymatous and perivascular infiltration in the gray matter of the medulla and cord, and in the subcortical region.

The organism from the brain and the spinal fluid of the rabbits yielded a pure culture of rather moist, flat, greenish colonies of streptococci. The strain in the second animal passage from rabbit 1 and one of the other positive rabbits, and from a mouse injected intraperitoneally with the washing from the throat, was injected into 16 rabbits and 1 monkey (table 1). The dose of the strain obtained from a single colony on blood agar in the primary culture, and in the 4th, 16th, 20th, and 29th rapidly made subcultures in glucose-brain-broth, ranged from 0.2 c c. of the undiluted culture to 1 c c. of a 1 : 1,000,000 dilution in sodium chlorid solution. Of the 16 rabbits injected, 15 succumbed in from 1 to 5 days, with symptoms and findings of meningo-encephalitis similar to those detailed in rabbit 1. Two of the rabbits and the monkey developed moderate lethargy, illustrated by the following protocol:

Monkey 1 (Macacus rhesus) was injected intracerebrally on June 17, 1920, with 0.5 c c. of the glucose-brain-broth culture, diluted 1 : 10, from the brain of rabbit 1 in the 16th rapidly made subculture. No symptoms developed. On June 29, the animal was reinjected with the same amount of the culture in the 29th rapidly made subculture. On June 30, at 3 p. m., it was excitable, and moved about slowly; respirations were moderately increased; vision was diminished, as evidenced by the animal bumping its head into the side of the cage; the knee jerks were equal, but slightly exaggerated; marked tremor over the entire body, moderate weakness and increased tonus of the muscles of the extremities, and occasional sharp twitching of the muscles of the upper lip were noted. On July 2, the condition was about the same. The animal responded slowly to stimuli; the weakness of the extremities, chiefly in the extensors, had grown worse, and ataxia was marked. On July 3, the weakness of the extremities was more marked on the right side than on the left. The left upper eyelid drooped, and there were fine twitchings of the muscles at the outer angle of the left eye. If thoroughly aroused, the animal would bite off a piece of bread, but would chew it only a few times, apparently forget to swallow, and go to sleep. When in this condition, moderate stimuli had no effect, but more severe stimulation aroused the animal. Thirty c c. of milk were given by stomach tube. In opening the animal's mouth, marked trismus of the muscles of the jaw was noted. On July 5, the condition was practically unchanged, but the lethargy had become more marked, and the animal could scarcely be aroused. It choked severely in attempting to swallow when milk was placed back in its mouth with a syringe, and it died a few minutes later. Gross lesions were not found in the brain or elsewhere.

Cultures from the blood, brain, and spinal fluid on blood-agar plates were negative, whereas cultures from the brain in glucose-brain-broth yielded a pure growth of the streptococcus.

Sections revealed a small area of necrosis surrounded by leukocytic and round-cell infiltration in the right frontal lobe at the point of injection, perivascular round-cell infiltration in the midbrain, mild edema and round-cell infiltration of the pia in the sulci over the base of the cerebrum, moderate neurophagocytosis and degeneration of ganglion cells in the medulla, and an occasional diplococcus in or adjacent to the lesions.

The strains from 2 positive rabbits which received the 16th culture generation, from monkey 1, and from one of the rabbits injected with the strain from a mouse, were injected intracerebrally (3rd animal passage) in various doses into 8 rabbits and 1 monkey (table 1). All of these succumbed to encephalitis. In four of the rabbits, and in the monkey, lethargic symptoms were prominent, as noted in the following experiments:

Rabbit 2, weighing 2,000 gm., was injected on June 22, 1920, with 0.75 c c. of the emulsion of the brain of one of the rabbits that succumbed to encephalitis

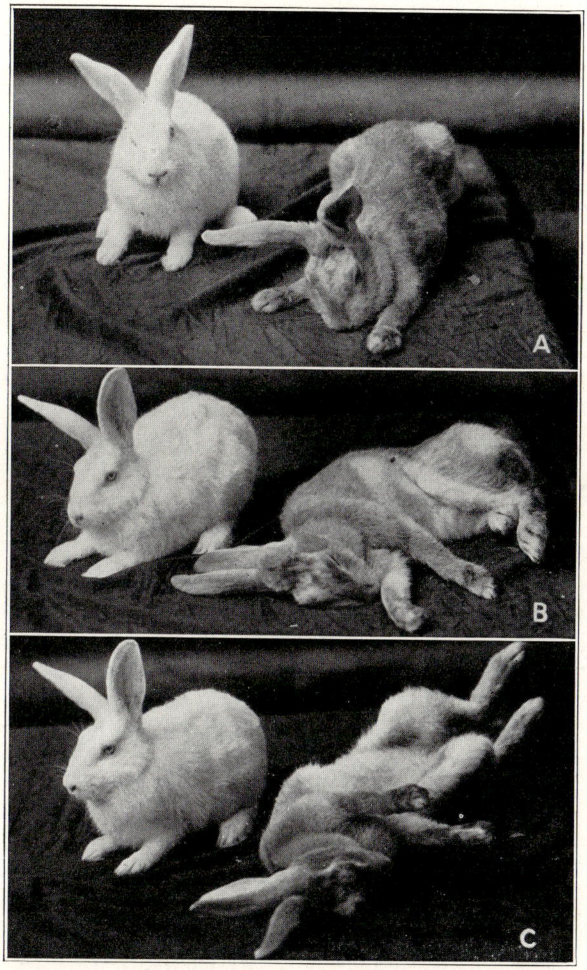

Fig. 1.—Normal rabbit, and rabbit 2, illustrating the lethargic state, *a*, in normal position; *b*, when placed on its side, and *c*, lethargy, and catatonic rigidity of muscles of extremities when placed on its back.

following injection of the strain from rabbit 1 after 16 rapidly made subcultures. On June 23, tremor of the anterior part of the body, associated with marked weakness of the fore extremities, and moderate ataxia, were noted. On June 24, the tremor, weakness, and ataxia were less marked. On June 25, at 10 a. m., the respirations were slow and the weakness had grown worse. The animal was unable to maintain its balance. It responded slowly to stimuli and appeared drowsy. At 4 p. m. the drowsiness had increased. The animal failed to respond to slight stimulation, and responded slowly to more severe prodding. It was photographed in various positions (fig. 1*a, b, c*). It refused food even when placed in its mouth. Twenty c c. of carrot emulsion were inserted into the stomach through a catheter. In doing this, marked spasms of the muscles of the jaw were noted. After this procedure, the animal became sufficiently aroused to eat bread soaked in water, but repeatedly forgot to chew and swallow its food. On June 26, the lethargy had become more marked, and the tonus of the muscles had increased. Emulsion of carrot was again introduced into the stomach by catheter, and the animal was aroused sufficiently to chew when crumbs of bread were placed in its mouth, but it would repeatedly fall asleep before swallowing. On June 27, the animal was found lying on its side, extremely lethargic, and some of the bread placed in its mouth the day before was still in place. While

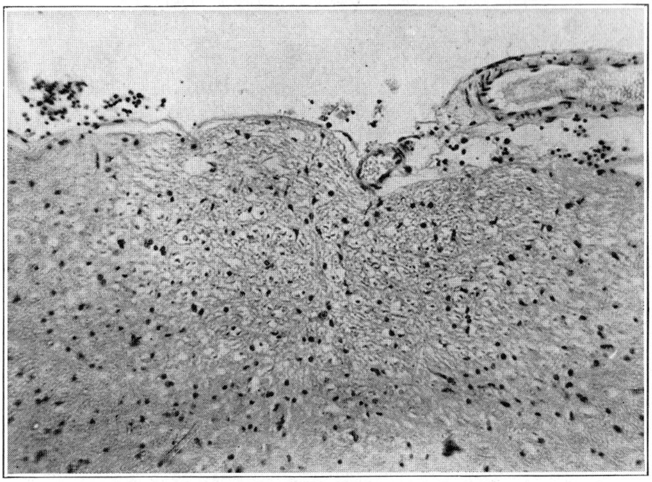

Fig. 2.—Slight round-cell infiltration in pia in sulci of brain of rabbit shown in fig. 1.

being watched during the forenoon, the animal died, without convulsion, from cessation of respiration. Necropsy revealed moderate congestion of the vessels of the meninges, and a small hemorrhagic area in the right frontal lobe at the point of injection, but no other gross lesions.

Blood-agar plate cultures of the blood, brain, spleen, liver, kidneys, and suprarenals were negative, as were also glucose-brain-broth cultures, except two tubes inoculated with pipetted material from the brain, which showed a pure growth of the streptococcus.

Sections revealed slight round-cell infiltration around vessels of the pia, and in the sulci of the cerebral cortex (fig. 2), perivascular round-cell infiltration in and adjacent to the basal nuclei (fig. 3), associated with areas of poorly staining nerve cells and neurophagocytosis, and scattered diplococci of varying size in or adjacent to lesions and in degenerating ganglion cells (fig. 4).

Monkey 2 (Macacus rhesus), weighing 3 kilos, was injected intracerebrally on July 5, 1920, with 1.5 c c. of the emulsion of the brain of monkey 1. No symptoms developed. On July 7, 2 c c. of a glucose-brain-broth culture of the brain of

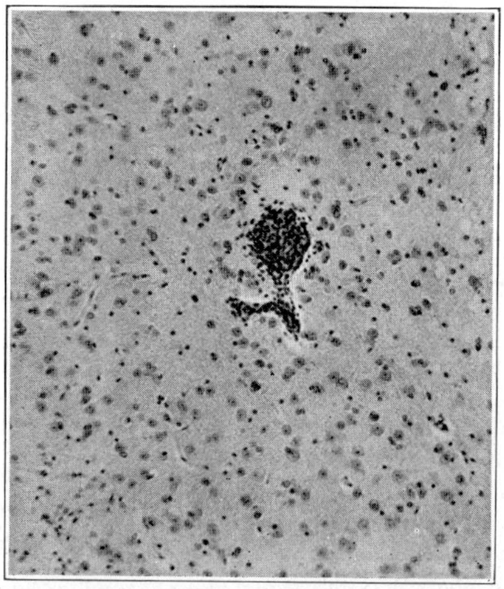

Fig. 3.—Marked perivascular round-cell infiltration in the midbrain of rabbit shown in fig. 1.

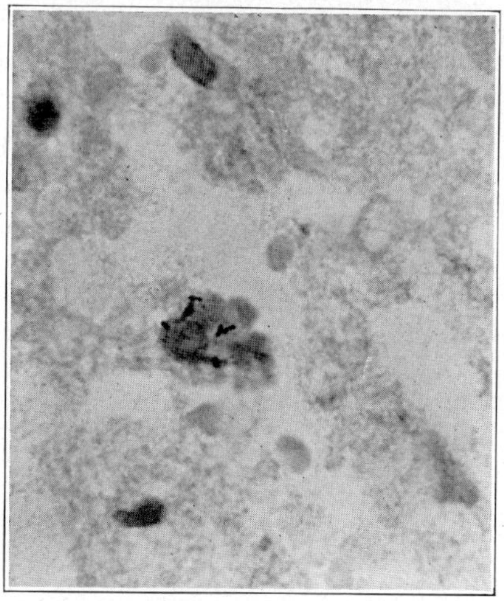

Fig. 4.—The streptococcus in a degenerating ganglion cell in the midbrain of rabbit shown in fig. 1.

monkey 1 in the third culture generation was injected intracerebrally. On July 8, no symptoms had developed, and blood-agar plates of the cultures injected showed only a few living organisms. The animal was reinjected with 1.5 c c. of the culture from the brain of monkey 1, derived from a single colony on blood-agar plate and in the fourth subculture. On July 9, the animal appeared well. On July 10, it moved a little slowly, but otherwise appeared well. On July 12, it was undoubtedly slow and lethargic. On July 14, the lethargy had become more marked, and weakness in the extremities and slight incoordination were noted. On July 22, at 9 a. m., the animal was found lying on its side, breathing slowly, with its eyes closed as in sleep. Slight stimulation failed to arouse it; more severe stimulation caused it to open its eyes. The knee jerks were diminished, the extremities flaccid. Forty c c. of milk were inserted into the stomach with a catheter. There was no rigidity of the masseters. There were continuous fine

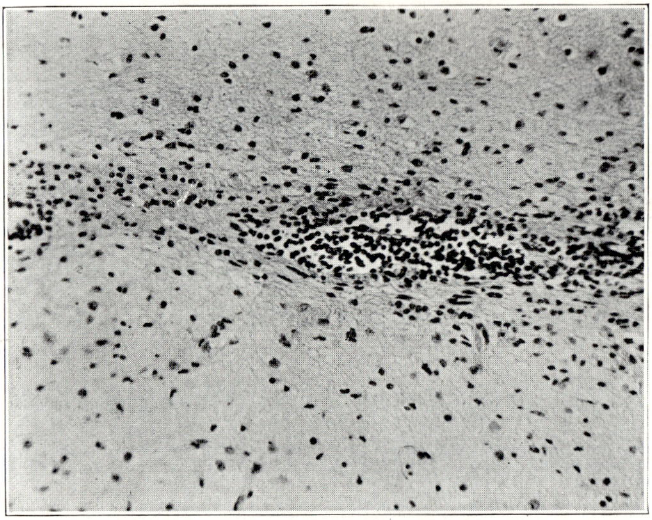

Fig. 5.—Localized round-cell infiltration adjacent to third ventricle in monkey 2. Hematoxylin and eosin (× 120).

tremor and twitchings of the muscles of the toes of both hind feet. At 2 p. m., the animal appeared to be in a deep sleep. When aroused, a slow horizontal nystagmus in both eyes was noted; the pupils were equal and of about normal size. All movements were very slow, and the animal repeatedly went to sleep after being aroused. At 5:30 p. m., it was found dead. Necropsy disclosed a small abscess at the point of inoculation, which contained a large number of gram-positive diplococci and leukocytes. There was no evidence of meningitis. Cultures on blood-agar plates from the brain abscess yielded a large number of indifferent streptococci. Cultures in glucose-brain broth of the streptococcus from the emulsion of the brain remote from the abscess yielded a pure growth of the organism, whereas those from the blood and other tissues remained sterile.

Sections revealed areas of localized and perivascular round-cell infiltration in the region corresponding to the corpus striatum, and surrounding the third ventricle (fig. 5), and moderate neurophagocytosis.

The strain from monkey 2 and from 3 positive rabbits was next injected (4th animal passage) into 6 rabbits and 2 monkeys (table 1). Three rabbits and 1 monkey, all of which had been injected with the highly diluted cultures or with emulsions of the brain, remained free from symptoms. The other 3 rabbits and the other monkey succumbed in from 1 to 4 days, with nystagmus, ataxia, and paralytic symptoms predominating. Only 2 developed lethargic symptoms. The turbidity of the spinal fluid was more marked than in the animals during the earlier animal passages, and 4 (50%) developed gross evidence of meningitis. The following experiment will suffice to illustrate:

Rabbit 3 was injected on June 11, 1920, with the emulsion of the brain of a rabbit that succumbed to encephalitis following injection of the strain in the 4th subculture and in the 3rd animal passage. On June 12 and 13 it appeared well. On June 14, at 8 a. m., there was marked ataxia; the animal stood with

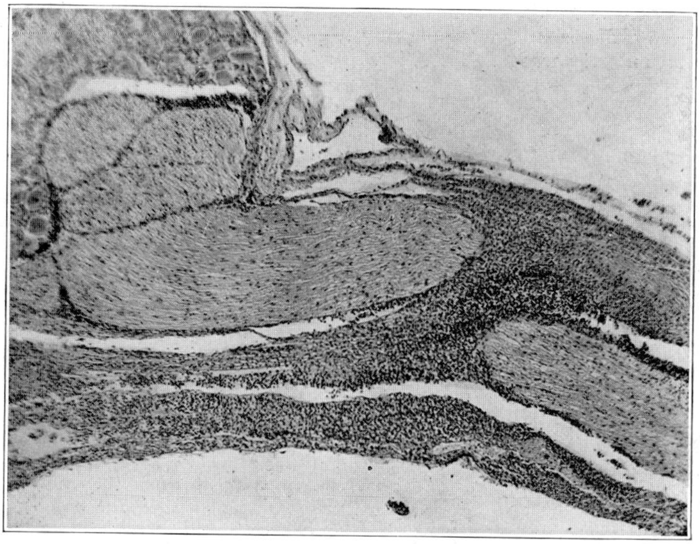

Fig. 6.—Leukocytic and round-cell infiltration of meninges and nerve roots over the anterior aspect of the cervical cord. Hematoxylin and eosin (× 75).

its legs widely separated, and when it hopped, it threw the fore part of the body high into the air, and had difficulty in maintaining its balance. There was slight tremor of the muscles of the fore extremities. At 4:30 p. m., the symptoms were more severe. The respirations had become rapid and labored, and weakness of the extremities, especially of the adductors, and a slow horizontal nystagmus of the left eye had developed. On June 15, at 8 a. m., the animal was found dead, with the extremities widely separated from under its body. The spinal fluid was increased in amount and decidedly turbid; the vessels of the meninges were markedly congested; the pia was dull, and the dura over the anterior aspect of the cord was edematous and infiltrated, especially along the nerve roots. Gross lesions of the brain were absent, but the cord revealed a number of linear hemorrhages in the enlargements in the lumbar and cervical levels. The lungs showed marked hemorrhagic edema. Blood-agar plate cultures of the blood and of the hemorrhagic fluid of the lung yielded a moderate number of large, moist, green-producing colonies of streptococci; those from the spinal fluid and brain, countless numbers of the same organism.

Sections revealed leukocytic and round-cell infiltration of the pia, and the dura, especially over the anterior aspect of the cord, along the sheaths and in the nerve trunks of the anterior roots (fig. 6), and in the perivascular spaces in the anterior aspect of the pons and medulla, and diplococci, singly and in short chains, in the lesions.

The 5% emulsion of the brain in sodium chlorid solution of rabbit 3, diluted 200 times, was injected intracerebrally into 4 rabbits, and the 2d culture generation from the brain into 2 rabbits (5th animal passage). Two of the former, and the two latter died of suppurative meningitis within 48 hours.

Of the 45 animals injected intracerebrally with this strain soon after isolation or after many rapidly made subcultures, 11 (24%) developed lethargy (table 1). That the incidence of this highly characteristic symptom was not accidental, but was due to changes in the streptococcus, is indicated by the fact that it varied greatly on animal passage. Thus, it was not observed in any of 5 rabbits in the

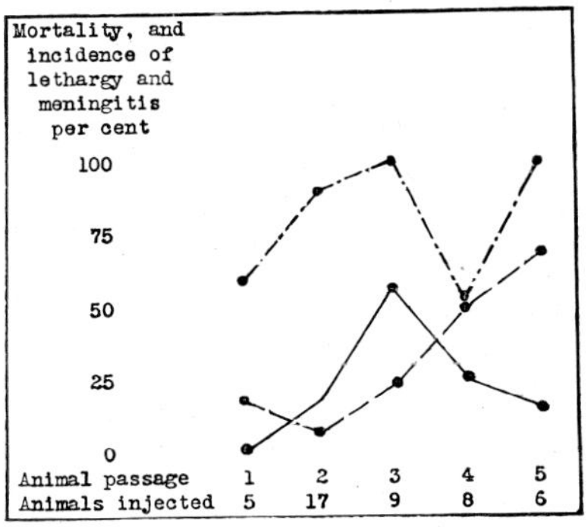

Fig. 7.—Results of intracerebral inoculations in rabbits according to animal passage. The dash and dot line indicates the mortality; the continuous line, incidence of lethargy; the dash line, incidence of meningitis.

1st passage, but developed in 3 (18%) of 17 animals in the 2d passage, in 5 (56%) of 9 animals in the 3d passage, in 2 (25%) of 8 animals in the 4th passage, and in 1 (17%) of 6 animals in the 5th passage (fig. 7). The incidence and degree of meningitis increased on animal passage. Thus, it was 20% in the 1st passage, 11% in the 2d, 22% in the 3rd, 50% in the 4th and 67% in the 5th. The mortality increased from 60% in the 1st passage to 100% in the 5th. The drop in the mortality curve in the 4th animal passage is attributable to the fact that extremely small doses were given to some of the animals.

Experiments on Intraperitoneal Injections in Mice

The washings from the patient's throat injected directly intraperitoneally into 2 mice, caused death from peritonitis in both. The strain in the second animal passage from rabbit 1 in the 4th, 16th, and 29th subcultures was injected intraperitoneally into 6 mice in doses ranging from 0.5 to 2 c.c. of the glucose-brain-broth culture. Of these, 2 remained well; 2 died during the night with mild peritonitis, with a pure culture of the streptococcus in blood and peritoneal fluid;

and 2 died in 8 days, with no evidence of peritonitis. Cultures from the blood and from the peritoneum of the last 2 remained sterile, whereas those from the brain yielded the streptococcus. Six mice were injected in the 3rd animal passage, 4 of which died of peritonitis; 4 were injected in the 4th animal passage, and 2 each in the 5th and 6th passages, all of which died of peritonitis, with or without pleuritis and pericarditis.

The strain from the brain of rabbit 1 was passed successively through 3 mice by injecting the primary culture in glucose-brain broth; and through 3 additional mice by injecting in turn a small amount of the peritoneal exudate, the blood, and the peritoneal exudate of the mouse preceding. During these passages, the strain markedly increased in virulency, producing exudative peritonitis, and acquired the power to produce a capsule and mucoid colonies on blood agar. The effect of the strain on intratracheal application in guinea-pigs was then tested by injecting pigs 24 and 25. The results are shown in table 2.

EXPERIMENTS WITH FILTRATES

It was assumed that an unknown filtrable virus, or one that could not be grown on artificial mediums, might be carried over with the cultures from animal to animal. In order to test this possibility, filtrates of the washings from the nasopharynx of the patient, of the emulsions of the brain of positive rabbits and monkeys, and of cultures of the streptococcus were made and injected intracerebrally into rabbits in doses ranging from 1.5 to 2.5 c c. Moreover, emulsions from animals with negative reactions following injection of filtrates were also injected.

Twenty-eight rabbits were injected with 8 filtrates, 1 of which was prepared from the nasopharyngeal washings of the patient, 5 from the emulsion of the brain of rabbits or monkeys with positive reactions, and 2 from cultures of the streptococcus in glucose-brain broth. Five rabbits were injected with the filtrate from the nasopharynx, 3 with filtrates prepared when the strain was in the 2d animal passage, 5 in the 3rd, 6 in the 5th, 7 in the 6th, and 2 in the 7th. Of these, 5 animals, representing 3 filtrates, developed symptoms of encephalitis, in 4 of which the characteristic streptococcus was isolated from the brain. The symptoms in general paralleled those noted following injection of the corresponding cultures or emulsions. Sections were made from the brain of 10 animals, including the 5 that developed symptoms. Of the latter, characteristic lesions were found in all. In the other 5, no lesions were found. Of the filtrates which gave positive results, 1 was prepared from emulsions of the brain of 2 monkeys and 2 rabbits that developed meningitis and encephalitis following intracerebral injection of the strain in the 4th animal passage and the 16th subculture; 1 from the emulsion of the brain of a monkey that developed meningitis and a brain abscess following injection of the strain in the 5th passage and the 29th subculture; and 1 from the glucose-brain-broth culture of the streptococcus from the filtrate of the emulsion of the brain of this same monkey.

The first of these filtrates which gave positive results was injected into 2 rabbits. Both developed progressive paralysis of the ascending type and died in 7 and 8 days, respectively. Cultures from the brain yielded the streptococcus, and sections revealed hemorrhages and round-cell infiltration in the basal nuclei of the brain, in the gray matter of the medulla, and surrounding the blood vessels. The second filtrate was injected into 2 rabbits. One remained well; the other developed a mild lethargy and died 17 days after injection. The streptococcus was isolated from the brain. The third filtrate was injected into 2 rabbits, both of which developed lethargic symptoms. One died 4 days, the other 34 days

TABLE 2

Summary of Results Following Intratracheal Injection in Guinea-pigs According to Animal Passage

Animal Passage	Animal No.	Clinical Findings	Leukocyte Count: Before Injection	Leukocyte Count: Twenty-Four Hours After	Leukocyte Count: Forty-Eight Hours After	Leukocyte Count: Seventy-Two Hours After	Necropsy Findings	Lung: Volume, C c.	Lung: Weight	Average of: Maximum Reduction in Leukocytes	Average of: Volume of Lung, C c.	Mortality Percentage
Second	P 1	Remained well; killed by blow on head 3 days after injection	7,000	7,400	10,900	8,500	Lungs and other organs normal......	6	3	0	6.25	0
	P 2	Remained well; killed by blow on head 3 days after injection	11,900	14,000	13,000	......	Lungs and other organs normal......	6.5	3.2			
	P 3	Remained well; not examined										
	P 4	Remained well; not examined										
Fourth	P 5	Remained well; not examined									18	20
	P 6	Remained well; not examined										
	P 7	Increased respiration; died in 4 days	......	......	......	......	Coalescing hemorrhagic bronchopneumonia; trachitis; tracheobronchitis; lymphadenitis; hemorrhagic pericarditis; flat, moist, green-producing streptococcus from lung and blood	18	19			
	P 8	Remained well; not examined										
	P 9	Remained well; not examined										
Fifth	P 10	Respirations increased and labored; died in 2 days	13,400	11,000	7,000	1,500	Coalescing hemorrhagic bronchopneumonia of most of lung; trachitis and bronchitis; moist, green-producing streptococcus from lung and blood (Fig. 8*b*)	25	30	32%	20.5	50
	P 11	Respirations increased and labored; died in 2 days	14,100	4,300	1,300	......	Coalescing hemorrhagic edema and bronchopneumonia of most of lung; trachitis; acute splenitis; hemorrhages in adrenals; moist, green-producing streptococcus from blood, lung, and brain	16	18			
	P 12	Remained well; not examined	18,300	22,600	21,400	......						
	P 13	Remained well; not examined	15,200	17,000	20,000	......						

Sixth	P 14	Respirations increased and labored; died in 2 days	28,700	6,900	12,300	......	Coalescing grayish bronchopneumonia; peribronchial lymphadenitis; acute splenitis; abortion; mucoid colonies of streptococcus from lung, blood and uterus	15	16	74%	15.3	66⅔
	P 15	Respirations increased and labored; died in 4 days	5,900	6,200	1,600	......	Bronchopneumonia; pericarditis; peribronchial lymphadenitis; acute splenitis; moist, green-producing streptococcus from lung, pericardium and blood	16	18			
	P 16	Respirations increased and labored; died in 2 days	31,000	9,400	......	......	Coalescing grayish bronchopneumonia and hemorrhagic edema; pleuritis; abortion; moist, green-producing streptococcus from lung, pleura, uterus, and blood	15	17			
	P 17	Respirations increased and labored; died in 6 days	19,000	4,100	4,600	......	Bronchopneumonia; serofibrinous pleuritis and pericarditis; "shaggy" heart; green-producing streptococcus from lung, pericardium, and pleura	15	17			
	P 18	Remained well; not examined										
	P 19	Remained well; not examined										
Seventh	P 20	Respirations increased; death from anaphylactic shock 3 weeks after injection	6,100	3,800	......	......	Adhesive and serofibrinous pleuritis and pericarditis; lung abscess; moist, green-producing streptococcus from lung abscess, pericardium and pleura	Moderate size		56%	14.5	83⅓
	P 21	Marked dyspnea; died in 3 days	9,300	5,800	......	3,000	Complete uniform grayish consolidation of left diaphragmatic lobe; serofibrinous and hemorrhagic pleuritis; green-producing streptococcus from pleura, blood, and brain	13	15			
	P 22	Moderate increase in respiration for 5 days; then recovery										
		Respirations moderately increased; died 17 days after injection	......	......	......	......	"Shaggy" heart; hemorrhagic and adhesive pleuritis; grayish red consolidation of right cardiac lobe; peribronchial lymphadenitis; acute splenitis; green-producing streptococcus from blood, lung, pericardium, pleura, and brain (Fig. 11)	Moderate size				
	P 23	Respirations rapid and shallow; died in 2 weeks	......	......	......	......	Serofibrinous peritonitis secondary to perforation of diaphragm from lung abscess; green-producing streptococcus from peritoneal fluid and lung abscess	Moderate size				

TABLE 2—*Continued*

SUMMARY OF RESULTS FOLLOWING INTRATRACHEAL INJECTION IN GUINEA-PIGS ACCORDING TO ANIMAL PASSAGE

Animal Passage	Animal No.	Clinical Findings	Leukocyte Count				Necropsy Findings	Lung		Average of		Mortality Percentage
			Before Injection	Twenty-Four Hours After	Forty-Eight Hours After	Seventy-Two Hours After		Volume, C c.	Weight	Maximum Reduction in Leukocytes	Volume of Lung, C c.	
Seventh (Cont.)	P 25	Respirations rapid; died 6 days after inoculation	......	......	......	......	Bronchopneumonia, with areas of hemorrhagic edema and necrosis; green-producing streptococcus from lung and blood	16	14			
Eighth	P 26	Remained well; not examined								20%	6.75	16⅔
	P 27	Remained well; not examined										
	P 28	Remained well; not examined										
	P 29	Remained well; not examined										
	P 30	Remained well; chloroformed 10 days after injection	16,000	14,500	16,700	......	Lungs normal	6.5	3			
	P 31	Respirations slightly increased; died 24 days after injection	9,800	6,100	......	......	Areas of bronchopneumonia; dry, green-producing streptococcus from lung and blood	7	6			
Fourth 1 year later	P 32	Remained well	8,800	10,200	6,200	7,100				7%	....	0
	P 33	Remained well; chloroformed 8 days after injection	10,300	9,700	9,150	11,500	Lungs normal	6.2	3.8			
Fifth 1 year later	P 34	Remained well	7,500	8,300	10,500					8%	....	0
	P 35	Remained well; chloroformed 10 days after injection	4,400	3,800	......	......	Lungs normal	6	3			
	P 36	Remained well; chloroformed 10 days after injection	7,500	6,100	6,200	5,700						
	P 37	Remained well; chloroformed 10 days after injection	12,300	12,600	......	11,200						

after injection. The streptococcus was isolated from the brain of both, and sections of the one that died in 4 days revealed localized hemorrhages, focal necrosis, and slight perivascular infiltration in the basal ganglion region of the midbrain, and in the anterior horns of the medulla.

The brains of rabbits and monkeys that died of encephalitis following intracerebral inoculation were placed in 50% glycerol in the ice chest. About one year later, cultures were made and animals were injected. The cultures of emulsions yielded the streptococcus in some instances; those from filtrates remained negative. Two sets of rabbits were injected intracerebrally, one of each set receiving 0.2 c c. of a mixture of the emulsion of the brain of 4 and 6 animals, respectively, and two 1.5 c c. of the corresponding filtrates. The 2 rabbits receiving the small amount of the emulsion remained well, and sections were negative; all of the 4 receiving the filtrates developed marked dyspnea and weakness immediately after

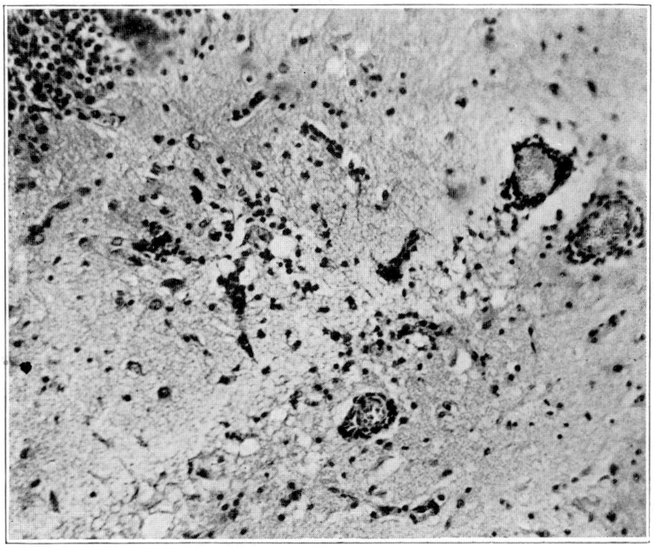

Fig. 8.—Localized and perivascular infiltration in the subcortical region of the brain of a rabbit that succumbed to encephalitis 6 days following intracerebral inoculation of a filtrate of the brain of positive rabbits after preservation in glycerol for one year and that yielded the streptococcus in pure culture. Hematoxylin and eosin (× 120).

injection, and the 2 injected with the filtrate of the mixture of the brains of 4 animals had tremor and twitching of muscles also. These 2 developed progressive symptoms of encephalitis, and marked weakness of the extremities, and died in 6 and 9 days, respectively. No gross lesions were found. Cultures of the brain yielded a pure growth of the streptococcus, and sections revealed widely disseminated perivascular round-cell infiltration, and other lesions (fig. 8). Cultures of the blood were sterile. The filtrate and emulsion of the brain of these rabbits were injected into 6 rabbits without apparent effect.

EXPERIMENTS ON INTRAVENOUS INJECTION

The effect of intravenous injection of this strain in various cultures was studied in rabbits and guinea-pigs. The primary culture from the nasopharynx of the patient was injected into one rabbit. In the 2d passage, 5 rabbits and 5 guinea-pigs were inoculated; in the 4th, 5 rabbits; and in the 5th, 1 rabbit. The culture generation ranged from the 1st to the 30th. The dose varied from 2.5 to 8 c c. In 5 rabbits, localization in the meninges and brain was facilitated by injecting 0.5 c c. of sterile distilled water into the brain at the time of the intravenous injection. In 4 of these, localization occurred, and death from meningo-encephalitis resulted in from 1 to 8 days. In one, no symptoms developed. Of the other 7 rabbits, and the 5 guinea-pigs, clinical evidence of encephalitis developed in 3 and 2 instances, respectively. In only 2 animals did lethargic symptoms develop, well illustrated in the following experiment:

Rabbit 4, weighing 900 gm., was injected intravenously on June 17, 1920, with 3 c c. of the glucose-brain-broth culture after 16 rapidly made subcultures and 2 animal passages. On June 22, the animal was ataxic and weak in the fore extremities. On June 23, it sat about quietly, slept most of the time, but could be aroused quite readily. In hopping, moderate ataxia was noted, the head and fore part of the body tending to bob up and down, but each time after prodding the animal sat quietly and appeared to fall fast asleep. On June 24, the condition was unchanged. On June 25, lethargy was more marked. Coarse tremor of the muscles of the neck, and undoubted weakness in the fore extremities had developed, and the animal tended to lose its balance on hopping. It was chloroformed. Necropsy disclosed a moderately turbid cerebrospinal fluid, increased in amount, congestion of the vessels of the pia, and slight edema of the pia over the anterior aspect of the medulla and the posterior portion of the cerebellum. There were no lesions of the viscera. Blood agar plate cultures were negative, but glucose-brain-broth cultures of the pipetted material from the brain and the spinal fluid yielded the characteristic streptococcus. The blood proved sterile.

Sections revealed perivascular hemorrhage, slight perivascular infiltration around several vessels, poorly staining nuclei of ganglion cells in the pons, edema, and mild round-cell infiltration of the pia, thrombosis of a fair sized artery in the anterior fissure in the medulla, and neurophagocytosis and infiltration by round-cells in the subcortical region in the lower rolandic area.

Sections were made of the brain of 6 other rabbits injected intravenously from 2 to 20 days previously. Characteristic lesions, with little or no involvement of the meninges, were found in the 3 that developed symptoms following intravenous injection only; meningitis, with invasion of the brain substance along the perivascular spaces, dominated the histologic picture in those that received sterile water intracerebrally to facilitate localization of the streptococcus injected intravenously.

Experiments on Intratracheal Injection Into Guinea-Pigs

The effect of intratracheal application in guinea-pigs of the green-producing streptococcus from influenza, which resembled the strain isolated in this case, was extensively studied by me during the pandemic of 1918-1919.[3]

The changes observed in the clinical and pathologic pictures of this disease at different periods in epidemic waves were closely simulated as the strains increased and then diminished in virulency from successive intratracheal passage. In view of these results, and the history of influenza prior to the patient's attack of encephalitis, I decided to test the effect of intratracheal application of this strain in this species of animal. The routine dose consisted of 0.5 c c. of the actively growing glucose-brain-broth cultures in tall tubes for each 100 gm. of body weight. Much of this material was expelled in coughing immediately after withdrawing the catheter.

[3] Ibid., 1920, 26, p. 567.

Transfers of the strain to the lungs of guinea-pigs were made from 1 positive rabbit (rabbit 1) in the second passage, from 2 rabbits in the 4th passage, from 1 rabbit and 1 guinea-pig in the 5th passage, from 2 guinea-pigs and 1 rabbit in the 6th passage, from 2 guinea-pigs and 1 mouse in the 7th passage, from 2 guinea-pigs in the 8th, and 1 year later, from 1 mouse in the 4th passage, and 1 rabbit in the 5th passage. The primary culture from the blood or the brain of animals in the preceding lower passage, or after one or more subcultures, was injected. In some instances, as many as 16 subcultures were made before injection. In all instances the cultures injected were controlled by plating on

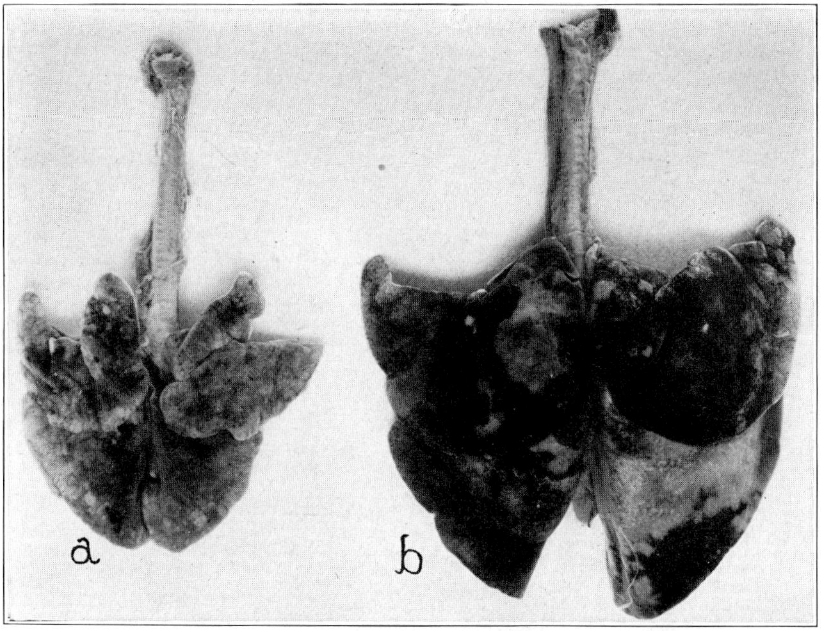

Fig. 9.—*a,* Lung of normal guinea-pig, volume 6 c c., weight 3 gm.; *b,* lung of guinea-pig 10 (table 2) that died 2 days after the intratracheal injection of the strain in the 5th animal passage, volume 25 c c., weight 30 gm. Note the coalescing areas of hemorrhagic edema, and bronchopneumonia.

blood agar. The important results are summarized in table 2. In the second animal passage, the power to invade the lungs of guinea-pigs was nil. The leukocyte count was not changed, the lung volume was normal, and all of the 4 guinea-pigs injected remained well.

As the virulency of the strain increased from successive passage through animals, manifested by its greater tendency to produce meningitis in the rabbit on intracerebral injection, and exudative peritonitis in mice following intraperitoneal inoculation, its power to invade the uninjured normal mucous membrane of the respiratory tract in guinea-pigs became more marked. This invasive power increased on successive intratracheal passage up to a certain point, and then disappeared. The findings in these guinea-pigs were almost similar to those which I obtained with morphologically and culturally similar streptococci isolated from patients with influenza during the pandemic of 1918-1919. The animals at the height of virulency became cyanotic; respirations were difficult and rapid, associated with coughing and anaphylactic spells; marked leukopenia developed; abortions occurred commonly, and the blood at postmortem was often liquid and dark. At the height of the invasive power, death occurred early, and hemorrhagic edema and coalescing areas of bronchopneumonia (fig. 9), usually lobar in distribution, were found side by side in the voluminous, heavy, wet lungs (figs. 10, 11, 14, 15, 16, 17). Necrosis of the alveolar epithelium and capillary endothelium, associated with hemorrhage and edema, and a relatively scant

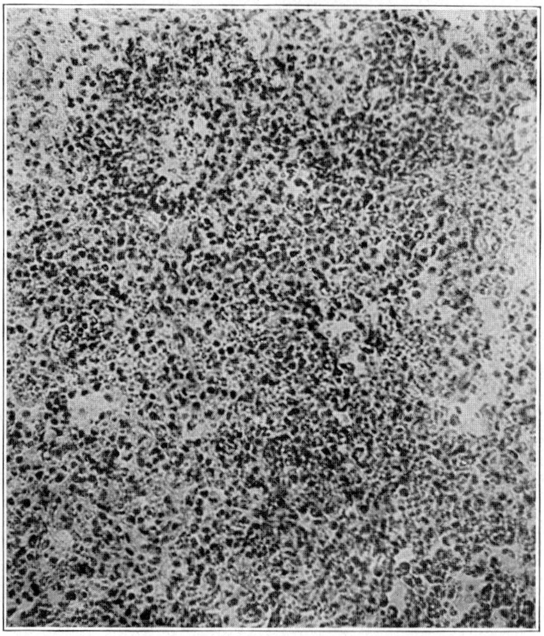

Fig. 10.—Section of lung of guinea-pig shown in fig. 8*b*. Note the marked edema and hemorrhage, the relatively slight and irregular leukocytic infiltration, and the area of necrosis of alveolar wall. Hematoxylin and eosin (× 120).

fibrin network, dominated the microscopic picture. Leukocytic exudation was relatively slight and irregular in distribution (fig. 10), and the bacteria were numerous, especially at the periphery of alveoli (fig. 11), as was the case following injection of the streptococcus from influenza. In short, the gross and microscopic changes were characteristic of those found in influenzal pnuemonia at the height of the epidemic waves during the pandemic of influenza, as emphasized especially by Le Count.[4] Moreover, in this series of animals, as in the influenzal series, the character of the lesions in the lung changed as the virulency decreased from further passage, and as the capsular substance and the mucoid character of growth of the organism on blood agar was lost. Leukopenia became

[4] Jour. Am. Med. Assn., 1919, 72, p. 1519.

less marked; the volume and weight of the lungs diminished; death occurred later, and dry, patchy areas of bronchopneumonia, associated at times with abscess formation and exudative pericarditis and pleuritis (fig. 12), dominated the postmortem findings (figs. 20, 23, 24, 25, 31). The relationship of lung volume, an index of severity of reaction, mortality rate and leukocyte counts, are given in fig. 13.

It will be seen that this organism, during its neurotropic or encephalitis phase (second passage), did not have power to produce pulmonary lesions. The leukocytes were not reduced, the lung volume remained normal, and no deaths occurred in any of 4 animals injected, but as the mortality and incidence of meningitis following successive intracerebral injection in rabbits, and the mortality and incidence of peritonitis following intraperitoneal injection in mice increased, this strain acquired the power to invade the respiratory tract (4th, 5th, and 6th

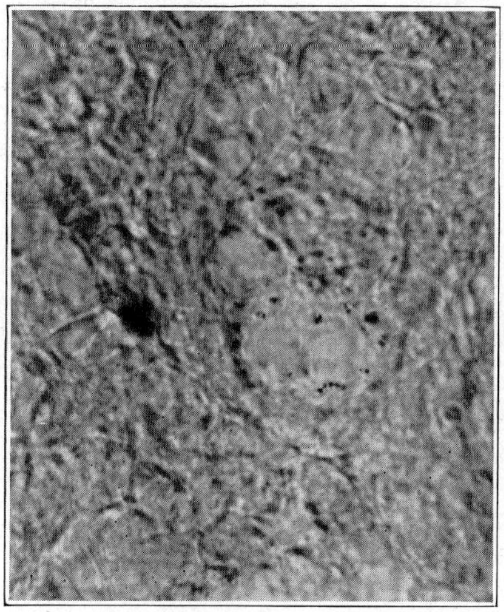

Fig. 11.—Diplococci in lung of guinea-pig shown in fig. 8*b*. Note the peripheral distribution in the alveolar exudate. Gram (× 1000).

passages). The lung volume became high, leukopenia became marked, and mortality increased, the pneumotropic or influenza phase. After further successive intratracheal injections, the strain lost the power to invade the uninjured respiratory epithelium, symptoms became less severe or absent, the lung volume and the reduction in leukocytes became progressively less marked, mortality disappeared, and the strain was lost (7th and 8th passages). As noted in fig. 13, the curve of the average lung volume in the guinea-pigs began to recede before the mortality curve, the peak of the former occurring in the 5th passage, of the latter in the 7th passage. This apparent discrepancy is explained when we consider the duration of the experiment in the animals that died, for the longer the experiment the less voluminous the lung. Thus, in the 4th passage the duration was 4 days; in the 5th, 2; in the 6th, 6; in the 7th, 10.2; and in the 8th, 24 days

The power of the strain to invade the uninjured mucous membrane of the respiratory tract in normal guinea-pigs was also lost on artificial cultivation. Two guinea-pigs injected in the 4th passage, and all of 4 in the 5th passage, after cultivation for 1 year, remained well and showed no noteworthy reduction in leukocytes. This loss of power to invade the pulmonary epithelium also occurred in strains that were isolated from animals that were chloroformed while recovering, or that died late following intravenous injection from causes other than overwhelming infection.

Experiments One Year Later

About one year later, after this strain had been on artificial mediums and had lost the power to produce mucoid colonies on blood-agar plates, but produced dry, green colonies instead, its infecting power was again tested. The dosage was

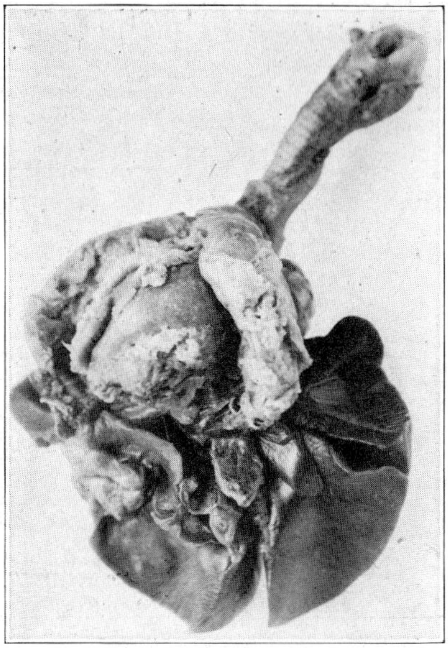

Fig. 12.—Heart, pericardium, and lung of guinea-pig 23 that died 17 days after intratracheal inoculation of this streptococcus in the 7th animal passage. Note the marked thickening and exudation of the visceral and parietal pericardium, and of the pleura over an area of bronchopneumonia in the right cardiac lobe.

comparable to that of a year before. Two mice were injected intraperitoneally, 2 guinea-pigs intratracheally, and 2 rabbits intracerebrally, with the strain from the blood of a mouse that had succumbed in 24 hours to an intraperitoneal injection in the 3rd animal passage a year previously; 4 mice intraperitoneally, 4 guinea-pigs intratracheally, and 4 rabbits intracerebrally with the strain in the 5th passage which had caused death in a rabbit in 4 days following intracerebral injection; and 2 mice intraperitoneally, 2 guinea-pigs intratracheally, and 2 rabbits intracerebrally with the strain in the 7th passage isolated from the blood of a guinea-pig that had died of hemorrhagic bronchopneumonia. All of the mice and guinea-pigs (table 2 and fig. 13) and 6 of the 8 rabbits remained well. One of the rabbits had tremor of the masseters for a few days, and then recovered. One rabbit, injected with 0.2 c c. of the glucose-brain-broth culture of the strain from the rabbit in the 5th passage, died of a rapidly progressing weakness that began in the hind extremities (table 1 and fig. 13). Marked softening of the brain and cord, without focal hemorrhages, was found at necropsy. Sections of the brain of 4 of the rabbits chloroformed 2 weeks after injection revealed no lesions.

FERMENTATIVE AND AGGLUTINATING PROPERTIES

The fermentative power of this strain was tested after 1, 2, 3, 5, and 7 animal passages. Dextrose, maltose, and lactose were fermented by the strain in all of the animal passages; inulin in the 1st passage only, raffinose in the 1st and 7th passages; whereas mannite and salicin were not fermented at all.

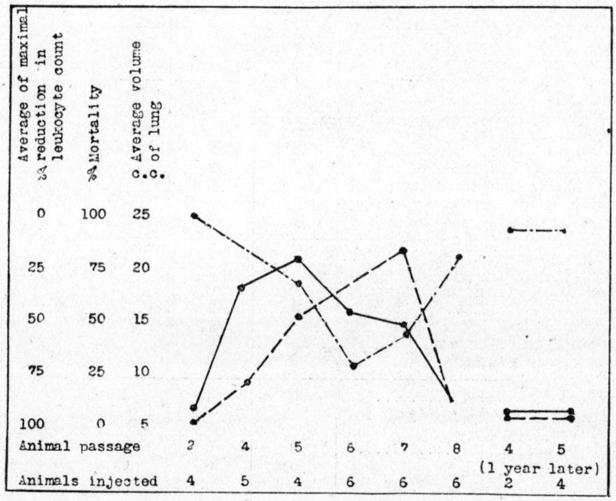

Fig. 13.—The effects of intratracheal application on leukocyte count, mortality rate and lung volume in guinea-pigs. The continuous line indicates the lung volume; the dash line, the mortality; the dash and dot line, the leukocyte count.

As the strain increased in virulency from successive animal passage, it acquired a capsule, and the power to produce moist mucoid colonies on blood agar, resembling those of type III pneumococcus.

A large number of agglutination experiments were made with the strain before and after a series of animal passages after preservation in glycerol and sodium chlorid solution, after preservation in latent life in cultures, and after repeated cultivation. Representative results are summarized in table 3. The bacteria used for agglutination experiments were grown usually in glucose broth or glucose-brain broth, and the centrifuged sediment placed in glycerol (2 parts) and 25% sodium chlorid solution (1 part) in dense suspension, and preserved in the ice chest. At the time of the agglutination tests, the dense suspensions were diluted with distilled water to about the density of a 24-hour glucose-broth culture. The cultures for agglutination were obtained from pure growths on blood-agar plates. The slide method was used as a routine. This consisted of mixing on a slide 1 drop of the undiluted serums with 2 drops of the antigen, tilting the slide repeatedly for about 10 minutes, and then recording the result. The results were frequently checked with those of the test tube method, using progressive dilutions of the serums up to 1:1,000, and were found to agree closely. Absorption experiments were performed in instances in which new agglutinating properties appeared, and in nearly all instances the results were in accord with the agglutination tests in the unabsorbed serum.

TABLE 3

ILLUSTRATIVE AGGLUTINATION EXPERIMENTS OF STRAIN 3947 ACCORDING TO ANIMAL PASSAGE

Animal Passage	Antigen (Dense Glycerol Sodium Chlorid Solution Suspension, Diluted at Time of Agglutination Test)	Serums						
		Anti-Encephalitis	Anti-Policmyelitis	Anti-Influenzal	Type Pneumococcus I	Type Pneumococcus II	Type Pneumococcus III	Normal Horse
0	Freshly made	2	3	1	0	0	0	0
	After 3 years	3	4	0	0	0	0	0
2	Freshly made	4	4	1	0	0	0	0
	After preservation on blood-agar for 1 year without transfer:							
	Freshly made	4	3	1	0	0	0	0
	Two years later	4	3	2	0	0	0	0
	After preservation on blood-agar for 1 year, and after 30 subcultures; freshly made	2	2	2	1	1	2	1
4	Freshly made	0	1	1	0	0	4	0
	After preservation on blood-agar for 1 year without transfer; freshly made	2	1	3	0	0	0	0
	After preservation on blood-agar for 1 year without transfer and then 20 subcultures; freshly made	3	3	3	3	3	3	3
5	Freshly made	0	1	1	0	0	4	0
	After preservation on blood-agar for 1 year without transfer:							
	Freshly made	0	0	2	0	0	4	0
	Two years later	0	0	0	0	0	3	0
	After preservation on blood-agar for 1 year without transfer, and then 20 subcultures; freshly made	2	2	2	2	2	2	2
6	Freshly made	0	1	0	0	0	4	0
	After preservation in meat infusion for 1 year without transfer; freshly made	0	0	0	0	0	4	0
	After preservation in meat infusion for 1 year without transfer, and then 15 subcultures; freshly made	3	3	2	2	2	2	2
7	Freshly made	2	2	1	0	0	4	0
	After preservation on blood-agar for 1 year without transfer:							
	Freshly made	0	0	0	0	2	3	0
	Two years later	0	0	0	0	2	4	0
	After preservation on blood-agar for 1 year without transfer, and then 25 subcultures; freshly made	3	2	2	2	2	2	2

The antiserums were prepared in the horse by repeated injections of pure cultures of the respective strains. The anti-encephalitis and antipoliomyelitis serums were freshly prepared. The anti-influenzal serum was prepared in 1919 with the green-producing streptococcus which was so prevalent during the pandemic of influenza, and it was found to have retained specific agglutinating properties. The type pneumococcus serums were procured from the New York State Health Department.

The results of the agglutination tests were in harmony with the changes in virulency, morphology, and growth characteristics. The experiments recorded in table 3 are representative of a large number of tests, many of which were kindly carried on by Miss Helen Minier, who worked with me as a Fellow. It will be seen that specificity is maintained to a marked degree by preserving the organism in latent life on the surface of blood-agar slants stoppered with paraffined corks, in tall tubes of meat infusion, and in dense suspension in glycerin-sodium chlorid solution, whereas cultivation in artificial mediums, especially alternately on blood-agar and in glucose-brain broth, and rapid animal passages, induce marked changes in agglutinating properties.

The strain as isolated from the nasopharynx of the patient in the primary culture in glucose-brain broth, and after 1, 2, and 3 animal passages, respectively, was agglutinated specifically by the encephalitis and the poliomyelitis serums. The specificity (table 3) of the strain as isolated was preserved in dense glycerol suspension for 3 years, in latent life on blood-agar for 1 year, and this subculture in dense glycerol suspension for 2 years. In the 4th animal passage, the strain had acquired a capsule and the power to produce distinctly mucoid colonies, and was agglutinated specifically by type III pneumococcus serum. This was true alike of the strain after passage through mice, rabbits, and guinea-pigs. After preservation in latent life on blood-agar for a year, followed by cultivation in glucose-brain broth, it was agglutinated most markedly by the "anti-influenza" serum. During 20 subcultures, the mucoid character of the colonies disappeared and agglutination occurred alike in all of the serums. During 3 additional passages, it continued to be agglutinated by type III pneumococcus serum on isolation, after preservation in latent life, and in glycerol. This newly acquired agglutinating property was lost when cultivated on artificial mediums, just as was found to be the case with the original agglutinating properties.

A series of agglutinin-absorption tests was made in the usual way with the encephalitis and the type III pneumococcus serums. In nearly all instances, the strain in the neurotropic phase, when agglutinated by the encephalitis serum, absorbed the agglutinin for other encephalitis strains and, vice versa, was not agglutinated by the serum from which the agglutinin had been absorbed with encephalitis strains. When agglutinated specifically by the type III pneumococcus serum (the pneumotropic phase), it absorbed the agglutinin for known type III pneumococcus strains and, vice versa, was not agglutinated by the serum from which the agglutinins were absorbed with type III pneumococcus.

Precipitin tests made with the cleared diluted glycerol extracts of various antigens corroborated the results of the agglutination experiments, precipitation occurring in the encephalitis and the poliomyelitis serums with the cleared extracts in the early animal passages, and in type III pneumococcus serum in the later passages.

SUMMARY AND DISCUSSION

The patient contracted influenza during an epidemic wave of the disease, with which his entire family had been ill, at a time (1920) and in a region in which the green-producing streptococcus was proved prevalent, and with which I produced the symptoms and lesions of influenza in guinea-pigs. The streptococcus isolated from the patient's throat several months later, during his attack of encephalitis, resembled morphologically but not in virulency the one isolated so commonly during the pandemic of influenza.

The symptoms produced in rabbits and monkeys on intracerebral inoculation of the streptococcus as isolated were characteristic of encephalitis, and similar in general to the type of the disease in the patient. The changing character of the disease induced on successive animal passage is in accord with different types of the disease as it occurs sporadically, in different epidemics and in different parts of epidemic waves, and with results (to be reported elsewhere) following inoculation of a similar streptococcus from a large number of other cases of encephalitis.

The neurotropic properties of this streptococcus were also noted following intravenous injection in rabbits, intraperitoneal injection in mice and guinea-pigs, and following the packing of the nose of rabbits and monkeys with gauze soaked in the culture. This neurotropism was found in freshly isolated strains from the throat of the patient, and from the brain of animals that died from encephalitis. It was noted also in cultures after many rapidly made transfers (monkey 1, rabbit 2, monkey 2), including strains derived from single colonies (monkey 2), and in the relatively few organisms in filtrates. Gross lesions at the point of inoculation and in the meninges were usually slight or absent; occasionally gross evidence of meningitis, and rarely abscess, were found, especially after the strain had increased in virulence from animal passage. The location and character of the microscopic changes in the brain corresponded roughly to the character of the symptoms and the duration of the experiment. Thus, in some lethargic animals, marked perivascular infiltration in the midbrain region was found (fig. 3), with little or no meningeal involvement (fig. 2). In others in which the disease ran a stormy course, with evidence of meningeal involvement, pachymeningitis and infiltration of nerve roots were the striking changes (fig. 6). In general, perivascular and localized infiltrations and other changes like those in the spontaneous lesions were most marked in basal ganglions in the midbrain region irrespective of the place of inoculation. The character of the infiltrating cells varied according to the duration of the experiment, leukocytes predominating in the animals that died soon after injection, and round cells in those that succumbed or were chloroformed a longer time after inoculation. No microscopic lesions were found in the brain of uninoculated rabbits, of those injected with sodium chlorid solution and sterile broth, nor of those which remained free from symptoms following inoculation of filtrates and the streptococcus after it had lost its virulency a year later.

The results on intratracheal injection in guinea-pigs were similar to those observed in the experiments with the green-producing streptococcus from influenza.[3] The symptoms, the leukopenia, and the lung findings of influenza as they occur in epidemic waves were reproduced so far as this is possible in this species of animal. The results were consistent on widely separated dates in different lots of healthy guinea-pigs, when spontaneous pneumonia among controls did not occur, with strains that were passed through three species of animals, in each of which a pure culture of the streptococcus was isolated, and with cultures proved pure on injection in each instance.

The conclusion that these various effects were due to changes induced in this streptococcus and were not the result of accidental isolation of contaminating organisms is warranted. The lack of invasive power of this strain as isolated when applied to the uninjured epithelium of the lower respiratory tract of guinea-pigs, its gradual acquirement of this power, which increased to a high point and then receded through successive intratracheal passage, the loss of all virulency from artificial cultivation, and the highly specific effects obtained even with filtrates and with cultures derived from single colonies of what appeared as pure cultures, effectively exclude the possibility that I was dealing with a mixture of strains.

The results of the agglutination and precipitation experiments are in accord with these conclusions and in agreement with the changes observed in morphology, virulence, and cultural characteristics.

Similar changes have been induced in a number of other strains from encephalitis, while in still others, original properties were so firmly fixed that increase in invasive power and other changes could not be induced. In the strain under consideration, experimental proof of the nature of the supposed causal relationship between influenza and encephalitis appears to have been discovered.

According to the results of these experiments, the same streptococcus may give rise to these widely different diseases, depending on whether it be in the virulent or pneumotropic phase, when influenza would result, or in the less virulent but neurotropic phase, when polioencephalitis and allied conditions would be prone to develop. Clinical studies indicate strongly that this is so. Since the changes induced in the microorganism include alterations in morphology, cultural characters, infecting power, and immunologic state similar to those noted in my studies,[5] and those of Clough [6] on mutations in the pneumococcus-streptococcus group, and to those noted by Walker [7] in the case of hemolytic streptococci, might it not be that members of this group of organisms, to which this strain belongs, which are normally present in the upper respiratory tract of humans, acquire under certain conditions these and other phases in their life cycle, and thus afford explanation for the occurrence of sporadic cases and the origin of epidemics in isolated regions? In any event, the consideration of specificity in this group in the light of particular and dominant but acquired properties of different strains would seem to be a good working hypothesis.

[5] Jour. Infect. Dis., 1914, 14, p. 1; 1912, 11, p. 338.
[6] Jour. Exper. Med., 1919, 30, p. 123
[7] Jour. Infect. Dis., 1923, 32, p. 287.

42

2/4 / 5/2

CAN ALL STRAINS OF A SPECIFIC ORGANISM BE RECOGNIZED BY AGGLUTINATION?

J. W. Stevens

From the Department of Agricultural Bacteriology. University of Wisconsin, Madison

The agglutination test has been used primarily in clinical diagnosis for the recognition of disease, as for example typhoid. It is realized that the reaction does not identify all cases of the disease. The reason ordinarily given is that some patients do not respond to the growth of the causal bacilli in the tissues by the production of agglutinins. Experimental proof of this error can easily be obtained through the injection of a series of animals with a specific strain of the organism and the testing of the serum against the strain in question.

I am not aware that errors in the opposite direction have been recognized; namely, that the agglutinins produced under the stimulus of a specific strain of an organism will not react with all other strains of the same organism. If this error exists, some cases of disease will not be recognized by the agglutination test, due to too great a specificity of the agglutinins.

It is recognized that different strains of an organism will not give quantitatively the same results with an immune serum. The culture which was used in immunizing the animal is usually agglutinated by a smaller amount of the serum than the other strains. The quantitative differences that have been noted are usually small.

The second application of the agglutination reaction has been for the identification of bacteria. An animal is immunized with a culture of a known organism, its serum is tested against the organism used in order to determine whether the animal has responded to the injections. If the serum of the treated animal is found to agglutinate suspensions of the organism injected, it is considered fit for use in making the final test as to the identity of suspected cultures. Errors in this application of the agglutination reaction are difficult to recognize. They can be recognized only by the use of an organism, the various strains of which can be identified with absolute certainty by other means than the agglutination test. The selection of such an organism is not an easy task. One cannot rely on morphology, on cultural characteristics, or on

Received for publication, Aug. 21, 1923.

physiology as determined by tests in various culture mediums. The agglutination reaction, which is being studied here, is possibly the only certain means of identification of the causal organisms of many diseases.

The bacteria which cause tubercles to develop on the roots of legumes would seem to be well fitted for the study of the value of the agglutination reaction in the identification of bacteria. Strains of the organism related to a particular group of legumes can be easily obtained from varied sources. The nodule itself represents a naturally pure culture of the organism. The purity of the cultures obtained can be further supported by the ordinary laboratory methods. The seeds of the legume can be treated so as to free them absolutely from the nodule-forming bacteria, a condition which can be tested out in the laboratory. The seed can be planted in sterile soil which is devoid of combined nitrogen. The bacteria to be tested can be brought into contact with the roots of this sterile plant. The ability of the pure culture to penetrate the roots of the plant, to produce nodules and to enable the plant to make a luxuriant growth in the absence of combined nitrogen in the soil is certainly as clear cut and as definite an answer as to the identity of the cultures as can possibly be obtained with any organism.

The common cultivated legumes of this country may be divided into 7 groups so far as their relation to the nodule-forming bacteria is concerned. The bacteria isolated from any one legume given in the following groups will inoculate any other legume in the same group, while cross inoculation between the various groups is apparently impossible.

1. Clover—Trifolium (all true clovers).

2. Alfalfa, sweet clover, bur clover, yellow trefoil, and fenugreek.

3. Garden pea, field pea, sweet pea, perennial pea, vetch, wild vetch, broad bean and lentil.

4. Cowpea, partridge pea, peanut, Japan clover, velvet bean, lima bean, and tick trefoil.

5. Garden bean, field bean, kidney bean, and scarlet runner bean.

6. Soy bean.

7. Lupine and serradella.

The legume bacteria have been studied from many points of view. Their morphology and their cultural and physiologic characteristics as determined by a study on culture mediums are nonspecific. Shunk[1] has studied the legume bacteria with reference to their flagellation. He found that they could be divided into two groups, depending on the

[1] Jour. Bacteriol., 1921, 6, p. 239.

number of flagella. The classification according to flagellation does not, however, agree with the natural classification as determined by the groups of legumes which will cross-inoculate. For example: the organism isolated from lima beans possesses a number of flagella, while those from the cowpea and the peanut have only one. The organism from any one of these 3 plants can be used for the inoculation of all. The difficulties encountered in determining the number of flagella lead one to place more confidence in the nodule-forming power of an organism on a specific legume than in its apparent flagellation when identification is concerned.

Löhnis and Hansen [2] were able to divide the legume bacteria into two groups according to their action on milk. One group, which included the organisms coming from clover, sweet clover, alfalfa, peas, vetch, navy bean, and lupine, produced a layer of clear serum from 2 to 5 mm. in depth on incubation from 1 to 4 weeks. The second group, which included primarily the organisms from soybean, cowpea, and peanut, produced no such serum zone.

It is to be noted from both of these investigations that it is possible to separate the legume bacteria into but 2 groups, while the legume plants themselves divide them into 7 or more groups.

Klimmer and Kruger [3] were the first to apply serologic tests to the study of legume bacteria. They used the agglutination test, the complement-fixation test, and the precipitin test. All gave similar results. They studied 18 cultures from as many different legumes and were able to divide them into 9 groups. Vogel and Zipfel [4] reported on similar studies. Their results agreed in general with those of Klimmer and Kruger.*

It was realized that the success of any study of these bacteria by serologic methods would depend more largely on the number of strains from a few species of legumes rather than on a study of a limited number of strains from many kinds of legumes. In the work herein reported, 55 different cultures were used, representing 7 natural groups of the nodule-forming bacteria. The greater number of these cultures belonged, however, to 3 principal groups: namely, the alfalfa and sweet clover group, the pea-vetch group and the soy bean group. The cultures were secured from widely separated sources. Some were freshly isolated while others had been cultivated in the laboratory for 10 years.

* Paine and Lacey (Annals of Applied Botany, 1923, 10, p. 204) have recently used the agglutination test for the differentiation of certain plant pathogens.

2 Jour. Agric. Res., 1921, 20, p. 543.

3 Centralbl. f. Bakteriol., II, 1914, 40, p. 256.

4 Ibid., 1921, 54, p. 13.

The purity of the cultures used was assured by a number of replatings and by a study of the cultures on the various types of culture mediums. The most frequent contaminating form is B. radiobacter. The mediums employed in the purity tests were designed especially to demonstrate the presence of this organism. Any culture showing non-characteristic growth on any of the mediums used was discarded. The ability of each culture to produce nodules on its characteristic legume was determined.

EXPERIMENTAL

It was desired to use a standard culture medium in the agglutination work with the legume bacteria in order to introduce as little variation as possible due to this factor. After several trials it was found impossible to use a single medium on which all of the strains would give a good growth. Some of the strains gave a meager growth on most of the common mediums, which was quite an obstacle in the preparation of heavy bacterial suspensions. With these slow-growing organisms, from cowpea, lima bean, soy bean and lupine, it was necessary to use a yeast water nitrate medium. Sucrose nitrate agar was used with the other strains. Stock cultures were kept on nitrogen-free mannitol agar. The formula for the two mediums used in the preparation of suspensions are given:

A. SUCROSE-NITRATE AGAR

Monobasic potassium phosphate	0.2 gm.
Magnesium sulphate	0.2 gm.
Sodium chloride	0.2 gm.
Potassium nitrate	0.2 gm.
Calcium sulphate	0.1 gm.
Ferrous chloride 1% solution	20 drops
Sucrose	20 gm.
Agar	15 gm.
Water (Distilled)	1000 c c.

The monobasic potassium phosphate was dissolved in about 50 c c. of water and neutralized with N/1 NaOH with phenolphthalein as the indicator before it was added to the medium.

B. MANNITOL YEAST-WATER AGAR

Mannitol	10.0	gm.
Monobasic potassium phosphate	0.2	gm.
Magnesium sulphate	0.2	gm.
Sodium chloride	0.2	gm.
Calcium sulphate	0.1	gm.
Potassium nitrate	0.5	gm.
Agar	15.0	gm.
Yeast water	100	c c.
Water (distilled)	900	c c.

(Adjusted to P_H 6.6 to 7.0)

One pound of Fleischmann's yeast was used to 4 liters of water. The mixture was sterilized at 20 pounds' pressure for at least an hour and allowed to stand over night. The liquid was then decanted off as used.

The method of obtaining an agglutinating serum was essentially the same as that followed by other investigators. Rabbits were injected intraperitoneally with a physiologic salt suspension of the desired organism washed from 4-day agar slants. Ten c c. of 0.85% salt solution was used with each slant to prepare the suspensions. Three injections were given at 3-day intervals of 1 c c., 2 c c. and 5 c c. of bacterial suspension. Usually 3 injections were sufficient to give a serum of high titer, but occasionally 4 and sometimes 5 injections were required.

One week after the last injection samples of blood were drawn directly from the heart by means of a sterilized syringe. The warm blood was placed in sterile test tubes and allowed to stand in the icebox for 24 hours. If the serum had not separated by this time, the blood was centrifuged. The clear fluid obtained in either way was pipetted into small tubes and kept in the icebox until used. It was found that serum treated in this manner would keep for several weeks and still retain a high titer.

The suspensions of bacteria used in testing the serum were prepared from cultures grown on sucrose nitrate agar, or mannitol yeast-water agar for 4 days at 28 C. The growth was removed from the slants with salt solution and the suspension then filtered to remove the clumps of bacteria. The suspensions were made of the same turbidity by comparing them with a suspension of barium sulphate, tube 3 made according to McFarland's[5] standard. Phenol, 0.5%, was used as a preservative, and the suspensions so treated would usually keep for several months. However, suspensions of the organisms would turn reddish brown in a short time in the presence of phenol, and fresh suspensions had to be prepared. The suspensions were kept in the icebox.

To test the agglutinating power of serum, the procedure was as follows: To a series of small test tubes (⅜" x 3") 1 c c. portions of a suspension of organisms were added. Pure serum and serum diluted 1 : 10, 1 : 100, and 1 : 1000 were added to the 1 c c. portions of antigen so that dilutions of 1 : 50, 1 : 100, 1 : 250, 1 : 500, 1 : 1000, 1 : 2000, 1 : 5000, 1 : 7500, 1 : 10000, 1 : 20000, 1 : 30000, and 1 : 40000 were obtained. The serum and antigen were well mixed before incubation. One c c. portions of the bacterial suspension without serum were used as controls. All tubes were incubated at 37 C., and the results were read after 24 hours. Agglutination was usually as far advanced after one day as after two.

Contrary to what might be expected from capsulated organism,[6] the legume bacteria are active in the production of agglutinins. Complete agglutination in dilutions of 1 : 20,000 to 1 : 30,000 was noted in several instances with alfalfa and clover strains.

However, there was considerable variation in the production of agglutinins among the various strains of nodule bacteria. As is found with other forms of bacteria, certain strains caused little response when injected into rabbits. The inability to produce agglutinins was not due to the animals used in the instances noted. Repeated injections of the same rabbit and the use of several different rabbits with the same strain were tried. The greatest difficulty was encountered with strains from cowpea, lima bean, soy bean and freshly isolated strains from red clover. These exceptions were rare and of little importance in the application of the agglutination test to the legume bacteria.

It should be noted that agglutination in dilutions of 1 : 10,000 with the legume bacteria have been reported by Klimmer and Kruger and by Vogel and Zipfel. The higher agglutinations that I obtained were probably due to the methods used.

[5] Jour. Am. Med. Assn., 1907, 49, p. 1176.

[6] Hess and Zinsser: Text Book of Bacteriology, 1918, p. 233.

Perhaps the age of the cultures may have been an important factor, as it is generally conceded that old strains are better than newly isolated ones for agglutination work.

The observations of previous workers show an immunologic grouping of the legume bacteria which is identical with the classification obtained by plant inoculations. The present work shows that this natural grouping of the bacteria, as determined by their relation to the legume, can be extended. Each of the natural groups can be divided into varying numbers of subgroups that manifest little relation to each other in their agglutinations.

TABLE 1

THE GROUPING OF THE ALFALFA AND SWEET CLOVER BACTERIA BY MEANS OF SERUM OF RABBIT IMMUNIZED WITH ALFALFA STRAIN 102

Antigens	Agglutinin Titers
Alfalfa 102, 103, 104	30,000
Alfalfa 101, 105	30,000
Alfalfa 108	10,000
Alfalfa 106	50
Alfalfa 100, 107, 109	0
Sweet clover 110	100
Sweet clover 111, 112	0
Red clover 122, 125	50
Red clover 121, 123, 124	0
Crimson clover 126	0
Garden pea 133, 135	50
Garden pea 130, 132	0
Vetch 134	50
Lima bean 142	50
Cowpea 143	0
Garden bean 140	0
Lupine 150	0
Soy bean 161, 163, 165	0

TABLE 2

THE GROUPING OF THE ALFALFA AND SWEET CLOVER BACTERIA BY MEANS OF SERUM OF RABBIT IMMUNIZED WITH ALFALFA STRAIN 107

Antigens	Agglutinin Titers
Alfalfa 107, 100	20,000
Alfalfa 106	5,000
Alfalfa 109	2,000
Sweet clover 110, 111	10,000
Sweet clover 112	2,000
Alfalfa 108	50
Alfalfa 101, 102, 103, 104 and 105	0
Red clover 121, 123, 124 and 125	0
Garden pea 131	0
Vetch 134	0
Lupine 150	0
Soy bean 161, 163, 164, 165 and 166	0

The 10 strains of nodule-forming bacteria from alfalfa and 3 from sweet clover, which according to their relation to the legume are of a single species, were found to be of two well defined groups, as will be seen in tables 1, 2, 3, and 4. It is sometimes true that serum for a specific strain of an organism[7] will not give the same quantitative results with other strains. But serum for specific alfalfa bacteria would agglutinate heterologous strains as rapidly and consistently and often to the same end titer as the homologous strain. As will be seen in table 1, serum from strain 102 agglutinated strains 103 and 104 to the full end titer.

[7] Jordan, E. O., and Sharp, W. B.: Jour. Infect. Dis., 1922, 31, p. 208.

There was little immunologic resemblance between the 2 groups. The cross-agglutinations were in low dilutions and were not as consistent as were the reactions among the strains of either group. In a majority of instances, there were no reactions between the 2 groups in a dilution of 1 : 50. Dilutions below 1 : 50 practically always gave a positive reaction with all of the strains of legume bacteria and hence were not considered in any of the studies. These reactions between strains of various species were due to normal agglutinins in the blood of the animals in the instances studied.

The strains of group A, with the exception of No. 108, gave a moderate growth on mannitol agar and reduced litmus slowly; strain 108 grew rapidly and

TABLE 3

THE GROUPING OF THE ALFALFA AND SWEET CLOVER BACTERIA BY MEANS OF SERUM OF RABBIT IMMUNIZED WITH ALFALFA STRAIN 103

Antigens	Agglutinin Titers
Alfalfa 103 and 104	30,000
Alfalfa 102 and 105	30,000
Alfalfa 101	20,000
Alfalfa 108	10,000
Alfalfa 106 and 107	50
Alfalfa 100	0
Sweet clover 110	500
Sweet clover 111	250
Sweet clover 112	100
Red clover 122, 121, 123, 124 and 125	0
Garden pea 132, 133	0
Vetch 134	0
Garden bean 140	0

TABLE 4

THE GROUPING OF THE ALFALFA AND SWEET CLOVER BACTERIA BY MEANS OF SERUM OF RABBIT IMMUNIZED WITH ALFALFA STRAIN 106

Antigens	Agglutinin Titers
Alfalfa 106	30,000
Alfalfa 100, 107	10,000
Alfalfa 109	5,000
Sweet clover 110 and 111	10,000
Sweet clover 112	5,000
Alfalfa 101	100
Alfalfa 102 and 104	500
Alfalfa 103, 105, 108	250
Red clover 121, 122, 123	0
Garden pea 131	0
Garden bean 140	0
Lima bean 142	0
Soy bean 161, 163, 164, 165 and 166	0

reduced litmus more quickly. All of the strains of group B grew rapidly on mannitol agar and reduced litmus quickly. The 5 slow-growing strains of group A not only produced serums of high titer, but agglutinated uniformly throughout (table 5).

A similar subgrouping was found with the other species studied. The number of these serologic groups did not seem to be limited to any definite number for any particular species. Four clear-cut serologic groups were found with the 8 strains from soy bean (table 6) ; the same was true with the 8 strains of clover organisms. Likewise, the 10 strains from pea-vetch were divided into 4 groups; the 3 strains from beans into at least 2, and the 4 strains from cowpea and lima bean into at least 3.

TABLE 5

THE GROUPING OF THE ALFALFA AND SWEET CLOVER BACTERIA BY MEANS OF IMMUNE SERUM

Antigens	Antiserums and Titers												
	101	102	103	104	105	108	100	106	107	109	110	111	112
Alfalfa 101	1:10000	1:20000	1:10000	1:5000	1:2000	1:250	1:100	0	0	0	0	0	0
Alfalfa 102	1:10000	1:30000	1:20000	1:10000	1:2000	1:500	0	1:50	0	0	0	0	0
Alfalfa 103	1:500	1:30000	1:30000	1:10000	1:2000	1:500	0	1:100	0	0	0	0	0
Alfalfa 104	1:10000	1:30000	1:30000	1:10000	1:2000	1:500	1:100	1:100	0	0	0	0	0
Alfalfa 105	1:10000	1:20000	1:20000	1:10000	1:2000	1:500	0	1:100	0	0	0	0	0
Alfalfa 108	1:2000	1:10000	1:2000	1:2000	1:500	1:2000	0	1:100	0	0	0	0	1:250
Alfalfa 100	0	0	0	1:100	0	0	1:20000	1:5000	1:10000	1:5000	1:500	1:2000	1:1000
Alfalfa 106	0	0	0	1:100	0	0	1:10000	1:10000	1:2000	1:2000	1:500	1:1000	1:500
Alfalfa 107	0	0	0	1:100	0	0	1:10000	1:5000	1:10000	1:7500	1:500	1:2000	1:2000
Alfalfa 109	0	0	0	0	0	0	1:20000	1:5000	1:2000	1:2000	1:500	1:1000	1:2000
Sweet clover 110	1:250	1:100	1:250	1:50	1:50	0	1:5000	1:5000	1:2000	1:7500	1:7500	1:20000	1:2000
Sweet clover 111	1:250	0	1:250	1:250	0	0	1:10000	1:5000	1:2000	1:2000	1:7500	1:20000	1:2000
Sweet clover 112	0	0	1:100	1:50	0	0	1:1000	1:2000	1:2000	1:250	1:250	1:1000	1:2000

The differentiation between the various natural groups or species was quite marked. Occasional agglutinations between strains of different species were noted; but these were in such low dilutions as to be of no practical importance in the differentiation between the various serologic groups. Indications were that the group agglutinations were due to normal agglutinative power of the serum rather than to a true serologic relationship. No attempt was made to make quantitative studies of these apparent relationships between the various species.

The most significant point brought out by this work is that by means of the agglutination test the legume bacteria, as they are commonly classified, may be further subdivided into groups which serologically are quite different.

The results herein reported not only extend the classification of the nodule-forming bacteria as previously reported, but verify the results of these investigations. Whether this difference in classification is due to the number of strains used in the respective investigations or to differences in the legume bacteria of this country and of Europe, remains to be seen.

TABLE 6

THE GROUPING OF THE SOY BEAN BACTERIA BY MEANS OF IMMUNE SERUMS

Antigens	Antiserums and Titers							
	161	164	166	168	163	162	160	165
Soy bean 161......	1:5000	1:2000	1:1000	1:7500	0	0	0	0
Soy bean 164......	1:2000	1:2000	1:1000	1:2000	0	0	0	0
Soy bean 166......	1:2000	1:2000	1:1000	1:7500	0	0	0	0
Soy bean 168......	0	1:2000	1:2000	1:7500	0	0	0	0
Soy bean 163......	0	0	0	0	1:20000	1:5000	0	0
Soy bean 162......	0	0	0	0	1:10000	1:5000	0	0
Soy bean 160......	0	0	0	0	0	0	1:20000	1:100
Soy bean 165......	0	0	0	0	0	0	1:50	1:5000

As was pointed out in the beginning of this paper, it is impossible by cultural and morphologic means to divide the nodule-forming bacteria of the commonly cultivated legumes into but 2 groups; while by the use of the host plants it is possible to divide them into 7 or more groups. By means of the agglutination test this natural grouping is further extended. The division of the natural groups into subgroups can be accomplished only by means of the agglutination test. Instead of a few serologic groups within each of the species, there may be many. The number of such groups for any particular species is not known and may never be known. As a consequence the infection of the host plant will probably be taken as the final proof of the identity of doubtful strains.

The agglutination test, although of limited value in the identification of the species of legume bacteria, may form a sound basis for further studies of these organisms. Serologic differences seem to be associated with other differences. Studies being made at this station indicate that different strains of the same species have different nitrogen-fixing powers. At present no means have been developed for differentiating between strains of low nitrogen-fixing power and those of high power. Further studies are being made of the nitrogen-fixing powers of representative strains of the various serologic groups from alfalfa, soy bean and peas.

SUMMARY

A total of 55 pure cultures representing 7 species of the legume bacteria were studied. These cultures were secured from widely separated sources. Freshly isolated cultures were compared with old ones, some as old as 10 years.

Immune serums from 40 different strains were used to group the organisms by means of the agglutination test. Most of the strains were sensitive to this test. Agglutinations of 1:500 to 1:30,000 were obtained with the various legume bacteria.

Agglutination differentiated the cultures studied into at least 18 serologic groups. Some strains were not agglutinated by any serum, and hence more groups were possible. Single species were found to be of as many as four well defined groups. The 7 species were subdivided as follows:

1. Clovers: agglutinations 1:500 to 1:30,000; four groups.
2. Alfalfa and sweet clover: agglutinations 1:2000 to 1:30,000; two groups.
3. Pea and vetch: agglutinations 1:1000 to 1:30,000; four groups.
4. Garden bean; agglutinations 1:7500; at least two groups.
5. Cowpea and lima bean: agglutinations 1:2000; two groups.
6. Soy bean: agglutinations 1:1000 to 1:20,000; four groups.
7. Lupine: agglutinations 1:5000; one group (one strain).

The agglutinations were highly specific. The minor agglutinations among the various groups were in low dilutions, rarely as high as 1:250.

The individual strains of any particular serologic group were always of the same species. Group agglutinations among strains of different species were in low dilutions and not frequent. Such agglutinations did not interfere with the differentiations among the various groups.

CONCLUSION

The result of these observations indicates the impossibility of identifying an organism by means of the agglutination test.

BACILLI OF THE PARATYPHOSUS B GROUP

DIFFERENTIATION OF THE PARATYPHOID-ENTERITIDIS GROUP. VII

Edwin O. Jordan

From the Department of Hygiene and Bacteriology, University of Chicago

The problem of the differentiation and variability of bacterial species, always acute in certain lines of work and of fundamental significance for most bacteriologic studies, has long been to the front in the paratyphoid-enteritidis group. Interpretation of "food poisoning" outbreaks, differentiation of "low" and "continued" fevers in various parts of the world, proper understanding of a wide variety of infections in domestic and laboratory animals, and the preparation of specific vaccines are all dependent on the identification and sure recognition of the micro-organisms concerned. In recent years numerous cultural and serologic studies of the whole paratyphoid-enteriditis group have dispelled some of the confusion that beset the earlier workers, but many questions still remain unanswered. Much uncertainty centers in the subdivision commonly known as the paratyphosus B group.[1]

Cultural Characters.—In another paper [2] I have discussed the salient cultural characteristics of these organisms, and I wish here to add further observations on a larger number of strains and on two additional fermentation tests. In all, 63 strains have been examined, 40 in addition to the 23 described in the first paper. All these agree in their action on arabinose, dulcite,[3] and xylose, as well as in the more general fermentative reactions of the paratyphoid-enteritidis group. All blacken lead acetate medium.[4]

An important differential disaccharide, trehalose, was first employed by Koser.[5] According to Koser, the bacilli of the paratyphosus B

Received for publication, Aug. 1, 1923.

[1] The specific name B. schottmülleri has been suggested (Winslow, Kligler and Rothberg: Jour. Bacteriol., 1919, 4, p. 429) for the paratyphoid B. bacilli. While there are many advantages in a definite nomenclature, we are not yet in a position to evaluate the agglutinative differences and host differences shown to exist among these strains. Perhaps the more general group designation may be usefully maintained for a time.

[2] Jordan: Jour. Infect. Dis., 1917, 20, p. 457.

[3] Winslow, Kligler and Rothberg designated B. schottmülleri (B. paratyphosus B) as a group of strains in part dulcite positive, in part dulcite negative. My own observations are not in accord with this. The 64 strains dealt with in this paper have all fermented dulcite promptly (acid and gas within 24 hours). Most of these have been tested several times, always with the same result.

[4] Jordan and Victorson: Jour. Infect. Dis., 1917, 21, p. 571.

[5] Ibid., 1921, 29, p. 67.

group fermented this carbohydrate (17 strains) while those of the suipestifer group (8 strains) did not. My own observations on 63 strains of B. paratyphosus B and 38 of B. suipestifer completely confirm Koser's observations. All paratyphosus B strains are trehalose positive, all suipestifer strains negative.

Inosite fermentation has also been suggested as a differential test,[6] but owing to the unsatisfactory results obtained by some workers,[7] it has not come into general use. Krumwiede, Kohn and Valentine,[8] while obtaining results generally comparable to those of Weiss, concluded that "inosite fermentation is evidently not a completely fixed characteristic, but has a high value where a positive result is obtained." My own earlier experiments, like those of most workers with this substance, yielded rather irregular results and hence were not included in previous papers. Gas formation in inosite medium, on which apparently some observers have relied as a criterion of fermentation, is quite variable and is an unsafe basis for judgment. I have obtained much more uniform results by determining the changes in P_H values in a 0.5% inosite nutrient broth of initial reaction P_H 7.5. Since acidity, when produced, is usually transient, the medium becoming alkaline after a few days, it is essential to make the P_H determination, always with adequate controls, after 24 hours of growth. The following tests are illustrative:

Culture No.	Type	P_H in Inosite (0.5%) Broth			
		Initial	24 Hours	48 Hours	7 Days
288	Paratyphosus B	7.5	5.9	6.7	8.2+
292	Paratyphosus B	7.5	6.6	7.0	8.2+
367	Enteritidis	7.5	7.6	7.7	8.2+
283	Suipestifer	7.5	8.0	8.1	8.2+

When all the cultures in my collection were subjected to examination in this way there was no doubt about the differential value of the inosite test. All the positive results occurred in the B. paratyphosus B group. It is significant that the 28 B. enteritidis strains which resemble B. paratyphosus B in all other cultural features now recognized, although sharply marked off agglutinatively, are uniformly inosite negative. The B. paratyphosus group itself, however, is not a complete

[6] Weiss and Rice: Jour. Med. Res., 1917, 35, p. 403; Weiss: Ibid., 36, p. 135.
[7] Tenbroeck: Jour. Exper. Med., 1920, 32, p. 19.
[8] Jour. Med. Res., 1918, 38, p. 89.

unit in this respect. Fifty-eight strains have proved able to ferment inosite, but five, although repeatedly tested, have always failed to ferment this substance. In summary:

	Inosite-Positive	Inosite-Negative
B. paratyphosus A	0	24
B. paratyphosus B	58	5
B. enteritidis	0	28
B. suipestifer	0	46

As will appear later, the five inosite-negative strains do not constitute a uniform group, as regards either source or agglutinative reactions.

Agglutinative Reactions.—The B. paratyphosus B group, as here characterized, is not homogeneous in its serologic reactions. This fact, together with the circumstance that some cultures obtained from swine belong to this group but because of their origin have been kept under the name B. suipestifer in certain laboratory collections, is responsible for much of the confusion that has existed. Furthermore, group agglutination with unabsorbed serum is often so pronounced as to give little definite information unless additional tests are made with properly absorbed serum. This difficulty is clearly recognized by many recent experimenters.[9]

At the present time it is relatively easy to distinguish the true B. suipestifer type from the B. paratyphosus B type by cultural reactions, the latter readily fermenting arabinose, trehalose and (in most instances) inosite, while the former does not attack these substances. The separation of B. enteritidis from B. paratyphosus B is also readily made, none of the former attacking inosite, while the agglutinative differences are sharp. B. enteritidis serums of high titer (5,000-10,000) rarely agglutinate B. paratyphosus B strains in 1:250 dilution, and vice versa. Thus, in one series a B. paratyphosus B serum (titer 1:10,000) in 1:250 dilution agglutinated 2 B. enteritidis B strains slightly, 2 in a trace and 60 others not at all.

About one-half of the 63 strains possessing the cultural and serologic characters described above have proved to belong to a single agglutination group. These strains have all been tested by the well-known absorption method. They not only agglutinate to the titer limit with the serum of 12, a representative strain, but the 12 immune serum,

[9] Krumwiede, Valentine and Kohn: Ibid., 1919, 39, p. 449. Schütze: Lancet, 1920, 1, p. 93; Jour. Hyg., 1921, 20, p. 330; Manteufel and Beger: Centralbl. f. Bakteriol., I. O., 1921, 87, p. 161.

when absorbed with any organism belonging to the group also loses completely its agglutinative power for 12 as well as for the absorbing organism. It seems unnecessary to tabulate all the tests made, since the methods are well standardized and the results are identical. The following examples illustrate the method and results:

12 Serum (Human blood strain)	Agglutinates	1:250	1:2,000	1:5,000	Control
Unabsorbed	12	+++	++	+	0
	288 (Porcine strain)	+++	++	+	0
Absorbed with 288	12	0	0	0	0
	288	0	0	0	0
Unabsorbed	12	+++	+++	+	0
	346 (Original Schottmüller strain)	+++	+++	+	0
Absorbed with 346	12	0	0	0	0
	346	0	0	0	0

The strains of this type are:

5 Stock strain, origin uncertain, probably human.
8 Human gallbladder (Theobald Smith, 1899).
12 Human blood, paratyphoid fever (Irons and Jordan: J. Infect. Dis., 1915, 17, p. 234).
47 Human feces, paratyphoid fever (C. J. Hunt: Arch. Int. Med., 1913, 12, p. 64).
149 Human feces, paratyphoid fever (W. G. Savage: Rept. Med. Off., Local Gov't Bd., 1908-9, p. 316).
169 Lung of virus hog (R. E. Buchanan, Ames, Iowa, 1915).
175 Lung of virus hog (R. E. Buchanan, Ames, Iowa, 1915).
209 Human blood, paratyphoid fever (Major Siler, U. S. A., San Antonio, Texas, 1916).
210 Human blood, paratyphoid fever (Major Siler, U. S. A., San Antonio, Texas, 1916).
211 Human feces, paratyphoid fever (Major Siler, U. S. A., San Antonio, Texas, 1916).
221 Human feces, paratyphoid carrier (A. B. Wadsworth: Bull. N. Y. State Dept. of Health, Oct., 1916, p. 252).
224 "Fatal case of paratyphoid fever" (E. J. McWeeney, 1908).
250 Human feces paratyphoid fever (W. E. Cary, Chicago, 1918).
251 Human feces paratyphoid fever (W. E. Cary, Chicago, 1918).
252 Stock culture of porcine origin, exact history unknown (W. E. Buchanan, 1917).
256 Feces of virus hog (R. E. Buchanan, 1917).
263 Feces of virus hog (R. E. Buchanan, 1917).
288 Mesenteric lymph gland of virus hog (R. S. Spray, Purdue Univ., 1919).
292 Liver of rabbit inoculated with hog cholera virus blood (R. S. Spray, 1919).
297 Heart blood of rabbit inoculated with hog cholera virus blood (R. S. Spray, 1919).
303 Blood of hog inoculated with hog cholera virus blood (R. S. Spray, 1919).
307 Human blood, clinical paratyphoid fever, Base Hospital in France (P. R. Cannon).
308 Human feces, German prisoner in France, 1918 diagnosis "acute colitis" (P. R. Cannon),
310 Human feces, case diagnosed as typhoid fever, Base Hospital in France (P. R. Cannon).
313 Human feces, paratyphoid fever, Japanese Hospital, Vladivostok, 1919 (T. T. Crooks).
315 Human urine, paratyphoid fever, Shkotova Epidemics, Siberia, 1919 (T. T. Crooks).
316 Human feces, paratyphoid fever, Shkotova Epidemics, Siberia, 1919 (T. T. Crooks).
325 Human blood, paratyphoid fever (H. J. Morgan: Johns Hopkins Hosp. Bull., 1921, 32, p. 195).
331 Human blood, paratyphoid fever (F. T. Foard and T. F. Walker: Public Health Repts., 1921, 36, p. 2095).
346 Stock culture original Schottmüller strain, Lister Institute.
347 Human blood (paratyphoid fever?) Lister Institute, King George Hospital, London, 1915.
348 Stock culture Original Achard strain, Lister Institute.
379 Meat sandwich (beef) probably contaminated by carrier (Jordan and Geiger: Jour. Infect. Dis., 1923, 32, p. 471.

33

One of these 33 strains (5, a stock strain of uncertain origin) was inosite negative, all the others were inosite positive. Since the original Schottmüller strain belongs to this group, I would suggest calling these organisms provisionally the Schottmüller type.

The origin of the strains of the Schottmüller type may be regarded as significant: nearly all, if not all, B. paratyphosus B strains from cases of undoubted human paratyphoid fever occurring in widely separated parts of the world—England, France, Siberia and many parts of the United States—fall here; all or most B. paratyphosus B strains of porcine origin fall in the same group. A possible exception may exist in two strains—116 and 161—long carried in my collection with their original labels of "hog cholera bacillus." One of these strains is of European origin, the other American. It has not been possible to determine the exact source of these strains. If they were isolated from rabbits, guinea-pigs or mice after these animals had been inoculated with material from diseased swine, they might have been derived from the former rather than the latter.

A second type, likewise agglutinatively distinct, comprises 27 strains. This group, which I shall call the Aertrycke type, is distinguished from the Schottmüller type by a difference in absorption tests.

12 Serum	Agglutinates	1:250	1:2,000	1:5,000	Control
(Schottmüller type) unabsorbed	12	+++	++	+	0
	180	+++	++	+	0
Absorbed with 180	12	+++	++	+	0
	180	0	0	0	0
355 Serum					
(Aertrycke type="Mutton") unabsorbed	355	+++	+++	+	0
	180	+++	+++	+	0
Absorbed with 180	355	0	0	0	0
	180	0	0	0	0

It is plain from these tables that the organisms of the Aertrycke type, as represented by 180, do not absorb the Schottmüller type agglutinin from the Schottmüller serums, but do absorb the Aertrycke agglutinin from Aertrycke serums.[10] The importance and frequency of occurrence of this group of paratyphoid bacilli were clearly brought out by Schütze,[11] who has called it the "mutton" group.

[10] All strains of the Schottmüller and Aertrycke types were tested with serums from at least two strains of each type; since the results were uniform and resemble those in the examples already given, it does not seem necessary to tabulate all the details.

[11] Lancet, 1920, 1, p. 93.

The strains in my collection that fall definitely into the Aertrycke or "mutton" type are:

116 "Hog cholera bacillus," W. E. King, 1904.
152 Organs of fatal food poisoning case (W. G. Savage, 1914; Savage and Gunson: Jour. Hyg., 1908, 8, p. 601).
161 "Hog cholera bacillus," Mich. Agr. College, 1915, from Ostertay.
179 Human feces, epidemic (typhoid and paratyphoid?) caused by sewage polluted water (G. H. Robinson: Jour. Infect. Dis., 1916, 16, p. 448).
180 Pie mixture implicated in food poisoning outbreak (H. S. Bernstein, J. A. M. A., 1916, 66, p. 167, and E. S. Fish).
185 Human lymph gland infection (C. L. Cole: Jour. Infect. Dis., 1916, 18, p. 349).
222 Fatal case of gastro enteritidis (E. J. McWeeney: Brit. Med. Jour., Sept. 30, 1916).
223 Stock culture of B. aertrycke (from the Lister Inst. through Prof. McWeeney, origin unknown).
{ 239 Intestine of cockroach (C. L. Cole, 1917).
{ 240 Liver of rabbit inoculated with 239 (C. L. Cole).
244 Spleen of guinea-pig dying after giving birth to young (C. L. Cole, 1917).
245 Heart blood of guinea-pig dying after giving birth to young (C. L. Cole, 1917).
273 Stock strain labeled "Meirelbeek" (W. G. Savage, 1919).
274 Guinea-pig epizootic—England (W. G. Savage, 1919).
275[12] Food poisoning outbreak (W. G. Savage, 1919).
327 Guinea-pig epizootic, Chicago (K. M. Howell and O. T. Schultz: Jour. Infect. Dis., 1922, 30, p. 516).
355 "Mutton" strain of English writers, food poisoning outbreak, Newcastle, 1911 (Lister Institute, 1922).
356 Human blood, food poisoning, France, epidemic 1918, Lister Institute (Martin: J. Roy. Army Med. Corps, 1919, 33, p. 37).
362 Guinea-pig epizootic (Lister Institute, 1920).
{ 370 Blood of guinea-pig dying from inoculation with aerobic growth (of unknown nature) from seized ripe olives (R. W. Pryer, Detroit, 1921).
{ 373 Blood of guinea-pig.
374 Spleen of rabbit: epizootic among rabbits and guinea-pigs, Panama Canal Zone, 1920-21 (Lewis B. Bates).
387 Spleen of Child dying with gastro-intestinal symptoms (R. E. Pleasance: Lancet, 1922, 203, p. 609).
388 Spleen of fatal case of food poisoning attributed to mutton (G. D. Dawson) Allen and Dawson: Lancet, 1922, 203, p. 609.
391 Human feces, food poisoning outbreak probably due to human carriers (C.-E. A. Winslow, J. V. Hiscock, O. F. Rogers and E. S. Robinson: Am. J. Hyg., 1923, 3, p. 238).
404 Guinea-pig epizootic, University of Pittsburgh (S. R. Haythorn, 1923).
409 Ice cream causing food poisoning Seattle, Washington (State Bd. of Health through Dr. Geiger, 1923).

27

Three of these Aertrycke strains (179, 180, 374) are inosite negative, all the others are inosite-positive. It is evident that there is a definite correlation between the source of the culture and the type to which it belongs. The human strains of the Aertrycke type are mostly either from undoubted "food poisoning" outbreaks (152, 180, 275, 355, 356, 388, 391, 409) or from cases of illness in which gastro-intestinal symptoms were prominent (179, 222, 387). One other strain (273) is presumably the Meirelbeek strain, isolated by van Ermengem[13] in a food poisoning outbreak due to the use of meat from an "emergency slaughtered" cow suffering from puerperal sepsis, and if so is of bovine origin. An organism found in a case of multiple lymphadenitis (185) also belongs here. Nine of the other strains are from outbreaks of

[12] Received by Dr. Savage from Delépine—probably the strain described by latter in Jour. Hyg., 1903, 3, p. 68.

[13] E. Hübener: Fleischvergiftungen und Paratyphusinfektionen, 1910, p. 34.

disease among guinea-pigs or rabbits in widely separated localities. One strain (239) sent me by the late Major Cole, was obtained from the intestine of a cockroach. Strain 240, from a rabbit inoculated with 239, is perhaps identical with 239, but since rabbits and guinea-pigs are frequently carriers of paratyphoid bacilli, it is not entirely certain that the strain isolated from internal organs after death is the one with which the animal was inoculated.

The fact that all the guinea-pig strains that have come into my hands belong to the Aertrycke or "mutton" type is in line with the results reported by Krumwiede, Valentine and Kohn [14] in their paper on "The Separation of a Distinct Paratyphoid Group Among Strains of Rodent Origin." These authors concluded that none of the rodent strains they studied belonged to the B. paratyphosus B group, or what I have called the Schottmüller type. All the guinea-pig strains, however, that I have worked with are, as here shown, closely related to other strains which are of distinctly human origin. Schütze includes one guinea-pig strain in his list of strains of the "mutton" type, most of which were derived from food poisoning outbreaks. I have not had any mouse strains of the B group in my collection, but Webster [15] has shown that a mouse typhoid strain that he has worked with is apparently similar to the type mutton strain of Schütze and is identical with the type B. pestis caviae strain of Krumwiede.[16] All the strains in the Aertrycke group agglutinate with the serum of a guinea-pig strain (244) as well as with the English "mutton" strain and also absorb all the agglutinin from the serum. It is possible that two strains in my collection (116 and 161) belonging to the Aertrycke type are of porcine origin, but since their exact manner of isolation is not known, there is a chance they may have come from inoculated rodents.

Besides the two main and rather clearly differentiated types already dealt with, I have several strains belonging to what I may call the free lance type. These, although conforming in the main to the cultural characters of the B. paratyphosus B group and showing agglutination in high dilutions with serums of either the Schottmüller or Aertrycke type or both, nevertheless fail to show any relationship with any other strains by the absorption test. The "Newport type" (363), received through the kindness of the Lister Institute, is one of these free lances.

[14] Jour. Med. Res., 1919, 39, p. 449.

[15] Jour. Exper. Med., 1922, 36, p. 97.

[16] In a footnote, Webster refers to unpublished studies of Krumwiede and Cooper which have "demonstrated a close relationship between the B. pestis caviae group and the 'mutton' types of Schütze."

Although agglutinating in fairly high dilations with 12 (Schottmüller type) serum, and also agglutinating almost as well with 244 (Aertrycke type—guinea-pig) and 355 (Aertrycke type—food poisoning) serums, it does not show true serologic affinity, as determined by the absorption test, to any one of these strains. The lack of relationship to all my other strains is further demonstrated by the results obtained with the immune serum of 363 itself, which, unabsorbed in 1:2,000 dilution, agglutinates many of the 63 B. paratyphosus B strains as strongly as it does the homologous strain, but after absorption by ony one of these strains still agglutinates the homologous suspension as strongly as before. So far as the absorption test may be taken to indicate close relationship, no such relationship exists between 363, the Newport type, and any other of the 63 strains tested. In Schütze's study of 46 strains (Lancet) the Newport type stands almost by itself, one other strain, however, being found by Schütze to sustain relations with it. In my collection it has no serologic double

Another strain (365), the "Stanley type" of the Lister Institute collection, is likewise a free lance and has no close agglutinative relationship with any other strain that I have examined. Schütze, however, found that a strain from a case of clinical paratyphoid fever was related to the Stanley strain. The Stanley strain is inosite negative, but otherwise like the predominant B. paratyphosus B type. It agglutinates fairly well with 12 serum, but 12 serum, after absorption with 365, agglutinates its homologous strain as powerfully as before. The same is true with the Aertrycke serums.

A third strain, possibly to be ranked as another free lance, is the "Reading type" of the Lister Institute collection (my number 360). It was obtained from a water supply and agglutinates in quite high dilutions with 12 serum. Unlike all the other B. paratyphosus B strains here considered, it does not produce gas from rhamnose, although it does give an acid reaction. Like 363 and 365, it shows no relationship to either the Schottmüller or Aertrycke types by the absorption test. This strain was the sole representative of its class in Schütze's grouping also. It is inosite positive.

DISCUSSION AND SUMMARY

The B. paratyphosus B bacilli may be regarded as a distinct division of the paratyphosus-enteritidis group; first, because they show essential unity in cultural characters, second, because their closest cultural relatives, the B. enteritidis type, stand sharply apart from them agglutinatively. There is, moreover, among the paratyphosus B bacilli themselves, an undoubted serologic as well as cultural resemblance. The unabsorbed immune serum of a member of the group selected at random (I have tested from 8 to 10 strains) will agglutinate more or less all the other strains. Some 63 strains, practically all of them of definite origin and many of them from recorded outbreaks of disease in man or animals, have been subjected to repeated cultural and serologic examination. Differences in degree of agglutinability with a particular serum appear among these strains, but as students of this group have generally found, these differences are often very slight and are not uniform if the immune serum of other strains be used. When, however, an immune serum is absorbed by the bacilli of another strain and tested against its own strain, a sharp distinction leaps into view. By the absorption method the majority of the strains fall into two groups, one of 33, the other of 27 strains. After the separation of these two agglutinative types had been accomplished, it was found that the former included all the strains isolated from typical paratyphoid fever in man and all or nearly all of the paratyphosus B strains of porcine origin. Since the original Achard and the original Schottmüller strains are of this type, I would suggest the name Schottmüller type for this division of the B. paratyphosus B group. The second type, which includes nearly all the strains of the group that have been isolated from food poisoning outbreaks together with all strains of rodent origin, may be called the Aertrycke type. In addition, 3 strains of the Lister Institute collection, two from food poisoning cases, one from a water supply, stand apart agglutinatively from both the main types and from one another, and I have suggested the term free lance for these seemingly independent, unallied forms

The correlation in the two main types of agglutinative behavior with origin is so close and striking as to seem significant, and may later be found to be accompanied by some cultural distinction at present unrecognized. The history of cultural differentiation within the paratyphosus-enteritidis group at least suggests that agglutinative divergence is usually associated with cultural dissimilarity.

There is good reason, however, at present for regarding the B. paratyphosus B group as composed of closely related organisms, since the Schottmüller and Aertrycke types are certainly more closely allied to one another than is either to the B. enteritidis type. Since our knowledge of cultural differential methods is probably still incomplete, there seems to be no ground for establishing any new types on the basis of one or two agglutinatively independent strains occasionally isolated.

GENERAL INDEX

A

PAGE

Acid agglutination of paratyphoid bacilli - - - - - - - 113
Acidity, titratable vs. hydrogen-ion concentration in culture mediums - 1
Agglutination, can all strains be recognized by - - - - - - 557
Agglutination of paratyphoid bacilli - - - - - - - - 113
Agglutination studies of clostridium botulinum - - - - - - 169
Agglutinins, typhoid - - - - - - - - - - - 142, 498
Antibody formation, effect of benzyl benzoate on - - - - - - 477
Anticomplementary action of fresh bovine serum - - - - - - 184
Ayers, S. Henry, and Mudge, Courtland S. Streptococci of feces and mouth of cows - - - - - - - - - - - - - 155
Ayers, S. Henry; Rupp, Philip, and Johnson, Jr., William T. The influence of surface tension depressants on the growth of streptococci. VI. Studies of the streptococci - - - - - - - - - 202

B

B. botulinus - - - - - - - - - - 169, 236, 274, 289, 384
B. botulinus spores - - - - - - - - - - - 274, 289
B. diphtheriae - - - - - - - - - - - - 124, 466
B. fusiformis - - - - - - - - - - - 134, 139, 147
B. paratyphosus - - - - - - - - - - - - - 113
B. paratyphosus B. - - - - - - - - - - - - 567
B. pestis - - - - - - - - - - - - - - 391
B. pestis-caviae - - - - - - - - - - - - - 269
B. sporogenes - - - - - - - - - - - - - 240
Bachmann, Freda M. Effect of spices on growth of clostridium botulinum 236
Bacteria, resistance of, from different habitats - - - - - - - 526
Bact. acidophilus - - - - - - - - - - - - - 482
Bact. typhosum - - - - - - - - - - - - - 269
Bact. pullorum - - - - - - - - - - - - - 331
Beaudette, F. R.; Bushnell, L. D., and Payne, L. F. Relation of Bacterium pullorum to hatchability of eggs - - - - - - - 331
Beckwith, T. D. Chemotherapy of experimental typhoid carrier conditions 457
Beckwith, T. D., and Jones, E. M. Typhoid agglutinins in rabbits - 142
Benzyl benzoate, effect on antibody formation - - - - - - - 477
Blood cells, foreign, in rabbit - - - - - - - - - - 230
Blood, identification of, by hemoglobin precipitins - - - - - - 224
Braafladt, Louis Henry. The effect of kaolin on the intestinal flora in normal and pathologic conditions - - - - - - - - - 434
Brams, J. See Pilot, I. - - - - - - - - - - - 134
Breinl, F. See Weil, E. - - - - - - - - - - - 60
Burke, Georgina S. Studies on the thermal death time of spores of Clostridium botulinum - - - - - - - - - - - - 274
Bushnell, L. D. See Beaudette, F. R. - - - - - - - - 331

C

PAGE
Cerebrospinal fluid, coagulum of fibrinogen nitrogen in - - - - 193
Chemotherapy of experimental typhoid carrier conditions - - - 457
Cholesterol, effect on phagocytosis - - - - - - - - - - - 285
Clasmatocytes - - - - - - - - - - - - - - - - 338
Clostridium botulinum - - - - - - - 169, 236, 274, 289, 384
Cold, common - - - - - - - - - - - - - - - - 416
COLEMAN, GEORGE E. Germination of spores of B. botulinus in colloidion sacs in abdomen of guinea-pigs and rabbits - - - - - - 384
Culture mediums, hydrogen-ion concentration vs. titratable acidity in - 1

D

DACK, GAIL M. See STARIN, WILLIAM A. - - - - - - - - - 169
D'AUNOY, RIGNEY. Studies on Bacillus pestis - - - - - - - 391
DIEHL, H. S. See SHEPARD, W. P. - - - - - - - - - - - 75
Diphtheria bacillus, Klein medium for isolation of - - - - - 466
Diphtheric vaginitis - - - - - - - - - - - - - - 124
Diplococcus associated with caseous lymphadenitis and pneumonia of sheep 161

E

ECKER, E. E., AND MEGRAIL, EMERSON. Immunologic alteration of Bacterium typhosum and of Bacillus pestis-caviae by growth in sterile fixation abscesses - - - - - - - - - - - - - - 269
Eggs, hatchability of and Bact. pullorum - - - - - - - - - 331
EMGE, LUDWIG. Effect of benzyl benzoate on antibody formation in rabbit 477
Encephalitis, epidemic - - - - - - - - - - - - - 531
Erythroprecipitins - - - - - - - - - - - - - - 224
ESTY, J. R. See SCHOENHOLZ, P. - - - - - - - - - - 289

F

FAWCETT, EDNA H. See QUIRK, AGNES J. - - - - - - - - - 1
FREUND, JULES. New method for increasing yield of therapeutic and diagnostic serum - - - - - - - - - - - - - - - - 328
FULMER, ELLIS I., AND NELSON, VICTOR E. Continuous growth of Saccharomyces cerevisiae in synthetic mediums - - - - - - 130
Fusiform facilli - - - - - - - - - - - - - 134, 139, 147

G

GAY, FREDERICK P., AND MORRISON, L. F. Clasmatocytes and resistance to streptococcus infection. Studies in streptococcus infection and immunity. V. - - - - - - - - - - - - - - - - 338
GOUWENS, WILLIS E. Acid agglutination of paratyphoid bacilli - - 113
GUYER, M. F., AND SMITH, E. A. Experiments in production of typhoid agglutinins in successive generations of rabbits - - - - - - 498

H

HALL, IVAN C., AND STARK, NAOMI. Serologic agglutination of Bacillus sporogenes - - - - - - - - - - - - - - - - 240
HASTINGS, E. G. Comparative resistance of bacteria from native habitats and from artificial cultures - - - - - - - - - - - 526

PAGE

Hektoen, Ludwig, and Schulhof, Kamil. On specific erythroprecipitins (hemoglobin precipitins?). II. Hemoglobin precipitins in identification of blood - - - 224
Hemoglobin precipitins - - - 224
Hemolysin formation in suprarenalectomized rabbits - - - 217
Hirsch, Edwin F. Hydrogen-ion studies. IX. The preparation of specific precipitin as dry powder - - - 470
Huddleson, I. Forest. Anticomplementary action of fresh bovine serum 184
Hydrogen-ion concentration vs. titratable acidity in culture mediums - 1
Hydrogen-ion studies. IX. Preparation of specific precepitin as dry powder - - - 470

I

Immunity, comparative - - - 230
Immunologic alteration of Bact. typhosum and B. pestis-caviae by growth in sterile fixation abscesses - - - 269
Infection, streptococcus - - - 338
Influenza - - - 416, 531
Intestinal flora, effect of kaolin on - - - 434

J

Jones, E. M. See Beckwith, T. D. - - - 142
Jordan, Edwin O. Bacilli of the paratyphosus B group. Differentiation of the paratyphoid-enteritidis group VII - - - 567
Jordan, Edwin O., Norton, John F., and Sharp, William B. The Common cold - - - 416
Johnson, Jr., William T. See Ayers, S. Henry. - - - 202

K

Kahn, Morton C. See Torrey, John C. - - - 482
Kaolin, effect of, on intestinal flora - - - 434
Kirschenbaum, Dora. See Levinson, A. - - - 193
Klein medim for isolation of diphtheria bacillus - - - 466

L

Levinson, A., and Kirschenbaum, Dora. A Study of the coagulum or pellicle and of the fibrinogen nitrogen in cerebrospinal fluid - - 193
Liver indestruction of foreign red cells - - - 230
Lymph adenitis in sheep - - - 161

M

Marine, David. See Take, N. Maximova - - - 217
Megrail, Emerson. See Ecker, E. E. - - - 269
Megrail, Emerson. Modification of Klein medium for isolation of the diphtheria bacillus - - - 466
Meyer, K. F. See Schoenholz, P. - - - 289
Morrison, L. F. See Gay, Frederick P. - - - 338
Mudge, Courtland S. See Ayers, S. Henry - - - 155

N

PAGE
NELSON, VICTOR E. See FULMER, ELLIS I. - - - - - - - - 130
NORTON, JOHN F. See JORDAN, ELWIN O. - - - - - - - - - 416

P

Paratyphoid bacilli - - - - - - - - - - - - - - 113
Paratyphoid-enteritidis - - - - - - - - - - - - 567
PARR, LELAND W. Intestinal spirochetes - - - - - - - - - 369
PAYNE, L. F. See BEAUDETTE, F. R. - - - - - - - - - - 331
PEARLMAN, S. J. See PILOT, I. - - - - - - - - - - - 139
Phagocytosis, effect of cholesterol on - - - - - - - - - 285
PICKOF, F. L. Studies in comparative immunity. II. Relative importance of the liver and spleen in destruction of foreign blood cells in rabbits 230
PILOT, I., AND BBAMS, J. Fusiform bacilli and spirochetes - - - - 134
PILOT, I., AND PEARLMAN, S. J. Fusiform bacilli and spirochetes - - 139
Pneumonia in sheep - - - - - - - - - - - - - 97, 161
Pneumococci, bactericidal action of blood of rabbits immunized against - 88
Precipitins, hemoglobin - - - - - - - - - - - - 224
Precipitin, preparation of specific; as dry powder - - - - - - 470

Q

QUIRK, AGNES J., AND FAWCETT, EDNA H. Hydrogen-ion concentration vs. titratable acidity in culture mediums - - - - - - - - - 1

R

ROSENOW, EDWARD C. Changes in streptococcus from encephalitis induced experimentally, and their significance in pathogenesis of epidemic encephalitis and influenza - - - - - - - - - - - - 531
ROSENOW, EDWARD C. The specificity of the streptococcus of gastro-duodenal ulcer and certain factors determining its localization - - 248
RUPP, PHILIP. See AYERS, S. HENRY - - - - - - - - - - 202

S

Saccharomyces cerevisiae growth of, in synthetic mediums - - - - 130
Scarlet fever, epidemiology of school - - - - - - - - - 75
SCHOENHOLZ, P.; ESTY, J. R., AND MEYER, K. F. Toxin production and signs of spoilage in commercially canned vegetables and fruits inoculated with detoxified spores of B. botulinus. XII - - - - - 289
SCHULHOF, KAMIL. See HEKTOEN, LUDWIG - - - - - - - 224
Serum, bovine, anticomplementary action of - - - - - - - 184
Serum, increasing yield of, therapeutic and diagnostic - - - - - 328
SHARP, WILLIAM B. See JORDAN, EDWIN O. - - - - - - - 416
Sheep, pneumonia and lymph adenitis - - - - - - - - 97, 161
SHEPARD, W. P., AND DIEHL, H. S. Studies on epidemiology of scarlet fever in a school outbreak - - - - - - - - - - - - - - 75
SMILEY, H. EVERETT. Bactericidal action of blood of rabbits immunized against pneumococci - - - - - - - - - - - - - 88
SMITH, E. A. See GUYER, M. F. - - - - - - - - - - - 498
Spirochetes - - - - - - - - - - - 134, 139, 147, 369

PAGE

Spirochetes, intestinal - - - - - - - - - - - - 369
Spores of B. botulinus in canned goods and toxin production - - - 289
SPRAY, ROBB SPALDING. A Diplococcus associated with caseous lymphadenitis and pneumonia of sheep - - - - - - - - - - 161
SPRAY, ROBB SPALDING. Bacteriologic study of pneumonia in sheep - - 97
STARIN, WILLIAM A., AND DACK, GAIL M. Agglutination studies of clostridium botulinum - - - - - - - - - - - - - 169
STARK, NAOMI. See HALL, IVAN C. - - - - - - - - - - 240
STEVENS, J. W. Can all strains of a specific orgainsm be recognized by agglutination? - - - - - - - - - - - - - - 557
Streptococcus from encephalitis, changes in - - - - - - - 531
Streptococci of feces and mouth of cows - - - - - - - - 155
Streptococci, tension depression and growth of, - - - - - - - 202
Streptococcus of gastroduodenal ulcer - - - - - - - - - 248
Streptococcus infection, clasmatocytes and resistance to - - - - 338
Spleen in destruction of foreign red cells - - - - - - - 230

T

TAKÉ, N. MAXIMOVA, AND MARINE, DAVID. The effect of suprarenalectomy in rabbits on hemolysin formation - - - - - - - - - 217
Thermal death time of clostridium botulinum spores - - - - - 274
TORREY, JOHN C., AND KAHN, MORTON C. Inhibition of putrefactive spore-bearing anaerobes by Bacterium acidophilus - - - - - - 482
Toxin production by botulinus spores - - - - - - - - - 289
TUNNICLIFF, RUTH. Life cycle of bacillus fusiformis - - - - - 147
TUNNICLIFF, RUTH. The influence of cholesterol on phagocytosis - - 285
Typhoid carrier - - - - - - - - - - - - - - - 457
Typhoid agglutinins in rabbits - - - - - - - - - - 142, 498
Typhus, infection and immunity in - - - - - - - - - - 60

U

Ulcer, streptococcus of gastroduodenal - - - - - - - - - 248

V

Vaginitis, diphtheric, in children - - - - - - - - - - 124
VAN SAUN, ANNA I. Diphtheric vaginitis in children - - - - - 124

W

WEIL, E., AND BREINL, F. Experimental studies on infection and immunity in typhus - - - - - - - - - - - - - - - 60